Praise for *Scenario-Focused Engineering*

"Breakthroughs often result when diverse disciplines collaborate to solve old problems using new perspectives. Scenario-Focused Engineering is just such a breakthrough. I'll never see software design the same."

—Eric Brechner, Development Manager, Microsoft Xbox, author of I.M. Wright's Hard Code

"If your team focus is dominated by what you want to make, without enough consideration of why or for whom, this book is for you. Revitalize your team and your product by using these rigorous techniques that put the customer at the center."

—Chris Pratley, Director of Program Management, Microsoft Office, creator of OneNote and Sway

"De Bonte and Fletcher have astute insight into how engineering teams build products today. They expertly lay out a compelling approach to the creation of desirable products and services through the embrace of Scenario-Focused Engineering. Read it and you'll want to start using Scenario-Focused Engineering in your development processes immediately."

—Gayna Williams, founder, Swash Consulting

"If you are new to customer-centricity or an expert with decades of experience, this book is a great addition to your library. It demonstrates that customer-centricity is the responsibility of everybody in the organization and gives readers strategies and ideas to make this happen."

—Charles Bennett, CEO, NextTen

"Microsoft has gradually shifted from a feature-focused approach to product engineering to a more user-centric, scenario-focused approach. The shift was both profound and difficult. The SFE training they drove was instrumental to Microsoft meeting these challenges. In this book you'll get the distilled lessons of that enormous undertaking."

—Charles Eliot, Head of Engineering Services, Skype

"In this impeccably organized book, Fletcher and De Bonte combine practical wisdom and highly refined techniques to produce a hands-on guide that will enrich the design room as well as the classroom. A smart, easy read."

—William Storage, Visiting Scholar, Center for Science, Technology, and Society, UC Berkeley

"One of the toughest challenges designers face is promoting the value behind building end-to-end scenarios rather than hundreds of glitzy, yet disconnected features. SFE throws the old engineering processes out the window and replaces them with a common language, tools, and techniques that enable development, test, program management, marketing, and design to work together to deliver a cohesive, end-to-end experience. The program transformed our organization from the top down."

—Bethany Kessen Doan, Principal Use

"The concepts of SFE are presented in a digestible and easily adopted way for people of all levels of experience. Having seen firsthand the impact the concepts can have on an engineering team, I am a big supporter of this way of thinking."

—Sheri Panabaker, Principal User Research Manager, Microsoft Surface

"Three years ago, we decided to pilot the use of Scenario-Focused Engineering for our division. The improvements were almost immediate, and customers love the outcome. There's no going back."

—Jeff Comstock, General Manager, Microsoft Dynamics R&D

"With great examples and a proven approach, this book provides a great roadmap for really learning about your customers and how to build great products for them."

—Mike Kelly, Managing Partner, Tech DNA

"Teams will greatly benefit from this book by shifting the primary focus from feature lists to 'who would use this product' (target customer) and 'why/how' (scenarios)."

—Raja Abburi, CEO, Navaraga Corporation

"I saw firsthand how engineers became more deeply involved with customers. SFE was a great step forward."

—Mike Tholfsen, Principal Engineering Manager, Microsoft Project

"Chockfull of common sense, SFE was controversial because taken as a whole it pushed for a much-needed culture shift at the company. We used to dream up scenarios to match the features we wanted to build. SFE helped teach the company how to start first with real customer needs and then design for the right scenarios."

—Kent Lowry, Principal Design Research Manager, Microsoft Office

"There are a handful of moments in life that make an indelible impression on one's memory. One of those moments for me was when Austina wrote at the top of the whiteboard, 'To help design a product customers crave.' SFE helped Microsoft transform, and it can help you as well."

—Michael Corning, Senior Data Scientist, Microsoft Skype

"This book will be a priceless asset in helping me apply SFE at my company."

—Arne de Booij, UX Strategist, SDL

"For those of you trying out SFE for the first time, trust that this system works. Trust that getting your engineers involved in the design process helps them understand the problem they are trying to solve. Trust that iterating and getting feedback on these iterations from customers can be done quickly. Trust that you will have that 'aha moment' when you show a design to customers and they are ecstatic. It's then that you realize that SFE works."

—Kevin Honeyman, User Experience Lead, Microsoft Dynamics

Scenario-Focused Engineering

A toolbox for innovation and customer-centricity

AUSTINA DE BONTE
DREW FLETCHER

PUBLISHED BY
Microsoft Press
A Division of Microsoft Corporation
One Microsoft Way
Redmond, Washington 98052-6399

Library of Congress Control Number: 2014946865
ISBN: 978-0-7356-7933-7

Printed and bound in the United States of America.

First Printing

Microsoft Press books are available through booksellers and distributors worldwide. If you need support related to this book, email Microsoft Press Book Support at mspinput@microsoft.com. Please tell us what you think of this book at http://www.microsoft.com/learning/booksurvey.

Acquisitions Editor: Devon Musgrave
Developmental Editor: Devon Musgrave
Project Editor: Devon Musgrave
Editorial Production: Rob Nance and John Pierce
Copyeditor: John Pierce
Indexer: Lucie Haskins
Cover: Twist Creative • Seattle

Contents at a glance

Contents

Chapter 3 Take an experimental approach 39

PART II THE FAST FEEDBACK CYCLE

Chapter 4 Identifying your target customer 65

Chapter 5   Observing customers: Building empathy   91

Chapter 8   Building prototypes and coding   261

Chapter 9   Observing customers: Getting feedback   311

Chapter 10   The importance of iteration   365

Foreword

As a leader of a large organization, I know that change is hard. Systems are built up over many years to prescribe the what and how of things. Organizational structure, design artifacts, and processes are all put in place with good intentions. Each individual decision is often the right one, but the cumulative effect can lead to interesting traps.

You might find yourself in a place where, despite your best intentions and years of wisdom, you and your organization have lost sight of what's most important to your customers. Worse, even when you find out what's important, your processes can be so rigorous that they thwart common sense. You still end up shipping a bad product.

After finding ourselves in just such a position in late 2011, my team and I set out to change everything. We started with the design process and adopted Scenario-Focused Engineering. Then we changed our processes to become more agile, adopting a team-wide cadence of four-week cycles with individual groups measuring their work day to day. Finally, we changed our organizational structure to eliminate artificial specialization of the development and test teams.

Figuring out what to do and implementing it across an organization of a thousand plus people took nearly a year. Mastering the new way of doing things took another 18 months on top of that. We had incremental gains at every step, but no one was certain that the new way was better than the old until near the end of the process. Then it became obvious that we were producing better products in less time and with less wasted effort.

At every step there was reluctance and even resistance, sometimes within the team, but just as often from outside—other organizations had a vested interest in defending the old way, and sometimes management feared what was new.

Perseverance is required if you intend to implement change at scale. Fixing products is easy. Fixing the processes and organizations that build them is hard. The tools and techniques in this book are a powerful starting point for change. Use them wisely on your teams.

Hal Howard
Corporate Vice President
Microsoft Corporation

Introduction

We are all too busy these days to do anything that doesn't add value to our lives in one way or another. So why are you spending your precious time with this book? Did somebody recommend it to you? Did you flip through the pages and see something that resonated with you? What added value are you expecting this book to provide?

If we've done our jobs well, the answer is simple. Circumstances in your life right now are urging you to improve your craft as a software engineer. You may want to improve the products and services you create for your customers. Perhaps you've noticed that your competitors are delivering solutions that seem to resonate with customers better than yours do. You may be thinking that there's a better way for your team to develop products, and you're looking to be a change agent for your team. Or you may be dreaming of creating the next breakthrough product—an offering that becomes so loved that it will have its own fan club. You aspire to get closer to your customers' needs and desires and to build products that they crave, products they use because they want to, not because they have to.

We think there is a better way to engineer software. We believe that innovation and creativity can be taught, and that there is science behind it, not just art. This book bridges the gap between the power of analytical, deductive reasoning and the seemingly unstructured world of creativity, innovation, and customer delight. It presents both the methods (things you do) and the mindsets (attitudes and points of view) that have been shown over time to be effective tools for creating desirable, innovative products.

Who are you?

You are an engineer. You think logically and systematically. You're smart, and you don't have a lot of patience for those who aren't. You value rigor, science, and efficiency. You strive toward finding elegant solutions to every problem. You like to get things done, to make visible progress, to cross items off your to-do list. You don't like to waste time, and you *hate* rework. And you certainly don't want to waste any more of your life writing code that no one appreciates.

You'd like to be more creative, to be more innovative, to do something that has never been done before, that no one has ever imagined. You aspire to invent something so groundbreaking that it will change the world. But all the things you've read about innovation and creativity feel a bit hollow to you. You sense a lot of hand waving and magic pixie dust and see no real substance; there's too much art, and too little science. But still, you have a nagging feeling that there has got to be a better way and that your current approaches aren't quite working as well as you'd like. This book is for you.

Or perhaps you lead a team of software engineers and want to shift the focus of your team from caring about the innovative details of the technology you're building to caring more about delighting the customers you want to serve. This book is especially for you.

Or maybe you're a designer, a user researcher, a product planner, a project manager, or a marketer and work with engineers who tend to influence big decisions on the basis of their technical knowledge. You wish those engineers knew better how to understand and use your expertise. This book is for you, too.

Our story

We are both engineers, who together have more than 35 years of experience designing, building, and shipping software products and online services at Microsoft. During our careers, we've witnessed a few teams that had great success in building innovative products that resonated with customers. These teams had a few things in common: a strong vision, a deep sense of empathy for their customers, and an iterative approach, sometimes trying tens or even a hundred alternatives over the course of a single release. One other common trait emerged—a healthy and productive relationship between the engineering team and the user-experience design and research team. Instead of working separately, with one team tossing ideas and designs over the wall for the other team to build, the engineering and design teams began to function as an integrated whole. Indeed, the very qualities that made those engineering teams so strong—their iterative approach and customer focus—were also core values of their user-experience partners.

With firsthand experience in using a highly iterative, customer-focused approach on several of our own projects—as well as living through some less-than-ideal situations—we knew how powerful this approach could be in developing outstanding products. Yet we also saw that some of our fellow engineers found this approach counterintuitive. Where we saw tremendous quality and efficiency in getting regular feedback from customers, we were surprised that others feared wasted effort. While some people saw long lists of features as a structured way to plan work, we feared that actual customer needs were being forgotten. Where we saw a rigor and science behind a customer-focused, iterative approach, some people saw only the artistic skills of craftspeople who knew how to make beautiful graphics. Both perspectives had their merits, but few teams found a middle ground to work from.

We also noticed that we weren't alone. A large number of engineers—as well as designers, researchers, marketers, and business people—also saw power in a customer-focused, iterative approach. Some of these people found one another and thrived as they helped their teams build innovative, groundbreaking products. However, many of these people felt increasingly alone on their teams—lone wolves unable to convince their pack to change its technology-focused approach. Most team members knew that they should be talking to customers more often, gathering more feedback, caring more about what customers thought, and striving for a higher level of quality, but the rhythm of daily work just didn't leave much room for this to happen.

We founded the Scenario-Focused Engineering (SFE) initiative in 2008 to help close this gap. On one side, we sought to help every engineer see the value of using a more customer-focused, iterative approach to developing software and realize that this approach is fundamentally logical, rigorous, and based on science. On the other side, we wanted to enlist and empower those who already understood these ideas and help them become leaders on their teams as they blazed a path to the future. It was a grassroots effort aimed at a pretty lofty goal: to fundamentally rethink how engineering teams go about designing products, services, and devices and to drive company-wide change. We were lucky to get to focus on this mission as our full-time jobs, as part of the Engineering Excellence team within Microsoft's Trustworthy Computing division. Over the next six years, we reached more than 22,000 engineers, and in the process learned a lot about what practices work in real life and how to catalyze significant change on a large scale.

What we discovered

We spent the first months conducting lots of interviews across the company. We had some hypotheses about the issues teams were facing, but we wanted to validate our assumptions by talking to lots of engineers on different product teams. The problems weren't difficult to identify, and we quickly noticed that the same stories were repeated over and over again:

> Each person on the team has a different idea about what's most important, what we're building, who we're building for.

> We do usability testing and betas, but the feedback comes back too late in the cycle to address it.

> We ended up having to make a huge design change late in the cycle and had to throw away a lot of code. We wasted a lot of effort.

> We had more features, but the competitor ate our lunch because their product had a better overall experience.

After a while, we began asking every team we worked with whether these statements sounded familiar. Their response was yes. But almost universally, very few teams had made any substantial progress in fixing these issues or even knowing where to start.

At the same time, the industry was rapidly accelerating toward online services, and with that shift came a desire for more frequent releases, even multiple releases each day, to provide new functionality to users as quickly as possible or to fix bugs as soon as they were found, not weeks or months later. This sea change intensified customer expectations, and we heard a growing voice within teams that we needed to find more efficient, effective ways to ship the right stuff, faster.

We already had the intuition that techniques such as the user-centered design methodology were an important missing link. Indeed, we weren't the first ones to discover this. Microsoft already had a long-running training course, offered every few weeks, that took students through the basic principles and techniques of user-centered design. The class was exhilarating to teach. Frequently, some students had breakthroughs during class and left feeling passionate and inspired. Yet, later on, we regularly heard from many of these same students that they weren't able to put any of the ideas they learned into practice. Between their manager, coworkers, project schedules, tools, performance-review commitments, and all the other realities of their work, these new approaches simply didn't fit.

Other students simply didn't understand what was being taught and occasionally became troublesome in class. These cases were rare (skeptics usually don't elect to take an optional course on a topic they don't believe in), but we certainly did get a taste of the depth of skepticism that could be found in our engineering community.

It became clear to us that to really light a fire would require much more than having individuals take a one-day class. We doubled down on our mission to catalyze change within the company and identified two central insights that drove our work for the next six years. First, while engineers are known for being intelligent and adept at solving complex problems, they tend to view the world differently from people in creative disciplines. A large gap exists in how these two groups naturally approach solving problems, in the processes they use, and in the mindsets they maintain. For example, imagine a designer at a creative brainstorming session. She embraces the most unusual ideas and encourages more of them, without restraint and regardless of any practical implications. She's comfortable following somewhat unpredictable paths of reasoning and has faith that the process will result in discovering a potentially innovative solution. Now envision an engineer at this same brainstorming session. He will likely look at the list of ideas and begin to prioritize them based on criteria such as market readiness, the cost of delivery, or the amount of effort required. He might ask for clarification of the problem statement and begin to do a root-cause analysis. The engineer will immediately begin to start *narrowing* the possibilities to get to an answer, but the designer will strive to *broaden* the possibilities. We believe that to optimize the chances for success, you need both approaches (or styles) to balance and complement each other. We've observed that most teams tend to strongly favor one style over the other, and at Microsoft that style almost always favored the engineer.

Second, to get any of our ideas adopted was going to require a whole team—a systemic effort that started with each team's leaders and moved down to every individual contributor. The reality is that it takes a team to build a product, and if you expect change to occur, you need to push the entire team toward change. Customer-focused, iterative product development is not something that can be delegated to someone else to do. It takes the entire team, especially those engineers whose first response to the ideas of SFE is deeply skeptical.

Where did SFE come from?

The general principles behind SFE are not new. They come from sources such as user-centered design (UCD), design thinking, customer-focused design (CFD), human-computer interaction (HCI), and practices we observed while working with Microsoft teams and from the industry. (Iteration and customer-centricity are both very hot ideas right now, and have only gotten hotter since we started teaching SFE in 2008. You can find many great books on these topics; we've listed some in Appendix C.)

If we had to choose the single largest influence behind SFE, it would be the ideas and practices of design thinking, a holistic method of problem solving that is based on the practices of user-centered design. It is not a stretch to say that SFE is an instantiation of design thinking wrapped in engineering terms and concepts.

However, during our journey of creating and refining Scenario-Focused Engineering, we were delighted to see other new approaches to software development gain traction and popularity. As SFE was first gaining momentum within Microsoft, Agile development was quickly becoming a mainstream practice. As we learned more about Agile and saw how compatible it was with SFE, we made some adjustments in the way we spoke about SFE to find the most natural way to present its concepts and practices in the context of Agile development. That adjustment came quite naturally because SFE also values a highly iterative process, and as such is well suited for teams that have already embraced Agile development practices. Throughout the book we mention Agile concepts and terminology and point out ways to incorporate SFE techniques into an Agile development environment.

In 2011, Eric Ries published *The Lean Startup,* and the ideas he describes have since gained tremendous popularity. *The Lean Startup* is also based on the notion that you want to learn quickly by trying out ideas. Ries's approach is generally focused on using actual customer behavior to determine the viability of the business ideas you are pursuing. It has a strong focus on experimentation and making adjustments based on what you learn. In Chapter 4, "Identifying the target customer," we discuss the importance of identifying specific target customers and honing in on a viable business strategy. *The Lean Startup* provides a wealth of ideas, stories, and examples for achieving these goals in ways that are highly synergistic with the activities SFE offers for thinking through complete end-to-end customer experiences.

About the SFE workshop

This book attempts to relay the content of our SFE workshop as well as the experience that a participant might have. It also passes along insights we've gained after working with teams on implementing SFE over the past six years, so it goes into much more detail than the original workshop.

There was no executive mandate at Microsoft for teams to go through SFE training. Every team engagement was driven at the grassroots level, and teams sought SFE training based on word-of-mouth reports. Leaders made an informed decision for their team, when and if the timing was right, which was often at the start of a major release cycle. Sometimes the engagement was scoped to an individual team, but it often involved an entire division of several hundred or several thousand people.

It's helpful to know a bit about how we run the workshop. Most importantly, the workshop is a team event, and the involvement of management is required before, during, and after the workshop. A single instance of the workshop is made up of four mandatory sessions:

- **Senior leader day**   This is an all-day session with the highest-level leaders of a team (vice presidents, general managers, development managers, and so on). This session typically involves 10–35 people. We present the content of the workshop and discuss implications for the leaders' organization. We also describe any customization of the workshop that's desired. At the end of this session, a decision is made whether to pursue training for the larger team or division.

- **Preworkshop meeting for group managers** In separate one-hour meetings, we preview the workshop for the three to five group-level managers on each individual engineering team. This session is required for each team. We discuss the expectations of the management team and the logistics for the daylong workshop. We've learned that even for very large organizations, it is crucial to get buy-in from managers for each engineering team separately.

- **The workshop itself** In a full-day, hands-on workshop, all members of each engineering team (and often key partners) are required to participate, including group managers, developers, testers, program managers, user-experience professionals, product planners, etc. We optimize the room, furniture layout, and training curriculum for a class size that accommodates a full engineering team of up to 120 people. By training together in the same room, team members can look around to see that the entire team is present and that leaders are fully engaged. When the energy and buzz of the room escalates and a promising change or action item for the team is discussed, the seeds for consensus are planted in real time.

- **Postworkshop meeting for group managers** We meet with each set of group managers a second time for two to three hours. We analyze and discuss feedback generated by their team during the team workshop. This "crowd-sourced" feedback gives the managers insights into which ideas are most relevant for their team, helping them settle on an initial set of techniques to adopt and put a plan in motion.

The hands-on exercises and content of the workshop are customized for each team's specific target customers, development practices, and market situation. Throughout this book, we introduce some of these exercises, with the intent to give you a sense of both the personal experience and the team dynamics that take place. You'll gain value from doing some of the exercises on your own, and others can serve as interesting thought experiments.

We have delivered the SFE workshop to hundreds of teams and worked alongside many of them as they put SFE concepts into practice. We've learned a lot, fine-tuned ideas that work, and abandoned those that don't. We've discovered many gotchas and pitfalls, and we've had the opportunity to observe and participate in large-scale change in teams of all shapes and sizes. Some teams we worked with made huge strides with the ideas in this book, and we'll share some of their stories and successes. However, we've also been humbled to see that some teams were not able to make the shift to adopt many of the ideas in this book, despite (in most cases) valiant efforts. The places they stumbled are noteworthy, provide important lessons, and are a reminder to future teams to take the change process seriously.

The workshop, however, is just the beginning of the journey. It serves as a catalyst to get the whole team on the same page, working with a common vocabulary and aligned to similar aspirations. The real work begins the day after the workshop, when the team must start to put these ideas into practice by adjusting tools, schedules, and roles and building new habits. Although the ideas in this book are straightforward, for most software engineering teams, they represent significant changes to day-to-day work habits and practices, as well as team culture, values, and habits. The change process is significant, and we'll discuss aspects throughout the book and in detail in Part III.

What will you get out of this book?

This book is about discovering how to put customers at the center of your engineering efforts. It describes effective and efficient ways to iterate and explore so that you can deliver solutions that customers will find deeply delightful, and deliver them as quickly and efficiently as possible. It's our hope and intent that this book will inspire you to reach out and connect with your customers in a richer way than you ever have before.

We also strive to arm you with enough data, tools, examples, tips, and gotchas that you have the confidence to take action and will be motivated to try out some of these ideas in your current project; in short, after reading this book, you will know just enough to be dangerous. We include references to our favorite books on each topic at the end of this book so that you can dig deeper into the techniques you choose to invest in. We expect that you will need to reach out to experts or to leverage some of the references we list to put these practices to full use. This book will help you figure out the menu of what's available and help you make informed choices about the most appropriate techniques for your individual situation. Finally, we hope that many of you are energized by this book and begin an effort on your team to put customers at the center of your work.

A special note to the user-experience community

Thanks for checking out this book. While you already know that it is not targeted directly at you, there is tremendous value in bridging the gap between what you know how to do and what engineers know how to do, and that is what we are aiming to do. As the saying goes, "It takes two to tango." We are trying to get the dance started.

Over the years, we've noticed that user experience (UX) designers and researchers have a few fairly predictable reactions to the idea of presenting a detailed workshop about customer focus, iteration, and design practices to engineers. We've spoken to other authors who have written books on the design process and have been fascinated to discover they have had the same experience with the UX community. Those reactions are worth a bit of discussion here so that you can bypass the anxiety and get directly to the value. Here are the three gut responses we tend to hear from UX professionals:

We learned all this early on in design school. These are the basics. This isn't even the meat of design work. It's not worth my time; there is nothing here for me to learn.

Hey, wait a minute! You can't just boil down these complicated and sophisticated concepts and skills and wrap them in warm fuzzies about collaboration and expect amateurs to get the same great design results I've produced for years! Sure, readers will learn some principles and buzzwords, but I don't want software engineers thinking they really know this stuff. And you know these engineers: when they learn a little, they think they know everything. I don't want to have to clean up more mess. I won't admit this publicly, but when it comes to budget crunch time, this will make me worried that the pointy-haired managers will see me as redundant!

We're BFFs at last! Is it possible that by learning more about the importance of the design process, engineers will finally see the value I can bring to the team? If I can be seen as a champion for a customer-centric effort using terminology and processes the team understands, maybe they'll stop throwing decorative UI projects over the fence and will actually engage with me from the product's conception through delivery.

We get it. We understand. We can say with some confidence that if you went to school for interaction design or user research, most of the principles and techniques described here will be well known to you. (To software developers: think about it as giving an "Introduction to Data Structures" class to someone who's never studied computer science.) And we know that we cannot represent the full scope of the research and design professions in a few chapters aimed at people who are trained in different skills.

However, our experience is that if an engineering team embraces the ideas in this book, several outcomes are likely. First, the demand for your skills and experience will increase, not decrease. The engineers will now understand the breadth of your experience and will understand that it's not quite as easy as it looks, and you will become very, very popular. Second, you will spend less time fighting for the right things to happen, as the entire team will be aligned on the customer's needs from the beginning. Third, if it does not exist already, the team will demand that you create and fill a reliable customer feedback pipeline. And finally, you will have more time to go deep on detailed research and design work. Other people on the engineering team will now be able to effectively contribute the basic elements that frequently spread your time too thin. You will be able to build on those elements and proceed with a newfound confidence, finally having the opportunity to use your true expertise. The really cool part is that once you make that shift, everyone on the team will have a shared vocabulary. Everyone is sitting at the same table, speaking the same language, able to work together more effectively than ever to create products that will delight your customers.

Organization of this book

This book is divided into three sections. Part I, "Overview," delves into the reasons why customer delight and end-to-end experiences are so important and introduces the Fast Feedback Cycle, which powers the Scenario-Focused Engineering approach. Part II, "The Fast Feedback Cycle," details each stage in the cycle, describing the principles and key considerations for each stage as well as techniques to choose from. In several "Deep dive" sections, we offer details about our favorite, most broadly useful techniques. Part III, "The day after," discusses insights we've gained from watching many teams adopt the practices of Scenario-Focused Engineering. The insights involve project management implications and the realities of shifting team culture.

This book also includes appendixes that provide resources and references. Appendix A presents the "SFE capability roadmap," a checklist teams can use to gauge their level of sophistication in 10 core capability areas. Appendix B provides a one-page diagram of the Fast Feedback Cycle along with the most essential ideas for each stage. It makes a great poster. Appendix C, "Further reading," provides a list of books and resources for further exploration. Appendix D offers two case studies of teams that used the SFE approach. Appendix E, "Desirability Toolkit," is a reference list of the words used in the Desirability Toolkit technique presented in Chapter 9.

How to read this book

This is a pretty long book, with a lot of varied content. Some sections read like hard-to-put-down stories, perhaps something you'd enjoy reading on an airplane. Other sections present encyclopedia-style descriptions of tools and techniques that are perfect as a reference guide. Still other sections give in-depth instruction on a specific technique that you could apply in your work.

While we certainly welcome you to read this book cover to cover, we know that different people have different needs from a book such as this one. We've organized the book so that it works for several different kinds of readers and situations. Here are a few suggestions for ways you might experience the content of this book:

- **The toe in the water**   You've always been interested in innovation, technology, creativity, and building products that customers' love. You suspect that you can do some things in your own work that would make a big difference. But you are super busy, don't have a lot of time to read, and certainly don't want to take on the task of plowing through a long, detailed reference. You'd love to take a couple of hours and learn some new things and perhaps feel energized to bring up a couple of new ideas at work.

  Read Chapters 1 through 3. These are fun, easy chapters and stand alone quite well. You'll get a great introduction to the ideas behind SFE—why it's important and what is involved—and come away with some good anecdotes to share at the water cooler.

- **The deeper read**   You are about to get on a coast-to-coast flight, and you're looking at the bestsellers in the airport bookstore. You're looking for something that will be an engaging read, that has the potential to add a lot of value to your work when you return. Wondering if this book might be helpful, you flip through a few pages and find yourself saying, "So true, so true. Oh, my gosh, that's my team," and your curiosity is piqued.

  Read Chapters 1-3 and the first half of each chapter in Part II, skipping the tools and techniques sections. Reading these portions of the book will give you a solid overview of SFE and the Fast Feedback Cycle, including the standout mindshifts and behaviors. If you have more time, take a look at Part III and Appendix A to crystallize your thoughts around the current state of your team, a few things you might like to try, and how you might go about doing so.

- **The student** You're in the middle of a university program, working toward a degree in computer science. You're taking a hot new class that claims to bridge the gap between the business, computer science, and design schools and this is the textbook.

  Focus your reading on Part II, Chapters 4-10, which describes the Fast Feedback Cycle and the techniques in detail. Parts I and III and the appendixes provide some real-world context, but the meat of the book is in Part II and includes all the how-to information and the specific techniques you'll draw from. We hope you have fun and that your class project yields a bazillion-dollar idea. Go forth and delight!

- **The change agent** You are already a fan of SFE and the Fast Feedback Cycle. Maybe you've taken a class, have used these ideas on a previous team, or have read through Part I and gotten inspired. Now you want to help your team gain proficiency in some of these practices.

  Start by reading Part III (Chapters 11 and 12) to get some perspective on how best to introduce a new practice to your team. Then, pick a chapter in Part II that covers an approach that you think will add the most immediate value to your team. Focus your team on trying out a few of the different tools and techniques presented in that chapter and gain some experience in that area. After some early success, you and a few of your cohorts might dig into the SFE capability roadmap in Appendix A to assess where you are and to figure out what areas you might work on next.

Contact us

SFE has grown beyond Microsoft. There is a large and growing community of SFE practitioners worldwide. Join in the conversation. We love to hear from readers. Please tell us how these ideas are working for you and what new techniques you've developed so that we can all continue to learn and iterate: http://www.scenariofocusedengineering.com.

Acknowledgments

Although this book was largely written by two people, it is the reflection of the hard work, passion, and dedication of hundreds of people—the Scenario-Focused Engineering community, whose members spent countless hours teaching, iterating, coaching, and practicing these techniques with their teams throughout the past six years.

First and foremost, we'd like to thank our families.

Austina: To Erik, Maja, and Viktor, thank you for your infinite patience, allowing me to sit in my chair and write—for what seemed like ages, and long into the wee hours. An enormous thank you to my parents, who lived with us this past year and helped so much with keeping the household running, feeding all of us, and delivering the kids wherever they needed to be. Thank you all for being there and for believing in me and in this crazy project.

Drew: To Kristy, Kylie, and Derek. I am so lucky to have each of you in my life. You have been my inspiration and my muse. Thank you for understanding when I didn't have time to cook a proper dinner (although I have learned how much you do like the frozen Chinese food from TJ's), was late picking you up from school, and why I was occasionally grumpy and tired after a long day of very deep thinking. But most, thank you for being you and for sharing your lives with me. I love you all dearly.

A handful of people have been instrumental in helping us write this book. Without them, this book would never have been finished. Thank you to Kent Sullivan for being our resident UX research guru and for providing data, countless interviews, and tireless reviews and for essentially ghost writing Chapter 5 and Chapter 9. Thank you to Norman Furlong, who was our official sidebar wrangler and who kept our spirits high. Many thanks to William Parkhurst, who provided inspiration and motivation, gave valuable feedback every step of the way, and, when we needed it the most, provided surfing lessons. Finally, thanks to Jeanine Spence, who did the lion's share of the work to conceive, build, and test the SFE capability roadmap (see Appendix A) and who synthesized data from more than 60 experts across Microsoft and the industry.

We'd like to offer a special note of gratitude to Dr. Indrė Viskontas, our resident neuroscientist and opera star. When we first approached Indrė, we had one topic in mind that we wanted her thoughts on. That initial idea quickly grew to a long list of topics, as it became clear how much overlap there was between our work and the available science to support it. We are deeply grateful to Indrė for her insights and contributions to this book.

In all, the book contains roughly 40 "SFE in action" sidebars. Thank you to everyone who contributed sidebars or provided their expert advice. Sadly, because of space constraints, we were not able to print all the sidebars that were contributed, but we are deeply thankful to all the people who took the time to suggest sidebars and other content proposals.

Many people offered their time and patience to help us test the concepts in this book and to review the text as it was drafted, rewritten, fine-tuned, edited, rewritten again, and finally sent to production. A special thank you for going above and beyond goes to Paula Bach, Bill Chiles, Steven Clark, Terrell Cox, David Deer, Bernie Duerr, David Duffy, Paul Elrif, Serguei Endrikhovski, Valentina Grigoreanu, Kevin Honeyman, Karl Melder, Susan Mings, Damien Newman, Bruce Nussbaum, William Parkhurst, Victor Robinson, Prashant Sridharan, Bill Storage, Mike Toot, Sam Zaiss, the entire SFE team, and the many other SFE champions within Microsoft.

Throughout the book, we talk about design as a team sport. The team that developed, taught, iterated, and coached SFE is no exception. We are ever grateful and humbled to have had the opportunity to work with the strong group of passionate engineers who made up the SFE team over the years:

- **SFE instructors and core team** Jeanine Spence, the synthesizer-conceptualizer extraordinaire; Kent Sullivan, our ultra-collaborator; Margie Clinton, who still holds the record for teaching the most classes; Ken Zick and Norman Furlong, who made the toolbox repository happen; Alex Blanton, who brought us "The Delighted Customer" blog; Ed Essey, who folded in Agile concepts and crucial platform team examples; Seth Eliot, who taught us about experimentation; Phillip Hunter, who taught us the nuances of the meaning of "delight"; and

Court Crawford, who was such a passionate champ that he joined the team. The early teaching team included Bill Begorre, Bill Hanlon, Richard Kleese, Marina Polishchuk, Alec Ramsey, and Surya Vanka. The international teaching team included Alex Cobb, Sven Hallauer, Antonio Palacios, Lior Moshaiov, and Jayashree Venkataraman. The early PM team was John Pennock, Li Lu-Porter, and Van Van. The founding team included Keith Bentley, Margie Clinton, and Michael Corning.

- **Instructional design team**   Robert Deupree, Fredrika Sprengle, and Brian Turner.

- **Operations team**   Robyn Brown, Joetta Bell, Kim Hargraves, Cristina Knecht, and LouAn Williams.

Thanks to Wendy Tapper for helping to get SFE off the ground by designing the "green card" in her spare time; our calling card has truly stood the test of time. Thanks also to Peter Moon, who saw the value in SFE early on and customized and adapted the SFE workshop for delivery to several thousand engineers in the IT departments at Microsoft. Gratitude also goes to Karl Haberl, Martin Plourde, and Brian Pulliam, who taught us how to measure and scorecard SFE's impact. Special thanks to Alec Ramsey for conceptualizing the first versions of the Fast Feedback Cycle model, which became the backbone of Scenario-Focused Engineering. Thanks also to Dean O'Neill, who taught us the value of good tooling and independently spearheaded the Microsoft Process Template in Team Foundation Server, which enabled SFE work-item tracking for many teams. We'd also like to thank a handful of expert Agile practitioners who helped us over the years: Bill Begorre, Arlo Belshee, Ed Essey, Sam Guckenheimer, Bill Hanlon, and Scot Kelly.

As we were developing the SFE program, Irada Sadykova and Eric Brechner were the leaders who created the space and budget in which we could operate. They battled for our cause in the metaphorical executive washrooms when SFE's success, popularity, and value were not immediately obvious to those who needed to care. Were it not for their hard work, we would never have gotten this project off the ground. More recently, thanks to Peter Loforte and Debbie Thiel for continuing to support SFE and especially for enabling the conditions to allow this book to be written. Thank you also to all our colleagues in Engineering Excellence for their support along the way. A special thank you goes to Surya Vanka, who represented SFE to the UX leadership community, served as our design guru, and helped recruit incredible talent to the SFE team.

Our first champion at Microsoft was Matt Kotler, who was instrumental in bringing the SFE workshop and ideas to the entire Microsoft Office team. Thank you, Matt, for being the first to believe and the first to champion SFE throughout such a large organization. Similarly, Ian Todd had a huge impact in making these ideas take root in Windows Phone. Susan Mings and Dean O'Neill had a similar impact in Windows Server, as did Lisa Mueller in Dynamics and Tracey Trewin in the Developer Division.

Throughout the years, a large and thriving community of SFE champions and change agents has developed, and each of them deserves big kudos for their work, passion, and perseverance: Bia Ambrosa, Gabe Aul, Paula Bach, Cyrus Balsara, Don Barnett, Richard Barnwell, Dan Barritt, Tom Baxter, Derrick Bazlen, Laura Bergstrom, Brijesh Bhatia, Safiya Bhojawala, Jeff Braaten, Tim Briggs, Adam Bronsther, Graham Bury, Jeremy Bye, John Cable, Ben Canning, Greg Chapman, Alison Clark,

Steven Clarke, Ken Coleman, Jeff Comstock, Matthew Cosner, Robin Counts, Clint Covington, Arne de Booij, Lance Delano, Shikha Desai, Tammy Dietz, Serguei Endrikhovski, Umer Farooq, Rob Farrow, Tricia Fejfar, James Fiduccia, Joseph Figueroa, Ned Friend, Bob Fries, Jim Fullmer, Jean Gabarra, Tyler Gibson, Stephen Giff, Valentina Grigoreanu, Carol Grojean, Sam Guckenheimer, Joe Hallock, Mark Hansen, Ed Harris, Geoff Harris, Steve Herbst, Steve Hoberecht, Kevin Honeyman, Christy Hughes Harder, Jeremy Jobling, Joe Kennebec, Alma Kharrat, Ruth Kikin-Gil, J. T. Kimbell, Bernhard Kohlmeier, Miki Konno, Kevin Lane, Sue Larson, Mikal Lewis, John Licata, Jane Liles, Ulzi Lobo, Derek Luhn, Craig Maitlen, Steve May, Michael McCormack, Ford McKinstry, Soni Meinke, Karl Melder, Trish Miner, Becky Morley, Cathy Moya, Lisa Mueller, Joe Munko, Mark Mydland, Dean O'Neill, Susan Palmer, Sheri Panabaker, Sachin Panvalkar, Milan Patel, Mike Pell, Ken Perilman, Nancy Perry, Mike Pietraszak, Barton Place, Chandra Prasad, Ed Price, TJ Rhoades, Lawrence Ripsher, Ramon Romero, Dona Sarkar, Joel Schaeffer, Ravi Shanker, Wenqi Shen, Jasdeep Singha, Shilpi Sinha, Cameron Skinner, Bill Stauber, Derik Stenerson, Christina Storm, Philip Su, Deannah Templeton, Mike Tholfsen, Robin Troy, Jonathan V. Smith, Kimberly Walters, Kim Wilton, Sam Zaiss, Brant Zwiefel, and so many more.

Thank you to all of the teams across Microsoft that put their trust in us to show them some new tricks. Special thanks to the entire Office team for living through our first big iterations of the workshop. It was a pretty rocky road in some regards, but we and your leaders learned a lot, SFE is now better for it, and Office has forged a great path forward. Thank you to the Dynamics team, which was the first large organization to figure out how to integrate SFE practices in an Agile environment at scale—and to demonstrate unquestionable business results from their investment. Thank you to Windows Phone for doubling down on SFE several times over the years and leading the way on the importance of brand, and to Windows Server for going the distance in building tools and infrastructure to support SFE. These and many other teams were the reason we continued investing in this work.

At Microsoft, senior leaders of user experience teams gather monthly as the User Experience Leadership Team (UXLT). That team provided valuable support, resources, encouragement, and course corrections throughout our journey. Thank you UXLT! We'd like to specifically call out appreciation to Lisa Anderson, Tom Bouchard, Andy Cargile, Terrell Cox, Monty Hammontree, Steve Kaneko, Laura Kern, Kent Lowry, Kartik Mithal, and Jakob Nielsen for their sponsorship.

One of the most rewarding aspects of driving the SFE initiative at Microsoft was that we developed close relationships with many senior leaders who provided mentorship for us as they brought SFE to their organizations. Thank you all so much for the invaluable contributions you've made to SFE and to both of us—Stuart Ashmun, Joe Belfiore, Erin Chapple, Andy Erlandson, Chuck Friedman, PJ Hough, Hal Howard, Bill Laing, Chris Pratley, Tara Roth, Zig Serafin, and Jeffrey Snover.

Finally, thank you to our developmental editor, Devon Musgrave, and to John Pierce and Rob Nance for their editorial and production work. We appreciate the patience they showed dealing with all of our funky, late, and ongoing requests. Thank you all for helping us make our dream happen!

Errata, updates, & book support

Microsoft Press has made every effort to ensure the accuracy of this book. If you discover an error, please submit it to us via mspinput@microsoft.com. You can also reach the Microsoft Press Book Support team for other support via the same alias. Please note that product support for Microsoft software and hardware is not offered through this address. For help with Microsoft software or hardware, go to *http://support.microsoft.com*.

Free ebooks from Microsoft Press

From technical overviews to in-depth information on special topics, the free ebooks from Microsoft Press cover a wide range of topics. These ebooks are available in PDF, EPUB, and Mobi for Kindle formats, ready for you to download at:

http://aka.ms/mspressfree

Check back often to see what is new!

We want to hear from you

At Microsoft Press, your satisfaction is our top priority, and your feedback our most valuable asset. Please tell us what you think of this book at:

http://aka.ms/tellpress

We know you're busy, so we've kept it short with just a few questions. Your answers go directly to the editors at Microsoft Press. (No personal information will be requested.) Thanks in advance for your input!

And let's keep the conversation going! We're on Twitter: *http://twitter.com/MicrosoftPress*

WHAT PRODUCT DO YOU RECOMMEND TO OTHERS? **Do customers love it?**

Resonates deeply with me   Is it easy to use?   useful

Emotions matter   # DELIGHT   IT'S MAGIC!

IT NEVER FAILS ME

simple   Deep desirability,   **IS IT SOLVING A REAL CUSTOMER NEED?**
           not just great aesthetics   usable   Zero hassle

What would YOUR customers say,   **easy**   CUSTOMERS ARE NOT WILLING
in their own words?   Always knows what I want   TO SETTLE FOR MEDIOCRITY

HELPS ME DO THINGS THAT   IT JUST WORKS
I DIDN'T KNOW WERE POSSIBLE   **desirable**

Functionality is not enough   Suits me perfectly
It makes me smile

CHAPTER 1

Why delight matters

Why does delight matter? For many human reasons, of course: the need for joy, as an antidote for loneliness or boredom, as a prompt for action or contemplation. And for software engineers, delight is also at play in their relationship with their customers. This chapter makes the case that satisfying customers with a solid, useful, usable product is no longer good enough. To compete effectively in today's marketplace, you have to take your work to the next level and delight your customers on an emotional level.

A car story

On my drive to work today, I looked in the rearview mirror and saw a smile on my face. Just a hint of a smile; it reminded me a bit of the Mona Lisa. You know the look: a little bit coy, implying that "I know something you don't know."

I realized that I was smiling simply because I was enjoying the experience of driving to work in a new car. Don't get me wrong—this wasn't a life-transforming experience, but I was really enjoying my commute, which is a little strange, isn't it? And quite honestly, I knew that when I got to work that little smile was going to evolve into a boasting session at the coffee machine. The first few colleagues I ran into were going to hear about how much I love that new car:

> "I bought a new car last week. I just love it. It's awesome. You know, I traded in my sports car to get this—did I tell you that already?"

> "No way—you got rid of that?! That was a sweet car. What possessed you?"

> "I know, it's crazy. But this new car is so awesome. I'm really happy I made the trade."

I wanted to share my joy with others. I wanted to tell people about this great car I had discovered because I thought they might like it, too. But why? What was it about that car that made me love it so much? What made it call to me as I passed by it in my garage? Why did I feel compelled to tell others about it?

The car has a set of features that are on par with most other cars in the same price range and category. It has satellite radio, automatic this 'n' that, and a sunroof, but so do lots of cars. It's not the features. I've purchased cars and other products with lots of features before, but those products don't necessarily end up being the ones that I love. It's got to be more than just the feature list.

So what is it that makes this particular car so endearing to me?

More data about me

Here's the story of what was going on in my life at the time. Maybe it will give some insight into why this car is so special to me.

Recently, I traveled to Europe with my children for our summer vacation. In lieu of the fantastic rail system, we chose to rent a car and drive around France, Germany, and Austria. The car I rented was quite small, at least by American standards. It maneuvered well along the narrow cobblestone streets, but it also held its own on the autobahn. It was extremely fuel-efficient. And as with one of those cartoon clown cars, somehow we were able to fit all our luggage in the trunk of this little car, with plenty of room in the passenger area. It defied physics, I don't know how.

So I learned to love this little car as we traveled throughout Europe. It was the perfect travel experience for our family. Toward the end of the trip I started doing some research to see whether I could purchase one back in the US. You see, back home I had been questioning my personal car strategy. I very much wanted to find a car (or cars) that would meet all of my needs. Every solution I drew up, every combination of cars I could imagine, forced compromises on me that I wasn't willing to make.

My criteria

When I returned home, I spent a remarkable amount of time on the Internet continuing my research about cars. I thought it would be easy, but the right car solution proved to be elusive. I decided to do some deep thinking and put together a list of my criteria. Surely, once I did that, the answer would become apparent.

I have two teenage children. Often, I need to cart them around, plus their friends and all their gear. My hobbies and passions often take me into the local mountains, which are quite rugged. Plus, I needed something fun—wind in the hair, midlife crisis kind of fun. I had a strong "I'll know it when I see it" feeling about the car, but I had a very difficult time communicating exactly what that was.

My current car setup included a convertible sports car (two-seater) and a large American four-wheel-drive truck. But this arrangement wasn't satisfying my needs. Both the kids can't fit in the sports car. The truck is a big gas-guzzler that can't fit into parking spots in the city and is just too expensive to use for commuting and soccer-mom duty. Morally, I'm opposed to owning three cars. Here's what my criteria looked like.

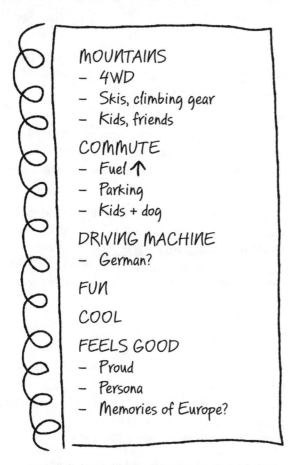

I was delighted with that little car in Europe. Between that and my truck, I knew all my needs would be met. But I quickly discovered that the car we had in Europe isn't sold in the US. And I couldn't find an equivalent.

This is a lot of detail, but I want to communicate how much having the wrong set of cars in my garage was bugging me. I had a taste of a great experience in Europe, but that solution wasn't available. Nothing available met my criteria. I was frustrated, and every time I got into one of my cars, I was reminded of my frustration.

The experience

Finally, I found my car.[1] I discovered a small, German-engineered hatchback. It could fit five people comfortably along with a bunch of gear. Its turbo-diesel engine gets up to 50 miles per gallon on the highway. The combination of this car, along with my truck, meets all of my criteria.

But this doesn't explain why I have an emotional connection with this car. Look at the words I listed on the bottom of my notes: fun, cool, feels good, proud, persona. Those words describe the experience I get when I drive this car. It's not all the features (50 MPG, room for my kids). And while the experience I had at the dealership was indeed a good one, it played a minor role (this time anyway) in my overall delight with this car.

You see, it's not just the car. It's all the stuff the car does that suits me perfectly. I feel as though whoever built that machine knew me, that they figured out what I needed and put it all together in a way that resonates deeply within me. And it's that positive end-to-end experience I continue to have—from discovering the car, to an easy and friendly purchase experience, to driving it off the lot, to getting my first free car wash (yeah, the car came with free car washes—for life!). No wonder I tell people about this experience—it's been awesome.

What do you recommend?

So the big question is . . . what about you? What is your "I have to tell you about this great car I found" story? Have you ever discovered yourself sounding like an unpaid sales rep for some product or service? I'm sure you have. Think about it. What was the last product you recommended to a friend just because you loved it so much and you wanted to tell someone about it?

When we teach our Scenario-Focused Engineering workshops, we start by asking people this very question:

> *What product or service do you love so much that you would unabashedly recommend it to your friends and colleagues? Discuss with your table group.*

The "What Product Do You Recommend to Others" exercise has been fascinating in several regards. First, it's typical that once the conversations begin, the room becomes quite noisy. It may take a few minutes for the ruckus to start, as some engineers are a bit introverted and not prone to spilling their emotional guts. But once a few people start talking about their favorite products, others start talking about theirs. People become excited and start speaking louder because they want to be heard and they really want to tell their stories about what they've discovered, what they love, and why. You would be amazed at how animated and boisterous these conversations become.

The level of engagement in this conversation is noteworthy, but it's also fascinating to see the lists of products these teams come up with. Here's a list of products that a class came up with during a recent recommendation exercise. At the time the list was created, these products and services resonated so well with the workshop participants that they were mentioned not just in the small discussion groups, but people felt compelled to brag about them to the whole room.

What would you recommend?

Fitbit

Pinterest

SousVide Supreme

iPad

Nordstrom

TED Talks

Spotify

BMW

Virgin Airlines

Waze

Minecraft

Uber

Khan Academy

Honda Lawnmowers

Evernote

The world moves quickly, so by the time this book is published, we're sure the list would be different. Your personal list will contain different products as well, of course. So think about it. Spend just a couple of minutes and think about what products or services you would recommend to a friend.

The common thread

Even though we know the products on this list change over time, the interesting question to explore next is "What are the qualities that these products or services all have in common?"

We ask this question as an exercise early on in the workshop, and it's not an easy question to answer. The list that any given class creates usually covers a wide variety of consumer products, automobiles, devices, and services as well as productivity applications, developer tools, and even favorite vacation spots. The common factor on these lists is not the market or demographic, nor is it the price point or set of features. What is it then that links these seemingly disparate items?

Here are the phrases that come up when participants describe these products:

What do the things you recommend have in common?

It just works	It does what I need it to, when I need it
Easy	I get the job done quicker
It's a good value	It makes me smile
It's cool	It's perfect for what I need
It never fails me	Always knows what I want
It's magic	It's there when I need it
Simple	No hassle, smooth
Powerful	Helps me do things that I didn't know were possible

The set of answers does not change every six months. It is remarkably consistent. Despite the fact that the list of recommendations changes over time, the characteristics of those products and services are fairly static.

Talking about cool things you love can be a lot of fun. Next time you're in an appropriate social situation, go ahead and start the conversation. Ask people what products and services they're using today that they love. Think hard about the qualities of those products and ask yourself why do people mention those and not others?

The reality check

The final questions we ask in this exercise involve a reality check: What do your customers say about the products and services you provide? What would they say, in their own words? We ask the class to think about these questions as well. The next illustration shows some common answers.

What would your customers say about YOUR product/service?

It's complicated

I don't have a choice, I have to use it for my work

It's powerful

Hard to use

It can import a lot of data formats, which is handy

It took a long time to learn

It's slow

It works, but it's not natural

It's glitchy. It crashes at just the wrong moments

It's tricky to install/administer

It doesn't integrate with the other software we use

I like the competitor's service better

It looks old

I like the automatic chart creation feature

Of course, every product has its bright spots. If it didn't, chances are that the team or company that produced it wouldn't be around anymore to talk about it. But when asked, most teams realize that their products and services are not eliciting the strong, positive emotional connection they strive for. They are not truly delighting their customers. And though this realization usually isn't a complete surprise to most engineering teams, most teams have a tough time figuring out how to go about solving that problem. Setting a goal or directive to "go build something that will delight our customers" does not lend itself to an actionable list of problems to solve.

While reading this book, if you ever need some motivation to do a better job for your customers, consider what your customers would say about your current offering, and challenge yourself to see whether you can do better. Can you build something your customers will truly love, so much so that they would go out of their way to recommend it to a friend?

Useful, usable, and desirable

The computer industry has matured quite a bit over the past few decades, and these days customers are demanding an ever-higher degree of sophistication, personalization, and polish. Customers are much more savvy and have had a taste of what truly outstanding solutions look like. Customers today are generally not willing to settle for mediocrity.

Useful

However, it wasn't always this way. At the beginning of the personal computing era, it was enough for new products simply to be useful—to solve a problem in a way that had never been done before. This was the era of the Commodore 64, the IBM Personal Computer, MS-DOS, VisiCalc, and the like. I have fond memories of manually typing in programs, line by line, from the back of *Games* magazine—and the all-important checksum in the right-hand column to prevent those insidious typos. Who were the predominant customers then? Like me, they were mostly computer geeks themselves, or geek wannabes—technology-savvy early adopters willing to put up with a sometimes steep learning curve and motivated to get the most out of this new technology, whether for work or play.

Consider this analogy: a traditional scale in a doctor's office is a useful and highly accurate tool, but you have to know how to work it—where to move the weights, how to read the result. In this case, the utility provided is well worth the training burden because the same person uses the scale over and over every day. But most average people aren't quite sure exactly how to work it—they could figure it out, but it isn't completely obvious.

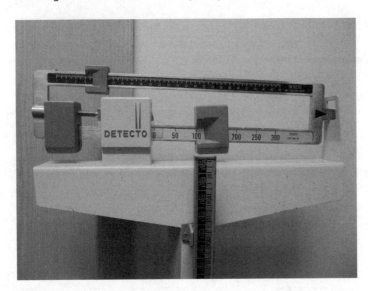

Usable

Then, in the mid-1990s, the computing market had a significant transformation. Windows 95 and Office 95 were released with new graphical user interfaces, Apple was gaining ground with the Power Mac, and the Internet was quickly becoming mainstream. Around this time it became important for products to be not just useful but usable, and most software companies began investing in usability testing to optimize their products for ease of use, efficiency, and especially discoverability for first-time usage situations. Technology had become simple and accessible enough to open up two major new customer bases: home users, who started buying personal computers for the living room, and the newly minted "knowledge workers," who started using productivity software—WYSIWYG[2] word processors such as Microsoft Word and spreadsheets such as Lotus 1-2-3.

Go back to our scale analogy: What would a more usable scale look like? Chances are you have one in your bathroom right now. This scale is dead simple to operate—just step on the scale and look down to read the number. No instruction booklet is needed.

Desirable

Over the past decade, we've seen the market change yet again. With the advent of mobile devices, tablet computers, connected gaming consoles, and ultraportable (and ultra-affordable) laptops, the customer base has broadened to include the far right end of the adoption curve, pulling in the vast majority of late adopters. As of 2011, fully 91 percent of American adults owned a computer, cell phone, MP3 player, game console, or tablet, and the majority of those who didn't own any of these devices are over the age of 66.[3]

While average customers are now less savvy about the inner workings of their computer, they are absolutely addicted to modern technology. With groundbreaking products now firmly established in people's minds, such as Apple's iPhone, Microsoft's Kinect, Facebook, Salesforce.com, and Ruby on Rails, customers in all demographics have gotten a good taste of what truly outstanding solutions look like, and they don't want to go back. These days, customers not only expect drop-dead simplicity, they also expect deep personalization—for solutions to magically anticipate their needs, and for their technology to follow them wherever they go. In short, they expect a smooth, seamless end-to-end experience.

Also relevant is the trend toward the consumerization of IT. IT departments are now bending once-sacred deployment and security rules because employees say they can't live without certain consumer products at the workplace, including iPhones, iPads, or Galaxy tablets. The pull of desirable computing solutions that is already highly visible in consumer behavior is now reaching work-oriented markets as well. Providing compelling end-to-end experiences is rapidly overtaking every corner of the market: consumer, developer, enterprise, and small business.

As we've already mentioned, truly outstanding solutions have some things in common. Great products go far beyond simplistic first-time usability. They stitch together functionality into end-to-end experiences that deeply resonate with customers. Tasks that used to require multiple applications and manual steps can now be performed in a simple, coordinated one-stop shop: sharing photos with friends on Facebook, fully integrated team-based development environments, collaborating on documents in the cloud with seamless access anywhere. The overall quality of offerings is better, with consistent reliability, availability, and polish. These great products feel as though they have a soul—a real purpose, mission, and personality—not just an impersonal collection of computational tools. When you have all these ingredients, the best of the best have an emergent quality—they evoke an emotional response from their users, just as I showed in the car story.

To stand out in today's market, products need to be genuinely desirable. However desirability isn't necessarily about flashy graphics or polished surfaces. We're talking about deep desirability, a quality that makes a product so good, so perfect, so "just right for me" that it evokes an emotional connection. Great aesthetics can certainly help, but the core of the solution is its desirability.

A desirable scale?

So getting back to our scale example, what would a deeply desirable scale look like? This is a bit tougher to answer. You see, the question you really need to ask is "Why do you want a scale in the first place?" Is it because you actually want to know the number: How much you weigh? Or is it because you are hoping that the number will change? Why do you want the number to change? Are you going on vacation soon and want to look good in a bathing suit? Have you just signed up for your first triathlon and the number is part of a fitness calibration? Just making the scale more visually beautiful won't address any of those needs. Here's another motivation, or scenario, for your use of a scale: Perhaps what you really want is a scale that lies, that tells you it's okay to eat that bacon cheeseburger? Or maybe what you really desire is something like this— the Nintendo Wii Balance Board, companion to the Nintendo Wii Fit.

Somewhat surprisingly, this was one of the best-selling console game peripherals for its time.[4] Nintendo was the first to capitalize on the fact that an awful lot of people are unhappy with their weight. Since then, the same insight has inspired the Fitbit, the Nike FuelBand, and many Microsoft Kinect titles. These companies built products that resonated with a deep-seated human vulnerability, giving customers new hope that they could finally get control of their body weight. Sure, the Nintendo Balance Board is a scale (it's actually two scales, one for each foot), and it will tell you your weight and even graph it over time. But more importantly, when combined with the Wii Fit software, it's part of an engaging exercise program that gets you up off the couch to start changing that number. The clean white color and high-quality industrial design of the Balance Board isn't why it sold so well. Rather, the end-to-end experience of the Wii Fit plus the Balance Board struck a chord—an emotional chord deep inside—about insecurity versus confidence, apathy versus motivation, weight versus beauty. It gave people hope that finally achieving the body shape they were longing for could be fun and easy. Again, deep desirability goes way beyond surface aesthetics.

Putting it together

Putting it all together, you get a pyramid (like the one shown on the next page) that rests on useful at the base, has usable as the middle tier, and desirable at the pinnacle. This useful-usable-desirable model was devised by Dr. Elizabeth Sanders in 1992,[5] and there have been many variations since. But the original terms and ideas are just as valid now as they were then.

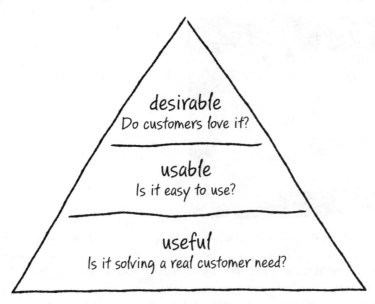

It's essential to start by solving a real customer problem. Solving a problem that no one cares about is the first, most painful mistake to make, and no amount of great usability or flashy paint jobs will save you from that.

Next, your solution needs to be usable. It needs to be easy to use, smooth, and seamless. No hassles, no hoops to jump through, ideally no need for documentation or help. It just does exactly what the customer expects at every step along the way.

Finally, your solution needs to be desirable. The customer needs to love it. What that love looks like may be different for different kinds of solutions and different types of customers, but to really hit it out of the park, you need to evoke that strong, positive emotional connection.

 MINDSHIFT

What is delight, exactly? Occasionally, the words "desirable" or "delight" or "love" provoke some controversy. When we say that products and services should delight customers, or that customers should love your solutions, what exactly do we mean? Are we saying that for absolutely everything that you build, customers need to be head over heels about it and think that it's the best thing that has ever been invented? Does there need to be an element of surprise or serendipity for it to count as delight? Should customers always have that warm, fuzzy feeling inside when they think about your solutions? No, not exactly.

While certainly you hope that some solutions will evoke those warm fuzzies in your customers, that's a much narrower definition of delight or desirability than we intend. The English language doesn't help here because there isn't an ideal word for the concept we mean. Delight and desirability come the closest, but they are imperfect.

When we say that a solution is delightful or desirable for a customer, what we mean is that it evokes some kind of nontrivial positive emotion. Sometimes that positive emotion will be a sense of satisfaction with getting a tough job done more easily than expected. Sometimes it will be relief at not looking stupid in front of an important colleague. Other times the feeling may be joy at being able to see a granddaughter's smiling face, and occasionally it may be a sense of wonder at an experience that truly seems magical. The important point is that customers have some kind of meaningful, positive emotional response about the software, not just a fleeting "That was cool" that is forgotten as quickly as it came. And this kind of deep, lasting delight simply cannot happen if you aren't first solving a real problem for a customer in a useful and usable way.

For the rest of this book, we use delight and desirability to refer to this idea, and we trust that you'll know what we mean.

The natural next questions are "How do you achieve desirability?" and "What's the formula for customer delight?"

Of course, there are some tricks and tips you can try. For instance, it's relatively easy to see how using more evocative language might make a customer smile, as in these screenshots of an empty music library on Windows Phone and Windows 8.1

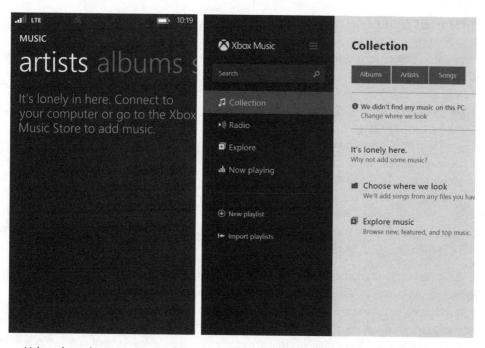

Using clever language and a friendly tone is one easy way to create a moment of surprise or serendipity. The right words can make the technology feel more human and more approachable. This is a great technique to use, but keep in mind that it produces customer delight primarily on a surface level. No one purchases a product on the basis of how welcoming the error messages are if the solution itself doesn't get the customer's job done. Similarly, beautiful aesthetics don't matter if the solution underneath is incomplete. Tone, language, and aesthetics all are good ways to polish a great offering, but they are not enough on their own.

Underneath it all, this music library is powered by OneDrive, which does have an incredibly compelling value proposition that is grounded in being genuinely useful—giving you access to all your music, videos, photos, and other files from any computer or mobile device, and even directly within Microsoft Office, is super valuable. Add to that the solid technical execution that makes the solution robust, an experience that works smoothly and seamlessly across all those different platforms, and a well-laid-out, easy-to-use interface, and you've got great usability as well. But the real delight of OneDrive is pulling these qualities together in one great package, and above all else, making sure that customers are never ever left in a lurch without access to their files, even if they don't happen to have Internet access at the moment. When you get to this point, the use of evocative language is a great finishing touch, the cherry on top of an already-delicious ice cream sundae—and the customer can't help but smile.

The next chapter discusses the most important factor you can plan for to build desirable solutions: solving an entire end-to-end problem and delivering that as a polished, high-quality, seamless experience.

Need more proof?

Think this doesn't apply to you and your business? Consider this data point from Bain & Company's research:

> Most companies assume they're consistently giving customers what they want. Usually, they're kidding themselves. When we recently surveyed 362 firms, we found that 80% believed they delivered a "superior experience" to their customers. But when we then asked customers about their own perceptions, we heard a very different story. They said that only 8% of companies were really delivering.[6]

This statistic is particularly notable when you consider that Bain also reported that "more than 95% of management teams we've surveyed claim to be customer focused." It seems that industry-wide, hearts are in the right place, but it's just not as easy as it looks to delight customers.

The good news is that your company is likely not the only one still learning. Forrester Research has been studying customer experience since 1998, and it also concludes that even today "mediocre customer experience is the norm, and that great customer experience is rare. What this means is that customer experience is a powerful differentiator for the very few companies that do it well."[7] So, there is still plenty of upside left for companies that are ready to make the investment in figuring out how to truly delight their customers.

What's even better is that Forrester has done the hard work to prove it. Every year since 2007, Forrester has conducted surveys asking customers to rate their experience with 160 top North American brands across 13 industries. From the results of those surveys, Forrester created a customer experience index for each brand. The punch line: in 2012, only 3 percent of companies they asked about were ranked "excellent" by customers, and 34 percent ranked "good." The rest of the companies ranked somewhere between "okay," "poor," and "very poor."

And lest you think those numbers are meaningless, Jon Picoult at Watermark Consulting took it to the next level to show how delivering a great customer experience correlates to financial results. Watermark used Forrester's index scores to investigate whether delivering a great customer experience could predict stock market performance. Boy, did it ever. His analysis showed that the five-year stock performance of the top 10 companies in the customer experience index for the years 2007 to 2011 had a net gain of 22.5 percent, whereas the laggards in the bottom 10 lost 46.3 percent. The S&P 500 Index dropped 1.3 percent over the same period.[8]

Harley Manning and Kerry Bodine summarize it best:

> For decades, companies have been paying lip service to the idea of delighting customers while simultaneously disappointing them. That approach won't cut it anymore. Recent market shifts have brought us into a new era, one Forrester calls the age of the customer—a time when focus on the customer matters more than any other strategic imperative.[9]

Summary

What does this mean for you? Competition is fierce, and the bar is high. To be successful in today's market you have to figure out how to achieve deep desirability within your customers. Customers now expect products to solve their problems completely and to do it in a delightful way, and this is becoming increasingly true across the industry, not just in consumer products. The goal is a product or service that customers would go out of their way to recommend to a friend.

The old technique of prioritizing a bunch of features and building as many as your schedule allows (in priority order, of course) just doesn't cut it anymore. Usability testing is still a great technique in the toolbox, mind you, but it's nowhere near sufficient on its own to compete in today's market. You need some new tools in your tool belt, and perhaps even more importantly, an adjustment in your philosophy of what software development is all about. This book will introduce you to an iterative, customer-focused approach to engineering that will dramatically increase your odds of creating products that will deeply delight your customers.

Notes

1. I am intentionally not revealing the make and model of the car. When I tell this story, people always ask what car I bought, but I find that the answer is largely irrelevant. The important part of this story is to recognize that there is an end-to-end experience and that the experience can evoke emotions (both positive and negative) in the user of a product.

2. WYSIWYG stands for "What you see is what you get."

3. Amy Gahran, "90% of Americans Own a Computerized Gadget," *CNN Tech*, February 3, 2011, http://www.cnn.com/2011/TECH/mobile/02/03/texting.photos.gahran/index.html.

4. "Nintendo Announces the Wii Balance Board Has Sold Over 32 Million Units Worldwide, Becomes a World Record," accessed August 27, 2014, http://www.qtegamers.com/2012/01/nintendo-announce-wii-balance-board-has.html.

5. Elizabeth B.-N. Sanders, "Converging Perspectives: Product Development Research for the 1990s," *Design Management Journal* 3, no. 4 (Fall 1992): 49–54, http://onlinelibrary.wiley.com/doi/10.1111/j.1948-7169.1992.tb00604.x/abstract.

6. James Allen et al. "Closing the Delivery Gap: How to Achieve True Customer-Led Growth" (Bain & Company, 2005), http://www.bain.com/bainweb/pdfs/cms/hotTopics/closingdeliverygap.pdf.

7. Harley Manning and Kerry Bodine, *Outside In: The Power of Putting Customers at the Center of Your Business* (New York: Houghton Mifflin Harcourt, 2012), 26.

8. Manning and Bodine, 204–6.

9. Manning and Bodine, 15.

Increase rigor and attention to experience

Features and functionality
are not enough

Customers want their problems solved
seamlessly and completely

CRADLE TO GRAVE

scope

EXPERIENCE

integrated

Get the details right

What job is your product actually doing? **Not a list of features**

Remember the ecosystem

Optimizing features doesn't
make an experience

Exceed customer expectations

seamless

Big picture first, **E2E** End-to-End Experiences

details later LESS IS MORE **ZOOM IN,
ZOOM OUT**

Experience of an API

GREAT END-TO-END EXPERIENCES CAN BE POLARIZING

It's fun. It's really, really fun. **Solve real-life customer problems**

CHAPTER 2

End-to-end experiences, not features

Emotional delight truly matters in getting the attention of customers in today's rapidly maturing technology market. The key to achieving a much deeper sense of connection and delight with a customer is to understand and satisfy the customer's real-world needs, which are inherently complex and multifaceted. To do that, you must focus on building end-to-end experiences, not individual features.[1]

What's wrong with features?

It's common to see a software team start a project with a list of features. To engineers, this may feel like a natural process—to approach a problem by first doing some data analysis (market, customer, competitive, and so on), and from that analysis generate a list of requirements, which is used to create a set of features that is expected to meet those requirements. The team then prioritizes those features by using some criteria (relative importance, cost to implement, risk), draws a cut line based on budget, and begins to build in priority order. That's simple enough, right?

But customers don't see the world that way. Customers have specific problems in specific contexts, and guess what, they just want their problems solved. The trouble is that technology is everywhere these days, so it is natural for a customer's real-life needs to require many pieces of technology just to get a simple task accomplished. Customers don't care whether a solution to their problem happens to cross organizational, architectural, or competitor boundaries—they just want the solution to work smoothly and seamlessly. Nor do they have patience for one-size-fits-all solutions—increasingly, customers expect products to meet them where they are and don't want to adapt their habits and reshape their mental model to match what the software happens to be able to do.

For example, let's say Ed wants to send a photo that he sees on his friend's Facebook wall to his sister in Germany who only has email. He expects that to be easily possible, in just one or two clicks, and will be frustrated if it isn't. Or consider Jeanine, who needs to book a business trip to Detroit and align her travel plans with a colleague who is also going to be in Detroit at the same time. She hopes that they can see each other's travel plans and arrange to sit next to each other on their shared flight home. Imagine how relieved and delighted she feels, having worried that the coordination might be awkward, when she learns that it was easy to arrange and is confident that it was all done correctly. Or consider Kent, who is collaborating on a research paper with three classmates, and the group needs to share their ideas, author the text, review their work with one another, and hand in a single document to their professor. A feature for emailing documents back and forth doesn't cut it anymore if what Kent really needs is a great tool set to support ongoing collaboration.

Even 10 years ago, customers didn't have the expectation that complete, ready-made solutions like these were possible. It used to be that our industry primarily built standalone products, and marketing campaigns focused on which feature list was longer. But as the shift to online services has intensified, it has both enabled and encouraged end-to-end solutions that aren't tied to just one piece of software sold in a box. With the advent of apps and services like Evernote, Dropbox, Salesforce.com, Zipcar, Nest, and countless others that continually push the boundaries of what is possible, people are expecting much more from technology. The startup market is vibrant and barriers to entry are low. If your solution doesn't support a customer's real-world, end-to-end needs, you can bet a competitor's will soon enough.

Of course, you will still build features as part of your product-development process. But you want to avoid building islands of individual features that don't interrelate with each other. To do that, you need to use your understanding of customer needs to determine which complete solutions you can build that stitch those features together to solve end-to-end problems. Individual features aren't bad; they're just too small in scope to address real-life usage scenarios. You need a bigger construct to capture the essence of your customer's situation.

 ## MINDSHIFT

Seamless experiences, not just integration. You might be tempted to think about this bigger construct as the need for integration across all parts of your system. But while you will almost definitely do some integration work, don't think of integration itself as the goal. *The goal is to create a seamless experience for the customer.* To achieve that, you will likely need to do some integration across your products, services, devices, and possibly with external partners or even competitors. But integrating with everyone and everything you can think of probably isn't the right approach.

For example, integrating your new photo-sharing service with every possible email service is a noble undertaking, but from your target customers' perspective, all they care about is the one email service they actually use. Your time may be better spent doing really tight, seamless integration with a few of the biggest email systems to cover the bulk of your target customer base.

Consider that when Nest started building a next-generation thermostat, the company explicitly chose to not interface with every kind of heating system; however, the ones they did support, they served extremely well. Then, over time, they broadened support to include more types of systems, but only if they could be sure of a high-quality end-to-end experience. The point is not integration for integration's sake, but to figure out which integration scenarios are most important for delivering a seamless, complete solution that solves your target customers' real-life needs.

Think end to end

A great way to think about building complete, seamless solutions is to think of the end-to-end experience that your solution enables. What is the customer's total experience with your solution, and how well does that experience match his or her needs and expectations?

 VOCAB

> An *end-to-end experience* is what the customer sees, feels, and does when he or she uses your product, device, or service in a real-life situation, from the very beginning to the very end.

A customer's end-to-end experience may be short and straightforward, such as a teenager reading a text message from a friend while standing in line at the grocery store, a developer writing a few lines of code to fix a bug, or an event planner sending an email to advertise a charity auction. An end-to-end experience can also have many moving parts and be quite complex, such as an event planner using a database, spreadsheets, email, online meetings, mobile phone, and word processor to organize and put on a charity auction event; or a software developer on a project team who uses bug-tracking tools, source control, API documentation, and a development environment to fix a bug, check it in, and mark it fixed. Or consider a teenager who buys a piece of music online and wants to listen to it and the rest of his music library first on his phone, later on his laptop, and again in the evening as background music in the living room as he plays his favorite Xbox game.

But what most assuredly is not an end-to-end experience is someone changing the view of his or her Word document from Draft to Print Layout. Clicking the button to buy an app in the Apple App Store is not an end-to-end experience either; the total purchase experience must include how that app is discovered, chosen, and then made available to use on the customer's devices. Individual actions like these are too small in scope to capture the essence of a customer's real-life usage situation; they are a part of a larger customer scenario.

However, these examples do illustrate that you can consider potentially multiple scopes of the same experience. You can zoom out to see the larger, end-to-end job being done, or you can zoom in to focus on a specific end-to-end task—but be careful that you don't zoom in so far that you no longer see the customer's real-life situation, context, and motivations. The important step is to align your perspective with the way the customer perceives the task at hand. If the customer sees it all as one connected job—or really wishes it could be all connected—then you should be thinking about it that way also. Zooming out to consider the larger job the customer is undertaking can help you see customer needs and identify opportunities for delight that you may not have noticed otherwise (and that your customer may not have considered either).

As the technology industry has matured, customers have also come to expect their experiences to flow seamlessly at larger and larger scopes. They want their end-to-end experience to hang together across their entire job, not just individual tasks. As more products and services deliver on this promise, this trend of rising customer expectations will only intensify.

What job is your product actually doing?

Harvard Business School professor Clayton Christensen, author of *The Innovator's Dilemma*, tells an insightful story about the need to zoom out to uncover a customer's actual end-to-end experience, which may not match what you initially thought.[2] The story conveys an important lesson about not assuming that you know what's going on in the customer's head and is particularly surprising because it's about people buying milk shakes. I mean, how complicated could the experience of buying a simple milk shake possibly be?

Christensen tells about a company he worked with that wanted to improve sales of their milk-shakes. They did all the usual demographics research of their current customers, and even sat down with individual customers to ask their preferences about flavor, texture, and other qualities. However, none of the changes inspired by this research improved sales one bit.

It was only when the company noticed the curious fact that nearly half of its milkshakes were sold during the morning commute that its customers' true end-to-end experience was revealed. It turned out that those milkshakes were being purchased by commuters who wanted a distraction during a boring drive. They needed something that they could handle in the car with one hand, with no mess, and would stave off their 10:00 a.m. hunger pangs. Christensen talks about this as understanding what "job" the customer is "hiring" your product to do. In this case, the job didn't have anything to do with milkshakes per se, it was much more about spicing up the morning commuting experience with the simultaneous constraint of needing to drive a car.

Armed with that insight, you might decide to make those morning milkshakes a bit thicker so that they take longer to drink, maybe throw in some bits of fruit for extra excitement, and certainly make sure they fit well in cup holders. And conversely, milkshakes sold in the afternoon to parents who are trying to placate their kids should probably be smoother and thinner so that the kids can easily gulp their treat through a straw and not take forever to finish.

Understanding a customer's true end-to-end experience requires insight into the customer's motivations and overall situation. Obtaining this insight requires you to zoom out to look beyond the immediate task at hand. With that understanding, new ideas for how to make a truly delightful experience for the customer become more apparent. This is true not just for milkshakes but for software as well.

For instance, you would optimize online credit card payments quite differently if you knew that instead of one-time purchases, the dominant usage pattern was for a customer to make several small purchases in quick succession as she browsed app listings looking for good games to try. This would allow you to minimize per-transaction fees and provide the user with a single, unified bill.

A customer's end-to-end experience with your product or service is deeply rooted in the real-life environment, situation, and motivation that surrounds its use. However, representing this all-important situational context is tough, with even the crispest list of requirements or features. Nor is it possible to enumerate every possible customer situation a product might need to address—that list is too long and unwieldy. You need some new tools and new ways of thinking to enable this kind of end-to-end approach.

Optimizing features doesn't make an experience

Around 2001, Procter & Gamble (P&G for short), the makers of products such as Pampers, Tide, and Oil of Olay, came to the realization that it needed to spend a lot more time understanding customers' real-world usage patterns, whether that was how families managed their laundry over the course of a week, how women chose skin-care products, or how parents of newborns approached diapering. However, the idea that an overall experience and the general aesthetics mattered more than any individual feature was a tough one for the company's more technically minded employees to grok.

Claudia Kotchka, the company's vice president of design innovation and strategy, would often tell a story about a hypothetical exercise to fold a competing brand, Altoids breath mints, into P&G's product line.[3] In the story, she shows the team a box of Altoids. She handles the old-fashioned tin with affection and opens it slowly. She wrinkles the paper inside and reveals a box of what look like old-fashioned homemade confectionaries, as the scent of 100 percent pure peppermint oil wafts through the room. She remarks that Altoids, with this old-time feel and great flavor, is able to charge a 400 percent price premium over its competitors.

She then asks the group of executives—as a thought experiment: What would they do with this product if P&G were to purchase the brand? The answers she got were almost always the same, regardless of audience—they would keep the 100 percent pure peppermint oil formula (taste tests show this is a clear winner), but replace the tin container (too expensive), remove the paper (serves no functional purpose), make the mints uniformly round (aids production, cleaner look and feel), and pack the mints tightly (optimize packaging—don't ship air).

"Exactly!" she says. "And this is what you will get . . . Proctoids!"[4] The room laughs as she reveals the new product packaging mockup, which utilizes a cheap white plastic container repurposed from P&G's line of baby wipes. The container is packed tightly with uniform rows of beige balls reminiscent of bleached rabbit pellets and has no paper.

Even though the Proctoids taste great (they still have 100 percent pure peppermint oil), she asks the people in the room, "Would you pay a 4X premium for this product? Would you even want to put one of these in your mouth?"

After telling this story, Kotchka says the light bulbs would go off. "The difference between these two products," says Kotchka, is that "while they both have 100 percent peppermint oil . . . the difference is design."

Let's step back and think about what's really going on here. Each change the executives proposed was a reasonable, logical decision that optimized some aspect of the product or process. And while each of the suggested optimizations made sense—make the packaging less expensive, remove the paper because it serves no function, don't ship air, pack the mints tightly, and so on—somehow, when they're all added up, the magic is lost. The story illustrates that it's quite possible to make a lot of sensible local optimizations and, in doing so, lose a meaningful end-to-end experience.

Big picture first, details later. Engineers are trained to look for the causes of problems, to break problems apart, to create abstraction layers, to compartmentalize, to fix issues at the root level, and then later reassemble the whole. This is also the approach that the engineers at P&G took when they thought about improving Altoids. But when designing for a great customer experience, and before you dive headlong into features, functionality, and requirements, you should be sure to broaden your approach and look at the end-to-end experience of your customers while they are using your product.

Take a few moments to consider your current team's engineering culture and results. What kind of product or service does your team deliver today? Is it more like Altoids or Proctoids?

Less—it's the new more

We've all heard this saying before: less is more. When you design for an end-to-end experience, the concept of using less to do more can be especially powerful. The reason is that it's all too easy for "extra" features in a product to get in the way of the overall experience. Yet, the instinct of engineers is that more must be better—and you can always find a customer who is asking for this capability or that feature or this other alternative view.

Many times, however, having fewer features and less functionality actually makes for a better customer experience, creating the streamlined, simple, and straightforward experience that customers desire. Focusing on features—how many, which ones, relative priority, and so on—is an upside-down way of thinking. Remember that the features in your product should serve the experience, not the other way around. And when you put customers and their experience at the center of your focus, you will often find that less really is more.

Bump is a popular smartphone application that was introduced in March 2009 as a simple way to share contacts between smartphones by physically touching, or "bumping," them together.[5] People thought that was pretty cool, and Bump quickly became one of the more popular downloads in the iPhone App Store. Subsequent versions of Bump began to expand on that idea by adding features for sharing additional file types, photos, and recommendations for apps and music. In 2011, Bump's CEO David Lieb said he ultimately wanted Bump to stand for "anything you want to do in the real world using your phone"—think near field communication (NFC), payments, and the like.[6]

But the Bump team started noticing that although customers would explore the different features of Bump, if they tried a feature that wasn't particularly useful to them (such as sharing a music recommendation), the customers most likely wouldn't return to the application at all. This data raised concerns and caused the team to make some tough decisions.

The team decided that it could get more customers to return by focusing on the few features that were being used the most. They decided to focus on those that seemed to have the most value to customers, that customers were actively using on a regular basis. As a result of this new strategy, the company made a drastic product change. It *removed* all extraneous features in the product and released Bump 3.0, which boasted a grand total of two features: the ability to exchange contact information with new acquaintances, and the ability to share photos with friends and family.

Before Bump 3.0 was released, the application had 75 million mobile-phone installations, but growth had stalled and the future looked uncertain. A year later, after Bump pared down to a simpler feature set, Bump had 125 million mobile-phone downloads and became one of the most popular programs in Apple's online store. It seems they made a pretty good decision.[7]

Bump's future was looking quite rosy. It won many awards, including *Fast Company*'s top 150 most innovative companies. So, perhaps it shouldn't be a surprise that Bump was acquired by Google in 2013. Sadly, the service was shut down soon after and has not yet resurfaced in Google's portfolio of services. We're curious to see how and if it reappears.

Easy, seamless, pain free

Even if there is nothing really new, having an experience flow seamlessly from beginning to end truly matters. You don't necessarily need to create some fancy new thing to win your customers' love. Just stitch the pieces together so that the experience actually works end to end. That alone counts for a whole lot. Especially if along the way you can proactively solve the key pain points that customers are likely to encounter, turning what could be an emotional disaster into a pleasantly painless surprise.

Have you flown on Delta Airlines recently? I had the pleasure of flying on Delta last summer and happened to make a stop in Minneapolis–St. Paul, where Delta has installed hundreds of iPads in its lounges throughout the terminal.

The sea of iPads was an instant draw for my kids, and I have to admit that my interest was piqued as well. Each iPad had the Fly Delta app installed and running. Not only did the app provide access to a few games the kids occupied themselves with while we waited, it also showed real-time information about our gate, that there was a slight delay, and a preview of the weather at our destination. If you left it idle, it rotated a tantalizing, full-picture menu for a nearby airport café.

It was certainly a nice touch for an airport waiting area, but that was nothing compared with what I got by installing the Fly Delta app on my own device for my next trip. That's when the experience really kicked in to high gear. The app handles the basics smoothly, allowing you to check in for your flight while you're on the go in a taxi or in your hotel room. And as expected, it shows real-time updates about your flight and serves as your boarding pass by displaying a code that the gate attendant can scan.

On an uneventful trip, the Fly Delta app provides all the little bits of info that help you get through the airport more smoothly, without the hassles of needing to print out your boarding pass or having to find your flight while you stare at the list on an airport monitor. But the clincher is that the Fly Delta app manages the single most dreaded aspect of air travel: cancelled flights. If your flight gets canceled, the app will likely notify you before the loudspeaker does. And it provides a quick and easy way to switch to a new flight, right from the app, in just a few taps. No waiting in line with a hundred other angry passengers, no worrying about whether there will still be space on the next flight by the time you get to the front of the line, no harried airport employee to interact with.

That's not rocket science. It's not even new functionality per se. It's actually a very simple, proactive solution to an age-old pain point. But Delta has clearly struck a nerve, and it's a good one. And the company was the first one to do it.

You can find gobs and gobs of reviews of the Fly Delta app that report experiences like "Never have to keep track of a boarding pass ever again" and "A much easier way to stay on track when traveling" and "Gives me the best chances of getting an upgrade" and "My flight was canceled, but the app told me this before the announcement and rather than wait to talk to the folks at the desk, the app had me rebooked in two minutes! LOVE IT!" Dealing with a canceled flight is never fun, but this new approach exceeded customer expectations so dramatically that it actually delivered customer delight. Ironically, the app's overall score is pulled down by consumer demand for this experience, with low-rated reviews that look like this: "Why isn't this app available on <platform> yet, because I really want it."

As a consumer, I hope that the other airlines don't take too long to figure out how to replicate this experience, and for Delta to port its app to the other mobile platforms. This may not be a competitive differentiator forever, but for now Delta has managed to smooth out and simplify what historically can be a nerve-racking experience, and that is making a lot of customers very happy. Airline travel is hardly the only domain that could use some end-to-end smoothing and solving of pain points. There's a lot to be gained just by pulling all the pieces together to provide an easy, seamless, hassle-free end-to-end experience.

Remember the ecosystem

Considering the larger ecosystem surrounding your solution is another way to make sure you're covering the user's complete experience. Often, after the initial purchase, the presence or absence of supporting elements makes the biggest difference in your customer's experience of your product, and often these are elements that are not directly under your company's control. Think about all the touch points a customer has with your solution. Does the customer interact with it via a single website, or are there third-party providers, retail partners, social media, and support channels the customer interacts with as well?

Let's take a look at Amazon's Kindle e-reader. It has an extensive customer experience that seamlessly integrates book publishers, public libraries, and application developers, in addition to what Amazon delivers with its device and retail website.

Most people's experience with a Kindle goes way beyond just ordering the device on Amazon's website. Sure, it starts with receiving a box in the mail, opening it, and reading a favorite book on a device with an amazing no-glare screen. But the end-to-end experience of using a Kindle goes much further. It also includes shopping for and downloading e-books, sometimes at a significant discount over conventional paper-based books, which required Amazon to develop special agreements with a multitude of publishers. Beyond those basics, Amazon considered a lot of other factors, too. How about the experience of reading reviews from other customers to help pick your next book to take on vacation? And if you like it, how do you recommend this e-book to someone else?

And how about being able to loan a book you've purchased to a friend so that she can read it, too? Oops, perhaps you've already loaned the book to someone else, but maybe your friend can check out the e-book from the local library? How does that work; are there partnerships between Amazon and the public library system? Who writes that library application, and what is that experience like? Is it easy to borrow an e-book from the library? What if I want to read an e-book on a different computer? Is it possible to do something else with a Kindle other than read books? Can I play games on a Kindle like I can on an iPad? If so, are the games any good? Are developers writing for this platform? How easy is it for a developer to get an application into the Kindle store?

It turns out that Amazon has steadily, over time, answered all of these questions and has built a powerful ecosystem around its popular Kindle reader to enable a complete user experience. That ecosystem goes beyond the walls of Amazon and involves book publishers, public libraries, and application developers. Not only is that ecosystem a powerful competitive advantage because it is so difficult for a competitor to replicate, but it also provides an incredibly smooth experience for customers. It's worth noting that Amazon is the top-rated technology company in Forrester's 2012 customer experience index, above even Apple.[8]

As you think about end-to-end experiences, don't think only about the one piece that your team delivers. Chances are that customers expect that piece to interface naturally with the rest of their lives as well, and that's going to require you to integrate with entities outside your company. *Making all those interfaces smooth and seamless is just as important a part of your job as getting your part of the experience done to a high degree of quality.*

Cradle to grave

Another way to think about an end-to-end experience is to think about the customer's experience over a longer period of time, from cradle to grave. That is, don't think just about the use of a device itself, also consider how the customer first heard about that device, how he purchased it, how he installed it, and what the first-run experience was like. And then think about what the support experience is like in the event of a problem, what happens when the device finally dies, and how the customer eventually replaces it. *Zooming out to consider the complete cradle-to-grave experience over time is another way to spot customer needs and opportunities for delight that you may not notice otherwise.*

Here's an example of applying cradle-to-grave thinking in a service business.

Amtrak hired the design consultancy IDEO and branding consultants OH&Co to help reimagine the Acela high-speed train route between Boston and Washington, DC, in an attempt to differentiate it from airline travel.[9] Imagine taking on that design challenge. Your first instinct might be to think about the train cabin experience—more comfortable seats, power outlets for business travelers, delicious food, sophisticated ambiance. This was Amtrak's first instinct as well.

Surprisingly, however, what the team found was that the customer's complete experience with train travel had 10 distinct steps, only one of which was riding on the train itself. The other steps happened before and after riding on the train—purchasing tickets, checking in, boarding, and collecting baggage had a significant impact on the total customer experience. In fact, these other areas were the ripest for making significant leaps forward; the cabin experience itself was secondary.

Toward that end, the team built a 60-foot-long walk-through prototype that served as a physical, tangible tool for thinking through the experience across all the steps of the customer's train experience. In the end, the team did create innovative train interiors, but it found that this aspect alone was not enough to deliver a great overall experience. It also designed station layouts, signage, and systems for handling ticketing and luggage, which together created an outstanding end-to-end experience for customers. Amtrak posted a tremendous increase in ridership and satisfaction, reaching one million riders of the new Acela line in less than a year, well ahead of its projections.[10]

Is it always necessary to consider the complete cradle-to-grave experience to have a successful product? No, sometimes it's fine to look more narrowly. But make that an intentional decision, consider the maturity of your particular market, and vet that decision with your competitive strategy. The last thing you want is a competitor who pops up and solves the entire cradle-to-grave scenario, making your solution look weak in comparison because you addressed only a piece of it.

Getting the details right

It is this sort of end-to-end thinking that leads you to consider not only the software experience for your service but also the specifics of the hardware it runs on. You would think not only about marketing but about where your device is placed on retail shelves and how it looks next to your competitor's product. You'd think about packaging for sales appeal and also about how that packaging might create a sense of anticipation when it is first opened. You'd think not only about whether all of the error conditions are covered but about how friendly the tone of voice is throughout the user interface. You'd think about performance and latency to ensure that the customer's perceived experience feels fast and fluid. In short, you'd think about how every aspect of your product could possibly affect the customer's end-to-end experience.

It turns out that considering these various aspects of the experience, and getting the details right, is what makes for a high-quality end-to-end experience for your customers. The vast majority of customers have no knowledge of the level of engineering quality under the hood. The elegance of the architecture, the efficiency of the algorithms, and the maintainability of the codebase means nothing to them. Rather, what customers see is what's on the outside, and human psychology is drawn to believe that beautiful packaging implies beautiful innards. So the user interface and the other visible parts of your software, device, or service matter quite a lot in conveying the level of quality and care that went into the rest of the solution as well.

However, it's going to take time to get the details right, to get feedback from real customers to learn which details they notice, to take a bit more care to polish the edges, to fix those fit-and-finish bugs, to get the performance to be not just acceptable but outstanding and responsive. Naturally, there are tradeoffs. This level of detail and customer empathy requires extra work. If you want to get your product to market in a timely manner so that you can actually make some money, *you need to choose to focus on delivering a smaller number of end-to-end experiences in order to have the time to execute each of them at a higher level of quality.*

What if there is no GUI?

It's fairly easy to imagine what a smooth, end-to-end customer experience for a consumer product might look like, especially for one that uses a lot of graphical user interface elements. However, we're often asked whether an end-to-end approach is relevant to more technical endeavors, like software platforms or APIs, software that has little or no visible user interface. Is there such a thing as an end-to-end experience with an API? Does delight really matter when the customer is a developer?

Perhaps the simplest way to answer this question is with another question: Have you ever been excited about using a programming language or an API? Have you ever witnessed an argument between two developers over their favorite programming language or model? The emotion displayed in those discussions can be very strong, and that emotion is evidence of a customer experience that has gone either very right or very wrong—we've witnessed both, and we're guessing you have as well.

As I think back to the early 1990s, I can recall a number of offerings that captured the hearts and minds of software developers. I was lucky enough to be part of the Visual Basic 1.0 team at Microsoft. I was able to experience firsthand what it's like to demonstrate a new product that customers (in this case, developers) love and to watch the creation and nurturing of a loyal fan base. It seems strange now to be using words like *love, nurturing,* and *fan base* when talking about a programming language and tools. However, in the early 1990s, when rapid application development (RAD) tools were becoming popular,[11] audiences commonly gave resounding standing ovations during demos. Typically, the presenter would say something evocative, like "Have you ever tried to finish a project only to discover you can't because of FOO?", and the whole audience would moan in agreement and empathy because most of them had suffered through that exact scenario. Then the presenter would type a couple of lines of code or drop a widget onto a UI element, and voilà—FOO was magically solved! Audiences would go crazy. It makes sense. The presenter would skillfully describe a real-life situation in which most of the audience had experienced frustration. And then, in front of their eyes, they would see how to solve that problem with ease.

 ## MINDSHIFT

I is for interface. To point out the obvious, the *I* in API stands for interface—not just the interface between one piece of code and another, but the interface between a piece of technology and a human being (the developer). The customer in this case is a developer who is writing code against an interface. A well-thought-out API that considers the end-to-end needs of the developer is a wonderful thing.

Sadly, many APIs are written in a utilitarian manner to serve the function of providing connections between two libraries or to expose the raw functionality of some technology to a developer. Perhaps because the customer's end-to-end experience is more remote, it's common to race through the design phase of GUI-less components. Have you ever seen the results of a quick API design captured as a whiteboard full of lollipop stick drawings?

But while an API built this way can be functional, it's rarely fun to use. Why? Because it doesn't intentionally account for the customer (you, the developer) and your needs. Instead, it focuses only on the technology and how to expose that technology externally.

Ruby—a love story

Visual Basic is not the only programming environment to have elicited strong emotions from customers. FoxPro, Delphi, Smalltalk, NeXTSTEP-Cocoa, and Lisp are all examples of integrated development environments (IDEs) that captured a large, loyal, and enthusiastic fan base. Remember how some developers reacted to the Java language? The early JavaOne conferences were reminiscent of something between a rock concert and a love-in.[12] Over the years, developers have doled out a lot of adoration for their beloved programming languages, frameworks, and tool sets. It's not solely the user interface that generates this affection; it's the combination of programming language, API framework, and IDE that allows developers to get on with the business of creating while minimizing unnecessary hassle and maximizing the fun, rewarding part of developing software.

A more contemporary love story between developers and a programming environment is Ruby on Rails. (Ruby is the programming language, and Rails is the application framework.) Ruby was created in 1993 by Yukihiro "Matz" Matsumoto, who said, "I wanted a scripting language that was more powerful than Perl, and more object-oriented than Python." He says that he designed Ruby for programmer productivity and fun, and stresses that systems design needs to emphasize human rather than computer needs. He had a very strong sense of focusing on the user rather than the technology:

> Often, people, especially computer engineers, focus on the machines. They think, "By doing this, the machine will run faster. By doing this, the machine will run more effectively. By doing this, the machine will something something something." They are focusing on machines. But in fact we need to focus on humans, on how humans care about doing programming or operating the application of the machines. We are the masters. They are the slaves.

Rails is an end-to-end (or *full-stack*) development framework for writing web applications using the Ruby language. It includes support for the web server, the database, business logic, the routing system, and test-driven development. In its design, Rails emphasizes a few key principles, which include:

- Model-view-controller (MVC) pattern

- Convention over Configuration (CoC)

- Don't Repeat Yourself (DRY)

Poke around the web a bit looking for information on Rails and you'll run into additional principles that people either attribute to Rails or apply when writing Rails applications. Search for "Ruby+Rails+Love," and you'll discover Ruby has a lot of fans. And as is often the case with great design, you'll also find a few anti-fans.

 MINDSHIFT

> **Great end-to-end experiences can be polarizing.** While a well-thought-out design can deeply delight the customers you have targeted, the customers you have not targeted may not see the value you have created—their needs are not being met by you. Consider the C++ language, which was designed for a very different type of user than Ruby was. C++ also has a lot of fans—and a lot of anti-fans. Its design principles are in stark contrast to those of Ruby. Instead of optimizing for productivity and fun, C++ optimizes for control,

choice, and zero overhead. These languages serve two different audiences, with two different sets of design principles, and two sets of fans (and anti-fans). Is it possible to optimize for both types of customers and usage patterns with the same solution? Usually, when you try, what you end up with is a mediocre solution that doesn't solve either set of needs particularly well, and neither customer is delighted. It's a tough decision, but if you strive to have passionate fans, you're going to have to live with the fact that not everyone will love what you build. We'll discuss strategies around how to maximize the quantity and business value of your target customers, and how to choose them, in Chapter 4, "Identifying your target customer."

It's interesting to look at the similarities between the design of a successful programming language and the design of other successful products.[13] Ruby had clear focus on customer needs and desires—it was all about developer productivity and fun. The Rails framework embraced an end-to-end philosophy that considered all the layers necessary to write a running web application. They were woven together into a great solution that really solved the end-to-end needs for the rapid application web developer. And the market responded with a large and loyal following. The point here isn't to delve into the design of programming languages, it's simply to state that it is absolutely possible for code that has no GUI to be designed with a target customer and an end-to-end experience in mind. And if that is done well, a non-GUI component can generate a strong emotional response from the user. With that context in mind, here's the rest of my Ruby story.

The things developers say

When writing this section, I reached out to a few friends who I know enjoy programming in Ruby. I asked them what they love about Ruby and why. I wanted to be able to summarize those attributes for you at a more detailed level than "Yeah, people really like Ruby—they say it's fun." I thought that providing details on the design philosophy of something like Ruby could be a valuable template for you to use when designing your own components. And so, to get feedback from Ruby programmers, I summarized my analysis like this:

> The Ruby language was highly principled from the very beginning, while Rails embraced an end-to-end strategy of creating a full-stack offering. I was excited to discover that, in fact, the early design of Ruby and Rails seemed to strongly support the thesis of this chapter—that an end-to-end design trumps a set of features every time, even in an API with no GUI.

When I contacted my Ruby-loving friends with this analysis, what I heard back was fascinating. I received plenty of affirmations of Ruby principles that my friends found important in their day-to-day programming, things like:

> "Ruby is a phenomenally expressive language."

> "I love that it favors convention over configuration."

"I think the cradle-to-grave concept of Ruby on Rails is very true."

"The Ruby [and GitHub] culture is that it is okay to make breaking changes if it makes the library better. So instead of people being scared of pushing a library too early and being stuck with a non-ideal interface, people push very early and see where it goes."

"It's inherently readable and expressive."

"Along with Python, [Ruby is] widely considered 'beautiful.'"

"Ruby on Rails gets out of my way so that I can be a great developer."

It was somewhat surprising but also encouraging to me how many of the comments were based on subjective emotion, not necessarily fact (which some might assume trumps emotion in programming). I also received this note, which is an insightful articulation of the deep connection developers sometimes have with their language:

> *As far as emotional connections between products and people, my very strong belief is that everyone has an artist in them. Sure, some people are legitimately great artists: writers, actors, painters, sculptors, etc. But all of us have an innate desire to create things, to marvel at our creation, to share our creations, and to revel in watching others enjoy our creation. It's what makes us human beings. We aren't just here to eat and sleep. We are here to create something that lives after us. When a product helps us create something AND makes the act of that creation enjoyable, people fall in love with it: they fall in love with the output of the product and they fall in love with using it.*

At the end of one particularly long email message, full of code examples describing why Ruby is so great, was this simple reminder: "But don't forget: it's fun. It's really, really fun."

Is delighting customers with an end-to-end experience indeed relevant to software that has little or no GUI? The answer is absolutely yes.

Don't forget what you already know

Building a set of end-to-end experiences that satisfy your customer's deepest needs is a wonderful thing. But it isn't everything. It's entirely possible to build the most beautiful, most compelling end-to-end experience ever that nobody actually cares about—or, rather, they care, but not enough to part with their hard-earned cash in exchange for that experience. You need to have a robust, realistic business plan behind your venture so that you will actually make money.

It's also possible to build a great experience on top of such poor technology that . . . well, it just doesn't work.

To build a successful product, you need to have a viable business strategy, technology that works, and a great end-to-end experience that meets customers' needs. You need all three, flawlessly executed. If any one of those components is missing, your chances for market success become severely limited.

You surely already have great methods and years of experience for how to build reliable, performant, secure, scalable software. Chances are you also have a business team or leaders who are experts at shepherding your business strategy.

The difference is that now you need to add a new capability to the mix. You need to develop your skills at building delightful, end-to-end customer experiences. It's likely that you are already trying to improve your abilities here. However, to do this well requires more than ad hoc efforts that rely on star individuals to lead a team (and that tend to fizzle when those people move on). To build great customer experiences, and to do that consistently on every project, requires the same level of rigor and attention that you are giving to technology execution and business strategy already, and this is usually a pretty big leap for most teams.

While there is some overlap and interplay between business, technology, and experience that we will mention along the way, this book focuses mostly on the new skills and approaches you need to develop to create great experiences. However, just to be sure we've said this out loud, the methods and mindsets we present in this book do not replace what you already know about delivering great software and managing a robust business. We hope this book helps you dramatically increase your skills in designing, iterating, and building great customer experiences, but don't forget all the things you've always been good at—you still need that stuff.

Summary

Customers want their problems solved, from their point of view, as seamless end-to-end experiences. By focusing on an end-to-end experience, you ensure that your features work together to provide a complete solution rather than isolated islands of individual functionality. Whether you go wide to consider cradle-to-grave situations or focus on specific pain points, thinking about end-to-end experiences as complete solutions to real customer problems helps you focus on solving them very, very well.

Notes

1. In Chapter 6, "Framing the problem," we describe in detail how to communicate end-to-end experiences using scenarios. For now, it's important to understand why the concept of providing an end-to-end experience is such a key part of achieving customer delight.

2. Clayton M. Christensen, Scott Cook, and Taddy Hall, "What Customers Want from Your Products," *HBS Working Knowledge,* January 16, 2006, http://hbswk.hbs.edu/item/5170.html.

3. Kotchka would tell this story as a way to start transforming technical leaders into design advocates. You can find videos of her presentation on the web: http://vimeo.com/5203345.

4. Get it? Pro**c**ter & Gamble + Al**toids** = **Proctoids**

5. Wikipedia, s.v. "Bump," last modified June 22, 2014, http://en.wikipedia.org/wiki/Bump_%28application%29.

6. Liz Gannes, "Bump Shares What Its 10 Million Users Share (Infographic)," *All Things D,* September 16, 2011, http://allthingsd.com/20110916/bump-shares-what-its-10-million-users-share-infographic/.

7. J. O'Dell, "Bump 3.0 Launches Today, Pared Down to Just 2 Features," *Venture Beat,* February 16, 2012, http://venturebeat.com/2012/02/16/bump-3/; Josh Constine, "Death to Feature Creep! Bump 3.0 Dumps All but Contacts and Photo Sharing," TechCrunch, February 16, 2012, http://techcrunch.com/2012/02/16/death-to-feature-creep-bump-3-0-dumps-all-but-contacts-and-photo-sharing/; Sarah Perez, "With Its Latest Update, Bump's Mobile App Replaces USB Flash Drives," TechCrunch, February 14, 2013, http://techcrunch.com/2013/02/14/with-its-latest-update-bumps-mobile-app-replaces-usb-flash-drives/.

8. Harley Manning and Kerry Bodine, *Outside In: The Power of Putting Customers at the Center of Your Business* (New York: Houghton Mifflin Harcourt, 2012).

9. "Amtrak Acela Express Accommodates All," case study, Center for Universal Design, College of Design, North Carolina State University, December 11, 2000, http://www.ncsu.edu/www/ncsu/design/sod5/cud/projserv_ps/projects/case_studies/acela.htm; "Acela for Amtrak: Interiors for High Speed Train," Ideo, http://www.ideo.com/work/acela.

10. It's worth noting that, coincidentally, Acela was launched at a particularly auspicious time, right after the 9/11 tragedy, when train travel enjoyed a surge in usage.

11. Prior to Visual Basic and the subsequent evolution of RAD tools, writing a Windows application required developers to program directly to the Windows API using the C programming language. This style of programming required a relatively high degree of programming skill and experience. The notion of drag-and-drop, event-driven programming was a revolutionary concept (well, except for NeXTSTEP with Interface Builder, along with a few others, which pioneered this style of programming years earlier . . . but that's another story). Many people viewed the introduction of Visual Basic as the democratization of programming for Windows because it allowed virtually anyone, regardless of technical training or experience, to write GUI applications.

12. The top-rated JavaOne speakers are literally referred to as "rock stars." See, for example, https://blogs.oracle.com/javaone/entry/congrats_to_the_2013_javaone.

13. Ruby is sometimes criticized by designers of programming languages as having a handful of quirky features—semantics based on names, capitalization, magic characters in names, etc. While some may argue that the Ruby language does not meet textbook standards for good programming-language semantics and design, Ruby did solve actual customer needs and has made its target customers productive and very happy.

SCIENTIFIC METHOD **Keep iterating**

NOT DECIDING, AGILE Understand vs. create
DISCOVERING Plan to get it wrong the first time frame

iterate **FAST FEEDBACK CYCLE**

Take an experimental approach Learning by making

scenarios 3 iterations before **Framing the problem**
finalizing the plan

Due diligence of generating User-centered design

brainstorm **multiple alternatives** build Observe customers

IDENTIFY TARGET CUSTOMERS **Get feedback early**

The Lean Startup Make a hypothesis Rhythm of iteration

science of iteration **GET CUSTOMER FEEDBACK**

CHAPTER 3

Take an experimental approach

To stand out in today's mature software market, you need to delight customers at an emotional level. A reliable way to delight customers is to deliver an end-to-end experience that solves a complete customer need, even if that means delivering less functionality overall. But how do you build those end-to-end experiences? And perhaps more importantly, how do you know which end-to-end experiences to build in the first place? The secret is staying focused on customers' real-world needs and desires and taking an iterative, experimental approach to zero in on great solutions for those needs.

In this chapter, we give you an overview of the customer-focused, iterative approach that we call the Fast Feedback Cycle. You will see what it looks like, what the basic activities are at each stage, and how the stages fit together. Subsequent chapters dive into more details and techniques for the work you do in each stage of the Fast Feedback Cycle.

Designing a new mouse

Let's start with an example of using the Fast Feedback Cycle to build a hardware device—a mouse. This is a case study of Project Bentley, a Microsoft hardware project that was chartered to build a highly ergonomic mouse.

The inspiration for the mouse was simple—when observing customers who were using Microsoft's ergonomic keyboards, the hardware team noticed that many customers used gel pads or other accessories to make their mice more comfortable to use.[1] A highly ergonomic mouse would be a natural extension to Microsoft's line of strong-selling ergonomic keyboards, and so the project was born.

With a bit of research about situations in which people used a mouse, which buttons and sliders got the most use, and the size of the average hand; a decision to focus exclusively on right-handed users; and a long history of designing mice and other hardware, the team began to brainstorm possible solutions. Here's what its first round of ideas looked like:

The team made many quick prototypes—about 50 of them in all. Each of the prototypes was made very quickly from inexpensive, easy-to-work modeling materials. None took more than 15 minutes to create, some much less. But take a closer look; many of the prototypes are not finished. In fact, some of them are downright strange. For instance, look at the gray one in the center: Which way do you hold it? Where do the buttons go? Look at the tall one just above the gray one and to the left—it's sharp on top. Would anyone ever ship a mouse that's sharp on top? Many of the mockups look like they were abandoned halfway through. Several have thin lips on the bottom that look destined to crack off and would never pass a manufacturing review.

The point is that the team tried out ideas that even in their mind's eye were going nowhere, just to see whether they might lead to a better idea.

At this stage in the project, it's cheap and fast to try out a new approach, so the team considered as many different shapes, configurations, and form factors that they could think of. *This is a classic brainstorming step, where you cast the net as wide as possible at the very beginning of the process, when your brain is most capable of generating many different ideas.* It turns out that some solid neuroscience lies behind why your brain is much more capable of generating lots of ideas when you brainstorm early, as the first step of a project, before you become too mentally committed to any single approach. We'll go into this in detail in Chapter 7, "Brainstorming alternatives."

To get some input as to which models were working best ergonomically, the team then showed them to a few customers to touch, feel, and hold. The team also began thinking through which approaches were most likely to be technically feasible. It's notable that this first round of customer feedback happened just a few weeks into the project.

After considering that feedback, they produced their second round of ideas:

Note that the team didn't choose just one of their initial ideas to work with in more detail—they were still working on nine alternatives in this round. But this time, instead of using foam and clay, they built CAD models for each mouse and "printed" them out using a 3-D printer to create the physical forms. At this point the details were starting to get worked out. The buttons and precise contours were all there, and you can see that each one now incorporates a scroll wheel, which turned out to be a key request from customers.

The team was now also considering the technical implications of each design. Would it work for manufacturing? Would all the gearing and components fit inside the case? What kind of plastics could be used? In parallel, they continued testing with users to get feedback about how the mouse felt in people's hands—because, after all, the ultimate goal was to build a mouse with superior ergonomics.

Here's what they produced for round three:

Again, the team didn't pick just one concept to move forward with. This time they selected four options to prototype more fully—now with functional buttons, real materials, and all the internal mechanisms. Just as before, they debated the technical feasibility of each design and had customers use these mice in real situations to get detailed feedback about what worked and what didn't.

In the end, here is what they finally shipped, the Microsoft Natural Mouse 6000, released in 2008:

Did you notice that the mouse they shipped is not the same as any of the final four prototypes? While it is most similar to H, look closely and you'll see that it incorporates aspects of all four of the final models. The same sort of combinatoric mixing of good ideas from multiple lines of thinking happened at every stage of this process. Go back and look at the 3-D models—none of them is exactly the same as any of the original foam models. Similarly, none of the four functional prototypes is the same as any one of the 3-D models. As the team iterated, it combined and recombined the best ideas from different prototypes to narrow in on the combination that worked the best—both for technical feasibility and for end-user ergonomics. In the end, they delivered a product that did well in the market, and really delighted their customers.[2]

Engineers naturally tend to iterate ideas. As you work through the issues and get feedback from others on the team, your solutions steadily get better and more refined. However, unlike in this example, you typically start with only one seed—one reasonably good idea of how to solve the problem, and you iterate from there, continually refining that idea until you get to a final solution.

However, if you think back to your mathematics background, starting with one seed is a really good way to find a local maximum in a complex plane. If you want a more statistically reliable way to find the global maximum, you need to start with more seeds. This is the magic behind the iterative approach illustrated by the mouse example—combining and recombining the best ideas from multiple lines of thinking within the Fast Feedback Cycle to give you the very best odds of finding the most optimal solution across all of your constraints.

Some of you may question whether this illustration is even relevant to software development. We chose this example because it provides a great visualization of what an ideal iterative process might look like. It's a good example precisely because it is so physical and easy to photograph and view step by step. For software projects, you don't prototype with clay and foam, but on paper, with wireframes, whiteboard drawings, storyboards, PowerPoint mockups, prototyping toolkits, flow diagrams, or even by writing prototype code. To capture a similar snapshot of the iterative stages in a software project would take stacks and stacks of paper, and the patterns would be much harder to see at a glance. But regardless of the form factor, the core ideas are exactly the same:

- Start with a clear idea of which target customers you are building for.

- Understand those customers' needs and desires in the context of their real-life situations.

- Explore many possible ideas, especially in visual ways.

- Build several rapid prototypes of the most promising ideas.

- Evaluate prototypes with customers to get feedback and learn, while working through technical feasibility in parallel.

- Refine prototypes, gradually focusing in on fewer ideas, adding more details at each successive round, and eventually writing production code once your plan has stabilized.

- Repeat as needed.

It's worth taking a short pause to ponder a quick thought experiment. What would it take to actually work with multiple ideas in an iterative approach in your software development process? How different would that be? How close are you to doing these things already in your current team and project? What would the implications be if you recentered your whole engineering system on this approach?

The Fast Feedback Cycle

The Fast Feedback Cycle is the heart of Scenario-Focused Engineering, and there's a clear science and rigor for how to do it well.

As the mouse example showed, you want to take a more experimental approach to building solutions. The key term here is *experimental*. This means that your job as an engineer is less about *deciding* what the product will do and more about *discovering* what is actually going to work in real time, in real usage, with real people, and with real technology constraints.

It's important to see how the different parts of the Fast Feedback Cycle fit together to achieve this goal. Together, the parts of this cycle form a general approach to problem solving; they aren't a specific prescribed tool set. In fact, you could (and should) apply lots of different tools at each stage in the cycle, depending on your situation and how far along you are in your project. We'll talk about the most common ones used for software projects throughout the book, and we'll also mention alternatives for more unusual situations or different domains. However, while you need to pick the most appropriate set of tools for your individual situation, the underlying rhythm and general approach shouldn't change. The science (and the power) of the Fast Feedback Cycle is in this rhythm, illustrated in Figure 3-1.

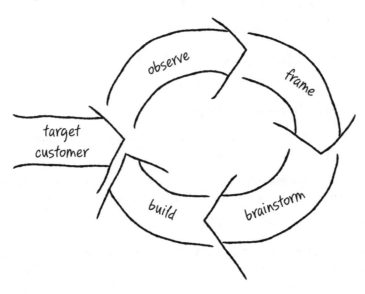

FIGURE 3-1 The Fast Feedback Cycle.

Let's walk through the Fast Feedback Cycle at a high level so that you can see the overall pattern. The chapters in Part II, "The Fast Feedback Cycle," go into each stage in detail.

Target customer

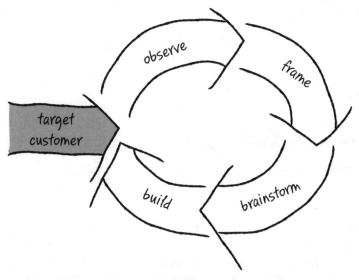

First, before you can start iterating, you need to know who your target customer is. That is, who do you intend to build this solution for? The choice of target customer is primarily a business-strategy decision—which customers are the most lucrative or most leveraged or most likely to drive long-term success?

Defining a target customer is essential because it acts as a lens through which all the other stages are focused. The target customer is the fuel that powers the cycle, and knowing your customer is the most important prerequisite before starting the iterative process.

Chapter 4, "Identifying your target customer," discusses this topic in more depth and describes why this focus is so essential.

Observe

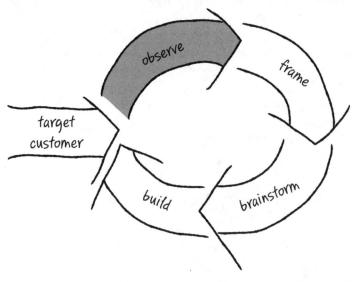

After your target customers are identified, you spend time researching them—looking for their un-articulated (or latent) needs: that is, what customers can't quite tell you themselves but which are the deep desires and underlying needs that drive their behaviors. Identifying an unarticulated need that your competition has not yet noticed, and then building an excellent solution for it, is a great way to achieve differentiation in a crowded market.

Site visits and other observational research approaches help ground you in customers' real-world situations—not in abstractions of what they should need, but in the reality of what they run into in their actual usage. By watching customers in their native habitats (on their couch, in their office, or walking in a crowded shopping mall), you learn things you wouldn't have thought to ask about. For example, "Why are you doing that eight-step workaround when this beautiful feature over here would do it for you? . . . Oh, you knew it was there, but it doesn't work with your company's procurement system? Hmm, you're right; oops, we didn't plan for that situation."

Your goal in observing customers is to gather data that will help you ferret out root causes—not the symptoms or the Band-Aids or the referred pain, but the original source of the problem or the deep human need that is driving the customers' behavior. You may uncover a critical detail—a prod-uct interaction you never noticed before. Or you may discover a surprising insight into what really matters for a knowledge worker. Perhaps for that worker deep delight comes not from getting the job done but from unobtrusively staying in touch with his family throughout the workday, which counter-intuitively improves productivity because he isn't worried about whether his kids got to school safely.

Collecting and analyzing more numerical, or quantitative, data adds another piece to the puzzle. Whether you are looking at statistics about your competitors or crunching massive amounts of usage data from your existing systems, quantitative data can help alert you to usage patterns, anomalies, or pain points that may help you find a new, unique opportunity to delight your customer.

> **Customers want to have input.** Too often there are many layers between the customer and the development team. Any feedback received is often diluted, distorted, and dismissed. Having a direct, real, and personal connection with customers can energize the team, as well as tell your customers that you really care about their needs.

After doing even a moderate amount of research, it's easy to collect a veritable mountain of data points, customer requests, ideas, and notes. These may come in a wide variety of formats: quotes, survey data, photos, video footage, competitive information, usage statistics, and so on. Unfortunately, the breakthrough opportunities you are looking for may not always be immediately obvious. As you get ready to exit this stage, it is vital to look across your research to identify patterns and themes that point to the most pressing customer needs and opportunities. Affinity diagramming is a straightforward and extremely effective technique for making sense of a large amount of unstructured customer data of this sort and will help you identify patterns and insights about your customers that might elude you otherwise.

Chapter 5, "Observing customers: Building empathy," discusses how to use a mix of subjective, objective, qualitative, and quantitative methods to uncover unarticulated customer needs and develop empathy for your customer. It also shows how to use affinity diagrams and other analysis techniques to distill a large set of data points into a small set of key insights.

Frame

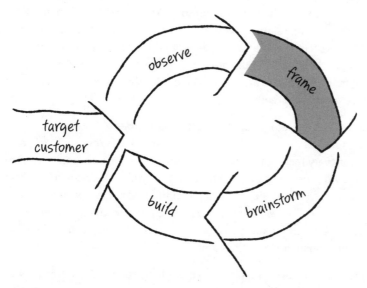

While observing customers, you will undoubtedly discover lots and lots of needs and potential opportunities. The next step is to make a judgment about which of those needs are the most important to address, and to precisely articulate what those needs are. This is called *framing the problem*.

Think of it like holding up an empty picture frame in front of an imaginary tapestry that depicts every aspect of your customers' needs, usage patterns, and desires. Depending on where you hold that picture frame, you determine which aspect of the customers' experience you are going to focus on. Will you hold it close and focus in on a specific, narrow situation? Or will you hold it farther away and zoom out to include a complete cradle-to-grave experience? Will you focus on this problem or on that one? On this situation or that other one?

Once you decide on a frame, this allows you to focus on how to fill out the inside of that frame—and not become distracted or continually debate why you are working on this particular need. In addition, framing encourages a bit of rigor to ensure that you articulate exactly which problem or situation you are trying to solve before launching into building solutions, which is vital for alignment when you have multiple people (or multiple teams) who need to contribute to a project.

One very helpful and broadly applicable framing technique is to write stories such as scenarios, epics, or user journeys that tell the story of what a customer is trying to accomplish that your product could help with. We have found the scenario technique to be a particularly effective tool for describing the kind of end-to-end experiences that we aspire to build with software. A scenario introduces the target customer, describes a real situation in which the customer has a need, and articulates what qualities a good solution would have—without saying anything about exactly how that solution would work.

Additionally, it is critical at this stage to establish a few metrics to track as key criteria for success and to embed these metrics in each scenario. Putting thought into specific, measurable goals for each scenario helps zero in on exactly what kind of experience you are aiming for. For instance, when looking for a photo of my daughter in my vast photo archive, is it more important to achieve a sense of magic (that the software somehow knows how to distinguish my daughter's face from my son's), or simply to get the job done quickly (where a simple text search for her name might be close enough—and much easier to build)? What aspects of a solution are going to drive customer delight in this situation? How might you measure them? Later in the project, these metrics can be listed on a scorecard to provide a view of how well you are achieving your goals across all of your scenarios and to help you know when you are "done" and ready to ship.

Scenarios are a popular and effective method for framing software projects, and they have some strong benefits. However, it's important to note that they are not the only possible approach, or even always the best method for every team. Other options include goals and non-goals, requirements, user journeys, outcomes, Agile user stories, and epics, some of which share characteristics with scenarios. Each tool has its pros and cons, but the essential job at this stage is to clearly frame the problem and define what success looks like *before* you jump into building anything. For the purposes of this book, we often refer to scenarios as the most typical framing tool, but you can easily substitute a different approach if that is appropriate for your situation.

Chapter 6, "Framing the problem," discusses framing and measuring against that frame in more detail.

Brainstorm

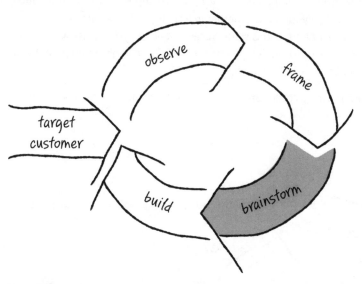

Now that you have the problem clearly framed, it's time to start considering possible solutions. You want to take the time to explore—to brainstorm and play around with lots of ideas before you make any decisions about which of those ideas you will pursue. At this point, you aren't concerned with finding the single perfect idea; rather, you're generating lots of ideas to give yourself plenty of choices that you can mix and match throughout the iterative process. There are many techniques to help you generate creative, innovative ideas—and it truly is possible to get better with practice.

 MINDSHIFT

Do the due diligence to generate multiple alternatives before deciding. Often you will find that the best concept emerges as a blend of multiple brainstormed ideas, and you might not have noticed this if you hadn't taken the time to come up with lots of alternatives first. Some companies embed this principle in a rule: you cannot make a decision about *anything* until you have done the due diligence to generate at least X number of alternatives first. The most common number we've heard is five—you need to generate at least five ideas before you are allowed to narrow down the choices and select one. We've heard house rules as high as nine or as few as three. Those are minimums, not maximums—in practice, some teams and companies regularly generate hundreds of ideas as a matter of course, especially in early turns of the iterative cycle. Note that this rule applies not just to deciding how many storyboards to generate or UI layouts to wireframe, but also to how to solve architectural problems or even what to have for lunch. Whatever minimum benchmark you set for yourself, the idea is to get serious about forcing yourself to generate multiple credible alternatives as part of the due diligence of doing engineering and to fully explore the problem space. Do not allow yourself to fall in love with your first good idea.

When you're brainstorming, it is important to think through "complete" solution ideas—that is, ones that solve the entire end-to-end scenario and are not just snapshots of one piece of functionality. It is also very helpful to visualize your ideas, whether in a sketch, a flow chart, or a comic strip. Storyboarding is a very popular technique at this stage because it allows you to visualize a sequence of events that map out a potential end-to-end experience, yet it is lightweight enough that you can sketch dozens of alternatives in an hour or two.

We'll discuss storyboarding as well as other brainstorming and visualization techniques in Chapter 7.

Build

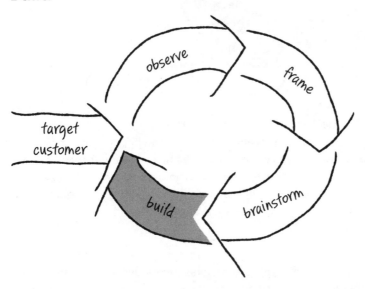

After you explore the range of possible end-to-end solutions, it's time to flesh out a few of those ideas in more detail—not all of them, but the ones that seem to have the most promise from a business, technical, and customer-experience perspective. It's essential to find very cheap, fast, lightweight ways to create prototypes for your first few iterations through the Fast Feedback Cycle—to be as efficient as possible and minimize wasted time on dead ends. You can often do this without writing any code, even when you're working on deeply technical platform components or APIs. The goal of these early prototypes is to get customer feedback on some specific approaches as quickly as possible so that you can make quick course corrections with a minimum of sunk cost.

Your prototypes can be paper drawings, wireframe mockups in PowerPoint, SketchFlow drawings in Expression Blend, an API interface written out on paper, flow charts or block diagrams in Visio, or a skit designed to work out a process workflow or customer-service scenario. The format of the prototype is much less important than how well it facilitates quick feedback from customers about whether you are on the right track. It's important to choose the prototyping technique that works best for you, depending on the type of solution you are working on and the feedback you are looking for. When you finish prototyping, write code in slices to enable continual customer feedback.

We'll discuss prototypes and coding techniques for many different kinds of situations in Chapter 8, "Building prototypes and coding."

Repeat: Observe customers again to get feedback

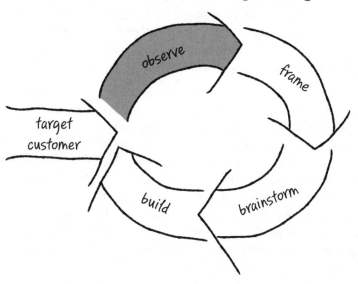

Now that you have a few prototypes, you start the cycle over again by observing customers using your prototypes. After all, the reason you built those prototypes is to get feedback from customers as quickly as possible so that you can learn and make course corrections while it is still cheap and easy to do so.

Ideally, your first prototypes are little more than simple sketches on paper. You want to learn as early as possible if you are on the right track or where your ideas are falling short. In the extreme, your first prototype for customer feedback could be the scenario you wrote earlier, to be sure that it rings true before you spend any time on solutions for an irrelevant problem.

 MINDSHIFT

Get feedback early, really early. Customers are actually much better at dealing with rough prototypes than they're often given credit for. In fact, counterintuitively, showing customers very early prototypes can often result in better-quality feedback because customers subconsciously see that you are still in the early stages of your project, you haven't decided yet, their feedback might actually be heard, and your feelings won't be hurt if they tell you that they don't like your approach. Some engineers tend to resist sharing their thinking until they've thought everything through, but this tendency makes it harder to get the immediate customer feedback needed to power a fast, efficient feedback cycle. *It is important to become comfortable showing early, half-baked ideas so that you have the opportunity to make a course correction before you have too much sunk cost that may end up being wasted effort.*

When you show rough, early prototypes to customers, you learn an amazing number of things. You may find out that your approaches resonate with the customer and that you're on the right track, so you can accelerate your team's work with confidence. You may identify a preference among the alternatives you're considering. Or you may discover that your solution doesn't make sense to customers at all, that you forgot to consider a key constraint, that you addressed only part of their end-to-end problem, or that the overall approach is flawed. It is not uncommon to discover in this first customer touch point that the problem you thought you were solving isn't really a problem—or that you misunderstood the essence of what needed to be solved. Or perhaps what you thought would be a key source of delight for your customers just doesn't resonate with them.

All of these possible outcomes have dramatic impact on the future of the project—and might even cause you to scrap it and focus on a different scenario altogether. Yet, in a typical software project, you wouldn't get this kind of feedback until the code is well on its way, and possibly already working. We've all been in situations where we discover way too late in a product cycle that we made a bad assumption somewhere along the line, that there was a crucial misunderstanding or a critical missing component. The idea here is to ferret out those big oversights much earlier, while it's still cheap and easy to recover. For highest efficiency, optimize your approach to verify that you've got the big picture correct first, before you spend too much time on the details, and certainly before you invest in writing production code. That way, if you find that you need to change direction, you haven't wasted much time or effort. Showing your early, incomplete thinking to customers is a powerful and effective way to catch these big bugs early.

We'll discuss ways to get customer feedback on your prototypes in more detail in Chapter 9, "Observing customers: Getting feedback."

 ## MINDSHIFT

Plan to get it wrong. One of the most important concepts in this book is to plan to get it wrong. Despite plenty of personal experience to the contrary, we all tend to be optimists and believe that this time we will finally get it right on the first try. A more realistic approach is to assume that your first attempt will be partly wrong, you just don't know which part. *The best insurance is to put a feedback loop in place to figure out as soon as possible where the problems are and build time into your project schedule to spend some cycles iterating.*

Think back in your history. Has any product you've ever shipped turned out exactly the way you first imagined it? No, you made plenty of adjustments along the way, sometimes even quite big ones. Those changes were expensive, too, and everyone knows that the later they happen, the more expensive they become to fix (and more work will have been wasted).

Yet we treat those changes as the exception, not the rule. We think that if only we were smarter, we would have come up with the right plan the first time. The problems seem preventable, yet the pattern seems to happen every time. We promise ourselves to do better next time. The trouble is that the world is so complex, and the problems we are solving now are much harder than they used to be—the easy problems were solved a long time ago. You can't predict everything, and even if you could, the landscape is always changing. So stop beating yourself up about it. Instead, plan for the fact that change will happen.

Assume that you will get it wrong the first time, and reserve the right to become smarter as the project progresses.

Keep iterating

You've surely noticed that this approach isn't a linear progression of steps but rather a cycle. In fact, the most important aspect of the Fast Feedback Cycle isn't any single step, but rather the fact that you repeat them. The faster you loop through the cycle, the better the results you are likely to get and the more efficient your team will be. We call each trip around the cycle an *iteration*.

 VOCAB

An *iteration* is a single trip around the Fast Feedback Cycle, starting with observing customers, then framing the problem, then exploring many ideas, and finally prototyping or building a few possible solutions to present for customer feedback in the next iteration of the cycle. We say that a team *iterates* as it makes multiple trips around the Fast Feedback Cycle, progressively narrowing in on an optimal solution as it gets customer feedback at the start of every iteration.

Here is a description of how your thinking might progress as you continue iterating after your first trip around the Fast Feedback Cycle:

- **Observe** So, what happens after you show your first prototypes to customers? Well, it all depends on what you learn from the customer feedback you receive. Perhaps customers loved what you showed them. More likely, they liked parts of it, but other parts didn't seem relevant to their needs or just plain didn't make sense.

- **Frame** Now compare the customer feedback against your scenario. This may be a very quick check to confirm that the feedback you received is consistent with the scenario you originally wrote. However, perhaps the feedback suggests that you need to adjust the scenario. Maybe your customers' actual needs or motivations are different from what you initially thought. Maybe their judgment of what a good solution looks like is different, which would suggest that you change the success metrics. Maybe there is a constraint that you didn't realize—for instance, you didn't consider that your customer might not have reliable access to the Internet when using your service on the road. Any of these things might cause you to edit your scenario to include these new needs and insights.

- **Brainstorm** Next, you move on to exploring some revised alternatives, this time with new information to inspire your idea generation in slightly different directions. Perhaps the solution alternatives you originally prototyped didn't quite hit the mark, so you need to try a different approach. Or, perhaps your high-level solutions were working fine with customers, so now your brainstorming is focused primarily on getting to the next level of detail, to bring your rough solutions to a higher level of fidelity. But still, the key behavior is to generate more ideas than you need so that you have done the due diligence to really explore the problem space before you decide which ideas are worth pursuing.

- **Build**   Then, as before, you move on to building or prototyping, but this time you create fewer alternatives and develop them in somewhat more detail than in the previous iteration. You still use the fastest prototyping techniques that are sufficient to get customer feedback. Perhaps after seeing what worked for customers, you can combine ideas from multiple approaches to create an even better prototype. At this stage you should also start exploring which alternatives not only delight customers but are also possible and reasonable from an engineering perspective and support your business plan. You also transition into writing production code.

- **Observe, again**   Then you get that second round of prototypes right back in front of customers, just as you did before, and so it continues. But be careful that you don't ask for feedback from just anyone—be sure that you prioritize getting feedback from your target customer.

- **Keep going**   The Fast Feedback Cycle can be repeated over and over, and, indeed, you should continue repeating it throughout your project, all the way until the endgame, when you have a final, shippable solution that customers find delightful and that works flawlessly.

As your project progresses, your iterations through the Fast Feedback Cycle will naturally shift their core activities, even though the essence of each stage remains the same. For instance, in early iterations, the framing stage is mostly about deciding which problem to solve and making sure you have described it correctly. As you start iterating, you might realize that your understanding of the problem is incomplete, so you normally update your framing once or twice. In later iterations, this stage becomes more about assessing your solution against that frame to be sure that you are still solving the problem you initially set out to address and assessing how close you are to achieving your metrics.

Similarly, in later iterations, the build stage becomes less about prototyping multiple alternatives and more about writing production code, fixing bugs, and fine-tuning the details. As you shift from showing mocked-up prototypes, to having customers attempt to use working code, to finalizing production code, the techniques you use to gather customer feedback will change as well.

 TIP

A rule of thumb for any good-size project is to iterate three times around the Fast Feedback Cycle before you commit to a spec, start writing large quantities of production-quality code, or otherwise finalize the plan. That gives you three opportunities to identify course corrections through customer feedback, even if that feedback happens in a lightweight, informal way. For most teams and most situations, this is the right tradeoff between taking sufficient time to ensure that you're on the right track before you invest too deeply and not getting stuck in analysis-paralysis in an effort to keep making the plan "just a little better." For very large projects, you may find that you need a few more initial iterations to solidify a plan.

After you go through the Fast Feedback Cycle a few times, you should have a concept for an end-to-end solution that you like—one that works from a feasibility perspective and is testing well with customers. Only then is it time to start breaking that solution down into the bits and parts of features and work items that will populate your product backlog, Team Foundation Server, or whatever system you use for tracking engineering work items. But even after you start writing production code, continue iterating: test your latest builds with customers, check against your scenario to be sure you are still solving the customers' core problem, and whenever you find that you have to make a design decision (addressing customer feedback, building the next feature, or fixing a bug), take a couple of minutes to brainstorm some alternatives and perhaps even quickly test them with customers before you pick an approach to move forward with.

 MINDSHIFT

> **Faster is better.** The Fast Feedback Cycle is most efficient and effective when you are able to iterate quickly. To make that happen, you need to let up on your inherent perfectionism and let the first couple of trips around the cycle be pretty loose. You don't have to have finished, statistically perfect, triple-checked customer research to start writing a scenario—a well-informed hunch based on talking with a few target customers could be plenty to start with. Nor does your scenario need to be perfect—take your best shot, brainstorm, and prototype against it, and you'll quickly see whether you're on the right track when you show it to customers. That first touch point with customers will give you the information you need to figure out what additional research you should do and where your scenario is not quite accurate, which will help you identify the root of the problem and the optimal solution that much faster.

It's important to note that the rhythm of constant and rapid iteration around the Fast Feedback Cycle should continue throughout the project, even during milestones that are primarily about implementation or stabilization. Iteration is not just for the early stages of a project. Obtaining continual customer feedback on your work in progress is essential for maximizing efficiency and minimizing wasted effort, and it may cause you to rethink the need for a separate implementation or stabilization milestone in the first place.

Looking deeper

An interesting pattern that's embedded in the Fast Feedback Cycle is worth pointing out. As Figure 3-2 shows, the top half of the cycle is all about clearly *understanding* the problem you are trying to solve. The bottom half of the cycle is all about *creating* an actual solution. As the cycle plays out over time, this split ends up being a sinusoidal sort of rhythm—identify a problem, try a solution, see whether it works, adjust based on what you learn, try a different solution, and keep on cycling. It's very powerful to go back and forth between understanding and creating based on that understanding, which then leads to deeper understanding, from which you can create something even better, and on and on. Expert practitioners sometimes call the creating phase *learning by making*, as compared with *learning by thinking*, and believe that it is a crucial skill to master to get the most out of an iterative approach.

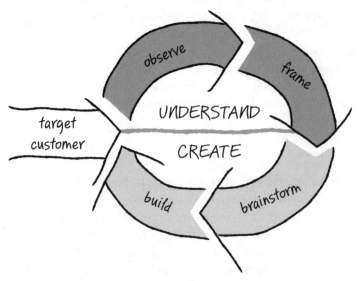

FIGURE 3-2 The top half of the Fast Feedback Cycle focuses on understanding the problem; the bottom half focuses on creating a solution.

Achieving a balanced rhythm across all stages of the cycle is ideal, though different teams will have natural strengths in different parts of the cycle. Predictably, most engineering teams are very strong at building. However, can they build rapid prototypes as well as they write code? And are they equally strong at generating and exploring multiple alternatives? Is the team practiced at identifying insights from customer research? Is the team good at framing a problem to identify the heart of the most important end-to-end experience to solve? What are the strengths of your team?

Haven't I met you somewhere before?

The fundamental concepts of the Fast Feedback Cycle have been around a long, long time. In fact, you can see a very similar cyclical rhythm in many other creative domains:

- Architects who draw and build foam core models to review before they finalize their plans.

- Artists who do pencil sketches before pulling out the paints, and who paint in layers, adding detail and refining as they go.

Or, bringing it to a more technology-oriented realm:

- Agilists who cap each weekly sprint with a demo or touch point to get feedback from their customer or product owner before starting the next sprint.

- Entrepreneurs who use the Lean Startup build-measure-learn cycle to quickly find and validate new business opportunities.

People from diverse backgrounds and disciplines have independently concluded that a fundamentally iterative, cyclical approach is the most effective, efficient way of developing new ideas.

The scientific method

We don't think this is a coincidence—at their core, all of these approaches stem from the scientific method.

While the scientific method is applied with some variation in different domains, it is generally accepted that it entails several key stages. First, you observe some phenomenon and notice something unusual or unexplainable about it. You then identify a specific question you want to answer. Next, you consider various hypotheses about how to answer that question to explain the phenomenon you observed and select a hypothesis to test. Then, you design an experiment and predict what you expect will happen, which outcome would give you the ability to prove or disprove your hypothesis. You then conduct the experiment and collect data. If the data disproves your hypothesis, you repeat the process, first confirming that you are asking the right question, then trying a different hypothesis and experiment, and on again until you land on a hypothesis that actually works to explain the phenomenon you observed. Scientific rigor is achieved by continually challenging the dominant hypothesis through other scientists repeating an experiment in a different lab and by designing new experiments to continue testing the validity of the hypothesis in other situations. The parallels to the Fast Feedback Cycle are plainly obvious, as you can see in Figure 3-3.

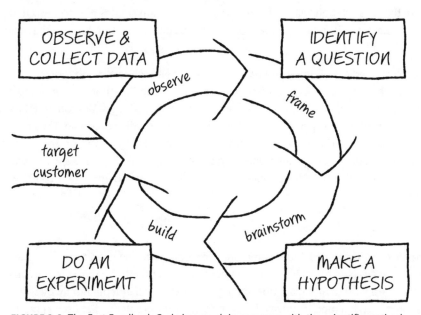

FIGURE 3-3 The Fast Feedback Cycle has much in common with the scientific method.

Historically, many groups of people have approached problem solving in a way that also has roots in the scientific method. Following is a brief survey of the main inspirations for the ideas behind

Scenario-Focused Engineering and the Fast Feedback Cycle, as well as related methodologies that have substantial overlap in methods and mindsets.

User-centered design (UCD)

The most substantial inspiration for Scenario-Focused Engineering comes from the field of user-centered design. Both academics and practitioners have been developing, studying, using, and applying user-centered design techniques for decades. Many universities offer degrees in interaction design, user research, and numerous related specialties.

The core ideas behind user-centered design are central to this book: develop empathy with your customers, use observation to discover unarticulated needs, use storytelling to frame the problems to be solved, brainstorm and visualize alternative solutions, test prototypes with customers to get feedback, iterate repeatedly at increasing levels of fidelity in response to customer need, and mindfully narrow the funnel of solutions at each iteration to ensure that the best amalgamated solution is delivered. The fundamentally experimental, cyclical nature of a user-centered design approach is a close analog of the scientific method and is embodied in the Fast Feedback Cycle.

A mainstay of user-centered design is a form of logic called *abductive reasoning*.[3] Unlike deductive or inductive logic, abduction is a form of logical inference that takes a set of data and creates a hypothesis that could possibly explain that data. When designing solutions, abduction is a logical leap of mind that suggests a reasonable design that could solve an attendant problem. Logically, you can't know for sure that this solution will work, but it might. Abduction creates a hypothesis that you can test, measure, validate, or disprove—just as a scientific hypothesis is tested through the scientific method.

In the past few years, the field of user-centered design has been broadened and is often referred to as *design thinking*, which is a recasting of the same core ideology and methods, recognizing its applicability to a much wider class of problems than just user-interface design. We concur that as a variant of the scientific method, these approaches are indeed very broadly applicable. They can be applied not just to designing products and services, but also to developing new business strategies, designing optimal organizations and systems, and even solving seemingly impossible world-scale problems, such as creating viable ways for people to get out of poverty and improving community access to clean water.

Agile

Agile was born from the software developer community in response to the need to build higher-quality software with less wasted effort in an environment in which precise customer requirements change over time and are hard to articulate upfront. Agile was invented independently by software engineers, but fascinatingly, it aimed to solve a lot of the same root problems that user-centered design aimed to tackle.

If you're working on an Agile team, a lot of this chapter probably feels familiar. You already loop quickly in sprints, likely somewhere from one to four weeks in length. It's easy to squint and see how one loop around the Fast Feedback Cycle could map to an Agile sprint, complete with a customer touch point at the end to get direct customer feedback on the increment you just delivered. It's likely that some of the same activities we discussed already occur during the course of your sprints.

Scenario-Focused Engineering differs from Agile in two main areas, which we believe help fill in some missing gaps. First, we believe that it's not necessary for every sprint to deliver shippable code. In early sprints, it's often more efficient to get customer feedback on a sketch, mockup, or prototype before investing in production code. However, we completely agree that getting customer feedback at the end of every sprint is absolutely essential, whether that sprint built prototypes or production code.

Second, we believe that the product owner is actually a mythical creature. We challenge the idea that any one person on the team, no matter how senior, no matter how often they talk with customers, can accurately channel exactly what real customers need and desire and provide accurate "customer" feedback at the end of a sprint. Agile oversimplified the whole business of understanding customers by giving that job to one person—the product owner. Anything beyond the most basic customer needs are too complex for that approach to work reliably in today's market. We hope you'll find that the ideas in this book give you practical ways to break out of that mold and actually talk to real customers.

Interestingly, most Agilists have concluded that shorter sprints work better than longer ones: sprints of one to two weeks are better than sprints of three to four weeks. We have come to a similar conclusion; you should probably aim to finish a single cycle within two weeks. Left to their own devices, most teams will spend too long on an iteration. Time boxing is key to keep people moving, and Agile sprints are a really natural way to time box on a software project.

Lean Startup

The ideas of Lean Startup were made popular by Eric Ries's book of the same name and are rooted in a combination of Steve Blank's "Four Steps to the Epiphany" approaches to entrepreneurship and the continuing evolution of lean approaches that started with "lean manufacturing" at Toyota in the 1990s.[4] The lean approach believes in finding ways to achieve equivalent value but with less work. Lean Startup takes this core belief and applies it from a business-minded entrepreneur's frame of mind to identifying and incubating successful new business ventures. However, the ideas in it are just as relevant to developing new services, products, and offerings in established companies as they are for an entrepreneurial startup.

There are particularly strong parallels between the Fast Feedback Cycle, the scientific method, and Lean Startup techniques. The build-measure-learn cycle is really just a simpler statement of the essence of the scientific method: experiment, collect data, create hypothesis. Lean Startup's focus on "innovation-accounting" measurement techniques emphasizes the importance of collecting data rigorously to prove or disprove your hypothesis, and to not allow "vanity metrics" or other psychological biases to get in the way of objectively assessing progress against your actual business results. The idea of a faked-up home page for your new offering is another form of a rapid, low-cost prototype intended to get customer feedback as quickly as possible to verify that you are on the right track with a minimum of sunk cost. As Ries would say, your goal is to reduce your "mean time to learning."

Similarly, a "minimum viable product" is a powerful concept to help keep a team focused, usually on solving a single scenario and seeing how it does in the market before branching out.

Mix and match your toolbox

At the core, these approaches are inherently compatible because they are fundamentally based on the rhythm of the scientific method. Therefore, it's ridiculous to say, "We have to decide whether to use Scenario-Focused Engineering or Agile for this project." Or "Is it better to go with user-centered design or Lean Startup?" It absolutely does not need to be an either/or proposition.

Rather, the questions to ask are "Which Agile techniques would be helpful for this project?" and "Which Scenario-Focused Engineering techniques would apply?" and "Which Lean Startup techniques would work?" Each methodology provides a set of techniques that enrich the toolbox; these techniques are born from different perspectives and emphasize different sets of expertise, but they are all fundamentally compatible. Use the tools and techniques that work for your situation and your team. When you consider them in the context of the Fast Feedback Cycle, you will find that they fit together nicely.

As we detail each stage in the Fast Feedback Cycle in the following chapters, you will see that you can choose from dozens of different specific techniques within each stage. In most cases, we encourage you to pick one or perhaps only a small handful of techniques to use at any given time—certainly don't feel as though you have to do it all, or even think that doing it all would be ideal. Actually, the idea is to select the fewest number of techniques and activities at each stage that give you just enough information to move forward to the next stage as quickly as possible. Remember that fast iterations are the key!

We have coached many different teams as they adopt an approach based on Scenario-Focused Engineering, often with a mix of Agile or Lean Startup (and sometimes both) mixed in. Our experience is that this is not a cookie-cutter process, and there is no single best recipe that works for everyone. Each team is responsible for building its toolbox to complement the scale of its project, its timeline, the skills already on the team, and all the other myriad factors that make each team unique. Each team's toolbox is different. However, we've found that a few tools are used more often than others, and these are the ones we elaborate on throughout the next chapters in sections that we call "Deep Dive."

If you aren't sure where to start, rest assured that experts are available for nearly every topic discussed in this book. We'll highlight the places where getting expert help is a particularly good idea.

 MINDSHIFT

You're probably noticing by now that there is some pretty heavy stuff embedded in Scenario-Focused Engineering. On the surface, the Fast Feedback Cycle looks easy and straightforward. But actually implementing it in an engineering team is far from simple, and there are many questions to answer. We've worked with a lot of teams, and there are common issues, questions, and tradeoffs that come up with nearly every one.

How do you schedule for iteration when you can't predict how many iterations you need to get to a great solution? How can you write scenarios when you're not sure what your customer really needs? Who is going to do all of that customer research anyway? Should every developer really go visit customers instead of writing code, or is reading a trip report sufficient? Who exactly is our target customer? How will we get access to customers to test early prototypes quickly without a lot of overhead? Realistically, can we actually plan out an entire engineering release without a feature list and focus on a small number of end-to-end scenarios instead? How can we keep focus on scenarios all the way to the endgame—what project reviews, status-tracking systems, or scorecards will we need to keep us honest? Will our leadership actually support this approach? Does our office space, performance-review process, and team culture support the kind of open collaboration we need for this approach to work?

Probably the most significant aspect beyond any individual question is the fact that you need the entire engineering team to use this approach for it to actually work. Indeed, this is one of our biggest insights from starting the Scenario-Focused Engineering initiative at Microsoft, and it has been reinforced over and over again as we've worked with countless teams to adopt these ideas. There are noteworthy changes in schedule, process, and tools, as well as significant shifts in mindset, leadership, and team culture that need to happen to make the Fast Feedback Cycle a reality, especially on a large scale.

If you are one developer on a larger team reading this book, what do you do? You can't change the whole organization, can you? Take heart, the good news is that you don't have to do the entire Fast Feedback Cycle to get some nice benefits—even just brainstorming more intentionally, or taking the time to write a scenario before you jump headlong into solutions, will give you plenty of incremental gains. You don't have to do everything; you can still get a lot of benefit by making use of just a few of these tools and techniques. Furthermore, as excellent as this book may be—we are sad to say that the chances of you reading this book and becoming an expert practitioner overnight are pretty slim. It takes most teams years to truly make this shift, so be patient with yourself. Appendix A includes the SFE capability roadmap, which is a checklist of skills and behaviors that can help you plan your team's progress over time and prioritize which skills are most important for your team to develop and improve on.

We have seen many teams get started very simply. A single champion on the team identifies a couple of practices that make sense to try in an incremental way. That champion recruits a few buddies on the team to help make it happen on one small project. After those first attempts show some success, the larger team becomes more receptive, the leaders agree to train the rest of the team, and the practice continues to develop from there. It's worth noting that even teams that have tried to "do it all" found that there was a practical limit to how much change their organization could absorb at one time. We'll continue discussing the team and cultural impacts of adopting Scenario-Focused Engineering throughout the book and in detail in Chapter 12, "Lessons learned."

Summary

Good product design follows a predictable, age-old pattern that can be learned and replicated. This pattern is encapsulated in the rhythm of the Fast Feedback Cycle, which is an application of the scientific method to the business of designing and delivering software products, services, or devices. By observing customers, framing their key scenarios, exploring multiple ideas, prototyping rapidly, and judging your progress against customer feedback and predetermined metrics, you can quickly discover whether you're on the right track to delight your target customers, with an absolute minimum of sunk cost.

Notes

1. Interestingly, better ergonomics wasn't something that customers were asking for per se, as people didn't seem to think it was possible to make a mouse more ergonomic. This is a great example of an unarticulated customer need.

2. The ergonomic mouse met all its sales targets, despite being released just at the start of the recession and despite being a high-end product for a niche market. But it didn't get universally great reviews—in fact, the reviews were somewhat polarized. There were many customers who absolutely loved this mouse. Then there were others who complained that it didn't work at all for lefties or that the buttons didn't work well for smaller hands or for very large hands. The product team made a conscious choice to focus on right-handed people of average size knowing that it couldn't do its ergonomic goals justice for a broader group, which was a key constraint the team figured into its business plan and sales targets. But for the target customer, this mouse was a dream come true and had a loyal following.

3. Abductive logic was originally coined by Charles Sanders Peirce (http://plato.stanford.edu/entries/peirce/) in the early 1900s as he described the interplay between abductive logic (making hypotheses), deductive logic, and inductive logic in the scientific method. More recently, Roger Martin discussed the role of abduction in design thinking in his books *Opposable Mind: Winning Through Integrative Thinking* (Harvard Business Review Press, 2009) and *The Design of Business: Why Design Thinking Is the Next Competitive Advantage* (Harvard Business Review Press, 2009).

4. Eric Reis, *The Lean Startup: How Today's Entrepreneurs Use Continuous Innovation to Create Radically Successful Businesses* (New York: Crown Business, 2011); Steve Blank, *The Four Steps to the Epiphany*, 2nd ed. (K&S Ranch, 2013).

PART II

The Fast Feedback Cycle

Emotionally delighted customers will forgive

WHO ARE YOU BUILDING A SOLUTION FOR? mistakes and missing features

Don't ship peanut butter **Who is your team's NORTH STAR?**

CUSTOMER Rowing in the
same direction

YOU CAN'T OPTIMIZE FOR EVERYONE

Decision about target customers is a You don't have time to
key deliverable of team leaders **be specific** build everything

you must **focus** WHICH CUSTOMER IS Get the team aligned
DRIVING YOUR MARKET?

CUT EARLY, MAXIMIZE CARRYOVER:
NOT LATE carryover 80% CASE, INFLUENCER, LEAD USER
gives you focus and breadth

MAP OUT YOUR **Lead users have deeper, sharper needs**

CUSTOMER ECOSYSTEM **that can be easier to spot**

Informed by a solid business strategy

CHAPTER 4

Identifying your target customer

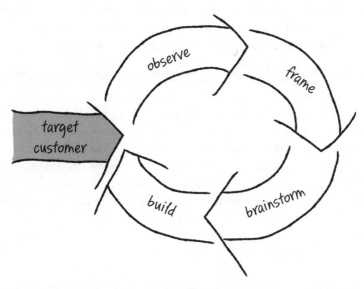

The chapters in the first part of this book explored customer delight. Today, customers expect and demand solutions that solve their real-world problems; they don't want a pile of loosely connected features and capabilities. In the current market, you need not only to deliver complete experiences, but to do so while connecting with your customers at an emotional level.

We introduced the Fast Feedback Cycle as a structured approach to building end-to-end experiences in a customer-focused, iterative way, with high efficiency and minimum risk. But how do you know which end-to-end experiences to build in the first place?

In this chapter, we go into detail about the most important prerequisite to the Fast Feedback Cycle: identifying your target customer.

Why you need a target customer

Before you can build an end-to-end experience, you need to know who you are building the experience for and what that customer needs—you need a target customer. You need to understand your target customer deeply enough to know what problems that customer faces, to figure out what motivates that customer, and to discover what a truly outstanding solution would look like from that customer's point of view.

You need to study customers in depth to start developing this understanding. This raises some immediate questions: Which customers do you study? If you have time to study only a few of them in depth, how do you ensure that the customers you talk with aren't outliers and aren't going to lead you astray? Who are your customers, anyway?

It turns out that selecting a target customer (and getting an entire team aligned on this customer) is a harder challenge than it first appears. Your current product likely serves many different customers who have different needs, motivations, and desires. For instance, Microsoft Office is used by many types of people: soccer moms organizing the snack schedule for weekly games, college students doing group projects, small-business owners promoting their businesses, research scientists capturing their findings, and, of course, knowledge workers in large enterprises. All of these market segments create documents, read email, and possibly also give presentations or make calculations in a spreadsheet. However, the situations in which they use this functionality differ substantially, as do the features they rely on the most. College students do a lot of group projects, so they want seamless ways to share documents, communicate status, and ensure that they don't accidentally overwrite one another's work. Scientists, on the other hand, care most about being able to embed graphs, charts, and mathematical equations in their research papers, and small-business owners get significant value from the ability to produce high-quality marketing collateral without having to hire an expert. All these groups are using Microsoft Word to do their work in this case, but the ways in which they use Word vary quite a bit.

You need to focus

It's tempting and natural to want to do everything for everyone. A common approach to product development is to start by building a flexible, general-purpose tool that can be used by a wide variety of people, figuring that it will fit 80 percent of people's needs and that will be close enough. This one-size-fits-all approach worked pretty well in the first couple of decades of the personal computer industry, when building a generally useful and reasonably usable solution was enough to distinguish yourself from competitors.

 MINDSHIFT

Learning from fast food. Even the stalwart McDonald's has realized that a one-size-fits-all approach no longer works with today's consumers. The company has shifted after a long history of its franchises using identical menus in cities around the world to introducing localized menus that reflect local needs, customs, and regional foods. From the McBaguette in France, to red-bean pies in China and Big Rösti in Germany, local specialties are the best-sellers that are driving McDonald's international success and are largely why McDonald's continues to survive overseas while Burger King has stalled.[1] McDonald's franchises in each locale are allowed to focus on what works for their specific market. The company has realized that today's customers expect more than the standard burger-and-fries formula that worked for generations.

However, the general-purpose-tool approach isn't really working anymore. Inevitably, you hear from customers that your default solution isn't quite hitting the mark—they're asking for this feature and that bug fix, compatibility with such-and-such format, and the list goes on. Product teams try to squeeze in as many of these requests as possible—a configurable parameter for this need, a fix for that issue—but even when you give customers exactly what they asked for, somehow it's still not enough. They might even start complaining that your product is now too complicated.

One approach to finding the next breakthrough solution is to "throw spaghetti at the wall and see what sticks." When it's not clear what will resonate with users, you opt to ship a bunch of different things and hope that at least one of them will end up being a runaway success. While you might get lucky, this approach is inefficient and likely means that you'll divide your team's time across many initiatives, most of which will not pan out. The sentiment here is good—be experimental and try different things—but the key is to find ways to experiment in a cheap, fast way that lets you quickly narrow in on which ideas are working long before you invest in production code and the full release process.

Whether your development philosophy is more traditional, or—more likely these days—uses some more Agile methods, it usually boils down to a protocol that looks something like this:

- Gather up a long list of all the possible things you could do. These ideas will come from all over: the engineers on the team will have suggestions, but you'll also have customer requests, new concepts generated in brainstorming sessions, and, of course, the myriad stuff that didn't make the cut in your last release cycle.

- Next, do a rough, T-shirt-size cost estimate (XS, S, M, L, XL, XXL) of how expensive each item would be to build. Then, debate that list to end up with a stack-ranked, prioritized backlog of work items.

- Finally, draw a cut line based on the number of man-hours available, and that's the list of stuff that you attempt to get done.

With this approach, there's never a shortage of ideas, but you can easily start arguing about the list because you don't have time to do everything. With rare exceptions you end up arguing about this feature versus that one—or this user story versus that one—and not about end-to-end experiences. It's easy to win a battle but lose the war, ending up with a plan that has lots of features—but without some intentional planning, very few of those features will naturally thread together into a complete end-to-end experience that delights customers.

What's worse is that throughout the product-development process, you'll find problems. Despite best intentions and a perennial feeling that "this time will be different," software projects are consistently hard to schedule and always take longer than you think. Estimates are overly aggressive, problems are harder to solve than you expected, and integration issues that no one anticipated pop up. Faced with a hard deadline when time to market is essential, you can be forced late in the cycle to cut features that just aren't coming together. What might even have started out as an end-to-end experience in the planning stages is weakened by the time it's released because the middle of your beautifully planned solution has been cut, leaving the customer hanging.

The trouble is that it's all too easy to reach the end of a big development push and hear that the marketing team is having a genuinely hard time figuring out how to talk about your new release. They just don't have much to say. None of the individual features you built are big enough or important enough to make much of a splash. The team did a lot of work across the codebase, fixed a lot of bugs and resolved a lot of open issues, and perhaps even substantially improved quality, but looking back, nothing really stands out.

We call this phenomenon shipping a "peanut butter" release—you spread a thin layer of peanut butter across your solution, and, unsurprisingly, no customer gets particularly excited about the result —nothing all that interesting or remarkable differentiates your offering from your competitors—or even from your previous version. From sprint to sprint, this kind of gradual, iterative improvement can be acceptable. But if you're trying to make a big splash with customers and end up shipping peanut butter, the results can be quite disheartening.

You can't optimize for everyone

Actually, it's even more complex than that—even with unlimited time and resources, building a solution for all potential customers is an unsolvable problem. Different types of customers often have conflicting needs. A soccer mom receives five email messages a day and would prefer a super-simple view in which to read her email without any confusing bells and whistles. A knowledge worker receives 150 emails per day and regularly uses folders, automatic sorting rules, and message flagging to stay on top of his daily workload. How do you build one email service that optimizes the experience for both usage patterns?

Without building a complex rat's nest of modes (or an entirely different offering) for every user situation, it's not possible to optimize a solution for every type of user. If you can find a win-win solution, of course that's ideal, but usually you find yourself with an unsolvable constraint equation. If you optimize for user A, you end up making it awkward for user B. If you optimize for user B, user A's experience isn't as smooth. If you aim for something in the middle, no one gets what they really need. You just can't make everyone happy all the time.

It's clear that if you want to achieve true delight for anyone, you have to focus. Thankfully, from past experience, you know that you can build a much higher-quality solution if you start with a clear, focused problem statement—so there is hope. But, as we said at the start of this chapter, who exactly should you focus on? How do you pick?

Carryover gives you focus and breadth

A concept we call *carryover* has proved to be very helpful to teams for wrapping their heads around the toughest nut in all of this—how can you focus on a small number of target customers yet achieve the broad market penetration that you are likely hoping for? Many teams aspire to build a product that will have broad, mass-market appeal—whether that market is consumers, developers, enterprises, or small businesses. But, if you're going for breadth, how can you possibly focus on a small set of target customers? It seems impossible.

> *Carryover* is achieving broad market appeal by focusing on and building a truly outstanding solution for a narrow target market, which then also appeals to a "halo" of similar customer segments.

A tale of two can openers

Let's explore this conundrum by looking at a specific, albeit unlikely, example: can openers.

The can opener on the left in Figure 4-1 was designed by a small company named Swing-a-Way (which was acquired in 2005 by Focus Products Group International). It was designed to be a general-purpose tool for anyone who needs to open a can and is found in many kitchen drawers. The can opener on the right is made by OXO Good Grips. You may have recognized it by the chunky, black plastic handles that distinguish the OXO product line. This can opener usually sells for around twice the price of a Swing-a-Way can opener.

FIGURE 4-1 The can opener on the left was made by Swing-a-Way. The can opener on the right was made by OXO Good Grips.

What you may not know about OXO is that it was founded by a man named Sam Farber, a mechanical engineer whose wife had arthritis in her hands. His inspiration was to build kitchen gadgets that were highly ergonomic—gadgets that his wife could use comfortably. As OXO introduced its line of ergonomic products, a funny thing happened. The market reacted surprisingly well to the company's innovative designs. It turns out that when you make a product ergonomic enough for someone with arthritis to use, it's remarkably comfortable for most other people as well. Even though its design made the product more bulky—which meant it did not always sit flat in a kitchen drawer—the benefit that it brought far outweighed that downside for many, many people. So much so that OXO is able to charge a premium for its products.

Getting this carryover from a narrow target market (arthritis sufferers) into a much broader market (anyone who appreciates ergonomics) was always part of Sam Farber's plan. The plan worked, and OXO has enjoyed strong business success. Since its founding in 1990, it has developed a portfolio of 800 products that are sold in 50 countries and has received more than 100 design awards.

Here's another example of carryover—travel suitcases with wheels. It may be hard to remember a time when suitcases didn't come with wheels, but those now-ubiquitous wheeled suitcases were first designed for pilots and crew members, who were constantly lugging bags around the airport. Even though mainstream consumers traveled much less frequently, the benefits of a small, portable travel bag with wheels were appealing enough that people were willing to buy a new suitcase for the convenience.

How does carryover work?

Carryover is the key principle that makes it possible to focus on a small set of customers but still achieve broad market appeal. Here's how it works. Imagine that this oval contains all the customers who might ever use your service or buy your product.

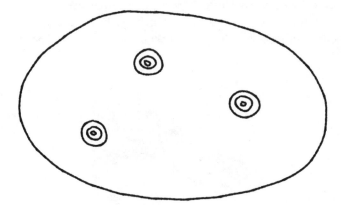

What you want to do is pick a few very specific customers to focus on and mark each with a bull's eye. Think of your target customers as the canonical cases around which you will optimize your solutions.

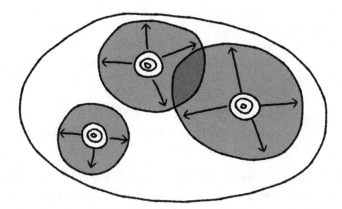

Now, for each of your target customers, you reason that if you fully solve their problems and make each specific customer truly, deeply delighted, there will also be a larger carryover population similar to that target customer who will also appreciate your solution. Your solution might not solve every one of these other customers' needs, but the needs it does address are handled completely and delightfully, so those carryover customers are also pretty satisfied. The carryover population for one target customer may be small but perhaps financially lucrative. For another target customer, the potential carryover may be very large because there is a large population of similar people. The idea is that if you choose your targets strategically, it's quite possible to get substantial market penetration by focusing on a few target customers who will give you the broadest possible carryover.

No, you won't be able to nail every single customer's needs with this approach, but you will be able to solve a lot of the most important ones. More importantly, you will be able to reach substantial market breadth while still providing clear focus for your team to ensure high-quality execution. And if you do your job right, the customers that you do reach will be those truly great customers we all dream about—*the ones who are loyal, passionate, and truly love your solution because it solves some of their real-life, end-to-end problems in a completely delightful way.*

Neuroscience break by Dr. Indrė Viskontas

Even before neuroscientists were able to peek inside the brain using neuroimaging, psychologists knew that the bulk of our decision-making computations were not available to our conscious minds. That is, most of the choices we make every day are the result of cognitive processes that are implicit, or outside our stream of consciousness. Indeed, the entire marketing industry is built on the observation that our decisions are often shaped by even the most subtle factors, like the music playing in the background while we shop for jeans.

Most of us remain blissfully unaware of the fact that conscious thoughts are only the tip of the iceberg, and what we feel is a rational, willful, and deliberate decision is actually the final step in a long series of calculations that our neurons have computed without our conscious help. In fact, more often than not, when we justify our reasons for having made a particular choice, we rely on the "interpreter" in our brain: the inner narrative voice that tries to make sense of our actions after the fact.

Neuroscientists first discovered the interpreter in action when they studied so-called split-brain patients—patients who underwent surgery to sever the connections between the two hemispheres of the brain to limit the spread of epileptic seizures. With these patients, neuroscientists could query each side of the brain independently, and they were shocked to find that when the right hemisphere made a decision, the left hemisphere, instead of admitting that it had no idea why the action was taken, made up a justification on the spot. Each of us displays the same type of confabulation—or "honest lying"—when we are asked to introspect and give a reason for why we made a particular choice. Study after study has shown that our interpreter weaves a narrative that makes sense of our actions, regardless of the actual reasons behind our choices.

In the past few decades, as neuroscience has permeated economics, scientists have begun to understand just how inaccurate our interpreter can be. In the 1970s and 1980s, the predecessors of modern neuroeconomists wanted to understand how shoppers chose between identical options. For example, in one famous study experimenters displayed identical nylon stockings on a table in a department store. They found that shoppers were more likely to choose the items on the right side of the table than on the left. But when the researchers asked the shoppers why they chose a particular set of stockings, the shoppers would talk about differences in quality, fabric, and other characteristics, never mentioning table position. Remember that all the items were identical.

In follow-up work, it became clear that the decision to buy is often driven by a gut instinct—an emotional or otherwise irrational reason that our rational frontal cortex doesn't have access to. Because we think of ourselves as rational people, our interpreter finds an explanation in line with that view of our personality. This tendency toward a rational explanation for an irrational choice even permeates our dating life: in another famous study, subjects were shown pictures of people of the opposite sex and asked to pick which one they found more attractive. Using sleight of hand in a portion of the trials, experimenters actually switched out the choices so that the participant had to justify a choice that he or she in fact did not make. And in a large portion of these trials, the participants didn't notice the switch and instead confabulated reasons for why that potential mate was more attractive than his or her partner. "I like her earrings" or "He has a nice smile," they would say, when, in fact, that particular photo was rejected initially in favor of another.

From neuroimaging, patient work, and other techniques, neuroscientists are beginning to finally see just how much power our unconscious mind yields over our decisions and just how late our rational, thoughtful frontal cortex is to the party.

How does the nature of our brain wiring affect your choice of target customers? It should reinforce the importance of delivering a high-quality, emotionally desirable experience. Ironically, when you solve a few of the most pressing end-to-end needs of a customer in a way that is deeply delightful for the irrational, emotional part of the brain, that customer will be quite willing to forgive many transgressions.

For example, even after many years of releases, the iPhone still had deficiencies, yet it maintained an incredibly loyal fan base because of its seamless integration of music, apps, games, and communication in a single, ultraportable package, which has become a hallmark of Apple's brand. Facebook's privacy rules are complex and default to sharing more openly than we might ordinarily choose—but the dopamine hit you get from seeing the picture of your sister winning the 5K seconds after it happens far outweighs those problems for most users.

What you do extremely well in your solution seems to count a lot more in the customer's mind than what you had to cut (despite the vocal complaints of a few power users who will try to convince you otherwise.) On the flip side, if you don't address the essence of what the customer needs, every minor nit will become magnified. Figuring out how to tickle the irrational, emotional brain to achieve delight really matters.

It's a complex ecosystem

So far we've talked mainly about end users, but they're only one piece of the puzzle. The reality is that your ecosystem is much more complex. For instance, if you are writing a developer platform, who are your customers then? The developers using your platform or the end users who will use the applications that those developers write? What if you are selling enterprise software? Is your customer the IT manager who makes the purchasing decision or the knowledge workers who will use your software every day? Which one is more important? Whose experience should you optimize? Where should you invest your limited resources?

Most businesses have not just one type of customer but many customers—that is, many different types of people and organizations that they deliver value to—and those customers are almost always connected into a larger value chain or ecosystem. The end user is surely important, but in today's markets, developer platforms, independent software vendors (ISVs), hardware vendors, service providers, and other partners can also play a big role in your ultimate success.

What is a customer, exactly?

Let's settle on some definitions. For the purposes of this book, we're going to use a very expansive definition of customer. A customer is any person, group, entity, company, and so on, that you need to interact with as part of the ecosystem of your business. Here are some common ones:

- **End users**   These people actually use the software and are usually the first group you think of when you think about customers. This group could include anyone from a consumer home user to a knowledge worker in a large enterprise. At the end of the day, if end users aren't delighted with your solution, you will definitely have problems.

- **Purchasers and IT managers**   This group comes up frequently if you are selling to larger businesses in which the person who makes the buying decision (and often also owns the deployment, rollout, and support costs) has very distinct needs from the end-user knowledge workers who will use the product day to day.

- **Developers and ISVs**   Many ecosystems rely on having other developers or independent software vendors build on top of a particular platform. The availability of apps that you can purchase on all the major mobile platforms is a great example. Developer platforms are common in larger software teams, even in businesses that aren't explicitly focused on building platforms per se, where, for example, a platform allows a crucial integration. Sometimes these developers are internal to your company—such as development teams outside your immediate workgroup. It's just as valid to consider internal developers to be your target customers as to focus on external developers.

- **External partners**   Other business partners in your ecosystem can frequently be important target customers, whether they are mobile phone carriers, hardware vendors, cloud service providers, or others.

No matter what role these customer groups play in your ecosystem, all of them can be considered customers. Depending on your business strategy, any of these groups could be your most important (highest-priority) target customer.

Getting specific about customers

How specific do you need to be when deciding on a target customer? Can't you just say that you're building a product for consumer end users rather than business users? While that's a great first-order decision, not all consumers are alike in their needs, motivations, and preferences (just like all developers aren't alike). It's obvious that different types of consumers have different needs—young and old, male and female, single and married, with or without kids, living in different parts of the world, and so on.

You need to consider finer-grained customer segments than just "consumer": each target customer should represent a segment of customers who are reasonably alike in their core needs, motivations, and preferences. When settling on a target customer, you need to boil down that segment into an actionable, single customer profile that can be easily used and internalized by the engineering team. It's hard to optimize for an entire group of people. It's much easier if you build out a profile of one person and use that single person as the representative of the larger group.

Many teams find that developing a target customer segment based on behavioral or attitudinal aspects is more useful than developing segments based purely on similar demographics. For instance, "novice software developers" could be young or old, male or female, and from many different locales, but everyone in this category has very similar needs for an easy-to-use software development environment. Or, in a consumer space, "trendy socialites" may represent a wide variety of demographic stats, but they all share common attitudes, needs, and behaviors in the use of mobile phones, social networks, and other communication technologies.

 TIP

As in all things, don't make assumptions when thinking about customer segments; do your homework. Research is needed to understand the complexities of your market. Product planners, marketers, and other business experts are great people to lean on to help create a customer segmentation.

How many target customers do I need?

Although we often use the singular term "target customer" in this book, you will hardly ever decide to focus on a single customer—markets and business ecosystems are more complex than that. However, many teams have found tremendous benefit in explicitly prioritizing some customers in their ecosystem more than others, both for clarifying the strategic direction and to communicate that direction clearly to the entire engineering team. In the end, you are aiming to identify three or four specific customers who are central to driving your business—along with a crisp notion of priority or the interrelationship between them, including what kind of carryover you can expect to get from each to the broader market.

In our experience, three or four target customers seem to be the practical maximum for good results, regardless of the size of your organization, and very small teams may opt to focus on only one or two customers. Think of your target customers as the primary cases that you will optimize for, and be confident that you will get carryover into broader markets if you choose your targets wisely. There are some specific strategies for how to choose targets to maximize carryover that we'll discuss in the next section.

Identify stage: Tools and techniques

Now that you see that having a clear target customer is important—and the complexity of the choices ahead of you—let's talk about how you figure out who your target customer should be. The first step is to get some clarity about your business strategy because your target customer should be tightly aligned with it.

While this is not a book about business strategy development, we do have to begin somewhere. This section lists a few techniques to help you get started choosing a target customer and developing a strategic direction. Don't get too hung up on this; you don't have to have perfect answers. But you do need to make some big-picture assertions about what business you are entering and whose problems you are trying to solve.

In the rest of this book, we urge you to collect real data and to modify your plans as the problems you are trying to solve and the solutions you are building are brought more crisply into focus through iteration and learning. The data you collect as you iterate will help you fine-tune your choice of target customer, or may even point you toward a different, more lucrative target customer.

Develop a business strategy

The choice of target customers quickly becomes a strategic question. Typically, there isn't only one possible answer: you have several viable target customers to focus on, each of which might be the key to your market success. What you should do is avoid the nightmare scenario in which you do a terrific job focusing on a target customer—and they indeed love your offering—but you find out much too late that they never had any intention of paying for your service, nor are they a particularly valuable target for advertising either.

Before your team spends any time writing code, it's important to ask how you are going to make money, and which customers are key to making that plan work. While the specific process behind building a business strategy is outside the scope of this book, one thing is very clear: you must have a business strategy that is in sync with your choice of target customer.

Settling on a strategy is a tough decision, and since none of us owns a functioning crystal ball, you can never be certain which road will be the right one. It's no surprise that when faced with this kind of situation, engineering leaders are apt to put off this decision. It's not at all unusual for one person to have a gut feeling for one path, while a peer has data to suggest another one, and since both approaches seem viable, it's hard to put the question to rest. Without clear direction, teams can end up executing against both strategies, or they ignore the business strategy altogether and instead focus on what seems to be a promising piece of technology. What results is an engineering team that is forced to operate in a world of shifting priorities—where the "most important things" are different depending on who you talk to. In a world of finite resources, this lack of clarity naturally causes a team to not execute particularly well on anything, and this is evident in the resulting solution.

Being clear about direction is important, and the responsibility sits with the team's leaders. They must provide a clear strategic direction to guide the team's work. For software engineering teams, one of the most tangible outputs of the strategy process is the decision of which target customers to focus on. Having a clear customer focus is an absolutely necessary precondition to delivering outstanding, high-quality end-to-end experiences.

So you know you need a business strategy, or at least a strong (and data-driven) idea about a market opportunity you want to pursue, but the question remains which strategy is actually the right one. There are so many factors to consider here, and this topic is well outside the scope of this book (and worthy of a book or two of its own!—we list a few of our favorite books on the topic of developing and iterating successful business strategies in Appendix C, "Further reading"). You must do your homework to understand the market, the competitive landscape, buying patterns, pricing models, trends, and the whole host of other factors that can affect your ultimate business success. We encourage you to seek the counsel of experts—though keep in mind that no one can predict the future.

Using the iterative approach described in this book will help you learn quickly whether your chosen strategy is working and will give you the feedback you need to change course before you have spent too much time pursuing a dead end. Especially when you're establishing new business models, iteration is key—expect to get it wrong the first time and be willing to shift approaches when needed and figure out what actually works in the real world.

It's no coincidence that the business strategy books we like share many similarities with the concepts underlying the Fast Feedback Cycle, especially with respect to the need to deeply understand your customer and then prototype, test, and iterate business strategies with real customer and market feedback. You may not pick the optimal strategy the first time, but as you iterate with customers, you will quickly learn and adjust. This doesn't mean that you can go without a plan, however—it is critical to have an initial plan, test it, measure it, and then see how it did and adjust accordingly. You know, just like the scientific method.

Map out your ecosystem

Once you have identified a business opportunity you want to pursue and have crafted the beginnings of a business strategy, you need to prioritize and crisply articulate the customer segment you're going to target. One way to better understand your customers and to help you decide which of them you want to target is to draw a diagram of your customer landscape. By doing so you can visualize the entire ecosystem and clarify the relationships and interdependencies between different customer types. Figure 4-2 shows three examples.

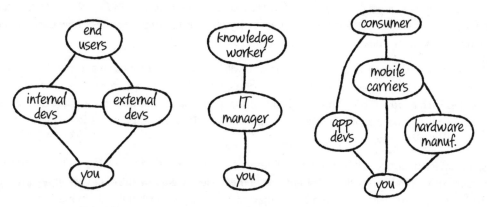

FIGURE 4-2 Three customer relationship diagrams: (left to right) a developer platform business, selling into enterprises, and a mobile phone business.

So which customer is really driving your market—who is holding the torch to lead the way? Which customer will give you the biggest leverage in the overall system? Is it the end user, who is demanding the service and will drive the market, making the intermediary developers and service providers merely cogs in the system? Or is the key factor the availability of apps on the platform, which means the developer is king and you should focus your primary efforts on enticing and retaining developers?

Multiple factors can easily be driving the market, and sometimes be in direct conflict with one another. Consider the mobile phone market. Who would you optimize for if you were entering that market today? Having a strong network of developers building lots of apps is crucial to attracting end users, but at the same time you also need a large, addressable market of end users to entice those developers to want to build on your platform in the first place. Will a large market of unique apps in fact be the best way to attract those end users, meaning you should focus on luring developers to your platform with a highly desirable developer experience? Or is having a beautiful, seamless user experience the key, so it matters less which apps are available or how many there are? These factors are clearly highly interdependent. But a third factor might actually be the most important—the availability of your device on different carriers, and perhaps even the pricing. Of all these complex factors, which one do you believe is the chicken and which is the egg, or must you split your energy and target both? Many paths are viable, and each represents very different business strategies.

This decision about who is driving the market will have a profound impact on your business strategy. It's worth doing some careful analysis and thinking through what-if scenarios as you decide which of the customers in your ecosystem are really driving the market, who you are going to bank on, and how to prioritize your efforts between them.

Strategies for maximizing carryover

Earlier in the chapter you learned about carryover and saw that it's theoretically possible to gain broad adoption by doing a great job for a few focused customers. You've also seen ways to gain an understanding of all the different customers who may play a role in your business, how they interact, and which of them may be more or less important to your success.

Obviously, you want to focus on customers who will be financially profitable and cull those who are unwilling or unable to pay for your solutions or are not valuable targets for indirect monetization approaches such as advertising. You may also find that particular customer segments are extremely profitable, so it can make a lot of sense to prioritize the needs of those segments so that you retain them as valuable customers.

Many times, though, you'll have a lot of different kinds of customers who all seem to be equally important, and it can be very difficult to prioritize them. Here are a few strategies we've seen teams use to prioritize target customers in order to maximize carryover, which helps them maximize their breadth in the market with a minimum number of target customers to worry about:

- **The 80 percent case**   If your business is lucky enough to have an 80 percent case, where the majority of your users are alike and have similar needs, that's a natural and obvious choice for a target customer. (No, it doesn't have to be fully 80 percent of your customer base, just a large enough bucket to matter business-wise.) However, be warned that this situation isn't particularly common—customer needs tend to be a lot more diverse than many may think.[2]

- **The influencer**   This situation surfaces in many different markets. The idea is to focus on a set of customers who are highly influential in your market. If you can get those influential customers to buy your solution, others will notice and follow. You can also approach this as a social strategy with which you focus on the users with the most connections or friends. Or you can focus on a high-profile customer with a lot of clout, where if that customer buys, others will trust your solution, too (that is, land the Mayo Clinic as a customer, and other smaller medical centers will likely buy, too). Focusing on getting great press reviews could be another approach, if those reviews will influence the buying behavior of others.

- **The lead user**   This is like the OXO can opener or wheeled-suitcase situation and is perhaps the most powerful approach. The lead user is a customer who has deeper or sharper needs than the rest of the market. Many other customers have some of these same needs, just not to as great a degree. As we mentioned, it's hard to remember a time when suitcases didn't come with wheels, but the first wheeled suitcases were designed for pilots and flight attendants, not consumers. A customer with arthritis needs great ergonomic products, but a user without that condition very much appreciates ergonomics as well. The novice developer needs inline SDK documentation as she is writing her first lines of code, but more-experienced programmers appreciate having the call signatures at their fingertips, too. One way to discover a potential lead-user opportunity is to study outliers in your population (novices, subject matter experts, people who use your tool in unusual ways)—their needs may be more obvious and easier to spot than the more subtle expression of those same needs in the larger population.

TIP

Beware the computer power user! Focusing on the computer power user is not a successful application of the lead-user strategy. The computer power user does indeed have deeper, sharper needs, but the rest of the population typically does not share any of those needs, so you should not expect much carryover.

The idea is to pick a set of target customers that will maximize carryover, and to be quite intentional about focusing on them. Which of these customers are the most important? Who is really driving your market, and therefore your business success? It comes right back to your business strategy. Whichever target customers you land on need to be 100 percent aligned with your business strategy.

Empower the team with a North Star

No matter how you develop your business strategy, or how you choose your target customer, your plan won't be effective unless the entire team can pragmatically understand it and apply it in its daily decision making. *From the perspective of the engineering team, the choice of target customer may be the most practical output of the leadership team's decisions about business strategy.*

Think of your target customer as your team's North Star. No matter what decision team members make, large or small, every team member should always take a moment to look up and verify that they are still heading for true north—that is, building something that your target customer is going to find deeply delightful because it solves an important problem for that customer.

Why do you need a North Star?

Why is it important for the whole team to internalize your strategy? Because at nearly every step of the product development process, and in every layer of the codebase, individuals on the team will be making tradeoffs as the product takes shape. While the big decisions may get discussed thoroughly, many more small decisions will be made in the solitude of a developer's office. Cumulatively, these small decisions can matter just as much as the big ones. Should this parameter be a user-configurable option or just a hard-coded, reasonable default? Is it more important to optimize this section of code for performance or for scale?

Consider this scenario about a late-night tradeoff. It's 9:00 p.m., and your star developer is the only one left in the office; she's on a roll and isn't ready to quit yet. A question occurs to her: Is it better to optimize this algorithm for performance or for accuracy? She can argue the issue both ways in her head, but it comes down to whether the target user cares more about getting a *complete* list of search results or getting an initial result set as *quickly* as possible. Because she knows that the target customer is a small-business owner who is shopping primarily for price, the decision is easy—you need the full set to be sure you are returning the lowest-price items at the top of the list. If she didn't know that, she could have just as easily coded the feature the other way or waited until tomorrow to bring it up in the daily standup.

It's clearly not efficient to hold a meeting whenever a question comes up, and indeed that's why companies hire smart, talented people who can make good decisions on their own. Some of these tradeoffs will be flagged as important enough for more formal attention from leaders, and spec and code reviews will provide a layer of review. However, many of these decisions tend to get made in the moment by relatively small groups or individuals. So, especially across a large project, it raises an important question: How will you ensure that these micro-tradeoffs are actually all aiming in the same direction?

Without some way to focus the team on a core set of goals, you risk having each person use his or her own best judgment when making decisions—but these decisions may not be aligned with one another across the project. For example, if I optimize my UI code for zippy responsiveness, but the underlying architecture is more focused on getting maximum throughput for a vendor's API that has some inherent latency, I might be unwittingly working at cross-purposes with others on my team. Both decisions are reasonable tradeoffs in isolation, but together they don't make sense. Multiplied by all the various decisions that need to be made across the architecture, platform, and user experience, this can result in an offering that seems a little muddy, like it was built by committee, without a clear vision or direction.

SFE in action: Rowing in the same direction

Panos Panay, Corporate Vice President, Microsoft Surface

Have you ever been on a team where you feel like you're accomplishing very little, that the work you do goes around in a circle instead of progressing toward the team's goals? The key to leading a team and driving it to success is to be sure that everyone is going in the same direction. Whether it's the right direction is a good question, but there can be no room for ambiguity, for a lack of decision making, for a lack of alignment.

To do this, leaders have to live the team's culture and show it in their daily actions. But almost as important, you need to talk about it, and talk about it a lot. My belief is that if you're willing to say something twice as a leader, people listen, and if you say it on a consistent basis, your team will understand how clearly important it is.

But finding the right words, the right way to keep a team aligned and moving forward isn't always easy, and leaders need to turn to many sources to find the inspiration. Everyone on the Surface team is familiar with a particular metaphor we use as the bedrock of our team's culture. This metaphor was originally inspired in a class I took many years ago, but I have evolved the idea into a much broader story over the years.

Imagine a picture of a massive ship, one that needs hundreds of people at its oars to move it through the water fluidly. When I first saw this picture in class, it was a thing of beauty. The image exuded harmony, a sense of power, planfulness, and organization at a massive scale—with all the ship's oars in the water, the ship would move gracefully through the ocean toward its destination. When showing this picture in class, the lecturer used terms such as *decision making, integrity,* and *dealing with ambiguity* to help describe leadership. It made sense. Yet, the closer and longer I looked at this ship, the more dysfunctional it appeared. Some of the oarsmen rowed in the opposite direction from others. Some had left their post, and left their oars dragging. A desk was placed strangely in the middle of the deck, with a group of people huddled around it arguing instead of rowing. The person who was supposed to bang the drum to keep everything in order and in rhythm was kicking back in a chair, asleep under a sign labeled "On Break." We were being taught a valuable lesson during this lecture—that although the ship was majestic and had all kinds of potential, at the end of the day, with its lack of leadership and clear direction, it did nothing but go in circles.

When we started Surface, we made it clear that anyone who wanted to join the Surface team had to get on the ship, grab an oar, put it in the water, and start moving in the same direction. If your teammate can't row, help out. And if you notice that someone is rowing in the wrong direction, point it out and turn them around. To win, to make the best products possible, and to be sure that the team has great energy—that the people on it love what they're doing—the team doesn't have time for cynics, and it doesn't have time for victims. Everyone needs to be on the boat and rowing in the same direction.

This metaphor is ever-present on our team. We use it to help drive the culture. Everybody together, everybody in the boat. We stay committed to fast decision making and clear direction. We even use *oar* in our day-to-day language. In the hallways, you'll often hear someone saying "My oar is in the water." One of the awards we give out is a large oar that's engraved with people's names and passed around from office to office. We might talk about how someone on the team grabbed an oar, and now look at how fast we're moving because of that person's initiative. While this might seem a bit over the top, it's a clear and simple way to align a team with its culture.

The leadership in Surface is committed to providing clear direction that leaves no room for ambiguity. And the metaphor of the ship gives the team absolute license to hold leadership accountable for making decisions that remove hurdles and keep the team moving forward. Our clarity of culture and purpose reflects back on what we do, and it reflects on the quality of our products. It also reflects in the pride we have as a team—working together, creating products together, and rowing together in the same direction.

Despite everyone working their hardest, a team's efforts can easily end up being scattered across multiple possible strategies and multiple target customers, with each member making the best local decision with the data they have on hand. The reality of resource constraints means that you won't end up doing a great job at executing on any one of these strategies, so the risk is high that you will end up shipping peanut butter.

Communicate your North Star broadly

In most cases, it's the job of the leadership team to make the decision about the high-level strategic direction of the team, and that direction setting won't make a bit of difference unless the team is aware of and has bought into that direction. You may think that the responsibility to make this happen lies solely on the top leaders, and while leaders certainly take on a large role in communicating and socializing a team's product strategy, it's everyone's job to turn that strategy into a living, breathing thing that ultimately gets transformed into a solution for your customers.

There are a lot of creative ways to communicate and socialize a strategy throughout a team. One tempting approach is to avoid doing so in the first place. Instead of relying on the broad team to understand the strategy, all decision making is routed through a gatekeeper. For example, a chief designer or architect makes it his business to oversee how things are coming together and to provide guidance and make course corrections as needed. While this can be an effective approach in smaller teams and in high-stakes situations, it breaks down quickly in larger teams where the gatekeeper (or guru) job is bigger than one brain can handle. This approach can also disempower the rest of the team, and that creates its own set of problems.

A better approach is to efficiently communicate the choice of target customers broadly across the team, and explicitly connect the choice of target customers to the business strategy you are pursuing. The goal is to make sure everyone on the team knows why you are focusing on these customers (and why you aren't focusing on others), and what kind of carryover you expect to get in the market. This enables every person on your team to make an informed judgment at every layer of the solution's architecture whenever a tradeoff must be made.

Here are a few ideas that we've found effective for socializing the business and customer strategy throughout the team:

- **Publish a business strategy or framing memo**   Write it and make it broadly available to the team (and probably your partners as well). Bonus points if you write it collaboratively and allow for iteration and feedback from the team. One great way to get buy-in on a strategy is to ask for help in creating it in the first place. We provide more details about creating a framing memo (and you can read a sidebar on the topic) later in the chapter.

- **Hold an all-hands meeting**   Assemble everyone together in a room (or hold a video conference), and present the essence of the team's strategy. These types of all-hands meetings can be incredibly boring, however, and from the team's perspective a brutal waste of time. Put some effort into making the meeting interesting, memorable, and educational for the team. If you can't do that, don't bother.

- **Schedule round-table luncheons**   Meet with every member of the team informally during lunch. It's a common practice to meet with a small group (5–10) each time until the entire team has had an opportunity to hear about and discuss the strategy (and air their points of view).

- **Hang posters in the halls**   Socialize the target customers by creating a poster that features them and their real-life issues. Hang up the posters everywhere, especially in high-traffic areas such as near the kitchen or restrooms.

- **Create a theme for the release**   More than just a code name, come up with some sort of theme that can be used throughout product development to make the main components of your strategy and target customer fun and memorable. For example, in the very early days of developing the C# programming language, the key target customer was nicknamed Elvis, which turned into a full-on, Graceland-inspired theme. Leaders dressed up as Elvis, T-shirts and coffee mugs were created, and there was a video floating around in which Elvis's hit song "C. C. Rider" morphed into "C# Rider." There's nothing like a popular rock song to keep the team abuzz with the target customer in mind.

■ **Invent a pithy acronym**   Assemble some of the key words of your strategy into a memorable acronym. This is a great way to build a shared understanding of a customer or a strategy that can be referenced over and over in shorthand.

Some of these ideas may seem a bit corny, and maybe they are. But the point is to create a shared understanding of your business strategy and target customer throughout the team. Make it memorable and fun and do something that the team can use to create a sense of tribe—and focus that tribal sense around your customers and their needs. Be creative in finding new ways to keep the target customer in sight as the team's North Star throughout the development process.

Write a business strategy memo

A specific tool that has been adopted by many of the leaders within Microsoft is a framing memo. The intent is for the leadership team to collaborate and consider the current business environment, discuss and explore the world of possible opportunities, and identify any key constraints facing the team, the product, or the business environment itself. This high-level business-strategy work is done well ahead of any detailed product planning.

For the team, it spells out clearly the opportunity, the target customer, the goals, the expectations, and the constraints in which the team must operate. Typically, a handful of events are held to socialize the framing memo and its content for every member of the team, thus aligning the team on high-level goals. It's important to understand that this memo does not specify any product features, nor does it say how the team or the product will achieve these goals. But it does a great job of explaining where the product is heading and why. The team is then empowered to figure out how to get there.

SFE in action: The framing memo

PJ Hough, Corporate Vice President, Microsoft Developer Division

I've had the opportunity to represent the Office leadership team and craft the framing memos for several versions of Office. The framing memo is a formalized planning document that is created to kick off a new project. It lays out the current business landscape for the product and describes the opportunities the leadership team would like the team to explore and deliver in the next version.

The notion of a framing memo is something that has evolved over time. In fact, the earliest drafts that I remember weren't formal, nor were they broadly distributed. These early incarnations were simply notes compiled to help the leadership team come together near the end of a release and decide what it was going to do next. Over time the memo developed into a formal practice that became a grounding for the entire team.

The framing memo decomposed

The purpose of the framing memo is to align and motivate the entire team. It contains just enough information to describe where the product needs to go and why, such that the team can use its genius and creativity to figure out specifically what to build in order to achieve those goals.

Over the years, the framing memo has taken on a more or less standardized structure. Or at least there are expectations by the team that the memo will cover certain types of information and answer certain questions. Here's what I consider to be the most salient sections of the framing memo:

- **State of the Union**   I typically begin each framing memo by literally presenting a light-weight retrospective of the product, the processes, and the team for the current release. I talk about what we have just delivered into the market, what customers are saying about it, and any initial reviews or feedback we have. In general I try to communicate a sense of what we've just built that the market is beginning to appreciate. I focus this section on what we have delivered, how it is landing with customers, the engineering processes we used, and how we had worked together as a team. This section is generally intended to be short and to show pride in what we have just accomplished. However, it also will highlight any major areas for improvement that the team had experienced along the way.

- **What has changed**   In this section of the memo, I take a hard look at what has changed, and I reframe the business, technical, and customer landscape for the team. I cover things like global changes that have occurred in the marketplace, new competitors, changes in customer expectations, trends, platform changes, and technology shifts. Sometimes, these changes represent major inflection points that are important to foresee and communicate, such as the emergence of mobile devices or the importance of web-based productivity tools.

- **Business data**   This is where I present the data that puts our team's business in the context of what the larger company is trying to accomplish. In this document, I'm not concerned with engineering metrics—we have plenty of that elsewhere. I include a lot of business metrics and data in this section, including data from analyst reports, competitive reviews, and observations from our field marketing teams. I'll also include hard business metrics, such as the rate at which the product is being deployed, or an analysis of the business value we are generating for the company. Sometimes, these business metrics illuminate clear direction on an engineering imperative we must tackle in the next release. An example is the time when the data revealed a gap between the number of copies of Office sold and the number of licenses actually deployed. This helped us realize that it was becoming much too difficult for customers to deploy Office. This would become a real business problem for us in the future because customers would have difficulty under-standing the value of any upgrade we would deliver if they hadn't even installed the cur-rent version. So we took those business metrics and framed it as an engineering challenge to the team. Something like *"Let's make our product more manageable, easier to deploy,* *more rapid to update and let's get more of our customers actually using the current version that they paid for."*

■ **Frame the business opportunity** Finally, based on all of those data sources, the framing memo outlines the business opportunities the leadership team would like to pursue. This includes describing the customer markets to focus on, taking advantage of new technology trends, and responding to emerging inflection points. Sometimes, the reframing of the business landscape is very focused on tightening the constraints in which the team must innovate and operate. But more often, the memo gives the team license to approach a new set of problems they may not have felt empowered to do previously. For example, this is the place where I would say something like *"The next version of Office needs to have a seamless mobile experience."* Or, *"The next version of Visual Studio needs to help developers build cross-platform applications."* These types of directional changes are usually a little bit of a surprise to the team because they reflect a change in the leaders' point of view about the direction the business is headed. Now, you can't have many of these directional changes, but by putting them into a framing memo, you send a very strong signal that as a team we are going to figure out some new dimension of the business, there is a new opportunity we are going after.

Aligning the team

I think there are two key aspects to getting the team aligned and engaged in the high-level direction presented in the framing memo. The first is follow-through. It is imperative after publishing such a memo that the leadership team continues to use the statements in the memo as benchmarks for measuring progress toward goals throughout the release. If the leadership takes these goals seriously and follows through on measurement and accountability, so will the team.

And finally, anytime I communicate broadly to a team about change, it's very important not to skip layers of management as you roll out that change. Before sending out the memo to the entire team, I give all levels of leaders an opportunity to participate in and to own the message, commit to it, and then personalize it for their own team. As the document gets rolled out, there are typically a series of team meetings where individual leaders in the organization take the memo, relay it in the context of their own team, and demonstrate the connection between what the business is trying to accomplish and what they, as an individual engineering team, are going to do within that context.

Final words

It's important to note that the interesting features and experiences that we build into any individual product are rarely, if ever, described in any framing memo that we write. It's the team's hard work to discover and design those customer experiences and product delighters. And the team does that work in the context of fulfilling the important business and customer goals that are laid out in the framing memo.

Finally, at no point is building the wrong product justified by the fact that you wrote something incorrect in a framing memo. Teams have to be smart; you have to be flexible and listen to customer feedback. You have to recognize when the world is shifting even faster than you thought, and you have to be able to adjust your plan and be able to balance the need to complete a set of experiences for a customer segment and the need to shift to meet a new opportunity. The existence of a document like a framing memo is no excuse for building the wrong product. This is especially true with long product cycles. As the industry has shifted to delivering with ever-shorter cycles, you can learn and adjust more quickly and integrate learning of what's happening in the market.

What if you pick the wrong North Star?

Don't get stuck in analysis paralysis trying to pick the perfect strategy or the most optimal target customer for carryover. Rather, trust in the Fast Feedback Cycle of rapid prototyping and early user testing to tell you whether you're on the right track. As you iterate with customers and learn what resonates with them (and what doesn't), you may find that you need to shift your focus to a different target customer or change strategies altogether. This is fine, and even expected, especially in newer businesses and more entrepreneurial ventures—and getting frequent customer feedback via the Fast Feedback Cycle will ensure that you don't linger too long on a bad plan.

Of course, if you do decide to make a big change, be intentional about it, and be sure the new plan gets communicated clearly to the entire team—your North Star might have just moved. Certainly beware of the temptation at the first sign of trouble to revert back to throwing spaghetti at the wall and seeing what sticks. There just aren't enough hours in the day for that approach to be viable in today's fast-moving markets, and you aren't likely to end up shipping a complete end-to-end experience. Make an intentional decision, communicate it clearly, and empower your team to iterate to give you the best odds of discovering the winning combination efficiently.

 MINDSHIFT

Focus, focus, focus. A common mistake is to not focus tightly enough, and it is probably the mistake that teams make most consistently when they adopt these practices for the first time. Trying to do everything for everyone is not a winning strategy in today's market. You really do want to settle on at most three or four target customers.

Sticking to the decision to focus on a few is genuinely hard, and team leaders need to set the tone here. Think back to your past experience—you can cut early, or you can cut late. If you cut late, you end up throwing out a lot of wasted work. The most efficient approach is to cut early.

Logically, we know this is true. But the beautiful thing about engineers is their nearly limitless ambition, a deep desire to build a breakthrough solution, and a strong cultural ideal of more must be better. It's excruciatingly hard to leave potentially world-changing ideas on the cutting-room floor, especially when the ideas that are chosen aren't a sure thing either. Later in a project, it is so tempting to add in "just one little feature." Yet, limiting scope is one of the most powerful levers a team has to influence the overall quality of the end product, to be sure that all your resources are focused on building and fine-tuning the product you will actually ship to customers.

Target customer stage: How do you know you're done?

The prerequisite to starting the Fast Feedback Cycle is that you identify a prioritized set of target customers that is aligned with a high-level business plan. You know you are ready to begin the next stage and start iterating when you have:

- A prioritized list of a (very) few target customers.

- A business plan, framing memo, or other written document that describes the current business environment you are working in, any real-world constraints the team faces, the opportunities you believe exist, and the rationale for how and why your chosen target customers fit into that overall picture.

- Communicated and socialized the business goals, strategic direction, and prioritized target customers with the entire team.

- Every member of the team can recite the list of target customers and refer to them naturally in conversation, in design discussions, and when making tradeoffs.

A word of warning: it's easy to become overly analytical about choosing your target customer. "Which customer has which percentage carryover? Why? Show me quantitative data to prove the case!" Identifying such a customer is nearly impossible to do, by the way, since it involves predicting the future, and even the most sophisticated models fail to predict the future on a regular basis.

But your gut still insists: "What if we pick the wrong target customer and focus in the wrong direction? Won't that be a disaster?" Focus feels like a risky decision. Having lots of irons in the fire feels intuitively like a much safer bet. However, remember that having lots of irons risks dividing your team's attention, making it that much less likely that you will deliver any complete end-to-end experiences that will delight anyone.

Think of your choice of target customers like making an informed hypothesis based on the best available data. Then manage the risk by relying on the Fast Feedback Cycle of prototyping and getting feedback to validate that hypothesis in the first few weeks (not months!) of your project—or to discover early on that you need to make a shift.

While it is true that picking your target customers is a very important strategic decision, don't lose the overall point of this chapter. A few end-to-end experiences will trump a large collection of features and capabilities, and you can't build a true end-to-end experience without having someone specific in mind. So pick someone and get going on building a product that will rock their world. In doing so, you will almost certainly rock other worlds as well.

Notes

1. Matt Goulding, "Why the French Secretly Love the Golden Arches," *Slate*, August 9, 2013, http://www.slate.com/articles/news_and_politics/roads/2013/08/mcdonald_s_global_expansion_the_american_fast_food_chain_has_become_an_unexpected.2.html.

2. Some engineers fall into the trap of believing that their users are homogenous. Read Chapter 5, "Observing customers: Building empathy," do some customer research, and you'll soon discover that customers often represent a diverse set of attitudes, behaviors, and needs.

MAKE A HYPOTHESIS **You are not the customer**

OBSERVE Big T Truth

WRITE IT DOWN AND KEEP IT RAW

empathy Wallow in data Personas & **QUANT**

INSIGHTS ANSWER "WHY" Don't overdo it Customer Profiles

Talk to real customers, not proxies **WATCH OUT FOR BIAS**

Look for patterns TELEMETRY & INSTRUMENTATION be curious

Look for the root cause **Customers can't always tell you what they need**

Social media & data mining the web **site visits** BUILD A MUSEUM

QUAL Contextual inquiry

User journey mapping

QUANT alone is not enough **What is the customer's motivation?**

SAY vs. DO data Don't make up stories

Unarticulated needs AFFINITY DIAGRAMMING **interviews**

Surveys & Questionnaires

CHAPTER 5

Observing customers: Building empathy

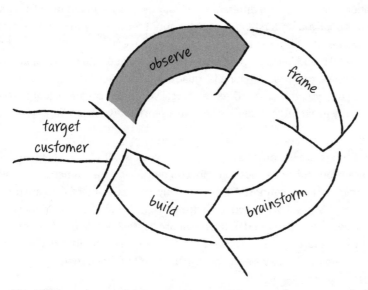

Now that you know who your target customers are, the next step is to learn all about them—to figure out what their needs are, what problems they have, and what motivates them. Having a deep understanding of your customers allows you to discover what an outstanding solution looks like from their point of view—a solution that meets their functional needs as well as their emotional wants.

In this first stage of the Fast Feedback Cycle, you do the research required to make data-based decisions about which experiences to build for your customers. This stage is all about data collection and the synthesis of that data. In gathering this data, stay grounded in observation, whether you are observing customers directly, observing customer behavior through instrumentation or A/B testing, or observing industrywide patterns and trends. Rather than basing decisions on opinions, judgments, or assumptions, you want to remain data-driven and base your decisions on actual customer research.

This chapter presents some of our favorite research techniques for collecting the data you need to kick off your project and inform your decisions. As in each stage of the Fast Feedback Cycle, there are many tools that you can use to achieve the intent of this stage. Remember that the tools and techniques presented in this chapter (and throughout this book, for that matter) are items in your toolbox, and you decide which techniques work best for you in any particular situation. By no means does this chapter list every available research technique. We just describe our favorites—those we've found most useful in our experience.

As with many of the techniques we discuss in this book, don't feel as though you have to be an expert in customer research techniques to get worthwhile results. Even small improvements in collecting valid customer data can have a tremendous impact on your product. In short, *don't let the perfect get in the way of the good enough.*

You are not the customer

To deeply understand your customers, you first have to accept that your customers' situation, background, experience, motivations, and needs are different from your own. Let's go out on a limb and posit that as a software professional you understand a lot more about technology than your customers do. You probably have a degree in computer science, math, or engineering (or the equivalent professional experience). You have firsthand knowledge of how software is made. You understand how 1s and 0s at the machine level relate to a programming language and compiler. When someone says that data is accessed "in the cloud," you have a good sense of local versus remote persistence. When using software you unconsciously avoid bugs because you have a sense for what software typically can and cannot do.

Now think about your customers. Do the qualities that describe you also describe them? What is their level of computer science experience or education? How do they spend their time, day in and day out? What are their priorities and motivations? Almost certainly, your customers' lives are quite different from yours. When it comes to software, you are a power user. (Remember the dangers associated with focusing on power users described in the previous chapter?) While building for power users is often tempting—because those needs are so familiar to you—solutions that address that audience likely won't generate much carryover to (or revenue from) broader, more mainstream customer segments.

Let's say, for example, that your customer is a tax accountant or a teenage gamer. Acknowledging that you are not the customer here is simple logic. You are not a tax accountant or a teenage gamer (sorry, as much as you'd like to be that person again, you aren't now). You went to a different school, you have a different degree and a different type of job. Your work schedule and cycle of output is different. The tools you use to get your job done are different, as is the style in which you communicate with your customers, peers, and managers. In cases where the customer's background is so obviously different from yours, it's not hard to accept that you are different from them.

However, internalizing that *you are not the customer* becomes more difficult when the domain you work in is well aligned with your target customer's domain. What if you are a regular user of the software you create? Or what if you are an avid photographer and your company is creating photo software? Or what if you work in what's mostly a consumer domain, where nearly everyone uses products such as mobile phones, televisions, game systems, refrigerators, and so on. In situations such as these, it is still extremely dangerous and short-sighted to assume that you are a mirror of your customer and that if you build software that you like, your customers will like it as well.

Sure, you may also have a smartphone, but unlike the average home user, you know exactly how to customize it, can debate whether syncing your mail with IMAP or POP3 is a better bet, and know what to do when your kid bricks it by mistake or a new app fails to install. In those cases, the average consumer probably heads to the Genius Bar to get help, or calls the teenager next door. Remember that you're getting paid to write this software, while your customers are paying to use it. Given that fact alone, the motivation gap is pretty huge.

Here's a short case study of a team whose target customer mirrored the team itself . . . or so they thought. The team named this quintessential customer Ellen and gave her the tagline "the vigilant tester." You'll learn more about Ellen later in this chapter.

SFE in action: Ellen, the vigilant tester

Steven Clarke, Principal UX Researcher, Microsoft Visual Studio

As part of the Visual Studio 2005 release, we integrated a set of test tools, code-named Camano, into the Visual Studio suite of developer tools. Prior to that release, Visual Studio had contained no significant support for testing software, as it was primarily used by software developers to write, compile, and debug code. Given a very short time frame, the Camano team set out to build what we believed would become a compelling set of test tools that would compete with the handful of sophisticated test-tool offerings already in the market.

We utilized multiple sources of information available to us at the time to figure out what we should build. We performed competitive analyses of existing tools, spent time talking to testers at Microsoft about the tools they used and why they used them, did extensive market research, and studied the work of recognized experts in the field. All of the information that we collected pointed us in the direction of building tools for automating the creation and running of test scripts and code. At that time, this was what almost all of the competitor tools did, and it was also what the vast majority of testers at Microsoft did. Given this information, we assumed that most customers would place a high value on tools that allowed them to easily create and manage their automated tests.

But after we shipped two releases of the Camano test tools, the product had not achieved the market share and revenue goals we had hoped for, so we started another round of analysis. We first brought in a handful of customers to the Microsoft usability lab. What we observed surprised us. Customers said things like, "Why are you making me do this? You are making me think like a developer!" And while the customers were able to perform their assigned tasks in the lab, when we listened carefully to what they were saying, the tone was not very complimentary, and it was clear that they were not having a good time completing their tasks.

We followed up these usability studies by observing professional software testers at work in their own environments—to observe their workflow, to see what tools they used, and to understand the context of their work. Previously we had observed testers at Microsoft to understand how testers work. Now we were looking outside Microsoft, and our observations were in stark contrast to what we had learned internally. In hindsight, it's interesting to see that though we felt like we had done enough solid research to get the first version completed quickly, we hadn't taken the time to talk to any external customers directly.

What we learned when we did talk to external customers was that testers outside Microsoft had different demands, worked in different situations, and required different tools. It wasn't that they were naïve or inexperienced—far from it! In fact, they were quite sophisticated in how they approached their jobs. It's just that their approach to testing software was different from the way the Microsoft testers worked. This was a pretty big new idea for us. Frankly, many of us were shocked to hear this because we had been thinking about the customer differently for such a long time.

There were certainly common attributes. We learned that great testers, no matter where they worked, were driven by raising the quality of the product they tested. They take pride in representing their customers and making their customers' lives easier. The big difference between our customers and testers at Microsoft was the type of team they worked on and the type of product they worked on. This had a large impact on the approach they took. For a variety of reasons (resources, type of application being built, etc.), testers outside Microsoft relied heavily on manual and exploratory testing to find product bugs. Occasionally they'd use automation to speed up the process for some often-repeated tasks, but, by and large, manual tests allowed the tester to focus on seeing the user's experience, which they found to be a more productive way to find bugs.

It was now clear why the previous releases had not been as successful as we had hoped. Customers who purchase and use Camano want to spend their time acting like their own end users, finding and removing bugs. They do not want to write automated tests. They seek out and use tools that make the process of finding and reporting good bugs easy. We learned that if the Camano team could find a way to make running and managing manual tests easier, and at the same time improve the communication flow between testers and developers, we would have a very good chance of creating a product that a large segment of the general testing community would genuinely want to use, and it would solve a real need for them.

Invariably, after presenting this case study in our workshops, someone shouts out, "But what about the C++ team?" You might think that surely Visual C++ is a product for which Microsoft engineers would make excellent proxies for the target customer, but it turns out even that's not true. One difference is in the libraries that are used. It's quite common for Visual C++ customers to use high-level libraries such as DirectX/Direct3D in their solutions. But the developers on the VC++ team don't typically use these libraries; instead they are authoring the libraries, as well as writing the low-level code for the compiler itself. Also, the build systems used inside Microsoft are often specialized (and optimized) for extremely large projects such as Windows and Office, whereas many VC++ customers use the Visual Studio build system or an open source system such as Git. Also, the developers working on the back end of the C++ optimizing compiler tend to spend much more time debugging assembly-level code than do typical VC++ customers. The list goes on and on. At the core, it's true that both Visual C++ developers at Microsoft and their customers are coding in C++, but the use of the C++ language, the available libraries, and the supporting tools are different enough that the VC++ team at Microsoft still has a very strong need for studying its customers—because they simply are not the customer.

Building empathy

After you accept the fact that you are not the customer and cannot rely on your own experiences to know what's important to build, the natural next question is, "How will I know what my customer wants?" The answer is that you need to do a bunch of customer research to figure that out. But as we explore in this chapter, doing extensive research alone is not enough. Research and data alone don't provide you with answers to all of your questions. Delighting a customer is not simply an equation, nor is there an algorithm to guide you. During the design and implementation of software, you are going to make judgment calls—many of them, every day—and you need empathy for your customer to inform your judgments.

 VOCAB

Empathy is the capacity to deeply understand the inner experience of another person, allowing you to see and understand from that person's point of view.

Scott Cook, founder and former CEO at Intuit, is largely credited with turning that company around from the brink of bankruptcy. Cook talks about gaining understanding by walking in your customers' shoes. Here's a wonderful excerpt from an interview with Scott Cook about what it takes to build customer empathy:[1]

> **How do you develop and nurture the kind of culture that can continue to innovate?**
>
> *First you have to understand the customers intimately, deeply, from observing them working in their offices. The key is face-to-face, regular close contact with the customer. It's crucial. You can't do it fly-by-wire, you can't do it by remote control. It's just got to be full frontal contact. Otherwise you misunderstand their needs. There's a proverb that I teach people in the company. It goes something like "Empathy is not just about walking in another's shoes. First you must remove your own shoes." You have to get past your own blinders and biases and assumptions before you can see with clear eyes what's really going on. And building a culture where that is valued, where engineers want to do that, where that's what's known to be valued, is very hard. Most companies don't have that culture. A company has to be willing to stop believing its own beliefs and believe what it's hearing from customers. Then you've got to translate that into products that are such a breakthrough that they transform business, and people can't imagine going back to the old way.*

The idea behind empathy is to become so immersed in your customers' perspective that you can imagine what they see, hear what they hear, and understand the world from their point of view. To do this, you must take off your own "shoes"—you must shed your own biases, attitudes, and preconceived notions, which are largely based on your own lifetime of personal experiences.

This deep level of understanding helps you predict what your customers would say or how they might react to various designs you consider, so empathy helps you streamline decision making. It helps you to narrow the places where you get feedback and to focus on a few concepts that you believe are most important to your customers. You need empathy because you simply can't collect conclusive data about every possible question that might emerge during the product-design process— you won't always have directly relevant data to inform each decision point. This isn't to say that you should make every decision from your empathetic gut instincts, but you need to become comfortable making progress using decisions based on empathy, trusting in the iterative process to provide course corrections if you get off track.

 TIP

> Talk to real customers, not proxies. Some teams hire employees to be a proxy for the end customer and to bring that perspective inside the company in an ever-present way. Their job is to talk to lots of customers and convey those needs to the development team. This approach has a nugget of potential value, but we have rarely seen it work well in practice —usually it results in a distorted view of what customers' needs are. If you want to be customer-focused and want to build empathy, the team needs to talk to real live customers, not proxies.

Evoking empathy across a team encourages people to do their best work, to really, deeply care about their customers not because their boss told them to or because their bonus depends on it, but because they genuinely want to help customers achieve their goals. This allows the team to be intrinsically motivated to solve a customer's problem, rather than feel as though it is simply earning a paycheck. And as the psychologist Mihaly Czikszentmihalyi suggests in his famous work on "flow," intrinsic motivation is linked to more creative and successful solutions.[2]

Empathy is not an inborn talent that only some people have. Rather, empathy can be developed in nearly everyone with a little time, experience, and effort. A curious, customer-focused mindset gets you started, and from there it is a continuous process of learning more and more about a customer to build up a body of knowledge and experience over time.

 TIP

> Everyone, not just the boss, needs to develop empathy for the customer. Every team member needs to be able to step into the customer's shoes from time to time to consider an alternative or evaluate a potential solution or decide whether to take a bug fix late in the project. Having empathy for the customer helps every individual person on the team make better decisions on the customer's behalf.

The data-gathering techniques described later in this chapter show how to collect information about your customers. As that customer data is compiled, shared, and analyzed, it becomes the basis for creating broadly based, deep empathy for your customers across the entire team.

SFE in action: Trading places

Susan Palmer, Program Manager, Microsoft Bing Advertising

As a program manager on the Bing Ads team, I saw a need to have our engineers connect more directly with our customers. I ended up creating a program called "Trade Places with an Advertiser," which was designed to provide our team's engineers with an opportunity to step into the shoes of a real small-business owner who has to figure out how to create, manage, and monitor paid search advertising using both the Bing Ads platform and Google AdWords, our main competitor.

Here's how it works. When engineers on the team sign up for the program, they're paired with a small business and are tasked with creating and managing a real ad campaign using Bing Ads and Google AdWords. The program takes place entirely in the live environment, where participants have a real budget and real deadlines. For a period of four weeks, participants behave as though they were the real owner of that business. During that time, our participating engineers must navigate the experience of paid search advertising across two different platforms in the same way our customers do—through trial and error. They're not allowed to use any internal Microsoft resources or support. They have access only to the same resources that our customers have access to. The engineers who participate in this program also have to continue to manage their very full-time jobs, just like our customers. This full immersion program is a great opportunity for our engineers to actually use the platform they work on in the same way that our customers do.

The results have been remarkable. Through weekly one-hour group discussions, engineers explain the challenges, frustrations, and surprises they experienced acting as customers, and they brainstorm ways they can make using our platform easier for our customers. It's not uncommon to hear participants request that everyone joining the Bing Ads platform team be required to participate in the Trade Places program because the experience is so eye opening. It's also not uncommon for a participant to reprioritize a feature request once he or she has gone through the program and truly understands the benefit and impact of the request on our customers. The Trade Places program has enabled our engineers to gain deep customer empathy by living through a real-world, end-to-end experience of what our customers do and feel every day.

What customers won't tell you

The obvious approach to gaining empathy is to ask customers what they want. And this does work to a degree. Customers are usually glad to answer your questions, share their experiences, complain about their pain points, and even suggest improvements that they'd like to see. But have you ever noticed that when you ask customers why they want what they're asking for, they tend to talk about their surface needs, most likely in the context of fixing or improving a specific task at hand? That's great information to have, but when you're looking for future needs and root causes, what customers say doesn't quite give you all the information you're looking for.

The truth is that customers usually find that articulating their deep needs is difficult or impossible. Often they fixate on their wish list, so you hear more about their surface-level wants than the real needs they forget to mention, or they take for granted that you already understand those basics. Sometimes, however, customers don't really know what they need, they just have a vague feeling that's difficult to put into words. (Remember the story about purchasing the car? Part of the criteria was "I'll know it when I see it?") Sometimes customers can't imagine the future, or they limit what they ask for on the basis of what they believe is technically feasible. Sometimes customers are trying their best to tell you, but because you don't understand their context, you don't understand the full implications of what they're saying.

People often see only what is broken in their individual situation and tend to miss the larger picture. Customers won't be able to tell you what is wrong with the entire end-to-end system because they see only what is broken with the portion they use. Deeper needs and more important problems become visible only when you zoom out to see issues and opportunities across several different roles or steps in a process, which gives you a more systemic perspective.

Furthermore, it may be difficult for customers to pinpoint their needs because, frankly, that need has not yet been discovered. People are so used to doing things the usual way that no one has noticed the opportunity to make something even better. Some of the most exciting needs might lie dormant, waiting for someone to do the digging necessary to reveal them.

Unearthing unarticulated needs

Henry Ford, the inventor of the Model T car that began the automobile age, has a famous quote about customers' ability to articulate their needs: "If I had asked people what they wanted, they would have said faster horses." You need to look beyond what people are saying and read between the lines to figure out what they really need. This is why many people say that listening to customers is dangerous, that giving them what they ask for is rarely the right plan. The answer, however, is not to stop asking but to listen more deeply, to watch customer behavior and read between the lines, and to be ready to analyze patterns and triangulate different sources to figure out what customers really need. The goal is to identify unarticulated needs.

VOCAB

Unarticulated needs, sometimes referred to as *latent needs*, are the deeper needs that customers can't quite tell you. They are the deep desires and underlying needs that drive customer behaviors.

An unarticulated need is one that is present but is hidden or not obvious. Customers are generally not aware of these needs on a conscious level. However, after you identify such a need and state it out loud, both the team and your customers usually recognize it as "obvious" and wonder why they did not notice it before. Identifying and solving a novel, unarticulated need is a great way to delight customers by solving a problem that they didn't even realize they had. Once they see the solution, they can't imagine how they've ever lived without it.

Think back to Chapter 2, "End-to-end experiences, not features." The Nintendo Wii Fit tapped into the unarticulated needs of customers by giving them not just a game but new hope for losing weight in a fast and fun way. The milk shake vendor discovered a surprising unarticulated need—that people purchased milk shakes to pass the time during a boring commute. 3M's invention of its ubiquitous Post-it notes also hinges on unarticulated needs, and it reminds us how hard those needs can be to notice. 3M unintentionally came up with a glue that was only a little bit sticky, but 10 years passed before the company found a use for it, when a 3M engineer carrying a dog-eared Bible with lots of paper tabs sticking out had the eureka moment that maybe those paper tabs would mark pages better if they were a little bit sticky.[3] Even needs that in hindsight are patently obvious weren't so obvious in the moment.

 TIP

Be careful about getting distracted by wants instead of needs. Even though customers can spin a passionate story, if what they are asking for is a surface-level desire or a nice-to-have feature, solving that problem may not really be your priority. You will likely find that customers are not as willing to pay for a solution that satisfies their wants if it doesn't also satisfy a true need.

It turns out that uncovering unarticulated needs can be one of the best ways to create a breakthrough product or service. If you can uncover a hidden need that your competition hasn't noticed yet, and can come up with a great solution that addresses that need, that can give you a significant competitive advantage in attracting customers to your offering.

That said, it's true that not every great product or service has based its success on unarticulated needs. Sometimes just getting the basics done, and done extremely well, with an eye toward fulfilling your customers' end-to-end problems, is all that you need. However, as the market continues to mature, we expect that an increasing number of major advances will be tied back to novel, unarticulated needs.

You won't end up acting on every unarticulated need that you discover. Instead, you will prioritize and probably blend some, winnow others, and synthesize your discoveries into a few highly meaningful needs—which you then combine with obvious, clearly stated needs—that you target in your solution.

Generating insights about customers

When you identify an important customer need, whether it's articulated or not, the crucial next step is to back up and understand why that need is so important. Good questions to ask are "What is the customer's motivation behind this need?" or "Why does the customer care about this?" Sometimes the answer is very obvious, while other times it requires some interpolation and triangulation between different data points for you to come up with a hypothesis. Other times you must go beyond identifying a pain point and take it a few steps further, looking for the root cause of that failure. Once you get to the reason for that need, and the reason explains something central about the customers you are targeting, those nuggets are referred to as insights.

 VOCAB

> An *insight* boils down customer needs and desires to a root cause—not a symptom or side effect, but the original motivation or deep need behind the customer's behavior. An insight tells you something new from observations, synthesis, or understanding. It is not a new fact, but a new meaning of the facts, derived from observations. Insights tell you why customers are doing what they're doing, not just what they are doing.

The deepest insights about your customers are the ones that are laced with what Annette Simmons, author of *The Story Factor*, calls "big T" truth.[4] That is, they pinpoint fundamental truths about human needs and desires that span cultures and epochs—the desire to belong to a community, to feel safe and secure, to express love, or to feel vengeful when wronged. As with an unarticulated need, when you hit upon one of these big-T truths, it can seem so obvious in retrospect. How could you have not ever realized that the reason teens spend hours texting each other well after they should be asleep is that they don't want to feel left out of something? That behavior is not about being addicted to technology, as parents might assume. Rather, it's about a teenager yearning to fit in with a group and to always be in the know.

The power of direct observation

Your first instinct may be to do research at arm's length—to make use of online discussion boards, email contacts, Twitter feeds, and analyst reports and to interview people over the phone. While these can be good sources of information and worthwhile activities, the richest source of unarticulated needs is often direct observation of customers in their native habitat, whether that is at work, at home, on the bus, or in a coffee shop. When you observe customers directly, you see their end-to-end needs in the context of their real-world situations. The Lean Startup movement has created a memorable acronym for this principle called "GOOB"—Get Out of the Building."[5] Don't just sit in your office building. You need to go to where your customers are.

While you observe customers, you likely won't be silent. You'll want to ask questions to understand their beliefs about what they do and their attitudes about those tasks. But many of those questions will be spurred by watching what your customers are doing and how they're doing it (which, by the way, will often not be what you predicted you'd see). You will notice things that people would never think to mention in an interview, such as the fact that they are using an awkward workaround to smooth the integration between two pieces of software (but they don't think of it as awkward—"That's just the way we've always done it"), or that they aren't using the new automation for a key task and continue doing it the old, laborious way ("I don't have time to figure it out," "It doesn't actually work because I need it to do this slightly different thing, and the old way still works fine").

Direct customer observation also gives you clues about the potentially biggest areas for delight—perhaps the customer has an irrational hatred for a particular part of your service, and fixing what appears to be a minor annoyance could yield huge delight for the customer, which you wouldn't have predicted. You will also learn more about your customers' context just by being in their space—seeing how much paper clutter is on the average kitchen counter or tacked to the fridge is an important piece of situational context if you are building a family calendar appliance, for instance. Or you notice how much of knowledge workers' desk space is taken up by family photos, helping you see where the workers' true emotional priorities are, despite the business software you are building for them. This style of observational customer research is sometimes called design ethnography.

VOCAB

Design ethnography is a style of customer research that relies heavily on observation to learn deeply about a particular individual in the context of that person's group, culture, environment, etc. The science of ethnography is rooted in anthropology and often includes detailed, in-depth descriptions of everyday life and practices.

The power of observing customers as a way to alert you to possible unarticulated needs is greatly underappreciated. Many teams tell us that they were skeptical at first but found that visiting just a handful of customers was transformative for helping the team unearth insights that they would not likely have found any other way.

TIP

If some team members are having particular difficulty establishing empathy with the chosen target customer, sending them on a visit to observe a customer is a particularly good way to help them refocus. It's tough to sit with live customers and not start seeing the world a bit more from their perspective. Site visits like this can be an eye-opening experience, and it's not uncommon for the experience to stimulate exhilarating discoveries and new insights, even from recalcitrant team members.

Here are a couple of examples illustrating the power of direct observation. When the company OXO looked at how to redesign measuring cups, customers never mentioned the biggest problem with a traditional glass measuring cup: that you have to bend down to check the level. But this problem was plainly visible when OXO observed customers in the kitchen. Based on this observation, OXO designed a new cup with a ramp along the inside edge of the cup, marked with graduated measurements. (See Figure 5-1.) The result is that users can measure liquid in the cup simply by looking down as they pour. This created a surprisingly simple solution that solved a problem the customer didn't even realize could be solved. The measuring cup OXO designed was a huge success and sold a couple of million units within the first 18 months after it launched.[6]

The power of observation isn't just for consumer products. While on a site visit, members of the Microsoft Visual Studio team observed a group of their customers, software developers, attempting to use instant messaging (IM) to communicate with each other. A member of the Visual Studio team took note of this behavior and got to thinking about what it might be like to incorporate some form of IM directly in the Visual Studio user interface.

FIGURE 5-1 A standard measuring cup (left) requires a user to bend down to check the level of the liquid being measured. In an OXO measuring cup (right), you can read the level of the liquid by looking down as you stand.

When the team went back to that same set of developers to explore this idea further, they asked them to demonstrate how they currently use IM in their work. The developers pointed out something that annoyed them greatly—when they copied code from Visual Studio into an IM window, the code became scrambled. The team probed further and asked why the developers were copying code into the IM window. They learned that these customers were trying to use IM to do informal code reviews. That was their primary use of IM in the first place.

After observing and interviewing this set of customers, the Visual Studio team concluded that the solution to the customer need was not to embed IM into Visual Studio. Rather, their customers needed to do code reviews and were looking for a better mechanism than looking over each other's shoulders to share and review sections of code, especially when they weren't located in the same place. Once the team realized that key insight, it shifted its approach to focus on supporting code reviews and code sharing rather than building a general purpose IM solution.

This is a great example of how building just what the customer asked for would never have solved the full, underlying need. In the end, the Visual Studio team built a rich suite of code-sharing features that was much simpler and more integrated with developers' natural workflow. Even the best embedded IM solution would have paled in comparison had the team not stopped to understand the reason behind their customers' behaviors.

Needs versus insights

We've talked a lot about the need to develop empathy with customers to truly understand them. You need to dig beyond surface-level needs to get to the insights that explain why those needs are important to solve. Take a look at the following table for some examples of companies that have capitalized on the powerful, motivating insights behind their customers' needs.

Example	Need (What)	Insight (Why)
Nike+iPod	Keep track of my running data	Tracking my running progress and seeing how I improve over time lights up my competitive spirit, makes running fun again, and keeps me motivated.
3M Post-it Notes	Stick a note anywhere, no tape or pushpins needed	My memory is not as good as I wish it was. I can quickly and easily put reminders and notes right where I need that information later, making me feel smarter and in control.
Sony Walkman	The original small, portable music player	Sometimes I just want to be alone, but that's hard to do in a crowded world. The Walkman allows me to have private time in public places.
Apple iPod	Bring my music anywhere	I like songs, not albums. I can pick exactly which songs I like across my whole collection of music and keep them with me all the time. It's super easy to get a single new song without having to pay for a whole album.
Callaway Big Bertha	A high-quality golf club that helps me hit farther and faster	The large sweet spot of the Big Bertha helps me be more successful at a very difficult game, helping me fit in with my golf buddies and not be embarrassed by my lack of skills.
Wii Fit	An exercise program for the living room	Turning exercise into a game helps me get motivated to actually do it, and watching my progress (weight loss) over time helps me keep doing it.
FitBit	A personal pedometer	Being able to see how my daily activities add up and comparing my stats with others motivates me to take the stairs more often, and push myself to continually do more and finally get fit in a way that suits my day-to-day life.
Kindle	Read books anywhere	Books are heavy, and I can never decide which ones I will want later. A lightweight device makes it easy to carry all of my books wherever I go (like, on a plane), so I don't have to make choices ahead of time. And, it's more comfortable to read in bed.
Netflix	Rent movies with no late fees	I always have a constant supply of movies in the house without having to think about it, and I get surprisingly good recommendations of movies that I would like from people like me.
Kinect	Play games without a controller	That's me on the screen! My TV sees me, and I actually see myself in the game!
Facebook	Share information among friends	It makes me feel good when I am validated ("liked" or "commented" on). And secretly, I like to "spy" on people and see what they are up to and compare my life with theirs.

This table illustrates the difference between a surface need and an insight. It's important to realize that these companies could have created other solutions that might have addressed the same identified need but been out of sync with the insight behind that need, and likely would not have been as successful. Each of these insights reveals why customers don't just appreciate a product's functionality but have an emotional connection with it. There is an element of deep surprise or delight or a big-T human truth embedded in every one of these insights.

The multiple dimensions of customer research

The good news is that there are decades of experience and practice on how to research customers quickly and efficiently and get valid information you can trust. You don't have to reinvent the wheel here or talk to hundreds of customers to find the patterns. It's a lot more doable than it looks, but there are a few gotchas to be aware of. In this section we take a high-level look at several approaches for how you find, record, and interpret customer data. Understanding how these different types of research fit together is critical to creating a balanced research plan—you need to use a rich mix of approaches to get the most accurate results.

Generative versus evaluative research

The first time through the Fast Feedback Cycle, you build empathy for customers so that you can start exploring ideas that are likely to resonate well with them. Gathering customer data with the intent of generating new ideas is called *generative research*. The insights that result from generative research provide the meat of the scenarios you'll write, which in turn help you create solution ideas that address the problems those scenarios describe.

 VOCAB

Generative research is used to collect data that helps create an understanding of customer needs and inspire solution ideas.

Later in the iterative cycle, another kind of customer research becomes important. Once you have a prototype, product, service, or website and you want to evaluate how well your proposed solutions are meeting customer needs and whether customers actually like them, you gather data with the intent of evaluating a specific solution, which is called *evaluative research*.

 VOCAB

Evaluative research is used to measure or evaluate something you have created.

In the rest of this chapter we focus mainly on generative research approaches. As we explore the Fast Feedback Cycle in the chapters that follow, we'll peel the onion to see how some of these same approaches can be used in an evaluative mode, and we'll discuss evaluative research in detail in Chapter 9, "Observing customers: Getting feedback."

Do as I SAY, or as I DO?

If you had some magic crystal ball and the ability to interact with any customer, any time, what do you think would be most effective? To interview a customer in depth? To track a customer's actions via software instrumentation? To observe the customer's behavior in person, maybe with the ability to interrupt in real time to ask questions? The common thread in all of these actions is observation, yet each approach is profoundly different in what you observe and what kind of data you collect.

Some of these techniques are about watching what a customer actually does, while others are about listening to what a customer says. Which is better? Of course, you already know the answer. Both approaches are valuable, and you ideally want a mix.

 VOCAB

> *DO data*, sometimes called *objective data*, focuses on watching what customers actually do when faced with a decision or a particular situation. *SAY data*, sometimes called *subjective data*, focuses on listening to what customers say about their experience, behavior, needs, or desires.

However, some researchers and businesspeople feel strongly that a customer taking action is ultimately the only thing that matters. Did the customer purchase the product or not? Was the customer able to complete the task or not? Did she use the new feature, or didn't she? It's true that customers often say that they would do one thing but actually do the other in a real situation, so DO data is pretty important. We've seen some teams go so far as to convince themselves that the only valid type of customer research is objective DO data, such as instrumentation, A/B testing, or other types of usage analytics.

On the other hand, SAY data is usually captured by asking questions during customer observations and interviews, as well as through surveys. By asking questions, you can learn about subtleties of your customers' behavior and attitudes, such as how they perform a task or why they like a particular feature so much or what annoys them about it. Remember that to generate insights, you need to understand why a customer is motivated to solve this problem in the first place. Because no one has figured out yet how to read minds, to get WHY data you need to be able to ask the customer some questions and get SAY data.

So what about those teams that believe DO data is all that matters? Although it's important to observe and measure a customer's actions, DO data on its own can hardly ever explain why customers did what they did and leaves you guessing. Relying exclusively on DO data makes it very easy to oversimplify cause and effect or to make assumptions that may or may not be true. Furthermore, by looking at your instrumentation, you might see the customer succeeding at the tasks you are watching, but if you don't question them, you might never realize that they were irritated the whole time because they found the experience unsatisfying, frustrating, or just plain annoying. You are aiming to build a positive emotional connection with your customers, so it's vitally important to understand their emotional state as well, and that requires getting robust SAY data. Luckily, some of the most powerful techniques inherently capture a mix of SAY and DO data at the same time. We'll highlight these in the "Observe stage: Key tools and techniques" section later.

QUANT versus QUAL

Another dimension that differentiates customer research techniques is whether the approach generates primarily quantitative data or qualitative data.

VOCAB

> *Quantitative data*, or *QUANT*, focuses on capturing measurements, usually in a numerical or other well-structured way.

Quantitative data is what many engineers are most familiar with, and it typically gets reported as graphs, charts, statistics, trends, and other types of numerical analysis. When applied to DO data, QUANT can answer questions such as "What is the customer doing?" or "How much are they doing it, and how often?" This is usually done by capturing and analyzing usage data to produce metrics. Many people assume that QUANT research is always focused on studying large numbers of participants so that you get statistically significant results. This is intensified by the current trend to harness and leverage the jewels hidden in "big data."

Big data refers to a data set that is so large it cannot easily be managed, queried, charted, and viewed using traditional data management tools such as spreadsheets and databases. While the term is applicable to many sciences—meteorology, genomics, and biology, for example—it is especially applicable to computer science because of the vast amounts of data captured through instrumentation of online services, otherwise known as "data exhaust." Think of the data that your mobile phone, your favorite apps, and the websites you visit are collecting about your actions every second of every day. As of 2012, it's estimated that we create 2.5 quintillion bytes of data daily.[7] The field of data science is emerging and is focused on extracting meaningful analysis from these extremely large data sets. Analyzing big data is a fundamentally quantitative technique.

However, QUANT approaches do not always need to rely on large data sets. Particularly when focusing on SAY data, you can use quantitative approaches to capture subjective data from customers, such as to ask about attitudes or overall satisfaction via a short survey at the end of a usability test. Customers could be asked to answer each question on a scale of 1 to 5, which would result in numerical data that can be graphed and trended over time. Those trends can serve as an early warning system for new problems that may have inadvertently been introduced (such as usability issues when multiple new experiences are integrated). Those statistics can also serve as a progress meter on how close your solution is to being ready to ship.

 VOCAB

> *Qualitative data*, or *QUAL*, focuses on gaining understanding by gathering and analyzing data such as descriptions, verbatim quotes, photos, videos, and other unstructured but rich data sources.

Qualitative data is typically gathered by doing research with a small number of participants, going deep with each participant to fully understand his or her situation. Qualitative research is about collecting detailed descriptions and narratives about an individual customer and is most often done through observations and interviews, which can capture both DO and SAY data. QUAL often answers questions such as "How is the customer doing that, and why is he doing it?"

Just like with DO data, teams can get into a bad habit of believing that QUANT is the only true source of valid data. But like DO data, QUANT rarely explains why things are happening—it only helps you quantify what is going on and how much it's happening. This means that QUANT will never be enough on its own for you to form insights about your customers, no matter how much big data is behind it. You need to use QUAL to figure out why. To get the best picture of what your customers are doing, and why they are doing it, you need to use QUANT and QUAL techniques together.

 MINDSHIFT

Data is data. We hear lots of stories from the user experience researcher, product planner, marketing guy, or field person that she is the lone voice in her company, desperately trying to get the engineers to add some qualitative research to the mix. This person should not have to be an underdog, the customer-focused David fighting the numbers-driven Goliath. Data is data, and qualitative data is just as valid and important as quantitative data. Each has its role in helping you figure out what customers are doing and what they might need in the future.

Using complementary research approaches

Have you heard the ancient Indian story of the group of blind men, each touching a different part of an elephant? The man touching the tusk proclaims the elephant is like a spear, while the one touching the skin says it is like a wall. Another, touching the tail, says it's like a rope, and the man touching the trunk says it is like a spout. Just like the men touching the elephant one part at a time, different research methods highlight different aspects of the same situation. The reality is that every research method is imperfect, so to see the whole elephant, you must have multiple data points from multiple sources using multiple research techniques. Only by triangulating those data points do you come away with a valid picture of what's really going on for the customer, and you can begin to see the whole elephant.

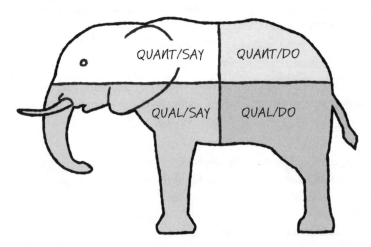

When you look at SAY versus DO and QUANT versus QUAL approaches, their cross-products combine to form a grid that describes four main classes of research activities:

	SAY	DO
QUAL	Interview	Direct observation
QUANT	Survey	Instrumentation, big data, A/B testing

Most research techniques boil down to applying one or more of these four basic approaches. The more important the decision you are making, the more important it is to get robust data from all four of these research quadrants. Some of the more powerful research techniques span these cells, and this greater coverage is the very reason they are so powerful. For instance, site visits often incorporate elements of both direct observation (QUAL/DO) and interview (QUAL/SAY)—you observe your customers in their native habitat and ask a few probing questions along the way. Similarly, usability testing can combine direct observation (QUAL/DO) of customers attempting to use a solution with a short questionnaire (QUANT/SAY) about their satisfaction afterward.

This grid is an excellent tool for making sure that you've chosen complementary research approaches and not just different forms of the same basic approach. For instance, consider a research plan that includes both a big-data analysis of instrumentation usage data and A/B testing of concepts on a live service. This plan seems good—until you realize that both of these techniques are fundamentally QUANT/DO techniques. Even though you are using two different techniques, you're still looking at only one-fourth of the elephant.

When complementary approaches are used together, they can help you find deep insights and give you the statistical confidence you need, and they do it in an efficient, cost-effective way. There are a couple of basic patterns that come up often. The classic approach is to start with QUAL/SAY and QUAL/DO methods, observe a small number of customers, and understand their specific situations in detail. When you do qualitative observation of a few customers, you're likely to develop several hypotheses about unarticulated needs that seem to be driving those customers' behavior. However, because you talked with only a handful of people, you can't be sure whether the patterns you see will hold with a larger population.

The next step is to use QUANT approaches to validate whether your hypotheses ring true to a statistically significant population of your target customers.[8] If the QUANT checks out, you can feel confident that you have unearthed a valid insight. Practically speaking, professional user researchers find that most insights generated through QUAL research are surprisingly correct and bear out in QUANT research with the larger population, despite the initially small sample size.

 TIP

Our personal experience concurs that even with small sample sizes, going deep with a few customers is the most efficient way to get insights that are almost always correct. If you have time for only one research approach, start with direct customer observation, which will get you both QUAL/DO and QUAL/SAY data.

However, if you already have some QUANT data on hand, you can start your research from a different direction. Perhaps you have usage data (DO) that you got through instrumentation, or perhaps you crawled through your database of customer support reports (SAY). Start by analyzing the existing data set for patterns. You may find some patterns about pain points, usage patterns, and the like, but also keep an eye out for anomalies in the data, for places where the data doesn't quite make sense. Sometimes you'll find outlying data points that you would just as soon throw out because they don't fit the curve. Sometimes a statistic that you expected to be high turns out low.

Instead of ignoring those cases, use the anomalies as jumping-off points to do some QUAL research to try to figure out what's going on. Go deep with a few people in your target segment, observe them, ask questions, and try to understand why customers might be behaving in a way that would generate that unusual statistic. Chances are you will learn something new, and maybe something that your competitors haven't noticed yet. Often these anomalies represent lead users, who can be very productive research subjects for identifying potential new unarticulated needs.

 ## MINDSHIFT

Addicted to QUANT? Gathering and analyzing quantitative data can be addictive, especially to someone with a strong engineering mindset. We've observed many teams, organizations, and companies that have recently adopted a strong data-driven culture, which is fantastic. Having a penchant for data is a great skill to have in the business world. And in the age of big data, having the ability to understand how to collect and synthesize massive amounts of data is transitioning from a "nice to have" to a "must-have" for our industry. But this focus on vast quantities of data can sometimes lead to problems. We've seen many teams fall into the trap of relying solely on quantitative data for most of their decision making, and that data usually represents only DO data. It is extremely easy to jump to incorrect conclusions based on quantitative data and analysis paired with your personal experience and opinions. This is a particularly insidious way to forget that *you are not the customer.*

Here's a final example that illustrates the need to go beyond QUANT. Several years ago, the Microsoft Exchange team collected email usage data from several large enterprise companies, as well as within Microsoft itself. The following table shows the average number of email messages that were received by each mailbox, in each of these companies (listed by industry for the sake of anonymity).

How many email messages do you receive each day?	
Microsoft	175
Banking company	20
Energy company	15
Mortgage company	95
State government	26
Private university	21

During our workshops, before we reveal this data, we ask the class to guess how many messages per day Microsoft employees receive on average. It turns out that Microsoft engineers have a pretty good idea about themselves and give pretty accurate estimates of their email usage patterns. However, it's consistently a surprise that other companies' use of email is dramatically lower in comparison.

Furthermore, when you look at the numbers, you can't just create an average and say something like "non-software companies use email one-fifth the time that software companies do." Because that's not what the data shows. Take a look at the mortgage company. Why is it that its employees receive almost four times as much email as the other companies? Is there a business reason? A cultural reason? Looking at this data also leads to other statements, such as "I'm pretty sure workers in government and academia communicate with each other regularly, yet their email traffic seems to be low. If they aren't relying on email so much, how are they communicating with each other?"

Then we look at how many messages the average employee sends each day, including original emails, replies, and forwards.

How many email messages do you send, reply to, and forward each day?	
Microsoft	34
Banking company	20
Energy company	12
Mortgage company	73
State government	17
Private university	18

Again, we ask the audience to guess the numbers. When we reveal the actual numbers, some people are again surprised. Despite the lower number of messages they receive per day, the companies studied still send almost as much email as a Microsoft employee. Most people notice a pattern that the number of messages received is roughly proportional to the number of messages sent—but this pattern isn't true for Microsoft, and there is still the anomaly of the mortgage company, which has a higher level of mail traffic overall.

At this point, after pausing to let the class consider the data, a discussion emerges. At first no one speaks, but then someone chimes in with an explanation for why these companies all send about the same amount of email as they receive: *"I think they must not use distribution lists like we do,"* and *"They must not get nearly as much automatically generated status emails as we do,"* and *"I bet they actually respond to all of their email!"* Someone points out the anomaly (the mortgage company), and another begins to explain to the class all of the business reasons why it makes sense that a mortgage company employee sends more than twice the amount of email in a day than someone at Microsoft. The class actually comes up with some very compelling reasons (at least they sound compelling), such as *"Mortgage companies have to send all of their documents around to be signed,"* or *"In a mortgage company you are dealing with financial transactions and you need to send email to all of the parties in order to have accurate records of intent."*

We then interrupt them and announce to the class that they are all liars. Bald-faced liars. We then plead with the class—don't tell lies. Don't make up stories to explain why the numbers are the way they are. It's so easy to jump to conclusions, to see a pattern and believe that you understand the reason for that pattern. In fact, you may be right about some of your hypotheses, but you simply do not know for sure, so don't make it up. Instead, notice anomalies like these and use them to trigger some QUAL research to help explain the WHY behind the data. You might generate some educated guesses, a point of view about what may be occurring based on the data as well as your empathy for the customer. You might even consider your own intuition and life experience if that is relevant and not too biased. But then it's essential to go do some further research to validate that what you think is happening is actually happening, and find out if you are correct.

We hope that everyone gets a laugh and egos remain intact. However, the point remains—don't make up lies. Be curious and use QUAL to understand what customers are actually doing and why. And be careful with quantitative analysis so that you don't interpret more than is there in the data.

Where do I find customers?

Gaining easy access to a robust pipeline of target customers to study is an activity where the value of having a strong user researcher or product planner on the team becomes apparent. If you have a researcher on your team already, he probably has a pretty good head start on understanding your customers and knowing where to find them. So if you have a researcher on your team, buy him a cup of coffee and see what he has to say. It may be the most valuable cup of coffee you've ever purchased.

If you don't have a researcher dedicated to your team, and you don't have the resources to hire a consultant, you need to do the work of creating a customer pipeline. Develop a list of people who match the profile of your target customers and who you can contact for ongoing research, whether that is the generative research that we're focused on right now, or evaluative research that you will do once you have some initial concepts and prototypes to show. It's important to have a deep bench of people available, because generally you don't want to go back to the same individuals over and over again. If you start using the same people repeatedly, you'll notice that they've learned too much about you and your offerings and can no longer provide unbiased, impartial, unvarnished feedback that is representative of the larger population of customers out there in the real world. Additionally, although most customers are flattered that you genuinely care what they think and that their feedback might make a difference, they will also become fatigued if you call on them too often.

Where do you find customers? Here are some good places to start looking:

- **Online groups**   Post a request online in a discussion forum, social network group, or Twitter hashtag related to your industry or specialty.

- **Go where your customers are**   If you are looking for skiers, go to a ski area. If you are looking for parents, try local PTA meetings. If you're looking for small-business owners, go to a conference that attracts lots of small businesses. You get the idea.

- **Ask around**   Use your network of friends, family, and colleagues to recommend people who match your target customer profile.

- **Get recommendations** Once you gather an initial base of customers, ask them to recommend friends or colleagues who they think might also be interested in providing feedback.

Be sure that you have a clear list of criteria that matches the profile of your target customer. This is sometimes called a *screener*. The screener typically consists of about a dozen questions that cover basic demographic information such as age and gender, as well as several specific questions that are unique to your target customer profile. When recruiting customers for research, you typically ask the screener questions over the phone before scheduling a time to meet, which ensures that it's worth your time (and theirs) to study them.

 ## MINDSHIFT

Make sure you're talking to the right people. One of the biggest mistakes teams make when they do their own customer research, without the help of an expert, is to start gathering data from people outside the target customer demographic. They don't do it intentionally—the people they talk with seem close enough, and time is of the essence, so they take what they can get. But later on they often regret not being more careful when they realize that some of their data was contradictory or actually pointed them in the wrong direction. It's easy to see how this could happen when you mistakenly interview a power-user photographer instead of a more novice point-and-shoot-camera user who is your intended target. A more subtle problem happens when you run an Internet survey that gets a strong response rate from a demographic you hadn't intended, but you forgot to include screener questions that would have alerted you to this fact. Take the time to build a screener and use it. If, after repeated attempts, you have trouble finding people who are a reasonable match for your target customer's profile, maybe that target customer doesn't actually exist. You may need to return to the activities described in Chapter 4, "Identifying your target customer," and reconsider your business strategy and target customer.

How many customers should I study?

Your instincts may lead you to want to do research with large numbers of people to maximize statistical significance and the validity of the data you find. However, doing deep, observational research with large numbers of people can easily become prohibitively expensive and time-consuming. Thankfully, it turns out that you can discover unarticulated needs extremely effectively by going deep with just a small number of research subjects. In fact, you need to observe only about a half-dozen customers, provided that each is aligned to your target segment. Once you start interviewing the seventh, eighth, or ninth customer in that same profile, it's very likely that you will have diminishing returns and not learn anything substantially new. The important thing is that you specify a customer profile based on your target customer segment and identify people who match that profile. Nonetheless, once engineers get bitten by the research bug, they tend to overdo research in an attempt to be "sure." Chances are that you don't need to do as much research as you think to inform any single iteration of the Fast Feedback Cycle.

Sometimes just having a strong and persistent curiosity can lead to valuable time with a customer. We know a former colleague, Prashant, who years ago traveled to New Orleans for a conference about some aspect of the latest version of Visual Basic. He was excited to travel to New Orleans because, it turns out, he had a few hidden tattoos and had made an appointment to get another from a well-known artist in the city. To his surprise and delight, the artist happened to be an avid part-time VB programmer, and as long as the tattoo session went on, Prashant had a captive audience of a terrific representative customer. Prashant shared his knowledge of the new product, and the artist engaged him in deep technical conversation. He filled Prashant with feedback, ideas, and a wealth of well-thought-out opinions on what he needed and why.

 ## MINDSHIFT

Lead users can be a gold mine for insights. Sometimes you may explicitly choose to study a lead user, even if she isn't exactly your target customer. As we mentioned in Chapter 4, lead users have deeper and sharper needs than others. But you'll find that "average" customers will have most of these same needs, just not to as great a degree. Because of this, spotting unarticulated needs by studying a lead user may be easier than by studying a more average customer. For instance, if you're aiming your service at a typical point-and-shoot photographer, you might study a complete beginner to notice more clearly what he stumbles on. An early adopter lead user may help you discover a new trend before it goes mainstream. A lead user may also help you uncover the true root cause behind a particular behavior. The flip side of studying lead users is that you need to carefully validate that the lead user's needs actually carry over and are representative of the larger target market you are going after. It's worth repeating: beware of studying power users who know the ins and outs of every bit of software they use and have figured out exactly how it was built. Their needs rarely carry over to a broader market.

How do you know you are done, that you have talked with enough customers? The answer is quite subjective. If you are looking for new insights, what you should hope occurs is that you hear something interesting within your first few customer encounters, something deep that leads you to a new possible insight about your customers. If you hear similar statements or see behaviors that point to the same insight from a few different people, that should be plenty of evidence to trigger your curiosity and excitement that you are on to something. You'll have opportunities in future iterations to further validate that insight with more customers, so you don't need to be completely sure, you just need a well-informed hunch. You might need only a few qualified people to develop a promising hypothesis that is worth moving forward with.

 ## TIP

If the data you're collecting doesn't seem rich enough for distilling interesting insights, instead of talking to more customers, focus on gathering different types of data and using different research techniques. Have you looked at all four quadrants of the elephant: QUANT/SAY, QUANT/DO, QUAL/SAY, QUAL/DO?

On the other hand, you may talk to plenty of customers, feel like you have lots of data, but still not see any clear patterns or insights. Or perhaps you see so many possible needs that it's hard to prioritize which are the most important. In this case, the synthesis techniques discussed later in this chapter will be of particular interest. These techniques help you find the needle in a haystack of data, help you make sense of what customers are telling you, and help you identify more subtle patterns in your data.

It's important to realize that collecting data and understanding customers is ongoing and cumulative. It's not a waterfall process where you stop everything, learn everything there is to know, and then proceed. You target your data gathering such that you learn enough to at least partially answer your current questions and move forward, but you remain open to new data and even new questions because you know you'll never have the complete picture. More data won't necessarily lead you to more or better insights, especially not right away, before you have explored some possible solutions and seen how customers react to them.

Do I need an expert?

A lot of science exists about how to do solid customer research, whether it's knowing exactly how many people you need to observe to get good coverage, how to interpret results, how many survey respondents you need to get statistical significance for a given target population, how best to capture data, or what inherent biases lurk in each technique. It's possible to hire a consultant to help you with your research, and many small and midsize companies go this route rather than employ their own full-time researchers. Professional researchers might have job titles such as user researcher, design researcher, ethnographer, market researcher, usability engineer, or product planner. The User Experience Professionals Association (UXPA) has consultancy listings on their website at *www.uxpa.org*. If you can afford it, it's well worth hiring a professional.

However, it is also possible to do research on your own. As we walk through the techniques later in this chapter, we'll point out some of the most salient gotchas to help you avoid pitfalls. The most common mistake is to introduce bias into your data without realizing it. One way to mitigate many biases is to simply be sure you have multiple observers. But every technique has inherent biases and blind spots, so picking the right technique for the job depends a lot on deciding which kinds of problems you can live with and which you can't. Despite the risks, we do strongly encourage you to give it a try. Getting started isn't as hard as it looks. You will gain some important benefits, even from an imperfect, first-time effort.

Conducting customer research is considered a branch of social science research in most contexts, and as such is subject to certain rules about the ethical treatment of research subjects. Generally, you have an obligation to inform research subjects about how their data will be used and that they have the right to decline to answer any question or to cease their participation at any point. You also are required to get the research subject's consent before recording them in any way, so no hidden cameras. Please learn your local laws and abide by them.

Will the real researcher please stand up? We often see teams of engineers fail to recognize the difference in approach used by two main types of customer-research experts. The crux lies between user researchers, who usually come from a social-science background, and market researchers or product planners, who often come from a business or marketing background. User researchers tend to focus more on ethnographic, qualitative approaches, whereas product planners tend to use more quantitative approaches, often starting from a business or competitive-landscape perspective. Both approaches are valid and important, but sometimes a bit of tension can arise between these two types of experts because they employ different points of view. Both are passionate about uncovering the deep insights about customers that should inform the project team's plans and strategies, and both have a tendency to think their methods are superior.

As the client who needs to make decisions based on research, ideally you want to be informed by both types of expertise and to take the time to understand the findings across both of them to gain the sharpest, most robust insights. If you decide to hire a consultant, clarify which approaches and techniques the consultant will use, and ideally draw from both schools of thought or link the consultant with staff in your company to bring in a complementary approach. It's worth the effort to help ensure that everyone works together and synthesizes their insights in harmony—otherwise, you might end up with two different sets of data that don't quite jibe, which could encourage an engineering team under stress to ignore both of them.

What is the engineering team's role in research?

Even if you hire some professional help, that doesn't mean the rest of the team is off the hook. It's vital for members of the engineering team to be involved in the research effort, including attending site visits, interviews, and focus groups; developing surveys; examining competitive data; and synthesizing the data into insights. But who exactly on the team should be involved, and how many people should participate firsthand?

Some teams we've worked with take the approach that every member of the project team needs to have a personal hand in some part of the customer research. These teams are more likely to dedicate a block of time at the beginning of a new project for the whole team to become familiar with the available research or do a consolidated push of interviews, site visits, and other studies. They might require every member of the team to attend at least one in-person research activity over the course of a project or during the year. These teams believe that there is no substitute for experience when it comes to developing deep empathy with your target customer.

Other teams have decided that it's better to have a small team of people, a mix of professional researchers and engineers, lead the research effort. It becomes that small group's job to keep everyone informed so that the rest of the team can also build empathy for its customers. Even if you have a dedicated research team, it is important that a few engineers be an intimate part of this group to help provide a translation layer when it is time to explain the insights to the rest of the team and also to bring their engineering mindset to bear on understanding the context or technical implications of comments customers may make during the course of an observation, interview, or other encounter.

Observe stage: Key tools and techniques

Now it's time to get to the nitty-gritty and talk about how to actually do generative research about customers. This section offers an overview of our favorite tools and techniques. The techniques are broken into two large categories: data-gathering techniques that help you collect generative customer data, and synthesis techniques that help you sort through and synthesize your data to find customer insights. The chapter finishes with a deep dive into one of our favorite techniques: affinity diagramming.

Of course, you won't use all the tools and techniques outlined here. Pick the ones (or one) that are most relevant to your situation, and remember that you probably don't have to do as much research as you think to kick off a rapid iterative process. Once you have a hypothesis for some key insights that seem promising, you are ready to move on to the next stage of the Fast Feedback Cycle.

 MINDSHIFT

Write it down and keep it raw. When doing customer research of any type, it's essential to capture the data that you collect in a robust way. For even a moderate amount of research, you will amass a lot of information, and you can easily forget the details if you don't write them down and keep them catalogued. Also, don't just go for rough impressions—you need all the details at your fingertips to do this well.

Data can come in a lot of forms. You might get multimedia data such as photos, video, or audio clips. You might also amass piles of quantitative data that will be processed into charts, graphs, and other visualizations. You should keep detailed notes of every customer encounter, which will give you transcripts, verbatim quotes, and other notes about what you've noticed about the customer's environment, motivation, or attitude. Think about what synthesis techniques you plan to use. This might affect how you capture your data—whether that means writing each separate quote or idea on its own sticky note or index card, capturing it electronically, or using a particular tool set.

The most important thing to remember when capturing data is to keep it as "raw" as possible. Especially when you talk with customers directly, write down as much as possible and exactly what the person says. Do not mix in your own interpretation of what was said or your ideas for what themes you see emerging at this stage. You can keep notes for potential hypotheses and insights separately, but it's better to spend your mental energy paying attention to the specific person or case at hand, capturing it as accurately as you can, and not try to draw conclusions. Save that for later when you can look across all of your data points. Also, don't zoom in too quickly on one specific case that may turn out to be fairly exclusive to a single individual. At the data collection stage, your primary attitude should be one of curiosity and of trying to understand your customers' environment, situation, tasks, pain points, and desires in as much detail as possible. Save the interpretation for later.

Data-gathering techniques

Here we'll introduce you to techniques that we find most useful for doing primary research, where you study your customers directly. These techniques represent a variety of DO and SAY approaches. Some approaches produce QUANT data, others produce QUAL data, and many produce a mix. We'll point out which techniques are best for different situations and where the major sources of potential bias stem from. Remember that no technique is perfect; each has its pros and cons.

Site visits and interviews

Primary usage: QUAL/DO data (observing behavior), QUAL/SAY data (interviews).

Best for: In-person observation to understand context, attitudes, and behaviors and to notice needs that customers may not be aware of.

The nice thing about watching customers in their own environment is that you may notice things that customers do that you would never have thought to ask about. When visiting with customers, you need to decide whether you are going to observe them quietly (as a fly on the wall) or engage in some contextual inquiry and ask them questions while you observe.

 VOCAB

Contextual inquiry is a research technique with which the researcher asks directed questions while observing a customer in the customer's environment.

Asking questions when you see a customer take a certain action can allow you to explore and gain deep insights that would have been impossible or difficult to deduce otherwise. You may find yourself in conversations like this: "Why did you just do that 10-step workaround? Did you know there is a feature that does that for you automatically? You did? Oh . . . it doesn't work exactly as you need it, and it's easier for you to do it by hand in 10 steps than it is to use the built-in feature and then fix it the way you want it?" However, when you visit customers in person, be aware that your presence alone can alter their behavior. A video camera or an audio tape can also cause people to be nervous or censor what they say, especially at first.

If you decide to engage in contextual inquiry, be sure that you don't ask leading questions. It is very easy to bias customers to behave the way you would like them to rather than the way they would naturally. To avoid influencing customers, it's often best to remain silent while a customer is working on a task and to save your questions for a natural pause. Also try to resist correcting their answers no matter how wrong they might be. Try not to complete their sentences; let a pause be a pause. And when they ask a question of you, turn it back on them by asking what they think the answer might be.

Not all customers are chatty. As you begin to interact directly with customers, you'll soon discover that humans have a wide range of styles and that they communicate differently. Some people talk a mile a minute and can tell you every thought that is running through their heads, moment to moment. Others find it difficult to reveal their thoughts, even to the most experienced interviewer. Perhaps they are shy and tend toward introversion, needing some processing time before they're ready to tell you what they think. Or, even more probably, they just haven't thought much about what you are asking them and aren't saying much because they're coming up blank—they just don't know.

You'll likely need to talk with several customers to find a few who are able to express their thoughts clearly in a way that you can understand and react to. But the fact that these customers are able to tell you what they think is inherently biasing as well. You're hearing from talkative extroverts, but it could be that more introverted customers have different opinions and preferences. This potential personality bias is a bigger factor with techniques that focus more on SAY than DO data, so keep this in mind as you select which techniques to use.

When on a site visit, be sure to get the most out of being in a customer's space. Aside from watching customers perform particular tasks or observing them go about their daily lives, use these other channels of information while you are there:

- What does the building look like? Observe the physical surroundings—the size, the walls, general decor, and so on.

- What kind of space does the customer bring you to? Is it a traditional workspace or a couch at home? What decorates the customer's personal space—what's on the desk, bulletin board, or walls or hanging on the fridge?

- What is the noise level like? If there is noise, what's causing it? People, machines, kids in the playroom, a TV playing in the distance?

- Is the environment crowded or sparsely populated? Will people overhear each other's conversations? What would people do if they needed privacy?

- While the customer is doing her thing, is she focused on a task or being interrupted by other people or tasks? How frequent are the interruptions?

Sometimes, you don't have the luxury of connecting with customers in their own environment. In this case, you can still learn a tremendous amount by interviewing a customer in a neutral environment or even on the phone. You just need to be a little bit more skilled in interview techniques because the context of the environment will not be aiding the customer to behave and answer most questions naturally.

Don't underestimate the amount of skill and practice required to interview customers in an unbiased manner. There are a handful of interview best practices that you can learn. These practices are valid regardless of whether you are on a site visit, in a studio, in a usability lab, trading emails, or talking on the phone.

 TIP

When doing interviews, make time immediately afterward to clean up your notes while they are fresh in your mind. A good practice is to schedule interviews with an hour in between so that you have the time to do this. Don't wait until the end of the day or, worse, another day and risk being unable to recall the details and nuances that might be important.

SFE in action: How to interact with customers

Karl Melder, UX Researcher, Microsoft Developer Division

Having worked in Microsoft's Developer Division for more than a dozen years and been a design researcher for more than 20, I've learned to never underestimate the challenges in asking users the right questions and correctly interpreting what I'm seeing and hearing. From those experiences I've derived a working set of basic principles that I teach and apply broadly in multiple products and contexts at Microsoft. I hope you find them equally useful for successfully engaging with customers to deeply understand their needs.

Code of conduct

First, understand that how we treat our customers dramatically affects our ability to get high-quality and honest feedback. In the past I've seen team members judge our users, talk over our users, and dismiss their feedback when it contradicted their assumptions. Code of conduct is about establishing genuine trust and creating an environment where customers feel comfortable enough to give you their honest feedback.

The code of conduct has four main components:

- **Acknowledging the customer's situation and emotions**   For example, for our users who are software developers, they may have made poor API choices and written suboptimal code. However, if they have a bug that has stalled progress for days and their stakeholders are panicking, you need to accept that perspective and validate their circumstances rather than lecture them on their choices.

- **Giving unqualified respect to everyone**   Seems like a "duh" point, but in our very technical industry I've seen a caste-like attitude where the more technically astute engineers are treated differently from the less-experienced or less-educated engineers.

- **Being modest**   When interacting with customers, people sometimes feel it necessary to proclaim their qualifications, power, and overall greatness to a customer—often leading to intimidation instead of creating a collaborative atmosphere where the customer feels welcomed to contribute.

- **Being patient**   Communication styles are varied. I've seen interviewers not slow down to the customer's pace and who stomp on their feedback. You need to pace yourself to your customer rather than the other way around.

Active Listening

Listening well can be a challenge for many. I like Active Listening as a framework for getting high-quality feedback. It is simple and sets a great tone. The basics are these:

- **Listening**   And I don't just mean with your ears. People communicate through many channels—their facial expressions, body movement, tone of voice, hesitations, etc. The words they use represent only a small part of that communication. Make sure you listen by observing more than just the words being spoken.

- **Probing**   Ask really great questions that drive toward understanding the root cause of a problem or the core of their underlying motivations. Phrase questions to get a more grounded, richer, and deeper understanding of your users and what they need. (See the next section for more information.)

- **Validating**   Mirroring what you think you heard is your chance to make sure you understand what is going on and demonstrate to your customer that you understand.

In a nutshell, you ask great questions, listen and watch intently, and keep checking back with your customer to make sure you understand what is going on. A critical component in this cycle is an environment of openness and trust. Trust and openness are qualities you need to actively work toward, not just by saying "trust me," but by being trustworthy and open in your actions.

Asking great questions

Asking great questions is about being open ended, nonleading, neutral, and grounded. What you want to achieve is a richer and deeper understanding of what your customers need and desire. Initially, you may ask whether your customers do X. However, the substance of what you learn comes about when you dig deeper and ask them to tell you more about X: When does X happen? How often? What happens right before X? What happens right after X? Walk me through the details of the last time X happened. How does it make you feel when X happens?

The last question (how does it make you feel) is an interesting one and a worthwhile tangent. A software development team is a bunch of engineers. We love facts. We tend to forget the emotional content. However, we do want our users to feel great when using our product. So don't shy away from asking them how using your product makes them feel. Did they feel nervous or not in control? Satisfied or underwhelmed? Understanding how they feel when they use your product versus how they feel when using a competitor's product can evoke game-changing ideas rather than lead just to feature parity.

Ask questions that are open, nonleading, and neutral. Avoid using biasing words or phrases in your questions. If you ask "What did you like about X," you basically invite the person to come up with something plausible about liking X. Similarly, if you ask "Was X better in version 7.0 than 6.0," you invite them to find something good to say. Instead, just ask them to tell you what they thought of X—giving them permission to tell you the good, the bad, and the ugly.

In contrast, a closed-ended question is one that can be answered with a simple yes or a no. They are typically good only for shutting down a conversation, not for engaging a customer in deeper conversation. Avoid these.

Asking for stories is important. Prompt for them by asking "Can you tell me about a time when . . ."If you don't have a long list of questions but have areas you're interested in, focus on asking questions that follow up from the initial prompt for a story. For people who need warming up, find where they're comfortable sharing: do they like to complain, do they like to promote themselves? Then change your prompts subtly. For the self-promoter, ask "Can you tell me about a time when you . . . " For the complainer, try "Can you tell me about a time when things failed?"

Finally, if you reinforce the privacy of the interviews and observations, people tend to be more willing to reveal themselves.

Show me!

Probably the most profitable action you can take when you're interacting with a user is to observe. In my experience, this is arguably the hardest technique for software teams to learn and remember to use. Mostly I see interviewers who want to ask questions and get answers. However, it can sometimes be difficult for a user to articulate what it is the user really wants or needs. It can be hard for a user to recall the details of how he or she uses your product. For our users, many of their actions are so automated that they don't think about them anymore.

The answer is to ask the user to "show me." It's about asking users to spin up the tools they use and walk you through how they do an activity. This can take the form of a usability study where you give a user a task to do or a site visit where the user walks you through some key activity. Regardless, watching people use a product makes for the easiest interview because their specific actions will help you know what to ask and when.

Where do most customer interactions go wrong? Engineers instinctually want to jump in and help. It is very hard to watch a customer struggle or be blocked. You want to make the pain stop. However, imagine the impact you might have if you can observe that painful event, uncover why it happened, and fix the core problem! Biting your tongue and letting the badness happen to uncover its root cause is an integral part of the observation process.

Diary and camera studies

Primary usage: QUAL/SAY data.

Best for: Getting customer data over time or when observing the customer in person is impractical.

Many times, it's difficult to capture the essence of a customer's day in a single interview or observation. For some customers, a more longitudinal approach to observing might be useful. A diary or camera study is an easy way to get observational data about a customer over a period of time.

VOCAB

Longitudinal research is research that is done over a longer time period, such as weeks or months, not just a couple of hours in a lab or a single snapshot of a point in time.

The idea of a diary study is simple. Give a diary to a customer and ask him to write in it daily. You might provide specific prompts to answer, which could be the same every day or vary. Or perhaps you give a camera to a customer and ask her to take a photo or video of the important parts of each day as well, or to take a snapshot at prescribed times to capture the moments that you're most interested in. The potential bias in a diary or camera study is obvious—customers have the leeway to be selective in what they choose to share with you, especially for more intimate or personal moments. However, this approach still raises the odds that you hear about things that are salient to a customer's everyday life and that are unlikely to come up in an interview, focus group, or even a site visit.

SFE in action: Customer safaris

Ulzi Lobo, Senior Software Engineer, Microsoft Office; Christine Bryant, Design Researcher, Microsoft Office

Our team had just taken the SFE workshop, and we were feeling inspired to go out and observe customers directly. Our challenge was to find a way to do this at a scale that would enable a large percentage of the team to participate. But more important, we had to figure out how to create a sense of empathy for the customer that the entire team would share. Our solution was to create a program we called "customer safaris." These safaris helped our team feel the pulse of our customers and understand their needs and pain points, and it provided an opportunity to share and extend customer communications with a large cross section of the product team, including program managers, testers, and developers.

Several important, and potentially nonobvious, components are part of a customer safari. First, each safari is led by a professional user researcher (the guide). The researcher (along with help from hired vendors) does all the work of locating and screening the target customers to observe. The researcher also establishes a focus for the safari by putting together a rough set of relevant topics and issues to be explored—essentially, what are we hunting for? In signing up for a safari, participants agree to spend a short amount of time with the researcher learning how to prepare for and conduct informal meetings with customers. During the day of observation, teammates are free to observe, ask questions, and generally do whatever they think makes for a productive use of time with the customers. But the safari leader is there, too, to provide guidance (perhaps restating a line of questioning to avoid bias, for example), take additional notes, and help the team get the most value from the day.

Team members use customer safaris to broaden their understanding of customers through one-on-one interactions and to help uncover and answer questions about products and trends. The scale and focus of a safari can be adjusted to fit team needs. On the Office team, we had 50 team members and 25 customers participating in safaris. Our primary goal was to expose the entire team to customers, with a secondary focus on specific product explorations. We found that meeting in a neutral location, like a coffee shop, created a more relaxed atmosphere for both customers and team members. It offered a comfortable and unbiased environment where the participants could more easily arrange to meet and have a discussion.

Once team members return from a safari, they present post-safari brown bag reports to the rest of their team. These sessions are very important, as they enable many different teams and groups of engineers (some who went on their own safari, others who didn't) to share their observations. These sharing sessions often unearth common patterns that teams saw with customers. Soon after we started the safari program, we began to hear statements in engineering meetings that quoted customers directly, and developers would offer observations that they either learned firsthand or learned through a post-safari brown bag. To the research team, hearing these statements was evidence that the safaris were having a direct impact on the daily routine and decision making of the engineering team.

Surveys and questionnaires

Primary usage: QUANT/SAY data.

Best for: Validating hypotheses and understanding attitudes and beliefs of the target population.

The basic idea behind a survey is to ask customers to answer a bunch of questions on paper or online. Surveys are a relatively easy and quick way to get data from a large population. A questionnaire is the same idea but asks only a handful of questions. A number of good websites are available where you can create, run, and administer online surveys or questionnaires.

Keep in mind that surveys are not observational. They are about SAY data—what people's attitudes and beliefs are. Surveys are most often thought about and used in a large-scale, quantitative setting, where you survey a large population of people to get statistically significant results. But not all surveys have to be that way. Many usability lab studies include a short survey, or questionnaire, at the end, asking a few questions about satisfaction. There are two reasons for doing this. The first is to stimulate a short conversation or interview before the participant leaves. The second is to collect data over time to establish a norm for successive rounds of usability tests. If the satisfaction results begin to stray too far to the right or the left of the norm, that tells you something.

As a quantitative research tool, surveys are well suited for validating hypotheses. You might be tempted to also use surveys as a qualitative, generative technique aimed at discovering new insights or unarticulated needs. But you really can't. The problem occurs when you assume that you can ask open-ended questions in an attempt to catch everything you forgot to ask directly in the survey. You can usually find some interesting patterns and themes by creating an affinity diagram from open-ended survey results. However, depending on the frame of mind of your participants, they may not think to tell you things that are actually relevant. Remember that you are hoping to find unarticulated needs that customers are largely unable to identify in the first place, never mind write cogently about while filling out a survey form.

However, if you already have a hypothesis about an unarticulated need, you absolutely can write up your hypothesis as a statement and ask survey respondents to rate their level of agreement, for instance, to give you some feedback about whether your hypothesis is on the right track. Validating and quantifying hypotheses is a great use for surveys.

Surveys are fairly simple to create and administer, but there are some issues and limitations that are important to understand. For example, as easy as it is to create a survey, it's even easier to create a bad survey. At best, a poorly designed survey will not give you the data you are looking for. Worse, a poorly designed survey will lead you to very wrong hypotheses. (Note that we didn't say conclusions, because you are always going to triangulate the results of your survey with other research approaches to validate it, right?)

People often ask how many responses they need from a survey for the data to be meaningful. The question of statistical significance of survey data is a particularly deep topic. A lot of smart people spend entire careers analyzing the details of survey data to get statistical significance. Our colleague Paul Elrif, who has been doing user research for more than 20 years, offers this advice as to how many responses you should target in a survey:

> Ideally, you will want 200–300 completed surveys per population segment. However, it's often impractical to survey very large groups of people. If a high degree of accuracy is not needed, you can get meaningful data from a survey if you collect 25 completed, valid surveys from customers that are in the same target audience. You should consider 15 survey respondents per segment as a bare minimum. If you have several different target customer segments, then you'll need to get this number of survey responses for each of the segments.

When you design a survey, understand that it may be difficult, if not impossible, to remove all bias. Are the respondents an accurate representation of your target population? Are they selected randomly? Will the respondents respond differently from the ones who opted out? Survey results can be easily biased based on who chooses to answer the survey. You may get a heavier representation of frequent Internet users or younger demographics if you do an online survey. Also, certain personality types are more likely to fill out surveys in general or for a modest reward. Depending on your target customer, this kind of selection bias may be a big issue to keep in mind.

It's also important to understand that people have a difficult time assessing themselves. Memories are not as strong as you might think, emotional state can inflict strong bias, it's difficult to observe and report on one's own habits and behavior, and many people will tend to answer questions in terms of what they think is socially desirable or expected. Furthermore, when looking at survey results, you are more likely to notice the data that confirms your current thinking and not notice or discount the data that contradicts it. We encourage you to find a professional to help you build an unbiased survey. But despite these issues, surveys can be helpful tools for confirming an insight with a larger population or sizing the relevance of that insight or opportunity.

Neuroscience break with Dr. Indrė Viskontas

Psychological studies are often conducted "double-blind," with neither the experimenter nor the subjects knowing which condition they have been assigned for very good reason: expectations change our behavior and how we interpret the results. Our minds have evolved such that we search for patterns in the environment—and our search is biased. We look for evidence that confirms what we already believe, instead of being good scientists and seeking only to disprove hypotheses.

This confirmation bias is particularly nefarious during remembering—what we remember, and how we remember it, depends on our current state of mind and on what it is that we expect to find. When we feel blue, we tend to remember the negative aspects of previous events. But in general, we see the world through rose-colored glasses: we're more likely to remember the good times than the bad.

What's more, most of us tend toward pleasing people in authoritative positions: experimenters, surveyors, anyone wearing a white coat. We want to meet or exceed expectations. So if you make your expectations known to your survey takers, you might bias them to respond just how you hope they will. That's why psychologists often ask the same questions twice in a survey, with opposite spins. For example, when trying to discover whether someone prefers function over fashion, the relevant questions might be posed as follows: "Do you agree with the statement 'Aesthetics are important to me and I am careful to choose only objects that are beautiful, even if I know they aren't practical'" and "Do you agree with the statement 'I'm a practical person—no matter how nice something looks, I care most about how it works and how durable it is.'"

In surveys, you want a range of responses, which is why psychologists often ask people to rate items on a scale. It's important to use an odd number for the rating system—5 or 7 works best—or else you are preventing your consumers from indicating that they are neutral or undecided on an item. In an even-numbered scale, people are forced to have an opinion, even if they really don't have one.

SFE in action: Seven steps for creating a survey

Robert Graf, PhD, Senior Design Researcher, Microsoft Engineering Excellence

In my work as a user researcher, I am often presented with a need to answer questions about our customers' demographics, attitudes, self-reported behaviors, or opinions. Surveys are a great tool for quickly and inexpensively collecting a large amount of data to answer these questions. Over the years, I've developed a process that I use to make sure surveys give you clear and actionable data. Here are seven guidelines that I've developed to help keep me on track:

1. What is the primary purpose of the survey? Make a list of what you want to learn. Prioritize the list. You will need to keep the survey short, so you probably can't ask everything. The shorter the survey, the higher the response rate you are likely to get.

2. For each item, write a simple question that asks just one thing. Otherwise, you will not know which thing people responded to.

   - Do not create compound questions—avoid use of "and" and "or."

   - Determine whether the question is (a) mutually exclusive, single response; (b) multiple response; or (c) completion (fill in the blank).

   - A common survey format is to ask the person's level of agreement with a particular statement on a scale of strongly agree, agree, neutral, disagree, strongly disagree.

   - Provide the user with the chance to select options such as none, not applicable, or don't know (as appropriate).

3. Create mock data for survey responses and generate a model report, table, chart, list, etc., to make sure that your reports work in the exact format in which your data will be returned.

4. For each question, determine how the results in step 3 would actually be used to make decisions about the customer, scenario, or solution. If it is not clear what you would actually do differently if you had that data, rework the question or eliminate it. It is remarkably common to ask survey questions that you only later realize don't produce actionable feedback, so the goal is to avoid that ahead of time.

5. Pilot the survey in person with three to five people to determine whether the questions are correctly understood and the respondents are interpreting the questions correctly. If not, rework or eliminate questions that aren't clear.

6. Stage the release of the survey by first sending it to a small, random subset of the intended audience. If you answer no to any of the following questions, rework the problematic questions and resend the survey to a different small subset. Repeat until you answer yes to all three questions.

   - Is the data returned in the format that you expect?

   - Can you analyze the data by using the procedure in step 3?

   - Are the results actionable?

7. Send the survey to the full intended audience.

Telemetry and instrumentation

Primary usage: QUANT/DO data.

Best for: Real-life usage analysis of existing applications and services with an active user base.

Instrumenting your code so that you can collect real-life usage data for your product or service is a great way to get a more detailed look at customer behavior. You might keep statistics on how many people use various features, how many attempts to purchase or complete a multistep action were abandoned midway through, or whether people are more likely to use the button or the menu item to access certain functionality. If you have an existing offering that is instrumented, analyzing this kind of data can be a great starting point for identifying current usage scenarios as well as pain points. Such data can also be a rich source of outliers—individual users or small groups of users whose usage patterns differ from the norm. Rather than discount these data points as irrelevant, you may discover a new user need by asking why they occur and digging into these situations with more qualitative approaches.

Microsoft has had a lot of success understanding how customers use its products with instrumentation programs such as Dr. Watson and SQM (software quality metrics). Dr. Watson is an error-detection tool that gathers information from a customer's computer when an error occurs. That error data is placed in a text file, and customers can then choose to automatically send that file to product support engineers for analysis and debugging. SQM is a tool used by some Microsoft teams (Office is one of them) to gather product usage data from customers. Typically, the team first identifies a handful of questions it wants answers for. When using Office, how do people use charts? Can we optimize the experience of the default set of chart types by understanding how the population is using them?

Recent advances in capturing data exhaust from online services means that more and more of this type of data is available. The volume of usage data can be very large, so be sure to budget the time for analysis. We will discuss big-data analysis in more detail in Chapter 9.

Web analytics

Primary usage: QUANT/DO data.

Best for: Existing websites with an active user base.

One specific kind of common telemetry is usage data for your website. Many tools are available for measuring the behavior of people using your website. Today, Google Analytics is one of the more popular web-analytics services. Typically, web-analytics tools and services provide web traffic information: how many hits did you get on your website, how many hits represent unique individuals, how did people get to your site, what search keywords were used, what length of time did a user spend on the site or page, what links did they click, and so on. These usage patterns can provide clues about what customers are doing that you may not have anticipated and what customers are not doing. They also might help identify areas for further qualitative research.

Customer support data

Primary usage: QUANT/DO data (incident metrics), QUAL/SAY data (verbatims).

Best for: Existing applications, services, etc., with an active user base.

Years ago, most customer support teams were organized as part of engineering groups. After all, if the customer support team is answering technically deep questions about the product, its members should sit close to the engineers who are creating the product. But it's becoming more common for customer support to be aligned with marketing teams rather than engineering teams. Why? Because many times customer support personnel are the first (and perhaps the only) direct human contact customers have with your company, and that contact point is usually at a critical moment of stress.

The opportunities to collect meaningful data from customer support are tremendous. One of the first and easiest to measure is data about your support activity and costs—how many reported incidents, how many hours, how many phone calls and emails sent and by whom? You can then look at the support activity data using different pivots: by territory, product, customer segment, time of day, product version, etc. You can also view the trend of support activity over time and see spikes or dips.

Use customer support data to try to understand what topics or problems people are calling about. Remember that people are much, much more likely to call support to complain about a problem than to provide kudos, so that introduces bias in what topics come up in your analysis. You can categorize each call and look at the percentage of calls in each category. You can use a textual analysis tool to analyze and extract verbatim statements, categorized by topics or keywords. You can interview or survey support engineers as proxies to learn what customers are concerned about. You can "instrument" the calls by having the support personnel finish each support call by asking a certain set of predesigned questions.

Another way to gather customer support data is to instrument and analyze the usage of your customer support website. The site may have solutions to high-frequency problems where you can use web analytics to measure activity across different problem areas. You can look at repeat usage per user on a particular topic and the amount of time a user spends on the website. Both of these measures are proxies for identifying the more challenging, frustrating problems that probably point to a customer pain point (or a bug in the software). You can analyze the conversations on a support forum to see the frequency and trends of what customers are asking about. You can also see whether certain categories of questions aren't getting answered or are getting answered within a very short or very long time period.

Listening to social media

Primary usage: QUAL/SAY data.

Best for: Creating hypotheses about the behavior, attitudes, and beliefs of the target population; identifying pain points.

You can get a constant stream of input about what customers think about various topics, whether it's your current offerings, your competitors' offerings, or just opinions about a topic in general. Tools and services can help you do sentiment analysis on a pile of unstructured text or use keywords to crawl particular websites or services looking for relevant information. Some companies even hang a monitor in the hallway that displays a real-time feed of relevant public comments. A couple of hours of manual labor is well spent reading what people cared enough about to take the time to actually post, write, tweet, or blog. For the long term, an automated system is a great investment to proactively identify problems in real time based on what people are saying on social media.

Keep in mind that the people who post online are likely to be a somewhat biased representation of the total population; be sure to consider whether they match your target customer profile. However, these avid posters are the ones whose opinions are being read, so they carry a somewhat larger megaphone than others. Word of mouth is an extremely powerful force, both positive and negative. You need to know what people are saying, and here are some places to look:

- **Facebook comments**   Certainly, if your company has a Facebook page or another site that collects comments or discussion, that's a great place to start.

- **Amazon reviews**   If you are selling something—a device or an app or a service—it's doubly good to sell through a marketplace such as Amazon because that gives you a channel for customer feedback. See what people say about your product in their reviews.

- **Twitter**   Be sure to establish a consistent hashtag for your company or your key products or services. Keep an eye on both your own hashtags as well as those of your competitors and related industry keywords.

- **Discussion and message boards**   These are a good place to hear what people are asking about and also what "expert" users say to answer those questions, which may or may not be what you would expect them to say. When even experts don't fully understand your offering, that's an important data point.

Usability testing

Primary usage: QUAL/DO data.

Best for: Evaluating an existing solution (yours or a competitor's); identifying problems in a solution.

Usability testing is when you observe customers trying to perform specific tasks using your product. Typically, this is done in a controlled environment, such as a usability lab, but it can also be done informally. Usability testing is commonly performed to see how customers react and make sense of a potential solution. It is generally considered an evaluative technique, but it can also be used with your current offering to help identify existing pain points or to study competitive products to see how they fare with customers. We'll discuss usability testing in more detail in Chapter 9, after you've read about the rest of the Fast Feedback Cycle.

Focus groups

Primary usage: QUAL/SAY data.

Best for: Getting a rough idea of customer perspectives on a topic.

Focus groups can be used for evaluative research, to hear what customers think about an existing product or an idea for a new service, as well as for generative research, to understand customer needs, perspectives, and pain points. The idea behind a focus group is to gather a reasonably homogenous group of target customers to have a guided discussion on a topic. You might ask questions such as "What kinds of problems do you run into when you use spreadsheets?" or "What are the most useful apps on your phone right now?" You might show pictures of people, situations, or products to get reactions. In a way, a focus group is like a giant group interview.

Focus groups can seem very efficient—you can talk to a dozen people in the same amount of time you might have needed to interview only one. However, there are many caveats and sources of bias for focus groups.

Focus groups are very often misused. People are misled to think that they can gather observational data about what people do via a focus group, and you just can't. Focus groups can tell you only what people say. Focus groups are good for collecting data about attitudes, beliefs, and preferences. They are also good for getting directional feedback about a concept, to know whether you are on the right track and whether your proposed concepts are resonating. However, you are not likely to get very deep insights from a focus group. A room with a dozen strangers is not a particularly comfortable environment for people to share their honest selves and innermost thoughts. Especially for more personal topics or where you are looking for the big-T truth that is motivating customer behavior, focus groups are not likely to reveal the information you're looking for.

By far the most insidious problem with focus groups is that they are highly susceptible to groupthink, a phenomenon that can introduce significant bias into the results. During the session, one or two people in the group may be particularly outspoken, and they may be perceived as leaders or experts. When this happens, others may begin to mimic and support their statements while suppressing their own beliefs and opinions. An expert facilitator knows how to recognize when this happens and can interpret the resulting data accordingly. It is only rarely possible to reverse groupthink, even with the best facilitator. Because of this, it is not uncommon to end up with pretty different feedback from a series of focus groups, and it can be hard to determine which data to listen to and which to ignore.

If you are going to gather data from a focus group, find an impartial third party who is experienced at this type of facilitation. It is nearly impossible to facilitate your own focus group without unintentionally introducing bias. If you can't engage an experienced facilitator, try to find another person on your team who doesn't have a vested interest or as much knowledge in the area you are asking about. The best way to include people who are connected to the team (and who have a vested interest in the outcome) is to allow them to watch but not to talk or participate in the conversation. For instance, have them sit behind a one-way mirror or watch a videotape of the session afterward.

Unfortunately, many organizations think of focus-group data as their primary source of qualitative data. This is really too bad, because the data gathered via focus groups is not particularly detailed and is more directional in nature. To build a quality product, getting deep insights is essential, and for that you need more observational approaches such as those mentioned earlier in this chapter. We strongly encourage teams not to use focus groups as their sole qualitative research approach. In our experience, going deep with a few customers is more efficient and gives more valuable data than a focus group.

Secondary research sources

Doing your own primary research is not the only way to learn about your customers. The modern world is full of data that can be helpful to you. Where and how you dig it up is limited only by your creativity. Here are a few ideas for secondary research sources that may be rich with information that can help you identify patterns or anomalies, make hypotheses, or validate hunches you already have.

Data mining the web

Best for: Hearing expert opinions, learning what topics are popular, identifying major pain points.

As we mentioned earlier, monitoring social media is a ripe source of primary data—what real customers are saying on the web. However, other places are ripe for data mining as well. Consider professional reviews and recommendations as one source. Mine what people are saying on the blogosphere. Read articles and reviews. Formal product reviews may not drive purchase decisions as much as they used to, but they are still read by some customer segments and represent an informed, external viewpoint. You can also track book sales data (which might indicate what people are interested in, not necessarily what they are currently using) or look through job websites to see who's hiring and what skills, experience, and expertise employers are looking for. You can examine academic sites to see what research papers are being written or how undergraduate curriculum in a particular field of study might be changing. A plain old web search can turn up information that you may not have realized was even out there.

Competitive data

Best for: Understanding what problems your competitors have already solved, as well as deficiencies and pain points in competitor solutions.

It's a good idea to learn more about your business and your customers by studying your competitors. By studying the public data available, you should be able to decipher what customer demographic your competitors are targeting and what assumptions they are making about their target audience. You can identify the needs they are attempting to satisfy and perhaps even get a glimpse of where they might be heading in the future.

You can get competitive data by looking at public records, financial statements, and annual reports. Even richer insights can be found by putting yourself in the position of being a prospective customer. Start searching the web, for example, and look for discussions on product forums, recommendations of which products to buy, and problems and solutions in product knowledge bases. (It may be interesting to you to objectively discover where your company turns up in this exercise.) Read your competitors' marketing materials carefully. Download and use their free trials, or purchase their product outright.[9] Get a feeling for their customers' end-to-end experience. Call their product support and ask some questions. Just as you would do with your own product, spend time on forums and discussion groups and read blogs to see what your competitors' customers are saying. You can even conduct a usability test on a competitor's product to better understand its strengths and weaknesses, especially if you measure your own product on the same tasks and benchmark yourself against the competition. Through the process of learning about your competitors, you will likely discover a lot about your own company as well.

 TIP

> Be careful about doing too much competitive research before you do your own customer research and investigations. Unconsciously, you can get locked into the way the industry is currently thinking about customer needs, end up following your competition's taillights, and not be open to a new pattern that may help you blaze a trail.

Analyst reports and other third-party sources

Best for: Learning the basics about a new industry or market.

Depending on your industry or market, analyst reports or other third-party research reports may be available. Often, these sources can be quite expensive because they are generated by professional researchers who have made use of many of the techniques mentioned in this chapter—with both depth and significant sample sizes, and that is expensive research to perform. While the methods they use to do their research often span qualitative and quantitative approaches, from your perspective as a reader of the report, the insights provided are largely quantitative in nature, with usually only a few illustrative case studies, a broad-brushstrokes explanation of why customers are behaving in some way, or what general trends are at play.

While third-party sources can help you become familiar with the basic mechanisms of a new market, they rarely contain the deep, unique insights you are looking for to build a solution that will be meaningfully differentiated from your competition. And when you consider whatever insights the reports do mention, realize that your competition is probably reading them too, so the insights are not unique. That said, reading these reports alongside your other research can sometimes give you a hint about a place to dig deeper or reveal data that can help support a pattern you've noticed in your own research. This kind of triangulation of insights from different data sources can help you feel more confident as you develop your first set of hypotheses.

Turning the corner: Synthesizing data into insights

The reason you have collected all this data is to give you clarity; to help you see your customers as they are, not as you wish them to be. Now your objective is to reason about the data and use inductive thinking to transform that data into insights that will inform the rest of the Fast Feedback Cycle. We call this "turning the corner" because it is a moment when you go from collecting lots of data to making decisions about which patterns in that data are most important.

After doing your research, you will likely have a mountain of data. Even if you did only a half-dozen interviews, if you were to print every quote from every customer interviewed, every photo, every video snippet, every audio clip, every diary entry and pile it onto a table, you would indeed have a formidable pile. Making sense of a large amount of data is tricky; it can feel like finding a needle in a haystack. But while it's not easy and does take some practice, it's not as hard as it looks once you get the hang of it.

Remember that you're looking for patterns across your data set. If you find that several different customers, asked in different ways, give a similar answer, that's a pattern. However, because customers are human beings, the patterns may not be immediately obvious—customers may have used different words, different examples, or different approaches to explain what they mean. But in the end, themes may emerge that boil down to roughly the same thing. For each pattern or theme you find, look at the relevant data more closely to see whether you can identify the root cause behind it. By triangulating data points, asking why, and looking for root causes, you can start making hypotheses about those patterns, to begin to reason about what's really driving your customers' behaviors, needs, and wants. These hypotheses are the first round of insights that you're looking for.

At this stage, you do not know for sure that a proposed insight is truly the reason behind the pattern you see, but you should have some evidence that points you in that direction. The rest of the Fast Feedback Cycle will quickly tell you if you are wrong, and if needed you can amend your thinking on the next iteration. Insights will be the backbone for telling stories about customers, which we cover in the next chapter.

 TIP

Sometimes the patterns and root causes you find are not so interesting, or your product already handles that need well or it is out of scope for your strategy. Not every pattern or insight you find will be important enough to carry forward. However, be careful that you don't discount a pattern too quickly. If it's important to the customer, it may point to an important insight that is ripe for the picking.

It's not always easy or straightforward to turn a set of qualitative data into a compelling set of hypotheses or insights. Because the data is not quantitative, you can't find insights by running calculations or by performing a query in a database—the data just isn't quantifiable or analyzable in that way. Much of the difficulty in finding insights lies in the fact that the data is not from your own personal experience; it's from your customers' experience. You have to do some work to discover the stories, the reasons, and the truths that are buried in your observational data. The synthesis techniques we describe are designed to help you discover and extract these patterns from your observations.

Wallowing in data

Best for: Finding patterns and insights that weren't obvious the first time you examined the data.

Spend some quality time with your data set, immerse yourself in it, and stay a while. Read everything, watch all the video footage again, look at the pictures, read the customer verbatim quotes, look at the analyst reports, and then read it all again a second time. Like a pig happily bathing in a mud puddle, you want to wallow in your data set.

To *wallow* is to look at a collection of customer data deeply by immersing yourself in it, looking at it from different angles and considering and reconsidering that data over a period of a few days or longer.

Aside from the obvious goal of becoming very familiar with all the data at your disposal, the larger goal of wallowing is to give yourself more opportunities to notice connections between different data points. Those connections might help you identify a pattern. Asking why that pattern is happening, and reading the data one more time with that in mind, can lead to making a hypothesis about a possible new insight. If you can, you should not wallow alone. Wallowing with others helps create alignment on what the data says and also improves the odds of finding more and deeper patterns.

Build a museum

Best for: Creating empathy for the customer, showing visible progress, wallowing in data over time, getting broad-based feedback, informally engaging the team and management in customer data.

One useful technique that allows teams to wallow in data a little better is to dedicate a room or a hallway to your data. Sometimes this is called "building a museum." Whenever new customer data comes in, print it out and hang it up on the wall. Whether it's a set of verbatim quotes, a blow-by-blow account of a customer's day, a graph of how long users spend doing particular tasks, or a series of photos documenting a task they are accomplishing, just make it all visible. If you have audio or video footage, play it in a constant loop on a monitor.

The room will be messy, and for this exercise it's better to keep it unorganized at first to avoid imposing an orthodoxy that will limit your ability to see patterns. Part of the magic of building a museum of data is that it allows you to see a wide variety of research results in the same eyeful, helping you see possible interrelationships between data points. As you amass more data, move things around to group similar ideas near each other and label the themes that start popping out. Use a location where team members will naturally walk during the course of the day. Make sticky notes and markers available, and encourage people to make a note if they see a connection or a particular hypothesis strikes them. This is a great technique to use while you are collecting data, before you are ready to do a larger, more intentional analysis. Building a museum allows you to engage the whole team in the exercise in a passive way, which doesn't take much focused time away from the members' daily work but still allows everyone to become familiar with the research as it is unfolding. An example of what part of a museum might look like is shown in Figure 5-2.

 TIP

You can build an effective museum when you work with teams in different locations in a couple of ways. One is to appoint a person in the other location to build a mirror-image museum. Keeping it organized the same way is not important. In fact, it may be beneficial to let different sortings emerge, which may reveal additional patterns. Just be sure that as new data becomes available, it makes it onto the wall in both sites. If you can't build a mirror museum, build an electronic variant that can be displayed in every office or even as a screen saver on team members' desktops. Do keep in mind that screen size will severely limit how much data you can see at the same time, which makes it harder to see patterns. For this activity, good old paper, sticky notes, and walls really are a better modality.

FIGURE 5-2 "We had customers take pictures of their home environment and then mounted the shots in a hallway, along with verbatim quotes and key insights. We called this hallway 'Customer Avenue.'"—Bernard Kohlmeier, Principal Group Program Manager, Microsoft Natural Language Group.

Affinity diagrams

Best for: Finding patterns and insights within a large volume of qualitative data.

Our favorite technique for synthesizing qualitative data is affinity diagraming. We've found this to be a particularly effective and easy-to-use approach for discovering the patterns, themes, and stories buried inside mountains of qualitative data. The basic strategy is to group similar ideas together—to affinitize them. The resulting quantity, size, and contents of those affinity groups help you identify patterns or themes that run through your data set. Analyzing those patterns often leads to insights. We'll cover the details on how to go about creating an affinity diagram later in this chapter, in the section "Deep dive: Creating an affinity diagram."

VOCAB

> An *affinity diagram* is a visual collage of your data in which similar ideas are grouped to-gether to make it easier to see patterns and trends in your data set. To *affinitize* is to group similar ideas together.

Case studies

Best for: Illustrating typical customer behavior or lessons to be learned from real world, factual stories.

A case study is a way to tell a meaningful story by using qualitative (and sometimes quantitative) data that has been collected through a variety of means. In the case study, you might use data gathered from interviews, observations, and surveys along with historical data, and you might also gather artifacts from the team that show specific tools or templates the members use. Typically, a case study focuses on a specific group (a team, company, and so on) and uses a lot of illustrative data to explain a situation that is representative of a larger class of people or groups. Case studies are particularly useful when your target customers are interrelated and exploring those relationships is more mean-ingful than looking at each customer individually.

Most often, a case study is written as a formal report that may range in length from a few pages to a hundred pages. For this reason, case studies can be expensive to produce. However, even a short written case study can be extremely valuable. Optionally, you can build a lighter-weight case study by building a museum, as described earlier, or as a series of PowerPoint slides.

Case studies can effectively communicate qualitative observations in a way that will help the team develop empathy for customers. Reading about an instance in detail can be easier to understand and relate to than is a set of more impersonal averages and patterns from the larger class of examples. The storytelling nature of case studies also makes them a good tool to help the team develop empa-thy. If you can, create several short case studies to begin to see the diversity of behavior, as well as the commonalities, behind the definition of a particular customer segment.

Personas and customer profiles

Best for: Communicating the most essential aspects of a target customer; aligning the team and partners on a target customer.

You can also write a case study about a single person, usually a target customer. Two different but related techniques are often used: personas and customer profiles. These can be a great way to com-municate information about your customer to the entire team.

 VOCAB

> A *persona* is a fictional character that generalizes the behavior, attitudes, and beliefs of a target customer, drawing from research across several people in that target group. A

customer profile (or *user profile*) is a report about an actual, real-life person who has been studied as a good representative of a particular target segment. The profile contains information about the behavior, attitudes, and beliefs of that specific individual.

Both personas and customer profiles seek to describe the most important qualities to know about a target customer. Common elements that you might see include these:

- **A photo of the customer**   This can be a formal headshot or a casual snapshot of the customer in the context of doing a relevant task, but either way it makes the customer feel real and human.

- **A day in the life**   Writing out a blow-by-blow description or a narrative story about a typical day in the life of a customer is essential to build empathy and will help team members tune in to the environment, task, and attitudinal factors that may be different from their own.

- **Bullet lists of key characteristics or insights**   Summarize key needs, desires, attitudes, and insights in a few bullet points.

 TIP

Include true stories with your insights. Without contextual information that humanizes the customer, a short list of insights may not make sense to team members if the customer's needs are very different from their own personal experience. Don't forget to include photos and true anecdotes about the customer's usage situations or needs if you want to build empathy. The trifecta of photo + stories + insights makes the customer easier to remember and is especially important when the target customer is very different from the members of the team.

Both personas and customer profiles are useful in a team setting to help ensure that every member of the team has a clear understanding of your customers' needs and to build team-wide empathy for your customers. Generally, a team would pick one technique or the other. A customer profile is a better choice when you have gone deep with a representative customer who matches your target extremely well, has a vivid story to tell, and is willing to share it with the team. However, this person may not be willing to be the poster child for your team. If you go the route of a customer profile, it is important for the research subject to agree to share his or her name, photo, and other details with your team. Be sure that you get explicit, formal permission from the customer you'd like to profile.

Personas are a bit more common because they allow you to combine learnings from multiple customers to build up a profile and are a bit more anonymous by nature. However, there are a few gotchas about writing personas, and these have caused the technique to catch a bit of flak in certain circles. When creating a persona that illustrates information about your target customer, it's vitally important that the information you convey is real and is backed up by data you have collected. And while it's usually a good idea to have some information about your persona that places him or her in a human context (with opinions, hobbies, passions, family, and the like), don't go overboard; keep those details grounded in what you observed during research. Make sure that the information you communicate about the persona is relevant to the task at hand—align the team around your target customer without getting confused about unnecessary distractions.

 TIP

One common mistake is to create what we refer to as a "franken-persona." A franken-persona is based on real data from a set of real people, but that data is mistakenly from different customer demographics. These divergent details are then blended into a single persona description. The problem is that by doing this, you create something completely fictitious. No human on the planet represents all of those qualities. A better idea is to create a few separate personas that each represent a different customer segment. Or better yet, don't be so wishy-washy and just focus on one of them.

Remember the story earlier in the chapter about the test team members who discovered that their customers' approach to testing code was different from their own? Here's the next installment . . .

SFE in action: Ellen, the vigilant tester (continued)

Steven Clarke, Principal UX Researcher, Microsoft Visual Studio

Through qualitative observation, the team learned that the customer's behavior was quite different from its own. But we needed a way to create a deep sense of empathy for the customer throughout the entire team, and we needed that transformation to occur quickly. To help achieve this goal, the team created a persona to represent the work style of the customers the team had observed. To make that person feel more real, the persona was given a name— Ellen—a background, a life story, and so on. We created a poster and hung it throughout the building.

While there was initial skepticism on the team that Ellen existed, the management team used the persona to drive a shift in the organization's mindset. The team held the general perception that it knew how to do things better than our customers, and therefore the customers should adapt to how our product works. Of course, we had to get to a place where we could abandon that type of thinking.

Team members were sent to conferences aimed at generalist testers so that they could spend time with real customers. I remember one great moment when we received a trip report from someone who said, "I met Ellen 150 times today!" The team began to believe in Ellen, and team members started to include real-life, external testers in their feedback loop. The team's mindset toward customers shifted to, "If we had ideas and we didn't know how to solve a particular problem, we'd ask them [the customers] what they think and which option we should pursue."

The persona helped to humanize the design process. It had a huge impact on customer empathy throughout the team and motivated members to drive change for the user. Instead of focusing on what the team considered cool, the team was able to focus on what its actual customer considered cool.

User-journey mapping

Best for: Identifying the major steps in a lengthy end-to-end experience.

Another approach to synthesizing and communicating customer data is to create a user-journey map that plots out the sequence of activities that happens across an end-to-end job that the customer is trying to do. You do this by analyzing the data you collected to identify the major stages in a customer's experience. This technique is excellent for analyzing existing experiences and helps you identify the biggest pain points, highlight possible causes of problems, and identify ways to optimize the overall experience. You might create a user journey for an existing experience that your company offers, to analyze a competitor's experience, or to map out your learnings from studying a more generic experience, such as the steps involved in going on a train trip. The Amtrak Acela case study mentioned in Chapter 2, used the user-journey technique to describe the 10 stages that a customer goes through when using train travel, from buying a ticket, to entering the station, to checking luggage, to boarding the train, and so on.

The purpose behind constructing a user journey is to show the steps of a customer's experience as a series of multiple stages. This lets you characterize the situation and problems at each stage separately yet also see how these stages thread together into a larger experience. Usually a journey map is linear and consists of 5 to 10 stages, but it may also have a few small decision points that create forks in the flow of the experience. Each stage may have different principal actors, locations, or problems to be solved. The key value of a user journey is to be able to stand back and see how all the individual factors in each of the individual stages connect to form the customer's end-to-end experience.

Kerry Bodine and Harley Manning's book *Outside In* details a variant of the user-journey technique that they developed at Forrester Research to help organizations identify the source of customer experience problems in an existing process or service experience.[10] They recommend making a variant of a user journey that graphically details each individual step of a process—both the steps that are visible to the customer and the steps in the internal processes that are invisible to customers. They mark each step in either green, yellow, or red to show how well that particular step is currently being delivered. After using this technique with many companies, the remarkable insight they report is that poor end-to-end customer experiences commonly become visible only near the end of the process, when customers complain about an incorrect bill or they arrive at a train that wasn't expecting them. But when they trace the root cause, the actual problem was caused many steps earlier in the process, often deep in the internal business of the company and, ironically, from internal processes that were believed to be working well and were rated "green." From the inside view, everything looks good, but the customer experience from the external perspective may have significant problems. This is yet another reminder of how important it is to look across the end-to-end customer experience, including at the infrastructure and back-end processes and components that enable it, and not look only at the individual pieces one at a time.

Synthesizing quantitative data

Synthesizing quantitative data requires different approaches from when you are working with qualitative data. Working with QUANT usually requires manipulation and then visualization of the data using tools such as spreadsheets, databases, and specialized programming languages. These tools focus on querying, slicing, dicing, and pivoting the data in many different ways and then using the results of those queries to identify patterns or anomalies.

Sorting, analyzing, and visualizing quantitative data is obviously a very broad and deep topic and is beyond the scope of this book. It is also an active area of continual innovation with the advent of big data. The new breed of data scientists is developing methods for sophisticated quantitative analysis on very large and often unstructured data sets. However, whether your quantitative data comes in the form of big data or in more modest data sets, visualizing the data in some sort of graph, chart, or other graphical form is one of the best ways for human brains to make sense of it. Still, the most important thing to remember is that no matter how much quantitative data you have, you should always balance it with observational, qualitative research. Perhaps the new generation of data science methods will unearth more sophisticated patterns and connections than ever before, but it will be a long while before statistical analyses figure out the deep human reasons behind why people do the things they do. Be sure you use QUANT for what it's good for, and keep it in balance with QUAL.

Deep dive: Creating an affinity diagram

Over the years we have gotten a lot of mileage out of creating affinity diagrams. It is a particularly approachable and straightforward technique that can yield some great benefits both in identifying patterns and insights and in helping a group of people wallow in data, build empathy, and develop a shared understanding about their needs. Creating an affinity diagram is a technique that helps you discern patterns and insights from a large set of qualitative data by physically sorting all of the data into groups, where each group is alike, or affinitized. Usually, affinity diagramming is a group activity.

It's important to understand that gaining insights by using an affinity diagram is a dynamic process. The full implications and meaning of the data may not be immediately apparent, even after you have created the affinity diagram. You will discover that with affinity diagramming, the meaning tends to emerge over a period of time. Perhaps you can think of the affinitized data as a primordial soup from which life will eventually emerge. Remember to be open to the idea that new insights may emerge from this activity, not just the ideas and insights that you've already been thinking about.

Preparation

First, there's a bit of prep work to do. However you collected the data, it needs to be printed on paper, with each individual quote, each separate thought, action, or behavior observed represented on a separate piece of paper. Do not attempt to summarize any of the data while doing this. If you come across the same idea in your notes multiple times, that's okay. Print each item on a separate piece of paper. One practical step is to simply print your observation notes. Then take some scissors and start cutting—per paragraph, per sentence, whatever makes sense—to end up with one idea on each piece of paper.

 TIP

When you observe customers, take notes so that each idea ends up on a separate sticky note. This practice makes affinity diagramming as simple as possible later on.

As we walk through the steps in affinity diagramming, we'll show examples that use data from a recent study we did of hikers on a trail in Washington State's Cascade Mountains. Figure 5-3 shows what our unsorted pile of data looked like.

Next, you need to set up a room in such a way that a handful of people can sort through that pile of paper. You need a table large enough to spread out the printed notes, and you need a whiteboard or, better, a large swath of butcher paper where you eventually tape up groups of notes. You also need a bunch of sticky notes, a lot of tape, and some Sharpie pens. A basic conference room should suffice for space.

FIGURE 5-3 Unsorted notes taken while we observed and interviewed hikers on the trail.

Step 1: Initial sorting

You are now ready to begin sorting through the data. Have everyone on the team pick up and read through individual notes. It doesn't matter where you start, just grab a few and get going. Soon, you'll begin to find notes that seem like they belong together. When that happens, shout out to the group "Hey, I'm starting a pile here that's kind of centered around people being too busy." Put those notes into a pile, labeling it with a sticky note that says *"I'm too busy."* Others will do the same, and in very short order you'll have a set of piles that represent an initial sorting taxonomy.

 TIP

> Do this initial affinity sort quickly. Don't stress about the categories or worry about not getting it right. It will work out, and you will have time later to adjust and re-sort. The first step is just an initial grouping. Most affinities will shift categories substantially after the initial sort.

After the initial sort, you will probably have a small pile of leftover notes that are oddballs and defy categorization. Just set those aside for now; you'll come back to them later. It's common and expected during this sorting routine that people discuss (or perhaps even argue a little) about the meaning of a particular pile and whether certain notes fit in. *"This pile is about people being too busy, it's not about the number of tasks they have to do . . . that's an entirely different thought . . . make a different pile!"* Raucous engagement from all corners of the room is a sign that the process is going well.

MINDSHIFT

Let the data guide the categories. An important word of caution is needed here. Affinity groupings often fail when people enter into them with a set of categories already in mind and then try to assign the data into the categories. It's okay and desirable to start having an opinion about how the different notes should be grouped. But the tendency will be to do this backward—to quickly come up with a handful of categories and then go through the data and assign each note to the closest-fitting category. This will not generate the results you want. Instead, you want the data itself to suggest the categories. Be open. Start some categories, and be open to changing them or breaking them up. Do not let the categories rule; let the data tell you what to do. This can take a little bit of time, and it can take a few passes. From personal experience, we know that it is particularly difficult to let go of your conclusions when you have deep domain knowledge of the customers you're observing. If you are feeling uncomfortable at this point or feel that you aren't doing it right, you're probably on the right track.

 TIP

Invite at least one person who has little to no domain knowledge into your affinitizing session. This person's view of the data may be much clearer and more objective than yours. Listen and don't worry; your domain knowledge, ideas, and the connections that occur during the affinity will be invaluable later when you try to make connections and discern the deeper meaning of the data.

Step 2: Summaries

The next step is to go back to each pile and look in more detail at which ideas ended up in them. Read through each item in the pile and attempt to summarize the essence, main thought, or theme of each pile on a single sticky note. You're aiming for a sentence or two at the most—less than a paragraph and more than just a couple of words. As you do this, you will surely find notes that are lost and that do not belong in the pile they're in after all. Move those notes to where they belong and adjust piles as needed.

Figure 5-3 shows an unsorted pile of qualitative data collected while observing and interviewing hikers on a trail outside Seattle. Here's a closer look at some of that data after the first round of sorting:

Gear/10 Essentials	GPS	We rely on experts	I did research ahead of time	How much farther?
10 essentials? I saw that on a sign down there	My phone GPS isn't showing us here	We need someone to tell us what to bring	I google stuff	The trail was longer than I thought
We have protein bars, sunscreen	We recently bought a GPS for Utah	I'm interested in contacting Pro Ski Service for a guide	I bought a guidebook	I want to know what elevation, how much farther
I always carry a cell phone	I carry a GPS if it's more than a short day hike	What would you do if you got lost? I'd ask him... (pointing)	I picked the hike based on difficulty	It seemed a lot longer than the trail description
Just water, it's a short hike		He's pretty good with a sense of direction (I rely on him)	Because of what I read; it was a pretty popular trail	

Did you notice that one of the summaries ("We rely on experts . . . ") is starting to look something like an insight? None of the hikers actually said, "Hey, I need a leader to feel safe" or "Yeah, we always rely on the expert to guide us." However, many of them indicated that in their hiking group, one person was indeed identified as the leader and expert who they all trusted to pick the trail, navigate to the summit, and make sure the group was prepared. That idea of "we rely on experts" is completely unarticulated, yet it shows up in a lot of the data.

 TIP

As you sort through the data, if you have aha moments where you discover a potential unarticulated need or make a connection between several seemingly disjointed groups of data, mention it to the group. Jot the idea down on a sticky note, preferably in a contrasting color, and stick it to your diagram for deeper discussion later.

Now take a look at the first column—"Gear/10 Essentials." All of the data sorted under that category relates in some way to what gear the hikers carried with them. Is this pile of data meaningful as it is? Probably not. The category "gear" doesn't tell you anything particularly insightful, but maybe something deeper is lurking in that list of what people were carrying in their packs that day. This category would be a great candidate to break up in the next round of sorting to see whether a deeper meaning exists beneath the specific data.

Step 3: Read out and re-sort

Once the first sort is done and each pile has a short summary, have each "summary author" read out loud what he or she wrote about the pile. Have each of them also read a few of the most relevant notes that led them to the meaning of the pile. Allow some time for team members to comment on what they hear and discuss ways that it might be related to other piles. Do this one pile at a time until you've covered all of them. This step helps the whole room become familiar with the total data set and will help people start making connections between ideas. At this point, some of those oddballs you set aside earlier may start to find a home.

As you continue the readout discussion, you might need to refine the statement of the pile's meaning. If necessary, modify or rewrite that statement. You might even create a new category for some of the notes that didn't quite fit in a group. With some group discussion, you will begin to have new clarity and precision around the meaning behind those notes. It's even more exciting when you discover through discussion that a deeper, underlying theme is running through several categories. You may choose to re-sort and relabel the piles based on this realization, or you may simply note a cross-category insight or meta-theme. You may also discover that two piles are really referring to the same thing, so you might merge them. Or the inverse might happen, so that you split a pile if you realize that it represents two distinct ideas.

 TIP

> At this point, summaries for each column should reflect an attitude or behavior of the customer. For example, "I can . . . ," "We try to . . . ," "We believe that . . . ," and "How does . . . " are all beginnings of descriptive statements. If you have a summary column that simply lists related facts, such as "Demographics," "Equipment used," or "Experience level," you need to do more work to find the meaning behind those factual lists. You may end up removing the list entirely and moving each entry to a different pile, or you may merge several related lists that share a meta-theme.

In the example, something needs to be done with the "Gear" pile from the first sort. Currently, it's just a list of related facts indicating what each hiker carried that day. Can you go one by one and move each of the stickies under "Gear" to find a new home? Or can you find a "why" behind the list of gear? For example, why is it that the hikers are carrying so few of the 10 essentials?[11] When we looked across the data, we noticed that while most of the hikers carried a minimal amount of gear, they did so intentionally. Check out the "I did research ahead of time" grouping. Other data also indicates the hikers' intention about the location, length, and difficulty of the trail they chose. In the GPS list (which is another fact-based list that needs to be reassigned), one hiker said, "I carry a GPS if it's more than a short day hike." Once we realized this connection, we combined the data in the "Gear," "GPS," and "I did research columns" and created a new heading that reads "I made a conscious decision about gear, safety, and route."

TIP

The only hard and fast rule for affinity diagramming is that you have to have at least three notes in a pile or grouping. Usually, the greatest value of an affinity sorting is finding the bigger themes that run through your data set. As such, it's usually counterproductive to make your piles too small, separating out each nuance of an idea into a separate grouping. This can make the larger themes harder to pick out. If it is essential to create microcategories, be sure to keep similar categories near each other so that you can see their common thread more readily.

Step 4: Tape it up

Once you are satisfied with the groupings, tape all the notes onto the butcher paper. Spread out each pile so that you can read the text on each note, and affix the summary sticky note on top. A good format for spreading out the piles is in long vertical lines, overlapping each square of paper so that the words are visible but without showing any additional white space. Lay out a category in a line on a tabletop. Then take a piece of tape and run it down the length of the category line top to bottom. Hang the whole category up as a unit. Particularly large categories can be laid out as several long lines next to each other. Figure 5-4 shows what the final affinity looks like.

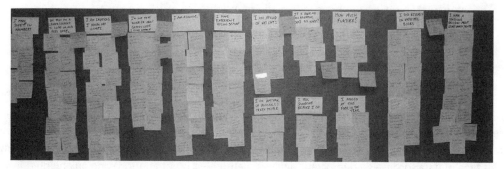

FIGURE 5-4 The final affinity diagram. Note the summaries in bold at the top of each column and some meta-themes (shown on a sticky note with a contrasting color) alongside several of the columns.

Step 5: Look for insights

At this point, you've probably already begun to identify some insights. In the hiker example, we've identified "I made a conscious decision" and "I rely on an expert" as insights. Now that you have the data spread out on the butcher paper, chances are you will continue seeing connections and themes among items. You might even rehang certain categories if you need to. However, the job for now is to look for unarticulated needs and especially insights that explain the WHY behind what you're hearing from customers. Look at each category and ask yourself, "What is the root cause from the customer's perspective that is motivating that category?" This is the time to refer back to any notes you made while sorting. Point out and discuss any thoughts, hidden connections, or big-T truths that might be underlying the categories you identified. Remember that you may not be sure about an insight at this stage in the Fast Feedback Cycle, so think of your insights more as hypotheses to consider and discuss. As you uncover potential insights, be sure to write them down and stick them to your affinity diagram as well. A sticky note of a contrasting color works well for these so that it's easy to scan the diagram to see them.

Here are the kind of insights you might glean from an affinity diagram:

- Some of the category summaries themselves may point to unarticulated needs or even an insight if your customers are particularly articulate. No single customer may have captured it fully, but once you see a whole bunch of customers talking about the same thing from multiple perspectives, the underlying need or desire becomes easier to identify and articulate.

- The relative size of each category may give an indication of relative need or priority with respect to other categories on the diagram. (Although be careful—depending on the questions you asked that spurred this data in the original research, some topics may be overrepresented in your diagram simply because you asked about them explicitly, whereas other topics were volunteered with a prompt.)

- You will likely notice themes that run across multiple categories, possibly pointing to deeper, more meta-level customer needs, trends, or insights.

- The lack of mention of certain topics might be interesting. Ask yourself what themes and categories you expected to see. If these aren't represented, maybe they aren't actually as important as you thought. Or maybe something about how you did the research kept a topic from coming up, which might inform a future round of research.

Affinity diagramming is a participatory technique. It is best done in groups of people who represent different points of view. Creating an affinity diagram is a great way to combine the perspectives of the participants and to get alignment about what problems are the most important ones to solve. This type of data sorting is a democratic analysis method—it is not about having an anointed few look at the data and decide what is valuable and what is not. There is no one right answer—any sufficiently interesting data set is complex enough to be able to be sorted in many different ways, but the same major insights should be visible whether they show up as explicit groupings or as meta-themes across groupings. By enlisting more brains, with different points of view, to digest and offer opinions on this data, you gain the ability to create a multidimensional view of the data. And having a multidimensional view is the best way to seek out the deepest insights from the data and to find the critical connections that are just out of sight.

Observe stage: How do you know when you are done?

Regardless of which techniques you used to research your customers, you know you're ready for the next stage when you have generated the following:

- A collection of fact-based customer data that helps the team develop empathy for the real-world lives of its target customers. Ideally, the customer data you collect contains a mix of QUANT, QUAL, SAY, and DO data.

- A few promising insights about your customers that explain why they want and need the things they do.

- Insights and data about the target customers is published and readily accessible to the entire team, either online or in a physical format such as a customer museum.

The big idea in this stage is empathy. If you have empathy for your customers and can begin to see from their eyes and hear with their ears, you will pick the right problems to solve for them and make better decisions. Empathy is perhaps the hardest thing for an engineering team to learn, but it is extremely powerful, and it's worth taking the time to get the hang of it.

 MINDSHIFT

Don't overdo it. There's one final piece of advice that applies to all the stages of the Fast Feedback Cycle but is particularly relevant to this first stage, especially early on in a new project. Don't get stuck in analysis paralysis. Your goal is to turn the cycle as fast as possible, not to execute each stage to perfection. Trust in the feedback loop that underlies the Fast Feedback Cycle. If you have gained some customer understanding and empathy and have a hypothesis (otherwise known as a good evidence-based hunch) about some proposed insights, then it is time to move on.

You don't have to be sure about your insights. Remember that you discovered them using abductive reasoning, which means you think they are probably true but can't yet be sure. That is perfectly okay. Rely on the Fast Feedback Cycle to quickly let you know if you are on the right track. Similarly, you won't have perfect customer empathy right away either. Like in a new relationship, you have much to learn about each other and you can't rush it. Get a good foundation going, share it broadly, and be ready to continue layering in more information and sharing it as you iterate and learn more about what really makes your customer tick.

Notes

1. David Lidsky, David Whitford, and Scott Cook, "Cook's Recipe," CNNMoney, February 1, 2004, http://money.cnn.com/magazines/fsb/fsb_archive/2004/02/01/360661/index.htm.

2. Mihaly Csikszentmihalyi, *Creativity: Flow and the Psychology of Discovery and Invention* (New York: HarperCollins, 1996); *Wikipedia*, c.s. "Mihaly Csikszentmihalyi," http://en.wikipedia.org/wiki/Mihaly_ Csikszentmihalyi.

3. The Great Idea Finder, Post-it Notes, http://www.ideafinder.com/history/inventions/postit.htm.

4. Annette Simmons, *The Story Factor*, 2nd rev. ed. (Cambridge, MA: Basic Books, 2006).

5. Steve Blank, *The Four Steps to the Epiphany*, 2nd ed. (K&S Ranch, 2013).

6. "Alex Lee at Gel 2008," accessed October 1, 2014, http://vimeo.com/3200945.

7. "Big Data at the Speed of Business, " IBM, accessed October 1, 2014, http://www-01.ibm.com/software/data/bigdata/.

8. You might test your hypothesis with your expected carryover segments to validate that the carryover you expected to get is actually likely to happen.

9. It is becoming more common for the end user license agreement (EULA) of software products to forbid the purchase of the product for competitive analysis. When you are evaluating competitor products, do your homework and make sure that you are operating within legal boundaries.

10. Harley Manning and Kerry Bodine, *Outside In: The Power of Putting Customers at the Center of Your Business* (New Harvest, 2012).

11. The 10 Essentials is a term used by the Seattle Mountaineers to describe the necessary gear one should always carry for safe backcountry travel.

Customer's real-world,
end-to-end situation

Align stakeholders **implementation-free**

SCENARIO
WHAT are customers trying to do?
WHY are they motivated to do it?

Understand the problem, don't rush into a solution

outcomes **SPICIER** BIG STORIES AND SMALL STORIES

Tell the customer's story, scoping **Clearly articulate the problem**
NOT the product story **you are about to solve**

A FEW CRISP USER
<magic happens> METRICS Kano analysis STORIES

Capture deep insights **epic** FRAME THE PROBLEM
from research

Performance metrics environment **Perception metrics**

EMOTION Narrative story, with a beginning, middle, and end

STORYTELLING User journey

Framing the problem

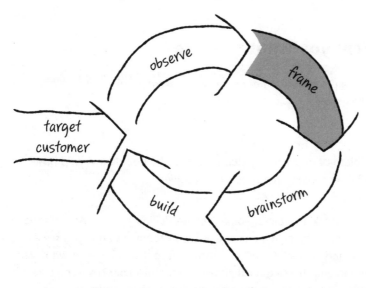

You leave the Observe stage with a short list of insights about your customers, as well as with lots of data about their habits, preferences, pain points, and desires. Many things you learned in your research naturally point to opportunities for surprising and delighting your customers by solving their unmet needs. Chances are that you uncovered many more possibilities than you have time to address in your current project timeline. You now need to make some decisions about which opportunities you'll pursue first.

In the Frame stage, you formalize the insights you discovered about your customers and capture that information in a way that can be used by the entire team throughout the development process. In doing so, you prioritize which customer problems and opportunities you're going to focus on. We call this *framing* the problem, and our favorite technique for framing these opportunities is to write scenarios, or real-world stories, about the target customers. By including quantifiable metrics in the scenarios you develop, you ensure that you have measurable goals that can be tracked during the entire project life cycle.

 VOCAB

A *scenario* is a story that introduces the target customer, describes a real situation in which the customer has a need, explains why that need is important, and articulates what qualities a good solution would have—but without saying anything about exactly how that solution would work.

While the target customer serves as your North Star, a prioritized list of scenarios provides the map that the team uses to navigate its way through the solution development process toward your North Star. Throughout the project, as you iterate through the Fast Feedback Cycle, you will continually refer to this map to ensure that you're solving the problems you originally set out to address.

Articulate the problem you want to solve

The crucial first step in solving a problem is to figure out exactly what problem you are going to solve—you need to *frame* the problem.

 VOCAB

Framing describes a problem or opportunity clearly so that the people involved have a similar understanding of the problem that needs to be solved.

Here's an analogy. Think about taking a picture or, better yet, filming a movie. As you shoot, you look for the best way to frame your subject in the image. Will you zoom in so that you see a close-up of the person's face, breathless and excited? Or will you zoom out so that you see his whole family standing together at a huge stadium, cheering for their favorite football team? Will you take a short video clip of someone checking email while she stands at the airport check-in counter, or will you take a video of her entire journey—waking up early and grabbing a quick breakfast, riding a shuttle to the airport, getting caught in rush-hour traffic, being dropped off at the door, checking in, going through a long security line, and finally boarding the plane?

Determining a frame is in large part determining the scope of the problem you're about to solve. Good framing is clear about what that problem is, how big it is, and what aspects of it are most important to address to achieve customer delight. The framing you use is referred to over successive iterations of the Fast Feedback Cycle. It serves as an anchor from which you measure progress toward your high-level customer goals and keeps the customer's needs and viewpoint embedded in the day-to-day activities and decisions of the team.

Get everyone on the same page

One of the most important goals of framing is to get everyone on the team on the same page about what you are aiming to build. This does not mean just the engineering and user experience teams; it also includes management, marketing, sales, and especially any internal or external partners. Whichever framing technique you use must be clear and useful for all of these disciplines and stakeholders so that they can all use the same map and navigate in harmony toward your North Star—your target customer.

You can trace the failure of many software teams to produce their intended results to a very simple cause—different people had a different interpretation of the problem they were collectively trying to solve for their customer. This problem isn't unique to software development—it shows up in hardware design, road construction, architecture, and other areas—wherever groups of people need to collaborate to build something, and the problem is complex enough that there isn't just one way to solve it. Whether or not a project fails outright, disconnects in communication and alignment make the road unnecessarily bumpy and unpleasant for everyone involved, and greatly decrease your chances of delivering a truly delightful solution.

Planning a software project, whether a brand-new service, version 5, or version 525, is akin to solving a system of interrelated, multivariable equations—with there being only one valid solution. You must figure out what customers need, what solution to build to meet that need, and what kinds of technology the solution requires, all while balancing the realities of schedules, resources, and technology constraints. In the rush to get the project started, it's natural to want to jump in and attempt to solve for all variables at the same time. But what can easily happen is that some people on the team argue about what technology to use, while others discuss what the solution should look like, and still others focus on understanding exactly what the customer's needs are.

Trying to make all these decisions in parallel is tough enough for one brain to do, but it becomes nearly impossible when you have an entire team that needs to work together. Furthermore, when all the factors are variable, there are too many possible valid solutions, and each have their merits—so discussions become circular, decisions don't seem to "stick," and you get the feeling that the project is being built on quicksand. It's really hard to fight against an invisible monster. This leads to a morale problem—an overwhelming sense of complexity and ambiguity during the planning phase of a project, which causes many people on the team to want to bury their heads in the sand until it's all over, which further inhibits the collaboration and consensus building that is so important in the project's early stages.

If you want to have a collaborative planning effort that makes use of the experiences and strengths of more than a handful of people, you need to add just a bit more structure. The key is to be disciplined enough to clearly frame the problem you're trying to solve *before* you launch into solutions. You are narrowing the complexity, not by defining a specific solution path, but by articulating a firm decision about who you're building for, what they need, and how you will define success. You must pause to get team-wide understanding and buy-in on the stated problem before you move on.

Once that's done, the engineering team can engage productively in brainstorming solution ideas and technologies with a clear goal in mind, and not argue anymore about whether this or that problem is the most important problem to solve. With a clear framing, the team is less likely to get sidetracked on tangents that may appear promising or interesting but that result in wasted effort because they don't align with your ultimate goals. *Strong framing enables a loosely coupled team to make fast progress* by providing team members with enough focus and direction that they can make decisions that consistently optimize for the same end-to-end customer needs.

> **Beware of putting a stake in the ground too soon.** Many engineering teams make the mistake of leaping into technical decisions too early, at least in terms of "broad brush-strokes" or to "put a stake in the ground." Unfortunately, deciding things too early can limit your ability to generate out-of-the-box ideas because your thinking quickly solidifies around that early plan and you have trouble seeing fresh alternatives.
>
> Additionally, defining solution specifics too soon tends to lead to contentious arguments between disciplines, stakeholders, and partner teams on issues such as which technology or platform to use—even before the problem is fully understood. Collaboration goes much more smoothly if you identify a specific end-to-end customer problem first and have everyone agree that it is a vital one to solve for the customer—and also agree on which things you will not try to address right now. Only after you have that agreement should you go to the next stage in the Fast Feedback Cycle and together brainstorm about technology options for how you can go about solving your chosen problem. It is much easier for teams to negotiate viable solutions that work for all stakeholders after the common ground for what is required to delight the customer is established. Engineers need to resist the temptation to skip the framing step.

You will still rely on the quick iterations and continual customer feedback of the Fast Feedback Cycle to validate whether the path you choose actually works. As you iterate and learn more about your customers' needs, desires, and preferences, you may need to adjust your framing. But it is essential to make any adjustments in a transparent way in order to keep the team aligned and pointed in the same direction and to not devolve into throwing spaghetti at a wall and seeing what sticks.

Maintain customer focus throughout the project

The second major benefit of a good frame is that it serves as a mechanism for focusing on your customers throughout the entire product cycle. A customer-focused framing should remain highly relevant even into the endgame of a project. The core customer need you describe isn't likely to change, even though your solutions might get better and better over time. As your project progresses, your focus on customer needs is helped by continually checking against your framing, including tracking against experience metrics. Continuing to track how well you are performing against your initial framing is an essential habit to foster to ensure that you actually ship a complete solution for the customer problems you identified.

We all know how easy it is to get sucked into thinking about execution and implementation details as a project progresses past its initial planning stages. Over the course of even a short project, thinking about what technology to use, wondering whether this partner will deliver on time, and tracking how many bugs you still have to fix can quickly occupy mind share. Furthermore, it's easy to be distracted by new discoveries, clever technology hacks, elegant algorithms, a competitor's new release, or any of a myriad of other shiny objects that might catch the team's attention and unintentionally distract you from your strategic goals. Even the best scenario-focused plan can easily turn into a disconnected set of features and functionality if the team forgets about its customers and scenarios midway through.

Building in regular and systematic checks of your work in progress against your framing is crucial for ensuring that you're still solving the problem you initially set out to address—and that you stay focused on solving customer needs. Everyone on the team must keep his or her eyes on the prize all the way to the end. Without a solid, customer-focused framing to measure against, you can easily be blown off course.

The basics of framing

Now that you know why framing is so important, let's talk about some of the most important considerations for how to build a good frame for your problem.

Capture the end-to-end experience with stories

While a problem can be framed in many ways, we've found that stories are particularly well suited for describing end-to-end experiences, which is why we prefer story-based framing techniques for most software projects. It is very powerful to tell the story of a customer's problem from the customer's point of view, showing both how a customer experiences the problem and what the customer's life is like after the problem has been resolved (we hope with the help of your innovative software solution). Stories naturally capture the essence of the real-world problem and the important constraints and contextual factors to consider, which are all important clues about how to evoke delight. By describing a real-world story about your customers in a particular situation, at a particular time, and with a particular problem, you can capture insights about what customers care about, identify what will truly delight them, and clarify the end-to-end path that needs to be traversed to deliver a complete solution.

One great benefit of customer-focused stories is that they do not require you to speculate about what technology choices you have to make, about how the product will look or act, or even about how expensive it will be to build. Quite truthfully, in the beginning of a new project, you simply don't have the answers to those questions yet. However, even in this early stage, stories can clearly articulate exactly what problem you are proposing to solve for your customers, how important that problem is to them, and how good the solution needs to be to evoke delight. Starting with a set of crisp stories ensures that everyone involved in the prioritization process has the same understanding of what you're setting out to achieve.

Neuroscience break, Dr. Indrė Viskontas

We may never know why our brains have evolved to behave as they do, but there are some compelling ideas that are supported at least by correlations, if not by definitive experimentation. One such idea points to the fact that around 1.7 million years ago, our skulls began an exponential expansion that suggests our brains inside got a lot bigger very quickly. Around the same time, our ancestors began living in groups, using tools to hunt and survive and eschewing solitary existences in favor of communities.

There's also evidence that what separates humans from other primates and other animals in general is the ratio of our brain to body size: comparatively, our brains are bigger than animals that we consider less intelligent. What's more, the ratio of neocortex, the newest part of the brain (phylogenetically speaking), to older regions correlates strongly with group size: that is, the larger the social group of a species, the greater proportion of the brain is neocortex. And it's the neocortex that is most active when we're trying to decipher the thoughts and feelings of others. Our brains were likely shaped by evolution to permit us to live in socially cohesive groups. That's the social-brain hypothesis.

So what do stories have to do with it? Well, it turns out that stories are how we learn to understand and predict the behaviors, thoughts, and feelings of others. Children love to listen to, read, and tell stories because stories help them make sense of the world around them— and the often complicated and nuanced behavior of the adults and children with whom they interact. Our conscious memory system has evolved such that we remember events by reenacting the narrative in our minds. We remember by associating new things with what we already know—and putting information into the context of a story is among the most effective ways of learning it.

Here's an example of our favorite story-based framing mechanism, writing a scenario. We'll go into detail about how to write scenarios in a deep dive at the end of this chapter. For now, you can study this as a good example of how to frame a customer's situation using a storytelling format:

> *Jessica is a sales specialist at a small European company that sells wind turbines internationally. One of her main responsibilities is collecting sales leads and sending out roughly 500 sales circulars per month to prospects. Her information comes from multiple sources: some leads she finds on her own via the web, others are provided to her by outside services and given to her in Excel files, and some come from other employees via individual emails. Each source uses different country formats, conventions, and layouts—who knew there were that many different ways of formatting an address and phone number!*

> *<magic happens>*

> *Jessica can easily get 500 international mailing addresses compiled in one place and standardized in a consistent format, ready to print mailing labels, without any manual editing and in under 10 minutes. Even better, she is able to repeat this task quickly in the future. Jessica is thrilled that she no longer has to spend countless hours manually editing her data, freeing her up to spend more time acquiring a greater quantity and quality of leads.*

Stories have many important benefits when they're used as a framing mechanism:

- **Stories are approachable**   Everyone on the team, regardless of discipline, can read a story about a customer and come away with a very similar idea about who the customer is, what problem the customer has, what that customer cares about, and what a good solution needs to accomplish. This reduces the chance of having different interpretations of the problem to be solved.

- **Anyone can write a story**   Everyone on the team is capable of writing, modifying, and debating the customer problems communicated in the story. No fancy techniques or skills are required.

- **Stories capture insights**   The insights you uncover in your research are documented in a way that remains relevant throughout the project life cycle, so team members can continually remind themselves who their customer is and what that customer cares most about.

- **Stories evoke empathy for the customer**   A well-told story captures the human element, making it much easier for everyone on the team to develop empathy for the customer and genuinely care about solving this customer's problem—and to do it in a way that will be delightful for that customer.

- **Stories are sticky**   An engineering team is much more likely to remember a complex set of needs if they are framed as a story instead of as a flat list of bulleted requirements.

- **Stories can pack a lot of information into a small package**   Stories contain the explicit needs and insights you learn about in your research but also enough context and subtext to convey subtler customer needs and attitudes that may be the key to achieving deep delight.

- **Stories are a reality check**   Writing stories helps keep you from trying to solve problems that don't actually exist or that no one cares about. If you can't write a compelling narrative that captures the need to solve a problem or just doesn't seem believable, that's a good indication that you need to do more research or that this may not be an actual customer need after all.

- **Customers understand stories too**   You can test your stories directly with customers. If you aren't sure whether your story is hitting the mark, take a super-quick loop through the Fast Feedback Cycle. Before you even have solution ideas, ask customers to read your stories and see if they resonate. Ask the customer, "Does this story sound like you?" By doing this quick round of feedback, you can verify that you are on the right track or perhaps uncover a missing link to help you nail down the most important aspect of the customer problem you're trying to solve.

 ## MINDSHIFT

Write specific "lighthouse" stories, not generic ones. We've noticed that when engineering teams set out to write stories, they often try to write generic ones. Rather than specifying an instance, they attempt to describe the class. For instance, instead of telling a story about Josephine using her phone to get a few things done and make the most of her spare moments while waiting in line at the grocery story, teams are tempted to broaden the story so that it applies to being productive in any location: home, work, or on the go.

It seems like the right approach because engineers want their solutions to be applicable in an array of situations, as general-purpose tools. However, the trouble with a generic story is that it leaves a lot of wiggle room in specifying what problem you're trying to solve, and hence doesn't give the team the focus it needs to make clear and efficient decisions.

Is Josephine sitting in traffic? Should we build a voice-activation system that can be used safely in a car? Or is she standing in line at the grocery store, where it may be too noisy and impolite to use a voice system? Maybe it's more important to focus on switching tasks and maximizing efficiency within the usual touch interface? How important is viewing the calendar mid-task without losing your state? These questions all become judgment calls, so they become the source of contentious arguments when the problem to be solved is left too open-ended.

Specific stories give a sharper focus for the team, are easier to prioritize, and ensure that everyone is aiming toward the same result. Just like choosing a specific target customer, writing a specific story relies on the principle of carryover, which we introduced in Chapter 4, "Identifying your target customer." You don't write every possible customer story, but instead you carefully choose specific, representative, canonical cases. In the context of writing stories, sometimes we call these *lighthouse stories* because they represent the tallest, brightest, most visible stories that the solution needs to satisfy.

By focusing the team on a specific canonical situation—a lighthouse story—you get a solution that is fully aligned, where everyone on the team is clear about what aspects of the story are the most important parts to optimize. Choose the stories you will focus on with care, knowing that if you solve those canonical situations, you'll have carryover into similar situations that will be solved as well. This requires that you recognize it's impossible to create a solution that is optimal for every customer situation at the same time. You need to make decisions about which situations and problems are the most critical for your customer, the solutions that will produce deep delight and satisfaction. Focus your energy on building those in a complete, high-quality end-to-end way.

Keep framing implementation-free

One of the most important aspects of any framing is that it be implementation-free. Your framing needs to articulate the problem to be solved, without describing how a solution will be built or what the solution will look like. Framing should not include any details about how the product, service, device, technology, or platform will actually work.

Whether you use scenarios, another story-based technique, or even old-school requirements to develop your framing, experts have long agreed that keeping implementation details out of framing is essential (aside from an occasional implementation constraint that is truly immutable, which we discuss later). However, many engineers find this principle counterintuitive at first, perhaps because an implementation-free framing feels as though it won't be specific and detailed enough to tell you what to build. But this line of reasoning leads to trouble.

Consider this example of a simple, implementation-free framing statement:

John wants to share the latest kid pictures with grandparents.

Let's play out this example and see where it leads. The next step in the Fast Feedback Cycle after framing is to brainstorm and generate as many ideas as you can think of in the hope of hitting on an out-of-the-box approach that no one has tried before. The following illustration shows a wide variety of ideas you might come up with when you're brainstorming about solutions for this small story. In fact, some of these ideas have proved over time to be very good ones and have even given rise to groundbreaking services like Flickr, Facebook, and Snapchat.

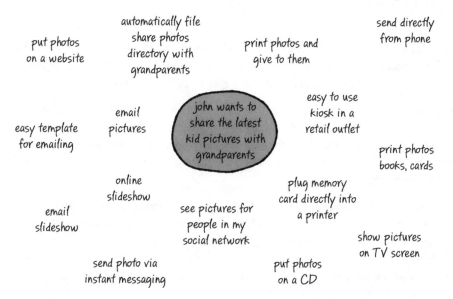

But think about it: What if we change the initial framing the tiniest bit? What if we change "share" to "email":

*John wants to **email** the latest kid pictures to grandparents.*

Given this framing, what kind of solutions would you think of now?

This is an interesting thought experiment. If you frame the problem to be about email, it's quite likely that you will never consider retail kiosks, social networks, or any of the myriad other ways to share a picture beyond the handful of ideas that directly relate to email. Your ideas would look something like this:

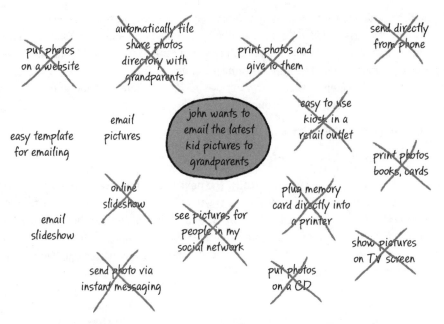

put photos on a website

automatically file share photos directory with grandparents

print photos and give to them

send directly from phone

john wants to email the latest kid pictures to grandparents

email pictures

easy to use kiosk in a retail outlet

easy template for emailing

print photos books, cards

online slideshow

email slideshow

plug memory card directly into a printer

see pictures for people in my social network

show pictures on TV screen

send photo via instant messaging

put photos on a CD

Yet it's easy to imagine how quickly you might fall into this trap and assume that the most likely photo-sharing solution would probably involve email. It would seem natural to start your thinking there and develop framing that mentions "emailing the latest pics."

This is why we say, over and over again, *don't let implementation details sneak in to your framing.* Engineers often have a strong desire to see the details, and this is another cause of their tendency to try to skip steps in their hurry to build, but this rush is counterproductive and will lead to conflict and suboptimal solutions. *Including implementation details is the single biggest mistake people make when attempting to frame a problem.*

Implementation details create two major problems. First, as the photo-sharing example shows, implementation details might constrain your thinking, making it less likely that you come up with a novel idea or an innovative approach that could differentiate your solution from competitors'. You want to have room to choose the optimal way to solve a problem and not be blocked in before you even get started brainstorming solution ideas. Including implementation details unintentionally is one of the biggest mistakes that will limit your creativity.

The second problem is a practical one. Implementation details will likely cause your framing to become out of date very quickly. A problem statement that is implementation-free can easily survive the entire engineering and development process—and be just as relevant a guide on release day as it was the day it was first penned. But if your framing includes implementation details, as soon as the inevitable twists, turns, and compromises of the engineering process force you to shift your implementation approach even slightly, your framing statement will be out of date, and the likelihood is that it will be forgotten rather than continually revised as your implementation approach evolves. An implementation-free framing is a much more durable guide and will last throughout the project life cycle, no updates needed.

Now, this isn't to say that you will get your framing right on your first try. As you loop around the Fast Feedback Cycle, you touch base with your framing in every iteration, and may even update it based on what you learn from customer feedback, especially in the first few iterations. In later cycles, however, your framing should be pretty solid, and you will focus more on tracking your progress against your framing to ensure that you are truly solving the problem you set out to solve. Tracking metrics on a scorecard is a key technique to help ensure that you haven't drifted away from your framing goals and that your solution is achieving the customer delight you intended. This brings us to our next characteristic of good framing: specifying metrics.

Metrics set the bar for how good the solution needs to be

Framing needs not only to describe the problem itself but to articulate what a successful resolution to the problem might achieve. But remember, this is not about describing how the solution works; it's about what will be accomplished by a good solution. What will your customers have accomplished if your product succeeds in solving their problem? What outcomes will they have achieved? As you iterate around the Fast Feedback Cycle, you need to know when your solution is good enough so that you can stop iterating and ship or move on to the next problem.

You express what a good solution would look like by incorporating a handful of specific, customer-focused metrics into your framing. The metrics should be tied to the factors that will produce the customer delight you are striving for—in that particular situation, with that particular target customer. Coming up with a dozen interesting and relevant experience metrics is easy, but this is a case where more is not better. Narrowing down the metrics to the one or two measures that are the most important is how the true intent and goal are articulated. The exercise of choosing key metrics often sharpens the framing considerably. Again, only with this level of precision in your goals does it become possible for a diverse engineering team to remain loosely coupled in their work but still optimize the end-to-end experience with alignment and consistency.

As the project progresses, these customer experience–focused metrics become critical as a way to measure and track whether your proposed solution is really solving the problem you set out to solve and keep you from convincing yourself that it's working when it really isn't. As Eric Ries warns in *The Lean Startup*, beware of creating "vanity" metrics that make you feel as though you're making progress but aren't actually measuring what customers really think about your solution.[1] For instance, tracking the number of downloads of your product on a website is not nearly as interesting as tracking customer satisfaction and sustained usage scores over time. Lots of downloads could be the result of great publicity or the fact that your solution is the only one available, but if customers aren't genuinely satisfied, they will quickly defect when a competitor ships a better alternative.

SFE in action: Don't believe your vanity metrics

Clint Covington, Principal Program Manager Lead, Microsoft Office

As a lead program manager on the Microsoft Access team, I was responsible for the Access templates. At the time, the team knew that it was difficult for many customers to start using a database product and to get it to do what they want. Access templates are designed to jump-start projects. One goal for the team was to grow the usage of Access, and these templates are a great way to help people get started faster. We had made a sizable investment in identifying new scenarios and building out a set of new templates while also improving some of our existing templates. We also changed the Start screen in Access to make it easier for people to find and discover the templates.

Most of us believed the work we had done was received positively by customers. Template downloads from Office Online grew from 1.1 million to over 8 million in about 18 months. Download trends looked like a hockey stick, ratings were above four stars, and comments were mostly all positive. I felt great about our progress.

Looking back on that now it is clear that the number of template downloads and associated ratings were "vanity metrics." After all, our team's goal was to increase overall usage. But at the time, my manager was skeptical that our template investment was driving overall usage. He doubted that we had made as much progress as those of us who were down in the weeds thought we had made. He asked me to look at metrics beyond downloads that pointed to overall usage growth. I had just read the book *The Ultimate Question: Driving Good Profits and True Growth* by Fred Reichheld, which inspired me to think hard about how we were measuring success. It seemed like a perfect application for what we were doing.

So we changed our approach to gathering usage metrics. This time, after a user had used a template four times, we gave the customer a standard Net Promoter Score (NPS) survey that asked questions such as "On a scale of 1 to 10, would you recommend this to your friends or your family or coworkers?"

The results were crystal clear—templates were not helping people get started faster with Access, nor did the templates generate greater satisfaction. Our total NPS score was terrible. There were more demoters than promoters and too many passive ratings—the NPS score did not match the type of growth we were seeing in the downloads of the templates. The verbatim comments from customers were brutal as demoters described their frustrations. Quite honestly, I was embarrassed by our Net Promoter Score. The clarity of our failure inspired us to make changes.

We categorized the negative feedback into buckets. In the NPS survey some people would voluntarily leave their email addresses, so we emailed them and arranged phone interviews. We spent several weeks calling people and digging into the color of the verbatim feedback. We learned that people were initially hopeful that the templates would save them time and help with their job. This hope is what led to the initial four-star ratings we had looked at earlier. But we now discovered that once a customer started to actually use the template, they hit a wall and became frustrated and dissatisfied. Through this new set of data and interviews it became clear to us that there were three or four design flaws in the product and there were gaps in users' knowledge that led to the majority of the frustration that people were experiencing.

Using our new insights, we redesigned several key flows in Access. We also produced a training video focused on helping people get past the problems we identified. We then brought people into the usability lab and watched them use the templates, after which we made further refinements. Several months after the first survey went out, we rereleased an update. The feedback to our updated templates came back far more positive. The Net Promoter Score increased by about 35 points and the help videos quickly became the most popular Access help assets.

The desire to change the template design was motivated by the clarity of the feedback the NPS survey generated. We used this to prioritize this work above other things we could have been doing. The NPS survey data combined with direct customer follow-up helped focus our efforts into the experiences that mattered most for people trying to use Access templates. The team found it inspiring to see such profound change in customer delight and quantifiable progress in creating a solution people loved.

Big stories and small stories

Over the years we have seen teams use different ways to frame their software projects. Many approaches rely on a multilayer hierarchy of priorities, starting with a few major areas of focus or themes that are then systematically broken down into smaller and smaller investment areas, eventually naming the deliverables, features, and tasks that represent the engineering work that needs to be done to deliver on those goals. Historically, these hierarchies of work, or work-breakdown charts, have consisted mostly of technology-focused investment areas, features, and work items.

As teams adopt more customer-focused approaches, we have seen these hierarchies shift to use customer stories as the primary nodes that both define and organize the engineering work to be done. There are roles for many types of stories within such a hierarchy, depending on the size and scale of the team, the type of project being undertaken, and the length of the milestones, iterations, or sprints. A team might write large-scale stories to recount the overall cradle-to-grave experience. It might write smaller stories that describe specific jobs or tasks the customer is trying to do. It might even include one-liners to describe slices of a larger story that can be implemented within a single Agile sprint.

Interestingly, nearly every team we've worked with, from small teams to thousand-person organizations, has ended up using a two-level hierarchy of stories: a small collection of larger scope, end-to-end narratives that each comprise stories that describe particular jobs, subtasks, or aspects of the larger end-to-end experience. Said another way, teams create big, end-to-end, or vision-level stories that articulate larger experiences, and these are then segmented into numerous small or task-level stories that align with the larger ones. (Some teams tried working with a single, flat list of stories, but found the list too long to manage, and the stories all had different sizes and scopes. A few teams tried a three-level hierarchy, but that became too complex and felt too process-heavy, for marginal benefit.)

This story hierarchy usually sits near the top of a team's work-breakdown chart and becomes the parent of the subsequent features, deliverables, tasks, and other work items that are needed to deliver those experiences. While each team we've worked with has its own system for accomplishing this, some repeatable patterns do emerge. We'll talk about where stories fit within a larger work-breakdown hierarchy, how to associate deliverables and tasks with stories, and the mechanics of how these pieces work together in Chapter 11, "The way you work."

 MINDSHIFT

Focus scenarios on defining the length of an experience not the width. One of the biggest traps we have seen teams fall into is writing way too many scenarios. With the intent of being complete and comprehensive, teams write a scenario to describe every single related situation and edge case. You will go crazy with that approach and end up with hundreds or thousands of scenarios, and this will be unmanageable.

Instead, think of your scenarios as guideposts, not as complete specifications. Your scenarios should capture the most important end-to-end experiences that you are optimizing your solutions for; you'll use good engineering practices to handle variations and edge cases as you get into the details of building solutions.

As our colleague Jeff Braaten would say, you can think about this as length versus width. Scenarios should focus on defining the length of the longest possible end-to-end experience, from start to finish, and should not try to cover the full width—the edge cases and possible variations within that scenario. Pick the canonical situations that describe the length you are going for, and focus on writing those scenarios. Many of the variations will be addressed naturally in the engineering process of building those long experiences.

Frame stage: Key tools and techniques

As in all of the stages in the Fast Feedback Cycle, you can choose from different tools and techniques to frame your problem. (There are many more than we cover here.) Depending on the nature of your project, its size and time frame, and the number of people involved, you should choose the techniques that best fit your needs. The techniques we highlight fall into three broad categories:

- Tools that help you capture key metrics

- Tools that help you tell the customer's story

■ Tools to help you prioritize your list of work

Tools that help you capture key metrics

All of the framing techniques we mention should be paired with metrics or have metrics embedded in them. For all the reasons described earlier in this chapter, it is critical to keep your success metrics focused on your customers' experience and to create metrics around specific customer outcomes. Metrics give you explicit, experience-oriented goals to reach, which are essential for keeping your focus on customer needs and scenarios through to the endgame of a project.

Generally, we have found that effective, customer-focused metrics break down into two broad categories:

■ **Performance metrics**   These metrics capture information such as how quickly a customer is able to perform a task, how many clicks are needed to buy a book, how many errors a customer makes when attempting to use a new API, what does a customer do after opening a browser, or how many customers successfully complete their task. Like DO data, these metrics are more objective in nature. For larger end-to-end experiences, a relevant performance metric may stretch across multiple systems, platforms, or teams. There may be substantial investment in building instrumentation and a tracking system that can collect these metrics in an automated way. You can also capture many performance metrics with a stopwatch and careful note taking during a series of user tests.

■ **Perception metrics**   These metrics capture data such as how satisfied a customer is with the overall experience, how frustrated she felt when something went wrong, how confident she was that she got the answer right, or how delighted she was to find a new way to solve an old problem. The typical approach for how to capture these types of metrics is to ask customers to rate a particular aspect of their experience on a 5-point or 7-point scale. For instance, "On a 5-point scale, please rate how difficult or easy it was to find the movie you were looking for (5 is very easy, 1 means very difficult, 3 means neutral)." Like SAY data, these metrics are more subjective in nature, though they are most often captured in a quantitative way for ease of tracking and measuring trends over time.

Whether you choose more performance-oriented or more perception-oriented metrics, you should set a specific numerical goal—for instance: "Customers can successfully send their first text message within three minutes" or "Customers rate their overall satisfaction at 4.5 or higher on a 5-point scale." This metric should be measured frequently so that a trend can be established and any regressions in the metric can be noticed promptly.

 TIP

> One great way to report metrics throughout your project's life cycle is to build a scorecard that rolls up your top metrics into one view. We'll discuss customer-experience reporting in more detail in Chapter 11.

Some teams rely so heavily on metrics and scorecards as tracking mechanisms that the metrics themselves act as a primary framing tool. However, even if the metrics take a primary framing role, they should always be paired with scenarios to illustrate the specific, canonical usage patterns for which that metric should be assessed and measured.

 MINDSHIFT

System metrics and test-case pass stats are not customer-focused metrics. Most engineering teams already use plenty of metrics in tracking their work, whether they are tracking bug counts, burndown charts, team velocity, or test-case pass rates. These are important measures of internal work completion that help teams manage execution, but they are not customer-focused metrics. Customers don't care how many bugs you fix, how many story points your team can achieve in a week, or how many lines of code you have written—they care only about how well their individual needs are being met by your solution right now and how fast a fix is available the next time they have a problem. It's certainly possible that even though a team reports that its test pass is complete and everything appears to be working according to plan, the customer is not satisfied with the solution that was delivered. Engineering metrics do not tell you about the customer's perspective.

Many teams also have system-level instrumentation to track server performance, availability, and so on. These are important metrics to track for engineering quality and system health—and failure in these areas will surely impact customer experience—but they tell you only whether something is wrong, not whether something is right. If the servers are down all the time, that will indeed create a bad customer experience. However, having a service that is reliable and performant does not tell you anything about whether the customer is delighted with the solution you provide. Again, for that you need to focus on measuring customer outcomes.

Tools that help you tell the customer's story

The following sections describe several techniques you can use to frame a problem. Some are more suited to big stories, others are better at small stories, and some are multipurpose.

Scenarios

Best for: Capturing an end-to-end situation with contextual information, metrics, and empathy for the customer in a single package. Appropriate for big or small stories.

The first framing technique we taught at Microsoft is writing scenarios. We developed a standard two-paragraph story format that captures the essence of the customer's perspective, the customer's needs as expressed in a specific situation, and the customer's contextual environment. This format also has one or two metrics embedded in the scenario that clarify the goals in a numerically succinct way. Everything you need to know to start working on solutions is captured in this one vehicle, making it a surprisingly efficient approach. Here's an example:

Josephine gets stuff done in the grocery line

Josephine is a busy mom of two school-age kids who has a dog and is always on the go. She feels like she never has enough time. Just yesterday she almost left her son at an empty soccer field when she missed the coach's email that practice was cancelled. Josephine is standing in the checkout line at the grocery store and realizes that she is going to be waiting a few minutes. She has so much to get done today and doesn't want to miss another important message or deadline. Could she get a few things done while she waits?

<magic happens>

While standing in line for six minutes, Josephine was able to check off a bunch of items from her to-do list: pay for her kids' music lessons, RSVP to a party (after checking that she and her husband are available that evening), schedule an appointment with the vet, answer her husband's text message to assure him that she did buy milk, scan her email to learn that her son's soccer practice was cancelled again this afternoon, and even squeeze in a quick peek at her favorite game, AlphaJax. The time waiting in line flew by. Josephine felt like she was able to maximize every second to help stay on top of her busy life and was able to give her full attention to her kids when she met them at the school bus later that afternoon.

We'll do a deep dive on how to write scenarios at the end of this chapter.

User-journey maps

Best for: Complete end-to-end or cradle-to-grave experiences. Capture multiple stages or steps that a customer goes through. Produce a good visual chart that shows all the steps, processes, systems, and partners touched by customers during their experience.

We discussed user-journey maps in Chapter 5, "Observing customers: Building empathy," as a way to show the steps that a customer goes through in an existing experience and analyze what is going well or poorly at each step. The user-journey technique is also great for describing the essential steps in a proposed end-to-end experience, especially for experiences with a larger scope. This technique is ideal for describing a cradle-to-grave experience that has multiple stages or steps that a customer goes through, usually over a longer period of time. User journeys are also good for describing extensive experiences that involve many different groups or stakeholders that each need to contribute in one or two steps but still be aligned to the larger whole.

Here is an example of what a simple user-journey map might look like for a cradle-to-grave experience for a mobile phone:

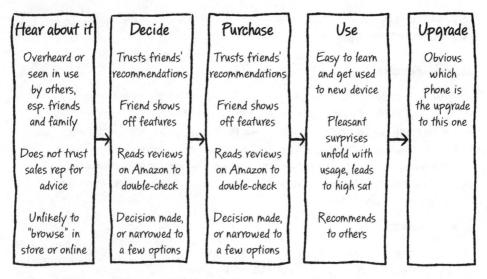

Hear about it	Decide	Purchase	Use	Upgrade
Overheard or seen in use by others, esp. friends and family	Trusts friends' recommendations	Trusts friends' recommendations	Easy to learn and get used to new device	Obvious which phone is the upgrade to this one
Does not trust sales rep for advice	Friend shows off features	Friend shows off features	Pleasant surprises unfold with usage, leads to high sat	
Unlikely to "browse" in store or online	Reads reviews on Amazon to double-check	Reads reviews on Amazon to double-check	Recommends to others	
	Decision made, or narrowed to a few options	Decision made, or narrowed to a few options		

If you find yourself stuck and can't quite figure out which scenarios to write, what jobs make up the experience, how it all connects, or which stakeholders are involved in which places, it may be worthwhile to put together a user-journey map to help identify the essential stages customers go through in their overall end-to-end experience.

User stories

Best for: Small stories or task-level scenarios. Articulate specific, individual paths or slices through a story or scenario. User stories are a mainstay technique for many Agile teams.

Teams who use Agile and Scrum-based approaches have been writing user stories to frame, manage, and track their work for a long time. User stories identify a single path or a slice that a user might take through a larger story. They represent atomic units of work that can be completed in a single sprint and that deliver a visible increment of functionality that the customer can see and experience. Agile teams demonstrate their latest working code to customers at the end of each sprint in order to get rapid customer feedback to inform the next sprint.

A user story has a very specific format:

As a <type of customer>

I can <achieve an outcome>

So that <reason or customer motivation>

Using our mobile phone example, you might write a user story such as the following to break down the larger story into several slices that you can start building one at a time:

As a busy mom, I can check my calendar and respond to an email while waiting in the grocery line so that I can maximize every second of my busy life.

When paired with a big scenario to provide end-to-end context, user stories are a great tool to help prioritize and order the actual work of the engineering team. While the user story guides the work of an individual sprint, the scenario is used to identify and track all of the user stories that need to be built until the complete end-to-end experience is reached. Many teams use an end-to-end scenario that is broken down into user stories as a way to understand and describe a minimum viable feature set.

The downside to user stories is that used alone, standard Agile approaches encourage teams to focus on one story at a time, and this can encourage teams to spend their time adding one piece of functionality after another without a lot of thought to the complete end-to-end experience. With shorter sprint lengths, user stories can also be broken down so finely to fit within a single sprint that the customer context may be lost. So beware that user stories that are unconnected to larger narratives can gradually devolve into a feature list, either by how they are used by the team or by incorporating actual implementation details into the user stories themselves in an attempt to scope and clarify the work for a given sprint.

 TIP

Don't mistake use cases for user stories. Use cases are a more formal way of describing customer requirements for a particular situation or sequence of events. A use case usually takes the form of a table in which you explicitly name the primary actor and stakeholders, the precondition (the state of the user and system at the beginning), triggers that start the action, the postcondition (the state of the user and system at the end), and a numbered list of detailed steps that the customer would take through a particular situation. Use cases tend to assume a particular implementation, and hence will embed implementation details in the list of steps. For this reason, we do not recommend this technique as an approach to framing, however it can be a useful way to describe a particular solution path in a specification.

Epics

Best for: Larger end-to-end stories within an Agile team. Similar in scope and usage to a scenario.

Another technique that is catching on in the Agile community is the epic. An epic is constructed at a higher level than a user story, which puts its focus on the end-to-end experience that's desired and the larger problem that is being solved. Some Agile teams write epics in narrative, paragraph form. As such, epics can be indistinguishable from scenarios, and the terms can be used synonymously.

We've also seen some teams formulate epics using the standard user-story format, but they write them with a broader scope. For example:

As a busy mom, I can get multiple tasks done while standing in line at the grocery store so that I can maximize every second of my busy life.

The division between epics and user stories aligns quite well with our experience that teams usually end up with a two-level hierarchy of stories—in this case, epics serve as the higher-level or big end-to-end story, and user stories act as the lower-level, small stories. Used in concert, epics and user stories are a good approach to framing as long as the epics are written in a narrative form and contain enough context about the customer and the situation. If not, they need to be paired with the key insights, motivations, and context about the customer to ensure that enough specifics are captured and empathy with the customer is not lost.

Neither user stories nor epics naturally include a specific success metric. Hence, it's also critical to pair this approach with some sort of mechanism to identify and track the metrics that determine what success looks like and help you to know when you have achieved the goals of the end-to-end experience.

SFE in action: The Storytelling Storyboard Toolkit

Susan Mings, PhD, Senior Design Researcher, Microsoft Windows Server Systems; Matt LaGrandeur, Designer II, Microsoft Windows Server Systems; Joe Hallock, Senior Design Manager, Microsoft Windows Server Systems; Ken Coleman, Designer II, Microsoft Windows Server Systems

As the SFE philosophy and practice has spread across Microsoft, it's been great to see colleagues in diverse disciplines become more excited about focusing on user-centered design. The concept of "storytelling" seems especially resonant—who doesn't like a good story? Learning about users through research, and then drafting stories about users' current frustrations and future goals has become standard steps when specs are first drafted.

The advantages of storytelling practices are obvious: team members gain empathy for customers, get excited imagining the "happy ending" our products can provide them, and rally around a common vision that everyone can grasp. But sometimes our written customer stories have not been as powerful or as easy to use as we hoped. Drafting the text of a story is a significant time investment for the author, who has to sweat about the precise words that describe the user's context, frustrations, and goals. And speed-reading long text blocks just before a review meeting takes time, plus there are language differences among global team members.

To address these drawbacks, and in the spirit of SFE iteration, a few brave teams decided to try picture stories. Another tenet of SFE is conveying ideas with quick sketches, so we added drawings to our storytelling. We started "small" with sketches, arranging simple drawings in a narrative sequence. Here's an example:

Teams adopted this "sketch storyboard" method quickly. These drawings were quick, easy, and fun to sketch—certainly faster to produce than a long narrative! Sketch storyboards worked great for sharing the essence of user stories within the team.

But again, there were drawbacks. Sketch storyboards were not great to use in presentations to key stakeholders or executives or to get feedback from customers. As hand-drawn artifacts, sketch storyboards were low quality, inconsistent across storytellers, and not digital. To address these issues, the UX team added another step to the process and started creating high-fidelity illustrations as in this example:

The high-fidelity illustrations did address some of the issues with the sketch storyboards. They worked great for presentations, they were high quality, and they had a consistent look and feel. However, they were time-consuming to produce and required a skilled artist. Most importantly, we had inadvertently moved away from the SFE philosophy of team participation in design.

To address these issues, we developed the Storytelling Storyboard Toolkit. It met our goals of standardizing and digitizing storyboard creation, and it was easy enough for anyone to use to create a storyboard. The first version of the toolkit (nicknamed the "Mr. Potato Head" version) was a PowerPoint file that contained storyboard elements that could be pieced together into a story. Here's an example of some pieces and a character created from them.

Put some characters together with some text, and you could create story frames like this one:

As teams adopted our toolkit, we realized that assembling the characters was rather tedious. Our second version of the toolkit (nicknamed the "Colorforms" version) solved this problem by providing larger elements to work with. Instead of elements such eyebrows, a nose, a mouth, and so on, the "Colorforms" version provided faces. Each face corresponded to a type of user and came with different expressions. It was easy to change faces to show different emotions. Here's an example of one such user.

This toolkit also included galleries of backgrounds, objects, and callouts for dialog. By combining multiple elements, anyone could easily construct a high-quality storyboard:

We've found storyboarding to be a powerful UX tool for motivating team members to create, review, and share user stories. Our teams have integrated storyboards effectively into the engineering process both to formalize user stories in specs, and to communicate those stories effectively at executive, stakeholder, and customer reviews.

"I can" statements

Best for: Very small stories, similar in scope to an Agile user story. "I can" statements are best when paired with an end-to-end story.

An "I can" statement is really just a shortened form of a user story that focuses on that middle line: *"I can <achieve an outcome>."* This approach is not normally advocated in the Agile community because it omits both the explicit definition of who the target customer is and the all-important reasoning or customer motivation for the story. However, as with user stories, we've seen teams successfully use "I can" statements as a detail-level small story in conjunction with a parent end-to-end narrative that clearly conveys the customer's situation and context. Sometimes it helps to name the customer instead of using "I" if the customer's identify isn't clear from the supporting story.

For our mobile phone example, you might write an "I can" statement such as this:

I can RSVP to a party invitation while standing in line at the grocery store.

Josephine can check her calendar while on the phone with the doctor's office.

Outcomes

Best for: Discrete jobs that make up an end-to-end scenario and associated metrics.

Outcomes have become more popular in the past few years. They were inspired by Clayton Christensen's idea, "What job is the customer hiring your product to do?"[2] Those jobs are the atomic units of the experience of your product and are expressed as the outcomes that customers hope your product will help them achieve. Said another way, outcomes enumerate all the actions your system must perform, along with a key metric that specifies how well the system needs to accomplish that specific job for the customer.

An outcome is typically structured in one of two ways:

<minimize/increase/etc. a key metric> + <to do this specific job> + (target: <goal>)

Example: *Minimize the time it takes for Marina to send a quick message while she's in the middle of doing another task. (Target: 30 seconds)*

<Customer> can <do this specific job> + <metric>

Example: *Marina can send a quick message while she's in the middle of doing another task within 30 seconds.*

Outcomes are best used in concert with scenarios or other story-based approaches. In fact, you can think about a scenario as a sequence of outcomes that the customer needs to accomplish. The atomic nature of outcomes makes them uniquely suited for helping to organize and prioritize metrics across a suite of scenarios.

Requirements

Best for: Documenting the technical constraints, policies, and implementation that are necessary for success and are nonnegotiable "must-haves."

The idea of writing software requirements has been around for decades. If you've ever studied the theory, you'll know that the key to a good requirement is for it to be implementation-free. However, in practice, this is very difficult to achieve, and most attempts at defining a list of short, crisp requirements end up with a laundry list of features, which are decidedly not implementation-free. It is tough to write a short, specific description of a customer need that is unambiguous, without also telling the customer's story or providing the context behind it.

Even if you are successful in keeping requirements implementation-free, they are still tricky to use: they end up as a list of product attributes (fast, easy) and jobs the customer needs to accomplish (copy, edit, send). However, without context about how and why the customer does these tasks, misunderstanding is inevitable between the person who writes the requirement and a person attempting to design a solution to meet that requirement. For this reason, requirements are our least favorite approach to framing. Even if requirements are truly implementation-free, this approach often devolves into creating a long list of hundreds of detailed items, with very little connective tissue for understanding how those requirements relate to each other or how they work together to form a coherent whole. It's very easy to get lost in the details and satisfy each of the requirements but not actually deliver an end-to-end solution.

However, although we are not big fans of using a requirements list as the sole way to frame a project, a requirements list is sometimes the right tool for the job. Sometimes, you have a set of business and technical constraints that are nonnegotiable. For example, say you are running an online business and want to expand globally. Your well-thought-out business strategy suggests that you should target Brazil as your next expansion market. In your research you discover a handful of tax, legal, and other implications for doing business and selling software in that market—issues such as how and who you make payments to, how you advertise, how you collect fees, how you do business with the banks, how you pay taxes. These are the technical and business constraints that you must implement correctly before you can even consider doing business in Brazil. In this case, it makes sense to have the legal and business requirements dutifully researched and listed in a requirements document, thus saving the engineering team the time and expense of figuring out exactly what it means to do business in Brazil.

Even though a well-researched list of requirements can be useful when you have a number of detailed business or technical constraints that are very specific, well understood, nonnegotiable, and must be implemented, don't fall into the trap and fool yourself into thinking that by implementing those requirements, you are finished. Meeting those requirements likely means you have paid the required dues of getting into that business . . . now, how are you going to beat your competition?

Goals and non-goals

Best for: Communicating the most important feature and performance tradeoffs in a technical component that does not directly face the customer.

Another non-story-based technique is to write a list of goals and non-goals. This technique can be good for framing deeply technical problems, where the target customer's experience is several layers away from the platform. In this case, the customer's needs can sometimes be captured as a set of key performance and functionality tradeoffs.

This isn't our preferred way of framing, but teams that are new to a customer-focused approach may have trouble thinking about how end-to-end scenarios feed down into the deep platform layer. This technique provides a reasonable compromise, especially when used in concert with customer-focused scenarios that describe the overall experience that a platform ultimately needs to support.

When writing goals and non-goals, keep in mind that the list of non-goals—the specific things that you are *not* trying to achieve—is a particularly powerful way to focus the team on the most important aspects to optimize and keep it from being distracted by tangents or details that are not as important. Writing down non-goals helps ensure that team members are on the same page about what the true goals are.

The press release

Best for: Aligning marketing claims with engineering plans.

Before you even know what the product looks like, write a press release detailing the marketing story you would tell on the day your product is released. In the style of a press release, describe what problems have been solved, what new opportunities have been realized, and what customers and reviewers would say to praise the product.

Writing a press release can be a great technique for aligning marketing plans with the development team and to clarify the business value of the proposed project. For one thing, it allows the marketing team to think through the key value propositions ahead of time and do a gut check on whether those really are differentiators and will resonate with customers. A press release can be tested with customers, analysts, and partners to gauge reactions and then fine-tuned based on that feedback. In addition, having the marketing messaging and key claims written out provides guidance to the engineering team about which aspects of the end-to-end experience are the most marketable, and hence most important to get right.

 TIP

Cross-reference the press release with your stories and then mark the stories that the marketing department cares most about to ensure that those stories are tracked carefully throughout the project. If a story is at risk or a component might need to be cut, the fact that it is a key element of a marketing campaign should enter into the decision.

The art of storytelling

At the end of the day, most of these techniques boil down to telling stories about human experiences. The ancient art of storytelling can teach you a lot about how to write a captivating and insightful narrative about a human being's experience. Various storytelling patterns and forms have emerged over the centuries. Here are a few that may provide some guidance for writing better end-to-end narratives:

- **Story arc** Most stories gradually build tension, starting with a small crisis or two, resolve those issues, then introduce a bigger crisis, work up to a major climax, and finally have a resolution. This gradual and measured progress through successively larger crises and resolutions helps keep the reader engaged but not overwhelmed. It's easy to see how a story arc might apply to game development, following the story of a character through multiple challenges until you meet the big boss. However, even though you are not generally trying to create crises for your customers, a similar pattern of gradual learning and successive accomplishments also applies to more productivity-oriented situations for which you want to build an end-to-end product or service experience that is engaging and productive, but not overwhelming. Sometimes the term "story arc" is used to refer to the overarching story that the smaller narratives can be tied to. In this sense, it can be used as a synonym for a user journey, epic, narrative, or big scenario.

- **Hero's journey**   This is a literary structure or analysis technique (coined by American mythologist Joseph Campbell) that identifies typical stages in stories that feature a main protagonist, or "hero," who undergoes a personal transformation through a special experience. Ancient stories that have survived the ages, as well as great modern-day stories, have an uncanny resonance to the Hero's Journey pattern, implying a deep connection to fundamental truths about human experiences. Key stages include the call to adventure, threshold, challenges, revelation, transformation, and return to normalcy. Again, these stages can be guideposts for framing an end-to-end experience that will engage customers and resonate at a deep human level.

- **Three-act structure**   This classic dramatic structure is frequently found in plays and screenplays and underlies most narrative stories. Act I provides background information, introduces the characters, sets the stage, and concludes with a significant moment of conflict or a turning point in the story. Act II develops that conflict and follows the emotional journey of the main characters until the conflict reaches a climax. Act III provides the resolution of the conflict. Generally, a story should spend 25 percent of its time in Act I, 50 percent in Act II, and 25 percent in Act III.

Turning the corner: Tools to help you prioritize your list of work

As you sort through your research and start writing stories, you will inevitably end up writing about more issues than you have time to solve. Just as in choosing a target customer, *it's more important to focus on a few end-to-end stories and execute on them with a high level of quality than to spread yourself too thin and end up delivering an unremarkable layer of peanut butter.*

As you start exploring your customer insights and developing stories to build, you will surely start forming opinions about which of these stories are the more important to pursue for your project. Your goal at this point is to prioritize your stories and decide which ones you will undertake. Whether that prioritization forms the beginning of your product backlog, a list of top-priority scenarios in your work-breakdown chart, or a spreadsheet that helps you schedule and sequence your work, it's important to have clear marching orders for your team.

Here are a few techniques for figuring out which end-to-end stories you should go after first.

Cut low-priority stories early

Get in the habit from the very start of looking for stories that are less important—less likely to carry impact for the customer—and cut them as soon as possible. You can cut early or you can cut late, but late cuts are way more expensive. Cut early. The single biggest lever a team has for improving overall quality is to focus on fewer stories. With fewer priorities, you have time to iterate each of them to a higher level of quality and polish.

Effort vs. value

A classic approach for prioritizing work is to estimate the approximate "bang for the buck." The idea is to generate very rough cost estimates, as well as estimates of how valuable each scenario is to the customer. Use that data to judge which stories might have the most impact but take the least amount of effort to build.

On the basis of your customer research, you should have some empathy-based judgment about how valuable each story would be to your customers if the problems it describes were solved well. Estimating the implementation cost is a bit trickier, however. Obviously, you don't have complete information about how much effort it will take to build a solution (after all, the stories are implementation-free), but you can still make your best guess as to whether this will likely be a long, complex, or difficult story to build, or something smaller and more tactical compared with the other proposed stories.

Rate value and effort for each proposed story on a scale of 1 to 5 and plot it. It doesn't matter exactly how you define 1 versus 2 versus 3, as long as your ratings are consistent. The resulting graph might look something like Figure 6-1.

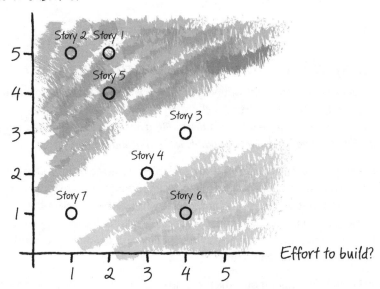

FIGURE 6-1 A chart that plots value to customer on one axis and effort to build on the other.

The top area represents the region of the graph where the value to the customer is high, especially in proportion to the amount of projected effort needed to deliver it. The stories that fall into this area offer a good bang for the buck and are generally worth doing. The middle area shows stories that are probably worthwhile, but you may need to trim how many of these you can take on because of time and resource availability, especially for high-effort stories. Stories in the bottom area should be avoided because they require high effort and have a comparably low value.

 TIP

Sometimes several stories require the same underlying infrastructure or will reuse key functionality. This is another way to judge "good bang for the buck"—to pursue several interrelated stories that would be expensive individually but whose cost goes down proportionally the more of them you do. However, beware of feature creep—just because building something is incrementally cheap, it might not be worth doing if it doesn't provide much additional customer value.

This is not a very sophisticated analysis, and it's only as good as the quality of the estimates, which by definition are going to be fuzzy at this point. But even so, it can be helpful as a way to initially think about a portfolio of stories. The greatest value of this analysis comes from the push it gives the team to start talking about the relative merits of various proposed stories and, in the process, to identify stories without as strong a value proposition, which should then be deprioritized. As such, it's a good first-level pass for prioritization, or at least an initial cut list.

Kano analysis

Kano analysis, although it was initially developed to prioritize requirements and feature sets, can easily be applied to prioritizing stories as well. The basic approach is to take the list of proposed stories and ask a representative group of target customers two key questions about each story:

- How satisfied would you be if we built that story?

- How dissatisfied would you be if we did *not* build that story?

Customers rate their satisfaction or dissatisfaction on a 3-point or 5-point scale. Then, you use those scores to group each story into one of five main buckets:

- **Must-haves**   These are the basics that customers expect in a product, but their presence does not increase satisfaction. Some people call these "table stakes"—or the minimum amount of functionality that a product must have to be a viable competitor to existing solutions.

- **One-dimensional**   Sometimes also referred to as "the more the better," these are the solid value stories. The more of these stories that you build, the more satisfied the customer will be. Also, customers will be dissatisfied if these stories are not built.

- **Delighters**   These are the things that the customer didn't expect but will satisfy the customer if you deliver them. A good check is to see whether the stories that feature unarticulated needs actually end up in this bucket (they should).

- **Indifferent**   This category is less common. If the customer doesn't care whether a story is delivered, it should end up here. Building these stories would be a waste of time.

- **Reverse** This is also uncommon, but it is very important if a story ends up here. Reverse is the unusual situation in which the customer rating indicates that a proposed story would actually cause dissatisfaction. Obviously, these stories should be cut, but also take the time to figure out why you originally thought the customer might like this idea and what insights about your customer might need to be revised in light of this new information.

The resulting chart is a nice way to visualize the differences between these kinds of stories and to give you some level of quantitative ranking between the stories within each bucket. If you want to pursue this approach, a quick web search will help you find the details for exactly how to tabulate results and create a Kano chart.

Despite the fact that a Kano analysis can be very helpful, it has a couple of downsides you should keep in mind. Strictly speaking, these problems aren't unique to Kano analysis, but because Kano analysis produces such tantalizingly specific numeric data, you can easy be lulled into a false sense of security, thinking you know a lot more than this analysis can actually tell you.

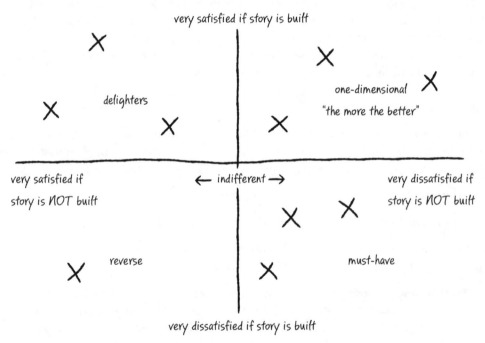

FIGURE 6-2 A simple Kano chart, showing how a set of stories (each marked with an X) might be distributed through the categories, after being scored and averaged across multiple target customers.

First, the whole system relies on you knowing which stories to ask about. Garbage in, garbage out. If you don't ask about the most important needs that a customer has, the Kano approach has no mechanism to tell you that you missed that opportunity. So, your Kano results will only be as good as the insights and scenarios you write in the first place.

Second, because Kano results are so precise, we've noticed a tendency for people to view them as the gospel—these are the "must-haves," therefore we absolutely must build every one of these stories before we can consider anything else. Remember, however, that Kano analysis is only getting SAY data from customers, which, as you know, is only part of the truth. In particular, customers are likely to overstate what stories are "must-haves." Also, the "delighters" bucket (things that are satisfying if they are present but not dissatisfying if they are absent) will also likely contain some less interesting "nice to haves" that may be satisfying on a surface level but not lead to deep desirability. So, when you look at results from a Kano analysis, be mindful that you probably need to fine-tune those lists based on what you have learned in your research about your customer's behavioral patterns (DO data).

Useful, usable, desirable

Another approach is to look at your portfolio of proposed stories and make a rough judgment of what each story's potential is for being useful, usable, and desirable for the target customer. Remember to put on your customer hat and use your hard-earned customer empathy instead of your personal opinions to estimate what customers might perceive. Even better, do some customer interviews and show them your proposed scenarios so that a few customers can rate how useful, usable, and desirable the scenarios might be from their perspective.

- **Useful**   On a scale of 1 to 5, how useful will this story be to the target customer? How pressing is this particular need for your customer?

- **Usable**   On a scale of 1 to 5, how usable do you expect your solution to be? Of course, you always aim to build easy, straightforward experiences, but if you already know of technical or resource limitations that will hamper your ability to build a highly usable experience, this would be the place to capture that.

- **Desirable**   On a scale of 1 to 5, how much potential is there to drive an emotional connection with the customer via this story?

Not every story you prioritize will be a key driver of delight—some may necessarily be focused on basic functionality and infrastructure that will enable more exciting stories later on. However, by rating your stories by potential desirability, you can be sure that your portfolio of stories includes some dazzling moments that provide emotional resonance with the customer. When you prioritize your stories, this is a helpful lens to use to ensure that you have a good mix of high desirability stories in your portfolio, balanced with solid usefulness and usability.

Competitive strengths and weaknesses

Understanding which stories are already well served by your key competitors, and which are still as yet unsolved, is another lens that you can use for prioritization. If you can identify a story that is genuinely important to your customer but is not addressed by any competitor, that is a natural platform for differentiation and can be a very powerful lever for success. This is especially true if the experience is something that your competition would have a hard time copying. In a rapidly maturing market, focusing on customer needs that your business is uniquely suited to provide may help secure some long-lasting competitive advantages.

Business strategy alignment

At the beginning of this book, we talked about understanding your business context and goals and determining a set of target customers to focus on. At this stage, it's also important to put on your business hat and make sure that the stories you prioritize resonate from the business, marketing, and sales points of view. Your marketing or sales experts will have data and opinions about which end-to-end scenarios are most saleable and most requested by customers, which ideas will benefit the most from network effects or word of mouth, or which are most conducive to feature in a catchy marketing campaign or social-network promotion. Depending on your business plan, any of these could be crucial input for prioritization.

Bottom line: Pick a few

It's worth reiterating: no matter how you prioritize, resist the temptation to choose too many stories to move forward with. Pick a few that you can focus on so that you have the time and energy to iterate and fine-tune all the details with continuous customer feedback and deliver a high-quality solution in the end. One of the phrases we find ourselves repeating to teams and leaders all the time is: *"Do a few things really right."*

Deep dive: Writing scenarios

Writing down real-world customer situations in the form of scenarios is a particularly effective way to frame the kind of problems that software is trying to solve. We recommend that you use scenarios as the primary description of the problems you will tackle, and then allow prioritization conversations to happen and a plan to emerge. As the Fast Feedback Cycle progresses, a small number of scenarios will form the backbone of the plan that the engineering team will work against throughout the development process.

Scenarios answer four key questions:

- Who are we building this solution for?

- What specific need or opportunity does this customer have?

- Why does the customer care about this?

- How good does a solution need to be in order to delight this customer?

The previous stage in the Fast Feedback Cycle, observing customers, gives you the raw material needed to answer these questions. If you've diligently done the work in that stage, you will have distilled a set of customer insights from your research data. You can now use the scenario technique to capture and communicate these customer insights in a durable way to use during the rest of the process.

This section provides a deep dive on the SPICIER scenario technique, including information about how to write a scenario, what makes a good scenario, and some tips and tricks for getting the most out of the scenario technique.

A good scenario is SPICIER

Several qualities of a good scenario can be used as a checklist to help ensure that you've covered your bases. These qualities form the anagram SPICIER, which is why we sometimes call narratives of this format *SPICIER scenarios*.

S tells a narrative STORY

P includes PERSONAL details

I is IMPLEMENTATION-FREE

C CUSTOMER's story, not the product story

I reveals deep INSIGHT about customer needs

E includes EMOTIONS & ENVIRONMENT

R based on RESEARCH

S: Tells a narrative Story

First and foremost, a good scenario is told as a narrative story. That is, it has a beginning, a middle, and an end. This means you should use sentences and paragraphs to write your story, not bullet points. The customer insights you distill from your research make for a good set of bullet points—and you should keep those. But now you are after something different. The job here is to develop those insights into a narrative about a real-world situation, ideally one you observed in your research. It's important to note that the story format helps you catch ideas that just don't hang together, that have something missing or don't feel real. A good, credible story that captures a viable opportunity or customer problem should resonate well with customers—it should sound like it is telling the truth. The customer's reaction to the story should be, "Yes, you understand me. Right on—please make this happen."

P: Includes Personal details

Next, a good scenario includes a few relevant personal details about the target customer that help you understand who the customer is, what he or she cares about, and why the customer is in this particular situation. It is often through these personal details that you evoke the empathy for the customer that is so essential to a good scenario. However, resist the urge to add personal details purely for humor or human interest. Be sure that the details you include tie directly to the customer's needs, motivation, or purpose. Details that illustrate the customer's motivation are often the most helpful. However, generally speaking, the shorter your scenario the better, so mention only the most essential personal bits.

I: Is Implementation-free

This is perhaps the most important quality of a good scenario. It should not include any details about how the product, service, device, technology, or platform will actually work. As we discussed earlier in this chapter, adding implementation details is the single biggest mistake people make when writing any kind of framing, including scenarios. Having implementation details in a scenario makes it less likely that you will consider other, potentially differentiating approaches to solving the problem and makes it more likely that your scenarios will become out of date.

C: Customer's story, not the product story

A good scenario is a story about your customer, not a story about your product or technology. It's a story about Ken or Margie or Court and their real-life situations as small-business owners, landscape designers, or struggling artists. A scenario is not a story about a new tablet device or a narrative about Microsoft Team Foundation Server or a tale about Ruby on Rails. In fact, you might not need to mention a specific product or service or brand name for a scenario to be valid and useful as a map for your team. The focus should be on the customer's situation, told from the customer's perspective.

Remember earlier in the chapter when we defined framing, when the camera zoomed out from a person standing at the airport ticket counter to show more and more detail about her end-to-end situation—waking up early and getting stuck in a traffic jam before she started waiting in line to check in? When you describe the customer's context in a scenario, you should zoom out and include just enough detail about the overall situation that you can then develop empathy and see the problems from the customer's point of view.

 TIP

Using the first-person when you write a scenario usually doesn't make practical sense. Almost every team will have multiple target customers, and writing your scenarios in the third-person helps everyone remain clear about which customer each scenario focuses on. It's also possible that you will end up describing more than one target customer in a single scenario, so you need names to keep everyone straight. For instance, imagine a scenario about the interaction between the director of marketing and an external ad agency.

I: Reveals deep Insight about customer needs

The best scenarios are the ones that highlight a deep insight about your target customer, preferably one that your competitors haven't noticed yet. Identifying a need or an opportunity ahead of your competition (and developing a good solution for that need) is a great way to achieve differentiation in the market. It's even better if you can develop that solution in a way that is not easily copied, thereby giving yourself a bit of a moat against fast-following competitors.

> **Insight spotting is not easy.** Recall from Chapter 5 that a lot of observation and synthesis is needed to reveal patterns and insights. The moment you finally see a pattern and can explain why it happens might feel like a sudden flash of intuition, but that moment comes only after you have been wallowing in customer data for some time. Insights may seem completely obvious with 20/20 hindsight, but they are rarely easy to spot in the first place. If you are lucky enough to have a talented insight-spotter on your team, remember to appreciate how buried an insight was before the spotter brought it to light, and how much work went into identifying and articulating it. Also, if you do happen to have any talented insight-spotters on your team, be sure to reward them and keep them around—this is a valuable and somewhat rare skill.

You could write an infinite number of potential scenarios, so where do you start? Your task is to focus on those that are likely to make the biggest difference for your customers, and for your business. If you find yourself writing boring scenarios about people's humdrum lives, chances are you're missing an opportunity to really delight your customer. Remember that building something useful and usable usually isn't enough in today's competitive marketplace. Even if you are working on a fairly straightforward experience, you still want to strive to do it in a way that will take your customer to a high level of emotional delight.

In general, you should write a single end-to-end scenario for each insight you target. Trying to address more than one insight in a single scenario usually makes the scenario unwieldy, and that makes it hard to know what to optimize for and how to measure success. However, if you have a particularly meaty or complex insight, or a couple of distinctly different cases that must be optimized, it's entirely possible that you'll end up writing multiple scenarios to address various aspects of that one insight. In Chapter 11, we'll cover more about how many scenarios to write, at what level to write them, and how to manage a portfolio of scenarios.

So where do you focus? Prioritize scenarios where you have an opportunity to solve a customer's problem that is already emotionally charged, where a fundamental human need is attached, or where you can tap into a strong customer motivation.

E: Includes Emotions and Environment

Moving toward your North Star is all about delighting your target customer. If you're aiming for an emotionally delightful experience, you better be clear about what kind of emotion you're trying to evoke with each scenario you undertake, and be sure that your metrics are aligned to measure whether you actually achieve that response with real users. Not every single scenario needs to be about a magical, gee-whiz kind of experience. Sometimes what the customer desires is simply to get the task done quickly and efficiently, especially if the task occurs multiple times per day and performing it smoothly and with zero hassle is itself emotionally satisfying. When considering a portfolio of scenarios, however, you want to think about which ones will be the amazing experiences that will surprise your customer in a delightful way, and which others will aim for an experience that's more sedate—"Check, got that crossed off my to-do list." This should be an intentional decision, part of the strategic design of your product and something you will measure and track as the engineering process continues.

We also add one more idea into the letter *E*, which is that you need to include enough details about the customers' environment that you understand the context of their situation. Where are they? What tools do they have available to them? What constraints are they working under? Again, the point here isn't to fill the story with arbitrary details but to include the environmental and contextual factors that will have a material impact on how the story is understood and what the shape of the solution might take. For instance, you could tell a story about an operations engineer's challenges in managing a data center, but the solution you build to address those challenges might be very different if that data center contains 300 servers instead of 30,000. This kind of context can provide important constraints about what scale the eventual solution should be optimized for.

R: Based on Research

Finally, it's essential that a scenario be based on real research, not on hearsay, assumptions, or biased viewpoints. Most certainly, do not write a story about the problems *you* would like to see solved, unless you are quite certain that those problems are shared by your target customer. Remember that you are not the customer, so be sure to climb into your customer's shoes (take yours off first!) when you write your scenarios and consider what the world looks like to your customer. If you are following the Fast Feedback Cycle and have already spent some time observing your customers and distilling key insights from those observations, this one is a no-brainer. However, it is so easy to lapse into believing that you already know what this customer needs—"It's obvious!"—that it bears repeating that you should always stay rooted in research with real live customers—not proxies, not assumptions.

Anatomy of a scenario

While there is no rigid format for a scenario, a standard formula has emerged that many people find to be a helpful starting point. Schematically, it looks like this:

> ***One-line headline***
>
> ***Introduction:*** *Who is the customer? What motivates him or her?*
>
> ***Situation:*** *What is the specific, real-world situation where there is a need or an opportunity?*
>
> ***<magic happens>***
>
> ***Outcomes:*** *What specific outcomes has the customer accomplished? What are the key metrics for success?*

Practically speaking, a scenario ends up having a two-paragraph format, where the first paragraph introduces the customer and the customer's situation, and the second paragraph describes the outcomes.

It's a bit goofy, but most people do find it helpful to write *<magic happens>* (or sometimes *<skip the implementation details>*) between the paragraphs as a tangible reminder to *skip the details about how the product will work.* You might be amazed at how well it works to have these two words as part of the team's vocabulary. Saying it out loud takes the pressure off teams so that they don't think about solutions right away. They give the team permission, at least for a brief period, to focus on customers and their needs, to spend time thinking deeply about what situations might give the team the best shot at delighting customers. Adding *<magic happens>* allows the team to put all the work of creating, building, and testing code into a box that can be dealt with later (albeit soon).

Here's another way to think about it. Composing a scenario is like writing the first paragraph and the last paragraph of a 10-page story. You write a great first paragraph to introduce the characters and the setting and the core problem. Then you skip to the last paragraph on page 10 and give away the ending. Everything in between—the magic—is your service, your device, your product, your solution, which will magically solve the customer's problem so well that you will achieve the outcomes. But at this point in your first iteration of the Fast Feedback Cycle, you don't know exactly what the solution is. Sure, you have some ideas, but at this stage you're being mindful to keep your options open, to give yourself the best possible chance of coming up with a game-changing concept. The next stages in the Fast Feedback Cycle, and the subsequent iterations around the cycle, are all about helping you write the rest of that story, to fill in the details of exactly how the magic will happen. Don't worry. We'll very quickly get to building creative ideas and solutions in the next step of the Fast Feedback Cycle. Just not quite yet.

Headline

It is important to write a memorable, one-line title or headline to capture the essence of each scenario. Practically speaking, this one-liner will be used a lot, so it's worth putting some effort into making sure that it is catchy and easily remembered. You will need to refer to a scenario in shorthand in multiple places; for instance, in your work-item tracking tools, bug database, and scorecards, or when discussing a scenario in email or in a hallway conversation. Strive to write a title that captures the essence of the customer problem you are trying to solve, such as "Norman's daughter gets sick at school" or "Marina worries about the quarterly tax filing." Some teams find that standardizing scenario titles by using the Agile user-story format or an "I can" statement works well. No matter what format you use, the title should be focused on the customer need and not on the product functionality.

Introduction

The scenario's introduction should identify a specific target customer for your product and provide enough personal and environmental detail that the engineering team can empathize with that person's needs. A powerful way to create that empathy is to explain the customer's motivation for doing this task in the first place. The introduction should answer questions such as:

> *Who is the target customer for this scenario?*

> *What is the customer's emotional state (frustrated, angry, anxious, confused)?*

> *What is the customer's motivation?*

An example might be something like, "Sarah has just begun working as a new nanny. The children's mother has left home on a business trip. Sarah is nervous about how the children may behave with their mother away and is intent on doing a great job and making a good first impression."

Situation

Next, you should describe a specific situation in enough detail to illustrate the key constraints of what a good solution would need to address. The situation should answer questions such as:

What specific problem does the customer have?

How big or complex is the situation?

What other things will the customer be doing at the same time?

What happened before and after this situation?

Resist the temptation to write about a general problem—the team needs enough specific details to actually land on an optimal solution, not just a "pretty good" general case. For instance, instead of writing a scenario about sending photos in general, write a scenario about sending three photos that the nanny just took of the kids to their mother who is currently on a business trip. This more detailed, specific description is much easier to design against and will help keep the whole team aligned. As we described earlier in the chapter, write a story about a canonical problem that can act as a "lighthouse" to represent a whole class of similar problems.

Outcomes

The last paragraph of a scenario should describe what the goal state looks like. When the end-to-end problem is solved, what will the outcome look like? What will the customer have accomplished? The outcomes paragraph answers questions such as:

What specific outcomes has the customer accomplished?

What are the best metrics to measure the success of those outcomes?

What does the solution need to accomplish for this customer to be delighted?

What is the customer's emotional state at the end of the experience?

As part of the outcomes, it's essential to include a specific metric that pinpoints a clear goal to optimize the solution around, especially if there is a key tradeoff to make. For instance, is it more important for this customer to finish a complex task in 5 minutes, or will the customer be more satisfied if the task takes 10 minutes to complete but he sees some progress within the first 30 seconds? Is it more important for this customer to feel safe that she won't get spam or for her to feel like she will never miss something important? Once you settle on a key metric or two and start measuring against them, those metrics will serve as the primary indicators of how close this scenario is to being done, and they can be tracked throughout the cycle as a scorecard benchmark. We'll discuss scorecarding in more detail in Chapter 11.

Scenario tips and tricks

The basic idea behind writing scenarios is straightforward. However, when you first start writing your own scenarios, you are likely to run into a few problems. This section points out some of the most likely issues you will run into and suggests some specific tips for how to avoid common pitfalls. At the end of this section, we included several sample scenarios demonstrating a variety of customer types, situations, and scopes.

What's wrong with this scenario?

Let's take a look at a few hypothetical scenarios. This first has some problems. Read through it and see whether you can identify the ways in which this scenario isn't SPICIER.

> *Gene regularly checks the amount of free disk space on servers that he manages.*
> *Currently he performs this task manually. He has to write a script for this task, but*
> *he is not a programmer and his scripting knowledge is limited. He opens a new*
> *script editor from the desktop. He immediately finds a Help button, which opens*
> *a help file describing how to get started. Within five minutes he can write his first*
> *script that runs on a local machine. When he tries to run it on multiple machines,*
> *however, he sees a red error message that the task failed and a line number for the*
> *error. He retypes one letter in a server name to run the task successfully.*

The first thing you probably noticed is all the implementation details—"He opens a new script editor," "finds a Help button," "sees a red error message . . . and a line number for the error." This scenario is brimming with implementation details. If you're unsure whether something is an implementation detail, ask yourself the question, "Who says the solution has to work this way?" If you can come up with a credible alternative, you've spotted an implementation detail that doesn't belong in the scenario. In fact, once you take the implementation details out of this example, not a whole lot is left. But other things are wrong with this scenario as well. What else did you notice?

Did you find yourself wondering who Gene really is and why he cares about free disk space on his servers anyway? The scenario is missing personal details about Gene that would give you a picture of his company or his role or how big a part this scenario plays in his overall job. Is it Gene's full-time job to manage these servers or is it something he does in between service calls? The scenario is also missing the context of how big this company is—how many servers is he managing? Is it 2, 200, or 20,000? The solution might be quite different depending on that scale.

The scenario also doesn't convey much emotion. Is Gene frustrated? Just plodding along? How does he feel when he finally gets his script working? Is he elated or just confident that he can move on to his next task for the day? Will he be rewarded if he succeeds, or is this a task hardly anyone notices unless there is a problem?

This scenario isn't all bad, however. On the plus side, this scenario does provide some nice insight into Gene with the fact that he doesn't like to write scripts, which is an important personal detail that would surely influence solution ideas.

A better scenario

Here's another version of the same scenario, rewritten to be SPICIER. Note how it avoids including implementation details yet still paints a vivid picture of Gene and his needs in a way that everyone on the team can understand and empathize with.

Gene learns how to automate

Gene, a system administrator at an online bank, must continually check the amount of free disk space and verify that logging is working on all 200 web servers. The bank's regulatory and compliance policies require extensive logging, and failures are a serious violation. Currently he performs this task manually several times a day. He wants this to be faster and more automatic, but he is not a programmer and he struggles with the few scripts he inherited from his predecessor. He is never totally sure if the right logging occurred.

<magic happens>

Gene discovers a new way to easily automate a common IT task and finds it straightforward despite his limited programming background. Within five minutes he is able to automate his first task, checking free disk space and logging, on a local machine. But when he tries to run it on multiple machines, it doesn't work. However, it helps him with troubleshooting, and within an hour he is able to check free disk space successfully across his entire cloud with a single keystroke. Gene is pleasantly surprised at how easy it was to achieve such a time savings in his day-to-day work and is confident that logging is happening consistently across the cloud.

Let's run through our SPICER checklist.

- **S**   Yes, this is told as a story in the standard two-paragraph format.

- **P**   Yes, this includes personal details about Gene, his company, his role, how often he needs to perform this task, how many servers he manages, and his limited programming knowledge. These personal details help the team empathize with Gene as well as have a common understanding for assessing what types of solutions might work well for him and which would not.

- **I**   Yes, this scenario is implementation-free. It uses general language such as "automate" to suggest a class of possible solutions rather than more solution-specific language such as "scripting" or "macros" or "C#."

- **C**   Yes, this is a customer-focused story, not a product story. In fact, this particular scenario doesn't mention any product or service name.

- **I**   Yes, there is a deep insight about Gene's discomfort with programming, but his clear need is to find a way to automate a common maintenance task.

- **E**   Yes, we see Gene go from struggling to get scripts working in the past to finding it straightforward and being pleasantly surprised. And we see that we will be optimizing our solution for Gene's environment of 200 servers.

- **R** Well, you're going to have trust us that this scenario was based on customer research. (Actually, a variant of this scenario was used in the development of one of Microsoft's server products.)

Can you spot the implementation detail?

Pop quiz! Which one of these phrases from a scenario about Gene is surely an implementation detail?

Gene uses Windows Server to . . .

Gene uses the drop-down to pick the right doc.

Gene has a mobile phone and a laptop.

The obvious implementation detail is the middle one, *Gene uses the drop-down to pick the right doc.* Under no circumstances would mentioning a drop-down list belong in a SPICIER scenario.

But what about the other two items? If you squint, they do look something like implementation details. Are they? Let's discuss each in turn.

The first, *Gene uses Windows Server to . . .* , mentions a specific product name. Is it okay to include a product, service, device, or brand name in a scenario? Yes, it is, and often this is very appropriate. But be sure that this is an intentional scoping decision. If you leave the product name out of the scenario, you are intentionally framing your problem more broadly—allowing for the possibility that you might define a new offering rather than stick to an existing product line, app, or service. On the other hand, if you include a specific—often already-existing—brand name in your scenario, you are making an intentional scoping decision to continue with your existing product line. With a narrower scope, you can discourage the team from wasting time considering options that are nonstarters from the beginning.

What about the last option, *Gene has a mobile phone and a laptop*? Is it an implementation detail to mention specific devices that your target customer carries with him? No, this is not an implementation detail. Having a laptop and mobile phone may be an important part of the customer's environment. Through the inclusion of key environmental factors in the scenario, you inform the team about what platforms and tools the customer has on hand as the team brainstorms various solution ideas. And, of course, the fact that this target customer has both a mobile phone and a laptop must come from customer research.

Sometimes, you do need to include some level of implementation detail in your scenario because it is nonnegotiable. You may face specific, immovable constraints that are based on business considerations, technology investments, or even the schedule. If this is true, there's no reason not to write the detail into your scenario—it simply becomes a constraint that the team will build around. This is the one case where it's okay to include an implementation detail in your scenario. Just be sure you are making an intentional decision. Don't let implementation details sneak in unawares.

Examples of big and small scenarios

Here are a few examples of SPICIER scenarios, including ones we've presented earlier in the chapter and additional examples that demonstrate some variation in format and scope. As we discussed previously, there are at least two levels of scenarios: higher-level, end-to-end stories that we call "big" scenarios, and lower-level, more task-oriented stories that we call "small" scenarios. Most teams find that they have stories to write at both levels, and they usually track them in separate categories or levels of a work-breakdown hierarchy. We'll discuss that hierarchy in more detail in Chapter 11.

Let's start with an example of a small scenario that focuses on a specific task, one we looked at briefly earlier in the chapter. This scenario is a particularly nice example of using a lead-user approach, which tells a story that demonstrates the most complex case the software should solve—being able to automatically standardize the format of mailing information, including international addresses, obtained from multiple sources of input.

Jessica's formatting hassles

Jessica is a sales specialist at a small European company that sells wind turbines internationally. One of her main responsibilities is collecting sales leads and sending out about 500 sales circulars per month to prospects. Her information comes from multiple sources: some leads she finds on her own via the web, others are provided to her by outside services and given to her in Excel files, and some come from other employees via individual emails. Each source uses different country formats, conventions, and layouts—who knew there were that many different ways of formatting an address or phone number!

<magic happens>

Jessica can easily get the data compiled in one place and standardized in a consistent format, ready to print mailing labels, without any manual editing. Even better, she is able to repeat this task quickly in the future. Jessica is thrilled that she no longer has to spend countless hours manually editing her data, freeing her up to spend more time acquiring a greater quantity and quality of leads.

In contrast, here's an example of a very big scenario, which is so broad in scope that it doesn't even make sense to explicitly write *<magic happens>* because there will need to be innovative solutions at each stage of this cradle-to-grave experience. This big scenario, about acquiring a mobile phone, would need to be broken down into smaller, more-focused scenarios to lay out the specifics about each of the major stages: hearing about a new phone, researching it, purchasing it, learning to use it, sharing with others, and eventually upgrading to a new phone. However, a scenario like this provides the big picture for how these pieces should fit together to create an overall customer experience, and a big scenario like this can help align the team to create a meaningful whole. An alternative representation for a big scenario like this is a user-journey map that would show the same stages of customer usage behavior in a more visual format.

Margie loves her new phone

Margie, a 25-year-old college grad, is in the market for a new mobile smartphone. She never really liked her current phone—and doesn't want to make another mistake by trusting a smooth-talking sales rep. One day, Margie overhears someone raving about a new phone. Then, the next day, she finds out her good friend recently purchased the same phone and also loves it. Margie asks her friend where she got it, and her friend shows off some of its best features. Margie trusts her friend's recommendation, but double-checks Amazon reviews just to be safe, and decides to get this phone. She goes to her mobile carrier's store and walks out 15 minutes later with a brand-new phone, and it has already downloaded her contacts and synced her email. Over the next few days and weeks, as she gets used to her new device and as she learns more about it, Margie runs into pleasant surprises that remind her how good a purchase this was. She eagerly tells her friends about her new phone, and several people also end up buying one and loving theirs. Two years later when it's time to upgrade, Margie knows exactly what brand of phone to look at first.

Here's an example of how you can break down that larger, cradle-to-grave experience by zooming in on one aspect in a small scenario. This small scenario expands on Margie's purchase experience of buying a new phone:

Margie, a 25-year-old college grad, has done her research and knows exactly what phone she wants to buy. She walks into her mobile carrier's store and goes straight to the display for the phone she wants. She is so ready to ditch her old phone; she never really liked it, and only got it because the sales rep talked her into it. Margie is determined not to let a smooth-talking salesman sway her again.

<magic happens>

Within 15 minutes, and with zero hassle, Margie walked out of the store with her brand-new phone in hand. Even better, no one pressured her—in fact, she felt supported with useful information that helped her finalize her choices. As she walked out the door, her new device was already set up with her contacts and email, and she placed a call to her friend from her new phone to tell her about her purchase. She couldn't wait to go home to play with her new toy.

Now let's take a second look at the scenario about getting stuff done in the grocery line, which we presented earlier in the chapter. This is another example of a small scenario that makes use of a lead-user situation—one that represents the most complex, longest path that a user would expect the system to handle. If you can build a solution that handles this complicated scenario smoothly, you're in good shape for many other, easier cases—such as just sending a quick email or checking a schedule—to make the most of a couple of free moments anywhere.

Josephine gets stuff done in the grocery line

Josephine is a busy mom of two school-age kids who has a dog and is always on the go. She feels like she never has enough time. Just yesterday she almost left her son at an empty soccer field when she missed the coach's email that practice was cancelled. Josephine is standing in the checkout line at the grocery store and realizes that she is going to be waiting a few minutes. She has so much to get done today and doesn't want to miss another important message or deadline. Could she get a few things done while she waits?

<magic happens>

While standing in line for six minutes, Josephine was able to check off a bunch of items from her to-do list: pay for her kids' music lessons, RSVP to a party (after checking that she and her husband are available that evening), schedule an appointment with the vet, answer her husband's text message to assure him that she did buy milk, scan her email to learn that her son's soccer practice was cancelled again this afternoon, and even squeeze in a quick peek at her favorite game, AlphaJax. The time waiting in line flew by. Josephine felt like she was able to maximize every second to help stay on top of her busy life and was able to give her full attention to her kids when she met them at the school bus later that afternoon.

Here's another scenario that was presented earlier in the chapter. It's a good example of a scenario that involves a customer in a business or enterprise environment. The big insight from customer research that drove this scenario is that getting something to work fast, albeit imperfectly, is crucial scaffolding to helping a nonprogrammer along the road toward learning to automate. Without that quick success, this system administrator is unlikely to stick with the task long enough to see it through, no matter how well the system guides him.

Gene learns how to automate

Gene, a system administrator at an online bank, must continually check the amount of free disk space and verify that logging is working on all 200 web servers. The bank's regulatory and compliance policies require extensive logging, and failures are a serious violation. Currently he performs this task manually several times a day. He wants this to be faster and more automatic, but he is not a programmer and he struggles with the few scripts he inherited from his predecessor. He is never totally sure if the right logging occurred.

<magic happens>

Gene discovers a new way to easily automate a common IT task and finds it straightforward despite his limited programming background. Within five minutes he is able to automate his first task, checking free disk space and logging, on a local machine. But when he tries to run it on multiple machines, the task fails. However, it helps him with troubleshooting, and within an hour he is able to check free disk space successfully across his entire cloud with a single keystroke. The system administrator is pleasantly surprised at how easy it was to achieve such a time savings in his day-to-day work and is confident that logging is happening consistently across the cloud.

The next scenario targets a developer who is looking for a better way to take advantage of multi-core and multiprocessor machines. It's very high level and could be considered a big scenario or a user promise. This scenario (or one just like it) provided direction to the Microsoft Parallel Computing Platform team when it was figuring out how to make parallel computing easier to access, while avoiding the traditional pitfalls of using multithreaded, parallel code. (More of this design story is told in a sidebar in Chapter 8, "Building prototypes and coding.")

Mark writes robust parallel code

Mark is a senior developer at a large software company. He's been a tech geek his entire life; exploring new technology is both a passion and a hobby. It was a natural decision for Mark to get a computer science degree and land a job as a programmer. Mark enjoys staying current on the latest programming languages, tools, and trends. He prides himself on being able to learn and adopt new techniques quickly. As such, Mark places a high value on using the right tool for the job. Recently, he's been reading about new parallel computing techniques. He sees the benefit of getting the most out of multiprocessor machines, and he'd like to figure out how to use parallel constructs in some of the server-side components he's responsible for. But he knows that these techniques can be difficult to use, that they're error prone, and that the subtleties of writing robust parallel code make it very time-consuming. In the past, he's not been willing to make the complexity versus value tradeoff that parallel computing has historically required.

<magic happens>

Mark finds a beta version of a parallel computing engine and API for the platform he's using. He downloads the beta and finds immediate benefit by simply decorating his code with some very simple constructs. His new parallelized components are on average 20 percent faster, and after rather extensive testing, Mark has not been able to detect any new bugs that result from parallel issues. Mark finds this to be very promising and reads more of the technical documentation. He discovers that the new parallel API provides customization points for him, in exactly the places where he thinks he'd like to have a bit more control over the behavior of his newly parallelized code.

The next scenario about George has a smaller scope than the scenario about Mark. This small scenario was subsequently broken down into a handful of user stories that were then prototyped and eventually coded.

George scales an existing application

George, a professional developer with expertise in the C# programming language, is fixing the responsiveness and scalability of an existing application. The application has a rich client UI that must remain responsive in the face of calls out to a server-side service. This service handles requests from a multitude of users concurrently and must achieve high scalability on a single box in order to best minimize hardware costs. The code is currently asynchronous to some degree, but the UI freezes now and again for various operations. The client code will run on various desktop machines, from single-core to quad-core, while the server code runs on manycore boxes. George is a longtime user of the ThreadPool and has some familiarity with the Task APIs in .NET 4.

<magic happens>

George easily improves the asynchrony of his application with more readable, functional, and maintainable code. Perf results show that the code can accomplish more in less time. He's proud of himself for the improvement to the architecture and eager to highlight his perf and scale gains.

Frame stage: How do you know when you are done?

The big idea of the Frame stage is to capture the essence of the customer's end-to-end experience—typically by writing specific customer stories called *scenarios*—before you start to work on solutions. Scenarios give the team a map that keeps everyone focused on solving the same problem and provide a way to check against the original customer goals all the way through to release. Embedded metrics create additional infrastructure for objective accountability and for tracking of both perception and performance goals.

Regardless of which techniques you use to frame your team's areas of focus, you know you are ready for the next stage when you have generated:

- A prioritized list of several customer scenarios (or other framing).

- One or two key metrics and targets for each scenario to track throughout the project.

Remember that your goal in the Fast Feedback Cycle is not to do a stellar job at each individual stage, but to do just enough and move on, relying on the fast iterative loop to let you know whether you're on the right track and what to focus on in the next iteration. Most teams spend too long writing and fine-tuning their scenarios. Instead, make a reasonable effort, prioritize the ones that seem most promising, and move on.

You don't have to be sure about your scenarios. In fact, most teams find that their first set of scenarios are not quite right—it's only in iterating them through the rest of the cycle that you realize how to fix them. Working longer in the framing stage won't solve the problem. You need customer feedback to see one layer deeper into the onion and realize that the real customer problem isn't quite where you thought it was.

Now it's time to move on and start thinking about solutions to solve the problems framed in these scenarios.

Notes

1. Eric Ries, *The Lean Startup* (New York: Crown Business, 2011), 128.

2. Clayton M. Christensen, Scott Cook, and Taddy Hall, "What Customers Want from Your Products," *HBS Working Knowledge*, January 16, 2006, http://hbswk.hbs.edu/item/5170.html.

Lots of potential solutions

STORYBOARDING   There is a science behind innovation

Don't fall in love with your first good idea

Suspend disbelief
about wild ideas   **EXPLORE**   QUIETSTORMING

Breadth before depth

YES, AND...   MANY ALTERNATIVES

Look for the blends

THINK QUANTITY,   **Patterns of successful innovation**
NOT QUALITY   **SKETCHING**

Allow time to marinate

Find fresh brains   Consider end-to-end sequences,   6 thinking hats
not just key frames
Embrace the cousins   **Are you in the tunnel?**

Defer judgment   **SCAMPER**   Mitigate tunnel vision

Use your whole brain   LEVERAGE DIVERSITY

fresh snow   **BRAINSTORMING**

THE MATH BEHIND INNOVATION

Lateral thinking techniques

CHAPTER 7

Brainstorming alternatives

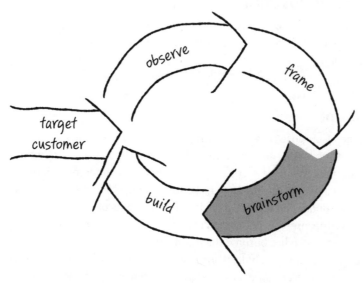

Now it's time to change gears and shift from the first half of the Fast Feedback Cycle, which is fundamentally about *understanding* the problem to be solved, into the second half of the cycle, which focuses on *creating* solutions. The first step in solving the problem you've identified is to explore a wide range of alternatives; then you narrow in on a few specific approaches to pursue.

The Brainstorm stage is one of the easiest ways to get a big bang for the buck with as little as a few hours of effort, and it should be an integral part of almost any problem-solving exercise, large or small, technical or not. However, we've found that this stage is where our intuition as analytical engineers is most likely to lead us astray, and some of our biggest mistakes and oversights can be traced back to this stage.

And note that while the last stage was about *converging*—making decisions about which problems you will focus on and at which scope—now you are going to switch gears and again *diverge* as you strive to generate lots of alternative ideas for a solution. This converge/diverge pattern happens repeatedly during the Fast Feedback Cycle, and we'll discuss it in more detail in Chapter 10, "The importance of iteration."

Where does innovation come from?

Deep down inside, every one of us dreams about having the next big, bold idea, an innovation so terrific that it will become a household name, make all our competitors jealous, and maybe even redefine the industry or disrupt a market. Ever the optimists, we see possibilities around every corner, and the ambitious among us gravitate toward projects that hold the potential for this kind of game-changing innovation.

Patterns of successful innovation

It's worthwhile to take a minute and think about where innovative, commercially successful ideas have actually come from. Is there a common lineage, a pattern of some sort, or even a secret formula that suggests a path for discovering the next big thing? Let's consider a few examples of industry-changing innovations in the history of computing.

Evolution over long time periods

Not too long ago, the first general-purpose computers with word processors became available to college students. Suddenly, students no longer needed to retype an entire chapter of their thesis when they had to insert a new paragraph in the middle of a page. Over the years, modern word processing has not just enabled greater ease in the act of writing; it has also fundamentally changed how we go about the writing process. It's no longer painful to reorganize your thoughts or to develop your ideas more deeply, with basic tools like the insertion point and cutting and pasting literally at your fingertips. Making repeated revisions on screen has become the norm—you no longer need to desperately hope that you'll get the job done with one rough draft and a single edit pass, and then hire a typist. Word processing has pervaded almost every aspect of modern life, from writing a Facebook post, to sending email, to jotting down a camping trip packing list. But where did the idea of word processing come from anyway? Was it a brand-new, revolutionary idea that had never been conceived of before, or did it have more evolutionary roots?

Going way, way back, of course, there was paper and ink. Then came the Gutenberg printing press in the 1400s, and a few centuries later the invention of the manual typewriter, popularized by the Remington in the 1870s, which introduced the QWERTY keyboard we still use today. In the modern age, widespread typewriting by secretaries and high standards in the business world spurred the invention of Liquid Paper correction fluid (originally called Mistake Out) in 1956. Then came a succession of electric typewriters, such as the IBM Selectric (1961), that helped people type even faster. In marketing for the Selectric, the term "word processing," or "W/P," was coined, which morphed in meaning over the following decades. And then came a very popular innovation, when a special-purpose whiteout tape was added to typewriters that allowed typists to back up a few characters to fix mistakes without having to pull out the paper and dab on whiteout. A slightly bigger transition to an electronic typewriter included a built-in, one-line LCD screen, where you could see and edit an entire line of text before it was actually committed to the page. This grew to a two-line screen and then a four-line screen. In parallel, the personal computer entered the scene, and it naturally evolved to take on the functionality already available on a typewriter and make it available on an even larger screen. Here, the first dedicated word-processing computers were born, such as the Digital DECmate, and this functionality soon became available on general-purpose personal computers as well. From there, steady improvement in command-line interfaces gradually evolved into better and better WYSIWYG (What You See Is What You Get) interfaces as the personal computer came of age, with floppy disks and printers growing up alongside. In the past couple of decades, rich-edit text boxes that embed word-processing functionality have become commonplace in nearly every modern computer application.

When you think about this progression, what ended up being a revolutionary innovation in modern computing was actually the result of steady evolutionary improvements from multiple, interconnected sources over a long period of time. It's hard to look at that historical progression and point to any single moment or transition and identify the single golden moment that changed the world, or exactly which step invented word processing. This is a great example of the first pattern of successful innovation: how *long-term, evolutionary improvements lead to important innovations.*

Combining ideas

Let's look at another example. Where did the idea for free web-based email come from? Hotmail was one of the first of these services. As with word processing, web-based email has deeply affected modern life, from how we do business, to how we communicate with friends, to how often we bother getting out an envelope and a stamp to send snail mail to pay a bill. But what was really innovative about Hotmail?

At the time of Hotmail's founding in 1996, the idea of email itself was hardly new. Universities and corporations had long had email systems, using proprietary clients such as Microsoft Mail, Lotus Notes, cc:Mail, or various UNIX or VAX systems. Home users could get email service as well through ISPs such as America Online or CompuServe. At that time, neither the Internet nor websites were brand-new, as the Internet revolution was already well underway. And certainly the idea of providing a web service for free was not new, as most of the nascent Internet industry at that time focused on attracting users and usage more than profits.

Hotmail is a great example of combining three already-existing ideas: email, a website, and free to consumers. None of the building blocks of Hotmail were in themselves brand-new, but the particular combination of these existing ideas turned out to be magical and resulted in a revolutionary innovation that has been copied by many. The same basic formula that Hotmail pioneered continues to be the norm almost two decades later. This example illustrates a second pattern: *combining existing ideas in new ways is a common path to innovation.*

Continuous improvement

How about a more recent success: Facebook? Where did Facebook come from? Again, you can trace an industrywide, evolutionary history, starting with UNIX bulletin boards and AOL member profiles back in the 1990s to the 1995 launch of Classmates.com for discovering old high school friends. All of these had a notion of a customizable webpage dedicated to one person's profile. Then, in 1997, SixDegrees.com popped up, showing how closely you were connected to the well-known actor Kevin Bacon. The degree of separation within a hierarchy of friends has been a widely used concept ever since, although SixDegrees itself didn't last long (it shut down in 2001). Then came the popular but irreverent "Am I Hot or Not?," an attractiveness voting site created by UC Berkeley students James Hong and Jim Young, later mimicked by Mark Zuckerberg at Harvard with a site called Facemash. Friendster was born in 2002 and was also wildly popular for a time, followed closely by LinkedIn and MySpace in 2003. Facebook was actually rather late on the scene, starting as an Ivy League–only social network in 2004, initially aimed at hooking you up with a friend of a friend for a date, before opening its doors to the general public in 2006.

When you examine the history, you see an evolutionary story behind the beginning of Facebook. Furthermore, even though many notable features have driven adoption and usage, none of them were actually universally loved ideas when they shipped, nor were they available in the very early versions, nor was Facebook always the first to ship them. For instance, Facebook's news feed was released to significant controversy about compromising personal privacy, and only in 2006, two full years after Facebook's launch.[1] The famous Facebook Like button was conceived by the development team in 2007 as the Awesome button, but shipped two years later, in 2009, as the Like button, after competitor FriendFeed independently released a similar "Like" feature in 2007 to minimal fanfare. (FriendFeed was eventually acquired by Facebook.)[2]

It's easy to think that Facebook sprang fully formed out of Mark Zuckerberg's head and has always been the way we see it today, but when you look at the timeline, its journey really was much slower and more evolutionary. The first version of Facebook was a great idea, and compelling for its time, but it lacked much of what we now recognize as the hallmarks of the Facebook experience. This, of course, in no way discounts Facebook's remarkable popularity, but it makes the point that brilliant and successful innovation does not need to be birthed from radically new ideas that are unlike anything that has come before. Nor does successful innovation need to happen all at once in a single big bang at the very first release. Nor is it one single killer feature that paves the way. In fact, innovation rarely happens that way.

Alongside an evolving industry and some deft combination of existing ideas, which follow the patterns of innovation we've already discussed, another factor behind Facebook's success was a steady stream of constant, small improvements that grew Facebook from a Harvard dorm project (2004) to a company that almost a billion people use every day (2014)—and it's worth pointing out that this journey took an entire decade. Tiny improvements like the color and placement of a link or the wording on a sign-up screen all affected usage and growth by some small amount. For instance, the news feed underwent a series of tweaking and privacy-control improvements to get the controls just right. When you add together each of the things that have had a positive effect, those little things tend to add up. And over not just a few years, but over a decade, they add up a lot. Facebook is very much a data-driven company. It has a culture of analyzing data, trying things out, measuring effectiveness, and iterating continually, and the company's management team tolerates risk as a necessary part of making these continuous improvements. Facebook is a great example of the third common pattern of successful innovation—*innovation is often achieved through persistent, continuous improvement over successive releases.*

Continuous improvement isn't a new idea, by the way, and it is very popular with online services, and increasingly so with the advent of big-data analysis and A/B testing that can power constant fine-tuning. Historically, Toyota has also relied heavily on continuous improvement in optimizing its manufacturing processes—a concept they call *kaizen*, which also led to the genesis of the Lean movement.

Innovation does not happen all at once

With those patterns in mind, take a moment to look around and notice all the technology success stories in the world around us today. On the surface, these innovations may seem to have dropped out of the sky, fully formed as breakthrough ideas that were conceived by a brilliant, creative genius, team, or company. But think about the history and the timeline behind those innovations—never mind the execution required to make those innovations a reality.

The fact is that all innovative ideas have a history, even those that end up revolutionizing a category or an industry. They all have a much more pedestrian, evolutionary path than appears on the surface—building on previous ideas, combining and recombining ideas, trying different approaches until a winning combination is found, and then building, optimizing, and continually improving. It's also important to remember that along the path to success were plenty of false starts, missteps, and failures, as well as plateaus, waiting for someone to take the idea one step further to find the magic combination. These ideas took a lot longer to go from concept to success story—years, not months— than we often think about.

Three important implications stem from the realization that successful innovation is a lot more evolutionary in nature.

Innovation may be closer than you think

The first implication is that people often reach too high when they're looking for an innovative, game-changing idea. We strive for a brand-new approach that no one has ever thought of before, that doesn't look anything like the current available technology—a radical, revolutionary invention. Yet there are plenty of examples of products that were too far out there, too far ahead of their time, which simply did not catch on.

The first touchscreen tablet was shipped by Microsoft 15 years ago, but it didn't sell very well at the time, which is quite surprising to contemplate today in the age of the iPad. Pitney Bowes executives anticipated the idea of the cashless society in the 1960s,[3] suggesting things like electronic fund transfers, barcode scanning, ATMs, and credit/debit cards, which are now commonplace, of course, but at the time seemed inconceivable and took decades to actually happen. The Segway was an amazing technological feat, but it still largely remains a curiosity, hardly the personal transportation revolution that its inventor, Dean Kamen, had predicted. These ideas were too different, too far ahead of their time to win mass-market approval and adoption when they first appeared.

On the other hand, many products and services that have been wildly successful commercially were initially criticized for not being particularly novel ideas or new technology, but they were the right combination at the right time. Practically speaking, this means that a more evolutionary style of innovation offers a lot more opportunity than you might realize. Just the right improvements, tweaks, and new combinations of existing ideas may be all you need to have a surprisingly large impact on utility and desirability for your customers.

Successful ideas satisfy deep human needs (that aren't obvious)

The second implication is that we mistakenly believe that we will instantly recognize a great solution when we see it. However, even the launch of the iPad came with its share of people saying, "Who needs a giant iPhone? It's a toy that will be used once, and will be a flash in the pan." The Facebook news feed, arguably the company's most important element for sustained, regular usage, was initially released to significant controversy. Even the release of a runaway success has a mixed chorus of prognosticators, some of whom love your solution and some of whom don't.

However, if you look more deeply, you see that successful innovations found a way to meet a deep customer need really well. And because unarticulated needs are tough to recognize, the power of these solutions was not universally predicted in advance or fully appreciated right away. Sometimes innovators are thoughtful about what deep needs they are solving, and sometimes it seems more like they just got lucky. But either way, satisfying the deep need was the root of their success and carried them through some mistakes, detours, and imperfect solutions.

For example, word processing served a huge population of students, professionals, and consumers who needed to write things down and who didn't always know ahead of time exactly what they wanted to say. At the time, it would have been easy to identify the surface needs of people using typewriters—they have poor spelling skills, they don't take time to plan their writing, they need to be able to rewrite quickly, and so on. However, in hindsight we know that the deep need was embedded in the cognitive complexity of the writing process itself, not in the gap in typing skills between professional secretaries and the general public, which was not at all obvious at the time.

Hotmail and other free web email services allowed people to communicate almost instantly with friends across the street or across the globe—a behavior borne of the deep-seated human need to communicate with others. But at the time, some argued that nothing would ever replace the intimacy of a handwritten letter, and email would be good only for doing business and never for personal communication. But it turned out that being able to instantly send pictures and greetings to a family member across the world was a deeply satisfying way to communicate, not to mention cheap and convenient.

Facebook and other social networks capitalize on numerous big-T human truths: from staying in touch with loved ones and getting advice from people you trust, to baser instincts like wanting to be visibly popular by collecting a large list of friends, comparing details of others' lives with your own, and even a touch of curiosity-driven voyeurism. Despite Facebook's popularity, people still argue over whether its news feed intrudes on privacy, or they denounce the addictive habit of constantly checking your feed for updates. But Facebook is addictive exactly because it satisfies a deep human desire to be part of a community and be in the know, and that turns out to be a pretty powerful driver of human behavior. Even though Facebook's culture of continuous improvement certainly helped spur things along, it would have gone nowhere if a core human need wasn't being filled in the first place.

The bottom line is that even unquestionably successful innovations have their doubters and detractors, and the extent of their success may have been far from obvious ahead of time. But whether premeditated or not, successful innovations are fueled by serving deep human needs extremely well.

SFE in action: Adding emoticons to MSN Messenger

Kelvin Chan, Business Evangelist, Microsoft Developer Partner Experience

When I was a program manager working on the MSN Messenger team in 2001, the engineering team was rushing to catch up to the feature set of its competitor at the time, AOL Instant Messenger (AIM), as well as having to make continual infrastructure improvements to support our exponentially growing user base. The list of work was long, and the team was small, so every feature proposed for addition was heavily scrutinized and debated.

We had an existing feature in the MSN Chat web app called *emoticons*, which allowed users to include graphical smiley faces in their messages alongside their text. I argued to port this feature to MSN Messenger. People had been using smiley faces of all sorts in their messages for years, with text characters such as these:

:-) ;) :) :(

The idea was to automatically convert these text-based smiley faces into tiny images that represented a graphical smiley (or frowny) face and to provide a drop-down menu that displayed a list of smileys you could include in your message. You could also select a number of other emoticons, from animals to musical notes to a little red devil.

Porting the code from MSN Chat to reuse it in MSN Messenger was pretty straightforward, so the cost was small. The work item was approved, and the feature shipped in the next release of MSN Messenger. Almost immediately, it became the headline feature for the release, eclipsing work items that the team had spent orders of magnitude more time and energy on but were nowhere near as popular or valued by users. How was it that this minor tweak of a feature resonated with users so deeply?

I wish I could say that we predicted that graphical emoticons would be so successful in MSN Messenger. In truth, we just got lucky. But as it turned out, the idea of emoticons spread rapidly across many different form factors over the years, from instant messaging, to email, to word processors, to mobile phones. And a full panoply of smileys was merged into the 2010 Unicode standards. Future versions of MSN Messenger added ever larger libraries of emoticons, including animated ones, hidden "secret" emoticons, and the ability to upload your own custom images. However, it was really the simple, facial-expression smileys that received the lion's share of use. Arguably, the others were merely a distraction, proving that we still didn't fully understand the true unarticulated needs that this feature was addressing.

But why were emoticons so successful? Because they helped people express emotions in the context of their textual messages, and emotions are core to the human communication experience. Both email and instant messaging can suffer from misinterpretation because the context isn't clear—a remark that was intended to be sarcastic is taken literally, a friendly suggestion is heard as criticism, a loving remark just doesn't seem all that intimate. Emoticons can alleviate some of the misinterpretation.

Simple text emoticons had already gotten the idea halfway there, but making emoticons graphical brought the idea mainstream, making them easily understandable and accessible to all users. Emoticons solved a deeper problem for users—avoiding the embarrassment of being misunderstood.

There is a science behind innovation

The third implication of innovation being evolutionary is perhaps the most important one: there is actually a science behind innovation, and there is a discipline around idea generation that can be learned and cultivated over time. Successful innovations are much less about a lone genius who suddenly has an inspiration and much more about a sustained effort, gradual improvement, and paying attention to and learning from feedback, which is the essence of the Fast Feedback Cycle. Even when a clever new idea is the seed, a lot of effort needs to go into tending and nurturing and pruning for the idea to be successful in the marketplace.

This chapter will help you learn the practical science and specific techniques behind how to unleash your gray matter to come up with better ideas to help fuel the Fast Feedback Cycle. Sometimes you will be hoping to find a magic new combination that will put you on a path to disrupting the competition, whereas more often you simply need to come up with a great solution to a reasonably tactical problem. Whatever your goal, there are techniques that will dramatically improve your odds of finding an optimal solution with high efficiency. The important thing, you'll find, is not to focus exclusively on generating a single killer idea, but to iterate several ideas in parallel and use feedback to combine and refine the most promising ideas into a truly innovative, winning solution.

 MINDSHIFT

Whose job is it to be creative? One myth about innovation is that the really good ideas all come from a very small set of creatively gifted souls, and your best bet is to make sure you have one of those people on your team and listen to what she or he says. While it's true that some people seem better than others at finding out-of-the-box ideas, it's not at all clear that this skill is innate or even that a "creative" person's ideas will always be golden.

Even for Apple, the biggest ideas did not actually start with Steve Jobs. At Apple, an elite team of industrial designers (which Jobs presumably helped recruit and hire) played that role. Jobs's main role was as gatekeeper, decreeing when an idea was "good enough." Steve Jobs consistently maintained incredibly high standards, blocking many products from releasing until they met his exacting scrutiny. He created and insisted on a strong culture around design, creativity, and putting the customer first. He identified the problems to be solved, but he did not generate many of the ideas for the solutions themselves. Those innovations came from a very strong design team, which, incidentally, made use of many of the techniques that we discuss in this book. The magic at Apple was a talented team that had a shared priority for customers, an iterative design process, and a gatekeeper with very high standards who was willing to wait for the right solution to emerge.

So whose job is it to be creative? It's the job of the team, and the job of leaders is to support an innovative culture. Prepare for iteration, let people try things, celebrate failure, measure results, and do it again. Creativity is not the job of any one person.

You have to get over the notion that you, or someone on your team, or someone you want to hire is going to suddenly receive a lightning bolt of supreme insight, the single, brilliantly creative, innovative, market-disruptive, billion-dollar idea. And even if this happened, you are not likely to recognize it as such, at least not right away. If you take the time to study the history of innovative products, you see that innovation just doesn't happen that way.

Explore lots of alternatives

Linus Pauling, the only person ever to win two undivided Nobel Prizes,[4] famously said,

> If you want to have good ideas you must have many ideas. Most of them will be wrong, and what you have to learn is which ones to throw away.

We wholeheartedly agree. To get started creating solutions, first you generate lots of ideas and explore as many alternatives as possible in an efficient, lightweight way, giving yourself the greatest chance at finding a new approach, combination, or improvement that may turn out to be wildly successful in the marketplace. Think of it as a numbers game. Your goal is to give yourself the best odds of discovering a promising new idea. Generating alternatives is the essence of this stage of the Fast Feedback Cycle.

Think about an architect who is helping you remodel your kitchen. Would you be satisfied if he drew only one floor plan for you to consider before construction began? Or would you expect to consider a few options, to see what happens if you move the door or put the stove in the corner instead of on the island or add a second sink? Architects have learned through experience that it's worth the effort to explore multiple ideas on paper, iterating a few times to ensure that both they and their clients have thought through as much of the plan as possible and thoughtfully considered several viable alternatives. Once the contractor starts building, the cost to change your mind skyrockets. The value of considering lots of alternatives up front when remodeling is obvious.

Is writing software so different? Yes, software is infinitely updateable, and you can make design changes, try different approaches, fix bugs, and often push updates almost instantly. However, those updates aren't free, especially when you consider all the time spent not just by development and testing but also in design and deployment, plus the impact on downstream operations, product support, and legacy support. Also, adding functionality is one thing, but taking a feature away can upset some of your customers, and even if they are only a minority, they may be quite vocal. Adding hardware devices into the mix complicates things dramatically, with physical constraints that dictate longer manufacturing timelines and hard limits to what you can change later in firmware or software.

One nightmare scenario is that you discover very late in the cycle that your architecture is fundamentally flawed. Or, after having invested in a hardware design, you find that customers think the device is simply too big. Or perhaps you discover that customers just don't seem to like your approach enough to switch from their current provider to your new service. You definitely want to avoid those nightmare scenarios. How best to do it?

Software development, too, can benefit from considering alternatives up front in a cheap and efficient way. Exploring and comparing alternatives can help you better predict which approaches are most likely to work and help eliminate the weaker options before you invest too much time. When you have only one solution under consideration, by definition it's your best idea. But once you have a few different ideas, the benefits and deficits of each approach come into sharper focus. Furthermore, getting feedback from customers not just on one idea at a time but on several that customers can compare and contrast helps make customer feedback more effective as well.

The power of blends

Remember the photographs of the three-dimensional mouse prototypes in Chapter 3, "Take an experimental approach"? One important phenomenon the mouse example highlights is that at every stage, the team didn't choose specific designs to move forward with in their design process. Rather, at each stage the team combined and recombined the best ideas from multiple prototypes based on feedback from users, while also considering hardware manufacturing constraints, and it used that feedback to inform its next generation of prototypes. This combinatorial mixing of ideas allowed the most promising aspects of a proposed solution to be retained, while swapping out other aspects that might not be working as well.

Many teams we've worked with have also commented on how the best ideas emerged from blending different approaches, and that they never would have considered that blend had they not taken the time to generate lots of alternatives. Looking for blends is a central approach behind implementing the innovation pattern we called "combining ideas" earlier.

 VOCAB

A *blend* is a combination of different aspects of multiple solution approaches that together create a new approach that is markedly better than any of the original alternatives that were considered.

Successful blends are all over the place. Consider Skype: it created the hybrid technical solution of a peer-to-peer infrastructure that keeps video chat bandwidth off its servers but still uses a web service for centralized services such as authentication. Or consider Snapchat, which combined existing technologies for sharing photos, video chat, and instant messaging in a unique way, making photos as ephemeral as a video chat stream. The best ideas don't often leap fully formed out of one person's head. Rather, they are more likely to be partly your idea and partly the ideas of others, plus other bits that no one on the team originally thought of but are obvious once you connect ideas together this way. By generating lots of alternatives, and spending some time wrestling with them, you give yourself a better opportunity to find ways to mix and match ideas to discover unique solutions like these.

If you remember back to your math classes in college, it turns out that setting yourself up to create blends of ideas is particularly important when you think about innovation in terms of finding mathematically optimal solutions. Read on.

The math behind innovation

Our intuition as software engineers often leads us to believe that if we find a good working solution to a problem, all we need to do is continually iterate and improve on that working solution to eventually reach the best, most-optimal solution. This is one area where the Agile philosophy of choosing the simplest possible solution for any problem can run you aground unintentionally—it is a reasonable heuristic that the simplest solution is often the best place to start, and we certainly don't want to overengineer for hypothetical future flexibility or architectural elegance. Sometimes, however, the simplest technical solution creates a suboptimal user experience or carries other hidden tradeoffs, and you may not realize those downsides until much later if you aren't looking out for them.

Your instincts might lead you to imagine the problem space to look something like what's shown in Figure 7-1.

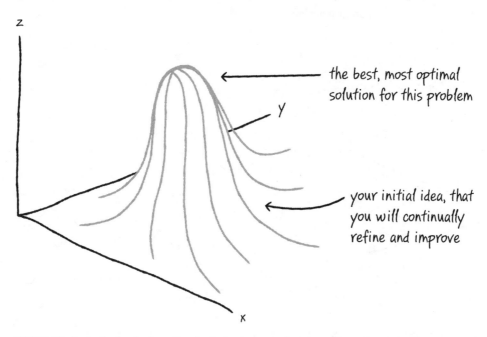

the best, most optimal solution for this problem

y

your initial idea, that you will continually refine and improve

FIGURE 7-1 A graph of a single, optimal solution in a complex, three-dimensional plane.

You imagine that all possible solutions are on the path to the one optimal solution. You figure that once you get going on building something, you're somewhere on the foothills of that mountain peak, and as long as you keep iterating and improving your solution, eventually you'll reach the top—that is, you'll land on a globally optimal solution. Engineers are natural iterators who constantly seek to improve their solutions by fixing bugs, adding functionality, integrating more partners, improving error handling, and so on. So, by and large, engineers do climb whatever hill they're on and make improvements little by little. However, most engineers typically iterate only one solution idea at a time, and that's where the trouble starts. The reason that iterating only one solution at a time is troublesome is that most problems are complex and multifaceted, and you're trying to solve for many variables at once. The landscape of possible solutions is much more complex than you often realize at first. There are actually many good solutions to any given problem, perhaps even more than one great solution, and those solutions may be quite different from one another both in concept and in implementation. Each potential solution may trade off key aspects of implementation elegance, performance, scalability, usefulness, usability, and desirability in dramatically different ways.

Consider a much more complex, three-dimensional mathematical plane, Figure 7-2, where the good solutions to a given scenario are represented by local maximums—small hills on the contour diagram.[5] There are also a handful of truly great solutions that have much higher peaks, and one outstanding approach that is the clear global maximum. If you start your project with a reasonably good, workable approach in mind, you can gradually improve your solution as you iterate and will likely climb to reach one of those small peaks, or local maxima. If you are very lucky, you might happen to start off on the foothills of that highest peak and reach the global maximum—because you picked a good starting point, or, in mathematical terms, a good seed.

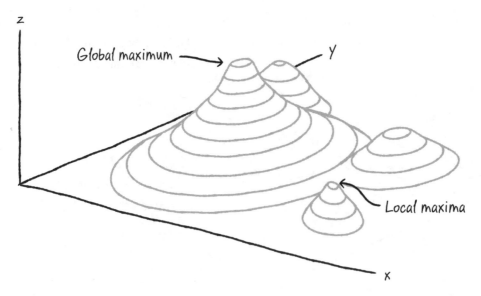

FIGURE 7-2 A graph of multiple possible solutions, some more optimal than others, in a complex three-dimensional plane.

But what if you are not so lucky? How do you give yourself the best odds at iterating toward the most globally optimal solution and not getting stuck at the top of a much smaller hill? Rather than enthusiastically rushing to code up the first good approach you come up with, what if you start off by exploring and iterating several diverse approaches, trying out ideas that represent several different regions of that plane? What if you combine and recombine the best aspects of those ideas to help you identify which neighborhood of solutions is most globally promising and provides the best balance of tradeoffs for your situation? As in mathematics, *the more diverse a set of seeds you start your iteration with, the better the odds you have for discovering a more globally optimal solution in a complex universe.*[6]

Why it's so hard to find a global maximum

Dr. Craig Wiegert, Associate Professor of Physics, University of Georgia

The task of optimizing a function (finding its maxima or minima) is ubiquitous in the sciences. For example, nature strongly favors minimum energy configurations of a system. So, chemists use this principle to describe molecular bonding in terms of the arrangement of atoms that minimizes the total energy of the molecule. Physicists model the physical properties of crystalline solids and amorphous glasses by seeking the lowest energy structures. In biology, protein chains spontaneously fold into their functional shape as the molecule lowers its overall energy in a complex aqueous environment.

Finding a local optimum is relatively easy, at least conceptually speaking. From a starting point, just go downhill (or uphill) until you can't go any farther! (This method is known, not surprisingly, as "hill climbing.") Algorithms such as gradient descent, the conjugate gradient method, and others generally improve the computational efficiency by carefully choosing directions in the search space. Many of these algorithms assume that, near the optimum, the function behaves quadratically (like a multidimensional parabola).

In most situations, though, it's important to determine the global energy minimum, the one that nature finds seemingly without effort. A local minimum might have almost the same value as the global minimum, but that's often not good enough to be useful. There's also no guarantee that this local minimum will be anywhere near the global minimum in the search space. That's especially problematic because even a small difference in the predicted atomic positions in a crystal can dramatically change material properties such as tensile strength, conductivity, or ferromagnetism.

The bad news for us all is that it's mathematically impossible to find the global optimum of any arbitrary function. In other words, any optimization algorithm, no matter how general, will fail on some classes of functions. The slightly better news is that, under certain assumptions about the function—for example, that it's smooth, bounded, and/or in a finite-sized search space—finding its global optimum becomes merely fiendishly difficult.

Much of the difficulty relates to the size of the search space. Each new coordinate or degree of freedom in the system adds another dimension to the search space. Consider a simple molecule such as water. To fully determine its molecular structure and properties from first principles, you need to minimize the energy function not just over the three atoms' positions, but also all 10 of the electrons. Naïvely, that's a 39-parameter search space (13 objects x 3 spatial dimensions)! Accounting for symmetries, and ignoring some of the nonbinding electrons, allows a considerable reduction of the dimensionality; that still leaves two atomic degrees of freedom and eight electrons that need to be optimized. Now imagine the computational complexity of putting thousands of molecules of water together and investigating their molecular interactions. This is why physicists still don't have a complete theoretical understanding of liquid water.

Without a universally applicable method of finding global optima, practical optimization procedures in huge search spaces rely on casting a wide-enough net. Some algorithms, like the Nelder-Mead simplex method, are deterministic but relatively inefficient. Many others are stochastic; they increase efficiency at the expense of introducing randomness into the search process. These include algorithms like simulated annealing (where a large initial search is gradually "frozen" into smaller and smaller regions) and evolutionary algorithms (where the best candidates from many small regions of the search space are remixed into new candidates). Fundamentally, all of these approaches are based on the same principle: evaluate a large variety of starting points across a complex search landscape, and narrow in on the optimum based on those results. Starting the optimization with only a few points, or with points that are too similar to each other, practically guarantees a nonoptimal solution.

Even for mathematicians and physicists, no matter which method they use, finding a true global optimum is a genuinely difficult endeavor. Thankfully, even though the software problems we work on are complex, finding the single, absolute maximum may not be as critical for us. In fact, there may be several comparable maximums, and practically speaking, we'd be pretty happy if we found any one of those truly great solutions and successfully avoided getting stuck on a smaller hill. To more reliably find a great, optimal (or nearly optimal) solution, you can take a lesson from the experts. To find optimal solutions in complex spaces, start out by casting a wide net and try multiple seeds as you narrow in on an optimal solution.

It's so easy to barrel down the wrong path, quickly picking an approach that looks reasonable, coding it up, and releasing it, only to find yourself fixing bugs and responding to customer feedback and pushing updates constantly, working hard but never realizing the success that seemed imminent with such an auspicious start. Later, when a competitor comes out with a variant that ends up gaining the popularity you hoped for, you may realize that the root problem was something more fundamental in your approach—the underlying architecture that defined the core performance characteristics, the user experience that needed to have been simpler and more streamlined, a key aspect of the customer's end-to-end experience that you didn't notice, the developer whose apps ended up driving customer adoption and purchase, or that you did a great job solving the wrong problem.

Looking back, the salient postmortem question often is "Did you ever consider alternative approaches that might have led to something similar to your competitor's winning solution?" Sometimes the answer is yes—that an intentional decision was made not to follow that path, and that will happen from time to time. But all too often the answer is no—that approach never occurred to you—you went down the first viable path that seemed to meet the customers' needs and didn't notice that there was an alternative to consider. Without a broad-enough set of inputs, no amount of iteration will lead you there. *That sort of failure lies not in the iterative process, but in not considering a broad- and diverse-enough set of alternatives from the very start.*

It's no surprise why people used to say wait for v3 before buying a Microsoft product. By the third version (that is, after the third cycle of iteration) Microsoft had finally explored enough of a complex solution space to find a more globally optimal solution—or, at the very least, it had reached the actual peak of a local maximum. These days, however, you want to get the iteration done well before the customer experiences a final solution, whether it's version 1 or version 15. Furthermore, in today's marketplace, customers demand not just good solutions but great ones, and they don't want to wait years to get there. So the bar is set higher than ever before.

The exploration stage is about giving yourself choices. You will never look as broadly at solution possibilities as you will at the start of a project, so take advantage of that time to generate lots of diverse ideas and explore the space of possibilities. Later in the project, you will naturally narrow your thinking and your choices. But at this early stage, you should explore as wide a variety of alternatives as possible and give yourself the best possible odds at combining them into a unique approach that leads to a globally optimal solution that will bring the success you're hoping for.

The problem with tunnel vision

The first step in exploration is to generate a lot of ideas. If only it were that easy. You see, there is a problem. The human brain is hardwired to lean in the opposite direction.

Let's illustrate with a story. Can you remember a time when you had a plan for something, you had written a spec perhaps, or worked out an architecture for a new component, or sketched a design for a new backyard deck? While you were pretty happy with your plan, you had a niggling thought in the back of your head that maybe that plan wasn't perfect, maybe you were forgetting something, maybe there was a better way. Perhaps you even sat down with a blank piece of paper and told yourself "Let's come up with a better idea," but all you could do was stare at the blank piece of paper?

We've all been in that situation at one time or another. You just can't seem to break out of your current mode of thinking to produce something new. The problem is that once you have a solution in mind, even if it isn't a particularly great solution, it's really, really hard for your brain to generate other alternatives. The longer you've thought about that solution, and the more you've explored it in detail, the harder it is to even imagine the possibility of viable alternatives.

What's going on? This isn't a personal character flaw, and additional time or brute-force effort will have little effect. It's actually a well-understood side effect of how our brain works, specifically how it learns. We call this phenomenon *tunnel vision*. Sometimes we refer to a person, or even a team, as being "stuck in the tunnel."

VOCAB

Tunnel vision is a neurological phenomenon where once you believe you have solved a problem and have a particular approach in mind, your brain becomes blind to the possibility that alternative solutions may exist, and your ability to generate new ideas becomes greatly compromised.

Neuroscience break by Dr. Indrė Viskontas

In the 1960s and 1970s, neuroscientists named Terje Lømo and Tim Bliss discovered that when two neurons connected by a synapse are stimulated at the same time, they become associated. This means that when one fires in the future, the other is more likely to fire, too. We say that the synapse has been "strengthened" because the connection between these two neurons is stronger.

You might have heard the adage "neurons that fire together, wire together," which is shorthand for this type of synaptic plasticity. Let's say that there's a set of neurons in your brain that turns on, or fires, when you see the refrigerator door. And there's another group nearby that fires when you see any type of food. Now, whenever you open the fridge, both sets of neurons fire because you see the door and you see the food at the same time.

Over time, these two groups of neurons fire together often enough that the connection between them, or the synapse, gets stronger. Just seeing the fridge door is enough to fire your food-detector neurons. The activity of these neurons is now connected, and the fridge door is associated with food.

Connecting cells through their wiring, and making these connections more efficient, is the very essence of learning: it's how the brain changes with experience. The capacity of neurons to connect to each other gives us the ability to learn, but it also has a downside. Much of what we learn over time gets ingrained in the wiring of our brains.

A common analogy for this side effect of our brain's wiring is to think of the brain as being a beautiful, pristine sledding hill, full of fresh, fluffy white snow. You are sitting in a sled at the top. The first couple of times you head down the hill, it's quite easy to lean this way or that way and cut new paths in the snow. However, once you have taken the same path in your sled a few times, a rut forms, and it's quite tough to get your sled to go anywhere else but in the rut. This is much like what happens at a neurological level. When the brain encounters a novel challenge, it can easily consider multiple potential solutions, recruiting different neural networks to the task, and it can quite flexibly consider different approaches. However, the longer you think about a particular solution, the stronger that particular neural pathway becomes, and the less likely it is that you can jump out of that neurological "rut" to see a different alternative.

VOCAB

Fresh snow is the mental state most conducive to creativity, when you haven't yet formed a clear opinion or decided on a solution to a given challenge. The term stems from the analogy of the brain being full of fresh, fluffy snow before a rut, or tunnel vision, forms.

As you can see, tunnel vision happens for a predictable neurological reason. When you start thinking about a particular idea a lot, you "learn" it—in neuroscience terms, the neural pathway gets reinforced every time you use it. Your brain can easily be convinced that there are no other options because the one you hold in your mind fits the pattern so well, and the more you think about it, the more ingrained your opinion becomes. Once that neurological rut is carved sufficiently deep, it becomes increasingly hard for your brain to generate a different idea, a different approach, a different solution. For some people, tunnel vision sets in faster than for others. Other people seem to tolerate ambiguity a bit longer. But no one is immune to the physiology of the brain.

 MINDSHIFT

Tunnel vision feels so good. One reason we are likely to fall so quickly into tunnel vision is that having a firm plan in mind is a powerful and satisfying feeling, especially because it replaces the much-less-pleasant feelings of ambiguity and anxiety about an uncertain future, which are inherent in the early stages of a project. Once we feel like we've hit upon the "perfect solution"—or even what looks to be a workable approach to a challenging problem—we can exhale, telling ourselves that it's all downhill from there. We quickly get caught up in the details of thinking through exactly how that approach might be implemented, naturally gravitating to our strengths in technical design and development and working through details. Tunnel vision can feel downright intoxicating, and it's easy to bring a team along with you, because everyone is eager for the clarity that a definite path forward brings.

In fact, the siren song of tunnel vision is so incredibly tempting that it can easily cause a team to entirely skip the first half of the Fast Feedback Cycle—clearly identifying their target customers, understanding their customer's unarticulated needs—and go directly to brainstorming product ideas without any regard to what problem the team is trying to solve, what is going to be desirable for its customers, or its business strategy. Skipping these steps is even more dangerous than not generating enough alternatives, because you will likely end up building a solution for a problem that your customers may not care about or for a fictional customer who doesn't exist in the real world.

Whatever the cause, remember that if you have zeroed-in on a solution approach too soon and left the complex plane unexplored, odds are that barreling down that well-worn rut in the snow will land you at a local maximum, not at the game-changing optimal solution you might have aspirations for.

Tunnel vision happens. It just does, it is part of the human condition. People and teams who understand what tunnel vision is, how it manifests, and how to mitigate it are able to generate more creative, innovative ideas. Those who can't, don't. It's that simple. Become self-aware, and learn to plan for and mitigate tunnel vision.

Mitigating tunnel vision

Your job is to predict that tunnel vision will happen and not let it surprise you. If you recognize that tunnel vision is inevitable because it's a fundamental property of our brain wiring, your best course of action is to delay tunnel vision as long as possible and take advantage of "fresh snow" by using the time when your brain is most able to think creatively to generate and explore a wide variety of alternatives. Remember that your instincts may be telling you to dig deep into the first promising idea you discover. You need to develop substantial discipline to combat those instinctual urges and delay tunnel vision from setting in before you are ready.

Neuroscience break by Dr. Indrė Viskontas

Have you ever noticed how young children, those under the age of five, can find very creative uses for everyday objects? A yogurt container becomes a drum. Mom's eyeglasses can double as a toothpick. A wall signifies a blank canvas, waiting to be drawn on. Then, by about age seven or so, as kids learn what the traditional purposes are for different objects, they lose the ability to dream up new functions. This is the point in their development when they begin to show evidence of a common cognitive bias: functional fixedness. Functional fixedness prevents us from finding novel uses for everyday objects—once we conceive of a tool's purpose, it's very hard to develop alternative ways to engage with it.

This bias likely helps us learn about our world, but it also can hamper creativity. The classic experiment during which the term was coined involved asking participants to solve a peculiar problem: they were given a candle, a book of matches, and a box of thumbtacks and asked to affix the candle to the wall such that no wax would drip on the table below it. The solution requires literally thinking outside the box: the thumbtacks have to be removed from the box so that the candle can be placed inside it, and a thumbtack then is used to pin the box to the wall.

Most participants failed to find the solution, but when they were presented with an empty tack box, the solution came easily. They needed a nudge to consider an alternative use for the objects. By the same token, when we generate only one potential solution to a problem, we tend to fixate on it—at the expense of other creative options. Generating a series of solutions is a great way to overcome fixedness and the functional equivalent of writer's block.

You can't delay tunnel vision forever, and indeed you benefit in other stages of the Fast Feedback Cycle from being in the tunnel, which helps you focus on the task at hand without constantly reopening decisions or questioning yourself. However, you don't want to go there until you have fully explored the space of alternatives. Here are some tactics you can use to delay or mitigate tunnel vision until you are ready for it.

Brainstorm early

The first tactic to mitigate tunnel vision is simply to recognize that there really is a time when you are at your most creative. Your brain will be dramatically more capable of generating a broad variety of alternative solutions in the very beginning of a project, before the tunnel begins to form.

Beware that some teams want to wait until the "right time" to brainstorm solution ideas—until all the right people can attend a key meeting or until a particular technical constraint is decided. There is truly a right time to brainstorm, but waiting is most likely the wrong call. Once you have identified the next set of customer problems to solve, whether in your first iteration or your fifteenth, your brain will start spinning on possible solution ideas and that will bring on tunnel vision, whether you intended it or not. It is essential to take the time up front to generate lots of diverse alternatives and go as broad as possible when you and your team are physically and psychologically most able to be creative.

Quantity, not quality

As Linus Pauling said, the goal at this point is to generate a large quantity of ideas. However, one of the quickest ways to turn off the flow of creativity is to start deciding whether the ideas you're generating are any good. As soon as someone hears that an idea he suggested "will never work" or "the customer wouldn't like that," it makes that person less likely to contribute again. It is so easy to unintentionally dampen or completely extinguish the fire behind an idea-generation exercise, simply with poor body language and offhand comments.

The problem starts when someone offers an out-of-the-box idea, which may understandably sound silly or impractical at first. (Remember that every new innovation probably sounded pretty crazy at first.) If the team accepts that unusual idea and builds from it, sometimes magical things can happen. But unfortunately, it's quite likely that a team member might roll his or her eyes or use other body language to unconsciously or subconsciously say, "That will never work" or "That's a stupid idea." Without really intending it, a team member might say something out loud that unwittingly carries the same message, such as "Anyway . . ." or "Moving right along . . ." Despite the usually neutral intent, the negative subtext is understood loud and clear by the recipient as well as by the other participants in the room, and can significantly reduce people's willingness to take a risk and contribute to the conversation, especially to share that wacky out-of-the-box idea rolling around in their head.

 TIP

> "Yes, and . . ." is a popular technique borrowed from improvisational comedy that can be very useful during idea generation to ensure that all ideas are valued and encouraged without judgment, either explicit or implicit. The idea is for each person to say "Yes, and . . ." at the beginning of every comment they make or any new idea they contribute. When consistently used in the context of a brainstorming activity, these two small words can make a world of difference in instituting a welcoming and nonjudgmental environment that encourages every team member to feel comfortable and participate fully.

The antidote is to make sure that every idea is welcomed and celebrated, no matter who says it, what it is, or where it comes from. There will be plenty of opportunities to sort through the ideas later.

For now the sole focus is on generating lots and lots of ideas, regardless of how crazy, unfeasible, or terrific they might turn out to be. At this moment, focus exclusively on quantity, not quality.

Breadth before depth

Another key tactic is to mindfully seek to generate a wide variety of ideas, exploring as much of the width of the solution space as you possibly can before talking about any ideas in depth. Think of it as doing a breadth-first search through the space, knowing that you can go back to think through an idea's depth later. Keep asking yourself, "How else could we solve this problem?" Your focus right now is purely to maximize the variety of ideas generated.

Imagine that as you generate ideas, you're creating a long, long list of pointers, with just bare minimum information attached, to help you remember what you were thinking as a jumping-off point. Your list may contain words and phrases, or it may also include visualizations like sketches and rough storyboards. You will come back to this long list several times in future iterations of the Fast Feedback Cycle and have many chances to continue brainstorming at a deeper level to explore the details of the most promising of those ideas.

Go fast

The trick to doing a breadth-first exploration is that you can't pause very long on any one idea, especially the good ones. You have to develop the habit to write down all of your ideas (practical or not, promising or not—don't try to decide now) and then force yourself to move on. Maintaining a fast pace helps to keep ideas fluid in your head, and you have a better chance of sparking new connections between different ideas when they are separated by seconds and not minutes.

Think of it like staying on your toes in soccer. Sure, you can stand on the field flat-footed, but you'll turn faster and react more nimbly to the game if you stay on your toes, ready to move at any moment. For this kind of exercise, intentionally go fast. Some teams even set explicit goals to generate a certain number of ideas per hour to help keep the pace up. Between 60 and 100 unique ideas per hour is considered a good rate for a group brainstorming session.

Keeping a fast pace is particularly difficult when someone comes up with what appears to be a brilliant idea . . . which leads us to the next tactic for mitigating tunnel vision.

Don't fall in love with your first good idea

You've just encountered a difficult problem that needs a creative solution. You understand that tunnel vision is going to set in soon, so you've kicked off a quick brainstorming session. After 10 minutes of slogging through a quagmire of irrelevant, impractical, and uninspiring ideas—BAM!, lightning strikes, and someone comes up with an approach that appears to be unique, exciting, pragmatic, and certain to delight your customers. What should you do?

Write it down and move on, asking yourself, "How else could we solve this problem?"

That promising idea won't go away. There is no reason (other than to invite the onset of tunnel vision) to linger on that idea or to start thinking about its details, implications, viability, or constraints.

Just write it down with all the other ideas and take comfort in the fact that you have captured it—it won't be forgotten, and you can come back to dig into it sometime later on.

But this is much easier said than done. This is exactly the situation in which your instincts will mislead you. Every bone in your body will want to chase this beautiful idea and discuss the possibilities—the way it might work, how it might look, what implications it might have for the architecture. The problem is that if you do that, tunnel vision will rapidly kick in. And once that happens, you will be much less able to generate any more alternatives, especially not meaningfully different approaches. In addition, it's very likely that an entire roomful of people will be brought into the tunnel with you.

Consider this. What if you discover that the first awesome idea you fell in love with doesn't work out for some reason? (You know, it's not as good as you thought it was at first . . . which is almost always the case with first ideas.) Because you didn't generate other viable alternatives yet, you have no options to fall back on, and you literally have to start from scratch. And starting from scratch will be extremely difficult this time, at least with this group of people, because you are all already in the tunnel. Likely, you will move forward with that idea and won't realize until quite a bit later that it has some fatal tradeoffs or that there was a fundamentally better approach that you never considered, but by then it will be too late (or at least very expensive) to change.

Avoid this problem by developing the discipline to write down the good idea and move on. Over time, you and your team will form the habit of doing this and it will become easier and easier. We've seen teams develop a culture and vocabulary around this approach. When they come across this situation, we hear people say things like:

> "Great idea. Write it down. We'll think about it more later."

> "Let's take advantage of the fresh snow. How else could we solve this problem?"

> "Awesome. Love it. What else?"

> "Yikes—tunnel vision is setting in . . . let's move!"

Instead of derailing the brainstorming to go deeper on that first great idea, you have to mindfully postpone that thought process until after you have done a complete breadth-first pass. As you take notes, don't write down a lot of details and don't have a lengthy conversation about every idea. Just capture enough of the idea that you can trigger your memory later. Aim for a sentence or a phrase or a very rough sketch; a paragraph is probably too much.

SFE in action: The algebra of ideas, or how two dumb ideas make a great idea

Bob Graf, Senior User Experience Researcher, Microsoft Engineering Excellence

Sandy, a program manager on my team, walked into my office to get input on the design of his feature from my UX perspective. Instead of just signing off on it, I asked him numerous questions about the users' roles, responsibilities, goals, and needs. I also asked him to describe our business needs and strategic needs and why the feature was important.

After our conversation, I was able to say with confidence that his design addressed everything we talked about. However, it was only one possible solution. I told him we should generate six ideas to make sure we explored all options.

I sketched his design on the whiteboard and labeled it "#1." Only five more to go. The next two ideas came fast, but then we got stuck. I looked at him; he looked at me. We shrugged. Stuck! I said we couldn't leave the office until we generated three more. To reach that goal, I told him I had a dumb idea and sketched it on the board. Two more to go. That dumb idea led to another, even dumber one. I personally created a safe environment for us to think creatively and without censoring our thought processes with premature evaluations.

Suddenly, magic happened. As we both looked at the two dumb ideas, the best solution simultaneously leaped into our minds. I quickly sketched it on the board. We felt we had the best solution, but we followed up with a pros-and-cons evaluation for each of the six possible solutions. When we were done, we knew idea #6 was the superior solution we needed to build. We would have never arrived at it had we not made a commitment to generate six ideas and allowed each idea to spark new ones.

I can summarize our experience into three principles for successful design thinking:

- Establish a safe, open environment, where free thinking is encouraged.

- The quantity of ideas is essential; there are no bad ideas.

- Keep interactions lightweight in both process and tone.

Employing these principles allows magic to happen.

It takes a village

It is unreasonable to expect that any one person can fully explore any solution space on his or her own. That is why many techniques for generating and exploring ideas involve multiple people in one way or another. It turns out that harvesting thoughts and energy from multiple brains—and perhaps more important, multiple points of view—is more than just a way to get out of a rut, it is a valuable and necessary ingredient to the creative process.

Ideally, you involve people with as much diversity as possible—consider different skill sets, different personal experiences, different career trajectories, different personality types, different backgrounds, different ages and life stages, different problem-solving styles, and even different motivations for solving the problem in the first place. Having people bounce ideas off one another, stimulating each other in unpredictable ways, is a key part of the formula for keeping ideas flowing and avoiding becoming stuck in a rut prematurely.

Team members also have a role to keep each other honest, to keep the discussion moving and not linger too long on any one idea. It's much easier to see when a teammate is drilling too deeply into an idea (and risking getting stuck in the tunnel) than it is to see that in yourself. Find a nonjudgmental way to communicate that it's time to move on. Anything from tossing a red bandanna to the offender, tagging them with a Nerf toy, or empowering anyone to cut off a discussion with a scripted reminder such as "too much detail" or "How else could we solve this?" can work. Define the plan ahead of time so that everyone knows the rules, and keep it positive, playful, and not confrontational.

Help! I'm in the tunnel

Now that you know about tunnel vision, you need to be vigilant and self-aware. Once you find yourself experiencing that intoxicating feeling of having found the perfect solution, you need to recognize that you may genuinely and firmly believe that no other alternative approach exists—even if one is plainly visible to others. If you have already generated plenty of alternatives, feel confident that you have explored the solution space, and have captured those ideas in a form that will trigger your thinking later, this is not necessarily a problem. But if you suspect that you have entered the tunnel too early, without having yet explored the space fully, or have simply run dry of ideas before you feel that you've generated enough, you need to find a way out of the tunnel. Here are some techniques that are pretty broadly useful when you need to get out of the tunnel.

One of the best steps to take is to solicit different ideas from a new set of people. Recruit people who have not yet been infected by your idea and use their "fresh brains" to see things that you may not. They may help you see alternatives, blends, and improvements that you likely would not find on your own. Even a few seemingly random new ideas can help unclog your thinking so that you notice alternatives you were not aware of before. Usually you can productively riff on an idea once it is suggested by someone else, even if you are too far in the tunnel to notice that alternative approach on your own.

 VOCAB

> Fresh brains? Sorry, this isn't a reference to the latest zombie craze. We use the term *fresh brains* to refer to people whose heads are still metaphorically full of fresh snow. They have not been exposed to your current thinking about the problem space and are better able to see ideas that you may not.

The first step to getting out of the tunnel is to acknowledge that you are in fact stuck. Something like this: "Hey gang, we've been spinning around this same idea for a while now. I think we're in the tunnel. Let's go find some fresh brains and see if we can get unstuck." Teammates who have not been deeply involved in your project are a good place to look for fresh brains. They are usually easy to find simply by walking down the hall or picking up the phone. A five-minute conversation by the water cooler may be all it takes to find a new perspective that gets you out of the tunnel.

Beware of limiting yourself to tossing around ideas only with others on your immediate team. You may readily convince each other that no other viable alternatives exist because you are all stuck in the same tunnel. It's very easy to bring teammates into the tunnel with you.

Even when you find some new people to brainstorm with, be sure you follow the rules and encourage new ideas. Don't try to sell or validate the ideas that took you into the tunnel in the first place.

You are still looking for quantity, not quality. You are looking for a new approach or blend of approaches that will get you out of the tunnel and able to explore new paths of thinking again.

An even better source of fresh brains is your customer base. Customers will almost always approach problems from a perspective different from yours. It is a good general practice to generate ideas with customers purely because of the different perspective they bring, which can be hard to replicate even with a diverse team.

Good ideas come from the strangest places

Regardless of the techniques you use to generate ideas, predictable patterns occur. In our workshop, to illustrate how these patterns emerge and what they look like, we conduct a little contest. It turns out that everyone loves a little competition, and the brainstorming contest really gets the post-lunch energy flowing again.

The room has already been set up with tables for four or five people, ideally with representatives from different disciplines at each table. We ask each table to nominate a scribe, and for a little added motivation we mention that a prize will be awarded to the winning team. The table that comes up with the greatest number of unique ideas wins. We set a timer for one minute and then announce:

> **Ready, set** . . . *the focus of the brainstorm is:*

> *"Name as many ways as you can to send a message to another person."*

> **Go!**

Immediately the energy in the room skyrockets. People shout, laugh, think, and write frantically. This is brainstorming. For most people, it's fun, engaging, exhilarating. But to use it as a productive and efficient ideation tool, it takes practice—intentional practice by the entire team, and not everyone is good at it at first.

After one minute we call time and ask people to count how many ideas their group came up with. We don't care whether the ideas are any good, it's just the raw number that matters right now. The average number of messaging ideas each table generates is about 20. The most ideas we've ever seen produced in a minute is 42—more than double the average. We've also seen plenty of tables barely get to a dozen in a minute's time; these teams get stuck on an idea and can't seem to get past it. We figure out which table came up with the most ideas and then announce the prize: the winners get the honor of reading their list of ideas to the group.

Here's an example of a typical winning list of ideas for how to send a message to another person:

> *Email, letter, text message, skywriting, smoke signals, airmail, carrier pigeon, Morse code, radio, television, webpage, discussion board, facial expression, frown, smile, spitting, walking away, handshake, kiss, hug, song, poem, ballad, haiku, limerick, gift, present, gift card, phone call, Skype, flaming arrow*

Diverse people create more diverse ideas

While you read through the list, did one of these entries trigger a new idea for you? Chances are that it did, and you have a couple of new contributions you could add to the end. Your ideas, in turn, might trigger additional ideas for other examples that hadn't occurred to you. That's the magic of brainstorming with multiple people, each coming from a different perspective and bringing multiple skills, life experiences, and backgrounds to help maximize the number and variety of alternatives generated.

In the classroom, people are always astounded at how many different ideas their own table came up with that are not on the list that was read out loud. It is an experiential reminder that *different people will often generate very different ideas, even given the same problem statement.*

Embrace the cousins

Do you notice any patterns in that list of ideas, and the order in which ideas are mentioned? The first three ideas—email, letter, text message— are all centered on typed or written text. It's very common for ideas to come out in spurts like this during a brainstorming session, producing a set of related ideas that are "cousins" of each other.

 VOCAB

> *Cousins* are a succession of similar ideas mentioned during an idea-generation session that all are closely related to one another.

Some people have trouble with cousins. Inwardly, they feel that a "cousin" idea might not be different enough from other ideas on the list to be worth saying out loud. For instance, in our example, a person might hear "email, letter, text message" and think about contributing "SMS," but she might second-guess herself because, well, isn't SMS just the same thing as a text message? This doubt is your inner perfectionist peeking through, worrying that someone will call you out for contributing an uninspired brainstorming idea, one that doesn't seem new or different enough from what is already on the list. You feel like you are cheating somehow.

Truthfully, you are better off saying your idea out loud no matter how similar or dissimilar it is. Otherwise, you'll spend a lot of mental energy censoring yourself. This makes it hard to stay in the fast-paced flow of the brainstorm so that you can keep riffing on ideas and contributing your unique perspective. Furthermore, saying "SMS" might have triggered someone to think of MMS messages, which might have led to sending videos, photos, Snapchat, photobombing, etc. (None of which are mentioned on the list, did you notice?)

You can make forward progress in your brainstorming with even the closest of cousins. And worst case, even if it goes nowhere, so what? You used only a few seconds of time, big deal. Bottom line: if the idea pops into your head, say it; don't self-censor. It's better for you, and it's better for the team's results overall.

Encourage lateral jumps

When we get to the end of a run of cousins, there's usually a short pause. Then, out of the blue, a new idea—skywriting—is suggested. Where did it come from? Note that skywriting is followed by another set of cousins: smoke signals, airmail, carrier pigeon. And when this run of cousins ends, there's another pause, and then a jump to another completely different line of ideas: Morse code, radio, television.

This pattern is typical of a healthy brainstorm. One idea starts a stream of thinking along a particular vein. When that vein runs dry, a different thought is suggested and it's followed for a while. There may be a pause between streams of thought, and then there's a jump to a new topic. Those jumps are called *lateral jumps*. They don't take a line of thought forward; they jump sideways, or laterally, to a different perspective on the problem or solution.

 VOCAB

> A *lateral jump* is a shift to a new topic while brainstorming that is seemingly unrelated to the previously generated ideas.

It turns out that lateral jumps are very powerful. The more lateral jumps that occur during idea generation, the more diverse a set of options you'll end up generating. The more that you can cultivate an environment that encourages and stimulates lateral jumps, the more ideas you will generate and the more likely that you will hit upon the raw materials for the winning combination you are searching for.

Suspend disbelief about wild ideas

One of our favorite techniques for encouraging lateral jumps is called *challenge assumptions*. The idea is to challenge a basic assumption about your problem and see whether by removing that constraint you can find an alternative through a side door that you might not have noticed while looking at your problem head-on.

For example, what if we suggested that you design a new kind of coffee cup, but we challenged the assumption that it would have a bottom. What would a coffee cup look like without a bottom? It's a basic assumption that all cups have some sort of a bottom. How would it stand on its own if it had no bottom to rest on? Your first instinct is to reject the whole notion and say, "That's impossible!"

But stay with us for a second. Suspend disbelief and think about it. What might a coffee cup look like if it had no bottom? What if it was a different shape? A rounded bottom, like a child's tip-free sippy cup? Perhaps a sphere? Or maybe a cone shape? A spinning cylinder that leveraged centrifugal force? An antigravity vortex? Maybe some sort of device that acts on vacuum pressure? What if it looked like a bag of intravenous (IV) fluids from a hospital—imagine, an IV drip of your morning coffee! Or what if the cup was like an IV bag but with a straw attached to the bottom? Hmm, I guess there might be some alternatives to consider after all.

But can you make the leap from there and imagine inventing the CamelBak, a water-containing backpack with a long straw meant for keeping you hydrated on hiking outings? Or perhaps you might leap in a different direction and imagine the beer hat, which comfortably perches two cans of beer on your head, with a long straw that lets you sip at will?

Both of these are actually pretty useful, intriguing concepts and have enjoyed commercial success in their time. How likely is it that you would have come up with these kinds of ideas just thinking about alternatives for regular old coffee cups? Forcing yourself to challenge an assumption allows you to think about the problem differently and open yourself to a different class of solutions you might not have noticed otherwise.

This example illustrates the importance of being playful in generating ideas, of not taking anything too seriously or at face value, and being willing to suspend disbelief and assume that, for just this one moment, anything is possible. Being willing to consider wild ideas, playing around with them, and letting cousins and lateral jumps happen are central behaviors to cultivate to get the most out of brainstorming.

Of course, not every wild idea will be practical or even possible. Many may feel downright crazy, ridiculous, corny, or foolish. However, it's only after following a string of wild ideas and seeing where that thread goes that you might stumble on an approach that proves to be a real winner, that is actually practical and implementable and perhaps not so crazy after all. And that idea probably would not have occurred to you otherwise. At this stage, ideas are cheap, so don't be pound wise and penny foolish. If you're willing to spend a few minutes of suspended disbelief to see where that wild idea might lead, you dramatically increase your chances of hitting on an out-of-the-box approach that no one has noticed before, not even your competition. And worst case? You spent only a few minutes on a dead end.

The point to remember is *that you are more likely to stumble onto a unique approach through a side door* rather than going at a problem head-on. This idea is so powerful that specific techniques, called *lateral thinking techniques,* have been developed that help spur lateral jumps in your idea generation. These encourage you to knock on those side doors and give you more chances to find new, unusual solutions. We'll discuss several lateral thinking techniques in more detail in the tools and techniques section later in this chapter.

 ## MINDSHIFT

Who gets credit for that good idea? If you witnessed hundreds of brainstorming sessions and idea-generation activities, you would notice that you can't predict where the best or craziest or most interesting ideas will come from. You can't predict who will initiate the lateral jumps in the group's thinking, and you can't give credit to any single person who comes up with what proves to be a brilliant idea—once you realize that this brilliant idea came at the end of a long string of related and unrelated ideas, all of which created the environment that stimulated the brilliant idea to surface at all.

The notion of who gets the credit becomes even more meaningless the more that a team becomes truly collaborative and operates as a unit rather than as a collection of individuals.

A strong, collaborative team shouldn't feel like they are competing with their colleagues for who gets the bigger bonus this year. Instead, everyone has skin in the game and is pulling together for a shared goal. When a team gets to that high level of interdependence and trust, its work becomes more about getting to the right decision for the customer (and not jockeying for whose idea is the best). In turn, this attitude makes it easier to admit and recover from failures and more fluidly take advantage of the unique skills of each team member at the right time. Developing team-wide trust and deep collaboration is essential for many of the practices we discuss in this book to take root, and brainstorming is a crucial place where it becomes very clear whether your team has that trust or not.

Marinating

When searching for new ideas, sometimes the best thing to do is walk away, or at least give yourself some space for a while. Marinating is a weird "anti-technique," but it is an extremely effective concept to keep in mind when you're generating ideas. You've worked on a problem for a while and perhaps gotten a bit stuck, overwhelmed, bored, or tired. Then you intentionally stop thinking about it and go do something else—work on a different problem, take a shower, go for a walk, play soccer, take a nap—and by some sort of magic, a new insight or connection or idea hits you hours or days later, when you least expect it, when you aren't even thinking about the problem. Or when you do come back to a problem hours or days later, you find that you have a much better understanding or think of ideas that you didn't have before.

 VOCAB

To *marinate* is to stop actively thinking about an idea to give your brain downtime for processing the idea in the background, making it more likely for your brain to notice unusual connections or new insights.

Most of us have experienced this at some point in our lives and have heard stories about it happening to famous people. Whether it's Watson and Crick dreaming about the DNA double helix or Archimedes's supposed eureka moment in the bathtub, it's a fascinating phenomenon of the human brain that it appears to keep working on a problem subconsciously long after the conscious mind has stopped.

> ## Neuroscience break by Dr. Indrė Viskontas
>
> Psychologists see the creative process as having four distinct stages: preparation, incubation, illumination, and verification. Because incubation, by definition, occurs outside our conscious awareness, it's hard to study. But there have been some interesting insights into its brain basis discovered recently by neuroscientists. In particular, sleep seems to be an important context for

incubation: studies have shown that a solution to a problem, or a new idea, can often present itself after a period of sleep.

During sleep, our brains replay what happened during the day, and important information is consolidated, while at the same time, the irrelevant things that we thought about or experienced get erased. There's even new evidence that the amount of fluid in your brain increases during sleep, washing away the metabolic byproducts of all the activity that your neurons were engaging in during the day. Cleaning up this waste prepares your brain for the next day's activities. If we skip or truncate our sleep, not only do we have trouble functioning the next day, but we also are more likely to forget what we were trying to learn the previous day.

If you don't have time for a full rest, however, just doing a relatively simple activity can also boost your incubation productivity. Studies have shown that a task that doesn't require your full attention, like a walk or an errand, can boost your chances of experiencing a eureka moment. And the longer the incubation period, within reason, of course, the more likely you are to find a solution unconsciously.

While marinating is not fully understood, it's well established that it does happen. So use it to your advantage. You can encourage better ideas by intentionally allowing ideas to marinate—giving time for ideas to ripen, like a fine red wine or an aged cheese.

There appear to be several ways to encourage marination—that is, to encourage brain states in which you are more likely to have a eureka idea through background processing. Some people say that activities that allow your brain and body to relax or get into a repetitive rhythm are more conducive to producing a flash of insight. Many people report experiencing an aha moment while showering, bathing, taking a walk, going for a run, or during other exercise. Similarly, meditation experts report that they achieve an altered, more creative state while meditating.

 TIP

Try using those precious few minutes of semiwakefulness in the morning as a time to gently call a particular problem or challenge to mind and encourage your brain to start chewing on it while your brain is feeling open and unhindered by full wakefulness. You may be surprised by the results.

Next time you need to schedule a work session, take care to consider whether breaking up the time over several days might be better than one long session. The marinating that naturally happens between each day might give you better results if you spread out the focused work sessions a bit. Also, the next time you feel blocked and tunnel vision is looming, or the team seems to be rehashing the same issue over and over, don't keep beating on the front door; stop and come back later. Sometimes, a little time or a trip to the coffee shop is all it takes to get back on track. If nothing else, taking some time might help you get out of the weeds, and you'll come back later with more of a balcony view.

SFE in action: Getting unstuck

Norman Furlong, Principal, Greenbook Inc.

When I worked for Boss Logic, a NeXTStep startup, I managed a group of developers in Silicon Valley. We worked out of a hillside house overlooking San Mateo. In those days there weren't many resources available for Objective-C developers, so we were pretty much on our own. Almost every day, sometimes more than once in a day, a cry of anguish would emanate from the other room. This would warn me that one of the devs had gotten blocked and was in need of a distraction. I would spring into action and drive said developer down the hill for a cuppa Joe. On the way, we'd talk about the coding problem, and sometimes I could offer some cogent insights. But most often, we'd change the subject and talk about music, women, cars—anything but code.

Usually within 10, but rarely more than 20, minutes after we'd get back to the house, I'd be rewarded with cries of "Eureka!" coming from the now-unstuck developer. This routine, with minor variations, repeated itself all summer. When I sensed the whole team needed a break, we'd all head down the hill. The summer we worked together in that house was extremely productive, due in part to our devs getting time to walk away from the problem and marinate, releasing their conscious mind from the burden of solving the problem and allowing their sub-conscious to step in and do some of the heavy lifting.

Explore stage: Key tools and techniques

In this section we go into more detail about different techniques you can use, individually or as a team, to generate solution alternatives. First, we'll talk about visualization techniques, such as sketching, storyboarding, and drawing flow charts and block diagrams. These are very powerful but lightweight ways to generate and explore alternatives. Then we'll discuss brainstorming approaches that can be used equally well in concert with sketching or with more traditional verbal techniques. We'll also introduce the broad topic of lateral thinking techniques and related approaches that help you supercharge your ideation by shifting perspectives to help generate more out-of-the-box ideas.

 ## MINDSHIFT

Use the whole brain. Remember when we talked about the power of including a diverse set of people when your team generates ideas? We suggested that a necessary step in the creative process is to harvest the brains of a diverse population, with different sets of experiences, backgrounds, perspectives, and so on. Well, the same approach applies to generating ideas with your own brain. To access the power of your whole brain, use idea-generation techniques that involve different types of thought processes and different parts of your brain.

You might write words, act out situations, draw pictures, or even use physical objects to explore different shapes and forms in physical space. You might brainstorm on the spur of the moment, or you might ask people to mull over the topic for a while before getting together to share their ideas. While not all of these modalities apply to any given problem or any given team, many of them will. By using different sets of techniques, you can bring more and different types of brainpower to bear on the problem at hand. The more modalities you use when you explore ideas, the larger the variety of ideas you are likely to uncover.

Visualization techniques

Among the many ways to express ideas as you generate and explore different approaches to solving your problem, the most obvious is to use words, creating long lists of ideas expressed as short phrases, sentences, or paragraphs. This is a valuable way to capture ideas, but it relies predominantly on the language functions of your brain, which are linked with logical, analytical thinking.

Visual and spatial approaches, such as building physical objects, sketching, and storyboarding, use other parts of your brain and have distinct advantages over verbal methods for many types of problems. Furthermore, some of the problems engineers encounter are highly visual in nature; they involve user interfaces, architectures, or physical devices that specifically lend themselves to a visual idea-generation approach.

Neuroscience break by Dr. Indrė Viskontas

The left brain/right brain distinction is a lot murkier than most people realize. There are many connections between the two hemispheres of the brain, and the idea that each hemisphere acts alone is not supported by neuroscience. What's more, creativity engages the left side of the brain just as much as the right, with a recent meta-analysis showing no clear evidence for a greater role played by the right side in creative thinking. But for most people, the conscious mind is dominated by language—we think in words more often than in pictures or other symbols. So the language centers in the left brain are sometimes thought of as "dominating" much of our thinking.

There is evidence that our frontal cortex can control neural activity in other parts of the brain, like our medial temporal lobes, where our long-term memories are stored. By switching approaches and engaging parts of the brain that are not involved in language processing, we might be able to release other parts of the brain that are inhibited by the dominant language areas and let them "speak" for themselves. In fact, in studies of dementia patients who lose the ability to communicate verbally because of a progressive neurodegenerative disease, we sometimes see an emergence of visual creativity: that is, as their language regions degenerate, other parts of their brains, like the parietal and visual cortices, can have a greater influence on behavior.

Let's explore a few ways to capture and explore ideas visually.

Sketching

A particularly versatile, but frequently overlooked, mode for generating ideas is to use some form of sketching. You might sketch different ways to depict an icon, draw several alternative flow charts to describe a workflow, whiteboard different architectural block diagrams, sketch alternative layouts for a user interface, or perhaps link several sketches in comic-book fashion to rough out an end-to-end experience in a storyboard.

The visual nature of drawings can help you notice connections and ideas that you would be very unlikely to see if you just described the same ideas in words. Many teams find that when they take the time to do some rough sketching as part of exploring alternatives, they discover ideas that they would not have found another way.

It's helpful to think of sketching as just another idea-generation tool; it's brainstorming with pictures instead of words. As such, tunnel vision applies to drawing just as much as to any other brainstorming technique. So keep in mind all the principles about why you should go broad first, not fall in love with your first good idea (or good picture), and not judge ideas until later. The ultimate goal of a visual idea-generation exercise is to sketch as many different ideas as you can in very rough form, mindfully postponing the details to generate the greatest diversity of ideas possible before tunnel vision sets in.

 TIP

> We strongly encourage people to sketch with a marker, which naturally writes with a broad line, helping you to keep detail to a minimum and your drawings rough and simple. This keeps you in the zone for idea generation, rather than straying into drawing with distracting details. Also, you can't erase a marker, which helps stop you from striving for a beautiful drawing and to just go with what you first put down, mess and all. The bold look of a drawing made with a marker is also ideal for sharing with others across a table or pinned on the wall. These drawings are much easier to see at a distance than a pen or pencil drawing.

It's important to understand that sketching is not about drawing beautiful pictures, it's about exploring different ideas. We don't care if our drawings aren't beautiful. In fact, they may be only semi-legible. But if a sketch means something to the person who drew it and helps him explore that idea, it's good enough. Simple sketches are the most effective at this point to focus on the essence of the idea being proposed. Sketches do not need to be pretty, or accurate, or complex. They just need to capture and communicate enough of the idea that you can return to it later to develop the idea more fully.

Beware of beautiful drawings (and great artists). Just because one person on your team happens to be an amazingly talented artist, and her sketches look light years better than everyone else's, does not mean that her idea is the best or that everyone else should sit back and let the team's artist do all the drawing. Remember that the goal of this stage of the Fast Feedback Cycle is to generate lots of alternative ideas and to leverage the diversity of perspectives of everyone on the team. If you're going to use everyone's visual brainpower, everyone needs to be holding a pen and drawing. A rough, messy, imperfect sketch is just as likely to carry a promising idea as a visually beautiful one.

Even a very rough sketch can help you better communicate your thinking to a teammate and create a shared understanding of an idea. With words, ideas can easily be misinterpreted or misunderstood, because different people unconsciously imagine very different implementations of the same basic idea yet still believe they are talking about the same thing. With ideas expressed as pictures, the gap between possible implementations begins to close. Drawings have much higher information density because they inherently include aspects like relationship, size, and proximity in addition to the specific content being drawn. As the old adage goes, a picture is worth a thousand words.

Unfortunately, many engineers believe that they can't draw, so they sometimes avoid sketching as an idea-generation technique and miss out on all its creative benefits. Some may happily sketch an architectural block diagram on a whiteboard but shy away from trying to draw anything more complicated than that. We see it in our workshop all the time; when we start talking about sketching, the room gets tense. If we don't start with a warm-up exercise, it's common for some people in the room to refuse to pick up a pen when we ask them to try sketching out ideas for their scenario.

In the workshop, after introducing the idea of sketching and how simple it can (and should) be, we have another timed contest. We ask everyone in the room to fill a page-size grid of 25 circles with a quick sketch, one drawing per circle. It can be a happy face, a sunset, a boat . . . it doesn't matter, as long as people don't use numbers or letters. The goal is to fill as many of the circles as possible in one minute. An example is shown in Figure 7-3.

When the minute is over, we ask everyone to hold up their drawings. Most are able to fill about half the sheet, but only a few fill in all of the circles. We ask the people who filled the page to share their secret to success. They say things like "keep it simple," "no details," and "follow a thread of cousins." At this point, most folks in the room are feeling a bit more confident in their ability, and many are itching for another chance. We give them a fresh sheet and set the timer for a minute. This second time, we observe that almost all the participants are able to fill the entire sheet with sketches.

After watching literally tens of thousands of engineers sketch their solution ideas in our workshops (not just this warm-up exercise), we can say with confidence that every engineer is capable of drawing the simple sketches needed to explore ideas. In fact, we are continually amazed at the quality of the sketches we see, and the quality of the ideas generated through sketching, especially from people who emphatically declare that they are terrible at drawing.

FIGURE 7-3 An example of the circle exercise.

SFE in action: But I can't draw!

Lisa Mueller, Senior User Experience Lead, Microsoft Corporation

On our team, after the scenarios were written and signed off, diverse teams (including UX, PM, Developers and Test) were put together to start on paper-and-pencil prototyping. In the beginning, these teams were very apprehensive about starting unless they knew that a UX team representative would attend. They felt this was the "drawing" phase, and since they didn't have any experience with drawing, their confidence was low and drawing was something these small teams of engineers just didn't feel comfortable doing. In the end, if a UX team member couldn't attend, many of these prototyping sessions were canceled and rescheduled.

We anticipated that our approach to paper prototyping was going to be to get into groups of two to three people to sketch out possible walk-throughs of each scenario. However, because so many people were so hesitant to draw, we changed our procedure. Instead of asking the small teams to sketch together, we directed the team members to work individually for one hour and to create their own walk-through sketches. Afterward, each person would present his or her sketch or drawing of the scenario to the rest of the team.

As each person presented his or her sketch, the team would highlight ideas that seemed particularly good with a sticky note and a star. By the time we got to the third presentation, the energy in the room was high and becoming very collaborative. Individuals began to notice and appreciate the different types of ideas that were coming from different people and that each team member brought a new strength to the table. The PM brought subject matter expertise. UX brought the UI framework. Developers brought the step-by-step plan, and testers brought detailed content. The combination of these strengths was very powerful. After this sketching-brainstorming meeting, everyone became much more engaged because they had the realization that this exercise wasn't about how well you could draw but about leveraging the strengths and perspectives from across the team.

SFE in action: How (and why) to draw anything

Dan Roam, international best-selling author of The Back of the Napkin *and* Show and Tell. *(All drawings © Dan Roam, 2014. Provided with the author's permission.)*

Here are two interesting data points:

- More of our brain is dedicated to processing vision than to any other mental task.

- More of our body's energy is consumed by our brain than by any other organ.

Adding those two facts together tells us something important: as humans, we are essentially walking, talking vision-processing machines.

For scenario-focused engineers, this offers a critical but overlooked insight: if we want to maximize our innate problem-solving skills, we should structure our problems visually. By intentionally enabling our visual mind to actively engage in defining, structuring, and formulating problems, we will discover that problem solving can be faster and more creative than ever.

The problem is that we rarely intentionally engage our visual mind. Why? Because we are afraid to draw. So step number one in becoming better visual thinkers is to relearn the simple art of drawing.

Here are six quick exercises to get you started:

1. All drawing starts with five simple shapes.

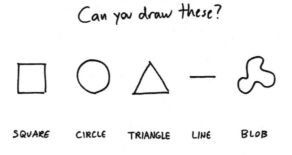

2. By combining these shapes, you can draw almost anything your mind can conceive. Can you draw these? What else can you draw?

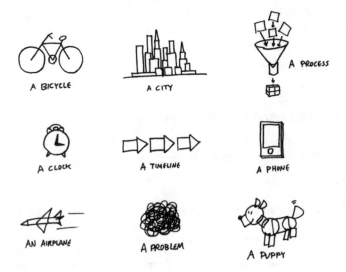

A BICYCLE

A CITY

A PROCESS

A CLOCK

A TIMELINE

A PHONE

AN AIRPLANE

A PROBLEM

A PUPPY

3. Since we usually find people at the center of most problems, it will be helpful to be able to draw them. Simple figures are good enough. Can you draw these?

-OK

4. Stick figures are ideal for showing individuals and emotion. Can you draw these?

Stick Figures = EMOTION

Yes!

FINE

OOPS.

ACK!

NOPE.

Snif.

Hmm...

REALLY.

5. Block figures are good for showing action. Can you draw more like these?

Block Figures = ACTION

Follow through...

Gone fishin'.

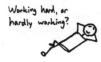
Working hard, or hardly working?

Outta here!

6. Blob figures are ideal for showing groups and relationships. Can you draw more like these?

I hope that by showing these simple examples, you can see how easy drawing can be. Now think about how you might apply this to clarifying your challenges.

Drawing and sketching is a very powerful technique, both for generating creative ideas and for communicating thoughts, ideas, and concepts to others. You do not need to be an artist, and your sketches do not need to be sophisticated or beautiful. By drawing the kinds of simple figures that Dan Roam demonstrates, you can describe just about anything visually.

Storyboarding

The specific sketching technique that we find most useful for generating ideas about an end-to-end experience is storyboarding. Instead of sketching a single picture, you string together several pictures into a sequence of actions or steps to form a storyboard.

Storyboarding originated in the film industry as a comic-book-style approach to drawing out sequences of movie scenes. Storyboards help filmmakers think through all the different camera angles, shots, and actions they need to capture to create the final film. It's very expensive to reshoot a scene if there is a mistake or a missing camera angle, so it behooves film directors to carefully consider all the pieces they need to thread together to form the final experience before they are on location with actors, gear, and staff.

Storyboarding is helpful for mapping out software experiences as well. It is particularly useful for the kinds of scenarios that engineers are typically solving because it encourages you to think through sequences of interactions, not just individual moments. If you're serious about building end-to-end experiences for your customers, storyboards are your first, best tool to start exploring different end-to-end sequences that might solve a given customer scenario. Just like in scenario writing, the storytelling nature of storyboarding helps you get to a deeper level of understanding and empathy with your customers, which may suggest new avenues for inspiration.

It's critical to approach storyboarding in your first couple iterations of the Fast Feedback Cycle as still being in idea-generation mode, trying to generate multiple diverse solution approaches before tunnel vision sets in. In later iterations, more-refined storyboards play a role in helping you fine-tune ideas and detail improvements to the experience, but the focus in the beginning should be on very quick, rough storyboards that explore as many different sequences of interaction as possible. Having alternatives will help you develop a feel for which ones flow most smoothly and best create the customer experience you are aiming for. Just like with other idea-generation techniques, only after you generate many divergent ideas do the relative merits of each approach become clear and the decision points become more obvious.

Figure 7-4 shows several different storyboards of a mobile app concept that would make it easy for friends who are physically near one another to find each other and meet up. Each storyboard shows a different sequence of how the user interface might be designed, in very rough form. These storyboards explore different ways to upsell a new feature and also manage privacy and consent for sharing your physical location with friends through a mobile app.

Here are some tips to keep in mind when storyboarding:

- **Storyboards show sequences**   A storyboard should have a minimum of three frames and can have many more. Frames can be a mix of comic-book drawings of stick figure customers in a situation, a sketch of a possible user interface flow, or a sequence of steps that the customer might interact with.

- **Keep the details to a minimum**   Notice that storyboard drawings are very simple and straightforward. They leave out a lot of details. We're talking line drawings, no artistic flourishes, no detailed pictures; just the core idea with a minimum of ink.

- **Brief captions are enough**   Writing a brief caption under each frame can be helpful to give context or communicate the story if it's not obvious. However, there's no need to write every single word in the user interface you are imagining. Some wavy lines to indicate where text might go and a keyword or two is generally enough to get the idea across. Remember that you're going for speed so that you can produce multiple ideas.

- **Show people and emotion**   While some storyboards focus directly on what is happening on the screen, many storyboards include frames that show the user before, during, or after the experience. Don't worry about having to draw people—simple stick figures are just fine, but adding a quick facial expression (smile, frown, etc.) or thought bubble can carry a lot of meaning about the customer's context, emotion, and state of mind.

- **Don't get attached**   The more effort you put into making a storyboard beautiful, the more you will like it. Indeed, you might fall in love with it. And that will lead to tunnel vision, making it hard for you to imagine that other ideas exist.

FIGURE 7-4 Four different storyboards exploring alternative user interface flows for a mobile app.

Flow charts and state diagrams

Some problems lend themselves to a flow chart or state diagram, showing the logic of how each state flows into the next. This approach is particularly useful for deeply technical problems, but it can also be used for drawing user interface flows to work out more detailed interactions or to fine-tune a proposed interaction in later iterations of the Fast Feedback Cycle. Some teams will develop their more-refined storyboards into user interface (UI) flow charts. These show how the UI might fork at various decision points in the interface: if the user chooses A versus B, what happens next for each of these choices.

This technique is not often the best choice in the first couple of iterations of the Fast Feedback Cycle. However, after you generate some ideas and get feedback, pulling your most promising ideas into a flow chart can help you refine those ideas and formalize the details and the flow at the next level of detail. Here are a few things to consider as you refine the flow:

- **Switch the order** If your proposed flow asks the user to log in first, flip the logic so that authentication happens later on or at the very end.

- **Challenge each branch** Is this decision fork absolutely necessary? What if you just don't ask? What happens if you pick a reasonable default instead?

- **Take different customer points of view** If your flow chart describes the experience of the end user, also draw the logic for how the experience might be for an administrator, purchaser, partner, or another customer type in your ecosystem.

Block diagrams, interfaces, and architectural drawings

The diagrams most often seen on the whiteboards of engineers are architectural block diagrams of one sort or another, often with lines, arrows, or lollipops connecting them. Block diagrams are excellent for describing modular components of software, abstraction layers, interfaces, APIs, and relationships between larger components such as servers, services, and databases. You already know how to draw these diagrams, and the finer points of formal architecture drawings are beyond the scope of this book.

However, many of the problems we've discussed in this chapter lurk beneath the surface for architecture diagrams as well. In particular, watch out for tunnel vision in your architecture diagrams and be open to true iteration, not just minor tweaks and fine-tuning. We hear too many stories of developers who create one reasonable architectural drawing and then, as they get feedback, start decorating their diagram with the parts they missed—a link to the authentication service here, a missing component there, a link between that component and this other one that will need to share data . . . and pretty soon you wind up with a spaghetti diagram. By that point, however, the proposed architecture is so firmly established in everyone's brains that it can be hard to see other alternatives. Indeed, it's easy to convince yourself that this is just a complex problem, so you resign yourself to building a complicated architecture as well. But is that really true, or is that tunnel vision talking?

We do an exercise in class in which we ask the groups at each table, after they have iterated on their storyboard concepts, to sketch out what a technical infrastructure to implement their concept might look like. We set a specific goal to draw three different architecture diagrams of whatever sort is most appropriate for the problem the participants' have identified. It's striking how few groups are able to come up with even a second architectural approach, never mind three. Yet as an instructor (with a fresh brain full of fluffy white snow), it's easy to walk over to a table, hear the basic idea, and suggest a few quick questions, such as, "Have you considered a peer-to-peer approach? Or a client-server approach? A cloud-service approach? A rich-client approach?" These are all familiar, basic architectural paradigms, but somehow the tendency is to zoom in to a particular approach right away and go so deeply into that idea that other options are forgotten.

What we observed was that teams that are able to come up with a few meaningfully different architectural diagrams also report that they didn't pick just one of the alternatives to move forward with. Rather, their favored implementation ended up being a blend of different ideas that were suggested. They often remark that *they would not have likely considered that blend had they not forced themselves to come up with multiple alternatives in the first place.*

Just as with user experiences, a good starting point for designing stronger architectures is to consider multiple options at the beginning. That means that when you sit down to draw some block diagrams of how your architecture might look in your next release, or some lollipops to work out the interface between this component and that one, the behavior to cultivate is to not stop after you work out one reasonably good approach. Keep drawing, and force yourself to come up with another credible alternative, and ideally more. Bring colleagues into that process to bring more perspectives and other approaches into consideration. The idea is to draw many possible architectures so that later you can compare and contrast their pros and cons and allow the simplest and most elegant blended solutions to emerge.

 ## MINDSHIFT

Think like an architect. One thing we've noticed working with teams is that expert software development architects naturally use a lot of the techniques we discuss in this book. However, they do it largely by instinct, not because they've been taught to. Perhaps it was precisely these instincts that led them to be architects in the first place.

For instance, expert architects believe that an architecture or an interface cannot be written in a vacuum—it's best to be paired with another team that will actually use your architecture or interface to be sure you're building something that works in real life. We've also observed that many expert-level architects intuitively think about customer and developer desires and needs as well as the end-to-end usage scenarios in which their architectures will be used. They intuitively generate multiple ideas, and before they pick an approach, they investigate the relative merits of those approaches (by researching documentation and discussion groups, networking with others who have experience, playing around with the code, or building functional or semifunctional prototypes). They are willing to iterate, sometimes many times, before settling on a final design.

The bummer is that many of these steps happen in their head, or when working solo on a whiteboard, making it hard for other, more-junior developers to observe and learn this craft and approach. This also means there are fewer opportunities for feedback and for incorporating diverse perspectives that might have enriched the plan. Over the years we've also heard occasional complaints from architects who did all the right things, yet had trouble convincing the team of their final recommended approach because they didn't bring the team along on the journey of their thought process.

We encourage architects who have this predisposition and skill set to practice their craft in a more public way, to teach others, better influence their teams, and ultimately build better architectures. And if you are a software developer who hopes to be an architect someday, pay attention: these are core skills to develop that will help you achieve your career goals.

Hold a sketchfest or charrette

Of course, all of these sketching techniques can be done solo or in groups, but it is a rare engineering team that has developed a strong habit of sketching to generate ideas. One productive technique to encourage more sketching and start building that muscle is to schedule dedicated time for a team a team "sketchfest," sometimes also called a "charrette." Get a broad group of team members together in a room, remind everyone of the current scenario or technical challenge, and have folks pick up markers and start sketching. After everyone has had time to sketch some ideas, have people present their more interesting concepts to each other, in pairs or in small groups, to allow ideas to mingle and encourage blends to emerge. Plan time for a second or third round of sketching, mix up the sharing groups, and be sure to collect the ideas that are generated as you select the most promising ideas to move into the next stage of the Fast Feedback Cycle.

Physical models

If you are aiming to build a physical product of some sort—a hardware device, a handheld gizmo, or a peripheral—it naturally makes sense to explore ideas physically in three-dimensional space. Whether you use modeling clay, paper, cardboard, foam core, wood, epoxy, plastic, or other materials, the goal here again is to explore many alternatives very quickly so that you can compare and contrast the best aspects of each possibility, consider blends of different approaches, and get a more visceral, physical sense of how these form factors might look and feel. (For an example of exploring ideas in a physical medium, using mostly rough-shaped clay and fiberglass models, review the Microsoft mouse example in Chapter 3.)

Using 3-D models is essential for building hardware or any kind of design for a physical object, but it is not a broad-purpose technique. An expert in designing 3-D objects (and all of the attendant complexities of structure, materials, function, and human factors) is called an industrial designer. So many technical details are involved in building a physical device of any sort that we strongly recommend that you employ a professional industrial designer.

Brainstorming techniques

Originally developed by marketing executive Alex Osborn in 1942,[7] brainstorming is a term that refers to a family of techniques that allow you to quickly generate a large number of ideas, usually taking advantage of the inherent diversity in a group of people. Unfortunately, the word "brainstorming" is often overloaded in its use and can refer to anything from sending email with some ideas to a couple of people, to chatting out by the water cooler, to a formalized ideation session with a facilitator.

When we begin the process of adapting our workshop for a new team, we first try to assess what iteration, research, and creativity techniques the team already embraces. It's been interesting to us to observe that virtually every team reports that they already engage in brainstorming activities. But, when we dig in, we soon discover that few teams have the knowledge (never mind the disciplined practice) of engaging in actual brainstorming techniques, other than in the loosest sense of the term.

 VOCAB

> *Brainstorming* is a family of structured, idea-generation techniques that can be used to generate a large set of divergent ideas for a given stimulus.

Group brainstorming

The classic brainstorming technique is to gather a group of people in a room and spend anywhere from 20 minutes to a couple of hours focused on generating ideas for a given topic. Meet in a comfortable place with lots of whiteboard space, have a facilitator to keep the conversation moving forward, and have a scribe write down all the ideas. Use your chosen scenario as the topic, and strive to fill the whiteboard with ideas. Sounds simple enough, but it's actually quite challenging if you've never done it before in a structured way. However, when it is done well, group brainstorming can be a tremendously valuable source of creative input to the Fast Feedback Cycle.

We go into detail about how to facilitate and lead a group brainstorming session in the "Deep dive" section later in this chapter.

Quietstorming

One piece of feedback we get about the "send a message" brainstorming exercise in our workshop is that it's not always fun for introverts. Verbalizing ideas doesn't get the creative juices flowing for some people, and we are sometimes asked questions like:

> *"I'm an introvert and I'm not comfortable shouting out my ideas that way. I like to think alone and mull things over. Does that mean I can't participate well in group ideation?"*

Given that many talented engineers lean toward being introverted, this is a great question to ponder. And while a traditional group brainstorming session is a valuable technique, it does tend to be more comfortable for extroverts and for people who are comfortable speaking off the top of their head. With people and teams who may be more introverted, you might generate more ideas if participants write down their ideas instead of speaking them out loud. It's also true that many of these people appreciate the opportunity to bounce ideas around with others, but only after they've had some time to gather their thoughts first. There are alternative ways to running a brainstorming session that rely less on extemporaneous talking but still take advantage of a diverse team's fresh brains. We call these variations *quietstorming*.

Here are a few quietstorming techniques you can try:

- **Entry tickets**   Have each participant show up with three to seven ideas as their ticket to enter the brainstorming session. Go around the room and have each person share his or her ideas. Allow others to jump in, and encourage piggybacking and new ideas to emerge. However, be sure to postpone judgment and discussion of the ideas until later; this is still about generating lots of ideas, not about investigating them.

- **Start with quiet time**   Set aside a specific amount of time at the beginning of the session for each participant to quietly write down his or her initial ideas, each on its own sticky note. Usually 5–10 minutes is plenty. Then, go around the room and ask participants to share those ideas one by one, and riff away. As each idea is presented, place the sticky note on a large piece of butcher paper on the wall to create a dynamic map of ideas, grouping similar ideas near each other. It's best to have each person share one idea at a time so that the latter part of the session doesn't degenerate into a "readout" of each person's private (and usually long) brainstorming list, which does not encourage piggyback ideas to emerge. When someone mentions an idea that another person also wrote down (or mentions a cousin idea of some sort), that person should speak up and go next.

- **Pass the paper**   Have the participants sit around a table, and give each person a piece of paper. Set a timer for a couple of minutes. Everyone then writes down a few ideas, and when the timer sounds, passes their paper to the left. Next, each person reads the ideas on the sheet they received, adds their thoughts to that list (stimulated by what is already there), and again passes to the left. Continue this for several rounds.

- **Computer mediated**   Use an online chat room, an instant messaging group, or other electronic tool in which many individuals can type their ideas in a visible, sequential way, each at his or her own computer. This technique is particularly good for large groups. It's impractical for more than about 20 people to brainstorm in a room without talking over one another or having to wait for a turn to talk, but they can all type at the same time. It's also a good approach for a distributed team that isn't located together. A computer-mediated approach can also mitigate some of the cultural issues that can impede group brainstorming, with its perceived anonymity and the emotional safety of typing rather than speaking. However, this technique does not work well for ideas that are better expressed with a quick sketch, an out-loud verbal description, or pantomime.

- **Solicit ideas over time**   Set up ways for customers, partners, or employees to submit a cool idea whenever it occurs to them, and leverage those ideas as inspiration when exploring alternatives. In this way you can create a pipeline of ideas that can incorporate the thinking of a large organization or community of users. However, expect that many of the ideas you capture in this way will not align with your business strategy, target customer, or chosen scenarios, especially if you do not limit ideas to a particular topic or challenge, so be careful that you don't get blown off track chasing a shiny object. Even so, some of the ideas will align with your goals, and occasionally one of these ideas might help uncover a potential customer need you hadn't noticed yet that inspires your future plans.

Individual brainstorming

A few techniques worth mentioning work best for individuals to generate ideas on their own. Of course, these can be used together with the more group-oriented ideas, but they tend to be better suited to individuals or a very small group.

- **Mindmapping** A mindmap is a popular way to brainstorm ideas, where you create a visual record of which ideas are connected to others as you brainstorm. Figure 7-5 shows an example.

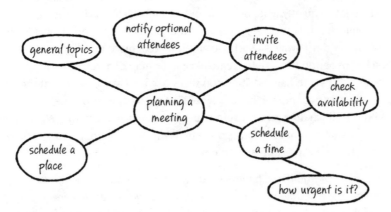

FIGURE 7-5 A simple mindmap. Large mindmaps can easily become complex enough to cover a large sheet of butcher paper.

- **Stream of consciousness** Write down your ideas as quickly as possible in a narrative form and don't stop—write down whatever pops into your head. If you prefer, you can do this orally, record the audio, and transcribe it later.

- **Keep a notebook** Keep a notebook with you at all times, and jot down ideas whenever they occur to you. If you see an interesting idea in the world, note it or draw a quick sketch of what you found interesting. If you wake up at 3:00 a.m. with a brilliant idea, note it and go back to sleep. You get the idea. Later, flipping through your notebook during a brainstorming activity can help trigger ideas for you.

- **Don't ignore serendipity** A chance meeting with an expert, an unusual flyer in your mailbox, a coincidental situation that helps you see from a new perspective can all provide unexpected inspiration. Be ready and open for what ideas are looking for you, and when a great opportunity happens to come by, don't be shy—speak up, ask questions, get involved— it might just be the missing piece you've been looking for.

Supercharging your idea generation

A few powerful techniques can help supercharge your idea generation. These techniques encourage diverse ideas and ensure that you don't miss anything obvious. They all work on the principle of shifting your perspective to look at problems from a different direction.

Practically speaking, these techniques are most useful when you start feeling dry, when you reach a point where you feel like you can't think of any more ideas. Whether you are in the middle of a raucous brainstorming session, quietstorming on paper, molding with clay, or sketching out storyboards, try one of these techniques when you get stuck to look at the problem from a different perspective.

Especially if you can suspend disbelief for a while and encourage wild ideas, these techniques can often open up a whole new line of thinking.

Lateral thinking techniques

First introduced by Edward de Bono in the 1960s, lateral thinking techniques are tools specifically designed to encourage more lateral jumps in your idea generation.[8] They force you to look at a problem from an unusual perspective, in a sense tricking your brain into looking at the same problem in a radically different way. By turning the problem upside down or inside out, you increase the chances that you will see a connection or notice a new way of approaching it that you may not have found by looking at the problem straight ahead.

Here are our favorite lateral thinking techniques that we call on again and again in our work with teams:

- **Challenge assumptions** Our example from earlier in the chapter about designing a coffee cup without a bottom is based on challenging a basic assumption about your problem space. What other kinds of assumptions can you challenge? Let's say you're building a user interface. Could you do it without asking the user to type anything? Could you build a website that never required the customer to log in? Could you build a compute-intensive game without using any local computer CPU? Remember, the point of challenging assumptions isn't to impose that restriction on your final solution. But by attempting to solve the problem in a more constrained space, you might notice a new approach that wouldn't have otherwise occurred to you.

- **Random input and association** Open the dictionary and pick a random word. Or use one of the random word generators you'll find on the Internet, built for this purpose (yes, they exist!). Force yourself to find an association between the word that comes up and your chosen problem. Sometimes (but not always) that association will open up a new way of thinking about your problem. For example, how is a company's performance review process like a canoe? Well, it involves two people, one who does the paddling, and one who does the steering, and if either person rocks the boat, the whole thing capsizes.

- **Reversal** This is one of our favorite techniques because it is so easy to do. Instead of brainstorming against the chosen problem, brainstorm against the opposite problem. For example, ideas could run dry pretty quickly if the problem is "design a great emergency room." However, if you turn the problem around and brainstorm all the ways you can make an emergency room terrible, the ideas flow like a geyser. Make the patients wait forever. Make the chairs uncomfortable. Give the patients nothing to do or nothing to look at. Insist on complete quiet. Keep it dirty. And so on. Now reverse those ideas and make sure that you are solving all of those problems.

There are many, many lateral thinking techniques besides these, as well as other resources available to develop lateral flexibility, from puzzles and games to workshops and worksheets. Just search for "lateral thinking," and you'll find tons of interesting options to try out.

SCAMPER

SCAMPER is an acronym that stands for Substitute, Combine, Adapt, Modify, Put to another use, Eliminate, and Reverse. It was invented by Bob Eberle, though it includes many ideas that were part of Alex Osborn's original conception of brainstorming. Very similar to lateral thinking techniques, each of the keywords within SCAMPER encourages you to modify your thinking in various ways to help you see other solution approaches. For instance, "Substitute" might trigger you to wonder whether there is a way to substitute an existing product for the one you're proposing to build, or if you might substitute a different type of material for the one you are considering. You can find many listings of SCAMPER-inspired questions on the Internet.

Six thinking hats

Six thinking hats is another idea developed by Edward de Bono. Each hat encourages you to look at a problem from one of six different perspectives. It is a helpful technique to ensure that you don't miss anything obvious and are complete in your exploration. Like the lateral thinking techniques, it can help get you moving again when you feel like your idea generation is slowing down.

The idea is to "wear" each of the six different color hats when exploring a problem: for example, the white hat focuses on gathering information, the red hat focuses on hunches or intuition, and the black hat plays devil's advocate. One of the benefits of devoting a specific block of time to each hat is that it limits a group from falling into habitual thought patterns, such as always playing devil's advocate, and forces the group to consider each of the perspectives in turn. A good description of the six thinking hats and training is available from the de Bono group at http://www.debonogroup.com/.

Turning the corner: Deciding which ideas to move forward

Once you've spent some time diverging and creating a pile of ideas, it's easy to get lost or even overwhelmed. Which ideas are the best ones? Do you start with the sketches or the brainstorming list? How do you pick the ideas to move forward with? Are any of the ideas any good? Are there patterns? Can you combine some to create something new and even more interesting?

Just as you did at the end of the Observe stage (see Chapter 5, "Observing customers: Building empathy"), when you had mountains of data (in that case, from research about customers), it's again time to *converge* and make some decisions about which ideas are the most promising. Several techniques can help you turn the corner and start sorting through and making sense of all the ideas you've generated, and this will help you forge a path forward.

The basic idea is to cull your list of ideas, identify a few that seem most promising for supporting your business, technical, and experience goals, and use those as input for the next stage of the Fast Feedback Cycle. In the next stage, you will rapidly prototype to flesh out those ideas just enough that you can get some customer feedback. Your goal here is not to pick a single idea to move forward with, but to winnow your list down to several good alternatives that you can rapidly prototype and then see how customers respond. Here are some approaches to help you figure out which ideas to move forward with.

Write it down

You can make the decision process a lot easier by being sure to write down your ideas all along, and archive them in a reasonable way. Use something as lightweight as a manila file folder full of sticky notes, or a folder in the cloud where you plunk all your notes, sketches, and photographs of whiteboards. Generally speaking, doing a lot of data entry and organization is not terribly useful at this stage, so keep it effective but lightweight. The important goal is to be able to scan through your ideas in one place. You don't want to have to dig around to locate them or, worse, try to recall your ideas from memory. You want these lists, sketches, and notes easily available because you might use them later for inspiration or to reconsider some alternatives if you find that your initial approaches aren't working as well as you hoped.

One particularly efficient way to capture ideas is to write them on sticky notes, one idea per note; for larger sketches, keep each sketch on a single sheet of paper. Whether you are sketching storyboards or flow charts, brainstorming ideas verbally, quietstorming, drawing mindmaps, or doing anything in between, putting each idea on its own piece of paper makes a lot of the processing we're about to talk about a ton easier. Sure, you can always transcribe each idea onto a sticky note later for sorting, but if you keep your notes on individual sticky notes in the first place, you'll maximize your overall efficiency.

Consider the feasibility

You are narrowing down a pile of ideas. It's time to get real. You need to take a hard look at the feasibility of those ideas, both for the technology involved (Can it be built and at a reasonable cost?) and for your business (Is it competitive; will anyone pay for it?). The first thing to do is sort out your ideas a bit so that you can see which ideas align to your business strategy, which support a great customer experience within your chosen scenario, and which are most feasible to build with available technology. The most promising ideas are those that support all three. Having a great customer experience supported by reasonable technology will get you nowhere if no one pays for it. Having a great business model and a terrific customer experience won't work either if the technology isn't reliable. You really need all three. Deciding which ideas to move forward with is the trigger to start bringing business and technology thinking into the solution and design process.

But this is not the time to do in-depth competitive analyses of each possible alternative, or to do serious development costing either—there are still too many ideas to consider. However, this is a good time to include a few senior people who can offer a rough judgment of whether a particular idea aligns with the business strategy or would support a compelling marketing message. In particular, you want people who can quickly identify ideas that are in direct conflict with your business plan. You should also include some senior technologists who can say whether an idea appears to be reasonably feasible. Ideas that are patently impossible or are in conflict with your strategy should be culled from active consideration.

One way to get this sort of input on the technical side is to do T-shirt-size estimations. For example, estimate whether a particular idea is small, medium, or large, where each size is an order of magnitude larger than the previous one. Small might mean that an idea could be implemented in an amount of time measured in days. Medium means it would take weeks, and large would be an investment of months. You'll be tempted to use extra-small for teeny-tiny ideas that are smaller than small, and extra-large for ideas that seem so impossibly huge that they appear to be unbounded. You can add these sizes if you like, but the intent is to keep it simple because these estimates should not be considered binding. Rather, they are very quick shorthand to help engineers convey to their leaders and the broader team the order of magnitude of work that is likely to be needed to deliver an idea.

 ## MINDSHIFT

T-shirt-size costing without guilt. Engineers often get quite nervous about T-shirt estimates because they don't have nearly enough data to make a true estimate at this stage in the process and do not want to have to guess. They rightly argue that many ideas can be implemented "the easy way," with minimal configuration and customization, or they can be implemented "the complicated way," with specialized algorithms, custom animations, and other added complexity. At this stage in the process, no one has any idea where on that continuum delivery of the final experience will be. On top of this, engineers really don't like being wrong, and they worry about the consequences of a bad estimate. They worry if they say that an idea is small but turns out to be much more involved than they realized that the team will hold them to that estimate, they'll be perpetually behind schedule, and they'll be blamed for slipping the schedule. It's no wonder that engineers are resistant to T-shirt-size costing.

The trick to making T-shirt-size costing work is never to use T-shirt estimates for building schedules and never hold individuals accountable to these estimates. The only value of a T-shirt-size estimate is to get a rough idea about whether an approach is buildable at all— to ensure that you are focusing on ideas that balance business, experience, and technology. Sometimes the answer is to give a range of sizes. To know that an idea is somewhere between medium and large is still useful information for prioritization.

If T-shirt-size estimates continue to give your engineering team heartburn, you could switch to using a yes/no format: yes, the idea is buildable; no, the idea is not buildable. However, in practice, almost everything is buildable given enough time, so the yes/no format leaves valuable information out of the equation. An order of magnitude of time is a pretty good proxy for technical complexity as long as you don't try to add more precision than that.

And, of course, we all know from long experience that estimates, even from the most senior engineers, tend to be wrong. It's a good bet to assume that everything will take longer than you imagine. That's another good reason to not use a T-shirt-size estimate for more than a super-quick gut check, which is after all, what it is.

A particularly productive way for a group of engineers to do T-shirt-size estimation is to have them vote in real time as a group. That way, no single person is responsible for the estimate, which helps reduce anxiety, and voting as a group also takes into consideration factors from different perspectives. The way to vote it is to announce an item, and then on

"Go" everyone holds up one (small), three (medium), or five (large) fingers to express their judgment for that item. If there are disagreements, the people with the largest or smallest estimates explain their reasoning, which sometimes brings an important consideration to the foreground, and usually a group consensus is quickly reached.

Affinity diagramming redux

Another helpful way to make sense of a large pile of ideas is to sort them into an affinity diagram. Just as with customer data, you can group ideas into ones that are similar to each other and see which buckets emerge. Having each idea on a separate piece of paper or sticky note makes this process dramatically easier. You can build an affinity diagram with ideas that are primarily textual, primarily sketches, or a mix. There is a detailed description of affinity diagramming in Chapter 5.

But affinitizing solution ideas has some differences from working with customer needs. With customer needs, an important channel of information is the size of the affinity group, which serves as a proxy for how loudly that need was heard. When you group solution ideas, even a category with one idea may turn out to be the most valuable. So don't pay too much attention to group size this time.

The primary value of an affinity diagram of solution ideas is to collapse into a single group all the ideas that are essentially variants of the same concept. Doing this helps show you which ideas are meaningfully different from one another. You want to avoid moving forward with several ideas that are really just cousins and are too similar. Rather, you want a diverse set so that you explore the solution space and give yourself the best mathematical odds at finding an optimal solution. Pick one approach (or a blend) from each of the most promising groupings to move into the next stage of the Fast Feedback Cycle.

Look for the blends

As you generate ideas, you should always be on the lookout for ways to blend or combine ideas to come up with a new approach or to improve an aspect of a given idea. Similarly, as you look over your ideas, you may notice blends that you didn't before. It's totally fair and, in fact, a really good practice, to propose that an idea you move forward into the next stage be a combination of one idea with another.

Update the museum

If you built a museum from your customer data in a room or a hallway, this is a good time to update it with the solution ideas from your brainstorming. Seeing multiple ideas in a single eyeful, walking by them every day on the way to the elevator, and exposing everyone to new ideas generated by other members of the team can all be helpful for making connections and noticing possible blends. An affinity diagram lends itself nicely to being posted in a hallway or other museum location.

Updating your museum is also a great way to collect feedback and focus attention on the latest ideas. Tack up pens and sticky notes so that passersby can add comments. You might be surprised at how often leaders (who are so pressed for time) walk by such a museum, have something catch their eye, ponder the wall, and leave comments or contact you in email. Think of your museum as a manager glue trap, except you aren't catching mice.

Collective decision making

Now that you've sorted and culled, you need to make some decisions about which ideas are the most promising and which should be moved forward into the next stage of the Fast Feedback Cycle. In collaborative project teams, usually no single person is charged with making the decision about which ideas move forward. The team is expected to come to consensus on most decisions and involve their managers or other leaders only at a significant decision point or if an irreconcilable disagreement occurs. This is generally a good thing because it means that you rely on the diversity of the team to make better-quality decisions. However, consensus-based decision making can also be very slow, and if there are strong opinions on the team, it can be hard to break a tie. (We discuss some techniques below that can make this easier.)

It's also really important at this point to be sure that you're getting input from stakeholders about all three key aspects of your project's success: business, technology, and customer experience. Be sure to involve people familiar with these areas in your decision making and use their background and insights to judge what will work best in the area of their expertise. Remember that a product that is terrific in two areas—say technology and experience—but weak in the third, will not be a commercial success. You are looking for ideas that resonate with all three areas: business, technology, and experience.

Here are a few tips and techniques that can be helpful in making collective decisions. Typically, these are not used for major strategy decisions but to unblock forward progress in an uncertain world, where no one on the team is entirely certain about the best course of action. But you won't know more until you do more iterating, so you need to pick some seeds to start with.

- First, realize that especially in the first few iterations of the Fast Feedback Cycle, you should not choose a single best idea to move forward with. Rather, you typically select three to five alternatives that seem the most promising to flesh out in more detail. Ideally, these ideas represent a range of relatively safe ideas as well as more novel or risky approaches. It's a lot easier to narrow and winnow to a small set than to decide on exactly one approach.

- This is not a one-time decision. Very quickly, you will get customer feedback, and if none of the first ideas pan out, you will have the opportunity to try some others in your next iteration.

- Keep the focus on ideas, not on people. The point is about trying to find the optimal solution for your customers' problem; it's not about having your idea win. It's actually best if the team takes the attitude that no individual is the owner or the creator of any of the ideas.

- If your team is relatively small and each member was personally part of every step in the idea-generation process, making a decision may be as easy as a quick conversation that reaches consensus about the most interesting ideas that emerged.

- If consensus does not come easily, dot voting is a very popular and easy way to use the diversity of a group to make better decisions. Allow a wide variety of people on the team to vote for their favorite alternatives, and then see which items get the most votes. You can do this with a whiteboard full of ideas or with a preculled list of the top 10 or 20 ideas. Give everyone on the team a small number of colored sticky dots (or a marker to draw their own), and ask them to put a dot next to the three or five ideas that they think are the most promising. It's helpful if the dots are somewhat anonymous—that is, show what you voted simply by marking a dot rather than by signing your initials or your name. Even when a discussion appears contentious, a dot-voting exercise can usually help the team settle on a path forward. The dots show where the real consensus is, which may be a bit different from what the most emphatic debaters are pushing for.

- Another way to get quick group consensus on a list of issues is to use your thumb. Announce an idea, and have people point thumbs up to indicate that they like that idea or thumbs down to indicate they don't (point sideways to show indifference or indecision). This works best on a team with a high degree of trust and for a decision that is not particularly contentious.

Deep dive: Group brainstorming

There's nothing quite like a good brainstorming session to generate a bunch of great ideas and elevate the energy of a team. Maybe you already engage in some level of brainstorming. Even so, this section is still worth reading. To get the most from your brainstorming, it's important to understand and follow some rules and guidelines.

Follow the ground rules

A set of "brainstorming ground rules" is commonly credited to IDEO, a design consultancy that's well known for using creative techniques to solve very difficult problems for their clients. The core of these guidelines dates back to the 1950s, when advertising executive Alex Osborn published the book *Applied Imagination*. These rules have since been widely circulated and adopted throughout the business world, and they have stayed remarkably true to Osborn's original list.

Brainstorming Rules
- Stay focused on the topic
- Go for quantity
- Defer judgment
- One conversation at a time
- Build on the ideas of others
- Encourage wild ideas
- Be physical or visual

Although these rules were conceived for brainstorming sessions, we believe they represent broad principles that apply to any sort of exercise whose main goal is idea generation, whether that's a raucous group brainstorming session at a whiteboard, a quiet sharing of ideas around a table, a sketch-fest, or a storyboarding exercise. Posting and following these rules helps create an environment that keeps the focus on generating ideas and helps postpone the onset of tunnel vision.

- **Stay focused on the topic**   A productive idea-generation exercise has a clear topic in mind, an open-ended question that has plenty of room for alternatives but isn't so broad in scope as to be unwieldy. A scenario, user journey, customer outcome, or technical challenge all work well as a starting topic. Keep idea generation from drifting too far off topic to ensure that you use your time to fully explore the given problem space.

- **Go for quantity**   Your goal at this stage is to generate lots and lots of ideas. Success for a brainstorming session should be measured purely by the number of ideas generated in a given amount of time. IDEO recommends numbering your ideas as they are captured to reinforce this goal and also setting an explicit target number to reach in a given amount of time. Sixty to a hundred ideas per hour is considered a good rate.

- **Defer judgment**   Originally stated by Osborn as "No criticism of ideas," this principle goes hand in hand with quantity. At this stage, your goal is lots of ideas, regardless of whether those ideas are any good. Wait until later to decide which ideas you will move forward with. Criticizing ideas, even in very subtle ways, can be extremely destructive to the activity, and will quickly stifle enthusiasm and keep participants from contributing for fear of critique.

- **One conversation at a time**   This practice is needed both to capture an accurate record of all the ideas generated and so that participants hear every idea and can be stimulated by them.

- **Build on the ideas of others**   Piggybacking, or building on another participant's idea, is expressly encouraged. In this way ideas bounce around the room and are often greatly shaped by this exchange. Ideas developed this way have no clear ownership, which is very desirable both for cultivating team buy-in and for discouraging personal ownership, which can impede collaboration. Be careful, however, that building ideas on one another aims at generating new variants or combinations of ideas, not just digging into the details of an idea, which can lead to tunnel vision.

- **Encourage wild ideas**   Creating a playful environment and team culture that explicitly encourages wild, impractical, or exaggerated ideas is ironically one of the most powerful ways to supercharge idea generation, as these unusual ideas can sometimes lead to a breakthrough that no one had ever considered before. This is critical behavior to develop, yet it is also one of the hardest for practicality-focused engineers to become comfortable with.

- **Be visual (or physical)**   Don't be afraid to sketch a picture, act out an idea, or grab a few items in the room to mock up a quick physical prototype. Sometimes words aren't the best medium with which to capture an idea. A rich, flexible environment, with toys, models, materials, and lots of drawing surfaces, helps stimulate ideas and the demonstration of ideas in other modes.

Facilitating a group brainstorming session

The secret to a successful brainstorming session is a great facilitator. With a skilled facilitator, a brainstorming session can be hugely productive, even with a fairly novice group of participants. However, with a poor or inexperienced facilitator, a session can easily go south for any number of factors. Here are the most important things for a facilitator to keep in mind:

- **Pick an appropriate space**   The environment can do a lot to both shape the mood and encourage divergent ideas. An informal room with couches and wall-to-wall whiteboards sets a mood quite different from a conference room dominated by a long table. Both environments can work, but we prefer using a more informal space when possible. Bring in physical artifacts that can serve as jumping-off points, inspiration for ideas, or fodder to explain an idea. These might be office supplies or even toys, such as Legos, building blocks, or plastic figurines. You may also bring in items related to your specific problem space, such as photos of your target customers or posters containing key insights from your research.

- **Invite the right people**   Get a good mix of experience, disciplines, backgrounds, and perspectives on the problem. Consider not including the manager or leader of the effort if their presence might prevent people from contributing wild ideas, especially until a brainstorming culture is well developed within the team. Keep in mind that given the limitation of 1 person talking at a time, having more than about 20 people in a room makes it hard for everyone to participate fully. For larger groups, schedule multiple sessions or encourage team members to vote with their feet to attend brainstorming sessions on certain topics but not others, based on their interests and passions.

- **Set the mood**   A productive brainstorming session is playful, informal, open to new ideas, and absolutely welcoming of every person and every idea, no matter how seemingly outlandish. Getting this wrong is the single biggest reason a brainstorming session fails—participants are unwilling to contribute because they fear criticism or worry that people will think their ideas are foolish.

- **Set the ground rules and enforce them**   Post rules visibly (see "Follow the ground rules," earlier). Firmly correct and redirect any comments that don't follow the rules, paying particular attention to anything that could be interpreted as even a subtle criticism. If left unchecked, this can cause many people to clam up and dramatically impact the effectiveness of the activity.

- **Keep the group focused on the chosen topic**   Start the session by reminding everyone who your target customer is and the scenario or problem statement. As the conversation progresses, allow some leeway for tangents, as sometimes these can be productive sources of alternative approaches and creative ideas, but a facilitator needs to be ready to pull the conversation back if it strays too far afield for more than a few minutes.

- **Capture every idea in a visible way**   Some facilitators will keep a running list by writing each idea on the whiteboard as it is contributed. Others will delegate the job to someone else, who writes on the whiteboard or types on a laptop that is projected onto a screen. Sometimes participants or a scribe capture each idea on a sticky note and post that on the wall or on butcher paper. If the idea is presented in visual form, the contributor should be the one sketching it on a sticky note or the whiteboard to capture it. The important thing is to capture all ideas so that everyone can see them. As the session progresses, being able to point to a previous idea and notice a connection or a possible blend is a powerful way to generate additional ideas.

- **Keep the pace up**   Encourage a fast pace, and make sure that your scribe can keep up with the conversation. Speed encourages more flexible thinking and a greater likelihood of seeing connections between ideas. Don't go longer than about an hour of focused work—you just can't keep up the pace much longer than that.

- **Constantly offer the reminder, "How else could we solve this?"**   Remember that the goal of a brainstorm is to generate as many ideas as possible. The facilitator needs to be vigilant to ward off tunnel vision and to not allow the group to discuss any idea in too much detail. Keep pushing the group to look for new approaches. Assume that there is always another approach you haven't considered. Even if you don't see it at the moment, someone else in the room invariably will.

- **Welcome offbeat ideas**   If an offbeat idea comes up, the facilitator should be extra supportive to help people suspend disbelief and give it due consideration. Play with it, extend the idea, see where the thread leads. Especially with a team that is new to brainstorming, it's important for the facilitator to encourage wild ideas—to hold open the door for novel, out-of-the-box ideas to emerge.

- **Manage a dry spell**   If the conversation stalls, inject a provocative question or a lateral thinking technique to get things moving again. Generally speaking, it's best for the facilitator to not contribute ideas to the brainstorming session, especially at the beginning. If the facilitator offers ideas early in the session, it can set the wrong tone and encourage people to sit back and let the facilitator take the lead rather than have everyone jump in and contribute. However, later in the session, if the well starts running dry, the facilitator might inject an unusual, thought-provoking idea to help get things moving again.

- **Save decisions for later**   Don't end a brainstorming session with a discussion or decision on which ideas will get pursued. And certainly don't allow tradeoff conversations to arise in the middle of your idea generation. Those are just other ways to judge ideas, and we know what happens when you unintentionally introduce judgment and criticism into brainstorming. Focus this time just on idea generation. Schedule a separate time to sort through them, make sense of your work, and pick a few ideas to flesh out in the next stage of the Fast Feedback Cycle.

- **Make sure the results get used**   One of the biggest problems with even a productive brainstorming session is that the results get forgotten or sidelined. Perhaps only one idea was actually chosen to move forward with, and the rest were forgotten. Or worse, the brainstorming session was a token activity to appease the team when the real plan was generated behind closed doors by the senior leaders, and may have little relationship to the brainstorming activity or its results. This is a sure way to tank any future attempts at brainstorming, not to mention team morale. Be sure results get saved in an accessible location. Be sure that they are used, both in the current iteration as well as when they're needed for inspiration in future iterations of the Fast Feedback Cycle. Communicate back to the participants how the ideas were used and what the next steps are.

Concluding a brainstorming session

You can use the end of a brainstorming session to get the opinions of the people who attended. As people leave the room, have everyone vote for three to five of the ideas that seem most promising to them. A vote could be as simple as a check mark on the whiteboard, or ideas can be flagged with a sticky note or a colored label. These votes aren't meant to be binding, but they help alert the facilitator or the owner of the decision area to promising ideas that might merit further investigation and more detailed exploration.

SFE in action: In defense of brainstorming

Scott Berkun, best-selling author of The Myths of Innovation (http://www.scottberkun.com)[9]

Periodically, popular articles arise decrying how flawed brainstorming is. Jonah Lehrer wrote a popular article in *The New Yorker*, "Groupthink: The Brainstorming Myth," but there have been, and will be, many others. Most of these articles have poor frameworks, miscasting what brainstorming was designed to do and how ideas in workplaces are actually developed.

I have no stake in brainstorming as a formalized thing. Even in my essay "How to Run a Brainstorming Meeting," I explain its strengths and weaknesses. It's a method, and I've studied many idea-generation methods. If done properly, in the right conditions, some of them help. I'm not bothered by valid critiques of any of them. However, sweeping claims based on bad logic and careless thinking need to be addressed.

Here are four key things Lehrer doesn't mention, which shatter his conclusion:

- Nothing matters if the room is filled with fools or strangers (or both). If you fill a room with thoughtless people who do not know each other, no method can help you. The method you pick is not as important as the quality of people in the room. The most important step in a brainstorming session is picking who will participate (based on intelligence, group chemistry, diversity, etc.). No method can instantly make fools smart, the dull creative, or acquaintances intimate. The people in [Charlan] Nemeth's research study, the one heavily referenced by Lehrer, had never met each other before and were chosen at random. A very different environment than any workplace.

- Brainstorming is designed for idea volume, not depth or quality. [Alex] Osborn's (the inventor of brainstorming) intention was to help groups create a long list of ideas in a short amount of time. The assumption was that a smaller group would review, critique, and debate, later on. He believed most work cultures are repressive, not open to ideas, and the primary thing needed was a safe zone, where the culture could be different. He believed if the session was led well, a positive and supportive attitude helped make a larger list of ideas. Osborn believed critique and criticism were critical, but there should be a (limited) period of time where critique is postponed. Other methods may generate more ideas than brainstorming, but that doesn't mean brainstorming fails at its goals.

- The person leading an idea-generation session matters. Using a technique is only as good as the person leading it. In Nemeth's research study, cited in Lehrer's article, there was no leader. Undergraduates were given a short list of instructions: that was the entirety of their training. Doing a "brainstorm" run by an fool, or a smart person who has no skill at it, will disappoint. This is not a scientific evaluation of a method. It's like saying "brain surgery is a sham; it doesn't work," based not on using trained surgeons, but instead undergraduates who were placed behind the operating table for the first time. (See Scott G. Isaksen and John P. Gaulin, "A Reexamination of Brainstorming Research: Implications for Research and Practice," http://www.cpsb.com/research/articles/creative-problem-solving/Reexamination-of-Brainstorming-Research.pdf.)

- Generating ideas is a small part of the process. The hard part in creative work isn't idea generation. It's making the hundreds of decisions needed to bring an idea to fruition as a product or thing. Brainstorming is an idea-generation technique and nothing more. No project ends when a brainstorming session ends, it's just beginning. Lehrer assumes that better idea generation guarantees better output of breakthrough ideas, but this is far from true. Many organizations have dozens of great ideas but fail to bring those ideas into active projects, or to bring those active projects successfully into the market.

Brainstorm stage: How do you know when you are done?

The Brainstorm stage is critical for generating and exploring many diverse ideas, giving you the best chance at hitting on a truly optimal solution that balances your business needs and technical abilities and delivers a great customer experience.

There are lots of techniques you can use to generate ideas, from brainstorming, to sketching storyboards, to modeling with clay. No matter which techniques you use, you know you are ready for the next stage when you have generated:

- A collection of the alternatives you have generated, which represent a dozen (or perhaps lots more) meaningfully different approaches to solving your problem or scenario, not just cousins of the same basic idea. Your collection should include some sketches or other visualizations, not just lists of words, and be archived in a lightweight way that you can refer to in future iterations.

- Three to five alternatives chosen from that larger collection as the most promising, which warrant deeper exploration in the next stage.

The good news is that the Brainstorm stage is the stage in the Fast Feedback Cycle that likely needs the least amount of total time investment. With as little as a few concerted hours of idea generation, you should be ready to move on to the next stage and start prototyping your most promising ideas so that you see whether they actually resonate with customers the way you thought they might.

Notes

1. Sam Biddle, "The Guy Who Invented Your Facebook News Feed Just Quit Facebook," Gizmodo, June 15, 2012, http://gizmodo.com/5918852/the-guy-who-invented-your-facebook-news-feed-just-quit-facebook; Farhad Manjoo, "Facebook News Feed Changed Everything," *Slate*, September 12, 2013, http://www.slate.com/articles/technology/technology/2013/09/facebook_news_feed_turns_7_why_it_s_the_most_influential_feature_on_the.html; http://en.wikipedia.org/wiki/Facebook.

2. Alexia Tsotsis, "Facebook's 'Like' Button Used to Be the 'Awesome' Button," TechCrunch, October 5, 2010, http://techcrunch.com/2010/10/05/awesome-this-post/; Om Malik, "Why Facebook Wants FriendFeed," August 10, 2009, http://gigaom.com/2009/08/10/why-facebook-wants-friend-feed/.

3. Pitney-Bowes judged that these would be a precursor to the paperless society, which would have deep implications to their core business of selling postage meters and paper-handling equipment for the mailroom and the post office.

4. Pauling was awarded the Nobel Prize in Chemistry in 1954 and the Peace Prize in 1962. Marie S. Curie also won two prizes, but she shared one of them (the Nobel Prize in Physics in 1903). http://www.nobelprize.org/nobel_prizes/peace/laureates/1962/pauling-bio.html#not_1.

5. Arguably, the complex problems we solve have many more dimensions, but that's tough to visualize, and three dimensions illustrate this concept well enough.

6. Stretching the analogy further, one could say that the complex plane is changing over time. What was an optimal solution five years ago is no longer as noteworthy, as new technologies and possibilities enter the market. Disruption becomes possible when a new global maximum appears that is not noticed by the incumbent.

7. Alex F. Osborn, Applied Imagination (New York, Scribner, 1979).

8. Edward de Bono, *The Use of Lateral Thinking* (London: Cape, 1967).

9. The full article is available at http://scottberkun.com/2012/in-defense-of-brainstorming-2/. A related article ("In Defense of Brainstorming") is at http://scottberkun.com/2007/in-defense-of-brainstorming/. You can read Lehrer's original article at http://www.newyorker.com/magazine/2012/01/30/groupthink.

Get used to showing
work early

BUILD MULTIPLE PROTOTYPES

Low-fidelity prototypes

IN PARALLEL

mockups

Make data-driven decisions

skits

Fail fast **BUILD** Your first design won't be perfect

Look for the blends Several potential solutions

Experiment! Don't let elegance win out over
customer needs **RAPID PROTOTYPING** **reduce risk**

Write code in slices Cheapest way to answer a question

**OPEN BOOK,
CLOSE BOOK** **Prototype with code** Minimize wasted effort

Paper prototyping PAY ME NOW OR
PAY ME LATER Expect to iterate

IMPLEMENTATION SPIKES WIREFRAMES

POWERPOINT PROTOTYPES **High-fidelity prototypes**

CHAPTER 8

Building prototypes and coding

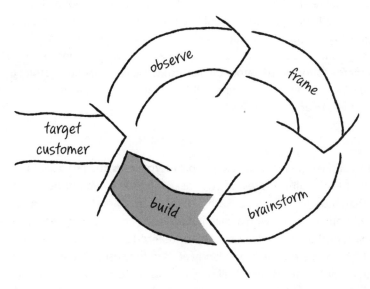

You've done the work to brainstorm a bunch of promising ideas. And you've narrowed those down to a few that you believe have the greatest potential for success. In this stage of the Fast Feedback Cycle, you turn those ideas into something concrete that a customer can see, use, feel, and experience—and then you test it to see whether you're on the right track. Until you actually try out an idea on real people, you won't know whether it will work or how good an idea it really is.

The key in this stage is to build out a few of your ideas as quickly and efficiently as you possibly can. This stage completes one trip around the Fast Feedback Cycle and gets you ready to start the next iterative cycle. The first step in that cycle is to show your customers what you've built and to get feedback, launching you into a continuous cycle of learning and improvement.

Experimentation: Make data-driven decisions

Here's a secret the professors probably didn't tell you in engineering school: failure is okay. As a matter of fact, failure is more than okay when you're doing it with a purpose, to learn. Learning what doesn't work is just as valuable as knowing what does work, especially in dealing with the complex, nuanced customer needs you are likely trying to satisfy. When you experiment as a scientist does, failure has a much different and more positive meaning; it is expected and desirable. At the beginning of a project, your understanding of the deep customer need is incomplete, so you have to experiment and learn, try and fail, and then try again in order to land on an optimal solution that solves your customer's needs. Your ideas may look great on paper, but will they work for real-life customers in the real world? In other words, you need to take an experimental approach to building software and use customer feedback to drive decisions every step of the way.

After all, wouldn't it be better to learn early on that customers don't really like what you're building, or only kind of like it (but still prefer your competitor's product), or that even though they love what you're building, they aren't willing to pay for it? Wouldn't it be nice to know this before you sink a lot of time and energy into creating your solution? And wouldn't it be nice to figure out which of your assumptions are wrong so that you can modify your approach as quickly as possible and still have the time, money, and energy to try again? Rather than investing weeks or months getting an idea coded and ready to ship, spend a few hours or days building a rapid prototype and then test it with customers to be sure that you're on the right track.

 ## MINDSHIFT

Expect to iterate. When you first present a concept, a prototype, or a build to a set of customers, don't think of it as the ultimate test of your design prowess and not be satisfied with anything less than a perfect outcome. Rather, think of every customer test as a learning opportunity that you enter into with a childlike curiosity, and expect to encounter rough spots and situations that you haven't noticed or realized before. What parts do your customers like? Which parts aren't really working yet? Are they using it the way you thought or does something different happen? Will they pay for it? Today? Would they like it better if you changed something? What are they telling you? By expecting imperfection, you leave room in your thinking to hear and learn from your customers' reactions.

By the same token, you should schedule your project knowing you will modify your plans as you learn. Building a project schedule that assumes your first design will work perfectly is a recipe for disaster. Have you ever worked on a project that shipped exactly what the first specification defined? Iteration will happen whether you like it or not. The point is whether you'll put yourself "behind schedule" and feel bad about it, or whether you've planned for iteration and left yourself some time to be nimble and respond to feedback.

Our advice: learn from experience. Don't be arrogant. Your first ideas probably won't work perfectly on the first go-around, so don't overinvest in production code or detailed prototypes until you have gotten some confirmation from customers that you're on the right track. Go into the process assuming that your plan is partially great and partially terrible—you just don't know which part is which yet. Make plans for feedback and iteration to figure this out.

Experimentation is fundamentally about gathering real, unbiased data to guide your decisions; it's about enabling data-driven decision making. Instead of relying on your own personal opinions and judgments about which alternative solutions will work the best, are most desirable, or have the best ease of use, get actual customer feedback into that feedback loop as much as possible. After all, you are not the target customer. You've already done a lot of customer research and observation, and you've used empathy for the customer to make well-informed decisions about the problem you want to solve and how to solve it. But this is just the beginning. For the remainder of your project you will use experimentation to continually gather feedback about how your target customers are responding to your work in progress, and you'll use that feedback to inform your decision making.

The best approach is to "fail fast." That is, if your idea is destined to fail, you want to learn that as quickly and efficiently as possible so that you can start on a better path right away. What you do not want to do is postpone failure, waiting until the product is complete, when you have already invested so much, before you realize that it won't work. Instead, test concepts and prototypes with customers as early as possible—even if you show only rough drawings or barely functional prototypes—to get directional feedback that lets you know what's working and what isn't.

Experimentation with rapid prototypes

The way that you get constant feedback and learning is by continually trying different ideas, seeing which ones work the best, and using that feedback to inform your next iteration. Sometimes you can do this easily by writing production code and testing with live users by running A/B tests or other real-time experiments. Often, however, it's much faster and more efficient to build out new ideas with lighter-weight approaches, such as paper prototypes, mockups, wireframes, implementation spikes, or other rapid prototyping approaches. You can even use a skit. (Really, you ask, a skit? Yeah, it sounds crazy, but you can prototype workflows and complicated processes by acting out the parts in a skit.) These rapid prototypes can help you determine much more quickly whether your ideas are on the right track for users, for the technology, and even for the business model. Customer feedback on your prototypes also gives you insights into both what customers find easy or confusing and why customers behave the way they do, which helps you refine your solution's usefulness and desirability as you iterate.

SFE in action: Getting early feedback changed direction

Bishara Kharoufeh, Principal Engineering Manager, Microsoft Dynamics

Several years ago, when we began thinking about the future goals for the Microsoft Dynamics product line, we knew we wanted to recognize the inflection point that was occurring in our industry toward cloud computing. Thinking about the possibilities of embracing the cloud immediately led many on the team to assume that we were going to write a mobile version of Dynamics for a smartphone. The team felt that creating a mobile version of Dynamics was an important business shift, but at the time we didn't know exactly what parts of the suite should be mobile, how to do it, or what the customers really wanted out of a mobile solution from us.

We did some initial research and identified a particular pain point about how long it takes to create a project that crosses organizational boundaries: getting a contract signed, setting it up, and getting work started even though the customer, account manager, and project manager are in different organizations. We wrote a short scenario for this customer problem and gave it the title "Prakash initiates a cross-organization project." The team did some focused brainstorming around this particular experience and came up with a promising set of both UI and technical solution ideas. One potential solution was to send the project manager (PM) a notification that the contract was signed and for the PM to then set up the project directly from his or her mobile device, no matter where the PM was at the time.

We quickly built a paper prototype based on the best of the current ideas. We were pretty excited by some of the ideas in this prototype and were ready to take it to some customers. In fact, we built three different prototypes for the customers to see—there was no shortage of brilliant ideas coming from the engineering team. The team was super excited to get validation that its ideas rocked and wanted to get on with fleshing out the real solution in code.

But we received some unexpected feedback. As we walked the customers through the flow of the paper prototype and asked them what they thought, the customers universally responded: *"Setting up a new project is too complicated to deal with on a small screen, with all these fields and actions I need to take. Really, I just need to know when the contract is signed. A text message would be perfect for that. Then I'll know that it's time for me to go set up the project, and I can get on it right away."*

We were fortunate that we received this very early feedback. Had we acted on the instincts and passion of the team, we would have headed down a path where we would have spent many months (or years) coding a complex mobile app, only to discover way too late that a much simpler and more delightful solution for our customer already existed: sending a simple text message.

Prototypes come in many flavors

You've likely built prototypes before. But there are a lot of misconceptions about prototyping, especially among software engineers. The term is often understood by software developers to mean a bunch of code that actually works, at least partially, to demonstrate some part of the platform, architecture, user experience, or other functional aspect of a software project. While developing working code prototypes can be very useful in some situations, writing and debugging code enough for it to actually function, even if only minimally, is a relatively labor-intensive job. This is especially true compared with some of the fastest rapid-prototyping techniques, which let you build a viable prototype in less than an hour.

> A *prototype* is a model of a concept, process, technology, or experience that is built for the purpose of learning whether the proposed solution is viable and meets the project's goals.

When we talk about prototyping in this book, we've broadened our scope to include many different types of prototypes, both code and noncode prototypes. We think of a prototype as anything you build that enables you to test an idea in real time and space with the intent of learning so that you can further refine your idea in subsequent iterations. Of particular note are rapid prototypes that can often be produced much more quickly and earlier in a product cycle, either with no code or within a simplified coding environment. Here are a few examples of different kinds of rapid prototypes:

- A paper prototype, consisting of sketches of a user interface drawn on sheets of paper, a stack of sticky notes, or even cocktail napkins. An example is shown in Figure 8-1. Each page shows what users would see at each step as they go through a particular experience.

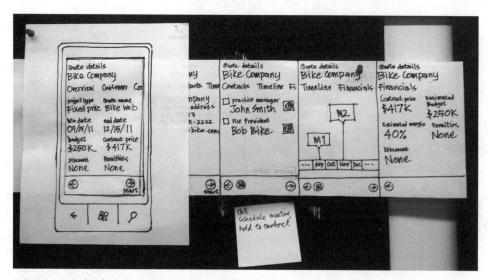

FIGURE 8-1 A simple paper prototype made with a sliding panel that changes the interface on the outlined mobile device as the customer interacts with it.

- Grayscale or wireframe drawings of a user interface produced with Microsoft PowerPoint, Microsoft Visio, Balsamiq, or a host of other simple prototyping tools. An example is shown in Figure 8-2.

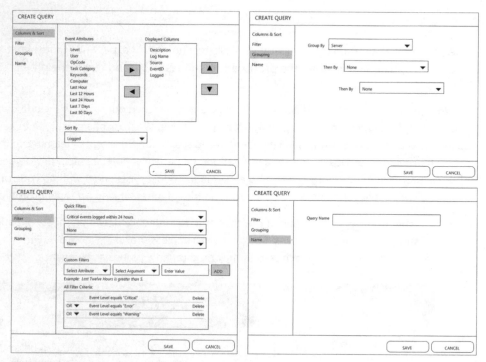

FIGURE 8-2 A wireframe prototype made with PowerPoint provides a quick way to mock up a user interface that can be tested with customers.

- A "Wizard of Oz" trial in which a customer interacts with a "computer" that is really just a person sitting behind a curtain who mimics what a voice- or text-based system might do.

- A sequence of screens built in SketchFlow (part of Blend for Visual Studio), perhaps with a bit of code embedded in a single control to mimic some crucial functionality of the proposed app.

- A written page listing the methods and call signatures for a potential API that has not yet been implemented. A developer-customer could attempt to write code against this API (but not compile it).

- A mockup created in Adobe Photoshop, Illustrator, or Flash that looks pixel-perfect but is actually just a set of pictures that show a canned example of a user interface, perhaps with a few buttons or hot spots wired up to click through the pictures.

- A simple HTML, Visual Basic, C#, or Ruby on Rails app that mimics the functionality and behavior of a solution that will eventually be built on a different platform.

Alberto Savoia, former director of engineering (and self-proclaimed "innovation agitator") at Google, has called these kinds of earlier, precode prototypes *pretotypes* to help underline the importance and value of prototyping before building functional prototypes or writing production code.[1] More commonly, approaches like these are referred to as *rapid prototypes*. Whether you call them pretotypes or rapid prototypes, the goal is the same: low-cost ways of making sure that you are solving a real problem and that your solution is the right one. Or, as Savoia would say, "Are you building the right '*It*'?"

In this book we recognize the value of many different types of prototypes, including rougher, early ones as well as more-detailed prototypes, in code and noncode formats.[2] Each type serves a different function at different iterations of the Fast Feedback Cycle throughout a project. The trick is to pick the right tool for the job. Exactly what you build, and what tool set you use, depends on what questions you have and what level of feedback you're looking for, and these will naturally change as you progress from your first trips around the Fast Feedback Cycle into subsequent iterations. Sometimes writing code is the best and most efficient way to get the customer feedback you need to make progress. But we hope that after you read this chapter, you'll find more efficient ways to reach your goal of enabling data-driven decisions using customer feedback with a minimum of sunk cost and risk.

 MINDSHIFT

Why not just start coding? In the early stages of a project, you might feel that the most efficient path forward is to get busy and start writing code. Why waste time with a prototype first, especially because anything that isn't code is going to be throw-away work? This way of thinking ends up being penny-wise but pound-foolish. You may make what feels like quick progress at first, but experienced developers know that almost always—after running into system constraints, integration issues, and customer complaints—you end up regretting your first idea, and then you have to throw it away or substantially change it. It can be particularly painful to hobble along, sometimes for years, with a suboptimal design that is the source of untold problems in legacy support, ongoing scalability or performance problems, or limitations in what end-to-end experiences the architecture can support without a major rewrite. We've seen countless teams genuinely believe that their first solution idea is flawless and inspired on paper, and yet, in its first user test, that same idea raises major issues that no one on the team anticipated.

Build multiple prototypes in parallel

In the first couple of iterations of the Fast Feedback Cycle, you should build out not one concept but several different potential solutions to test with customers. Building multiple prototypes in parallel is a good practice for three main reasons.

The first reason to build multiple prototypes is to allow the team to explore diverse approaches in enough detail that the relative strengths and weaknesses of each approach become more apparent. As you start thinking through how the solution will work in a bit more detail than in the quick brainstorming sketches you made in the previous stage, you'll see possibilities that weren't obvious before, and ideas that seemed great at first may now look pale in comparison with better alternatives.

Second, when you explore several sufficiently different approaches in detail, you have another chance to blend ideas. As we discussed in Chapter 7, "Brainstorming alternatives," the path to the solution that best optimizes your goals is often not choosing just one of your prototyped alternatives over the others but combining aspects of several prototypes to create a blend or a new approach that you had not considered initially.

The third reason to build multiple prototypes is that customers give better feedback and comment more on the relative merits of different approaches when they can compare and contrast a small number of options.[3] When you show customers a single approach, they too can quickly develop tunnel vision and have trouble imagining any other possible solution. They might have trouble giving feedback other than, *"Looks all right to me."* However, if you show some alternatives, those same customers can become quite chatty and will be much more opinionated about what parts they find useful, which places are confusing or straightforward, and, importantly, what aspects tickle their fancy. All of this data provides important clues for what you might need to change and where you should focus to create that emotionally desirable experience you're ultimately striving for.

Also, writing code for one approach is expensive enough, but writing code for multiple approaches, even if it's throw-away code, is almost always too costly in the earliest stages of a project. A noncode approach is usually a more lightweight, efficient way to produce multiple prototypes in the first few iterations, where your primary goal is to validate that you are solving the right problem, one that customers care about and that will support your business model. Showing a few different solutions that highlight different aspects of your customers' situation and needs is one way to stimulate feedback on which parts of the problem are indeed the most important to address.

A group of computer scientists, designers, and education researchers at Stanford University put the value of creating multiple prototypes to the test. They conducted a study to compare the efficacy of iterating on one prototype in a serial fashion with iterating on multiple prototypes in parallel. They had 33 web designers create online advertisements for a new website. Each designer created five prototypes before settling on a final design. Some of the subjects received feedback after showing one prototype, before generating the next one—serial prototyping. Other subjects created three prototypes and received feedback on all three before going on to create one more prototype, receiving feedback on it, refining that prototype, getting feedback again, and settling on a final design—parallel prototyping. The researchers found that every measure—from independent experts' review of the resulting advertisements, to actual click-through rates, to the length of time visitors spent on the website—was higher for the ads produced through the parallel prototyping approach.[4]

Rough prototypes stimulate more valuable feedback

It might seem a bit crazy for us to suggest that you can get better customer feedback from a rough prototype than from a detailed, picture-perfect one. However, in practice, when you present something that looks like a finished product, that encourages customers to give you feedback on the details: things like the color scheme, the specific words on a page, or the icons you used. A prototype that looks finished lures the customer away from engaging with the more structural issues and concepts you are working through in your first couple of iterations.

Even if it is trivially easy for you to mock up a pixel-perfect prototype using something like HTML, you have to ask yourself whether you really want that type of feedback right now. Do you want feedback on the words you used, the color scheme, what your logo looks like, or the way you laid out graphics? Probably not yet. Instead, you should be more concerned about confirming whether the basic idea makes sense, whether the experience's flow and sequence feel smooth and natural, and whether you've even addressed a problem that customers want solved.

 ## MINDSHIFT

Get used to showing work early. It will feel uncomfortable at first to show customers half-baked work. Engineers can have trouble sharing their early ideas with teammates, never mind with external customers, often out of fear and insecurity that their ideas will be criticized. But if you want to be efficient and avoid wasting work, you need to get used to it. Remember that getting feedback is not about you, it's about the idea and whether that particular idea works for this particular situation. Likely, you will have to try a bunch of approaches before you hit on one that works, so go in with the expectation that not every idea will pan out. Show your ideas to customers before you are comfortable or have even worked out all the mechanics yourself, and remember to keep it simple and focused. Do not wait until your solution is working or until it is beta quality—that is much too late. The sooner you get feedback, and the less you are experiencing tunnel vision about how it should work, the easier it is for you to adapt to feedback and meaningfully shift your approach to something that your customers will really love.

Furthermore, it's natural for customers to not want to hurt your feelings. When you show them a prototype that looks finished, reviewers may be quite reluctant to tell you that they don't find your solution very useful, that the whole concept doesn't make sense to them, or that they would have reordered the experience a wholly different way. Subconsciously, they might assume that you are already committed to this approach because it looks so finished, so they will give you feedback on little things they think you may actually be able to change at this stage of product development.

However, if you show a prototype that looks obviously rough, and especially if you present alternatives, that opens the door for a much richer and more open conversation and makes it much easier for customers to tell you what they honestly think. A prototype that is obviously unfinished makes for a natural two-way conversation about how your solution could or should work. A more polished prototype, on the other hand, subliminally challenges the customer simply to spot the flaws.

In fact, several sophisticated prototyping tools intentionally use fonts that look like handwritten text and lines that look hand-drawn to help customers feel comfortable about giving honest feedback on prototypes that still don't look "done."

SFE in action: A "sketchy" toolkit made us more efficient

Lisa Mueller, Senior User Experience Lead, Microsoft Dynamics

When our team began to explore ideas and designs for a new version of Microsoft Dynamics, the UX team wanted to help the engineers explore solution ideas as efficiently as possible. Our idea was to create a toolkit that the program managers (PMs) would use to mock up rough ideas that we could show to customers and get early feedback. We ended up building a PowerPoint toolkit that provided individual UI components, experience patterns, photos, and links to supporting documents (things like text guidelines and persona information). This customized toolkit had extensive functionality for building detailed wireframes and UI mockups with a ton of high-fidelity patterns and detailed data that were easy to access and manipulate.

After a few months of using the toolkit we discovered that the mockups coming from the PMs were taking more time to produce than we (or the schedule) had expected. Turns out that the PMs were spending way too much time thinking about and iterating on UI details. We found the PMs "pixel pushing" in preparation for the upcoming scenario reviews with the leadership team.

As we were still in the early stages of the project, we wanted to help teams create rough drafts of their solution ideas. The current toolkit led them down the path of working on too much detail. Once we realized this, we updated the toolkit to be more "sketchy." This sketchy toolkit contained the same basic patterns and components as before, but this time it offered a more limited set of rough-looking components and used the Buxton Sketch font, which looks more like handwriting. The idea behind providing rough-looking UI components in the toolkit was to discourage the PMs from spending a lot of time working on details, and to encourage them to get the big ideas across quickly, with just enough (rough) fidelity that we could test it with customers. As UX professionals, we were well aware of the dynamic with customers where they tend to give feedback at a level of fidelity similar to what you show them. Give them high-level fidelity, and they'll assume the decisions are already made on an almost-finished product. Give them low fidelity, and they assume the team still has time for feedback.

Once we "sketchified" the toolkit, the PMs were able to more quickly create rough prototypes and mockups that we could show to customers to get early, high-level feedback. We still needed higher-fidelity tools for later stages, like redlines, but for early mockups, this "sketchy" toolkit was exactly what we needed to get customer feedback on ideas faster.

Prototyping: More than just a feedback tool

This book is focused on using the Fast Feedback Cycle to get iteration to work for you so that you build things your customers will love. In this context, the primary purpose of prototyping is to build out ideas in order to get rapid customer feedback to fuel that cycle, particularly in the first several iterations. But prototyping has other notable benefits that can be very helpful to your project as well.

Thinking it through

Prototyping allows you to try out ideas in physical space, in real time, with real people, and sometimes even in real situations—but in a very fast way. Building a prototype is a great way to think through a problem and consider the real-world interactions and constraints that need to be negotiated to create a functional, understandable solution. Rather than learning by thinking, this is learning by doing. And for an engineer, prototyping is an extremely productive way to make quick progress and find the bugs in your own thinking. Whether you are working out the technical details, the implementation of the business plan, or the customer experience, moving out of the abstract and starting to actually put pieces together helps you work through the constraints and see whether your solution is viable.

Communication

A good prototype can be an effective communication tool. It can elicit a visceral response about the direction you are taking and how you are approaching the key problems you are taking on. You can use a prototype to communicate to the team, to customers, to partners, to management, and to any other stakeholders you may have on the project. A prototype also helps unify the team on the direction and key decisions for a project, and it does more than describe what you are doing; it allows someone to experience what you intend to build. Unlike a written specification or a long list of requirements, a prototype is difficult to misinterpret. To this end, even a storyboard or series of rough sketches can be enough to align a team and partners on the direction you are taking. Indeed, a rough prototype can serve these needs quite effectively.

For similar reasons, including mockups, screenshots, and other prototypes in specifications is very useful, and they may become a primary tool for spec writing. Prototypes on their own are usually insufficient for completely replacing specs, however, because even fairly detailed prototypes do not usually include all of the error conditions and other edge cases that will ultimately need to be handled by the software. We'll discuss this in more detail in Chapter 11, "The way you work."

Soliciting support

If a picture is worth a thousand words, a prototype is worth . . . we don't know, a lot more than that.

Prototypes are often used to get buy-in from managers or investors who control the resources you need to complete a project. Whether you are pitching a product idea to an investor, trying to win a lucrative contract, or getting a green light from management, a good prototype can be pivotal to convincing others that your ideas are good ones and that they are achievable.

When you use a prototype to sell your ideas, you want to show two things. Be sure that people see the "aha moments," where you demonstrate that you've solved a deep technical, business, or customer need. You should also show any customer data and feedback you've collected that communicates what target customers think about your prototype or what customer insights initially inspired the idea. It's really easy to get caught up in the whiz-bang flash of a good prototype or demo. Keep it grounded and real by backing up your hopes with actual customer feedback.

Technical exploration

There are clear benefits of using prototypes to investigate technical and architectural problems and to refine approaches before you write production code. But you can go a step further and explore technical areas not just for the sake of discovering creative solutions to technical problems, but also to get a deep understanding of the breadth and depth of the technical challenges ahead. You can use prototyping techniques such as spiking to better understand the resources that are needed to complete the project, as well as to get an early handle on the performance, scalability, and other key characteristics of various implementation approaches that may in turn have material impact on the resulting end-to-end customer experience. We'll discuss this in more detail later in this chapter.

What makes a good prototype?

In the iterative process, a prototype is the stimulus for an experiment. Just as with the scientific method, you have a hypothesis, some idea that you want to test. You use a prototype to test the hypothesis and get answers to related questions, either about the problem you've identified or the solution you're proposing. It's natural that in the very beginning, the questions you have will be quite broad: Is your approach appealing to customers? Are you solving a real need? Is the form factor appropriate? As you iterate, the questions become more and more detailed and specific: Is the user interaction intuitive? Is the color scheme appealing? Does the application meet specific performance benchmarks?

Regardless of where you are in the Fast Feedback Cycle, a good prototype has some common characteristics:

- **Rapid**   Don't spend a lot of time building the prototype. Be as efficient as possible. Your goal is to learn exactly what you set out to learn and no more, as quickly as possible. Don't waste your time on unnecessary details or on areas you're not questioning. A good prototype uses the least amount of work required to answer a specific question.

- **Disposable**   By definition a prototype is meant to be thrown away.[5] Remember that the point of prototyping is not to build a beautiful, elegant prototype; the point is to experiment, to get customer input, and to get data to inform your decision making with a minimum of effort. Often this means building something inherently disposable because taking the time to make it real doesn't make sense, especially in your first iterations through the Fast Feedback Cycle.

- **Focused**   Concentrate the prototype on what you don't know, on what you want to learn, on whatever you aren't sure about. Generally, you would not attempt to prototype the whole system, just a portion of the experience or the technology that you have the most questions about or that seems the riskiest.

 MINDSHIFT

A good prototype looks like a patchwork quilt. The implication of building rapid, disposable, focused prototypes is that your prototypes, especially early ones, will most likely not be visually or architecturally beautiful. They will look more like a patchwork quilt, a mix of formats, styles, and materials, possibly forged from a variety of different tools, that quickly stitches together just enough of the ideas to make sense. A prototype is a rough approximation for the purpose of getting feedback, nothing more. Nor will your prototypes feel complete. They will usually zoom in on a few aspects or threads of the solution, not the entire system. They will probably completely ignore error conditions and edge cases. The perfectionist in you may rebel at the idea of producing work that looks so blatantly unfinished, but this is usually the right tradeoff because for now you are focused on speed, on getting feedback so that you can correct your course to maximize efficiency and minimize wasted effort.

Lean Startup offers another term for what makes a good prototype: minimum viable product, often abbreviated MVP. Agile development also has names for this idea: minimum marketable feature (MMF) or minimum marketable product (MMP). Whatever you call it, the underlying idea of an MVP, MMF, or MMP is the same—what is the smallest thing you can put together most quickly that is sufficient for learning whether customers find it valuable. Sometimes an MVP will be a mockup or prototype, but it can also be a live, functional service with an absolute minimum feature set, intended to prove whether actual customer demand is strong enough to make pursuing that direction any further worthwhile. One clever idea proposed by Eric Ries is to create a faked-up homepage for an offering that hasn't been built yet, just to see how many people click the Buy button. He also suggests that an MVP could be a concierge service that manually provides a new service to a handful of customers but could be scaled out to serve a larger number of people if the feedback is positive. Some good arguments can be made to suggest that the Apple iPhone was originally built as an MVP, with only enough features to test whether this new paradigm for a smartphone with a touchscreen instead of a keypad was actually workable and valuable for customers.[6]

SFE in action: But we don't have time for a prototype!

Mike Pietraszak, Adjunct Instructor, DigiPen Institute of Technology

I teach a game design and production class to freshmen at DigiPen Institute of Technology. The students, many of whom have never written code, work in teams of three over 10 weeks to design and build their own game using C++. Students start the semester overflowing with feature and gameplay ideas ("Let's have zombie aliens! With missiles for eyeballs! And laser swords! And . . ."). But the whole point of a game is "fun," not features. Games that are feature-rich but also tedious or frustrating are not successful. So how do you "make fun"? You get feedback.

Department chair Doug Schilling and computer science instructor Elie Abi-Chahine came up with a great way to introduce fast feedback cycles to students. During a lab session in the first few weeks of the semester, the three-person teams are given a game engine and are instructed to code a working game prototype in 45 minutes (!!!)—including placeholder art (sound is optional). When time is up, students demo their game to the rest of the class, which provides verbal feedback. Many teams are unable to produce a complete "game," but no team has ever wound up without anything to demo.

Completing a feedback iteration in less than one hour is powerful. Students quickly learn a lot about what others find fun in their games—and it's often not even remotely what they expected. Placeholder art and sound—or even coding errors—that embarrass a game's creators often wind up being features that players love most. One military-strategy game substituted a jaguar roar for an explosion sound as a placeholder. People loved it! The positive feedback was so enthusiastic that the jaguar stayed in the final game, becoming its unexpected mascot.

Creating a time box for students forced severe scoping. The scoped prototypes, even though they had few features, were able to be coded very quickly and stimulated valuable customer feedback. After students have this initial experience, the value of customer feedback becomes clear. In addition to receiving feedback every three weeks during milestone reviews, many teams seek out more frequent, informal feedback from friends throughout the semester.

Go from low fidelity to high fidelity

Generally speaking, you should focus your first few iterations of the Fast Feedback Cycle on big-picture ideas and gradually work your way toward details as plans solidify. This usually means starting with lower-fidelity approaches, such as paper prototypes, and working your way up to higher-fidelity prototypes, such as detailed wireframes or coded prototypes, until you're sure enough of your approach that it's time to shift to writing production code.

 VOCAB

Low-fidelity, or *lo-fi,* prototyping shows just enough detail to communicate big ideas or concepts and get directional feedback. Lo-fi prototyping is characterized by very rapid iterations using low-tech tools (paper, whiteboard, sticky notes).

High-fidelity, or *hi-fi,* prototyping shows lots of details with the intent of testing some portion of a more complete, more polished solution. Hi-fi prototypes are characterized by having some level of implemented functionality or a lot of visual detail, especially animations, sounds, and other design elements that are important to an interface. These prototypes are usually created by using more sophisticated tools and programming languages.

Many people think about lo-fi and hi-fi prototypes as a binary decision—you create one or the other. In reality, a broad spectrum spans very lo-fi prototypes (such as a paper prototype drawn using fat markers) to very hi-fi prototypes (a code prototype that mimics a fully functional application). Many of the most broadly useful prototypes fall somewhere in between, and in practice you will use a variety of prototyping techniques along this spectrum.

The choice of tools is not a binary decision either. A single tool can support a range of lo-fi and hi-fi prototypes along the spectrum. For example, depending on how much work you put into it, a PowerPoint prototype can be very rough or extremely detailed, with a branching click-through sequence. The tool you use doesn't completely define the fidelity of your prototype. The questions you want to test should define the level of detail your prototype implements. Many tools, while they have a sweet spot, also have the ability to span different levels of fidelity.

Where do I focus my experiments?

So where do you begin? Especially at the start of a project, with so many ideas and hypotheses, how do you know where to turn your attention first? Do you test the end-to-end experience, the underlying technology, or the business model itself?

In general, you should prioritize by deciding which areas represent the most risk. Is there risk in your business model or do you already have evidence that customers will pay for what you are building? Is the deeper risk about your technology? Can you actually build your solution and make it scale? Or is the risk centered on the end-to-end customer experience? Will customers use it and love it? Quite possibly your biggest risk will be finding the right combination of these—can you build the technology that creates an experience that will delight customers and that they're willing to buy? You will likely have questions about and experiment in all three domains—the business model, the technical architecture and implementation, and the end-to-end customer experience. And the good news is that you can usually do these experiments in parallel.

The focus of your experiments will change depending on where you are in your project. You should let your highest-priority questions and concerns guide you. The answers to some questions will greatly affect the next round of design decisions, and these questions must be answered before you can move on. Early in a project, in your first round of testing rough prototypes with customers, your mindset shouldn't be so much on refining specific design ideas for your solution but on verifying your understanding of your customers' needs. As we've said before, the most meaningful result from the first round of prototyping and user testing may be the realization that the problem you are attempting to solve isn't really that important or that one seemingly minor aspect of your proposed solution is much more valuable to your customer than you realized.

Next, you need to make some informed decisions about the basic shape of the solution you envision, which gives rise to a different set of questions to explore and also impacts (and is impacted by) decisions about which technologies to use. At the end, your questions are much more detail-oriented, aimed at fine-tuning specific aspects of your solution to get it just right.

We break up a project into three major phases: the needs phase, which encompasses the early iterations of a project; the solution tradeoffs phase, which is the main work of the middle of the project; and the details phase at the endgame of a project. The following sections offer some sample questions that you might ask in each of these major phases and give you an idea of how your focus will shift over time. You will have business questions, technology questions, and user-experience questions that can be answered through testing noncode prototypes at first and then, when you are ready, with production code. Often you can answer several types of questions at one time. It is ideal to iterate not just on the user experience, but on your business and technology plans in parallel. Depending on the scope of your project, you might rocket from early stages to the endgame in just a few weeks, or, for larger projects, you might spend weeks or even months iterating to answer each set of questions.

The needs phase

Early in a new project, during the first couple of iterations, you are probably working with noncode prototypes or very rough code prototypes and are testing concepts and developing your initial ideas. You haven't figured out the details yet, nor are you trying to. Rather, your focus is on making sure that you're in the right neighborhood for solving a problem the customer cares about, in a way that you can monetize and with technology that is feasible to build. If you remember the mountain peaks we described in Chapter 7, you're looking for the foothills of a solution that appears to lead to a global maximum.

These are the sorts of questions you should explore with your first prototypes:

- **Experience**   Does the basic idea make sense to customers? Do they find it valuable and useful? Does some aspect of it excite them, does it validate that you're on the path to achieving deep desirability? Does your framing of the problem accurately describe its most important aspects to your customers?

- **Business**   Would customers be willing to pay for this functionality directly, or engage with advertisements, or do whatever you plan for monetizing the solution? Will each part of the ecosystem find enough value to play its part to make the approach successful? Can you secure contracts with key partners?

- **Technology**   Is this rough plan feasible to build within a reasonable amount of time? What resources will this take to complete? Are there technology boundaries that limit what you can achieve in the user experience? What are the hardest technical challenges you will need to overcome?

The solution-tradeoffs phase

After the early stages of a project, once you have narrowed in on the right path for the customer experience, business, and technology, you need to work through all the interactions. At this point you focus on getting the high-level flow right and on ensuring that the solution matches the users' expectations and mental model. Most of the time people think of testing customer interactions with the system in an end-to-end manner. Don't forget that your solution likely has other interactions as well, such as how the different technical components interact and how the partner ecosystem functions. Be sure that those interactions are meeting your goals as well. You may also start working through the visual and aesthetic design of your interface at this point, but be sure that your basic solution approach is working for customers first before you start working on refining visuals or optimizing performance. If you haven't already started writing code, you definitely will during this phase.

This phase is where you do the activities that most engineers associate with design and development work, and they are vitally important, but it's a mistake to start a project with these activities and inadvertently skip the needs phase. Be sure you have answered the questions above before moving into detailed design work—lest you end up spending a lot of time solving the wrong problem or on a dead-end solution path.

Here are the kinds of questions you might ask midgame:

- **Experience**   Is the end-to-end experience compelling? Can users navigate the flow of the experience? Is it usable? Do users understand where to click, how to interact with the UI, what steps to take to complete their goal? Is the API platform easy to use for developers? Do the target customers find the experience desirable?

- **Business**   Is the solution meaningfully differentiated from your competition? Are there lighthouse moments that will enable strong marketing messages? Does the detailed business model meet the needs of all partners? Are you getting the carryover you expected from your chosen target customer into adjacent segments?

- **Technology**   Is the technical solution scalable, performant, and secure enough to support the delightful end-to-end experience you are striving for? Have you solved the hardest algorithms and do they work as well as they need to?

The details phase

During the project's endgame, your solution is now refined enough for you to focus on the small details, fine-tuning various aspects of the solution so that it is polished and has high quality. Here are the kinds of questions you should be asking now:

- **Experience**   Have you achieved deep desirability? Is the user experience smooth, fast, and fluid? When someone is using the product, do they get tripped up anywhere? Are there annoyances you can fix? Are there places you can further optimize for the most common user tasks and situations? Is the end result visually beautiful in your customers' eyes?

- **Business**   Exactly how much should you charge for a monthly subscription? Are there tweaks you can make in the user experience that make a customer more likely to go through with a purchase? Would an incentive help? Are your partners fully aligned and ready to launch?

- **Technology**   Are there ways to optimize the performance or scalability or to improve maintainability or operability?

I don't have a GUI, why prototype?

Don't be fooled into thinking that prototyping is always about visual experiences and user interfaces. It's easiest to imagine what a prototype might look like in those domains because they are inherently visual. However, prototyping can be just as useful when you are responsible for deeply technical work that may have no user interface at all, such as building architectural or platform components, an API, or a new compiler. You might think of DLLs, APIs, and compilers as not having a user interface. Of course, they actually do, but they just aren't graphical interfaces.

Technical component design can also benefit from the ideas entailed in the Fast Feedback Cycle—know your customer (who is probably a developer, and may even be a teammate); articulate the end-to-end scenario you're trying to solve; explore ideas and visualize multiple approaches; try out several potential approaches in a lightweight, rapid way; get feedback from your customer on your ideas before you commit to a plan; keep iterating. As we discussed in the last chapter, many seasoned software architects intuitively do many of these things already.

More importantly, don't forget that most, if not all, deep technical work does meaningfully affect how your customers experience your solution. The engineering team should be very much aware of this value and how and when it plays out for the user, business, or ecosystem. If the system relies on transactions with a remote back-end database, for instance, that inherent latency can easily impact the user experience, making the system seem slow to respond. An algorithm that optimizes for minimum memory footprint rather than performance might have a similar affect. However, if the planned user experience requires lengthy customer input at that stage, it may not matter, and optimizing for memory footprint and not latency may well be the best tradeoff—but this should be an intentional decision and not a lucky near miss. Or if your cloud system does not support in-place deployments (and rollbacks, if needed), frequent maintenance outages will inevitably impact the customer experience, as well as your business relationship with partners. Is this the right tradeoff, or should you invest in improving your operations system? Good architecture and technical design is needed not just for the technology to work from an engineering and operations perspective, but also for the end-to-end user experience to be smooth, and ultimately to support your business plan.

Consider the following story about a team that built a compelling user experience and wrote a ton of complicated code in doing so, but only exposed two words to their end users, who were actually fellow software developers.

SFE in action: Prototyping parallel computing

Ed Essey, Senior Program Manager, Microsoft Developer Division

Parallel computing techniques have historically been very challenging for most developers. Our research showed that even the 5 percent of developers who were comfortable writing programs using parallel constructs still considered parallel computing to be a time-consuming, error-prone programming paradigm fraught with subtle perils. As a senior program manager in the Parallel Computing Platform, I was part of a group tasked with creating the programming experiences that would enable developers to more easily access the power of parallelism and concurrency on Microsoft's platforms.

My team sought to make an easy, error-free programming model that could leverage the parallel capabilities of the multicore CPUs that were rapidly becoming status quo in the PC industry. Our goal was to provide a model with which developers no longer needed to create any threads, tasks, locks, semaphores, monitors, critical sections, or anything like that in their own code. This would all happen under the covers. We thought this would be a total win for developers, and that they would love it. With the key technical decisions made, we were ready to build and test the first prototype of our framework, called PLINQ.

In our very first prototype, we just wanted to test the PLINQ engine—did it work and would people use it? We didn't yet have a design for a programming model to access the functionality, but we released an early code prototype of the PLINQ engine to a small set of our best and most skilled customers to try out. We received a ton of positive feedback; customers loved it and told us that PLINQ was exciting and powerful. Word got out in the developer community, and PLINQ quickly received a lot of attention. Now we needed to figure out exactly how it was going to be exposed to the developer.

We wanted to enable a programming model as simple as this:

```
var query = from num in nums.AsParallel()
    where someExpensiveOperation(num) == true
    select num;
```

"Just add *AsParallel*" became a rallying cry for the team. It summed up the value proposition we created and became a mantra that the team would use to guide our decisions.

But sticking to this simple mantra meant that we had to do a lot of work. It opened up questions like "Do we parallelize if the left data source is marked *AsParallel*? The right data source? Both? Or is *AsParallel* about the query instead of the data?" These were complex design questions, and it was really the iterations with customers that helped us hone the answers. Eventually, we were able to take care of all the complicated stuff regarding parallel-izing algorithms and primitives. We would partition, merge, divide and conquer, handle locality, handle thread scheduling—all of that. We could handle various types of hardware and manage resources across various loads on the system. The developer no longer had to worry about any of that tedious and demanding code.

But the next set of customer feedback surfaced a problem. It was now possible to achieve 4 times, 16 times, or greater speedups with just a simple function call, but there was a catch. That simple function call also made it possible to introduce the most insidious of all code defects: race conditions, deadlocks, and other intermittent run-time errors. At this point, we learned that we had a new target customer, a group far outside the 5 percent who had traditionally used parallelism, and they were now stumbling into a world of hurt. We had big decisions to make in terms of our user scenarios, the amount of safety we would provide, and so on.

We tried several different approaches. For one prototype we focused on our original audi-ence of skilled developers by adding more imperative steps to the declarative model, making it harder to turn on PLINQ unless the developer knew it would be safe to parallelize. We backed off from the "Just add *AsParallel*" vision and tested it with a small, close circle of advanced developers. Customers were not happy, and the backlash was strong.

We then proposed a number of alternative designs, and eventually widened our brainstorm-ing and prototyping with others outside our team. This larger group quickly grokked our situ-ation, and being untainted by the deep knowledge we had of our users, came up with a very elegant solution. Their idea returned to the "Just add *AsParallel*" plan, but also included a safety check. Under the covers the code would analyze the safety of the query first and only parallelize if it was absolutely safe to do so; otherwise, it would run the sequential version. This was a deep mental shift for us parallel-computing folks—to optimize for absolute safety instead of trying to run as parallel as much of the time as possible.

This new approach tested really well with users and could be seamlessly extended in future releases to add in new common query shapes we learned about through user feedback and telemetry that we could guarantee to be safe to parallelize. By the end of the project, we had solved many mainline scenarios for our customers in a very simple and delightful way, by adding only one visible function call that was guaranteed to be safe, and would seamlessly improve code performance. The final design looked like this:

```
var query = Parallel.Foreach(nums, num => someExpensiveOperation(num))
```

After we shipped this last iteration, we rarely received unsolicited user feedback on PLINQ again. This was worrisome, until we analyzed our telemetry and marketing data. The data showed that this was the most common form of parallelism in the market, and that users understood it without the need for support. There are many wrong turns we might have made, but the ultimate success of this model came about through constant prototyping and iteration with our customers and partners.

When to transition from prototypes to production code

A question that comes up a lot is how do you know when you've done enough prototyping and it's time to start writing production code? Closely related is the question of whether you should really always throw away your prototype code, or can you successfully iterate your prototype into production-quality code?

While the predominant view of prototyping is that you build with the intention of throwing the prototype away, it doesn't always need to be that way. However, there are some important tradeoffs to be aware of. Planning to throw away a prototype does allow you to write code a lot faster, without having to worry about long-term architectural implications, performance, scale, operability, security, localization, or any of the long list of requirements that need to be satisfied for production-quality code. So there are definitely potential efficiency benefits to intentionally writing throw-away prototype code, especially if you are still exploring several different approaches in an early iteration.

However, sometimes it makes sense to begin a project with the intent of iterating on production code from the very beginning. Perhaps the technical architecture is already defined and unchangeable (a platform you inherited or purchased), or the changes you intend to make are so surgical that it's just as easy to code them in production as not. Regardless of how much time you spend prototyping, at some point you have to make the decision to transition to writing production code. How do you decide when is the right time to make that transition? Here are the key factors to consider in this decision.

Where are you in the project?

How much have you learned about your target customers and their reactions to your plans and early designs? Early on you will have broad-based questions, and you'll want to get them answered quickly. At the early stages of a project, you usually stick to noncode prototypes; however, perhaps you have a solution that really needs code to explore it, even at the high level. Either way, the idea is to use the fastest techniques possible for getting your broad questions answered, and when writing code, faster almost always means throw away—focus on the rough idea of the concept you want to test, not on the quality of the prototype.

As a general rule, however, after you have experimented with several prototypes, your solution is converging, and your big questions about the business, technology, and end-to-end experience have been answered, that's the time to start serious development and begin iterating on production code. Once production coding begins, you will still iterate and get regular feedback from customers, so the Fast Feedback Cycle keeps going, but you will be feeding changes directly into your production code.

As the project progresses, new problems and issues may arise that you haven't anticipated. At times throughout the project, it may make sense for you to answer some questions by forking off small prototyping efforts (using throw-away code), trying out a few approaches and getting feedback before adding a production-code task to the backlog. Prototyping work tends to happen on a sliding scale, where noncode prototypes and throw-away code are heavily weighted toward the beginning of the project, and smaller, tactical prototypes, or "investigations" with possible production code, are more heavily weighted toward the end.

What is the nature of the problem you are trying to solve?

Is the biggest challenge in your project fundamentally about designing an architecture or algorithm that will be the basis of your solution? Or do you need to investigate the relative merits of different components, platforms, or tool sets before choosing a technology approach to move forward with? Is it critical to work with a live customer data set (such as an email inbox or an actual stockpile of digital photos) to get valid customer feedback on your approach? Is the nature of the interaction so complex that customers really need to have it functioning for it to make sense? Does the interface rely heavily on animations or a particularly novel user interface? Those are all cases where you will probably want to start prototyping with code, and perhaps even write production code, earlier than usual, possibly within your first few iterations of the Fast Feedback Cycle.

However, when your project is more focused on designing a flow through a multistep process, and you're not quite sure which order of the steps will be optimal, you probably want to stick to noncode prototypes. Or perhaps you are working through the business implications of a particular end-to-end solution. For instance, you want to know whether a customer can smoothly make a purchase, whether a customer notices (but is not aggravated by) your advertising, or whether a customer is compelled to pay for your service to begin with. Perhaps this experience will flow across not just your software but through a partner's software as well. These are situations in which you will likely get tremendous value from using noncode prototyping approaches to quickly iterate multiple ideas. These rapid prototypes let you assess whether customers find your approach useful, usable, and desirable, and whether your proposed business model is going to work, before you take on the expense of code and integrating with a partner's system.

Of course, rarely are projects so straightforward that this is an either/or decision. Most likely you will have portions of your project that you can prototype productively without code, very rapidly and with extremely tight iterations. Other parts of your project may require that you use code sooner, with that work happening in parallel with your other efforts. Again, let the nature of the question you are trying to answer drive the approach you take.

Which skills or tools are your team members most comfortable with?

How comfortable or fluent a team is with a particular language or set of tools can also be a factor in deciding which prototyping tools to use. It would be a mistake for us to blindly tell a team what tools or prototyping methods to use because we think they are faster. If the goal is to get feedback quickly, individuals and teams should pick the tools that they're skilled with and that are well suited to their project in order to get feedback most efficiently. Paper prototyping may be faster, or using a high-level wireframe tool may be faster, or coding in an object-oriented language may be faster . . . or not. It depends on the skills of the team as well as the nature of the problems the team is trying to solve.

Think of an experienced designer who is fluent and practiced in HTML. It may be faster for that person to prototype a webpage by writing HTML than by using some web mockup tool. As long as the details don't get in the way, why not use the same platform from the get-go to iterate with customers and the rest of the development team?

However, you need to consider the skill set of both the people building the prototype and whoever on the team is asked to help iterate the prototype. The reason is that allowing everyone to edit the prototype directly is an extremely effective way to collaborate and get feedback from peers. In this way, team members can demonstrate their thoughts and any alternative ideas they have. If the prototype is built using a highly technical tool by a single whiz on the team, you may lose an avenue for team collaboration because no one else can contribute to, extend, or edit that prototype.

This is one of the arguments for using rapid, noncode prototyping approaches as long as you can, because they often create a more accessible playing field on which the larger team can collaborate, including marketing, planning, and management personnel. Many teams have told us that using PowerPoint to create early-stage wireframe prototypes has been transformative because it is a tool that is rich enough to satisfy expert designers but simple enough that everyone on the team can meaningfully participate in the hands-on prototyping process by creating and editing the same prototypes that the designers produced.

Most teams have relatively little background in using noncode prototyping approaches, so the initial startup cost can make them hesitant to use these approaches the first time. Although you do need to invest in learning techniques and tools to productively use paper prototyping, PowerPoint, and other lightweight prototyping tools, we've found that most of them are easy to learn and well worth the investment. More importantly, the efficiency gains are tremendous—once you can produce credible, testable prototypes in hours, rather than in days, weeks, or longer.

Throw away code or production?

In both cases, dangers lurk. The danger in prototyping with production code is that you might lose sight of the original goal of the prototype, which is to quickly answer a question to inform your decision making. If you write production code, it's highly likely that you will overengineer the prototype and end up writing a lot more code than you need to get the feedback you desire. It's a balance. Perhaps it's worth taking more time so that you have good enough code for reuse. But what if the feedback is negative? What if customers reject the ideas in your prototype? What if your prototype proves that this approach is impractical from an engineering perspective? All that extra time making sure the code is reusable has been wasted.

Perhaps more importantly, when you put time and energy into the craft of quality coding, tunnel vision is close by. The more time you spend caring about the code you write, the more difficult it will be to hear customer feedback or feedback from your fellow developers that your solution is junk.[7] There is a danger that you will go deeper and deeper into the tunnel emotionally, and it will be harder and harder for you to throw out your expensive investment and look for a better solution.

On the other hand, let's say you decide to quickly write lots of throw-away code and test different ideas with customers. You do this a bunch of times with rapid iterations, and your throw-away prototype looks better and better and is getting fantastic feedback from customers. Now you demo your awesome, somewhat-functional, throw-away prototype to management and they say . . . drum roll please . . .

> "We love it! Customers love it! You are an amazing team! Now ship it in production immediately, full steam ahead!"

Yikes! What do you do? Thus, the danger of building great-looking, working prototypes with throw-away code. Everybody falls in love with it, including you, and you want to get it out to customers as soon as you can. With a bad case of group amnesia setting in, you forget about the shortcuts you've taken in the implementation, everything from security and memory footprint to operability and long-term maintainability. You risk taking on a huge coding debt for the next version, if you are lucky enough that the solution survives that long.

 TIP

If you choose to write throw-away code or build noncode prototypes, be sure they don't look finished so that casual observers don't get the wrong impression about how close you are to shipping. One way to do this is to use fonts that mimic a person's handwriting. Also, consider using hand-drawn sketches instead of dropping in actual UI controls or graphics. Show line-drawing wireframes rather than pixel-perfect renditions of a user interface. You might also add a watermark in the background that specifically says "PROTOTYPE" or "DRAFT." Many prototyping tools use these techniques by default for exactly this reason.

Remember that the point of prototyping, regardless of your intention for the future of the codebase, is to learn something—to answer a question that moves your project forward with the minimum amount of sunk cost. You need to find a balance between noncode prototypes, prototyping with throw-away code, and writing production code that makes the most sense for your team and project.

Building code in slices

When time comes to build production code, it's critical to sequence the work appropriately to get the most out of the Fast Feedback Cycle. The order in which you do your coding and integration will have a significant effect on how well you can continue to validate your work in progress with customers. This affects how quickly you will detect mistakes and, hence, how efficient your overall process is in minimizing wasted effort.

Most pieces of software can be represented by some sort of block diagram, stacked in abstraction layers from the lowest primitives and platforms to the presentation layer, something like the following illustration. It can be tempting to look at a block diagram like this and decide to write the code one component at a time. It can be even more tempting to assign individual developers on the team to "own" each component.

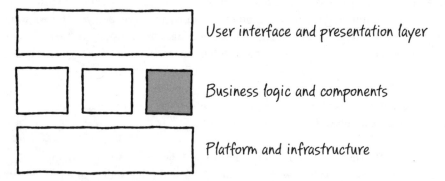

However, this creates a problem. Implementing all the components to a certain level of completeness so that you can see the end-to-end system work can take a lot of time. You carry a lot of risk that your approach (user experience, business, or architectural) has some sort of mistake, which you will not discover until quite late in the project when you first attempt to integrate.

This kind of late integration is well known to be problematic for engineering quality, and engineering teams commonly use continuous integration approaches to try to avoid these problems. It turns out that a late integration approach is bad for user experience quality, too.

Instead, you want to sequence your work and continually integrate so that you see the end-to-end performance characteristics of your code from the start, which allows you to detect architectural problems and integration issues early. Similarly, you want to continue to get customer feedback on a regular basis so that you can verify that you are still squarely solving the right problem, that your solution works for them, and that your monetization plan is on track. Ideally, you should get customer feedback on your work in progress at every iteration of the Fast Feedback Cycle. If you are an Agile team, the end of each sprint is a natural time to do this.

Being able to test with customers throughout coding has profound implications on how you sequence your development work. If you want to test a work in progress with customers, you have to build things in such a way that you will have something to show that makes sense to them. You need to sequence the implementation work so that you have some reasonable increment of working code to show customers—not an internal component or some unintegrated platforms, but functionality that works from a customer's point of view. To accomplish this, an Agile approach known as "slicing" is a particularly useful construct to think about as you sequence and assign development work.

 VOCAB

Slicing is implementing a single, vertical path through a multilayered system so that you can test the resulting end-to-end experience with a customer right away.

Instead of building one component at a time, sequence your development work so that you build slices through your multilayered stack vertically to create a complete path through an end-to-end experience.[8] Your slice may not touch every component, but it needs to make it all the way to the top layer so that it is exposed to the end user. The approach is illustrated in Figure 8-3.

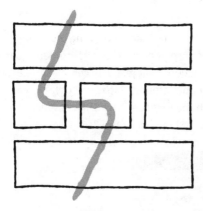

FIGURE 8-3 Building a single slice through a layered architecture.

As you build each slice, test with customers to ensure that what you are building is still resonating and is on track to meet their needs. The first few slices may require stubbing out a particular component temporarily, or faking up a database or server call with dummy data. The first few slices may also be quite simplistic in functionality, such as creating and naming a shopping list but not yet allowing any items to be added to it. Even trivially basic functionality like this is worth testing with customers. It is remarkable how just seeing something semifunctional can trigger customers to mention a requirement or an expectation that had not occurred to them before, or help you realize that this implementation approach is not going to work because of a fundamental limitation of screen size, form factor, or another basic constraint you may have taken for granted.

Over time, as you build more slices and widen existing ones by adding more-complete functionality, error handling, and so on, you naturally fill out the full functionality of each component yet still always have your system in a state where virtually all of the code can be demonstrated and tested with customers early and often. Sequencing your implementation work in this manner not only allows you to get constant customer feedback but also tends to flesh out any architectural issues much sooner because of the earlier integration of components. All of this helps you reduce risk, since you can be continuously verifying your latest work with your customers. We will discuss how slices grow to become complete experiences across multiple iterations in Chapter 11.

Build stage: Tools and techniques

All sorts of tools and techniques are available for developing concepts to get good customer feedback. You can use anything from the extra napkin you're served on an airplane to writing thousands of lines of compiled code. In this section we present a handful of our favorite tools and techniques for building prototypes. Remember that this is just a short, static list. Many other tools and techniques are available that are not listed here, and new ones are showing up all of the time. And, of course, not all of those we discuss will make sense for every kind of problem; use this list as a reference, and pick the approach that is most suited to your particular situation.

Paper prototyping

A paper prototype is exactly what it sounds like—a prototype that's built by drawing a user interface on paper. By using various colors and kinds of paper, clear transparencies, sticky notes, pens, markers, scissors, and tape, it's fairly easy to mock up complete interactions, where a user can make selections and see how the software responds just by shuffling some paper around. Paper prototyping can be extremely efficient and effective for early iterations through the Fast Feedback Cycle, especially for getting feedback on user interface approaches. An example is shown in Figure 8-4.

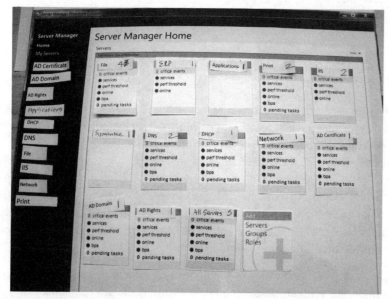

FIGURE 8-4 An example of a paper prototype built to test out early ideas for Windows Server 8.

Don't underestimate the power of using very simple, low-tech tools like this for getting your ideas and concepts into a form that you can share with customers. You might even be able to change a prototype on the fly as a customer's feedback sparks new ideas.

We'll dig into paper prototyping in more detail in the deep dive section at the end of this chapter.

Software for rapid prototyping

If you're ready to include more detail than you can easily do on paper, or you need to show basic animations or transitions or simply need to share your prototype electronically (rather than in person), consider using a software tool. Various software programs can be used to create prototypes—some that were intended specifically for prototyping and others that just happen to work well for that purpose.

More engineers are recognizing the power of getting early customer feedback every day. It's not surprising then that the marketplace is reacting, and we are beginning to see more and more prototyping tools and support offered to software developers. Here is a list of our favorites tools, which we've seen many teams use quite productively. Plenty of other tools are out there as well.

Microsoft PowerPoint

Most people think of Microsoft PowerPoint as a tool for creating slides and slide shows. However, in the past few years PowerPoint has gained popularity as a tool for creating wireframe mockups of user interfaces; it's our favorite software tool for this purpose. Search the web, and you will find many downloadable templates containing common elements that you can use to create wireframes for different form factors, including webpages and mobile devices. Microsoft Visual Studio 2012 comes with a particularly rich PowerPoint "storyboarding" add-in that provides a ribbon and a complete library of common controls to use in your PowerPoint prototypes.

The basic idea is to copy and paste common controls from a template or library and then arrange them to mimic a proposed user experience. For instance, copy the blank mobile phone template, and then paste in several buttons and check boxes; add some headings and some text, and voilà, you have something that looks just like a settings screen on a mobile device. Or create a full-screen application like this early iteration of Windows Server 8 shown in Figure 8-5. Notice the Storyboarding tab in the ribbon and the Storyboard Shapes panel on the right, which provides an extensive library of elements and icons as well as starter backgrounds for the Windows desktop, Windows applications, and Windows Phone apps.

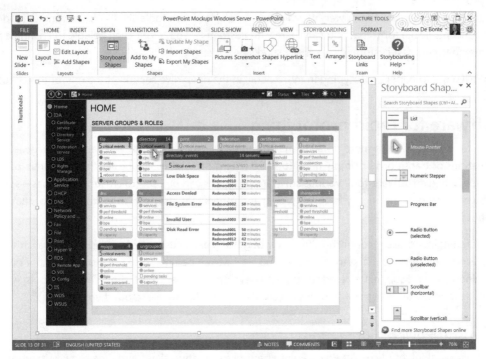

FIGURE 8-5 A detailed prototype of the proposed Windows Server 8 dashboard, built in PowerPoint.

None of the common controls in a PowerPoint prototype actually work functionally, but visually they are close enough to get the idea across. However, PowerPoint also has the ability to turn any element into a clickable hot spot, which makes it possible to simulate simple user interactions by hyperlinking multiple slides. For example, you can make the Close button on a pop-up dialog return you to an earlier slide (thereby "closing" the dialog). To do this, right-click the Close button element and select Hyperlink. In the dialog that appears, shown in Figure 8-6, select Place In This Document, and choose which slide to link to.

Once you have linked all your slides together to mock up the interface transitions you are interested in, switch to Slide Show view for a live session in which customers can click items on the screen to explore the prototype. For more complex interactions, PowerPoint also has a full macro scripting language and debugger.

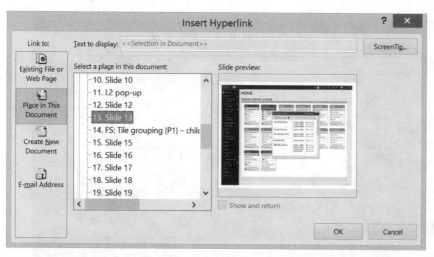

FIGURE 8-6 The Insert Hyperlink dialog box in PowerPoint allows you to create hot spots that link slides to create a click-through prototype.

Microsoft Visio

Visio has been around for a long time. It was introduced in the mid-1990s as a diagramming and flow-chart tool. It became very popular for architectural design, with its strong support for UML (unified modeling language) and code generation.

Visio has also become a popular tool for prototyping application user interfaces. Despite the influx of new, innovative prototyping tools in the market, Visio remains one of the most widespread prototyping tools within the design community.[9] Visio has a built-in library of common controls, cursors, dialogs, and other primitives that you can use to mock up your application's interface. You can create simple click-through prototypes by hyperlinking the shapes. For more complex interactions, you can use the Visual Basic programming language that is embedded as part of Visio.

Microsoft Blend for Visual Studio with SketchFlow

SketchFlow is a visual drag-and-drop tool for creating interactive prototypes. It's housed within the larger Microsoft Blend developer suite and is now part of the Visual Studio 2012 developer tools (in update 2).

Like PowerPoint and Visio, SketchFlow provides a set of reusable common controls that can be used to create many common types of user-interface layouts. However, the controls in SketchFlow are automatically backed by live code and provide basic functionality as soon as you drag them into place. Because SketchFlow resides within Microsoft Blend for Visual Studio, the full programming power of the Windows Presentation Framework (WPF) is available as well, enabling you to create arbitrarily complex prototypes with animation, motion, transitions, data sources, and application logic. (See Figure 8-7.) This means that you can populate a list box with actual data (such as the snowboard boot you want customers to purchase), and remove the item from the list when the user clicks Remove.

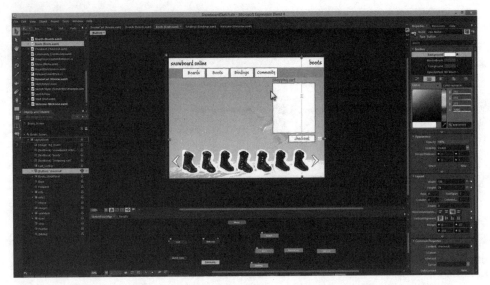

FIGURE 8-7 Interactive prototype in Microsoft SketchFlow of an online shopping app.

One of the nice features of SketchFlow is its use of wiggly lines throughout its wire-framing tool set to help convey that what you've created is a prototype and not a finished implementation. Also notice the handwritten font the app uses, Buxton Sketch, which further underscores that impression.[10] While learning SketchFlow is not quite as easy as learning PowerPoint or Visio, SketchFlow is dramatically more powerful. Notably, we know teams that have started a project by building lower-fidelity prototypes in SketchFlow; gradually added functionality and detail into that prototype; swapped in production-quality fonts, controls, and graphics; and continued to build production code in the same environment. Especially if you are writing production code for the Windows Presentation Framework, SketchFlow is worth checking out for prototyping.

 ## MINDSHIFT

Meet the devigner. The popularity of using languages such as HTML, CSS, XAML, and WPF has created an opportunity for design teams and engineering teams to work more closely together than ever before. Some design teams are gaining the technical proficiency to mock up proposed UI designs and to be responsible for some of the final production code as well, particularly when a tool set such as Microsoft Blend for Visual Studio helps separate the code from the presentation-layer markup.

People with both the design and tech skills to do this are sometimes called *devigners*, a combination of *dev*eloper and des*igner*. This arrangement gives devigners the flexibility to implement design details exactly as they envision them, without the potential for misinterpretation by the development team. Of course, with this responsibility comes many of the same issues development teams have faced over the years. How do you handle fixing and tracking bugs? In early iterations, do you prototype with final product quality or build it to throw away? In later iterations, how much time and energy do you spend to get that last few percentage points of perfection? When hiring a devigner, what skills are required? How are devigners rewarded and compensated with respect to their developer counterparts?

Balsamiq mockups

This tool allows you to build lo-fi wireframes that look and feel like sketches on a whiteboard or on paper, with a charmingly hand-drawn aesthetic—except these sketches are on a computer and provide linking and other quick functionality that allow you to create click-through prototypes with ease. Find it at www.balsamiq.com.

POP (prototyping on paper)

POP is an app for mobile devices that uses your phone's camera to snap a picture of a user interface you draw on paper and then allows you to link the pictures through hot spots. Very quickly you have an interactive, lo-fi, click-through prototype running on your mobile phone or tablet. You can find it on https://popapp.in/. It is currently available for iPhone, Android, and Windows 8.

Time will tell if this tool becomes popular, but we like it for its simplicity and for the idea of merging two ideas (paper and interactive-wireframe mockups) in a new way. (What a brilliant example of innovating through combining existing ideas, too).

 MINDSHIFT

The downside of pixel-perfect visual prototypes. Many designers have spent years learning the ins and outs of tools such as Adobe Photoshop or Adobe Illustrator in order to draw user interfaces whose looks are indistinguishable from the real thing. You can even link UI elements together with active hot spots that trigger changes in a picture (often implemented by hiding and showing layers), which imitates a user clicking through some part of the experience. These pixel-perfect visual prototypes are beautiful to look at, and can show exactly what an interface should look like in minute detail. They can be used to work out some detailed visual elements, such as animated transitions, or to excite a team about a new visual motif for its solution. Exciting visuals can sometimes be just the thing you need to sell an idea to an investor or a partner.

However, these pixel-perfect prototypes are very time-consuming to produce, even for an expert, and require a particular skill set that takes some time to master. Unfortunately, leaders can become very excited about these kinds of prototypes and may not realize how much work goes into making them. This points to a major downside of these types of prototypes—if only a few people on the team know how to make them, and iterating them is difficult and time-consuming, it makes it a lot harder for the larger team to meaningfully collaborate, edit, and consider alternatives as part of the Fast Feedback Cycle. This tends to lock in ideas and cause the team to be less responsive to feedback.

For your first few iterations, you almost always want a lower-fidelity approach so that you can explore a few alternatives more quickly. For later iterations, sometimes there's a good reason to build a pixel-perfect visual prototype. But our experience is that you often don't need to bother building a pixel-perfect prototype at all. Once you have explored some ideas in low-fidelity ways and narrowed in on an approach that seems to work, most teams find it more productive to move to code at that point. However, if you need a detailed, pixel-perfect prototype, you're better off having a professional do it than trying to learn these tools yourself.

Three-dimensional prototypes

If you are seeking to build a device or other three-dimensional object, you can use cardboard, woodblocks, foam, clay, fiberglass, or other physical objects to approximate the size and shape of the object you are imagining. You might also use a 3-D printer to mock up a physical object. By carrying a device-shaped woodblock in your pocket for a few days, you get a feel for whether an extra millimeter of thickness really matters. There's a famous story about a bunch of designers from IDEO who were consulting with a group of surgeons about a new surgical tool the designers envisioned that would solve a specific problem the surgeons were running into. Rather than trying to draw or describe the idea, the designers grabbed a whiteboard marker and taped it to a black film canister and a clothespin to physically demonstrate how the tool might look.[11]

Prototyping with skits

If the solution you are trying to prototype is a service, process, or workflow of some sort—a situation that includes a sequence of steps that multiple people need to do across a period of time—sometimes a skit can be a useful prototyping tool. Perhaps you are designing a system for getting three departments in a media business to approve a new article before it is published. Or perhaps you're imagining a retail kiosk where a customer can plug in her cell phone to create a custom-printed mug, wait for it to be made, and pay for the finished item at a cashier. Or maybe you're designing a bug-tracking solution that helps developers and testers collaborate to find and fix bugs. Perhaps you are thinking through how customer service calls will work for your new online service. Any of these sorts of problem spaces are conducive to using a skit as your prototyping tool.

Of course, you can also draw flow charts and process diagrams to think through how a process would work. But the benefit of a skit is that by physically walking through a process, you get a more visceral sense of whether that workflow is smooth and feels natural and comfortable to the people involved, especially if there are different actors with different perspectives. By acting out the process, you see more clearly what information is needed at each step and can identify where redundancy or confusion occurs. You might also notice spots with bigger lags in time or processing or where the process might be optimized by reordering the steps or perhaps omitting a step entirely.

Here's how to do it. Recruit team members to play different roles in the skit or to represent the different steps of your workflow. Use a piece of paper or another token to carry "information" from one step to the next. Build some simple props or UI mockups to model what the customer would see at each step. Place each step in a different location so that customers need to walk from place to place to accomplish their task. But as with any type of prototype, don't try just one skit. Try reordering the steps or making other changes, and then run through the skit again to see how that affects the end-to-end experience.

Prototyping an idea with skits is a great technique for enabling the team to think through its ideas in real time and space, but it can be even more productive when you bring in a customer to take part in the skit to make sure that the process is smooth and understandable from the customer's perspective as well.

Prototyping an API

Changing an API after developers have begun to code against it is perhaps one of the most disruptive things you can ever do to those customers. And those customers are your fellow software developers. Have a heart and prototype the end-to-end usage of your API and get feedback before you commit the resources to writing any code and releasing the API to the world. When you think about it, an API is probably the easiest thing in the world to prototype. Do you have Notepad installed on your computer? Here are a couple of techniques you can use to rapidly prototype an API.

Gather around the whiteboard

When you are ready to work out the details of an API, gathering a few team members around a whiteboard can be very productive. You can even invite a few customers who would use the API you're designing. Write out what the class structure would look like, what the methods would be called, what arguments they would take. Draw sketches of how different classes relate to one another, and which functionality appears where. Consider different alternatives and discuss the pros and cons of each choice.

 MINDSHIFT

Don't let elegance win out over customer needs. Just as with any other customer scenario, you need to keep developers' needs, desires, and preferences in mind when you're designing an API for them to use. When prototyping an API, take a minute to remind everyone about the customer scenario. What are customers trying to accomplish? What role does this API play in the larger system? This may be a single scenario (my customer needs to perform analytical data analysis on large data sets), or it may be a laundry list of smaller scenarios (print to a file, sort lists, etc.). Try to adopt that customer's point of view as you work, and don't ever forget that the beautiful class design you're creating is in service to your customer, who is trying to solve a problem or complete a task. All too often, we've seen the elegance of the class design take center stage over the customers' needs, and the result is an API that is elegant on paper but awkward to use in practice.

Write the documentation

An easy but very effective way to prototype an API is to start writing the documentation for it. You can use a simple text editor or word processor to write up the essentials of your API—the object hierarchy, classes, methods, arguments, and so on. Along with that, you can also write some sample code against that API and see how the methods you defined feel in actual use. Ideally, your sample code would demonstrate how your API might be used for the specific customer scenarios you've identified.

This prototyping approach is lightweight enough that it's quite reasonable to write up a few alternative APIs that you can show to customers, ask them to compare the alternatives and comment on the differences, and then adjust and perhaps merge the best ideas based on their feedback.

SFE in action: Using demo.txt

Jeffrey Snover, Distinguished Engineer, Microsoft Windows Server

The PowerShell team uses SFE techniques for command-line interfaces and APIs and considers it critical to our success. Before we used SFE, we had a few experiences where we had developed something that made sense in a functional specification but then failed when we used the feature to accomplish a task. It was too complicated or was missing steps or information. We adopted a technique we called "demo.txt," which required people to simply write down what the user experience of a feature would be. This technique transformed our development, and the payback was immediate and profound.

A developer or program manager would produce a demo.txt for a feature area. The form of the document was a PowerShell-session transcript file. It had a number of sections. Each section declares what the user is trying to accomplish and then shows what commands a user typed and what the command results were. For example, here's the sequence of commands that a customer would type to schedule a new job to happen at 3:00 a.m.

```
# Register the scheduled job (Every day at 3am, wake up the computer)
$trigger = New-JobTrigger -Daily -At 3am
$options = New-ScheduledJobOption -WakeToRun
Register-ScheduledJob -Name SyncAndBuild -Trigger $trigger -ScheduledJobOption $options
  -ScriptBlock { cd $enlistmentLocation; sdx sync; .tools\build.cmd }
```

After writing the document, we would all get in a room and walk through the experience. Writing the demo.txt file forced the author to get out of his head and put himself in the customer's shoes. That alone improved the design, but it was the peer review that had the largest impact. The most frequent phrases used in those meetings were "Wait, what?" and "How would I . . .?" and "Why do I have to. . .?" and "What happens when . . .?" and "This is going to rock!" Having lots of people walk through the experience fleshed out the different assumptions, mindsets, and approaches and forced us to make sure that we were designing a coherent, complete, and cogent experience. It was a turning point in the project.

The success of the early demo.txt approach for command-line interfaces led us to adopt a similar approach for APIs, where the developer would write sample programs showing how someone would use a proposed API.

It needs to be stressed that thinking through the experience for an API or a command-line interface has to be done before any code is written. We didn't always do that, and we learned our lesson. For a while, we allowed someone to write the feature and then do a review of the demo.txt afterward. The problem is that once someone writes the code, any feedback means changing the code that already works. People were fine changing things that were really broken, but they resisted making big changes just to improve the user experience. We switched pretty quickly based on that learning and insisted that the review take place prior to any coding so that we could change anything and everything in order to deliver an optimal customer experience.

We did all this years before SFE training was available, so we made it up ourselves and learned from our mistakes. Here are some of the key things we learned in applying these techniques to APIs and command-line interfaces:

1. Start by declaring a target customer persona and skill level.

2. Have individual scenarios for how customers will use the feature area.

   a. Declare what they are trying to accomplish and then show what they need to do.

   b. Stack rank these scenarios by frequency of usage.

   c. Make sure that the things that people do the most require the least effort.

3. Have scenarios for errors and stack rank them by probability.

   a. To paraphrase Dostoyevsky, "Errors, like the poor, will be with us always." The cloud means networks; networks mean failures.

   b. The error experience is when customers need our help the most and is a great opportunity to delight them.

4. Design your nouns and group your verbs.

   a. Nouns define the conceptual model for your feature. Once someone understands your nouns, he or she should understand your feature. If that isn't true, chances are that your design needs work.

   b. Pick the verbs to perform on those nouns from a well-defined set of verbs grouped by activity (e.g., Data, Life Cycle, Diagnostic, Communications, Security, Common, and Other).

5. Write the actual code that your users would write.

6. Do a peer review of the scenarios and the code the user would write to accomplish them.

   a. Pay particular attention to the flow of things that a user has to type and whether the output of one command contains the information necessary for the next step.

For PowerShell, we look to ensure that one command can be piped to another to accomplish a task.

    b. If you can review it with actual target customers, do so.

7. Adopt an 80/20 approach to complexity.

    a. Provide a simple command to deal with 80 percent of the user scenarios and provide an –OPTIONS parameter that takes an object created by another command, which can be as complex as needed to deal with all the corner scenarios.

    b. If your high-frequency command can't be explained with a crayon, consider refactoring it.

The cookbook approach

A clever variant of writing the documentation is the cookbook approach, which is featured in a series of books from O'Reilly Media. The idea is to not just write the documentation for a new API, but to also create a cookbook that shows the new API being used in various ways. With this technique, you create a cookbook that is a collection of recipes (or useful tasks) that demonstrate how the API would be used.

Each recipe contains three ingredients:

- **Problem**   A description of the problem being solved.
- **Solution**   A code example showing how to solve that problem.
- **Discussion**   Any relevant notes or comments about using the API to solve that problem.

Prototyping an API with a cookbook provides several benefits. A cookbook serves as a mechanism for both thinking through how a particular API design would play out in actual use and for getting feedback on your design. Because the cookbook shows the API in various usage scenarios, it's easier for customers to evaluate on paper. Once coding of the API begins, keep the cookbook up to date, and you'll be able to use it to test any proposed additions or changes prior to coding the new features.

As you test various proposed cookbooks, you will also learn about new tasks customers want to perform or discover that some of the problems you anticipated as being common aren't so common. You'll add, delete, and merge new recipes until your cookbook contains a set of recipes optimized for your customers' needs. A cookbook can also be a good tool for comparing different APIs. What does a cookbook of similar recipes look like for your competitor platforms or for other APIs in your system?

Finally, by keeping the cookbook's recipes current as you develop the API, at release time you'll have a valuable set of documentation and sample code ready-made for your broad set of customers.

Open book, close book

Once you start narrowing in on one or two API designs, you can use a technique we call "open book, close book" to test the design a bit more rigorously with some customers. Have them use the new API, take away the documentation ("close the book"), and then see what parts of the API they remember. This is a fancy way of doing usability testing for APIs that gives you even more information about how customers internalize your proposed API. Here's how you do it.

Start by writing some code examples that show how to perform the tasks of your API that you want to test with customers. Try to make the examples look just as they would in a development tool, with syntax coloring and other adornments. You can use a text editor, word processor, PowerPoint, whatever—just write out an example of what the actual code should look like. You'll also need some basic documentation for the API or perhaps even a cookbook if you have one already. The documentation doesn't have to be complete, just a quick reference with an object hierarchy, header file, and some brief descriptions of the essential classes and methods you want to test.

Invite some customers to review and analyze your API. It's helpful to have them review the API two at a time—the conversation between the two customers will be extremely helpful because it forces them to vocalize what they are thinking. Ask the first pair into a room, and without giving them any documentation, show them the first code example. Ask them to read the code and tell you what it does. Your job is to listen to them react and encourage them to talk out loud. With a pair of reviewers, one of them is usually more knowledgeable than the other. It's typical for that person to begin to "teach" the other one how the code example works. Listen very carefully to that conversation because it may provide you with some useful customer insights. After all, that expert customer has not seen the documentation or even the class object model. She's seen only the snippet of sample code you have provided, and she will project all sorts of ideas onto your API that she believes to be true.

After the pair has analyzed and discussed the code example, give them the documentation along with any code examples they have evaluated so far (paper printouts are fine). You then give them an open-book test and ask them to code a few things using your API. Observe them working and notice how well they do or don't do. Take note of how they use the documentation, where they went for more help, and what was intuitive and not intuitive to them. If the documentation is light (which is okay, this should be a quick prototype), the facilitator can play the role of the virtual online help system for anything you forgot to write down.

Once they finish with the open-book coding, close the book. Remove the code examples and any documentation. Ask them to code the same set of tasks or a similar set, but this time as a closed-book test. Again, watch them work and notice what they do, this time as they attempt to use this new API from memory.

When concepts in your API map to the customers' mental model, the customer will remember the API and will be able to recode those sections. But when the customer forgets something, they will code up a mix of what they remember, along with what makes sense to them. They will fill in the gaps with something they made up. It's important to pay attention to the things they make up because quite often the made-up parts will be an improvement on your original idea and provide a window into what makes the most sense from your customer's point of view.

Prototyping with code

Writing code is usually the most expensive way to build an idea to test with customers. Because using code is much more resource intensive than other prototyping techniques, if you are going to build a functional prototype using code, be sure you are doing so for a good reason. The classic criteria for building a functional prototype is simple—do it when you want to get feedback on something that can't be mocked up adequately using less expensive alternatives. Here are some of the common situations where teams have found writing code to be the best way to test out their ideas.

An easy, surgical change

If the idea you want to try is small and easy to code in a few hours or less, by all means just write the code. This usually is the case for minor adjustments to an existing service, for aesthetic tweaks, or for other minor changes to the interface. While you can test code with customers by using all of the usual approaches, these types of changes are often the sort of thing you want to use an A/B test with to see whether a new idea might improve the use of a feature or your ability to monetize your live service. A/B testing allows you to test two variants of your code to see which works better for the system, for the business, or for the customer experience. For instance, you might try two different layouts of your "buy a subscription" page to see which one converts more visitors into buyers.

A/B testing

A/B testing isn't just for quick-and-easy code changes. If getting live usage data is important for knowing whether an idea will truly work, there is no substitute for A/B testing. This is often the case for aspects of your software that affect monetization or the usage patterns of specific features or services. While the code you write for an A/B test might not need to be fully and completely production quality, it needs to be awfully close if you are going to make it available on your live service without jeopardizing service quality and operability, so there are some additional costs to consider. We'll discuss A/B testing in more detail in Chapter 9, "Observing customers: Getting feedback."

Complex interactions

As you iterate through the Fast Feedback Cycle, you will come to the point where your questions become much more specific. At that point you already know what problems you are solving and how you are approaching them. And you may already have begun writing production code toward those goals. But now you are trying out something new that involves a very specific set of interrelated and complex interactions that would be unwieldy to mock up using a high-level tool set.

A simple example is a situation where the exact method of user input, either mouse or touch, makes a big difference in the experience. A solution that tries to perfect the experience of dragging two windows to dock them together would be difficult to prototype adequately without writing code. Dialing in the exact touch motion to initiate a swipe is another example. For these kinds of complex interface interactions, customers can't give you valid feedback from a paper prototype, so you need functional code for customers to try.

Animation

Sometimes, the details matter. And when it comes to animation, the details are usually important. You might experiment to see whether any higher-level tools can get the job done more quickly, but many times with animation you have to write code, especially if you need to factor in any server latency to the animation's feel and performance. Do a quick Internet search for "animation prototyping," and you'll find some options for quickly prototyping animation (most of them require some level of scripting).

Personal data

Sometimes, to get good feedback, it's best when customers can try out your solution using their own data (email, photos, songs, etc.), perhaps even in their own environment. For example, you are working on a photo app and wonder about how a particular sorting or tagging scheme will work. In this case, you may get better data if users try out your ideas with their own photos of their kids, dogs, and vacation spots, rather than with a pile of stock photos that they don't recognize and don't care about.

The test drive

At times, you can't get real, deep, informative feedback unless customers have the ability to use your solution in their own environment, with their own data, and over a few days, weeks, or even months. Getting longitudinal feedback like this requires the most complete, fully functional, and highest-fidelity code—you can't expect customers to use something in their daily lives that isn't substantially complete. It goes without saying that you should do a significant amount of iteration with lower-fidelity methods to fine-tune your ideas before you get to this point. Often this kind of test drive is less of a prototype and more a prerelease version of the code, sometimes called a preview, alpha, or beta.

One example is in the development of Microsoft Kinect. The best way for that team to see how customers used the Kinect games and interface in a realistic family environment was to find a way for a handful of homes to use the system and to observe that usage over a period of time. By doing this, the Kinect team was able to discover all sorts of valuable insights, such as how the system worked with home furniture and layout (was proximity a problem?), what happened when friends came over who had never seen or heard of Kinect before (could they figure it out?), or how the family reacted to the system after its newness wore off (did they still use it and, if so, was the usage different?).

Similarly, many development teams work with enterprise partners to deploy prerelease code in their environments in order to get real-world feedback that helps fine-tune the final release. The systems found in larger corporations are almost always very complex. And while many enterprise systems have a lot of basics in common, the actual systems vary greatly in the number and type of legacy systems, code, and data that they integrate. Legacy integration and data can make it difficult, impossible, or prohibitively expensive to replicate different types of enterprise systems or topologies in a lab setting, so this kind of real-world testing is essential.

Technical investigations

As a developer, you probably already do a reasonable amount of code prototyping in the course of your regular work. Some development teams call these "investigations." If there are a couple of technical approaches to solving a problem, a developer might play around with the code, trying out each approach to see which one works the best. Sometimes this happens when you're working on a particularly difficult bug, where there is no clear, easy fix. An investigation is just another way to do a quick round of code prototyping with the intent to answer a question about which is the best technical solution for the given problem.

Auditioning components

"Buy, borrow, or build?" is a common question that teams ask (or should ask) frequently. Can I purchase a component that solves my needs, can I use an open source component, or do I need to build it myself?

When beginning a project, you may have choices to make as to which API, which components, which libraries, and even which programming language you will use. To answer these questions, teams need to write code that exercises the key component interactions and all of the architectural layers so that they can make well-informed decisions about which option offers the flexibility, ease of use, and maintainability that's needed. In Agile development, this practice is one application of the technique called *spiking*.

 VOCAB

A *spike* is an experiment that cuts through the technical and architectural layers of a solution with the intent of learning about technical characteristics and tradeoffs rather than assessing the end-to-end experience. Spikes are done with the intention and expectation that any resulting code will be thrown away.

Spikes are often quite divergent, where different developers go off and try something and then get back together in a day or two to compare notes and decide upon an approach. It's common to use spiking as a technique to inform buy, borrow, or build decisions on specific components to be used in a solution. Spikes are also used to answer questions such as which language or API best suits the problem domain, which data structures are optimal, what the basic performance characteristics of a particular implementation might be, or whether to put certain code on the client or the server.

Testing the -ilities

Most projects have specific goals and metrics for the system related to performance, scalability, security, reliability, maintainability, operability, accessibility, localizability, and the like. If you have several architectural approaches you're considering that may impact these "-ilities," you may find value in writing code to test a few approaches to see which solution works best for optimizing these factors.

Deep dive: Paper prototyping

Paper prototyping is well suited for detailing user interface ideas and making modifications early in the design phase. You can use this technique for testing ideas with customers as well as for thinking through your own ideas. Sometimes, ideas that look good in your mind's eye end up not working so well in real life. Paper prototyping is an easy way to explore many alternatives over a short period of time.

Paper prototyping tends to work best when the UI is composed of elements and controls that people are familiar with, because customers already have reasonably accurate expectations about how these elements work. You can create a paper prototype that uses these common elements and then test to see how the user interacts with your system. However, with new types of interactions and metaphors (think about swiping a touchscreen or how a user interacts with a product like Microsoft's Kinect), paper prototyping probably isn't a very accurate way of judging how customers will interact. To represent and test new UI metaphors, you probably need a higher-fidelity prototype.

Paper prototyping is also a good tool for including lots of team members and for building bridges between them. You can use rapidly made paper prototypes to set expectations and to get everyone on the same page with regard to direction, proposed plans, and what you've learned about your customers. Paper prototypes also lend themselves to having more team members play around with them, mocking up new, creative, and potentially innovative ideas regardless of the team members' skill sets or expertise.

You can create remarkably detailed and complex user interfaces using only paper and other basic office supplies. For instance, consider Figure 8-8 and Figure 8-9, which show a prototype built by a group of design students from Sao Paulo State University.

This paper prototype uses a black cardboard backing to hold a fixed, unchanging background for the mobile device the students are designing for. All of the "screens" they want to test are placed as separate pieces of paper on top of that model, which lets the students quickly change what users see as the users interact with the device by pushing a button or selecting a menu item with a finger or, in this case, a stylus. We encourage you to view a short video that demonstrates this paper prototype in action: https://www.youtube.com/watch?v=5Ch3VsautWQ (turn on English subtitles; the video was originally produced in Portuguese).[12]

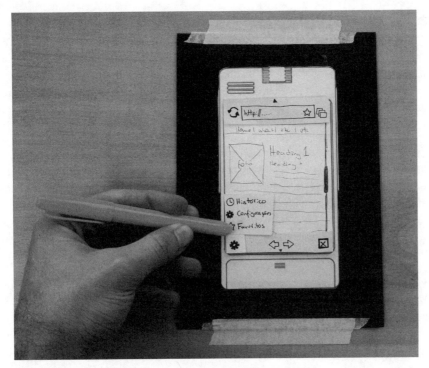

FIGURE 8-8 A detailed paper prototype, being used for a user test.

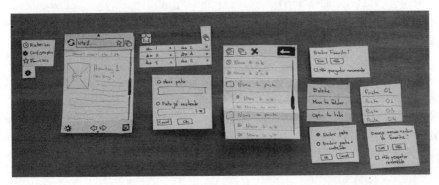

FIGURE 8-9 All of the individual elements that were used to create that paper prototype.

 MINDSHIFT

Don't overdo it. More than anything, paper prototyping works because it is extremely fast while also being flexible. If you lose the speed, a lot of the efficiency you gain through paper prototypes is eroded. Be willing to let your paper prototype look a little rough around the edges. If the customer can understand it, it's good enough.

Building a paper prototype

The following sections give some brief tips for how to use common materials to build a paper prototype. While we list the materials that we have found the most useful in our experience, there is almost a limitless variety of office supplies, toys, and other doodads to choose from. There are not hard-and-fast rules about what raw materials to use in a paper prototype, other than to keep the prototype quick and simple. It is a good idea to gather a set of paper prototyping materials to make a supplies box that you can easily pull out when you need it.

Backdrop

The place to start is by creating a backdrop or frame for your paper prototype. A backdrop keeps you from having to redraw the basic shape, size, and layout of the desktop, mobile device, application window, or whatever other form factor you're designing for. There are two basic ways to accomplish this:

- Make photocopies of the master version of your backdrop, and use those photocopies as your starting point for all the "screens" you create.

- Mount a single copy of your backdrop on a piece of cardboard or foam core, and place the "screens" on top of that frame.

 TIP

Laminate your backdrop so that you can write on it with wet-erase pens. This also makes it more durable, which is helpful if you use it often or share it across projects.

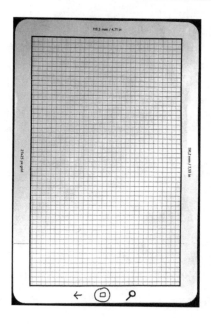

Paper and scissors

In a paper prototype, most of your designs are drawn on paper that you cut to various sizes and shapes. Use different colors to help distinguish areas of a prototype. For instance, cut a small square of brightly colored paper to stand in for a fly-out menu. The menu can then easily appear and disappear during a user test without disturbing the rest of the prototype.

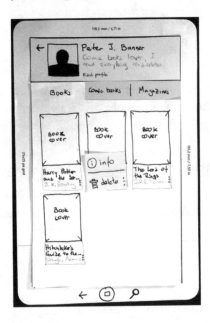

Sticky notes

Sticky notes are particularly helpful when you want a small bit of your UI model to stay put for a little while. Making a fly-out menu from sticky paper is even better than using plain paper because a sticky note is easier to manage during testing and won't blow away with the slightest breeze or hand movement. Sticky notes can be folded into an accordion shape to mimic a drop-down menu; fix one edge to the prototype and keep the other edge loose so that it can be pulled open or folded shut. A glue stick also works to make something a little sticky or to more permanently glue pieces of the UI together.

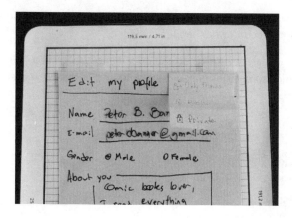

Index cards

Index cards make very good dialog boxes and provide a consistent size and shape. Both 3x5 and 4x6 cards are useful, depending on the scale of your prototype.

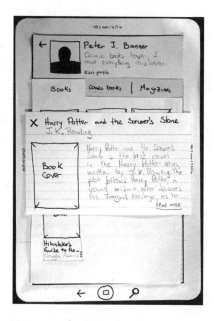

Transparencies

Transparency sheets can be amazingly useful in a paper prototype. A common step is to lay a transparency over the entire mocked-up interface so that a user can enter input into a field, for instance, by writing with a marker directly on the transparency, without messing up the prototype underneath. When that test is over, just wipe the transparency clean, and the same prototype can be tested with other customers.

Transparencies can also be helpful for showing an overlay of some sort, such as a box to highlight a selected photo in a slide show app, without affecting what happens below it.

Remember that you can stack multiple transparency sheets on top of one another to keep different UI elements on separate layers, which sometimes makes it easier to demonstrate the user interface you are envisioning.

Pens, pencils, and markers

Use various colors and line weights to mimic different fonts and to distinguish different types of text. For instance, use a big black felt marker for the heading of a page, but use a pen for the majority of the text. Use a blue pen to indicate hyperlinks. Write lightly with a pencil if you need to represent a grayed-out UI control.

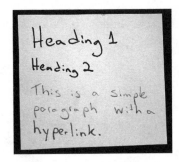

Tape

A little bit of transparent tape can be very useful for connecting parts of your prototype or to temporarily attach a new dialog box, control, or other element to the top of a larger piece of paper. We especially like gift-wrapping tape, which is easier to peel up and reapply without tearing the paper underneath.

Fishing line and dental floss

To mock up a simple animation or transition in a paper prototype, one clever trick is to use a piece of fishing line or dental floss to drag an element across the page.

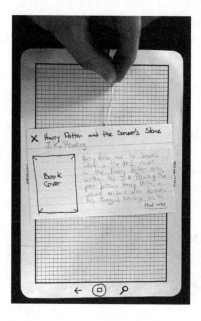

Common shapes

A relatively small number of common controls show up frequently in paper prototypes. Here are some that appear frequently, with examples of simple ways to draw them so that most people will readily understand.

Screenshots and printouts

Although drawing is usually faster, paper prototypes don't always need to be hand drawn. It might be easier to print a screenshot and modify it a bit to demonstrate what you envision. On a small piece of paper, draw an alternative for the place you want to modify, and then just tape it on top of the screenshot. Or take a screenshot of an existing control and use that within a hand-drawn paper prototype. You can even use a printout as your master backdrop. Feel free to mix and match hand-drawn prototypes with printouts as needed. Remember that your goal is to create something as quickly as possible that reasonably approximates your idea, not to make something beautiful. It's okay for your prototype to be a bit of a Frankenstein. Just remember that screenshots may give you more fidelity (and details) than you really want in your prototype, which may invite detailed feedback too early. Keep an eye on this.

Stay organized

Paper prototypes almost always involve stacks of paper and sometimes small bits of paper that are layered on top of one another. Keeping track of which bits go together is important, especially in a more complex or extensive prototype. Try using ziplock bags, manila folders, paper clips, binder clips, or other containers to keep yourself organized.

Build stage: How do you know you're done?

The goal of using the Fast Feedback Cycle is to learn from real customers as quickly and efficiently as possible. The Build stage is about building something tangible so that you're ready to get feedback from customers and test whether you're on the right track.

Although the character of what you build and how you build it changes between early and later iterations, you know you are finished with this stage and are ready to get customer feedback when you have:

- Something concrete to show to customers, with the intent of getting feedback. Very early on, this may be as simple as a few paper prototypes. As you make progress, you may build higher-fidelity prototypes to show customers and eventually demonstrate working code.

- An understanding of the level of feedback you want to get from customers. Are you looking to validate the direction you are taking, to see whether customers are wowed in their first impression, or to see whether they are able to perform a task without any hints?

We touched on a number of principles in this chapter that are worth repeating. First of all, get into the habit of prototyping your ideas early, before investing a lot of time and energy. To adopt this mindset, you need to lose any fear you might have of testing rough, early prototypes. Oftentimes, the first rugged, bumpy prototypes stimulate the best feedback. If you feel uncomfortable showing unfinished work, get over it. Finally, remember that you should not rely on your first good idea. Make sure that you create and test multiple alternatives, especially in your first few iterations. It's likely that you will find an even better solution by combining the best aspects of several ideas.

It shouldn't be a surprise that these principles are also key principles of Agile development, Lean Startup, as well as the scientific method. Iteration and feedback are the driving forces behind all of these methods.

Notes

1. Savoia makes a distinction between prototyping and "pretotyping" to focus on precoding prototypes. We don't necessarily see a significant benefit to this distinction in nomenclature, as many modern prototyping tools blur the line between code and noncode prototypes, and all prototypes should be produced as rapidly as possible. However, we absolutely agree with Savoia's emphasis on the value of early prototyping before writing production code. You can read more here: http://www.pretotyping.org/.

2. Some people ask what the difference is between a prototype and the various types of exploratory drawings we described in Chapter 7, "Brainstorming alternatives," such as storyboards, flow charts, architecture diagrams, and so on. Both a prototype and an exploratory drawing can take the form of simple hand-drawn sketches, yet they are fundamentally different. Exploration-oriented drawings provide a bird's-eye view of the system, showing an end-to-end user flow in a storyboard sequence, an entire process in a flow chart, or a whole layer cake in an architectural-system diagram. On the other hand, prototypes mimic the actual behavior of the system, acting as the software would depending on the input that's provided. Practically speaking, a prototype shows only one state at a time. Then, as a customer interacts with it, it displays what changes, just as the software might once it's fully built.

3. Although when you present a few options, you do need to mitigate order effects because people typically report that the last option they see is the one they like the best. More on this in Chapter 9, "Observing customers: Getting feedback."

4. Stephen P. Dow et al., "Parallel Prototyping Leads to Better Design Results, More Divergence, and Increased Self-Efficacy," http://hci.stanford.edu/publications/2010/parallel-prototyping/ParallelPrototyping2010.pdf.

5. While "disposable" is often listed as a principle of prototyping, it is not true that you will always throw away your prototype code. As with many things, there are shades of gray in the "disposable or not" question. We discuss the pros and cons of writing production code or disposable code in the section "Prototyping with code."

6. Eric Reis, *The Lean Startup* (New York: Crown Business, 2011); Brendan Sterne, "The Original iPhone Was a Minimum Viable Product (MVP)," http://brendansterne.com/2014/04/10/the-original-iphone-was-a-minimum-viable-product-mvp/.

7. Sorry, but this happens. In the Fast Feedback Cycle, getting bad feedback from time to time is an expected part of the process, especially if you're pushing the envelope of innovation. If you aren't occasionally hearing customers tell you that your idea is junk, you probably aren't trying out enough ideas.

8. Agilists will recognize the slicing approach as another way of describing what naturally happens when you build code one user story at a time.

9. According to the data in Todd Warfel's book *Prototyping: A Practical Guide* (Rosenfeld Media, 2009), Visio is the second most popular tool among the designers he surveyed. Paper prototyping is the most popular prototyping tool (among the designers surveyed). It will be interesting to see how the availability of prototyping tools and their usage changes over time.

10. We intentionally used hand-drawn illustrations in this book to reinforce the point that rough sketches can carry plenty of information, with a minimum of overhead and effort.

11. You can read more about this and other IDEO projects at http://www.ideo.com/images/uploads/news/pdfs/USNews_2006-09-24.pdf.

12. Many thanks to Henrique Perticarati for producing the paper prototype examples featured in this deep dive. (See www.perticarati.com.) Henrique also was part of the team of students who created the paper prototype video.

Continuous feedback
from customers   A/B testing   Are you solving the right problem?

Your first idea is probably wrong   Conduct surveys

Customer feedback helps you make
early course corrections   **FEEDBACK**

big data   Test multiple alternatives   LISTEN, DON'T EXPLAIN

EXPERIMENTS ARE SUCCESSFUL ONLY   **Quick Pulse Study**
1/3 OF THE TIME   instrumentation   Cogwalk

Do you understand the   Concept testing   WAIT FOR ROCK STAR FEEDBACK
customer need?   & focus groups
Informal vs.   Wait until tomorrow
Evaluative research   formal testing   **Longitudinal study**   to decide

ASK OPEN-ENDED QUESTIONS   HEURISTIC EVALUATION

Discount usability   DON'T SPEND TIME ON A   Usability testing
PROBLEM NO ONE CARES ABOUT   QUESTIONNAIRES

CHAPTER 9

Observing customers: Getting feedback

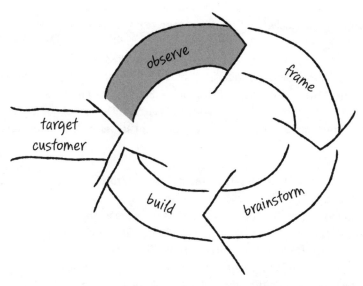

Congratulations. You've completed your first iteration of the Fast Feedback Cycle and built something that you expect will delight your customers. Now you repeat the cycle, and it's time to check in again with customers. It's time to find out what customers think of your ideas. It's time for you to be objective and listen to what they have to say.

This chapter returns to the first stage of the Fast Feedback Cycle, "Observe." In Chapter 5, "Observing customers: Building empathy," we explored *generative* research techniques for building empathy and identifying new customer insights; the focus of this chapter is on how to use *evaluative* research techniques to get customer feedback on what you've built, whether that's a prototype or a functional solution.[1]

Why get feedback?

Remember the tunnel? You may be in it. You've invested a lot of time, energy, and emotion in your solution idea up to this point. You've researched your customers and developed empathy for them. You've made decisions on their behalf and now have something to show them. You've built it for them, and you love it. Of course your customers are going to love it as well . . . or are they?

The fact is, as hard as you try and as smart as you are, you don't own a functioning crystal ball. And cold, hard data shows that even when you start with great customer research and build something based on that, you rarely achieve your goals on the first attempt. This is why we believe so strongly in iteration.

So what are the odds of getting it right the first time, without any feedback from your customers? Dr. Ron Kohavi, general manager of the Analysis & Experimentation team in Microsoft's Applications & Services Group, has made a career of testing ideas through online controlled experimentation, otherwise known as A/B testing. After performing countless experiments at Microsoft, starting before 2007, he concludes, "We are poor at assessing the value of ideas. Only one-third of the ideas tested at Microsoft improved the metric(s) they were designed to improve. Success is even harder to find in well-optimized domains like Bing." This problem is not unique to Microsoft. Dr. Kohavi gathered data from many other sources to demonstrate that this is a systemic problem across the entire software industry:

> Jim Manzi wrote that at Google, only "about 10 percent of these [controlled experiments, were] leading to business changes." Avinash Kaushik wrote in his Experimentation and Testing *primer that "80% of the time you/we are wrong about what a customer wants." Mike Moran wrote that Netflix considers 90% of what they try to be wrong. Regis Hadiaris from Quicken Loans wrote that "in the five years I've been running tests, I'm only about as correct in guessing the results as a major league baseball player is in hitting the ball. That's right—I've been doing this for five years, and I can only "guess" the outcome of a test about 33% of the time!" Dan McKinley at Etsy wrote "nearly everything fails" and "it's been humbling to realize how rare it is for them [features] to succeed on the first attempt. I strongly suspect that this experience is universal, but it is not universally recognized or acknowledged." Finally, Colin McFarland wrote in the book* Experiment!, *"No matter how much you think it's a no-brainer, how much research you've done, or how many competitors are doing it, sometimes, more often than you might think, experiment ideas simply fail."*[2]

Don't be depressed by these statistics, getting it wrong isn't all bad news. In the process of running an experiment, you almost always learn something that helps you adjust your approach, and then you are that much more likely to nail it on your next iteration. By using some of the techniques listed in this chapter, you'll figure out which of your ideas work and which don't. You will get a much better idea of what customers really want by watching how they react to your proposed solutions, deepening your customer insights. You'll usually leave with inspiration for what new ideas (or what blend of existing ideas) might work better. And you will weed out bad ideas instead of carrying their costs through the longer development and delivery process.

 MINDSHIFT

Many engineers tell us that they have lightning-bolt moments when they finally get to watch customers use the stuff they've worked so hard to build. As soon as you sit down with a customer, a magical thing happens—all of a sudden, you start to see the problem space through the customer's eyes. You may notice problems in your approach that you didn't see at all during the long hours you spent designing or coding your solution. That profound shift in perspective is quite easy to achieve and can make all the difference in helping you see what isn't quite working, to notice where your customer is stumbling, and to know where to focus your energy next.

User testing comes in many flavors

Now that you have developed some ideas, the main goal of the Observe stage in the Fast Feedback Cycle is to put customers in front of your prototypes, your working code, or whatever your latest progress is and see how they react and what they do with it. Is their response enthusiastic? Does your solution actually solve the problem you've set out to solve? Do they intuitively navigate through the user interface? Did they do what you expected? Can you measure improvement in the key metrics you're trying to move? You may be surprised by what you learn.

You can discover many different kinds of things in user testing, from whether you are solving a problem that your customers care about to whether you picked the right solution for the problem you addressed. You can also compile real-world usage data about your solution. The focus of your testing and what you are seeking to learn progresses in a predictable pattern throughout a project's phases, from early to midgame to endgame. It's worth thinking about what you're trying to learn at any given phase of your project so that you can pick the right approach for getting feedback.

Testing whether you fully understand the customer need

In the first couple of iterations of the Fast Feedback Cycle, you want to make sure that customers actually care about the problems you decided to solve for them, and that you fully understand all the nuances of their needs. To do this, you show customers your latest thinking and look primarily for confirmation that the problems your solutions are trying to solve resonate with them. You should also listen for how you might adjust your framing to describe the customer need more directly. Do you understand the customer problem deeply and thoroughly, in all its complexities? Are you thinking about solving that problem in a way that your customers understand and appreciate? Is this problem important enough that they will pay for a solution to it? Do you have a clear understanding of what you need to deliver to make a useful and desirable solution?

Since you are primarily interested in testing your overall direction and customer insights, it's quite likely that you can get feedback long before you have any working code. As we've mentioned, it's usually most efficient in the first iteration or two to use low-fidelity, rapid prototyping techniques such as sketches, storyboards, or paper prototypes, or just have customers read and react to written customer scenario narratives. The goal is to get directional feedback that tells you whether you are on the right track before you get too far along in selecting, building, and fine-tuning a specific solution, which prevents you from wasting time on a dead end.

For example, imagine that you decided to build a new service that provides a way for small businesses to establish a web presence. At this stage, you show customers some early concepts, perhaps prototypes of tools to help build a website, or easily establish a business-oriented Facebook presence, or create a blog, or more easily post and respond to Twitter messages. Showing these early concepts helps customers describe what additional aspects of the solution they were expecting or perhaps triggers them to mention more-subtle problems you haven't heard from them before, or they might comment on where your ideas haven't really met their goals. You might simply show the scenario your team developed and ask whether the story sounds familiar or how they might change it to better reflect their situation.

After showing customers your early ideas, you might ask them again how they currently do these tasks, what it would take for a solution to be better enough that they would switch to it, and what would be involved in switching. You might also do some price testing at this stage to see what customers would be willing to pay for or how they react to advertising.

In doing all this, you might better understand that even though most small-business customers aren't totally satisfied with their current web presence, they're also loath to put their energy into rebuilding it, and their most pressing needs are actually in managing their social-network presence and communicating with their customers. In deeper conversations, you now discover that the biggest issue for these business owners turns out to be how to reach their customers without having their emails land in the junk mail folder, which was not what you first assumed. It's common for teams to find that the problem they thought was most important really wasn't as important as they thought. If you went full steam ahead and delivered a fancy new tool set for establishing a website presence for small businesses, you might have been disappointed by poor sales, regardless of how well the solution worked or how innovative it was, because this just wasn't an important problem for them to solve right now.

Remember, that to validate your direction and confirm whether you fully understand your customers' needs and are on a path to delight them, it's vital that you test with customers who are representative of your target market. Only your target customers can answer the question "Is this device, service, or app solving a problem that I care about?"

MINDSHIFT

Don't spend time on a problem no one cares about. It can be very tempting to skip customer feedback and move on based on your intuition. However, remember that you are trying to avoid spending a lot of effort on a problem, only to realize later that your target customers don't actually care enough about that problem to switch providers, pay money, or actually engage with your product. Sadly, this mistake happens a lot in our industry, so it's worth making a quick iteration to avoid having to throw out a lot of work later on—or worse, end up shipping something you later realize isn't the right thing but is the only thing you've got.

Thankfully, getting feedback doesn't have to take much time. In fact, because you're only looking for directional feedback, you don't have to have a complete, buttoned-up prototype to get started talking to customers about your ideas. The sooner you float your half-baked, early concepts with customers to see whether you are on the right track, the quicker you'll be able to make crucial course corrections that point you in the right direction.

SFE in action: You're wrong

Jeff Derstadt, Principal Development Lead, Microsoft Azure

For nine months, starting in the fall of 2013, I participated in an incubation experiment within Microsoft where we adopted "lean startup" techniques to find new business value for the Azure platform. Our team developed a three-day workshop to give other engineers at Microsoft a taste of what it is like to practice lean techniques and the kind of customer development that mirrors that of successful startups.

At the start of the workshop, attendees form groups of four around an idea for a new consumer product that all team members are passionate about (such as a wearable device for children or a movie recommendation service). Each team starts by developing a pitch about their idea and then delivers the pitch to the entire group on the morning of the first day. As pitches go on, we ask team members whether they believe in their idea and think it's a winner. Everyone raises their hands in affirmation: customers will love their idea and product.

Following the pitches, we provide a brief overview of lean techniques and make the point that in today's technology markets, the most significant business risks have shifted from *Can we build this* to *Have we built the right thing and achieved successful product-market fit*. Halfway through the first day, the learning begins when we kick everyone out of the building and have them go talk to customers about their product idea and record what they learn. Each team is tasked with interviewing 15–20 real customers—that is, people who do not work for Microsoft and aren't friends or family members.

On the morning of day two, teams come with a readout of their idea and their learnings from the customer interviews. As though following the same playbook, each team delivers a scarily similar message: not many people liked their solution, the team is a little depressed, and talking with customers is hard stuff! What we've observed is that teams typically spend that first customer outing talking to people about their solution and its features ("Do you want music with your workout reminder app?"). From this experience, most of the attendees get a good taste of being wrong, and being proven wrong by people who were supposed to buy their product.

To get teams back on track, the day-two readouts are followed by a discussion about customer development, which is the process of learning about customers, their activities, and their problems and leaving out any mention of a solution. Teams regroup and come up with a line of questioning that allows them to inquire about a day in the life of their customers, how they spend their time, and the problems they have trying to achieve something. At midday, teams again head out of the building to talk to 15–20 new customers and prepare a readout for the next day.

Day three is about promise and hope. Teams again present their readouts, but the sentiment is always very different: people are reinvigorated and full of new ideas. From their new line of questioning, teams have learned why people rejected their initial solution and why it may not have fit for their customers, and they have usually discovered a new problem that their customers wish could be solved. The creative gears are turning again, innovation is happening, and people are excited about how easy it seems to now get to a right answer.

Regardless of engineering position or level, people start the workshop by raising their hands and saying they are right, and they end the workshop knowing they were wrong. They learn to fail fast and that gathering data about all aspects of their customers can lead to something customers will love. Being wrong isn't so bad after all, and learning how to get to being right and then delivering that value is the action we all have to take.

Testing whether you've got the right solution

As you gain confidence that you've focused on the right problems, your attention shifts to identifying an optimal solution that strikes the right balance between great customer experience, technology feasibility, and business strategy. At this point you want to get feedback that helps you make the big tradeoffs between what is ideal versus what is feasible and helps you balance multiple, sometimes conflicting, goals.

To get this type of feedback, you test the alternative solution ideas you developed in the prototyping stage. If the ideas are relatively easy to code, then A/B testing several different approaches can be a good option. But the more you are facing a larger or newer problem or exploring an unknown solution space, the more you should lean toward rough, noncode prototypes that you test with customers in person.

Remember from the last chapter: While you explore alternatives, don't let your prototypes become unnecessarily detailed, which distracts you from the main decision points. At this point you care mostly about the rough flow of your solution, whether it makes sense to the customer, and whether it feels good to them. Again, if your prototype has too many bells and whistles, your customers can easily be distracted and start telling you about how they don't care for that animation or that they really prefer blue rather than orange—small details that are not really central to the essence of your solution.

Following along with our small-business example, you might use early feedback to reframe your scenario to focus on social networking and customer communication as the problems your customers care most about. In the next round of user testing (with a fresh group of representative customers), you might show some paper prototypes of several approaches for how to manage Twitter, Facebook, and email communications. A few of the prototypes might propose out-of-the-box ideas for how to ensure that email doesn't get junked, or new approaches for how to communicate with customers in ways that don't involve email, which avoids the junk mail perception to begin with. You carefully listen to feedback about which aspects of the updated solutions resonate with customers and which don't. You notice where customers say that key functionality is still missing and use that feedback to create a smaller set of revised alternatives that you test with another set of customers.

 ## MINDSHIFT

Keep iterating until you get rock-star feedback. It's easy to convince yourself that customers love your solution, so beware of feedback that sounds like this:

"Well, that's kind of cool, but it's not for me. But I like it. Good job. You know I think I have a friend who might really like it . . ."

The feedback you receive when you have solved a well-understood, articulated need will be generally positive. You'll get encouraging and optimistic feedback from your customers. After all, you are solving a pain point for them, and people mostly want to be nice and tell you that they like your work.

However, when you solve an *unarticulated* need exceptionally well, when you have found a way to address a problem that customers might not even know they had, your customers are surprised and deeply delighted, and the feedback you receive cannot be misread. When you rock your customers' world, you know it. And you will know this very early on when you give customers a first glimpse of your ideas in prototype form, or even in a simple sketch. If you are not getting extremely positive, glowing feedback that shows that customers think you are a magician or a rock star, you probably haven't hit the optimal solution yet—or you aren't yet solving an important problem—and need to continue trying out ideas. Don't be impatient: it may take a few iterations before you find the sweet spot that truly resonates with your customers.

SFE in action: Testing early prototypes of Kinect

Ramon Romero, Senior Design Research Lead, Microsoft Kinect

With Kinect we were able to successfully predict the device's appeal and potential well in advance of release. The key was to understand the questions we wanted to answer with our prototypes. Early testing of Kinect experiences focused on two parallel questions, both fundamental to the ultimate success of the accessory:

- First and foremost, could consumers adapt to controlling Kinect?

- Second, could we create a set of experiences that would be fun, attractive, and novel while sufficiently demonstrating the potential of the technology?

Kinect prototype testing with consumers began in early 2009, 22 months prior to release. Before shipping, Kinect would be experienced by hundreds of participants, but in those first few months we conducted only a few simple tests of prototypes as they were updated. Testing was undertaken in the utmost secrecy. Participants were led to believe that an existing Xbox video camera was the active device. The early Kinect prototype was hidden within a PC chassis.

We followed standard usability protocols with the exception that we gave the Kinect itself only a limited introduction—"Imagine controlling a game system without using a controller"—and required that customers figure out how to control their interaction with the game without further instruction. This was our success criteria: Kinect's success hinged on it being instantly understandable.

The answer to our first question was clear almost immediately. Consumers readily adapted to Kinect in even the earliest versions of its prototype. We had the answer to our experience question as well. In these earliest tests we saw success in one of the mini-games that ultimately shipped as part of Kinect Adventures!: Rally Ball, a game that requires the user to bounce a virtual ball against a wall at the end of a hallway to clear tiles.

Interestingly, Kinect looked good in all phases of its testing, even when it ostensibly should not have. Prototypes were rough, failed frequently, and often contained only the seed of a coherent game design. Nonetheless, the potential shined through and participants expressed their excitement directly. This is not a common thing, even for games.

We should use this experience to teach ourselves something. Ultimately, the release of Kinect was highly successful. Microsoft announced 24 million units sold by 2013, meaning about one in three Xbox 360 owners bought a Kinect attached to go with it.[3] We cannot conclusively state that we predicted this level of success in prototype. But we do know one thing. True potential shined, and we could see it well before the final experiences were created.

Testing whether your solution works well

As you start winnowing your options down toward a single solution, the fidelity of your solution prototypes needs to increase. If you haven't already, you should switch from testing prototypes to building end-to-end slices of functionality and testing working code. As you do this, you'll use the feedback you receive to shift from deciding which solution to implement toward tuning the interaction and usability of your implementation. Is the experience smooth, fluid, and easy to use? Does it flow? Is it aesthetically pleasing? Is it meeting your experience metrics?

This is the time when you might take a few shortcuts in recruiting customers for in-person testing. It can take a lot of effort to locate, recruit, and screen for target customers who are willing to take the time to give you early feedback. Especially if your contact list of target customers is small, you need to use your customer pool wisely. Because obvious usability problems often mask nonobvious ones, you want to take care of the obvious problems before you recruit actual target customers to give you detailed feedback.

Big usability issues that you uncover first—such as can users find the command, can they follow the steps, does the UI follow well-known standards, can users remember what to do, does the language make sense, does the experience flow naturally, and so on—tend to be universal. When fleshing out these types of early issues, it's okay to get feedback from a teammate (someone who did not work on the product) or from people who are not directly in your target market, as long as they are about as savvy with technology as your target customers are. You might even make the code available to the engineering team for "dogfooding"—Microsoft's lingo for "eating your own dog food," meaning to use your own prerelease software, which helps identify obvious problems quickly without the expense of customer testing.

Asking a user experience expert to do a heuristic evaluation of your proposed design is another way to flesh out the more obvious problems. Or try asking a few team members to put on their user hats and do a cognitive walk-through to predict what customers might be thinking at each stage and where possible confusions might lie. These are good techniques not only for identifying obvious usability problems but also for identifying blocking issues such as logic problems, gaps in the end-to-end experience, or written text that makes no sense to anyone. We'll discuss these techniques in more detail later in the chapter.

 MINDSHIFT

You are (still) not the customer. Be careful at this stage not to overuse feedback from teammates and other tech-savvy members of your company. Self-hosting your code and getting quick feedback on prototypes give you a good gut check about whether your solutions basically make sense, but internal feedback tells you little about whether those solutions are truly tuned to your customers' needs and preferences. Getting a thumbs-up from your colleagues is the easy part, but it definitely doesn't tell you whether you've achieved delight for your real-world customers. You have to take your testing to the next level and bring your solutions to target customers, see what areas need adjustments, and keep iterating to get to finished, polished, thoroughly tuned solutions.

Fine-tuning the details of your solution

Once you've smoked out and resolved the big problems, you need to test with customers in your target demographic again and watch those customers use your solution. At this point, you are almost always testing live, functioning code. As your solution matures, your focus moves from optimizing the basic flow for your customer to finding more-subtle problems and fine-tuning the details of usability and aesthetics, all as the team continues to write code in parallel.

You might conduct an A/B test with a percentage of your user base by hosting your idea on your live service to see what happens in actual usage. You can also get feedback in person by asking customers to perform a series of specific tasks while you observe and pay attention to what they do, what they say, and what they have trouble with. Usability testing is a good mechanism for doing this. It can be done informally with good results to fuel quick iterations, or formally if you need to get more statistically reliable results for benchmarking.

Testing real-world usage over time

Sometimes it's advantageous to do longitudinal research to track a set of customers using your product over a period of time to see how their behavior changes. Do they hate your product at first but then, after day three, realize they can't live without it? Or perhaps their first impression is delight, but they discover that what first delighted them becomes annoying later on as they become more fluent with the system and want a more streamlined experience? What features and functions do they discover right away and which do they discover later or never? Which do they continue to use and how often? Are they using your solution for the scenarios you expected and optimized for?

 VOCAB

> *Longitudinal* research is when you give your solution to customers and track their behavior as they use the solution over a period of days, weeks, or months.

Longitudinal studies take more effort to do effectively. You first have to build something robust enough that someone can use it under real circumstances, and you need to devise ways to get regular feedback from your participants throughout the study. However, the big advantage to doing a longitudinal study is that you get feedback about how the product is being used in the customer's context—home, workplace, automobile, or wherever you expect your solution will be used in real life. Sure, you can always try hard to re-create a real-life situation in a usability lab, but there's nothing like the real thing. It's very difficult to simulate environmental inputs such as the phone ringing during dinner, the crazy driver cutting you off at the intersection, or your boss popping into your office to say hi while you're deep in thought about a gnarly coding problem.

Although conducting a longitudinal study outside the lab—for example, in the customer's real-world environment—is usually preferable, it's not always possible. Sometimes, the specific environment is difficult to use for firsthand observation. An IT server environment is one example. What IT pro would expose the live corporate network to early, potentially unstable prototype code? In these cases, do your best to mimic the real-world situation in the lab, and then bring customers into the lab for several sessions over a period of time.

Formal versus informal testing approaches

You can make use of a continuum of approaches for user testing, from formalized, to informal, to ad hoc. For almost all of the techniques we describe in this chapter, you can adjust the level of formality to best suit your situation. If you're an engineer who is very close to the implementation of the project, you'll usually want to engage in informal user research techniques that allow you to get frequent, quick feedback, and then use that input to rapidly iterate ideas and continue to build on your sense of customer empathy.

An informal user test is done quickly and easily, with little to no setup or planning costs. Informal user tests are highly influenced by the intuition, knowledge, and communication style of the researcher (in this case, that would be you). You just go out and show your stuff to a few customers, watch what they do, listen to what they have to say, make observations, and take notes. You can do this type of informal user testing with a prototype, an early build, a sketch, working code, or whatever work output you have created. You are looking for problems in your design, to see what works and what doesn't and how customers react to your ideas. Quick, informal methods usually let you find most of the big problems in your early solution ideas after interacting with just a few customers. However, be attentive that you don't introduce bias into the feedback by trying to sell your ideas; be sure you create an environment for honest feedback.

 MINDSHIFT

Be opportunistic about gathering informal feedback. Don't be shy about engaging people and getting quick, informal feedback about your product or the early ideas you are considering. Remember the story about the marketing manager who got great customer insights while being tattooed? If you have that level of customer desire, curiosity, and connection, you'll be able to get brilliant feedback on your ideas every day, armed with nothing more than a piece of paper and a Sharpie. Taking a trip on an airplane? Don't think of the airplane as a mode of travel, think of it as your personal customer feedback lab. Open your laptop, and get quick feedback from your row mates about what you are working on. Go ahead and carry a paper prototype, folded up in your pocket, and show it to people when you go to a café or keep an interactive prototype installed on your smartphone. You never know when you'll have a great opportunity for a quick user test.[4] But be sure that you ask enough questions to determine whether you're talking to an actual target customer so that you can interpret the feedback accordingly.

As your solution matures, you may want to add more formality to your user testing. By formality, we mean the structure and rigor around which you run your user tests and collect and report on the resulting data. You might conduct an A/B test online with a large number of participants, tracking specific metrics with telemetry and with careful attention to the experiment's design and the statistical validity of the results. For more-formal usability tests, you would determine how many customers you need to test ahead of time, write down a specific set of tasks for the user to perform, and ask each user to perform the same set of tasks in the same order, in the same environment, and with the same facilitator. You might even time the customers' actions with a stopwatch so that you can create a mathematical model of user behavior and learn how long it takes customers to do a particular task. With formal testing, observations are recorded in a structured format that allows the data to be merged and analyzed after all the tests have been completed, and the data is usually compiled in a written report.

The advantage of increasing the formality and rigor of your user testing is that it increases the reliability of the data you collect—you gain the ability to extrapolate your findings more reliably to your target population. Many teams use a more formal user-testing approach to help them understand when their experience metrics have been met, to tell them when they are "done," or for benchmarking against a competitor. While you can conduct formal testing at any time, it typically begins after the project's direction is well understood and the big usability issues have been uncovered and fixed. This kind of testing tends to be more expensive, so you should use it sparingly. Because of the need for an impartial facilitator, formal user testing is another area where you would be well served to hire a professional.

Testing for improvement versus confirmation

While it is generally true that informal user-testing techniques are great for quick iterations and getting feedback to further develop and refine your ideas, and that more-formalized user tests are employed to answer questions about experience metrics, this isn't always the case—formal and informal methods simply refer to how you approach the user test; they don't define why or what you are testing. To help you communicate clearly with user researchers (and the product team in general), there's one more concept to learn that helps make the definition of different kinds of user testing more precise.

In the world of user research, evaluative techniques are often classified as *formative* (you are looking to make improvements that will help shape or "form" the product) or *summative* (you are measuring results against a benchmark, answering the question "Are we done yet?").

 VOCAB

> *Formative* research techniques are used to determine what works well and what doesn't, with the goal of making improvements or validating your ideas. Your intent is to uncover problems so that you can fix them. *Summative* research techniques provide a systematic and objective way to gather measurable feedback data about a specific problem, product, scenario, or hypothesis you want to test. Summative research gives you statistical power and allows you to make statements such as "90% of people were successful in winning a pink bunny within the first 10 minutes of play."

Summative approaches are much more rigorous and require a deeper level of expertise than do formative approaches. They also take more time to prepare, execute, analyze, and report. It is overkill to use summative methods during early iterations. Because summative research involves quite a bit more science and statistical knowledge, it is another area where hiring a professional is extremely helpful.

In this chapter we focus mostly on formative techniques for validating customer delight and finding issues. In Chapter 11, "The way you work," we offer a bit more about summative approaches that help you track the progress of your solution against user-experience metrics, using tools such as scorecarding and benchmarking.

The Zen of giving and receiving feedback

Hearing feedback about your work can be painful. It's hard to be critiqued. It's hard to remain objective and continue listening when a customer finds fault with something you built for them, something you thought they would love. Thankfully, accepting feedback becomes easier with practice. It especially helps if you can keep a Zen frame of mind about receiving feedback: the process is not about you being right, but about finding an optimal solution, which is everyone's common goal. The more you understand how hard it is to pinpoint another person's true needs, the easier you will be on yourself when you inevitably discover that your first set of ideas isn't perfect and you need to adjust.

How to listen for feedback

Receiving feedback can be really hard on a lot of people. But this is just another instance of tunnel vision. Your idea makes so much sense in your own mind, and seems like the only viable approach, that you can't imagine how another person might not understand it or see how wonderful it is. As soon as someone challenges an idea, suggests that it might not be working, or suggests an alternative, our overwhelming tendency is to jump in and argue, often before the reviewer even finishes a sentence. Or, if you're feeling charitable, you might not so much argue as explain: "Clearly, they aren't understanding my idea," you think, "so if I just explain it a little bit better, then they'll get it and appreciate how great my idea is."

The trouble is that software doesn't come prepackaged with an engineer who sits on your shoulder, ready to explain anything that doesn't make sense. If you have to explain how your solution is supposed to work, then by definition it isn't working yet. And if you're spending so much of your energy explaining and arguing, then you really aren't listening to the feedback and may miss out on valuable clues for how you might improve your solution. Remember that feedback is not about you, it's about the solution. It's not personal. As such, everyone, including team members and customers, is on the same side, trying to find the absolute best solution possible.

So whether you are getting feedback from a teammate or from a customer, develop the self-discipline to just listen and not speak, other than to say "Uh huh" every now and again. You may be tempted to, but don't explain anything or argue or justify. Just listen. As Karl Melder discussed in his sidebar "How to interact with customers" in Chapter 5, body language is an important part of listening. Be open to the feedback and present a body language that conveys that you are actively listening and that you value what the reviewer is saying, no matter what.

If you are a solution-oriented problem solver, which is generally a good trait to have as an engineer, it may be particularly hard for you to listen for very long because you so much want to apply a fix to everything the customer is telling you—you want to get on with it and build a better solution. Other times, the feedback might cause your head to spin and make you worry about how the heck you're ever going to fix your solution or if it's even possible. It's really easy for your mind to take over and lose focus on what the customer is telling you right now.

The antidote to these mind games is to get back into your Zen frame of mind. Remember that your immediate job is to listen to the feedback and understand what the customer is telling you. Remind yourself that you can wait until tomorrow to decide whether to act on that feedback. In other words, to make the best decisions about what to do, you need to marinate the feedback. By the next day, the feedback often makes a lot more sense than it did in the moment. Acting right away often produces a poorer result.

When you listen to a customer who is giving you feedback on your solution, remember that the value of listening doesn't only come from hearing customers tell you that they adore your solution. The value lies in hearing the good and the bad together, because they are often intertwined. Pay special attention to the places where the customer is confused, frustrated, or doesn't use your solution in the way you anticipated. Those rough spots give you clues to what you should focus on next.

Ask open-ended questions

Any time you observe a customer using your solution, it's tempting to try to help them out, give them hints, tell them what you know, or give them the context you have so that they'll come to the same conclusions you have. But you'll get much better feedback if you can learn to use the language of psychologists.

Limit your speech. If a customer asks for help, pause and let him work it out himself. If he continues to struggle, try to respond first by asking a question. Finally, when you ask the customer for information (versus helping the customer get through a task), ask open-ended questions. If he answers you with a question, put the question back to him and have the customer, not you, answer. Doing this may seem awkward or rude, but customers quickly understand that this is not a normal conversational setting. You will be amazed how often a single question from you will help customers become unstuck (which usually indicates that the problem is probably not a large one, by the way).

Here are some phrases you can practice using:

- Interesting, tell me more about that.

- Yes, I understand.

- What would you have expected?

- What do you think you should do next?

- How do you think it works?

- What do you expect this component to do?

Sometimes, it's productive to simply have a frank conversation with a customer as she is experiencing your solution. But oftentimes your talking can actually get in the way of hearing the customer's feedback (or it changes the flow of how she is experiencing your product and thus alters her experience and feedback). In a semiformal setting, such as a usability test, it's a best practice for everyone but the facilitator to keep quiet and for you to ask any questions you have at the very end.

But if you find that you can't resist, that you must ask users questions as they experience your solution ("Why did you do that? Any idea what would work better for you right now?"), you can do so as long as you are intentional about having an investigative conversation (not just constantly interrupting). A useful technique is to define breakpoints as part of the user test and ask your questions when the user reaches those moments. Asking questions in this manner helps you avoid contaminating the customer's behavior on any subsequent task.

You may think that holding an informal conversation while walking a customer through your solution is one of the easiest ways to get feedback. But, in fact, it's actually one of the more difficult techniques to do well without introducing significant bias, and it requires practice.[5]

Present multiple options

It's easier for most people to give richer feedback when they have multiple options to compare and contrast. If you present only one idea, the only possibility is for customers to like or dislike that idea. Perhaps customers dislike some aspect of a particular implementation but would still find a solution valuable. Perhaps customers like one aspect of this solution but another aspect of a second solution. When you present only one option, it can be hard to tease apart these sorts of things.

> ### Neuroscience break by Dr. Indrė Viskontas
>
> For most of the decisions we make, we go through a step-wise process of evaluating alternatives, and we feel much more satisfied about our decision when we have had the opportunity to compare multiple options. Marketing companies have known this for years: it's why you see several options whenever you shop, whether you're buying magazine subscriptions ($24.99 for 1 year, $29.99 for 2 years), trying on running shoes, or ordering lunch. It's hard to evaluate the worth of something on its own—we assign value by comparing things. What's more, we find it easier to compare like with like, and that comparison influences our decision making.
>
> For example, if we are in the process of buying a house, any good real-estate agent knows that to encourage us to buy house A, say a three-bedroom, two-bath, ranch-style home in an up-and-coming neighborhood, she should show us two other options—a very similar house B, the decoy, say a two-bedroom, two-bath home in the same neighborhood, and house C, a totally different style of home in a different neighborhood. Our natural tendency is to fixate on comparing house A with house B and then put an offer on A. However, when there are too many differences between options, or too many options to consider, we tend to find it much more difficult to make a decision.

Remember that even though you have been thinking long and hard about this problem space, you can almost be certain that the customer has not been and that this user test is probably the very first time the customer is seeing your solution. When you first explore the solution space by showing multiple ideas or approaches to customers, you expose them a little bit to the universe of what is possible. This allows customers to give you deeper and broader feedback rather than limiting them to the path you already chose. Customers might even suggest a different path, one you haven't considered.

How to give feedback (to teammates)

Before we get into the details about methods of customer feedback, there's one more topic to touch on. When teammates ask you to comment on their work, how do you give productive feedback?

Teams that put the customer at the center of their work tend to be highly collaborative in nature. When working on such a team, it's especially important to learn how to give constructive feedback that is easy to swallow so that it really gets heard and considered by your teammates.

When you're the one giving feedback, you can make it easier for the recipient to hear your perspective. Here are a few tips for giving feedback:

- **Offer your thoughts**   Don't claim to be right, just offer your opinions as you see them. Remind yourself that diversity helps teams be more effective in the long run. If you see something differently from the rest of the group, don't be shy—you owe it to the team to speak up. The recipient gets to decide whether to act on your feedback. Your job is to make sure that your teammate hears the feedback so that he or she gets the benefit of your perspective and can make an informed decision.

- **Say what you see**   Providing a running commentary about which parts of the user interface you've noticed first and what thoughts are going through your head can be extremely helpful. You may not have noticed the crucial interface item that was added, for instance, which is valuable feedback for the designer. Or you may have misunderstood what it was for. Or you may have noticed something on the page that confused you but that the designer hadn't given a second thought to. If all those thoughts are locked in your head, people aren't getting the full benefit of your feedback. Say it out loud.

- **Don't try to convince anyone**   This is not the time to drive for a decision. Give the other person time and space to marinate on your feedback. Wait until tomorrow to plan your next steps.

- **Remember to point out the positives**   It's easy to zoom in on the problems, but pointing out things that are working well is equally important so that they don't get lost inadvertently in the next iteration. Sandwiching negative feedback between two positive comments can also make the negatives a bit easier to hear.

- **Be genuine**   Don't compliment something that you don't really like, just to have something nice to say. Similarly, don't go looking for problems to quibble about. It's okay to say, "Hmm, this looks pretty good to me, nothing is jumping out at me right now."

- **Remember that you're on the same team, with the same goals**   Everyone is trying to get to an optimal solution for your customers. Try not to let personal egos drive decisions. If in doubt, instead of going head-to-head and debating your opinion with others, suggest doing a user test to see what works better.

Observe stage (feedback): Key tools and techniques

In this section, we present a handful of specific research methods for getting customer feedback and also make some suggestions for which techniques best fit different situations and phases of your project. These methods are presented roughly in the order in which you might use them in a project, starting with techniques for early iterations and ending with techniques you would use against real code as you fine-tune your solutions getting ready for release.

Just like the generative feedback techniques we discussed in Chapter 5, these evaluative research techniques break down into SAY, DO, QUANT, and QUAL. You still want a good mix of all four quadrants of the research elephant for the best validity of your results. Also, it's customary to refer to the people who take part in customer research studies as *participants*, and we've used that nomenclature in this section.

Scenario interview

Primary usage: QUAL/SAY data.

Best for: Testing whether you fully understand the customer need.

Many teams find it useful to get a quick round of feedback on their scenarios before they start building prototypes. This is a particularly good idea when you are in a brand-new solution space or don't have a lot of experience with your target customers. Getting feedback on your scenario helps ensure that your scenario is correct, that it reflects your customers' reality, and that it captures the most important nuances and motivations of your customers. Taking the time to test your scenario helps you move forward with confidence that you are on the right path to solving a problem your customers care about, even before you start generating solution ideas and prototypes.

Instead of just handing a written scenario to a customer and asking, "What do you think?" create a structured interview and ask questions such as these:

Does this scenario ever happen to you?

Can you talk about the problems the scenario presents and how it affects you or someone else?

Is there anything left out that's important?

Did we get any of the details wrong?

If we were to build a solution for this, on a scale of 1–5, how important would that be to you? Why?

Which of these two scenarios would you rather we focus on?

Lean Startup "fake homepage" approach

Primary usage: QUANT/DO data.

Best for: Testing whether you've got the right solution; testing marketing messages and pricing.

In *The Lean Startup*, Eric Ries underlines the importance of testing with customers before you commit to a business plan or solution, to make sure that demand for your solution exists before you invest in building it. One of the central techniques that Ries suggests is based on a very simple rapid prototype.

The idea is to publish a single webpage that acts as the home page of your new service. It should display the marketing message that conveys the core value proposition of your solution, including pricing or other terms. Put a "Buy" or "Download" button at the bottom, and see if anyone clicks it. (Be sure you have web analytics enabled so that you get reports of page views as well as clicks.) If a customer does click to purchase your service, the next page might show a 404 error (page not found) or perhaps say "Coming soon" and ask for information about how to notify customers when the product is available. These customers would make great candidates for future customer testing, by the way.

Ries makes the point that if no one clicks the "Buy" button, you know that you need to try something else. Either you're solving the wrong problem or your pricing or business model needs to be rethought. In any case, don't bother building the solution until you can see that enough people are actually clicking "Buy."

This is a very simple idea, but it's profoundly useful to know what percentage of visitors to your website would actually want to buy your solution—not just in a lab setting, but in real life. You can imagine extending this approach to other domains as well. This is one of the few ways we've seen to test an early concept with a QUANT/DO approach, so it's well worth having in your toolbox.

Concept testing and focus groups

Primary usage: QUAL/SAY data.

Best for: Testing whether you've fully understood the customer need, testing whether you've got the right solution, testing marketing messages and pricing.

The idea behind concept testing is to get feedback on your initial solution ideas very early in your project, often before you have anything that looks like a user interface. This is another approach to take in early iterations to see whether you are solving a problem customers actually have and whether customers respond well to your rough ideas. The goal isn't to nail down a specific solution but to see whether you're in the right ballpark and engage customers in a conversation that would help you deepen your understanding of their needs—and thereby learn how to improve your solution ideas to better meet their needs.

The basic approach to concept testing is to show customers both the original scenarios as well as a few possible ideas for solutions that might address the problem or situation raised in each scenario. If you have sketches or mockups for some or all of your ideas, you might show those. You might show some key marketing messages or pricing ideas to get feedback in those areas as well.[6]

Ask customers which solution ideas they would prefer for each scenario and why. Ask how they might use such a solution in their daily life. We strongly recommend asking customers how they think the solution would work; this can be illuminating and may identify hidden assumptions, both yours and theirs. Encourage customers to share ideas they have for how to improve your solution. You might ask customers to rank the scenarios or the solutions you show over the course of the session. Or, to elicit a finer-grained prioritization, give them $100 of fake money and ask them to spend it on the ideas or scenarios they would find the most valuable. A couple of ideas may be dramatically more valuable than the rest, which would not be as evident if you asked them simply to rank the ideas in priority order.

To do concept testing, you might meet with one customer at a time or with a group of customers to gather feedback in a focus-group format. However, remember the caveats about focus groups from Chapter 5. Even with an experienced facilitator, focus groups often result in biased feedback because of groupthink, when some participants heavily lead the discussion and others yield to their opinions. Our experience is that testing concepts with a few individuals is usually more efficient and reliable than a focus group, and you're likely to elicit deeper, more personal feedback with that approach.

SFE in action: The case against focus groups

Paul Elrif, PhD, Principal at Caelus LLC, Owner of Dragonfly Nutrition LLC

Focus groups are often used by trained and untrained researchers without regard to the tradeoffs of the method. I assert that there are more useful and efficient methods for data collection than running focus groups. I find that one-to-one interviews, surveys, and some lesser-known methods are much more robust and, more importantly, more reproducible than focus groups are.

Robert K. Merton is largely credited with developing the idea of focused interviews and focus groups. One interesting thing about Merton is that he viewed focus groups as a method to test known hypotheses rather than to tease out new hypotheses or features from participants. When run well, a focus group can contribute to a product development idea. The problem is that a properly run focus group requires expert skill as a facilitator, and expert skill as a study designer, to know what is appropriate for a focus group and what is not.

The main problem with focus groups is the influence of groupthink. Several studies demonstrate that individuals tend to conform to what the group expresses rather than be seen as disagreeing. For example, Solomon Asch (1951)[7] ran some interesting studies that demonstrated that even when participants were asked to judge the difference between the lengths of lines drawn on a piece of paper, they often conform when they don't agree with others in the group. This relatively benign difference highlights that even for small disagreements, individuals are eager to conform.

Focus groups are often made up of people who are unfamiliar with one another. This poses a number of concerns. For instance, if you have people who are under NDA with their own employers, they will likely not provide honest answers if they believe they will be in violation by talking about their work with competitors in the room. Also, many people will become reticent in the presence of their managers or coworkers, especially if they do not want to be seen as disagreeing.

The many personality types in focus groups can direct an entire room in ways that are not repeatable. Based on my own observations, at least five types of participants will negatively affect your study: the agreeable, the contrarian, the loudmouth, the one-upper, and the quiet polite guy (similar to "the agreeable," except he may not agree but will remain silent).

You will often find that focus groups do not allow nearly enough time to get through an entire structured question list. It's difficult to give every person in a focus group an opportunity to provide complete answers to your questions. How will you know whether individuals had time to fully provide data?

Two of the hallmarks of good research are reproducibility of results and accuracy of the data collected. To assert that a study is both reproducible and accurate, one must try to reduce the number of confounding variables. It can be very tricky to acquire both reproducible and accurate data from a focus group conversation.

Even though focus groups are very difficult to administer well, there are indeed some specific cases where a focus group may be the right tool for the job. The classic case is when you want to discover how a group of people will react to an idea, or you want to observe how a group of people will interact when they are presented with an idea. Another situation is one where you expect that multiple customers will be using the hardware or software at the same time, or when there is workflow involving multiple users. These are all situations where hosting focus group conversations would be a good additional exercise to conduct. The same goes for families that share a computer or some kind of system.

If you want to gather feedback from multiple customers and you are not an expert facilitator, I highly recommend that you put the time and energy into scheduling a series of one-to-one interviews. One-to-one interviews are a much easier method for collecting independent and unbiased customer observations.

Surveys and questionnaires

Primary usage: QUANT/SAY data.

Best for: Testing whether you fully understand the customer need, testing whether you've got the right solution, testing whether your solution works well, fine-tuning the details of your solution.

We talked about surveys in detail in Chapter 5. Surveys are commonly used for generative research, although you can also use this technique to gather feedback about solution ideas. The difference is in the types of questions you ask. Generative surveys focus on a customer's attitudes and preferences before any solution is available. Now that you have a solution and are looking for feedback, your survey questions will focus on evaluating how well customers believe your solution ideas will satisfy their needs. As we mentioned earlier, while surveys are easy to create and administer, they are deceptively difficult to do well. Many bad decisions have been made based on the data coming from flawed surveys. Professionals are plentiful; leverage one to help you build an unbiased survey.

The most common form of survey used for getting feedback is a questionnaire, a small set of survey questions that is administered at the end of a usability test. You can also implement an online survey with a percentage of your live customers during their regular use of your service or after the customers finish a particular experience such as sending an online invitation to a party or placing an order. The value of using a questionnaire after a customer experiences your solution is that it gives you an easy way to collect some numerical preference data about that experience, which you can then track and trend over time. Keep the number of questions to a minimum, on the order of 5 to 10. The most common types of questions provide structured answers that allow for straightforward numerical analysis afterward:

- Yes/No questions on a Likert scale of 1-Definitely No, 2-Probably No, 3-Maybe, 4-Probably Yes, 5-Definitely Yes.

- Rate the level of agreement to a statement on a Likert scale of 1-Strongly Disagree to 3-Neutral to 5-Strongly Agree.

- Goldilocks questions that use a slightly different scale: 1-Too much, to 3-Just Right, to 5-Too Little. Goldilocks questions create a slightly more complicated analysis because the optimal answer is at the middle of the range; they don't offer a simple "higher is better" calculation.

- You may also want to include an open-ended question at the end to capture anything that is top-of-mind for the customer that you hadn't thought to ask about.

The results of a questionnaire may provide you with hints for questions to ask customers during a post–usability study interview. For example, perhaps a customer gave a high satisfaction rating to a task that you noticed he was struggling with, or a very low satisfaction rating to a task he seemed to do quickly and easily. Often, task performance and satisfaction are not congruent, and you may not recognize the disconnect unless you ask. It's important to discover these discrepancies and then probe with the customer to find out why. Also, be sure to provide the questionnaire to customers after they are done with their task so that you don't interrupt their flow or influence their opinions during a task.

Questionnaires are commonly administered following both informal and formal usability testing. Because this is such a common practice, there are a handful of industry-recognized and standardized usability questionnaires that you may consider using. These include QUIS (Questionnaire for User Interface Satisfaction) and SUS (System Usability Scale). Some of these questionnaires are so widely used that you can get industry data about how customers have responded to similar products, which lets you set some benchmarks for how usable your product is relative to others in your industry. Note that you are required to pay a license fee to use many of these questionnaires. A more detailed introduction to the world of questionnaires, along with a list of commonly available questionnaires (with links to the specific questions/forms) can be found at http://hcibib.org/perlman/question.html.

Another way to use a questionnaire is to embed it in your product or service. At some point in the customer's experience, pop up a questionnaire that asks about the customer's perception or satisfaction right when she is using your solution. This approach is common in web experiences these days, but it can also be used in a desktop application. For example, the Send-a-Smile feedback program was implemented during the beta for Office 2010. In the beta release, the feedback team added two icons to the Windows taskbar in the lower-right corner of the desktop—a smiley face and a frowny face. The idea was to encourage beta users to click the smiley face when something in the beta product made them happy, and to click the frowny face when something in the product made them unhappy. The tool automatically took a picture of the screen that the user was working on at the time and also prompted the user to type in a reason for his or her response. Send a Smile generated a tremendous amount of beta feedback and identified key areas where the product was missing the mark as well as validating that places built for delight were actually having the desired effect.

Cognitive walk-through

Primary usage: QUAL/SAY data.

Best for: Testing whether your solution works well, identifying more commonly found problems without needing real customers.

A cognitive walk-through, or a *cogwalk* for short, is a straightforward, informal evaluation method that focuses on the interaction and flow of a solution.[8] It's a good technique to use early on when you are ferreting out problems with concepts and mental-model issues and making sure that you catch bigger issues before you test with customers directly, which is more expensive.

When doing a cogwalk, you don't need actual customers. Instead, you gather several teammates or colleagues together to evaluate the flow of a prototype. The team starts out with a set of tasks to achieve. Together, the group's members put on their metaphorical customer hats and walk through the prototype one screen at a time, putting themselves in the place of the customer and imagining what the customer might do, think, or wonder about at each stage. They run through the specific set of tasks to simulate how users will experience the flow of the application. You aren't so concerned about the total time needed to perform each task; rather, you want to observe whether people can easily navigate through the system, find what they need, figure out what to do when they need to do it, and most especially, predict where customers might get stuck. In short, you want to see whether your solution makes sense to human beings.

Practically speaking, cognitive walk-throughs usually involve showing a series of static screens in some sort of slide show, a PowerPoint prototype, or a paper prototype. This helps the team focus on the right level of feedback (concepts and flow rather than small details) and also makes it doable very early on in a project, before the team spends a lot of time making more elaborate prototypes or investing in functional code.

As team members walk through each screen in the experience, they answer some standard sets of questions.[9] By using the same set of questions for each stage, you can calibrate the responses you get over time:

Do users know what to do at this step?

Do users feel like they are making progress toward a specific goal?

At each screen, the group's members collectively discuss the steps they would take to achieve the set of tasks presented to them. You want to predict where customers might get stuck, and what they might misunderstand. For example, will they know what to do with the big blue button on the Update screen? As you walk through the prototype, a scribe takes notes on any potential problems to be addressed in the next iteration.

Heuristic evaluation

Primary usage: QUAL/SAY data.

Best for: Testing whether your solution works well, identifying more commonly found problems without needing real customers.

Another method that is often used to identify early usability issues is a heuristic evaluation.[10] In contrast to a cognitive walk-through, which addresses interaction and flow, a heuristic evaluation assesses the user interface against a set of established principles, or heuristics, to look for well-understood gotchas and common mistakes that are known to make interfaces hard to use. Like a cogwalk, this evaluation is a good way to identify the bigger, more obvious problems in an interface before you go to the trouble of recruiting customers for testing.

In his book *Usability Engineering* (1993), Jakob Nielsen (who's often considered the father of usability testing) explains in detail how you go about doing a heuristic evaluation. He's also written many articles on the subject that are easily discovered on the web.[11] We'll present a condensed version of his thoughts here.

Heuristic evaluations are typically done by a reviewer who has a lot of experience observing customers and who is very familiar with common usability issues. Before the evaluation takes place, though, teams must decide upon a set of heuristics on which the application will be evaluated. Those heuristics are usually a set of user interface guidelines or a set of platform-specific user experience principles. Examples of user interface principles include consistency (Are similar actions performed in the same way?) and user control (Can the user back out, or escape, from any step or application state?).

In running the evaluation, a best practice is to have the reviewer go through the prototype twice. The first time through, the reviewer becomes familiar with the prototype. She gets a feel for what the system does, how it works, and how the user interface flows. Once she's familiar with the system, she goes through the prototype a second time with the intent of providing feedback, stepping through the application and evaluating each screen against the heuristics.

Remember that a heuristic evaluation is a bit different from a usability study. In a usability study you really want users to try to make sense of the system, even if they have to struggle to do so. In a heuristic evaluation, you are primarily focused on discovering usability issues by systematically judging the user interface against a set of established principles, so if the reviewer gets stuck, it's okay to move her along quickly through the application by helping, answering questions, or providing hints. However, definitely note those stumbling blocks and address them in your next iteration.

While a heuristic evaluation is typically performed by a single reviewer, it's understandable that no single person is likely to find the majority of usability issues in a system. When you use this method, it's ideal to recruit a few people to do the evaluations and then merge their feedback afterward. According to Nielsen, to get the best return on your investment, heuristic evaluations work best with three to five reviewers.

For a heuristic evaluation, you can use either low- or high-fidelity prototypes and even recruit teammates and others who do not perfectly match your target audience to do the evaluations. However, it is important that the reviewer or reviewers have expertise in good user interface design practices in addition to being familiar with the intended customer for the solution.

A quick Internet search for "usability heuristics" provides a long list of papers, articles, and information on guidelines and rules of thumb for usability and evaluation. Jakob Nielsen publishes a particularly useful and widely used set of usability heuristics.[12]

Wizard of Oz test

Primary usage: QUAL/DO data.

Best for: Testing whether you have the right solution, testing whether your solution works well; especially appropriate for voice- or text-based interfaces.

One clever approach to user testing is called a Wizard of Oz test. Instead of building a paper or other visual prototype, have a "man behind the curtain" make an experience magically work by responding to the customer manually. This technique is most natural if you are testing a voice-based interface, where the person behind the curtain speaks aloud to mimic an automated voice system. For example, if you were building a service such as Siri or Cortana or redesigning an automated telephone menu, you might do some Wizard of Oz testing to try out different voice commands and interaction patterns to see which are most natural and understandable for customers. This approach can also work well for a simple text interface or a command-line interface, where the person behind the curtain simply types the response to each command.

You might imagine using a Wizard of Oz approach for a visual interface to test the magic of desktop sharing or something similar, with someone sitting behind a curtain manually changing what appears on the customer's screen. This is more work to set up, however, and less common. By the time you have enough visual material to show on a screen, not much more effort is needed to link it up into a click-through prototype.

Informal testing and observation

Primary usage: QUAL/SAY data.

Best for: All stages, for quickly testing to see whether you are on the right track.

Informal observation can very quickly and easily provide you with customer feedback about your solution and your customer. With informal testing, you have a great deal of discretion in what you show, say, and ask, and it can be applied at nearly any phase of the project.

The important step in an informal test is to show customers some sort of artifact representing your solution and let them react to it. You might just ask them to comment on it, but it is helpful to have a few questions in mind to make sure you are getting feedback on the aspects you are most interested in. And whether you are sitting in a usability lab or in a café, you want to pay attention to minimizing bias, which means you want to keep your tone as neutral as possible and generally ask open-ended questions and then just listen. Although tempting, explaining your idea to customers does little in telling you whether they would understand it on their own or find it useful. The more you explain, the less likely customers are to offer their own thoughts. The hardest part about doing any kind of user research is often just listening, and this is particularly true for informal testing because you don't have an impartial facilitator running the test.

One way to get more frequent and earlier feedback is to think more about *what* you are testing than *how* you are testing it. Go ahead and test your earliest work. Remember the outputs you created in the earlier stages of the iterative cycle—insights, scenarios, sketches, and storyboards? In addition to prototypes, these are also relatively well-formalized bodies of work that you and your team have created. They all represent some amount of teamwork, consensus building, and decision making and are all well suited for getting very quick, informal feedback. The goal of this feedback is not to know definitively that you've found the right solution, but to get directional feedback that confirms you're on the right track or to help you find an appropriate course correction.

Even though you can get a lot of great data from informal testing, be sure that the people you talk with are target customers—or ask enough questions to understand how far away from your target they are. You don't want to get blown off course by getting conflicting feedback from people who are not your target customer.

Here are some ideas for getting quick, informal feedback on a customer insight, scenario, sketch, or early product design:

- **Read your scenario (or list of insights) to customers and ask them what they think** Do they tell you something like, "Oh man, that is so me. I can totally relate to that person. Please let me know when you solve that problem. Can I be on your beta test?" Or do they tell you something more like, "Hmmm . . . yes, that's interesting. It's not me, but I guess I can see how someone else would have that problem." But beware of an answer like this: "Yeah, that sounds like an important problem for person X, and I bet they want this, this, and this." This suggestion is no more based in data than your own guesses about that customer's needs, and this kind of statement also confirms that a person who makes it is either not your customer or isn't all that excited about your proposed scenario, or both.

- **Get on an airplane (or sit in Starbucks, or ride a gondola, or get a tattoo, you get the idea)** Take advantage of all the people you meet in your daily life, and strike up a conversation. Make a judgment as to how close they are to your target market (it's okay to get their feedback if they're not in your target, just weigh the feedback accordingly). See if you can get them interested in the problem you are trying to solve (test your insights to see whether the problem framing you chose resonates). If they show real interest, sketch out some of your proposed solutions and get their feedback. The serendipity of who you happen to talk to and what new perspectives they might bring to your problem can sometimes unlock new insights, so it's worth talking to people even if they aren't always your specific target customer.

- **Find a place where your target market hangs out**   Try a local coffee shop or a professional conference, for example. Go there, sit down, and watch people for a while. Take notes. Use that common area as a place to find potential research subjects, ask them to take a look at your scenario or prototype, and see what they think.

- **Walk the halls of your company**   Bring cookies. You'd be amazed at how much goodwill a box of chocolate chip cookies can buy for getting some quick feedback on an idea. Keep in mind, however, that your company probably isn't inhabited by your target customer segment. But you can still get useful feedback that can help you find the larger usability problems in an idea or feedback that inspires a new alternative to consider. Just don't rely on people in your company to gauge usefulness or desirability or detailed usage patterns. For those, you need real target customers.

It's true that a single reaction from the person sitting next to you on an airplane might not give you much data. On the other hand, you might receive a ton of data from that person, and it may indeed be very useful data. But don't make the mistake of thinking that you can take data from a single source and generalize your findings across the entire target market with any level of confidence. When you are doing informal testing, look for patterns that emerge after talking with multiple people in the same target customer group. If you talk to five different target customers, draw the same sketch on a napkin, and four of the five tell you the same thing, that's good qualitative data that can be used to make a hypothesis about your target population.

 TIP

> We don't recommend videotaping informal tests. Reviewing and analyzing video footage is very time-consuming and can easily take up all the time you saved doing this kind of informal testing rather than a more structured study.

Finally, just do it. Go find some users, see what they have to say, and leverage their brains for the betterment of your product.

SFE in action: Fast iteration in the (un)usual places

Ed Essey, Group Manager, Microsoft Garage; George Engelbeck, Senior Design Researcher, Microsoft Developer Division

We had each just taken on new roles on a team that was building tools for a highly technical developer market. The team was focused on an area that until now had been the realm of the most hardcore of performance and research developers: parallel computing using GPG PUs (which are essentially used to make graphics chips do complex math really, really fast). This was very tricky stuff, and the team wanted to be sure that it got it right for the hardest-core developers, yet kept it simple enough for mainstream developers to leverage as well.

Because of the complexity and technical depth of the project, it was very hard to find users who were willing and qualified to give us feedback. And when we did, very few of them were within driving distance of our offices in Redmond. Having exhausted all of our existing customer connections, we were beginning to wonder if we'd be able to find reliable feedback. We knew that it's typically a red flag when you cannot find target users for your technology (Are you building something nobody cares about?). In this case, we knew this was a "strategic" project that didn't have customers right now. The project was trying to support a big future technological bet, and we were challenged to find the early adopters who would help guide us.

Several months in, we were able to find only three qualified users to provide feedback. However, there was a big conference coming up (Nvidia's GPU Tech Conference), and we had a hunch that we'd be able to find some qualified target customers there. So treating that conference's dates as a deadline, we pulled together a user study, arranged to have some invitations inserted into attendee swag bags, and two of us boarded a plane with a flip cam, two laptops, and a few copies of the Microsoft NDA. Our goal was to find three to five developers to give us feedback.

At the conference we set up a makeshift user lab in a hotel meeting space attached to the conference center and posted sign-up sheets inside the conference proper. As it was too late for us to sign up to attend the conference ourselves (where maybe, just maybe, we could have recruited folks attending the sessions), we waited nervously in the hotel room to see if anyone would show up. Ten minutes before the first time slot, a developer showed up. He passed our screener, and we began the user study. Minutes later, there were eight qualified participants in our little hotel room, and we scrambled to parallelize our study. As a program manager, Ed had never previously run a user study. Ed was supposed to be there to take notes and to help George, the user researcher. That day, under George's tutelage, Ed learned quickly and was able to run a few user tests on his own, while George did the majority.

We soon got a phone call from the sign-up desk saying that the sign-up sheets were filling up. They asked if we could do multiple sessions at once. Having found a wealth of qualified customers, we arranged for more folks from our team to fly down and join us in a week of intense user testing.

Now that we had found our customers, we got creative in getting their feedback. We also made sure we had representatives from the dev team watch these customers' interactions to be sure that they built empathy firsthand, rather than relying on our data later. To engage all of these customers, we added late-afternoon discussion/focus group sessions and often ran through the user studies with two or more people at a time. The pace was so fast that week that the dev team didn't bother trying to code or spec details. Instead, we built quick mockups and experimented with customers on lots of ideas—sometimes with obvious ideas, sometimes with wild ideas. We were often surprised by what the customers came up with.

During that week we ran nearly 30 user tests, performed 10–12 iterations of the main product theme, and experimented with numerous side trials. Over the course of the week, we received feedback that spanned the conceptual level to the user model—all the way to fit-n-finish-level feedback.

The team now had everything that it needed to lock in the major design of the product. The team also gained a tremendous amount of knowledge and empathy for the target audience. And we all experienced the power and excitement of getting into a tight feedback loop with qualified customers. Because our target customers represented such a narrow niche in the developer market, they were difficult to locate. But by figuring out where they hang out, our efforts to connect with them and get feedback yielded a very high return on our investment.

Usability testing

Primary usage: QUAL/DO data.

Best for: Testing whether you've got the right solution, testing whether your solution works well, fine-tuning the details.

Usability testing is the classic form of user testing, where you observe customers trying to complete a set of tasks with your solution. Exactly how usability tests are conducted can vary greatly. They can be run as anything from a loosely structured conversation at a coffee shop to a more formal test in a lab setting in which you use a predefined set of methods and procedures.

In all usability testing, the general pattern is that you identify a handful of specific tasks that you'd like customers to accomplish. You then give customers your latest solution, whether it's a paper prototype, fully functional code, or something in between, and direct the customers to accomplish those tasks. You carefully observe them as they work, encouraging them to think out loud and verbalize what they are thinking and noticing, unless absolute measures of time on task are critical. You take notes about places where customers have problems or any interesting comments they make. For some tasks, you might measure the customer's performance (e.g., the amount of time it takes them to accomplish a particular task, the number of clicks, or the number of mistakes they make).

Most large software companies have usability labs that include tools like computerized recording and behavior monitoring, one-way mirrors for team observation, and eye-tracking devices. These labs are usually run by a group of professional user researchers and can provide invaluable data about your solutions and your customers. You can also rent time in a usability lab in most major cities.

However, you don't need a fancy facility to do usability. You can reap a ton of value by running small, informal studies, often called discount usability. All you need is a customer, you, and something to test. Because the value can be so high and the cost so low, it's worthwhile to spend some time learning how to run an effective, informal usability test on your own. We will discuss usability testing in more detail in the deep dive section later in this chapter.

Eye tracking

Primary usage: QUAL/DO data.

Best for: Fine-tuning the details of your solution.

It's unlikely that you'll ever do an eye-tracking study on your own, but it's a really cool method and has recently become much more affordable (in terms of equipment cost), so we thought we'd mention it briefly just to make you aware that it is available.

Eye tracking is almost always done in a usability lab. During a usability test, the eye-tracking device is able to detect minute eye movements and determine what a person is looking at. The device generates different types of reports that show the location and frequency with which the user looked at different parts of the screen. Eye tracking is mostly used with code or higher-fidelity prototypes to test and optimize different screen layouts.

Two report types are most common. "Gaze paths" show in order the different areas of the screen the eyes rested on. You can also generate a "heat map" that shows the areas of the screen where the eyes spent the most time looking. However, you may need as many as 39 test subjects to get a stable heat map.[13] The Nielsen Norman Group website has a great free report available for how to conduct eye-tracking studies: http://www.nngroup.com/reports/how-to-conduct-eyetracking-studies/.

Eye trackers are more commonly used by user experience teams inside medium and large companies. If you don't have a user experience team, it's possible to hire out eye-tracking services. You'll find that most major cities now have vendors who will do this for you. We are also starting to see some people use Microsoft Kinect as an eye-tracking tool. If that becomes a commercial reality, it could make for a very inexpensive way to do something that has traditionally been quite expensive.

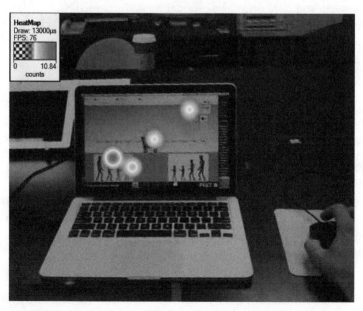

FIGURE 9-1 Heat map. Photo courtesy of Dr. David Rosengrant, Associate Professor of Physics Education, Kennesaw State University.

SFE in action: Desirability Toolkit

Trish Miner, Principal UX Researcher, Microsoft Windows

The Desirability Toolkit is a set of 118 cards with words on them. It provides a quick, easy-to-use way to tap into customers' emotional response to products or experiences. The idea is to capture how people would naturally talk about products, how they react to them, and what they feel is important. You provide the word cards and ask the participants to choose the cards that best describe the product or their experience using it. They then narrow down the set to the five cards that best describe the product. The most important part is a follow-up discussion about why they picked the cards they did.

confusing
clear
compelling
disruptive
efficient
annoying

It's tempting to count the number of times participants choose a particular word, but, in fact, the words themselves are not important. The critical feedback is the reason behind the chosen word. For example, words like *fun* or *frustrating* can be related to completely different feedback depending on the person who chose the word. You need to look through the reasons your users give for selecting words and search for both themes and specific examples, highlighting how your product is creating both negative and positive emotions in your users.

Teams can use the feedback from the toolkit in a variety of ways and during all phases of the development cycle. The feedback can be particularly useful in assessing an existing product to determine what aspects to retain and build on in a subsequent version and what issues are critical to address. I have seen teams make good use of the output to define themes to investigate further with quantitative research such as a survey. It has also worked well in the development of an international version of a product to assess local cultural differences in tastes and perspectives.

An interesting alternative is to have team members use the toolkit to describe the reactions they would like their customers to have. This activity is very useful for making sure the team has the same goals and objectives. Also, the words a team chooses can be used as goals, which can be tested against later when user feedback is obtained.

The output of the toolkit is qualitative. It will not give you statistically significant results or tell you which theme or reaction is most important. If you need to prioritize next steps, you can use the data from the toolkit to create a survey to get quantitative data. The advantage of starting with the toolkit (rather than starting with a survey) is that you are sure that the topics you are including are based on what your users feel is important, which can often be very different from what we think is important.

The list of words in the Desirability Toolkit is available in Appendix E.

Card sorting

Primary usage: QUANT/SAY, QUAL/SAY data.

Best for: Testing whether your solution works well, fine-tuning the details of your solution; especially appropriate when you need to organize a long list of items.

Card sorting is used when you have a large number of links, commands, methods, or other bits that need to be organized, most often by grouping these items into categories. Instead of defining the categories yourself, ask a bunch of customers to create the most natural and logical categories from their perspective. They may not be the same categories that you would come up with, but remember that they need to make sense to your customers, not to you. This work comes up frequently in designing websites, such as when you're deciding the placement of links on a page or organizing a set of commands into categories or drop-down menus on a toolbar.

Here's how you do a card sort:

1.   Take a set of index cards and write the name (and maybe a brief description) of each command, link, or item you want to organize on a separate card.

2.   Hand the stack of cards to a participant, and ask him to organize the cards into groups of related cards on the table.

3.   Ask the participant to then create a name or label for each group of related cards.

4.   Do this with a bunch of people, but have them work individually. Jakob Nielsen's rule of thumb is that you need at least 15 participants to produce reliable results.[14]

5.   Analyze the results and see what patterns emerge.

Interestingly, this method can also be used to create an organizational scheme or to see how well existing categories are working. To come up with new ideas, you use "open" card sorting, as described in the preceding steps. (That is, you let the user make up the names of the categories where they place related cards.) You can also use "closed" card sorting, where you give the user the names of the existing categories and ask the user to sort the cards into those categories.

As with online surveys, a good number of tools are emerging that let you do card sorting remotely over the Internet. These tools are typically quite easy to use and administer and allow you to more easily recruit a large number of participants. The downside is that by doing the card sorting online, you get only quantitative data because you can't observe customers doing the sorting and hear their comments or what they say aloud as they sort.

A/B testing

Primary usage: QUANT/DO data.

Best for: Testing whether you've got the right solution, testing whether your solution works well, fine-tuning the details of a solution; generally most appropriate when you already have a production service with an active user base.

The basic idea behind controlled online experimentation, more commonly called A/B testing, is to expose a fraction of your live user base to a proposed solution and see whether it performs better than the existing solution. You identify ahead of time what metrics to track and what change you expect to see—perhaps a higher percentage of users who complete a purchase, more click-throughs to a particular link, or an increase in the time each user spends on the website overall—and make sure that you have built instrumentation to measure the specific outcomes you've identified. Then you see whether you are right: you compare what customers did in the A case (the "control" group, the group of users who saw the old experience) with the B case (the "treatment" group, the group of users who saw the proposed experience). It's also possible to do an A/B/C/D/ . . . test and trial multiple options at the same time, but this adds some complexity.[15] Careful experiment design and statistical analysis of the results will tell you whether any difference in the outcomes is significant and to what level. As we noted at the beginning of this chapter, the experience of Dr. Ron Kohavi and other researchers indicates that two-thirds of the time A/B tests show that a change you make does not create the intended outcome, so it really is worth testing these things.

A/B testing is an incredibly powerful technique because it can tell you unequivocally what real customers would do in real-life usage, and you can get a tremendous amount of quantitative data all at once. Even better, the results are not ambiguous—you can see exactly how well your idea worked or not, based on the outcome you are trying to change. This provides the team a laser focus on achieving specific and measureable goals. Organizations that embrace online experimentation tend to give ample leeway to the team to try out different ideas, measure the results of each, keep what works, and get rid of what doesn't. A/B testing goes a long way toward developing an engineering culture that supports and values iteration. It's been used broadly by Amazon, Google, Facebook, Microsoft, Netflix, and many other online services. These days, the A/B testing approach is starting to spread beyond services and websites, with some teams adapting the technique for testing mobile apps and even desktop applications.

If your production environment supports it, and the solution you are proposing is relatively small and inexpensive to code, sometimes the most efficient way to get customer feedback is to do an A/B test quite early in the project. Or, even if your solution is not that small or easy to code, it's possible that testing noncode prototypes won't tell you what you need to know; it may be vitally important to see exactly how real user behavior changes before you invest further in design and development work or deploy the new solution fully.

Historically, A/B testing was developed to fine-tune the details of an experience or to gain confidence about a design change or new layout, especially where the proposed design might change how well you monetize the solution or how well it engages its users. The A/B technique is particularly well suited for optimizing content and layouts, such as trialing different page layouts to see which one maximizes click-throughs, fine-tuning fonts and colors, or trying several different marketing messages to see which one gets more buyers. The MSN homepage has used A/B testing for more than a decade to trial multiple versions of news articles each morning. The team sees which topics and specific versions of headlines get the most interest from visitors and uses that input to pick the day's headlines. The Bing search engine team has been using A/B testing for years to trial all sorts of feature improvements and optimizations and is typically running hundreds of tests at a time. More than 90 percent of Bing users are participating in an average of 15 or more concurrent experiments at any given moment.[16]

Over time, A/B testing has grown to become an integral part of the core design process for websites and other services teams, who regularly test minimum viable products (MVPs) to get feedback on new ideas. As we discussed in Chapter 8, "Building prototypes and coding," an MVP can be anything from a website touting a new feature (that may lead to a "coming soon" message whose only purpose is to see how many people click), all the way to a functional implementation of a proposed experience. Either way, the idea is to get feedback about how live customers engage with an idea and see whether it's worth investing in further.[17]

To do A/B testing, you need to make some up-front investment in an infrastructure that can redirect a portion of your user traffic to the proposed improvement while others continue to see the existing site's functionality. This work would seem relatively straightforward to accomplish for websites that are served by a farm of stateless servers: simply load your test code onto a single web server, while the others continue to run the existing service, and ensure that you can query your analytics by server. However, that simplistic approach doesn't really work. If you want to run multiple A/B tests in parallel over different lengths of time; keep track of which users were in which tests; allocate users in a random, unbiased way to ensure statistically equivalent populations; and ensure that there's no overlap between concurrent tests that could affect the results, you need to build an experimentation platform. Most large services have developed extensive A/B testing platforms over the years.

It may surprise you that A/B testing is actually remarkably difficult to do well with statistical validity. Careful experiment design is required to get valid, statistically significant results, and many pitfalls can cause you to get bad data that may mislead you. This is another place where enlisting the help of an expert—a data scientist, experimental scientist, or statistician—is a really good idea, both to set up an experimentation system as well as to ensure that each individual experiment will have valid results. Here are a few of the more important factors to consider:[18]

- Make sure that you are getting a true random sampling of users, and that the way you are splitting traffic doesn't inherently create bias between your A and B populations.

- Most ideas don't improve your core metrics very much even if they are "successful," so you really do need sophisticated statistical analysis to detect whether your experiment worked—you probably won't be able to just spot it. A really striking result might occasionally be accurate, but this is much more commonly a sign of a bug in your experiment or experimentation system.

- One of the most common causes of incorrect results is bugs in the instrumentation code that collects the metrics you are looking for. It's important to test the instrumentation code itself, as well as to run A/A testing to ensure that no statistically different results are detected.

- Robots are prolific on the web, and their automated use of websites can throw off your results; identifying robot usage patterns is nontrivial but is essential to get clean data.

- You may find that your experimental treatment improved one metric or outcome at the expense of another, and sometimes this can be missed if you aren't watching out for it.

- Probably the most counterintuitive gotcha is that well-formulated, statistically valid A/B testing takes time—the current state of the art is to run experiments for two days to two weeks to control for novelty effects, and sometimes even longer. This means that unless the results are stark, which is rare, A/B testing is not a great choice for getting feedback to fuel super-fast iterations. That said, you don't always need full statistical validity. If you're just looking to see which version of the daily headline gets the most hits or whether a server is running acceptably when it's loaded with the latest build, a quick A/B test may be good enough.

Dr. Ron Kohavi and others offer many more great insights and practical advice about online experimentation in several papers published on the website http://www.exp-platform.com/.

SFE in action: A/B testing is great, but you still need QUAL

Rob Farrow, Senior User Experience Researcher, Microsoft Bing

Bing was going through a brand and UI redesign that would have broad implications throughout the site. Since the changes were much more involved than those in typical A/B tests, some initial work was done with prototypes to gauge user preference for the new look across the different areas of Bing. The early research data consistently showed that people had a preference for the new designs, so the redesign went forward and a lot of resources were committed to building out the new UI.

However, when the new designs were released within an A/B test, everyone was surprised that many of our core metrics went down substantially. Since these results were so unexpected, everything was double-checked and additional tests were run that confirmed the deficits associated with the new design. The team struggled to figure out why the metrics were down—it was clear that the "preference" metric that was used to support the redesign didn't lead to improvements in our actual, live business metrics.

Since the A/B tests didn't provide any insights into the observed changes and the team had already invested substantial resources in the work, we wanted to figure out what was causing the problems and understand if they could be fixed. To figure it out, the Bing user research team used traditional qualitative methods, including a diary study and user interviews to better understand the user response to the new design. The new research confirmed that users had a preference for the new UI but also uncovered that the bold color scheme was somewhat distracting. Specifically, the colors drew people's attention away from the core parts of the page toward areas that had less opportunity for engagement. The new designs didn't shift the clicks away from the core to the periphery but simply resulted in fewer clicks overall. Armed with a qualitative understanding of why the new designs were affecting people's behaviors, the team was able to more effectively explore alternate designs that could meet the redesign and brand goals without adversely affecting the overall metrics.

A/B testing is a great way of evaluating the effectiveness of designs, but it doesn't give insights into why you see the observed effects. Why did it fail? Why did it succeed? Do differences in user goals or intent affect their approach and the effectiveness of designs? Any time

---

someone makes a statement that a test was successful (or failed) because of *X*, they are just stating a hypothesis. It is especially easy for people who are new to A/B tests to forget this and believe they have a deeper understanding of what is going on than they really do.

Coupling qualitative "why" research with A/B tests can provide the deep insights needed to better understand what's going on in the behavior you observe. It isn't practical or realistic to do qualitative research on all or even many A/B designs, but in some cases, spending time to gain an understanding of why things happened makes business sense, especially when development costs are significant—what can you learn to salvage your investment? Engaging in traditional qualitative research can provide the insights you need to understand whether changes can be made to achieve the effects you want or the idea should be discarded in total.

Just as the Bing team found out, it's important to realize that A/B testing does not give you much insight into why customers are behaving the way they are. It's possible that with your new design, customers are clicking the "Buy" button more often, but maybe that's because they mistook it for something else. Perhaps they did actually complete a purchase, but they were unsatisfied with the product they bought and will not be a return customer. Or perhaps what they really want isn't something that you're providing at all, and as soon as a competitor figures that out, you'll be in trouble. A/B testing alone provides QUANT/DO data, which as you learned in Chapter 5 represents only one quadrant of the four major types of customer research. Be careful that you don't rely too much on A/B testing at the exclusion of other approaches.

Furthermore, for a lot of solutions, it's too expensive to get all the way to writing production-quality code only to find out through an A/B test that your idea doesn't work at all or you're solving the wrong problem to begin with. If you can figure out your approach faster with a noncode prototype, or at least gain higher confidence that you're on the right track without having to write code, that's usually more efficient. A/B testing should not be the first way that you test a big new concept or idea that requires significant development time. However, A/B testing is a great way to confirm that what appears to work for customers in the lab is also providing the expected benefit in real life.

Still, when you are in a situation where the coding effort is relatively small, A/B testing is a great choice. Likewise, it's worth doing when collecting real-world usage data is of material importance to the direction of a solution that simply cannot be adequately mocked up and tested with other methods. If you go this route, you should create the smallest workable MVP to use in an A/B test to get feedback with a minimum of sunk cost.

Big data, usage telemetry, and continuous feedback

Primary usage: QUANT/DO data.

Best for: Testing whether your solution works, fine-tuning the details of your solution, identifying pain points that might lead to a new scenario.

Many apps and services these days have a server or cloud component that has the capacity to capture huge amounts of aggregate data about how customers are using those services. Whether that big data is captured via web analytics, custom-built instrumentation, or a log of server events, the data exhaust from these services is vast and growing every day. With this volume of usage data available, it becomes possible to know, often in real time or with minimal delay, how effective a particular advertisement is at prompting click-throughs, how many customers are using a particular feature, or, conversely, what features or areas of your solution are being used surprisingly little or not at all.

Big companies such as Amazon, Facebook, Microsoft, and Netflix spend a lot of engineering effort on being able to efficiently collect and synthesize the data available to them and to make decisions based on that data to continuously improve their solutions and their understanding of their customers' needs. A new role is emerging in our industry, the data scientist, an expert who can analyze and find insights in this huge morass of often unstructured data. Leveraging large data sets effectively is easier said than done, but the promise is that by using the data that's already on hand, engineering teams can have a dramatically deeper and more accurate view of what customers are really doing with their solutions. As the collection and analysis of these massive data sets become more tractable, companies are starting to analyze the entire data set instead of just a statistically valid sampling, which allows you to see outliers (who may be potential lead users) as well as the dominant usage patterns. Collectively, this data provides a continuous flow of information about how real people are using a system, which encourages and enables teams to make changes to continuously improve the service they are providing.

A lot of benefit can be had by using this data to drive direction and decision making. In addition to providing for an ongoing and current understanding of customers and how they interact with your system, it extends some of the benefits of A/B testing from individual, discrete experiments to the whole system, letting you watch how real customers interact with it in detail all the time. This usage data can identify places for improvement or investment and confirm what is going well and where customers are spending their time most. Perhaps the most immediate value of this kind of usage data analysis is to proactively detect where customers are having trouble and alert the engineering team to fix it, even before someone calls customer support. All of these opportunities encourage teams to become serious about iterating their solutions for continual improvement.

The frontier of usage data analysis lies in seeing what customers do not just at a single moment in time but across an entire experience. For instance, imagine if you could see how many users are actually using a solution you built for a particular end-to-end scenario? How long does it take the average customer to complete the entire job, end to end, not just individual tasks? Minutes, hours, days? Early versions of this kind of scenario usage analysis are already in place, but these analyses will only get more sophisticated in the future.

It is important to understand that usage data must be collected in a way that respects customer privacy, removing all personally identifying information so that you use the data in aggregate only. Your goal is not to snoop on what individuals are doing but to make sure that the system is working as it should be and that the things you expect customers to be doing are available, functional, and being used. You want to notice problems early on so that you can fix them right away. This prevents expensive calls to customer support, but more importantly, it also prevents any more users from being exposed to frustrating experiences that will make them dissatisfied.

By definition, this kind of big-data usage analysis gives you summative data: that is, usage data from telemetry is quantitative and statistically robust. This kind of data is very powerful because it reflects what people actually do. But remember, as we discussed earlier with A/B testing, usage data gives you little to no information about why customers did what they did, so you'll get a better picture of your customers if you can triangulate usage data along with QUAL and SAY data. Also, this data is available only for solutions in active use on your live service. As with A/B testing, it is expensive to wait until the code is written and live, even with a beta audience, to get feedback. Usage telemetry should never be the first customer feedback you get on a new solution.

Can big data help us design new products and services?

Kerry Bodine, coauthor of Outside In: The Power of Putting Customers at the Center of Your Business

Human-centered designers have a long history of integrating qualitative research techniques into their work. Ethnographic research, one-on-one interviews, and participatory design sessions are the research tools of the trade—and the resulting data sets are often conference rooms filled floor to ceiling with sticky notes. The objective, of course, is to find patterns that reveal people's behaviors and unmet needs and spur the ideation of new or improved products and services.

But a change is among us. In recent years, designers at mega corporations, marketing agencies, and tech startups have joined forces with data scientists and turned their focus to quantitative data.

For example, [24]7, a provider of software and services for customer engagement, uses predictive analytics and big data to improve conversion rates in digital channels. When a major telecom company wanted to increase conversion of its online chat invitation, [24]7 created eight different design treatments for the invitation widget. Each treatment fit within the telecom's brand standards but had a unique combination of icon style, typeface, background color, message, and placement.

After two weeks of live testing, the company was able to mathematically determine the best widget design—even though the winning combination of elements was not one of the eight tested treatments. The new widget design produced a 19 percent incremental lift over the existing chat invitation, a result that would have been impossible to produce with designer intuition alone.

Design optimization such as this—and the resulting generation of new interfaces—is a great step forward in getting designers to consider and actually use big data. But the data sets available to designers aren't limited to digital analytics. Designers can now tap into information as diverse as social media content, call center conversations, biometrics, credit scores, disease transmission, energy use, driving behaviors, and parking ticket issuance. If that's not enough, just wait a few years. As sensors become increasingly embedded in the everyday objects we use—from coffee pots to tennis shoes—the amount of available data will become mind-bogglingly large.

Big data sets like these will never be able to replace the qualitative data on which designers currently rely to develop empathy for people and uncover deep insights about why people think, feel, and act the way they do. But big data has the potential to play a much bigger role in the design process, as it can reveal what people do in ways that observation and conversation simply can't. Those quantitatively driven insights have the potential to lead designers down new paths and to the creation of ever more effective products, services, and experiences.

Teams that learn to embrace big data will lead us into a new era of design—one that sits at the intersection of quantitative and qualitative research techniques.

 ## MINDSHIFT

Collecting internal telemetry is not enough. The biggest mistake we've seen teams make with usage telemetry happens when they test their prerelease "dogfood" code with some of their internal colleagues. At the same time, they test the telemetry system and analyze usage data based on their colleagues' usage patterns. So far this is all good; it's wise engineering practice to ensure that the system is working end to end and there are no major problems. The difficulty comes next, when a team concludes that the usage patterns it's seeing are indicative of what will happen when the solution is released externally. A team might even be tempted to optimize the experience based on this internal usage data, putting the most commonly used menu items at the top of the list, for instance. This is another case of "you are not the customer." It is very likely that external customers will use the software quite differently from how your engineering team would.

Be careful. Even daily usage by your colleagues isn't going to tell you much about what the patterns of daily usage by your target population will look like. And certainly don't view this exercise as getting feedback from customers. Other than providing a basic smoke test—confirming that your solution works at all for any human being—you learn little else. Usage telemetry is tantalizingly numerical and very precise, but don't let it lure you into thinking that you know something that you don't. Who you get the usage data from is what really matters.

A note about confidentiality

When engineering teams start showing ideas to customers, whether in a rapid prototype or with functional code, we've found that teams tend to get nervous about sharing their ideas with people outside their company: "What if a competitor gets a hold of the idea and ships it before we do?" "What if they steal our idea and improve on it?" "What if the press hears about it and it leaks in the news? Will we still be able to make a big splash on release day?"

It's a real issue. There are good reasons to keep a big new idea under wraps. Competition is fierce, and you don't want to give anything away. While it's possible that your competitors are already working on a similar problem or idea, there is definitely an advantage to getting as much of a head start as possible.[19]

Thankfully, you don't need to worry about confidentiality in most projects. If you are working on incremental improvements to an existing product or service or in a market that is not particularly competitive or visible, confidentiality may not be a critical concern. However, you still might feel that you want to keep your ideas under wraps, "just in case." You never know what could happen, right?

No matter what your competitive situation, securing total confidentiality by not doing any user testing is foolhardy. You need customer feedback. Remember the stats from the beginning of this chapter? You are likely to be right only a third of the time. Those are pretty tough odds. So you need the feedback and iteration, but you still want to maintain confidentiality. How do you do it?

The standard way to manage confidentiality is with a nondisclosure agreement (NDA). An NDA is a legal document that clearly spells out what participants may or may not talk about after they leave the testing situation.[20] When you begin a user test, before you show anything, ask the participants to sign an NDA and follow up with a stern talk about the consequences if they violate the agreement. As you recruit participants, inform them ahead of time that they will be required to sign an NDA. It's also a good idea to check whether prospective participants have family or friends tied to your competitors or to the media, and if they do, exclude those prospects from your testing.

All of these precautions are reasonable and not terribly expensive, so they are worth doing. However, our experience is that although leaks do happen, they don't usually happen through customer-testing participants who violate their NDA. Your idea is much more likely to be leaked by an employee, contractor, or vendor who shares a crucial document or prototype with someone they shouldn't, either intentionally or accidentally. If you're really worried about leaks, you would be wise to think about internal security.

If you want to add an additional layer of protection before doing user tests, consider removing your branding and identifying details from any prototype you show so that it is unclear what company or existing service this prototype is connected to. If you make your prototype anonymous, be sure to conduct any studies at a different site, away from your company's offices. You might travel to another city to conduct a study—this is a good idea for getting a richer view of any regional differences as well. You can rent usability lab space, focus group rooms, or other research spaces in most cities.

If you provide a copy of the software to participants to use at home, say for a longer-term trial, be sure that the interface includes an obvious reminder that this is prerelease software and the terms of their NDA. A clever technique is to display the participant's name clearly in the software to dissuade people from sending around videos or screenshots—and possibly to also subtly encode their name elsewhere that may not be so visible. Participants could edit their name out of a screenshot, so this is hardly foolproof, but it does provide something of a barrier and demonstrates clear malicious intent rather than an accidental leak.

And, needless to say, providing actual software to customers is the riskiest step to take and still hope to maintain confidentiality. However, it is extremely useful and is sometimes worth the risk, but choose your research subjects carefully, or conduct this kind of research only after a public announcement is made. Keep in mind that preventing other people from noticing something new over someone else's shoulder is nearly impossible.

Some teams feel more comfortable doing user testing with family and friends, who they feel are more trustworthy. However, depending on your project, friends and relatives may not be good representatives of your target customer. Also, the familiarity that friends and family have with your company may cause them to not always take an NDA as seriously as a stranger would.

Despite all of this, some teams may feel that any risk to confidentiality is unacceptable. Some rare moments in the industry have benefitted from a big surprise announcement, though it's helpful to remember that even most of Apple's famous launches were leaked or predicted in some way or another. Some teams have a deep cultural and business priority for keeping everything an iron-clad secret. If you do go this route, recognize that it is a very serious strategic decision that adds tremendous risk to your plans. Without getting real feedback from anyone outside the walls of your company, you carry a high risk of shipping something that bombs, and you will have no early warning system.

Deep dive: Usability testing

Usability testing is the workhorse of most teams' iterations, so we provide a deep dive here on this method, including some important variants, nuances, and biases. The term *usability test* refers to a class of similar techniques for getting feedback from real customers on something you have built, typically by observing the user perform a set of tasks with your solution. The technique was first developed to identify problems that prevented people from being able to use a solution easily or naturally (hence, the name), and it is indeed the gold standard for finding ease-of-use bugs. However, usability testing can also be productively used to gauge a broader range of customer reactions to a solution than just whether people find the solution easy to use, especially when usability tests are conducted in concert with a post-test interview or questionnaire.

Usability tests can be, but do not have to be, large, highly organized productions. In fact, the vast majority of usability testing that teams do is more properly termed *discount usability testing,* meaning that the testing uses fewer participants and is primarily focused on getting just enough feedback to inform a rapid iteration of solutions as efficiently as possible. The prototype to be tested doesn't have to be coded or functional; it's fine to use a low-fidelity prototype such as a paper prototype or a PowerPoint mockup. Anything that simulates your application well enough that you can observe the user trying to make sense of it will work (for tests using a noncode prototype, customers simply speak or point to tell you what they would do in each situation). Of course, as your solution progresses, you will have working code, and at that stage you'll be able to watch customers use your software and get feedback on more and more of the details.

Companies that hire user experience professionals and who build out dedicated usability labs sometimes engage in more formal testing, where a lot more rigor is applied to how the test is designed, administered, and analyzed. These cases may involve larger numbers of participants, especially to capture specific performance metrics or benchmarks. A usability lab may be outfitted with one-way mirrors, video recording equipment, real-time commenting tools, and maybe even an eye-tracking camera. However, most of the usability testing you'll want to do does not need a deeply formal approach or special equipment (though if you have the facilities handy, they are helpful). A usability expert can help you decide between a discount approach and a formal one, depending on your goals.

Discount usability testing

Discount usability tests often use very few participants, so they are cheap and quick to run. You can expect to find about 85 percent of the biggest issues after testing with five participants, which is usually plenty of input to direct the team's next iteration on the most important aspects to solve.[21]

A typical usability test

A typical discount usability test takes place in a dedicated usability lab (when one is available), which provides a relatively controlled environment for the test. The participant sits in a room outfitted with a computer or whatever equipment is being tested. Team members watch from another room through a one-way mirror, and cameras capture the test on video.

 TIP

> Recording usability tests on video is a really good idea. It lets you hear a second time what customers said and also often provides really good video clips to show to the entire engineering team to illustrate pain points or customer viewpoints caught on camera.

In a typical test, a usability engineer or user researcher facilitates the test. In a usability lab, the facilitator usually sits behind the one-way mirror and speaks to the participant via a microphone and speaker set up in the lab. The testing may span several days or perhaps a week to accommodate a half-dozen individual participants, each in a 1–2 hour time slot. It's likely that at least one or two participants will cancel at the last minute, so it's a good idea to overbook slightly.

Ahead of time, the facilitator works with the engineering team to develop a task list and become familiar with the prototype to be tested—and to ensure that the areas to be tested are smooth and working without any obvious bugs. The task list is written up on a sheet of paper and placed next to the participant's computer in the usability lab.

When the participant arrives, the facilitator greets him, has him sign a nondisclosure agreement and a Consent for Research Subjects form, and has him sit at the computer. As part of the facilitator's greeting, she encourages the participant to speak his thoughts aloud throughout the test and reiterates that this is a test of the software, not the person. If the participant can't figure something out, it's the software's fault, not his, and this is very valuable data for the engineering team. The facilitator then leaves the participant alone in the room and enters the control booth on the other side of the one-way mirror.

The facilitator gets settled, turns on the recording system, and speaks into the microphone to instruct the participant to start the first task. She reminds the participant to read the task aloud and to think out loud as he performs the task. The participant uses the computer, which has been loaded with a click-through prototype or working code, and clicks and types as needed in an attempt to complete the task. The facilitator generally stays silent while the participant is actively working on a task and take notes of her observations throughout the test.

Unsurprisingly, sometimes the participant gets stuck. If the participant asks for help, the facilitator will often ask the participant what he thinks he should do or what he expected to happen that didn't. Generally, the facilitator will try to give the smallest possible hint, and only when absolutely needed, in order to learn the most about what the participant would try in his attempts to perform the task.

The test continues this way until all the tasks are completed. The facilitator may ask a few specific questions at the end of a task to clarify the participant's understanding of the system. It can be powerful to simply ask "Are you done?" because sometimes participants aren't sure whether they've completed the task or not, even if they have done what you expected. This is also valuable feedback for the engineering team.

At the end, the facilitator asks the participant to open up a standard satisfaction questionnaire on the computer to give some specific ratings about the experience he just had. Based on the participant's answers to that questionnaire, the facilitator may probe for more details. The facilitator will also ask if the participant has any questions or ideas to offer. Sometimes participants have interesting insights to share at the conclusion of a test, stimulated by what they have experienced.

After the test, the facilitator saves all of her observation notes and videos for later reference. After all of the participants have been tested for this particular study, the facilitator uses those notes as input for a brief report that's shared with the engineering team. The report is saved in an archive along with the usability reports. A facilitator may also make some short video clips of highlights or particularly insightful moments during the test to share with the engineering team.

RITE

The RITE method, or Rapid Iterative Testing and Evaluation, is a variant of usability testing in which the engineering team works alongside the usability test in progress.[22] As problems are discovered in the prototype, the engineering team is there to discuss them. If a problem appears to be important to address and a clear fix is available, the team revises the prototype, hoping to do so in time to present the updated prototype to the next usability participant. In this manner, a prototype can be iterated extremely quickly over the course of a few days. In the early stages of refining a specific solution, RITE can be a very useful technique for identifying and addressing issues.

SFE in action: The quick pulse study

Miki Konno, Senior UX Researcher, Microsoft Team Foundation Server

A quick pulse study (QPS) is a weekly study with three to six participants, which teams can use to get data about customers and to iterate designs rapidly. It provides quick customer feedback on specific features that are part of scenarios.

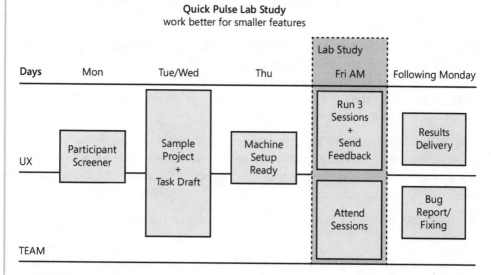

Quick Pulse Lab Study
work better for smaller features

A QPS takes place over a week from start to finish. On Monday, the UX team screens customers and sets up one-hour time slots for Friday. On Tuesday and Wednesday the team plans the tasks to be studied. On Thursday the team sets up the machines to be used. On Friday morning the team runs the sessions with the customers, and on Friday afternoon the whole team does a short debrief. The UX team distributes the results on Monday.

A QPS has several benefits. It is flexible, agile, and collaborative (the entire engineering team is invited to attend). It requires minimal advance planning, can have immediate product impact, and can meet urgent needs. The nature of the QPS means that it is not a replacement for formal lab studies.

We use quick pulse studies in Team Foundation Server to ensure that our UX team can make recommendations that actually have an impact on our product. Because our engineering team works in an Agile environment, we had to develop UX processes that were agile as well—the weekly cadence of the QPS allows us to integrate with the monthly sprints of the engineering team. And the QPS also helps us deliver on our team philosophy that "we have to test before implementation." Team members know that customers will be coming in every Friday, so they get frequent opportunities to get their ideas in front of customers. Our UX team works with 13 different feature teams, so this approach allows us to provide results across these teams, focusing on the most critical needs at any point in time.

Testing with paper prototypes

We love building, using, and testing with paper prototypes. They can be built quickly and easily, and they are perfectly suited for many types of user testing (informal, formal, cognitive walk-throughs, concept testing, and so on). They are also easily modified, and as such they can be used to explore new ideas quickly.

In Chapter 8 we talked about how to go about building a paper prototype, and we suggest that you watch the video we recommended if you haven't already; it demonstrates how to do a user test with a paper prototype: https://www.youtube.com/watch?v=5Ch3VsautWQ. Because a paper prototype can't automatically react as a customer interacts with it, the way a PowerPoint mockup or code prototype can, there are a few special considerations.

First, it's important to identify the different roles that need to be played during a usability test using paper. A single person can play all (or any combination) of these roles, but it's easiest if you have a separate person perform each of these roles. Here's what you need (of course, you also need a participant to try out your solution):

- **The facilitator**   Same as with any usability test, this person talks with the user and directs the test.

- **The computer**   This person manipulates the paper prototype based on the user's actions, to mimic what a computer would do.

- **The observer(s)**   Because running a paper prototype test is a manual process, it can be very helpful to have a dedicated observer and note taker.

The basics of running the test are the same as for any usability test, but you don't need a one-way mirror because you will all be in the same room. You create a set of tasks for the user to perform. The facilitator introduces everyone, puts the participant at ease, and begins the test.

When the participant is ready, the facilitator shows the first paper prototype screen and describes the first task. The facilitator might say, "Please send an email to your friend Suzy." The facilitator tells the user to use her finger to indicate where she would click or touch the screen.

Based on the user's actions, the person playing the role of the computer changes the paper prototype as needed, shuffling paper around to show what the screen looks like after the participant's action. For example, if the participant touches a drop-down menu with her finger (simulating a click), the person playing the computer unfolds the paper to show the drop-down choices. Or if the customer touches an OK button, the person in the role of the computer removes the current sheet and replaces it with one showing what would now be on the screen.

As with any usability test, any observers sit silently and take notes on the customer's actions, focusing on any mistakes or troubles she encounters.

While using multiple individuals to perform these roles is ideal, it is certainly possible to do a paper usability test with just you and a customer. In this case, you'll be pretty busy because you'll perform the roles of the facilitator, the computer, and the observer. Videotaping the test is also particularly helpful in this situation and allows you to review the footage later to capture notes and insights you might have missed the first time.

Formal usability testing

A lot of the feedback you want from customers can be done informally, often by members of the engineering team or through discount usability testing. For hunches and validation of big ideas or to sort out early usability issues, a formal usability lab study is almost definitely overkill. But when you want to gather valid statistics about how customers behave when they're trying to accomplish a task or work through a scenario using your software or live prototype, a formal usability study is a great way to collect both DO data and SAY data in a way that can be measured quantitatively. One of the most common reasons to do a formal usability test is to capture summative data, such as benchmarking data, to compare against your own scenario metrics, to compare your product against competitors, or to compare a new release against your previous version.

If your company has invested in a usability lab, chances are it has also hired a professional user research team. To best use that lab for formal testing, and to maximize the reliability of the resulting test data, the research team will pay attention to a lot of details and perform the usability tests using an appropriate amount of rigor. It's a really good idea to use a professional to do formal usability testing. The intent of this section isn't to enable you to design a highly reliable usability test (there are a lot of books and courses available on that topic if you're interested in digging deeper), but to give you some insight into what and why the professionals do what they do.

How to add rigor to a usability test

Here are a few examples of what it means to add rigor to a usability test (roughly in increasing order of rigor). Many of the first few items are commonly incorporated into discount usability testing as well when appropriate and feasible.

- **Customer recruiting and screening**   Use a screener questionnaire to ensure that the customers participating in the usability test represent the target customer segment. Participants may even be rescreened when they arrive for the usability test to confirm their fit, ensuring that there haven't been recent changes in a participant's background or experience. This might be important for maintaining the validity of the metrics gathered in a benchmarking usability test for the launch of a new game, when it's vital that participants have not yet played the game.

- **Number of participants**   The researcher determines the number of customers needed to achieve the desired level of reliability. Typically, the researcher will schedule more participants than needed to be sure that the level of reliability is achieved even if a few participants drop out at the last minute. Where a discount usability test would include 5–8 participants, a formal test might use a dozen, and a benchmarking study might use 15 or 25.

- **Prepared handouts** Consistency is added to the test by preparing a handout for participants that includes a short description of the target customer, a paragraph or two about the experience being testing, and the set of tasks they are being asked to complete.

- **Mitigate the order effect** People tend to have a strong reaction the first time they are exposed to something new. That reaction can be either positive or negative. The *order effect* refers to the phenomenon that the order of questions in a survey or the order in which you present solution alternatives can influence how a participant responds. Participants often prefer the last alternative they see. It's good practice to rotate the order in which you show alternative solutions across the slate of participants.

- **Clear roles** Each person in the room with the participant has a clearly defined role that is explained to the participant. The facilitator is identified. Everyone else in the room should remain silent and just observe and take notes (or whatever their role requires). Ideally, all the observers are behind a one-way mirror to minimize bias.

- **Consistency** Formal usability tests strive for consistency by using the same facilitator, the same facility setup, and the same set of tasks.

- **Time on task** If performance is an important metric, the time spent on a task is measured and recorded in the same way for the same tasks every time.

- **Benchmark against competitors** Design a test that allows you to collect multiple metrics during the usability test for both your company's solution and your key competitor's solution, and compare relative strengths and weaknesses. These metrics might include length of time to complete a task, the number of errors when completing a task, preference ratings in a questionnaire given at the end of the study, and many others.

- **Objectivity** In measuring time or getting benchmarking data, a priority is placed on objectivity. To this end, little to no extraneous conversation takes place with the participant, and nothing is spoken "off script." The facilitator maintains complete objectivity throughout the test.

- **Simulate reality** The more real a usability test is, the better. The tasks tested are actual tasks that the participant would be expected to perform. The participant should fit the target customer. The situation presented to the participant is as real as is practical. For example, is the task regularly done under stress? If so, can stress be created by giving the participant an aggressive time limit or other constraint? Does the physical appearance of the usability lab represent the environment where the user will typically perform the tasks? For example, for testing Microsoft Kinect, the usability lab was built to look like a family room.

- **Remove branding** When the source company might create a preference bias, prototypes can be modified to remove the company name or replace it with a dummy. This is the usability equivalent to a blind taste test.

- **Video recording, with indexing** Record the entire session on video so that it can be reviewed and analyzed later as needed. Special tools can be used to embed notes in the video at the time of the observed behavior to create a custom index in the video. The observer's notes can be queried to locate video evidence that supports any conclusions, insights, or discoveries.

- **Data analysis and formalized reporting** After all participants have been tested, a team of knowledgeable researchers uses a variety of techniques to synthesize and report on the resulting data. A more formal usability study could result in a substantial written report.

The usability lab: What is your role?

We've noticed that after a user research team spends the time and money to set up a study, there can be an avalanche of interest from the engineering team in hearing directly what customers say. This is a good thing, but it's important to limit the number of people in the room with customers during a usability test. To this end, most usability labs come equipped with an observation room that is outfitted with a one-way mirror, from where other people who attend can watch. However, being stuck behind the one-way mirror without a way to participate in the test directly can be frustrating.

Remember that your job as an engineer is to bring your knowledge of the product, the technology, and the customer . . . and to observe. You have a unique perspective, and it's important to note any insights you see, which might be different from what the facilitator notices. As you watch customers stumble on a task or fail to find an obvious link, you may desperately want to talk to them, to understand what they were confused about or help them get unstuck—but find that you aren't allowed to.[23] As a general rule, only the facilitator is allowed to speak during the test, no matter what happens. Even if the facilitator makes a mistake and says something that's completely incorrect, the team members in attendance must remain silent and deal with any discrepancies after the test. Once the test is complete, you'll have an opportunity to get together to debrief and share the insights from all of the observers and clarify any questions before the next participant.

We've seen another phenomenon that's worth mentioning here. The story goes like this: An influential person (the manager, the architect, the engineering guru) finally clears his schedule to observe a usability test. He only has time to watch two subjects, and halfway through the second test he has to leave. But the first test was full of great information and insight. The influential person goes back to his office and whips out an email to the team about these insights, proposes some changes, and begins to write code based on his newly discovered customer insight.

And just maybe, the insights that influential person derived from a single customer test are completely accurate. But maybe not. Maybe that one participant was an outlier compared with the rest of the group. While the energy and enthusiasm of the engineering team to want to act on the users' behalf is awesome, it's probably best to wait until all the data is in and the patterns are clear before making any judgments or taking any actions. Having a strong, influential engineer or manager make a snap judgment on a small slice of the data is common and can lead to troublesome, albeit well-meaning, results.

How many people do I test?

The good news is that you may not need to test as many people as you think.

Jakob Nielsen believes that most usability studies use too many participants. How many users should you test in a usability study? Nielsen says that number is five.[24] And for formative, qualitative studies, where you are looking to identify the biggest problems to fix and use customer insights to guide your product's design, that number makes a lot of sense to us. With that level of research, the cost/benefit ratio is quite high, and that encourages both quick turnaround and early testing, which are fundamental to the principles we present in this book.

SFE in action: Why you only need to test with five users[25]

Dr. Jakob Nielsen, Principal, Nielsen Norman Group

Some people think that usability is very costly and complex and that user tests should be reserved for the rare web design project with a huge budget and a lavish time schedule. Not true. Elaborate usability tests are a waste of resources. The best results come from testing no more than five users and running as many small tests as you can afford.

In earlier research, Tom Landauer and I showed that the number of usability problems found in a usability test with n users is:

$$N (1-(1- L) n)$$

where N is the total number of usability problems in the design and L is the proportion of usability problems discovered while testing a single user. The typical value of L is 31 percent, averaged across a large number of projects we studied. Plotting the curve for L =31% gives the following result:

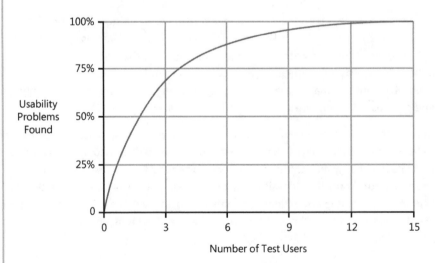

The most striking truth of the curve is that zero users give zero insights. As soon as you collect data from a single test user, your insights shoot up and you have already learned almost a third of all there is to know about the usability of the design. The difference between zero and even a little bit of data is astounding.

When you test the second user, you will discover that this person does some of the same things the first user did, so there is some overlap in what you learn. People are definitely different, so there will also be something new that the second user does that you did not observe with the first user. So the second user adds some amount of new insight, but not nearly as much as the first user did.

The third user will do many things that you already observed with the first user or with the second user and even some things that you have already seen twice. Plus, of course, the third user will generate a small amount of new data, even if not as much as the first and the second user did.

As you add more and more users, you learn less and less because you keep seeing the same things again and again. There is no real need to keep observing the same thing multiple times, and you will be very motivated to go back to the drawing board and redesign the site to eliminate the usability problems.

After the fifth user, you are wasting your time by observing the same findings repeatedly but not learning much new.

Iterative design

The curve clearly shows that you need to test with at least 15 users to discover all the usability problems in the design. So why do I recommend testing with a much smaller number of users?

The main reason is that it is better to distribute your budget for user testing across many small tests instead of blowing everything on a single, elaborate study. Let us say that you do have the funding to recruit 15 representative customers and have them test your design. Great. Spend this budget on three tests with five users each!

You want to run multiple tests because the real goal of usability engineering is to improve the design and not just to document its weaknesses. After the first study with five users has found 85 percent of the usability problems, you should fix these problems in a redesign.

After creating the new design, you need to test again. Even though I said that the redesign should "fix" the problems found in the first study, the truth is that you think the new design overcomes the problems. But since nobody can design the perfect user interface, there is no guarantee that the new design does in fact fix the problems. A second test will discover whether the fixes worked or whether they didn't. Also, in introducing a new design, there is always the risk of introducing a new usability problem, even if the old one did get fixed.

Also, the second test with five users will discover most of the remaining 15 percent of the original usability problems that were not found in the first test. (There will still be 2 percent of the original problems left—they will have to wait until the third test to be identified.)

Finally, the second test will be able to probe deeper into the usability of the fundamental structure of the site, assessing issues like information architecture, task flow, and match with user needs. These important issues are often obscured in initial studies where the users are stumped by stupid, surface-level usability problems that prevent them from really digging into the site.

So the second test will both serve as quality assurance of the outcome of the first study and help provide deeper insights as well. The second test will always lead to a new (but smaller) list of usability problems to fix in a redesign. And the same insight applies to this redesign: not all the fixes will work; some deeper issues will be uncovered after cleaning up the interface. Thus, a third test is needed as well.

The ultimate user experience is improved much more by three tests with five users than by a single test with 15 users.

However, whenever you are trying to capture summative, quantitative results, such as numerical statistics, you need to get more data points to have a reasonable level of reliability. Valid quantitative metrics need data from at least 20 users, captured in a rigorous way in a usability lab. An example would be measuring exactly how long it takes a participant to do a particular task and computing the average time on task. These kinds of summative metrics are best collected after the implementation has stabilized near the end of a project and can help you formally assess whether you are achieving your scenario metrics.

If you are using quantitative data to benchmark your solution's performance against a competitor's or against your existing solution, you may need even more participants. The Studios User Research group in Microsoft Game Studios did a power analysis and discovered that they needed between 25 and 35 participants to create statistically significant metrics that let them benchmark a new game against their portfolio of past games.[26]

Of course, the need for more participants makes capturing these kinds of statistics more expensive. However, often it's enough to have cumulative metrics collected over multiple studies, which can work if you are consistently using the same measures or asking the same questions on a post-test questionnaire. We will discuss this in more detail in Chapter 11.

Biases of usability testing

Usability testing is a great technique and can be adapted for many uses. Discount usability testing is an especially powerful way to quickly smoke out big issues with your solution. But as with all research techniques, usability testing has a few biases that you should be aware of. Thankfully, many of them can be mitigated, at least partially, if you are thoughtful about how to design your study.

- **Usability testing overemphasizes first-time use**   Because usability testing almost always uses a fresh set of users, you're usually watching a first-timer's view of your system. However, in the real world, first-time use represents only a very small slice of a customer's interaction with your solutions, so you'd be wise to incorporate more longitudinal approaches to get a broader picture. For example, you could invite customers to a series of usability tests and perhaps give them a prototype or a prerelease build to use at home in the meantime, but this requires extra planning and willing customers.

- **Where will real customers use your product?** A usability lab, your company's office, or even the line at a coffee shop are all probably fake environments for your solution. These aren't where your customers will ultimately be using your product. In a customer's own environment, many factors and complexities become relevant, from environmental distractions such as ambient noise and light from the window, to specifics about how the customer's computer is configured or organized, which makes it easier (or harder) for the customer to find files. In a usability test, you're usually not using the customer's computer, cell phone, camera, or other device. To this end, if you can design a test that lets customers use their own computer and devices, even if it's in your usability lab, that helps mitigate this bias. Or if you can bring a laptop loaded with a prototype (or even a prototype on a USB stick) to a customer's environment, that can be a productive approach as well.

- **Remember that usability testing on its own is designed for finding problems, not assessing delight** Even if your prototype passes usability without any blocking concerns and the users can do the tasks, that doesn't mean they are enjoying it or that they would choose to use your solution at home or at work. While you can get a lot of informal indications of usefulness and delight from listening to the participants' comments during the testing, this is not a rigorous way to measure these factors on its own. However, if you end every usability test with a questionnaire that delves into measures of satisfaction, delight, and desirability, that will help tremendously, and we highly recommend doing so. Still, be aware of the inherent bias of customers wanting to tell you that they like your work more than they actually do—they don't want to hurt your feelings.

Getting feedback: How do you know when you are done?

How do you know when you have enough feedback and it's time to move on? It's really quite simple. You are done when you have enough data to act on. Either you have identified some problems to work on in your next iteration, or you've gotten confirmation that your plan is on the right track, and you can dig into the next level of detail.

Practically speaking, you almost always have opportunities to both fix and fine-tune, as well as areas that are ready for the next level of detail. This input will start your next iteration of the Fast Feedback Cycle: adjust your framing if needed, brainstorm how to solve the problems you found, and build some new ideas to test . . . and then test with customers again. Unless, of course, you have data that verifies that you have met your experience metrics, and you are ready to ship.

Aside from very formal or summative testing approaches through which you're trying to generate hard metrics, a good rule of thumb is to get feedback from five customers during this stage, whether you are testing early concepts or fine-tuning final builds. That should give you a clear-enough picture to see what the common issues are and what you should iterate on next. If you feel like you aren't getting a distinct picture, by all means talk to more customers. But most teams find that by the time they've talked with a handful of people in their target customer demographic, the feedback is clear, and they are eager to start addressing it.

How do you know when you are done observing and getting feedback? In a sense, you are never done with this stage. In an ideal world, you (and your entire team) adopt a mindset that makes you always curious—you are always observing customers and looking for their feedback. You should strive to build a team culture and process with which you can continuously incorporate that feedback into your next generation of products, services, and devices.

Notes

1. Some techniques are useful for both generative and evaluative research, so this chapter overlaps with Chapter 5 to some degree.

2. Ron Kohavi et al., "Online Controlled Experiments at Large Scale," http://www.exp-platform.com/Documents/2013%20controlledExperimentsAtScale.pdf.

3. Tom Phillips, "Kinect Sales Equal the Original Xbox, Higher Than GameCube," Eurogamer.net, December 12, 2013, http://www.eurogamer.net/articles/2013-02-12-xbox-360-worldwide-sales-top-76-million.

4. Caveat: you might need the customer to sign some sort of nondisclosure or confidentiality agreement before sharing your prototype.

5. The technical term for asking questions while observing a customer is "contextual inquiry." You can read more about it in the book by Hugh Beyer and Karen Holtzblatt: *Contextual Design: Designing Customer-Centered Systems* (Morgan Kaufmann, 1998).

6. Although you can get some feedback on price points in a concept test, this is a case where you can't fully trust what customers say. Setting optimal price points is remarkably complicated and worthy of its own book. We strongly encourage you to hire an expert for detailed pricing studies.

7. *Wikipedia*, s.v. "Asch conformity experiments," last modified May 16, 2014, http://en.wikipedia.org/wiki/Asch_conformity_experiments.

8. The cognitive walk-through was first developed by Wharton and others. It grew in popularity when Jakob Nielsen published his book *Usability Inspection Methods* (Wiley, 1994). In 2000, Microsoft's Rick Spencer published a well-read paper at the Conference on Human Factors in Computing Systems that greatly streamlined the cognitive-walk-through process ("The Streamlined Cognitive Walkthrough Method, Working Around Social Constraints in a Software Development Company," CHI 2000, http://wiki.fluidproject.org/download/attachments/1704853/p353-spencer.pdf).

9. These two questions are part of the streamlined cognitive walk-through that Rick Spencer describes in his CHI 2000 paper.

10. Jakob Nielsen and Rolf Molich, "Heuristic Evaluation of User Interfaces," Proceedings of SIGCHI Conference on Human Factors in Computing Systems, CHI 90, 249–56.

11. Jakob Nielsen, "How to Conduct a Heuristic Evaluation," Nielsen Norman Group, January 1, 1995, http://www.nngroup.com/articles/how-to-conduct-a-heuristic-evaluation/.

12. Jakob Nielsen, "10 Usability Heuristics for User Interface Design," Nielsen Norman Group, January 1, 1995, http://www.nngroup.com/articles/ten-usability-heuristics/.

13. Jakob Nielsen, "How Many Test Users in a Usability Study?" Nielsen Norman Group, June 4, 2012, http://www.nngroup.com/articles/how-many-test-users/.

14. Nielsen, "How Many Test Users in a Usability Study?"

15. Alex Deng, Tianxi Li, and Yu Guo, "Statistical Inference in Two-Stage Online Controlled Experiments with Treatment Selection and Validation," http://www.exp-platform.com/Documents/p609-deng.pdf.

16. Kohavi et al., "Online Controlled Experiments at Large Scale."

17. Another use of A/B testing is to stage rollouts by presenting new code to a portion of the user base and verifying key metrics before fully deploying it, which helps reduce risk of unintended regressions with frequent code releases.

18. Ron Kohavi et al., "Seven Rules of Thumb for Web Site Experimenters, "http://www.exp-platform.com/Documents/2014%20experimentersRulesOfThumb.pdf.

19. Remember, however, that lasting competitive advantage will come not exclusively from being first. If your idea is easily copied, competitors will quickly do so, and your early advantage may not last long. It's worth thinking about what kinds of problems and kinds of solutions your company is uniquely suited to deliver, that would be tough for competitors to copy.

20. It's worth hiring an attorney to draw up an NDA for you to ensure that you've got all the right elements covered for your unique business and competitive situation.

21. Jakob Nielsen, "Why You Only Need to Test with 5 Users," Nielsen Norman Group, March 19, 2000, http://www.nngroup.com/articles/why-you-only-need-to-test-with-5-users/.

22. *Wikipedia*, s.v. "RITE Method," last modified April 28, 2014, http://en.wikipedia.org/wiki/RITE_Method.

23. However, the facilitator may stop to ask observers if they have any questions for the participant at appropriate times during the test. The facilitator then relays that question to the participant, and the observers remain silent (and, in the best case, invisible behind a one-way mirror).

24. Nielsen, "How Many Test Users in a Usability Study?"

25. Nielsen, ""Why You Only Need to Test with 5 Users." Reprinted with permission. The full article is available at http://www.nngroup.com/articles/why-you-only-need-to-test-with-5-users/.

26. Pagulayan, R. et al., "User-Centered Design in Games," in *Human–Computer Interaction Handbook: Fundamentals, Evolving Technologies, and Emerging Applications*, ed. Julie A. Jacko, 3rd edition, Boca Raton, FL: CRC Press, 2012, 795–822.

Cyclical feedback system, not a linear sequence of events

Diverge vs. converge

Let go of perfectionism

ITERATE

winnow

Experience architect

The magic comes from the repetition

NO MATTER HOW MUCH LIPSTICK YOU PUT ON A PIG, IT'S STILL A PIG

Avoid Big Design Up Front (BDUF)

NEEDS PHASE

Tiny iterations

TIME BOXING IS YOUR FRIEND

Turning the corner

3 times around before committing

Details phase

Iterative rhythm

Solution-tradeoffs phase

SMOOTH FUNNEL SHAPE

ITERATE QUICKLY

Fail fast

Get to the first prototype ASAP

THE SCIENCE OF ITERATION

External vs. internal

Understand vs. create

sawtooth

Iteration is a feedback system

CHAPTER 10

The importance of iteration

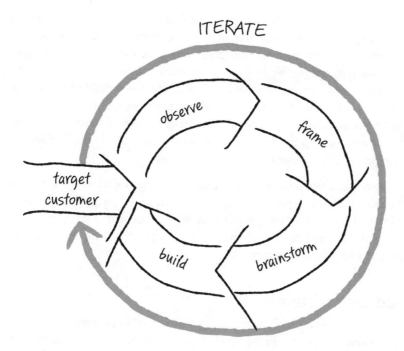

ITERATE

observe — frame — brainstorm — build — target customer

Iterating is the key to delivering great solutions that customers love. Our experience is that the biggest benefits don't come from any one stage in the Fast Feedback Cycle, or any single "must-do" technique. Rather, the magic comes from the repetition and continual improvement enabled by the iterative cycle itself. The more iterations, the more opportunities for feedback, the more chances to adjust and fine-tune, the better the overall result will be. Fast, lightweight iterations are the key.

Up until now, we've dug in deep. We've taken a very close and detailed look at the Fast Feedback Cycle and the activities that you might do during each stage, focusing in particular on the first couple of trips around the cycle. Let's pop up to 50,000 feet now and take a look at iteration from that perspective to see how the rhythm of iteration continues throughout a project and how the activities in each stage shift as you move from identifying the problem to finding a solution to fine-tuning and getting ready to ship.

Interesting patterns emerge when you look at iteration as a cyclical feedback system instead of as a linear sequence of events. Internalizing this cadence allows a team to gain the full benefit of the

Fast Feedback Cycle—an iterative rhythm that can be extremely productive, allowing different team member's strengths to shine at different stages as the team iterates.

What does (good) iteration look like?

We've used the word *iteration* throughout this book, but now it's time to unpack the term a bit more thoroughly. When we say that you should iterate, what exactly do we mean? What does it look like to iterate well? Is it possible to do it poorly?

At the most basic level, an iteration is a single trip around the Fast Feedback Cycle, doing the work involved in each of the four stages: observe, frame, brainstorm, build. First, observe customers, then develop and check your problem framing, then brainstorm solution ideas, then build or prototype some of those alternatives, which makes you ready to show those ideas to customers in your next trip around. As you make successive iterations, you gradually turn rough ideas into detailed plans, with customer feedback guiding you along the way. As a rule of thumb, teams should strive to iterate at least three times around the Fast Feedback Cycle before committing to a spec, a specific design, or production code, and for more complex projects, you'll potentially iterate much more. The idea is to continue iterating throughout the entire project, from concept to release.

But the science behind iteration is much more sophisticated and nuanced than the basic concept we've used to explain the parts of the Fast Feedback Cycle so far. In fact, you can go through the motions of each stage of the Fast Feedback Cycle yet gain only marginal benefits if you don't attend to the overall shape, pace, and rhythm of iteration across your project's lifetime. The next sections describe the characteristics of a healthy iterative process.

Iteration is a feedback system

The Fast Feedback Cycle is a loop. You work around the loop again and again, repeating the stages of the Fast Feedback Cycle over and over during the lifetime of a project. As you finish one iteration, the results of that iteration become the input for the next cycle. Each iteration does not stand on its own. Instead, each depends on the work that's gone on before and is deeply informed by the learning that happens in previous iterations.

In this way, the Fast Feedback Cycle is a type of feedback system in which you collect both positive and negative feedback from customers on every iteration, and that feedback is used to shape and direct subsequent iterations. Similar to what happens in other feedback systems in biology or economics or engineering, positive feedback reinforces the signal—that is, it encourages you to continue on your current path. Negative feedback causes you to reconsider your approach and perhaps to back up and try some other alternatives. Iterating in a fast feedback loop that is alert to both positive and negative feedback helps you narrow in on a solution that represents the "truth," or perhaps an "equilibrium," or (you hope) an "optimal solution" to meet your customer's needs reliably and efficiently.

However, for this feedback system to work, you have to actually listen to the feedback and be willing to make substantive shifts in your approach, depending on what you hear from customers. Teams that gather customer feedback but pick and choose which areas to listen to are not taking advantage of all the benefits of iteration. Similarly, teams that look at the Fast Feedback Cycle as simply a linear set of steps will never get the full benefit of iteration either. It is crucial to understand iteration as a continuous, cyclical system that requires lots of repetition and constant input from customer feedback to do its job.

Iterate quickly

This brings us to one of the most important characteristics of a healthy iterative process: keep iterations short so that you can fit in more iterations in a given amount of time. The greater the number of iterations, the more opportunities you have to react to feedback and fine-tune your plans. Our experience shows us that shorter, faster iterations are much more valuable than long ones. The magic is not in the individual activities and artifacts, but in the repetition and constant feedback. For most teams, you should be shooting for iterations of about two weeks, and for small teams and smaller-scale projects, possibly even shorter durations. Yes, that means that you need to be ready to show customers a few very rough prototypes of your first ideas a mere two weeks after you start a project. When we call it the Fast Feedback Cycle, we really do mean *fast*.

As we said in Chapter 9, "Observing customers: Getting feedback," you are often going to be wrong. The idea is to find out if you are wrong as quickly as possible so that you can recover as quickly as possible, and this means getting your ideas in front of customers as quickly as you can.

Several teams we've worked with made the mistake of initially moving slowly through each stage of the Fast Feedback Cycle, with the goal of doing the work in each step with care and attention to detail. First, they made sure that they did a thorough job of collecting customer research and schooling all team members in that customer data. Then, they spent weeks drafting, polishing, and prioritizing their scenario narratives. With a few chosen scenarios in mind, they involved carefully culled groups of team members in brainstorming and visualizing ideas. Finally, they built some rapid prototypes to show to customers. You know what that very conscientious approach meant? They did *one* iteration of the Fast Feedback Cycle over the course of a couple months (not weeks). In retrospect, it's no surprise that when these teams finally showed customers their first round of ideas, many of them did not resonate with the customers, and the teams had to scramble to adjust. That's better than finding this out after you've already written code, but the teams that took this approach still wasted the better part of two months.

The well-intentioned desire to do each step "right" can overwhelm the competing need to keep iterations fast. A funny thing can happen, though. As soon as a team gets customer feedback and starts becoming aware of the bugs in its thinking, the team naturally starts moving a lot faster. Partially that's because iterating is much easier once you have actual solution alternatives to think about. Also, by that point, the project-management clock is ticking loudly, and the urgency to begin coding becomes very strong. Unfortunately, this urgency can be so great that it tempts a team to move forward and start coding what it knows may be a suboptimal solution, simply to have built something—the details can be tweaked later. If a team's approach to the customer problem is already on the right track, and the issues in the early builds are minor, this approach can work perfectly well. But often, if not most of the time, the problems discovered in early iterations are much more fundamental and tend to alter the team's growing understanding of its customers' actual (versus hypothesized) problems and needs. If you don't clearly understand the problem you're trying to solve, tweaking the details and aesthetics of your initial idea will never really satisfy the customer. No matter how much lipstick you put on a pig, it's still a pig.

 MINDSHIFT

Avoid Big Design Up Front. Historically, computer scientists have argued that because bugs are much easier to fix on paper than in code, it's best to thoroughly think through solutions ahead of time. If you can prevent a problem, that's better than incurring the expense of coding up a bad solution, finding the bug, filing it, and fixing it. Even worse, for large problems, sometimes a fix isn't really feasible without substantially rewriting the code.

Agile teams argue strenuously against this Big Design Up Front (BDUF) philosophy. Their primary rationale is that designing a system on paper wastes too much time. In practice, nearly every software project team ends up having to change its initial designs as the code is written. Teams discover new customer requirements or find integration problems between components that invalidate the original design.

We see value in both perspectives, but we fundamentally agree that you want to avoid BDUF and instead start building prototypes and testing them with customers as soon as possible. However, an important nuance we stress is that you don't launch straight into writing code until you are on solid ground about what problem you are trying to solve. By clearly understanding the customer problem first, you avoid many of the most insidious problems that BDUF was trying to solve in the first place, and you also get the benefit of a more iterative, Agile approach.

A better approach is to iterate quickly from the very start. Get to the first prototype as soon as possible. The immediate customer feedback you get from even a couple of rough, half-baked ideas is almost always more valuable than spending another week trying to identify other unarticulated needs from more customer observation, or trying to write the perfect scenario, or brainstorming a few more ideas. In fact, getting feedback early is so important that some people evaluate a team's performance level by measuring and tracking its "time to first prototype" and doing whatever is possible to reduce that time.

 MINDSHIFT

Let go of perfectionism. To iterate quickly, a team has to let go of a certain amount of its innate desire for perfectionism—a point we've stressed before. You have to be comfortable sharing ideas that aren't fully thought through, showing prototypes that are rough and not picture-perfect, and moving forward with a few well-informed hunches about unarticulated customer needs without having talked to a statistically significant number of people. Relinquishing this desire is one of the most important cultural shifts that a team needs to make to get the highest efficiency from an iterative approach. You have to truly believe that your first ideas will likely be wrong and shift your mindset so that getting early feedback is more important than just about everything else. In fact, we encourage teams that have no ready source of generative customer data to make their best guess and start the iterative process by showing a prototype to a customer and then using that feedback to kick off the iterative cycle.

Time boxing is your best friend

To sustain a rapid pace of iteration, you need to find ways to beat the drum and keep people moving. Many teams find that time boxing is a good approach for managing the iterative process and keeping things moving along.

VOCAB

Time boxing is when you assign a fixed and limited amount of time in which to accomplish a specific goal.

Creating a more structured system to keep a team on a rapid cadence is especially important during the first year of the team's transition to our approach, when team members are learning new behaviors and trying to unlearn old habits. One way to time box is to create a forcing function, such as a series of regular scenario reviews or checkpoints that force a specific length of time on an iteration. Our favorite approach is to schedule weekly or biweekly user-testing sessions and use each session as the point for finishing an iteration and moving forward. If the team is expected to show three alternative prototypes to a customer on Friday, you won't make that deadline if you linger too long on any one stage of the iterative cycle. Time boxing and creating forcing functions to achieve small (and reviewable) outputs helps prevent analysis paralysis and keeps the focus on experimentation. Try something, see how it goes, and don't be afraid to fail: know that the feedback will tell you where to go next. Frequent, regular, and predictable opportunities to put ideas in front of customers are extremely helpful in keeping a team iterating quickly. We'll discuss these systems in more detail in the next chapter.

But it is possible to overdo it, to focus too much on the speed of iteration that you miss the point of getting feedback. We've seen some teams create a cadence in which they iterate so quickly that they don't bother to get feedback from actual customers before they refine and finalize their ideas. Instead of using customer feedback, these teams use heuristic evaluations, cognitive walk-throughs, dogfooding, and other feedback techniques that use the engineering team, not customers, to provide feedback for fueling iterations. However, if you read the last chapter carefully, you know that these approaches are appropriate only for identifying the more obvious usability issues and don't reveal much about usefulness or desirability. Don't be in so much of a hurry to iterate that you forget to talk to customers. Without actual customer feedback to power your iterations, you're violating the first rule of customer focus: "You are not the customer."

Iterate throughout the entire project life cycle

It's easy to imagine how continual iteration works in the context of an online service that a team is designing, building, and deploying to customers with small improvements on a daily or weekly basis. In those cases, it's clear that you can use a couple of rapid iterations to develop an idea, build the code, and release the service as quickly as possible, often as an A/B test. If the customer feedback is positive, and server performance looks good, the update is made available to the whole customer population.

It's also easy to see how iterations work at the beginning of a large yearlong project, when you use multiple turns of the Fast Feedback Cycle to identify the right scenarios, find good solutions, and fine-tune those solutions. But once the plan is more or less clear, the specs are locked, and coding in earnest is underway, do you really need to keep iterating?

In our experience, many teams want to stop iterating after they start coding, especially in larger, longer-term engineering projects. They believe that they have everything more or less figured out and that the main focus now is on execution. To some extent this is true—the team has to focus on the more technical functions of writing, debugging, and testing code to ensure the solution will work as planned. But that shouldn't mean the end of user testing and getting customer feedback. As the different parts of your solution come together, it's important to remain mindful of the customer's entire end-to-end experiences and track them using the metrics you defined in your framing. In Chapter 8, "Building prototypes and coding," we mentioned that some experiences can be tested only with running code. For example, experiences that rely heavily on animations and complex visual transitions, that work with variable kinds of user data (such as managing a personal photo library), or that involve responding to daily email in an active inbox are all situations that probably require that you test with production code.

Also, when several subteams work on different scenarios within a larger project, it's common to encounter unanticipated confusion that results from bringing together the various scenarios and experiences into the same UI. In your production code you may also discover unexpected latency between client and server components or other complexities that arise in execution. These can throw curve balls into the experience and are discovered only as scenarios begin to function in the code-base. When you bring components together, keep a close eye on how the end-to-end experience is coming together across all the pieces.

Finally, remember tunnel vision? That concept applies here as well. After immersing yourself in a project for any length of time, you (and the team) tend to see the solution through your own eyes, not as customers do—you become blind to the customer-experience issues lurking in your solution. To overcome this blindness you need to continue testing with customers to ferret out these issues as the code is being written and throughout the entire product cycle.

Iterating through the project's life cycle seems like a straightforward, common-sense idea, but as you will see in Chapter 11, "The way you work," adopting this habit is possible only when everyone on the team adapts their behavior.

Iterate in a funnel shape

Think back to the example of the ergonomic Microsoft mouse in Chapter 3. In that team's first iteration, team members used materials such as clay and fiberglass to mock up dozens of rough shapes for mice. In the second iteration, the number was winnowed down to nine ideas that the team worked out in enough detail that the concepts could be drawn in a CAD program and printed on a 3-D printer. In the third iteration, the number of alternatives was winnowed some more, and the team turned these into functional prototypes. Finally, in the fourth and subsequent iterations, the team came down to one final design that it tweaked and fine-tuned and ultimately shipped. This sequence is shown in Figure 10-1.

FIGURE 10-1 The funnel shape of iteration.

 VOCAB

To *winnow* is to reduce the number of items under consideration from a greater number to a smaller number but still more than one.

The mouse example is a great illustration of the "funnel" of iteration, and specifically it shows the shape that you want an iteration funnel to have—an overall cone shape.

A good iteration funnel starts with a lot of rough ideas, and over time the solutions become more detailed, more refined, and less numerous. Eventually you narrow options down to one solution, which you then continue to fine-tune through further iterations until it meets all your metrics. Then you declare it done and release it to customers.

The funnel shape allows the best ideas from multiple prototypes to be combined and recombined, giving you the best chances at finding a globally optimal solution, as we discussed in Chapter 7, "Brainstorming alternatives." You need multiple ideas to hang around for a while during the early iterations of your project to enable this. Showing multiple ideas to customers enables them to give you the feedback you need to identify the best aspects from each of the ideas you've prototyped. You can then combine and recombine those winning ideas into an even better solution. If you decide on a single approach too early, you cut off your chances of finding that magic combination that not only meets your customer experience goals but balances your business and technical goals as well. You might get lucky with an early decision and pick the optimal direction to follow, but statistically that's unlikely.

Maintaining the shape of the funnel is vital for gaining the most from the iterative process and consistently getting good results. You want a funnel like funnel A, at the left of Figure 10-2—a funnel that has smooth, curved sides, that you use to gradually winnow down the number of ideas, keeping multiple ideas in play long enough to find the right combination of ideas to form an optimal solution. Good iteration follows an asymptotic curve, but practically speaking (just as with an asymptote), you will never reach the truly optimal solution—it's too time-consuming, and you will get to a point of diminishing returns. At some point you will declare your solution good enough and ready to ship because it solves the scenario and meets the metrics you set out to address.

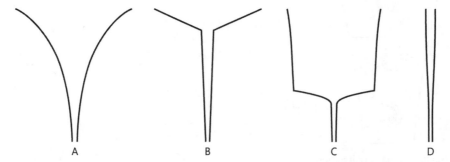

A   B   C   D

FIGURE 10-2 Different iteration funnel shapes. A is an ideal shape for iteration. B, C, and D represent flawed approaches to iteration.

In contrast, look at funnel B, which starts out with room for lots of ideas—probably from a robust initial set of customer research or a brainstorming session—but from here the team took a sharp turn and winnowed down too quickly to a single solution. We call this the "martini glass" shape. It's a suboptimal approach because it doesn't allow for much cross-pollination of ideas during the iterative process, and therefore you risk landing on a local maximum rather than a more globally optimal solution.

Funnel C is another common variant, where teams iterate a large variety of ideas for an extended period of time and do not winnow as they go. Sometimes this is referred to as "letting a thousand flowers bloom" or "throwing spaghetti against the wall and seeing what sticks." Often, this shape applies to cases where many branches of a larger team are working on different aspects of a problem but not talking with one another about how to integrate their ideas. The clock is ticking, however, and eventually the pressure to make a decision heats up. Usually, with some pain, the team moves into decision mode, choosing a single solution approach to pursue. Funnel C can lead to good results if a team integrates and mixes ideas along the way, but it results in a lot of waste and is slow, which makes it an expensive and inefficient approach.

Funnel D is the absolutely worst approach, where you consider maybe only one idea or a small set of cousin ideas, narrow in on a single approach right away, and subsequently "iterate" only that one solution concept. Unfortunately, this approach is typically what many engineers call "iterating," where you pick one reasonably good idea and then get feedback from the team and from customers to make that idea progressively better and better. It's a great approach for finding a local maximum, but if you are looking for a globally optimal solution, it's not a reliable technique for attaining consistently optimal results.

How many alternatives are enough?

Up to this point, we've talked a lot about the best funnel shape—one that requires you to explore many alternatives at the top of the funnel. But there's a big question—how many alternatives are we talking about?

The answer depends on how many iterative cycles you have done already, as well as on the depth and scope of the problem you are trying to solve. A good rule of thumb is that in your first trip around the Fast Feedback Cycle, for an average scenario, you should generate a large number of initial solution ideas, at least 50 or 100 or more. These ideas can take many forms and may have been generated in a few different forums—for example, a long list of brainstormed ideas plus a few dozen sketches, diagrams, or rough storyboards. As you continue around the cycle, you should narrow substantially at every iteration.

 MINDSHIFT

Require alternatives before making a decision. Some teams take the idea of exploring alternatives very seriously and apply it with rigor at every decision point in their ongoing work, whether they're considering how the user experience will look, what technology stack to use, or what to do for their next morale event. A team might make a rule not to make a decision of any sort until at least three or five or maybe even as many as nine different, viable alternatives are considered. This is one way to be sure that team members do the due diligence to really think through a problem before making a decision, especially a decision that can be painful to unwind later. The reasoning is that if you cannot generate several alternatives, chances are your understanding of the problem is one-sided or superficial, so this is a way to combat that.

Unpacking the Fast Feedback Cycle

In fact, we can peel back another layer of the onion. While it's true that some properties emerge from a sequence of iterations that are important to manage, there are also fascinating and elegant patterns within the Fast Feedback Cycle itself. The rhythms of these patterns are vital to embed in the day-to-day functioning of a team.

Understand versus create

As we mentioned in Chapter 3, "Take an experimental approach," the Fast Feedback Cycle can be split in half, top and bottom. The top of the Fast Feedback Cycle is about understanding—understanding customers, understanding their unarticulated needs, capturing those needs with good framing, and knowing how to measure and track against that framing to stay on course. In this half of the Fast Feedback Cycle, you aren't actually building anything. In a way, the top half of the cycle is about auditing or governance, continually checking back to be sure that customers still like what you're doing, that you're still solving the problems you set out to solve, that you're meeting the success metrics you laid out—or adjusting your framing based on what you learn.

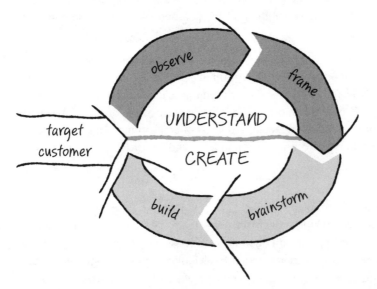

The bottom half of the Fast Feedback Cycle is all about creating solutions—brainstorming specific solution ideas, visualizing possible solutions with sketches or storyboards, creating prototypes or writing code to make those solutions come to life. The bottom half is about generating specific solutions. Here, you learn by making—you don't just think about the problem, but you get your hands dirty and build something.

As you travel around the Fast Feedback Cycle, you continually move between the top half and bottom half of the cycle. In the top half, you check in with your customers and verify your framing. Then you shift to the bottom half to do more work on your solutions. Then you shift again and check back with customers to see whether you're on the right track. Identify the problem, work on the solution, gather feedback, then adjust your understanding of the problem, and repeat. First understand, then create, then check your understanding, then create some more. Problem, solution, problem, solution. Understand, create, understand, create.

External versus internal

You can also split the Fast Feedback Cycle vertically, down the middle, and look at the cycle that way. The left side of the Fast Feedback Cycle is about going outside the team to engage with the external world—building something expressly for customers to use and getting their feedback on it. From a customer's perspective, all he or she usually sees of your work is the stuff you create when you're working in the stages on the left side of the cycle—the prototypes and products and services that you build for customers to use, plus the usability tests and conversations and surveys that ask them to tell you what they think of your solutions.

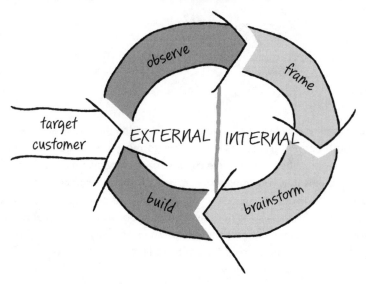

The rest of your work happens inside your offices, internal to the team and invisible to anyone outside your company, during the stages on the right side of the Fast Feedback Cycle. This side is about the team's internal work—writing down your best understanding of your customers' needs, tracking metrics, coming up with your best ideas for how you might satisfy those needs, relying on your current understanding of those needs as well as technical feasibility and business constraints. Those are all internal team concerns that you don't share with customers directly, but they are important to consider and are tools that help guide and structure your work.

You cycle back and forth between building something expressly for customers and seeing how they like it and taking what you learn inside the team and working through it as best you can. Then you're ready for another shot at showing your latest thinking to the outside world again. You move between doing work internally and building things that you show to customers externally. After that, it's back to your private, internal team processes, and then back to external customers again. External, internal, external, internal. Outside, inside, outside, inside. Customer, team, customer, team.

Diverge versus converge

The last pattern within the Fast Feedback Cycle is the most interesting—and also the most powerful. Take a look at the diagonals in the Fast Feedback Cycle; they also have something in common.

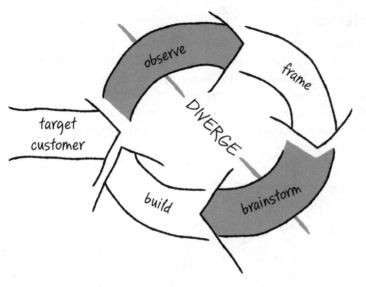

One diagonal focuses on diverging activities; that is, activities that widen the funnel and create more alternatives to consider. Both observing customers and brainstorming alternatives are fundamentally about creating more options. When you observe customers, you uncover more and more customer needs and possible problems that you could solve. When you are showing customers solution ideas to get their feedback, their responses will cause you to see various places where you need to change your solutions or may even inspire you to notice yet more opportunities for other problems you could tackle in the future. Similarly, when brainstorming solution ideas, you are by definition creating more alternatives, widening your funnel of options to consider.

 VOCAB

When you *diverge*, you create more options and alternatives to consider, broadening your scope.

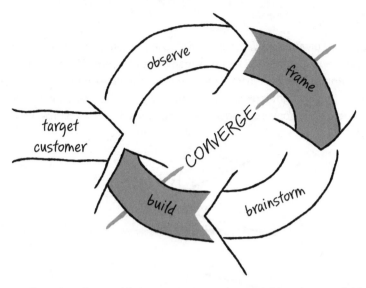

The other diagonal focuses on converging activities; these activities narrow the funnel and winnow the field to fewer choices. When you frame, you make decisions about which specific problems you're going to go after and choose the success metrics that are going to best indicate that you've solved that problem well. Similarly, in the build stage, whether you are building code or noncode prototypes, you don't work on every single idea that you came up with. Instead, you pick the handful of the most promising ideas to build and make some judgments about which ones are likely going to work the best. This diagonal is all about making decisions.

 VOCAB

> When you *converge*, you winnow from more options to fewer, making decisions about which problems and solutions are the most promising to move forward with.

As you travel around the Fast Feedback Cycle, at every stage in the cycle, you switch from diverging to converging and back to diverging again. Notice that the pace of the diverge-converge rhythm is twice as fast as either the understand-create rhythm or the external-internal rhythm. Practically speaking, diverge-converge is the dominant rhythm that team members notice as they do their day-to-day work, and as such, it is the most important one to integrate into the team's language, culture, and practices.

Having a team internalize the diverge-converge rhythm is a mark of a team at the top of its game—a team that can smoothly diverge to consider many problems, converge on a few of those problems to focus on them, diverge again to consider possible solution alternatives, converge to pick a few alternatives to get in front of customers for feedback, and then use that feedback to diverge again. Diverge, converge, diverge, converge. Alternatives, winnow, alternatives, winnow.

The sawtooth

When you take a closer look at the diverge-converge rhythm, you'll notice that the iteration funnel isn't strictly a smooth cone shape that gradually funnels many ideas to fewer. The constant cycle of diverging and converging within the funnel creates jagged edges—"teeth"—in the sides. A more precise drawing of the iteration funnel might look like Figure 10-3. We call this shape the sawtooth. It arises when you repeatedly diverge and converge and at the same time continually narrow your focus from one iteration to the next.

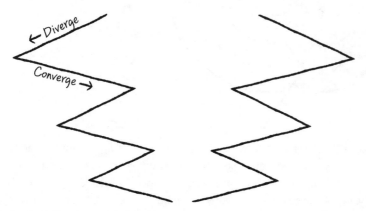

FIGURE 10-3 The sawtooth shape created by diverging and converging within the iteration funnel.

In practice, a team that is diverging looks, acts, and feels very different from how it behaves when the team is converging. If the team is not in sync about what stage it's in, you can find that some team members are trying to converge while others are trying to diverge. This can lead to a lot of confusion and frustration, as neither job is accomplished.

Aligning the vocabulary across the team is critical here. As the team moves through an iteration, team members need to be verbal and overt with each other about which stage the team is in and what frame of mind that stage brings to the tasks at hand. The team needs to be able to remind itself: "This meeting is about diverging" or "It's time to stop considering alternatives; time to converge." People need to instantly understand what that means and be able to align their approach appropriately. Understanding the science behind iteration, and internalizing the rhythms that govern it, helps everyone become comfortable with the idea that there is a time for diverging and a time for converging, but just not at the same time.

 TIP

> In meetings, be clear about whether the primary activity of that meeting is diverging or converging. Meetings designed for diverging might be about brainstorming, generating alternatives, hashing through ideas, investigating possibilities, discussing options. Meetings related to converging might be about making decisions, prioritizing, winnowing, or creating a plan of record. Whenever possible, schedule separate times for activities related to

diverging and converging, even if you separate them by only an hour or so. People need time to switch context.

All the activities we've discussed in this book fit into the Fast Feedback Cycle as either a divergent or a convergent activity. Figure 10-4 shows another view of some early activities and the artifacts you would likely produce at the convergence points, where you turn the corner from diverging to converging.

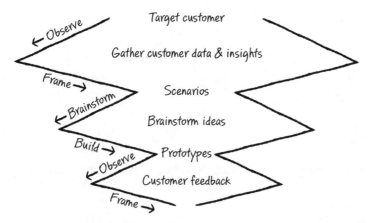

FIGURE 10-4 The sawtooth shape, overlaid with the stages of the Fast Feedback Cycle and typical deliverables at each stage.

Figures 10-3 and 10-4 show only a few teeth, representing just one and a half iterations of the Fast Feedback Cycle. But in reality, you'll iterate many times, and a sawtooth diagram of your entire process will have many more teeth. When you take a bird's-eye view and consider the sawtooth diagram for an entire project, you'll notice that the funnel shape becomes clearer. The sawtooth pattern happens throughout the project, but the teeth become smaller and smaller as you progress. When you consider the sawtooth pattern across the whole funnel of a project, it looks something like Figure 10-5.

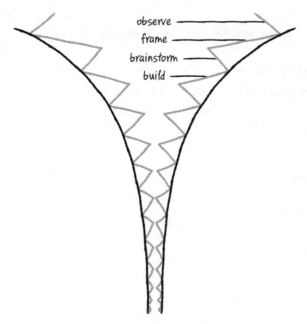

observe ———
frame ———
brainstorm ———
build ———

FIGURE 10-5 The whole iterative cycle follows a sawtooth shape, inscribed inside a smooth, curved funnel.

Turning the corner

We consistently hear from teams that the hardest part of this rhythm is the "turning points" in the sawtooth, when you shift between diverging and converging and back again. Yet, these turning points are essential to making progress—if teams have trouble turning the corner, then they may get stuck in a stage for too long and their iterations will become slow and inefficient.

Some people and teams find that turning the corner from diverging to converging is easier, especially teams that have a natural proclivity toward making decisions, picking a plan, and moving forward. Others find that type of turn difficult, feeling that if they had just a few more days they'd find a better insight or a more revolutionary solution idea. These teams might resist having to make a decision based on what feels like an incomplete set of choices.

On the other hand, some teams and individuals find turning the corner from converging to diverging easier. Typically, these are more creative sorts, who enjoy thinking through various alternatives or hearing the nuances of customer feedback; they look forward to diverging activities. But at the same time, others on the team might encounter difficulty going from what seemed like a solid plan to considering alternatives again, albeit on a smaller scale. This can feel like a step backward without understanding the larger wisdom of the sawtooth funnel.

These preferences highlight the reality that you have diverse individuals on your team, each with different strengths and comfort levels in different parts of the iterative cycle. You can expect that different people on your team will come to the forefront to lead different stages of the iterative process, and you should encourage this to happen. However, this should look less like handing off a baton in a relay race and more like a change in the leader in a V of geese as the flock flies south for the winter.

Regardless of who takes the lead at any given moment, the project team needs to remain engaged throughout.

TIP

Consider organizing some activities with your team to better understand where different individuals are best suited to contribute in the iterative cycle. One option is the Basadur Creative Problem Solving Profile (www.basadurprofile.com), which is a self-assessment tool that can help identify these different styles and preferences. You may be surprised at how diverse your team's preferences are, even between people with the same job title. In Chapter 12, "Lessons learned," you'll find a sidebar that discusses the Basadur CPSP technique in more detail.

While every team will have a mix of preferences and strengths, a team typically also has a general leaning toward diverging or converging. Most engineering teams lean toward converging, and certainly most managers have a bias in that direction, because converging is fundamentally about deciding a plan for the future and shipping a product. But while shipping is important, so is shipping the right thing, and without a proper balance of diverging and converging, you risk shipping the wrong product. For most engineering teams, particular emphasis needs to be placed on not shortchanging diverging, at the right points in the cycle, to give yourself the best odds at discovering a winning combination. Many designers tend to have a bias toward diverging, so adding staff with that skill and natural preference is one way to help balance a team, as long as that staff is treated as a full-fledged member of the project team and not as a "consultant" that can be easily ignored.

MINDSHIFT

Managers need to change their behaviors, too. Managers of teams have a role to play in making sure that the full iterative process is supported and reinforced. We see managers new to the Fast Feedback Cycle become nervous when their team picks not just one but a few ideas to move forward with, worrying that their team is indecisive or stuck in analysis paralysis. Managers need to realize that, especially in the first few iterations of the Fast Feedback Cycle, working on multiple ideas in parallel is expected and winnowing represents solid progress, even if the final solution hasn't been chosen yet.

Managers need to get used to the idea of a gradual funneling process, which does not yield an exact plan right away but, in the long view, is a more efficient and reliable approach to finding a solution that will genuinely meet customers' needs with a minimum of risk. Some time is needed for both teams and leaders to trust an iterative funneling process, so don't expect this mindshift to happen right away. Having a few projects successfully use this approach helps build confidence and develop a sense for what the funneling progression looks and feels like in practice. Until then, teams and leaders need to keep reminding themselves of the science of iteration and know that it's important to live with ambiguity a bit longer than they may be used to.

Turning the corner requires a good degree of coordination across the team, as well as mental agility to be able to change your frame of mind. Trouble turning the corner comes in a few forms. Some teams don't turn soon enough. A feeling of "just a little bit more" keeps the team from switching gears. For other teams, not everyone agrees to turn at the same time, so you end up with part of the team moving on to the next stage and some laggards having trouble letting go. The cure for both problems is the same: get the religion that your first ideas are likely to be wrong, but you just don't know which parts. The only way to find out what you need to do to improve is to get customer feedback as soon as possible. Teams that truly internalize this frame of mind will have a much easier time turning the corner quickly, because they view the whole iterative process not as a series of irrevocable decisions but as a series of experiments, where any decision that doesn't pan out can always be reconsidered.

SFE in action: Turning the corner doesn't happen by itself

Ian Todd, Principal Program Manager, Windows Phone

Our team had a history of success on Windows Phone 7 and 7.5 and was in the zone. We had forty people—program managers mixed with designers—collaborating on scenario-oriented specifications for the communications features in our next release. As usual, we had a strong set of scenarios and a smorgasbord of design concepts—we had enough material to hunker down and write those specifications. The engineers were finishing up a quality milestone and were going to start coding features in a month. We didn't have any specs yet, but no worries, right? Wrong. That last month came and went, and somehow the team never actually made the detailed design and functional decisions necessary to finish specs and be ready for coding. Deadlines came and went with very little to show for them.

What happened? The team had experience doing this kind of work and hitting deadlines. Yet we were also trying out some new things. We'd read the latest books on the benefits of being design-led and had taken the Scenario-Focused Engineering course. We had established a series of planning milestones to focus first on insights and scenarios, then on concepting, then on final designs, and finally on specs. The problem was that even after hitting the final-designs milestone, the team wanted to keep iterating, to get the design just right. At the same time, not enough pressure was being applied to get the team to turn the corner and get started building the product. That combination resulted in a team that wasn't motivated to converge. There was no tension in the team culture that made the imperfect prospect of convergence seem like the right place to go. Why *not* delight your customer just a little bit more with extra design time?

The team recovered over the next few weeks and finished a set of functional specifications. Sure, we probably got to a better set of designs than if we hadn't spent that extra month, but the incremental increase in the quality of the design was outweighed by a larger incremental reduction in how much time we had to iterate in actual code, with real customers. That's why regular convergence is so important to strive toward, even when it seems like less fun than spending more time designing.

These turning points are great places to pause and take stock of the work you've done. After a diverging activity, stop a minute to take pride in the amount of data or number of insights you've collected or in the sheer number of ideas the team generated. After converging activities, you'll naturally have work that represents the team's hard-earned decisions and reflects the team's intentions and focus moving forward. Artifacts from these converging points can and should be saved, discussed, communicated, and celebrated. In addition, focusing on the artifacts you create at converging points can help give managers what they need to know that the team is making progress so that they can confidently support the project over the long haul, especially during the first set of iterations, before the team has narrowed in on a single solution approach.

Phases of iteration

In Chapter 8, we explained how the prototypes you create—and the questions you are trying to answer with your prototypes—are different depending on how far along in development a project is. You saw in Chapter 9 the many different kinds of customer feedback you can gather, from feedback on whether you've identified an important customer need, to testing whether the solution works well, to fine-tuning the details. In this section, we follow those thoughts a bit more and explore how the activities in the stages of the Fast Feedback Cycle change as the product matures from concept to rough implementation to detailed production code.

When you put it all together, three distinct phases of iteration emerge across the life cycle of a project. A project starts in the needs phase, which is primarily about identifying customer needs. It continues into the solution-tradeoffs phase to narrow in on a specific solution approach, and finally settles into the details phase to fine-tune that solution. This phase finishes when the solution ships. Production coding typically starts midway into the solution-tradeoffs phase. Figure 10-6 shows how the phases overlay on the sawtooth diagram.

The activities you do at each stage of the Fast Feedback Cycle can look quite different in each of these phases. For instance, during the needs phase, the Frame stage is mostly about writing scenarios and metrics, but by the time you get to the details phase, the Frame stage has become mostly about assessing how well your solutions are doing, with your scenarios and metrics as a reference point.

The activities you undertake in each stage might also look different depending on whether your project finishes in a matter of days or weeks, versus a much bigger project that continues for months or even years. For example, a short, small-scale project might use only discount usability testing in the Observe stage, whereas a larger-scale project might use a mix of surveys, various levels of usability testing, and site visits to get feedback from customers.

Furthermore, whether you are working on a large project or a small one, the overall goal is still to keep iterations fast, so you will probably only have time to use one or a very small number of techniques during each stage within a single iteration of the Fast Feedback Cycle. Given all these complexities, a natural question is, "Which techniques are the best ones to use at different phases of my project?"

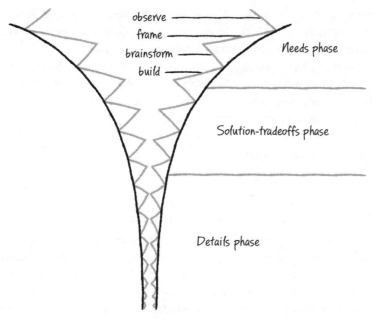

observe ——————
frame ——————
brainstorm ——————
build ——————

Needs phase

Solution-tradeoffs phase

Details phase

FIGURE 10-6 The phases of a project, and how they relate to the sawtooth funnel.

As you've seen in the previous chapters, you can consider using many different techniques at each stage of the Fast Feedback Cycle. Even after you focus in on just the techniques that make sense for your specific problem domain (hardware, software, API, user experience, etc.), it can be tricky at first to see which techniques are optimal for which situations and at which stages in the project. Thinking about the main phases of a project and how iterations proceed within those phases can help you select which techniques are most appropriate for each iteration and will also give you a more practical feeling for what a series of iterations might look like over the duration of a full project, especially for a larger-scale project.

The following sections provide more details about each phase, including which techniques are most commonly used in those phases, how long that phase should last, and what each phase is trying to accomplish. These guidelines refer to medium- and large-scale projects. Some special characteristics of small-scale projects are offered in a separate section; significant parts of the iterative cycle and various phases can collapse and overlap for small-scope projects.

Needs phase

What are the most important real-world needs of my customer, and do I understand them fully?

The needs phase entails the first few iterations of the Fast Feedback Cycle, where you focus on identifying customer needs, seeking to deeply understand your customers' perspective, constraints, desires, and frustrations. The needs phase starts at the top of the iteration funnel, its widest part. You may be simultaneously considering a large number of diverse customer problems or a large number of different aspects of a problem, and possibly even narrowing in on exactly which customer to target. The goal of the needs phase is to figure out which of those areas to focus on, which are the most important aspects to solve from your customers' point of view, and what factors are going to be important in a truly delightful solution. In this phase, you are more concerned with identifying a problem whose solution would be useful and desirable to a specific target customer; at this point, it's too early to think about usability or craftsmanship.

During the needs phase you iterate through all four stages of the Fast Feedback Cycle, including showing your proposed solution ideas, but for now you're most interested in getting confirmation that you're solving the right problems. In this phase you are not yet concerned with figuring out which solution is the best one. Instead, you use the tactic of showing the customer a wide variety of possible solution ideas to help spur feedback and conversation, with the goal that this will clarify and ferret out the true customer needs. Until you are sure that you've identified your customers' most important problems, specific solutions don't matter per se. The needs phase is akin to the approach in Lean Startup of testing an MVP to validate your basic value proposition and target customer.

Typically the needs phase involves one to three iterations. It occurs at the widest part of the funnel, where you consider the largest variety of alternatives. You exit the needs phase when you are confident that you have identified your customers' deep needs, know exactly which problems are most valuable to solve, know how good the solution needs to be to delight customers, and have captured that knowledge in a solid scenario (or other framing device) that can be shared with the entire team. When you finish this phase, the funnel is still fairly broad, as there are many possible solution paths that could be followed, but it is significantly more focused than when you started.

Here are some details about each stage in the Fast Feedback Cycle during the needs phase of a project and which specific techniques make the most sense during this phase:

- **Observe stage**   During the needs phase, start with the generative research approaches outlined in Chapter 5, "Observing customers: Building empathy." Site visits are a particularly good technique for the very first iteration. You can hear pain points and learn about needs directly from customers in the context of their real-world situation. After you have your first round of rough ideas to show, switch to the lighter-weight evaluative approaches found in Chapter 9, such as scenario interviews, concept tests, or informal usability tests using paper prototypes. In the needs phase, you always show multiple alternatives to customers because comparisons lead to understanding customer preferences more clearly. It's absolutely essential during the needs phase to test with target customers and not proxies.

- **Frame stage**   The focus during the needs phase is on writing and editing scenarios (or another framing mechanism) to capture what you've learned about your customers. As you write scenarios, you should also begin identifying which success metrics are the most important indicators of deep delight. In your first iterative cycle, you will draft scenarios, and in subsequent iterations you will revise, fine-tune, and finalize your scenarios based on what you learn from your customers, making them more accurately reflect your customers' real-world situation and your latest insights about their motivations and desires.

- **Brainstorm stage**   During the needs phase, you brainstorm many ideas. You look for as much diversity in solution alternatives as possible, explore many diverse directions, and cast a wide net. This breadth of alternatives helps stimulate customers to mention ideas, needs, desires, details, or constraints that have not yet surfaced. Focus on open-ended brainstorming techniques with groups of people to generate many diverse ideas quickly, and be sure to encourage the unusual, wacky, and seemingly impractical ideas. These can lead to breakthroughs in solution concepts and also suggest potential customer needs you might not have noticed in direct research. At this phase, you're not interested in thoroughness in your brainstorming, you are merely exploring the edges of the space, so the more rigorous techniques such as six thinking hats or SCAMPER are not worth the effort yet. Visualize ideas with sketches, but don't bother to refine them. Rough storyboards are great to quickly sketch out the flow of how different solution alternatives might play out. The focus on sketching and storyboarding at this stage is not about refining ideas into something practical or optimal, but about getting a rough idea on paper so that it can be shared with others for directional feedback.

- **Build stage** In these first iterations, you should stick to extremely low-fidelity, rapid prototypes, such as rough paper prototypes. Take the storyboards and sketches you generated while brainstorming and pick a half dozen to clean up just enough that you can show them to customers in an initial round of evaluative customer feedback. Your prototypes don't need to work in any form yet, or even fully make sense, they just need to get the idea across well enough that you can get directional feedback from customers or engage them in a participatory design exercise to have them extend the prototype with their own ideas. Ask them whether it looks interesting and how they would change it to be even better.

In the needs phase, you do something at every stage of the Fast Feedback Cycle, but you spend proportionally more time in the Observe and Frame stages. This emphasis shifts in future phases of iteration.

SFE in action: We forgot to check for usefulness

Tracey Trewin, Partner Program Manager, Microsoft Developer Division

We were on our way to shipping Progression/CodeMap a third time, and yet we were still missing something. The product demoed well. It had even tested well in usability studies for certain scenarios. Everyone agreed that visualizing relationships between code was a compelling concept. It seemed like it had so much potential, but somehow it just wasn't hitting a chord with our developer audience.

We decided to do another user study. Truthfully, our usability researcher, Paula Bach, and I were preparing the team for a pivot. We were going to conduct a rapid iteration study, where we have the developers on hand make adjustments in real time. After all, there is no point in continuing to test the same prototype over and over when your users are clearly struggling.

We had our first users come in, and we started to walk them through the script. It was a disaster. They struggled and didn't make it through the tasks without a lot of help.

That is when we regrouped. Paula and I looked at each other and said, "Dang, we are busy testing whether this is usable, but we are not even sure that this is useful." I know it sounds obvious, but in hindsight, it is a very common mistake. This realization caused us to do a reset of the study and focus on validating the key scenario. We needed to determine whether the problem we were trying to solve was interesting and important to our users in the first place.

Through the study, we determined that our users did find CodeMap useful in understanding and navigating code, but the surprise was that users gained the most value from CodeMap when they were debugging and wanted to jump around in a debugging stack. You can certainly do this in the debugger window, but in general people found it helpful to have a visualization of the code and its relationships.

During this study we had an aha moment where we realized that if we built a CodeMap automatically as users debugged their code, rather than requiring them to manually add elements to the map, that users intuitively understood what they were looking at and were immediately able to navigate the map. Truthfully, this was a relatively small change, but it fundamentally changed how we were thinking about this functionality. Showing the map of the code during debugging dramatically increased the usefulness of the feature.

Looking back, we made the classic mistake of assuming the feature we imagined was useful, jumped ahead to build solutions, and then tested our solutions for usability before we had verified the problem was the right one to solve or fully understood the customer need. So, in short, the moral of the story is always check usefulness first.

Solution-tradeoffs phase

Which solution provides the most optimal tradeoff between great customer experience, technical feasibility, and enabling the business plan?

Once you confirm that you've chosen the right set of problems, you focus on identifying the best end-to-end solutions to those problems, including making decisions about key tradeoffs. You will get feedback on various solution approaches from customers and then narrow in on a single, specific solution that strikes the right balance between great customer experience, technical feasibility, and enabling your business plan. This phase is characterized by making tradeoffs between what would be ideal and what is practical and balancing multiple, sometimes conflicting, goals.

This phase represents the middle section of the funnel. You start with a reasonably clear description of customer needs, but you still have a broad set of possible solution alternatives. Over multiple iterations, you gradually narrow this set down to a single proposed solution. To accomplish this, you blend multiple solution ideas together, informed by regular doses of customer feedback and ongoing feasibility investigation that provides course corrections and directional guidance.

You should start considering technical feasibility during this phase, providing feedback about the solutions being considered and whether they are reasonable to build in an appropriate time frame with the resources you have available. You will be doing technical design work in this stage, working in parallel to define the underlying architecture as the end-to-end solution is iterated. As you progress through the solution-tradeoffs phase, you make the transition from building rapid, noncode prototypes, to writing prototype or investigatory code, to writing production code. Some projects make the transition to coding faster than others, especially if creating multiple alternatives to test in code is easier for the architecture or platform you chose. However, regardless of whether you are building paper prototypes, functional code, or some of each, you will continue to test your latest ideas with customers at each iteration so that you have a continuous stream of feedback into the iterative process.

You also need to think through the business plan in detail during this phase and confirm with your target customers exactly how your monetization plan is going to work. This customer feedback is needed whether you plan to monetize directly—such as by selling devices, subscriptions, or services to customers—or indirectly through advertisements, developer licensing, partner deals, or other means. Obviously, if customers aren't willing to click the "Buy" button to pay for your service, you are in trouble. But even for an ad-supported model, if your customers aren't willing to tolerate and en-gage with advertisements, you need to know that now and figure out an alternative—it could have a big impact on the overall solution you build. You need to put whichever customer in your ecosystem is going to be financing your business on your list of customers to get feedback from and iterate with, even if they are not a direct consumer. This might include partners, OEMs, developers, device manu-facturers, as well as end users.

An often-forgotten aspect of the solution-tradeoffs phase in a larger project is the need to integrate the solutions being iterated in parallel by multiple teams, each of which is focused on solv-ing different scenarios but whose solutions will ultimately appear within the same parts of the user interface or in a set of APIs. Integrating the user experience of these solutions, resolving conflicts, and making tradeoffs between them is an important aspect of winnowing down to a single solution approach. These steps should happen before solutions are locked and before they are implemented with final ship-quality code. Trying to integrate experiences across a product after you see collisions and surprises appear in the build is much more difficult than resolving these problems earlier, when plans are more fluid and adaptable.

 TIP

An experience architect can be extremely helpful throughout this phase. This team mem-ber provides structures to prevent collisions and inconsistencies by establishing visual guidelines, layout templates, interface metaphors, design principles, and other elements of a user experience architecture. An experience architect can also be instrumental in re-solving integration collisions when they do happen, and he or she ideally provides over-sight throughout the iterative process by proactively checking in with each team to help plans grow together in a complementary way and to ensure that discoveries and ideas are shared broadly. The skills of an experience architect to be able to zoom in to the details as well as zoom out to see a cohesive big picture are rare, but they're essential to have on any large team.

The solution-tradeoffs phase typically lasts anywhere from two to six iterations, depending on the size and scope of the project and the difficulty or novelty of the problem space, and may vary significantly for individual projects depending on how long the team takes to hit on a solution that meets all the goals and critical constraints.

 ## MINDSHIFT

Allow for the flexibility to iterate. It's true. Iterating based on feedback and waiting until you get it right makes predicting a development schedule up front more difficult. But in the big picture, it's much more important to increase your predictability of commercial success than it is to increase the predictability of the development schedule. By providing room in your schedule for iteration, you can avoid the situation where you prematurely decide on a suboptimal solution and ship something that the customer doesn't understand, need, or like.

Balancing iteration, feedback, and the creative process against real-world pressures to ship is an art, not a science. You need to find a balance that satisfies both the need to delight your customer and the need to bring a product to market. One way to gain more scheduling flexibility is to do fewer things in the first place. And remember, inside the creative process, time boxing is your friend. It is possible to fuel iterations and creativity while still maintaining the respect and discipline for the need to finish.

You are ready to exit the solution-tradeoffs phase when you've gotten to a single proposed end-to-end solution that meets experience, business, and technology constraints and all of the related scenarios are well integrated and rationalized. With competing constraints and practical limitations to balance, it's easy to forget that achieving a delightful user experience is your ultimate goal. If customers aren't finding your solution deeply delightful by the end of this phase, it's too late to fix this in the details phase, so be sure you keep your eyes focused on delight throughout the solution-tradeoffs phase.

Here are some details about each stage in the Fast Feedback Cycle during the solution-tradeoffs phase of a project and which specific techniques make the most sense during this phase:

- **Observe stage** By the time you start this phase, you are typically using evaluative research approaches, starting mostly with rapid, lightweight, qualitative approaches, and still evaluating multiple solution alternatives at each iteration. Usability testing with all manner of prototypes or functional code tends to be the workhorse in this phase, often paired with a questionnaire or brief interview at the end of the test to gather preferences, satisfaction, and other attitudinal data. A/B testing may be possible in some situations where infrastructure is readily available. You are listening for which aspects of each solution alternative are working well and which aren't and for the preferences that people express. This feedback helps direct your efforts to fix those problems in future iterations and recombine the best aspects of multiple alternatives. As you gather feedback, be sure to listen not just for validation about usefulness and usability but also for desirability. If you hear doubts in the solution-tradeoffs phase about the overall usefulness of your solution, instead of trying out a new solution, consider reframing the problem—it's likely you're not focused on a valuable customer problem yet. It is still important to use actual target customers when assessing usefulness and desirability, but this is the phase when it is reasonable to use customer proxies during initial rounds of usability tuning or to do heuristic evaluations or cognitive walk-throughs to ferret out bigger usability issues.

- **Frame stage** At this point, your scenario and metrics should be written and fairly well refined, so your first job is simply to briefly check in and remind yourself of your scenario and its key success metrics. Use this checkpoint to make sure that you haven't drifted away from your initial problem statement and to make small edits to your scenario based on ongoing learnings, when appropriate. Large edits to your scenario at this point will reset the clock and put you back in the needs phase temporarily. For this phase, your new work in the Frame stage is to start reporting on your progress via scorecards or other reports. You need to figure out how you're going to actually measure and report on your key metrics, start putting telemetry or other infrastructure in place, collect preliminary data as it becomes available, and collate that information into scenario scorecards or reports to track your progress toward shipping. In this phase, your first report will likely contain summaries of qualitative feedback that was heard in user testing and data points from end-of-test questionnaires, but your reports will gradually include more quantitative metrics when they become available. Collecting and reporting on this data at every iteration is important so that you can establish trends over time.

- **Brainstorm stage** The beginning of the solution-tradeoffs phase is your last chance to brainstorm broadly, looking for new approaches and wild ideas. Be sure that you have thoroughly explored the entire problem space before you start to winnow, so include some of the more structured brainstorming techniques, such as the six thinking hats or SCAMPER, or the rigorous use of lateral thinking techniques, especially paired with sketching. Holding a sketch-fest is a great way to generate a lot of storyboards that explore multiple end-to-end solution alternatives and to bring fresh brains into the brainstorming. You are looking for as many divergent ideas as possible, as well as cousins of current proposals so that you can compare their relative merits. As feedback on your solution ideas starts coming in during the solution-tradeoffs phase and feasibility and business constraints begin to surface, your brainstorming becomes increasingly constrained. You now generate alternatives for solving a particular problem discovered within the context of a given set of solutions rather than reimagining the solution set from the beginning. The latter part of this phase should have a big focus on blends of ideas, combining and recombining the best aspects of different solutions to fine-tune your solution.

- **Build stage** You start the solution-tradeoffs phase with low-fidelity prototypes of the most promising end-to-end solution ideas generated in the previous stage. As you iterate in this phase, you gradually increase fidelity, moving from rapid prototypes to writing code, as you winnow your ideas and become more confident about which solutions to pursue. Your prototypes should play out the full length of the end-to-end experience, to ensure that you're delivering a complete solution for your scenario. However, it is rarely worth your time to consider errors or other corner cases in prototypes, unless these are somehow central to the experience. Be careful not to skip to high-fidelity prototypes or code too quickly, before you've allowed an iteration or two for the best ideas to be identified by customers and then blended those ideas. Spikes or code prototypes investigate the feasibility of various approaches and can happen in parallel with rapid UX prototypes for a time. Write code as a series of slices of the end-to-end experience, which gives you a double-header of value: insight into feasibility and performance characteristics of the proposed technical architecture, and a slice of functional code that you can use in usability tests to get customer feedback. By the end of this phase, you should certainly have done enough technical investigation to feel confident about the feasibility of your approach, have settled on a technical architecture, and be well underway writing production code.

In the solution-tradeoffs phase, you still do something at each stage of the Fast Feedback Cycle, but you spend proportionally more of your time in the Brainstorm and Build stages.

 TIP

> If you want to super-power your iterations, consider doing a week of co-located iteration with your customers. Bring your development team to live with a customer for a week, do rapid iterations with customer feedback the moment you need it, and maximize your speed and efficiency. A terrific video by Nordstrom's Innovation Lab demonstrates what this might look like: http://www.nordstrominnovationlab.com/#case_study.

Details phase

Which details of my solution need to be fine-tuned before I can ship a high-quality release?

Once you have narrowed in on a single solution that meets all your core constraints, you switch your attention to fine-tuning the details. Your goals are to optimize usability, performance, and aesthetic appeal and to ensure flawless execution in the final shipping code. Along with creating a great end-to-end experience for your customers and enabling a viable business plan, the production solution must also be robust, scalable, performant, maintainable, and generally executed with a high degree of craftsmanship. Thankfully, all those aspects of technical craftsmanship (and more) are pretty familiar to most engineers, so we won't belabor those points. However, that same level of craftsmanship and attention to detail is just as important for fine-tuning the customer experience.

The details phase represents the bottom, straight-down part of the funnel. Here, you take a single proposed solution and fine-tune the details in a fairly linear fashion. You should already have high confidence that your chosen solution is useful for the target customer, reasonably usable, and desirable, so there isn't much risk of finding surprising, new problems by this point.

You won't make big changes in your solution from iteration to iteration in this phase, just small adjustments to fix minor problems or confusions or to add small touches that enhance the experience, improving customer delight. As you make those adjustments, you will still try some alternative approaches, but they will be different only in the details. For instance, to enhance the discoverability of a link on a page, you might propose changing its font color, adding a box around it, or underlining it. To improve aesthetics, you might try a couple of different visual motifs and get feedback on which one customers like best.

MINDSHIFT

You don't have to test everything. It may surprise you that we recommend that you not test every single change. You can overdo it by subjecting every change in color to a usability test or an A/B test, which is clearly overkill and inefficient. A team needs to apply some judgment about which changes are significant enough to merit developing alternatives and running a test. Discount usability is cheap, but it's not free. Neither are A/B tests. Focus your iterations and data gathering on the places most important for your key success metrics and the places where you have the biggest risks or visible problems.

The details phase can take anywhere from three to as many as dozens of iterations, depending on the size of the project and how long it takes to write the production code and fine-tune the details to meet your success metrics. You are done with the details phase when you're ready to ship your solution to customers.

Here are some details about each stage in the Fast Feedback Cycle during the details phase of a project and which specific techniques make the most sense during this phase:

- **Observe stage**   Usability testing is still the go-to approach for evaluating code. Detailed testing always needs to be done with true customers to be sure you catch any differences with your target population and stay connected to what they find pleasing and desirable. But, from time to time, you can get away with using customer proxies if all you need to know is whether the solution works at all, especially as new code comes online. As your solution stabilizes and is performing well in qualitative usability testing, you may consider adding a formal usability test to capture quantitative metrics with statistical reliability or for benchmarking your solution against a competitor. However, realize that these quantitative tests are expensive and are valid only if you use target customers. If you have the infrastructure, A/B testing is great in this phase to quantitatively test aspects of the design you may need real-world usage data on.

- **Frame stage**   You continue to check in on your scenario and metrics to be sure you haven't drifted off path and to capture the latest round of metrics on the scorecard or scenario report. You should pay particular attention in the details phase to trends you see on your scorecard to ensure that there aren't any regressions in your key metrics and to identify the areas that need the most work to meet your goals. The Frame stage is when you look at your scorecards and scenario reports and decide whether a solution is good enough to send out to beta testers, to reviewers, or ultimately for release. You'll also undoubtedly make some hard decisions about whether a scenario is still complete enough to ship when not all the pieces are on track for release, or whether larger cuts need to be made.

- **Brainstorm stage**   In this phase, brainstorming is limited to specific targeted fixes to identified problems in your solution. Typically, it's not worth conducting a big group brainstorm for these types of problems (unless something is really stumping you). However, you should still generate multiple credible alternatives as part of the due diligence of thinking through any problem before you pick which solution to implement. Individual or small-group brainstorming in short bursts when a problem crops up is typical for this phase.

- **Build stage**   You should definitely be well into building production code by this point. If a trickier problem comes up, you may perhaps build a few targeted prototypes to explore alternatives, but the vast majority of building is done directly in code at this point. It's important to build code in slices so that you can continue to test your work in progress with users and ensure that the live code is resonating as well as your initial prototypes did. If there is a problem with how your ideas are being translated into code, you want to find out sooner rather than later, so be sure to sequence your coding so that you can keep testing end-to-end paths as they come online.

In the details phase, although you do something at each stage of the Fast Feedback Cycle, you spend the majority of your time in the Build and Frame stages.

After the project ships, you may do a final usability test to capture final benchmark information, and you certainly will be monitoring new kinds of feedback channels now—live feedback from product support, social media, discussion groups, and any telemetry that might be coming in. This is all great data to inform your next project, whether that is a small update to address some feedback right away or a larger project to figure out the next major release.

What about small projects?

For small projects, especially incremental additions to an existing system, you certainly don't need to do as many iterations. Also, small projects with small teams typically iterate faster because they have less complexity to manage. Weeklong iterations are not uncommon. Here's what a three-day iteration might look like:

- **Day 1**   Wallow in available data, draft scenario and metrics.

- **Day 2**   Hold a one-hour to two-hour brainstorming session, create an affinity diagram, and then sketch four to eight storyboards.

- **Day 3**   Build rapid prototypes for two to four of the most promising storyboards, and get ready to start the next iteration by testing the prototypes with customers the next day.

For a small change, where the code revision is trivial, you might go from idea to release in a single iteration and in a single day. However, before you go live to your whole user base, you should probably do an A/B test or partial rollout to confirm that nothing is broken and, ideally, that your key metrics did what you expected when the change was exposed to a smaller set of customers.

Although managing quick iterations for a small project might seem easy, it requires that you already have a firm intuitive grasp of the iterative process and can exercise judgment on which parts you can safely collapse or downplay at each phase in your project. Probably the biggest mistake in small projects is doing too few iterations because the solution seems obvious. Unfortunately, this may well lead you to discover that people didn't find your change useful or desirable at all, and you end up having to do more work to back it out. Just because the code is easy to write doesn't mean that you're doing the right thing. Take enough time to be sure that the change will be well received before you suffer the embarrassment and the brand damage of exposing a worthless feature to your customers.

SFE in action: Tiny iterations

Ed Essey, Group Manager, Microsoft Garage

As a practitioner of design thinking, and more recently as a teacher and coach of Scenario-Focused Engineering, I often come across resistance from engineers who feel that the process is too time-consuming and simply too heavy for the problems they are tackling. When I teach classes, I like to counter that impression and demonstrate how SFE principles can easily be applied to the smallest of situations.

SFE is a fractal process, and it is just as applicable to a problem at the tiniest scope as it is at the grandest scale. Most people can envision using SFE on a large scale, to suss out the biggest customer problems and to prioritize the big business ideas. But it can be elusive to think about how to apply these principles when you're doing something as small as drafting a convincing piece of email.

I sometimes walk through an example of using SFE concepts in a typical product meeting. We've all been in meetings that begin with someone proposing a solution to a problem, and then the rest of the time is spent riffing on that solution until the hour is up. The amazing thing is how often this occurs without anyone actually articulating the problem that is being solved.

To take the class through an example of following SFE in the small, I play out such a meeting. In the meeting, the organizer is talking about building a bridge. As soon as that solution is mentioned, I go up to the whiteboard and write "Build a bridge." As the conversation and debates about the bridge ensue, I capture those specific notes. After a few minutes, I ask, "Well, what else could we try, if the bridge doesn't work out? You know, it's too expensive or we can't get it done in time?" At the whiteboard I add an "Options" header, showing that building a bridge is just one option, perhaps of many.

Options:
A. Build a bridge
B. ...

I then turn the discussion to divergent thinking and get the room to quickly list a bunch of additional, nonbridge options. After we capture a few, I write two new headings on the whiteboard and ask: "What problem are we solving?" and "Who is the target customer?" Once these questions are answered, the class can even capture what we know as a brief scenario, further clarifying the problem, and then solicit more options, now with a specific target in mind.

Options:

A. Bridge
B. Tunnel
C. Ferry
D. Another lane
   on the old bridge

Problem:

Get across the water quickly, reliably, and inexpensively

Customer:

People driving cars between Seattle and Bainbridge Island

Incidentally, I've led teams down this path many times in actual meetings. I find it a good backdoor technique to get people to think more clearly about framing the precise problem that is being tackled, and to then free themselves to consider a bunch of different options. I'm always amazed to see how often there was little agreement or understanding in the room of what the actual problem was or who it was being solved for. Over time, once teams experience this pattern of getting in sync on the customer and the problem being solved, they can quickly get to the most promising solution and begin working on the details, but this time in the context of a customer, with everyone aligned on the same problem.

After talking about how I use SFE in the context of a one-hour meeting, I'll ask the people in the class how they might approach writing a particularly sensitive and difficult email communication. And there is an aha moment when the class sees that yes, indeed, it would be valuable to understand who the email is being written to (the customer) and exactly what the desired results are, and then to come up with a handful of different approaches and collaborate with a few colleagues. This can all be done in a matter of minutes; it doesn't have to be time intensive or process heavy.

Finally, I remind my students that SFE is about applying intention to what you're solving, and the formula is simple and repeatable.

- Crisply articulate the problem you are trying to solve.

- Identify who you are solving it for (and, ideally, gather data).

- Come up with a few options.

- Pick the most promising one and try it out.

The main point is to keep it lightweight—save time solving the problem by focusing on the problem to be solved. It is entirely possible to follow an SFE cycle in just a few minutes. And often, these few minutes will save you a lot of time later on.

Final thoughts on iteration

This chapter has examined some patterns, rhythms, and phases involved in the Fast Feedback Cycle. The key is going around the iterative cycle many times, as quickly as possible, throughout the design process and continuing through development. A sequence of rapid iterations should create a funnel-shaped winnowing of ideas, as you search for the optimal solution to a given scenario. Along the way, there are times to diverge and be creative in the iterative funnel, when you consider more options, as well as times to converge, when you must make difficult decisions and narrow in, and there's a consistent rhythm that governs both. A progression of iterative phases goes from understanding customer needs, to working through tradeoffs to finding an optimal solution, to fine-tuning the details and getting ready to ship. The really breakthrough ideas come through combinatorial blends of ideas from different lines of thinking, which are iterated with continual customer feedback as you progress through this iterative cycle.

Knowing all this, you might conclude that following the Fast Feedback Cycle produces a very regimented and predictable process. However, this isn't exactly true. While there is definitely a rigor and science to doing iteration well, it's also important to be flexible, to roll with the punches, and to allow the process to feel a little messy. Being able to live with ambiguity a bit longer than usual is an important ingredient. In reality, it's not smooth or orderly, it looks more like the scribble in Figure 10-7.

Sometimes to go forward, you go backward. And sometimes the nature of the funnel might not be apparent in the moment ("Hey, why are we diverging. I thought we were converging at this point?"). In the middle of it all, it really does feel quite messy. But with experience, you gain confidence and learn that this messy process is quite predictable, and in the end it will lead you to great results.

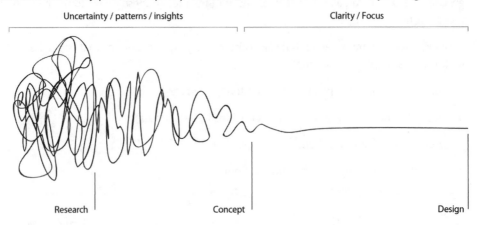

FIGURE 10-7 The design squiggle by Damien Newman.

SFE in action: The design squiggle

Damien Newman, CEO, Central; Lecturer, Stanford University School of Engineering

Years ago I found myself having to explain the design process to a billionaire with an unbelievably short attention span. He had never considered putting design into software, let alone thought it was needed. He was committed to spending a lot of money to build some software and had been told to bring me on to make the software pretty. So I had a split second to capture his attention and then hold it long enough to convince him to spend money on design in the right way, not just the "let's make it pretty at the end" way. It was a challenge I accepted, and it required me to update my approach to explaining the value of design.

Some 12 years before, I had the great fortune to work as a graphic designer at the Cambridge, UK, office of Xerox PARC (known as EuroPARC). I had started my working life as a graphic illustrator, so some of my work at EuroPARC was to illustrate scenarios found in their research. And it was there that I first learned about the process of design and how to describe it.

For the researchers and scientists at Xerox PARC, their process began with research, from which they created prototypes and then a final iteration of a solution. I learned that there were three distinct phases of design: an abstract phase, when ideas and thinking come from research; a concept phase, when ideas are turned into something physical; and a design phase, when a final prototype or working version is created. Each phase contributed to the next, helping to refine the team's understanding as a single point of focus.

So for 12 years I successfully pitched the three phases of design as abstract, concept, and design. I explained to my clients at the time that we had to begin with an abstract notion of what our problem might be, and through a phase of exploration we would refine our understanding and generate several possible concepts to solve it. This was a tough sell more than 20 years ago. I didn't have books like this to help me. Developing empathy for users was quite an alien concept. But at least I was armed with a reasonable-sounding, intellectual way of selling the process of design, which worked until I met the billionaire.

I had three things to communicate about the design process to my easily distracted and impatient new client: what the process is, how you move from uncertainty to focus as you progress, and that the design phase is actually in the process, right there toward the end. And I also had to explain the three fundamental phases of design. An added bonus would be if I could somehow also explain the magic of design, which is synthesis—how one makes sense of the research.

One of the points I wanted to convey was that the process would not always be comfortable because of the nature of how we go about it. One whole phase, when we're learning and understanding, would feel like trying to clear a fog or untangle a mess of cables and wires. But we would untangle the wires and become more certain of our direction as we proceeded. What the design process makes possible is the space to collect information, either through observations or other methods, and to methodically synthesize that knowledge into meaningful insights. The effort taken to create insights from research before generating ideas for design is what makes this process unique. Any self-respecting illustration of the process of design has to provide the means to explain this. There is, in fact, a noticeable line going backward in the design squiggle, which is to suggest that sometimes you have to go back to earlier stuff to make sense of what you have. In my thinking, if I could explain to my client that the upfront parts of the process would feel uncomfortable, then when the time came and he felt discomfort, he might remember that the feeling would pass as we progress and he didn't need to panic. This is similar to telling people at the beginning of a workshop that energy will dip, everyone will feel uncomfortable, but that this will pass, and they will leave with far more energy than when they started. This helps prevent anyone from freaking out when they feel that dip.

I use the design squiggle constantly. Even during my days at IDEO. As widely known as the term *design thinking* is, many people don't understand the process behind it. If you present the story of a process inside a corporate conference room, many people think of a Gantt chart or a straight-line experience. Instead, by using the squiggle, you're able to show that the process is a little different. When I display a slide that shows the squiggle along with an image of rampant Post-It notes, that usually conveys the nature of the process quite well.

Back to the billionaire. The squiggle made sense to him. I landed the project and spent a very interesting 10 months or so designing software for him. Doing the upfront work to adequately explain the nature of the design process to the person in charge allowed us the space we needed to proceed during the project.

The squiggle is free for you to use. If it helps you explain the process of design thinking, big D design, or SFE and the Fast Feedback Cycle, then by all means use it. Search for "design squiggle," and you'll find many different versions you can download. It's been adopted widely—printed on a wall of an Australian consultancy, referenced in books and on T-shirts, and seen in a TED Talk. People frequently send me pictures of it where it's seen in the wild. Do let me know if it works or doesn't; I'm always interested to hear the stories.

Breaking up the iterative process into patterns and phases and distinct stages within each iteration makes the process of design easier for new practitioners to understand and conceptualize. But the truth is that design is not a linear process and there is no prescriptive stepwise process. Expert teams skip around between the stages of the Fast Feedback Cycle at times, or may collapse some aspects of the phases together when it's efficient and appropriate to do so. A mature team may split into parts, with some people conducting user tests while the rest of the team starts to work on the next level of detail in the solution as they wait for test results to react to. Experts may do faster iterations at the beginning of a project and then slow down the iteration cadence as they get into the details phase, once there is high confidence that only tweaks remain. They will use judgment about which kinds of changes require them to generate alternatives and do customer testing and which changes aren't worth that level of work.

So even though the squiggle diagram may seem messy, it actually isn't that far from the truth, at least when you watch a high-performing team operate. With time and persistence, you will get there.

The day after

Outcome-based metrics

Science of change management

swarming RELEASE CODE MORE OFTEN

Task-level stories

SHIFTS

Shift from work-item lists
to story hierarchies

**What to do
the day after?**

**Shift from building components
to building experience slices**

Beware the HiPPO Weekly customer testing

SHIFT FROM DOING MANY THINGS
TO FOCUSING ON A FEW

VISION-LEVEL STORIES

Two-week iterations **pairing**

AGILE SPRINTS **Customer satisfaction metrics**

Shift from bug counts
to experience metrics

SHIFT FROM INDIVIDUAL FOCUS Performance metrics
TO TEAM FOCUS Customer experience health **Perception metrics**

Shift from upfront specs
to alts, prototypes & docs

STORY HIERARCHIES

EXPERIENCE SCORECARDS

**Regular customer
touch points**

SUMMATIVE DATA Track progress against stories

CHAPTER 11

The way you work

The last couple of chapters (and a few of the appendixes) focus on what we call "the day after." We've noticed a consistent pattern in teaching the Scenario-Focused Engineering workshop. Teams spend a day in our workshop, learn some techniques and approaches, and leave inspired to try some of these ideas in their own projects. But the next morning, team members wake up, get to work, and find that they aren't quite sure what to do next. They find themselves in the same old office, with the same computer, same tools, same performance-review goals, same specs, and the same project schedule.

All of a sudden, the task of using some of the techniques and principles they just learned seems daunting. After all, the context and boundaries we set up in class do not currently exist on their team. These team members are now back in the real world, facing real problems, with real constraints and an established team culture and set of practices.

Now, the day after the workshop, they realize that the team doesn't really have a unified notion of who the customer is, other than "someone with a computer." They sit down to write a scenario and realize, "Hey, we don't have real customer data to tell us which situations are most important to optimize for. Should we go get some? How? When? How much time can we take to do this?" Or, if data is available and a few team members write up a killer scenario, take a couple of hours to brainstorm, and discover a few inspiring ideas, they then realize, "We don't have time to prototype and test, the schedule says we have to start writing code today. What do we do?"

The trouble is that the ideas in this book are pretty straightforward, and reading about them or trying them out in a controlled classroom environment can be deceivingly easy. However, in real life, putting the Fast Feedback Cycle into practice is surprisingly difficult. Many teams' existing systems, tools, processes, and culture are optimized for the old approach to building software, in a more or less linear and hierarchical manner, and long-established habits are tough to break. For these same reasons, Agile and Lean practices can also be difficult to establish on a team, as we'll explore in this chapter.

Adopting the Fast Feedback Cycle requires teams to change their behavior. The ideas are straightforward, and the resources and techniques exist if you know where to look for them, but until a team's attitudes and beliefs change, it's tough to make much progress. Motivating a group of people to collectively change their approach and start using these new methods is a classic problem of change management. As we've observed teams adopting new customer-focused practices, we've developed a deep appreciation for the extreme difficulty of changing behaviors, processes, culture, and beliefs across large groups of people.

TIP

> The science of change management provides models and guidelines for how best to effect change in groups of people. We discuss these in more detail in Chapter 12, "Lessons learned," and provide a reading list of our favorite change-management texts in Appendix C.

In a way, this entire book is about changing the way you work. In previous chapters we've talked about how to make some of these shifts when they are relevant to a particular stage or set of activities. The focus of this chapter is on how these changes affect the meta-level systems that govern the overall management of a software project. We have seen teams make substantial overhauls of fundamental team processes and tools, such as work-item tracking, project reviews, performance-review systems, and rethinking the structure and milestones of the team's project schedule. Teams that bake an iterative rhythm and customer focus into their process and tooling are much more successful sustaining the shift over the long term.

That said, no single tooling or project-management system works for every team. Different teams are just, well, different. A family-owned small business is very different from a multithousand-person software company. Teams building online services with rapid release cycles are very different from teams shipping a device with hard manufacturing constraints and longer lead times. Maintaining and improving a successful legacy product is very different from starting a version 1 project. One approach to tooling and project management can't possibly serve all those needs. However, we have noticed some issues that come up in most team situations and can share a few patterns about how teams have successfully addressed them.

In this chapter we summarize these patterns as a set of nine shifts in how to manage your software project. We think these are the most important steps for enabling the Fast Feedback Cycle to fully take root in your team. Some of them require you to make a distinct change: stop doing the old thing, and start doing a new thing instead. Some of them are more subtle—keep doing what you are already doing, but consider a few more inputs or optimize for a slightly different factor. Different teams may find that some of these shifts are more important for their situation than others, or that they have already addressed some through previous investments in Lean or Agile approaches. You don't have to make all of these shifts, or implement them all at the same time, to get good value, but they do build on one another. Keep in mind that most of our experience is with teams that range in size from 100 to as many as 3,000 people. These shifts may surface differently on smaller teams, although we suspect there will be plenty of similarities.

Shift from doing many things to focusing on a few

One of the first places that teams get stuck adopting new practices is simply finding the time to do it. Many teams, especially those working in the world of online services, are running so fast that the thought of stopping to consider who their target customer is, or doing customer testing before writing code, or even doing customer testing on their live service before shipping broadly may seem patently impossible given their fast-paced schedule and the competitive pressure they feel. Furthermore, many, many teams are so busy that stopping to learn a new set of techniques or to take on the overhead of learning a new rhythm of working can be difficult, if not impossible, to justify.

If you've read this book to this point, you recognize this as a penny-wise, pound-foolish attitude. Do not underestimate the cost of discovering after months of work that you've spent all your precious development time writing code for something that nobody wants, isn't solving a real customer problem, or no one is willing to pay for. These are truly painful, expensive (and avoidable!) wastes of time that you should be guarding against. Plus, the extreme hurry is often unjustified. Remember the stories in Chapter 6, "Framing the problem," about the roots and pace of innovation? We described how some of the most influential innovations of the past decade took time—usually years—to evolve from an idea to a successful implementation and were not even necessarily first to market in their categories.

What is the root cause of being too busy? Is it a scheduling problem? Yes, partly, and we'll cover that in the next section. And certainly, a natural amount of firefighting takes place for any services business, dealing with live site issues and providing responsive customer service. But a far bigger problem is allowing a team to take on too much work in the first place, so that no matter how creatively you arrange the schedule, there just isn't enough time to get everything done—never mind achieving high quality from the customer's point of view or accomplishing this without burning out your team.

Of course, this isn't obvious at the start of a project. Whether a team follows an Agile, a waterfall, or some hybrid approach to project management, teams tend to be very optimistic at the beginning. They have a lot of great ideas and an infinite amount of passion, and all the customer promises the team envisions just seem to fit. As a former colleague, Howie Dickerman, once quipped, "All plans are perfect at the start." But any seasoned engineer knows that there will always be unforeseen problems, and the actual effort for even a modest task will take much longer than you expect. A project's true time and effort won't become clear until you're deep enough into the project to be very committed, both emotionally and physically. New code becomes increasingly difficult to back out, so you are effectively trapped by all the great ideas you aspired to build but that you now find you don't have time to finish.

All this brings us to the first shift in how to manage your project differently. You simply need to make more time and space by choosing to do less overall and put fewer things on the schedule. This allows the team to concentrate more on each area of focus and to produce a high-quality result that optimizes technical quality, customer experience, as well as business results. Choose fewer scenarios to deliver, choose fewer target customers to focus on, choose to actively work on just a few big ideas at a time. Don't spread the team's attention across many different, unrelated investment areas. Having a narrower focus will naturally create more buffer time to account for iteration, learning, dealing with unforeseen issues, and responding to customer feedback in a meaningful way. *Focusing a team on fewer things is the single biggest lever that leaders have for improving the quality of the resulting product. When it comes to delighting customers, less really is more.*

It can be scary to commit to only a few investments, but remember that the Fast Feedback Cycle will give you early and constant feedback about whether you've made the right choice or whether it's time to change course. Getting a few things done with high quality is more important than getting a whole lot of things done with marginal quality.

The key behavior to introduce here is for all team leaders to commit to agreeing on a small set of focus areas and to not allow a project's scope to creep and become larger as it progresses by adding "just one more thing." This requires a sharp knife when you prioritize and that you stay committed to that focus. It helps to think more of sequencing than of prioritizing. What you are deciding are which areas you will focus on for now; there will be time for others later.

One way to force yourself to do less is by shortening your release cycle. A fast cycle makes it easier to say that it's okay to do less. Plan a three-month release cycle instead of a one-year cycle, or for a one-month release instead of three months. To help control scope, focus on one change or one new area in each release cycle. Combine the shorter cycle and the "do less" mantra to catalyze the shift to happen.

SFE in action: Getting an A versus pass/fail

Joe Belfiore, Corporate Vice President, Microsoft PC, Phone, Tablet

In my job running the PC, Phone, Tablet team at Microsoft, I've offered a refrain that people have heard so many times in meetings or reviews that they often recite it for me in anticipation: "Is that list prioritized?"

In my view, the most critical piece of thinking you can do for yourself or your team is to become *clear on priorities*, and I insist that the "prioritized list" is the way to do it. At the end of the day, your focus and effort are allocated linearly, and that's the best way to ensure that you're spending energy where it matters most.

When we built Windows Phone 8, we had a ton of great features planned—an Action Center, new shape writing in our Word Flow keyboard, massive improvements for developers, better Live Tile flexibility, and Cortana, our new personal digital assistant. At a critical point halfway through the product cycle, we decided to help the team by clearly and loudly picking where we wanted to place our bet, and the way we communicated that decision was with a prioritized list of "where we want to get an A." At the top of the list was Cortana, and the message was to work on this with top priority, aiming to get an A. After that item, everything else was listed in priority order, with the message that we could view the rest of the items as needing pass/fail grades instead.

The result: people did what was necessary to get a "pass" in the features that were important but weren't our core story—and they were excited to spend all their extra effort and hours on Cortana, which really paid off in having Cortana turn out great and land well for Windows Phone 8.1. Understanding which investments needed to be good enough to pass and those for which we really needed to get an A turned out to be a great way to communicate priorities and align the focus of the entire team.

Shift from milestones to sprints

A project's schedule can exert a powerful force on a team, setting expectations for team members for what they should be doing, how long it should take, and when they should move on to the next thing. If you want a team to start doing something new, one of the best ways you can make that happen is to build that new behavior into the team's schedule. You are seeking to change the culture and practices of the team so that they become more iterative, and one of the best ways to do this is to enforce a baseline level of iteration in the schedule itself.

If you haven't noticed already, most of the development world has been moving (or has already moved) toward using some flavor of Agile methodology. The reason, we believe, is quite powerful and is one of the cornerstones of this book. To be responsive to customers and solve complex needs well, you need to iterate continually, and the Agile community has done a terrific job of creating a platform and mechanisms for development teams to manage and schedule an iterative process. Typically, the basic unit of schedule in an Agile system is a sprint. A sprint, having a length of one to four weeks, is the right scale for completing an entire iteration of the Fast Feedback Cycle. The key value of a sprint is to finish it by getting customer feedback on something you've built so that the feedback can inform the next sprint. We recommend using Agile sprints as the underlying mechanism for managing your iterations.

You want to instill in a team the habit of thinking of its work in the context of an iteration, and that an iteration represents a full turn of the Fast Feedback Cycle. This means that even at the start of a project, the team should aim to produce something at the end of its first iteration with the expectation of getting a very quick round of customer feedback.

From a scheduling perspective, you should think of a single iteration as an atomic unit that is absolutely indivisible. Do not try to schedule dedicated time for each individual stage within the Fast Feedback Cycle, and do not try to align the entire organization to do the same activity at the same time. In a healthy iterative cadence, the stages in the Fast Feedback Cycle should happen naturally in the context of each time-boxed sprint.

But more profoundly, teams need the latitude to adjust the percentage of time within each sprint that they spend on each stage of the Fast Feedback Cycle. This depends on where they are in the project and what the most recent customer feedback says (for example, do they need to focus this iteration mostly on rewriting their scenario or on exploring lots of solutions to address the feedback they heard). And from a management perspective, you often do more harm than good if you try to get a status update from a team in the middle of an iteration. The best time to ask about status is after the team has received customer feedback and you can have a conversation that's grounded in data about how the last iteration went and then discuss options for what directions the team might try next.

There are some nonobvious implications to the idea of handling iterations as an atomic unit. Don't put milestones on your schedule that are linked to different phases of development. For example, don't have any milestones called "coding start" or "design" or "feedback" or "stabilization." Don't encourage teams to think about the time they spend in design versus coding work. Instead, expect that at the end of their first iteration, teams should start testing concepts with customers in whatever form is most convenient, and that teams will continue iterating as quickly as they can to zoom in on the right thing, starting to code only when they have confidence about the direction. Some teams may start writing code on their very first iteration, whereas others may be able to make solid progress for several iterations without writing code. When you start writing code is highly variable across teams and depends on what scenario a team is working on and what kind of feedback it's getting.

Here are a few ways that we've seen teams build iteration into their schedules:

- Use Agile sprints as the baseline rhythm of the schedule. Teams are expected to complete an iteration of the Fast Feedback Cycle within a single sprint and should plan to get customer feedback at the close of each sprint.

- Schedule customer touch points in advance at a regular interval, such as every week or every other week, and encourage teams to use those opportunities to show their latest work to customers for feedback. The regular opportunity for customer feedback forces a certain rhythm to emerge—a team will manage its time so that it has something to show to the customer for the next time. After a team receives customer feedback, that naturally kicks off the next iteration, in which the team will address whatever it learned from that round of feedback. *Customer touch points create the drumbeat of iterations.*

- Set project reviews at regular intervals, and set the expectation that teams will present the results of an entire iteration, including customer feedback, at that review. We'll discuss how to conduct project reviews (or, should we say, experience reviews) in more detail later in this chapter, but the important point for now is that having them on the schedule can encourage the team to develop an iterative habit. The project review acts as a forcing function to make sure that a full iteration, with the right activities, happens before the review.

- Release code to customers more often. Iterative habits are helped by building in frequent opportunities for releasing code to users, instead of scheduling release windows only a few times per year or even monthly. Even once or twice a week might be insufficient for some services and apps for which customers expect faster turnarounds. Teams need to feel as though they can do as much iteration as needed to get to a high-quality result and not be tempted to release a solution before it's ready just so they don't miss a particular release window.

If you're not sure how long your iterations should be, a good rule of thumb is to start with two weeks. That time period is short enough that you will get customer feedback in time to avoid wasting a lot of effort on a possible dead end, but it's long enough to give a team new to the Fast Feedback Cycle the time it needs to get through the entire cycle. It also keeps the overhead of testing with customers from becoming overwhelming as you set up a system and pipeline for regular customer feedback.

Kick-starting a significant new project deserves special attention. Especially when you are aiming to build something that's brand-new or are making a big change to an existing product, there's often an extra dose of ambiguity about target customers and their most important problems. In these situations, you may find it helpful to schedule your first couple of iterations to be a bit longer, which allows for more time to do in-person research to get your project rolling with solid footing in customer data. Another approach is to have a small team do some observational research ahead of time so that the broader team can begin from a good seed and can make a running start at solving those customer needs. However, remember to resist the urge to spend months preplanning. You'll gain the biggest benefits as soon as you get through your first iteration and show your first rough prototypes to customers.

Shift from work-item lists to scenario hierarchies

One of the fundamental ways that a team manages its engineering work is with some sort of work-item tracking system. Many Agile teams use a burndown list—an ordered list of user stories that is worked on in priority order. Conventional teams are used to working with feature lists, which are usually organized under some unifying themes, priorities, or other categories. Features or other work items might be tracked during a project with tools ranging from sticky notes on the wall to a spreadsheet or a software-based work–item management system such as JIRA, Pivotal Tracker, Team Foundation Server, or many others.

While a system for tracking engineering deliverables and work items is a necessity for managing a software project that involves more than a handful of people, if your goal is to build end-to-end experiences, you actually need to be tracking more information than just the individual work items and their completion status. With the Fast Feedback Cycle, after your first few iterations (or whenever you transition to writing production code), one of the biggest challenges is to keep your focus on building complete scenarios and to be sure that the complete experiences survive intact through to shipping. The more that different teams are involved, the more important it is to track work and progress in terms of complete experiences. If a team's primary, day-to-day view into a project shows only the atomic, technology-focused work items and not the experiences that connect them, the team will inevitably revert to its old habits and focus on building just the technology. It is very easy for a team to zoom into the task-level work and forget to keep an eye on the full end-to-end experience it's aiming for—to stay true to the original scenarios and customer insights defined by your research.

You want everyone as they are writing code to remain mindful about which deliverables and work items need to be integrated to deliver a smooth, end-to-end experience and which situations and customers you are optimizing for. The team writing the UI code has probably been iterating with mockups all along and can see the connection points more easily. But think about the platform teams whose deliverables are a few layers away from the end-user's experience. They also need to remember the customer experience that their work will ultimately support and should be optimized for. Also, if you find that a deliverable is at risk, you need to consider its role relative to the overall experience as you decide whether to double-down, pare back, or cut the entire scenario. If this deliverable is a crucial piece of the user experience, cutting the entire scenario is almost always better than delivering an incomplete experience. However, that is a very tough decision to make, especially if it means that you also have to cut pieces of work that are already done or are not at risk in any way. Bottom line—if you are trying to deliver end-to-end experiences, you better be tracking your work not as individual work items but within the context of those end-to-end experiences.

Story hierarchies

The first hurdle in tracking experiences is to figure out how to represent the end-to-end experiences themselves so that you can write them down and track them. How do you make experiences robust and able to be tracked and also associate them with the baseline engineering deliverables and work items? If you are using the scenario technique, or any of the other story-based framing techniques, you will craft a set of scenarios or other stories to capture the customer needs and goals you want to achieve. However, when we've seen teams set out to describe their customer problems and business opportunities with stories, they usually come across the same set of questions:

> *How many scenarios should we have? How many is too many, or too few?*

> *How much overlap should there be between different scenarios?*

> *What is the right level of scope for a single scenario to cover—should it cover a five-year business opportunity or describe a need that can be solved with a few well-designed features?*

Remember the story about the airport, where we talked about framing—zooming in and zooming out? Should you write the scenario about the check-in process, or do you zoom out to include the customer's entire end-to-end experience, including the early wake-up call, the traffic on the way to the airport, and the delay at the gate? Scenarios are ultimately about framing problems through storytelling, and as such they entail nearly infinite possibilities for defining the scope of the problem to focus on.

It helps a lot to think about what scope, or altitude, you are aiming for so that you can align the stories across your project at a similar elevation. Talking in a consistent way about the different levels of scope your stories cover makes it possible to track and manage the work without losing your sanity, and it helps you manage and prioritize apples with apples and oranges with oranges.

Nearly all of the teams we've worked with have landed on a two-level hierarchy as a way to balance large- and small-scope impact and to organize their stories into a more manageable, logical structure. This two-level story hierarchy acts as the translation layer that bridges the high-level themes—or global priorities for the project—and the specific deliverables and work items that the engineering team needs to execute.

We've seen a couple of teams try to make a three-level story hierarchy work, but in the end this was deemed too unwieldy and too heavy. We've also seen teams attempt to use a single, flat list of scenarios. However, they found it very difficult to make sense of a long, unstructured list that mixed huge scenarios (that described an extensive end-to-end situation) with unrelated, tactical scenarios of a much smaller scope. They found that some sort of organization was needed, so most of these teams added a hierarchical structure later on.

These days, most teams start with a two-level story hierarchy. In fact, we recently audited 16 of the largest Microsoft teams and found that all but two now use scenarios as standard items in their work-item hierarchies and the vast majority use a two-level hierarchy of stories of one form or another. Although different teams use different terminology, the general pattern we've seen is that teams build a pyramid-shaped hierarchy of stories to describe their business and customer opportunities, and use those stories to break down opportunities into actual product deliverables. The top of this framing hierarchy describes the high-level business and customer goals (themes, for example), and the bottom describes customer deliverables with enough detail that code can be written. Figure 11-1 shows an example.

		Huge Team (2000+)	Large Team (200-1500)	Small Team (20-150)
1	Themes	6-8 themes	3-4 themes	1-2 themes
5	Vision-Level Stories	30-40 vision-level	15-20 vision-level	3-7 vision-level
50	Task-Level Stories	300-400 task-level	150-200 task-level	30-70 task-level
500	Deliverables	3,000+	1,500+	300+
	Tasks, Bugs, Etc.			

FIGURE 11-1 The breakdown of a scenario hierarchy.

We've observed a ratio of approximately 1:5:50:500 as the typical shape of this hierarchy. That is, 1 theme breaks down to about 5 vision-level stories, and those 5 vision-level stories break down to about 50 task-level stories, and about 500 engineering deliverables in total, and perhaps thousands of individual tasks and other work items. There is no hard and fast rule about these numbers, of course, but the general shape seems to hold. We've also noticed that even for the largest teams, the number of vision-level stories must be small enough that everyone on the team, especially the team's management, can keep them at the top of their mind throughout the project's lifetime. In light of this, there seems to be a practical cap of about 8 themes and 40 vision-level stories for even the very largest of teams (but very large teams do seem to broaden the definition of both vision-level and task-level stories to compensate for this).

MINDSHIFT

Too much of a good thing. The most common mistake for a team to make is to define too many vision-level scenarios. We have all experienced how difficult it is to decide not to invest in an idea that appears to be viable, even if it is clear that we have too many promising ideas to realistically pursue all of them. The reality is that the cuts will need to be made, and the sooner the better to maximize the team's efficiency and the quality of the final solution. We have observed many teams that start out with a larger number of vision-level scenarios, but they invariably end up paring this list down to a more manageable number that aligns more closely to the ratios in the pyramid shown in Figure 11-1.

Let's discuss each of the core layers of the scenario hierarchy in more detail.

Themes

Most teams, especially larger teams, find it useful to start a project with a small set of themes, which might also be referred to as pillars, big bets, priorities, or investment areas. A theme is typically stated as a broad goal, such as "Improve operational supportability," "Reduce customer support calls," or "Ship a new SDK." Usually, these are tightly linked to strategic business goals or predetermined technology investments and serve to provide a certain amount of scoping and anchoring that helps prevent an overly broad framing at the highest level. Themes are often featured in a framing memo (see the sidebar "The framing memo" in Chapter 4, "Identifying your target customer"), along with the designations of target customers, that is issued at the very start of a project or even sometime before the bulk of the engineering team has rolled off the previous project. You can see in Figure 11-1 that the number of themes can vary quite a bit by the size of an organization. The smallest teams probably don't need to name a theme explicitly, whereas very large teams have as many as a half-dozen themes that define a particular release horizon or a multiyear road map.

Vision-level customer stories

After themes are defined, teams write a small number of vision-level stories about their customers. Vision-level stories typically represent the broadest end-to-end scenarios that are likely to capture a cradle-to-grave customer experience and feature a significant customer insight. In practice, this layer of the pyramid is usually given a name such as Experiences, Customer Promises, User Journeys, or Meta-Scenarios. Vision-level customer stories are usually completed and delivered within a major release cycle.

Vision-level stories might use any of a number of different framing techniques. We've seen a few teams write full scenario narratives, user journeys, or epics at this level, and these teams benefit from using these more expansive narratives to align and clarify goals for the team. While we prefer a longer narrative at this level, some teams keep this layer of the pyramid short and sweet, with a single, inspirational one-liner that captures the core value proposition for a particular customer. This can be written as an "I can" statement or an outcome or a user story. Whether it is a short description or a full narrative, a vision-level story should be paired with a few key metrics that specify what success looks like, as well as references to the grounding research and insights about the target customer.

These bigger-scope stories are typically authored by top-level leaders in the organization, in partnership with planning, user experience, and business-strategy experts. Vision-level stories may be identified and articulated before a large new project kicks off or may be added anywhere along the way. The bulk of these stories are usually identified by small advance teams that zero in on investigating a potential area of focus for target customers and their needs.

These large-scope stories are the ones that describe the major customer problems the organization seeks to solve, and they often require that multiple engineering teams or subteams work together to deliver a complete solution. A vision-level scenario describes what kind of customer experience the final product should be able to achieve at the highest level and is closely linked with the core value proposition for the entire offering.

Vision-level scenarios are very useful for marketing teams in developing marketing plans well in advance of implementation. They are also excellent for articulating a common vision about the target customers and their needs and can be used as a North Star for getting stakeholders aligned around a common goal. Finally, as the North Star for the customer's experience, vision-level stories should contain top-line metrics that are used in scorecards to measure how and when you have met the business and experience goals for your solution.

 MINDSHIFT

Vision-level stories help align partners and stakeholders. Vision-level customer stories are an extremely effective tool for describing and negotiating strategic partnerships. Starting with a vision-level customer story allows different teams to find common ground more easily and avoid jumping into technical details or getting into contentious arguments about whether to use this component or that platform. These conversations are much more productive when they center on working together to meet a particular customer need that is strategically valuable for all parties. It helps to use a more complete, narrative-based approach in a vision-level story if coordinating work between multiple teams is the goal. If that vision-level story is constructed well, the customers' motivation and personal details, their context, and the successful outcomes will all help provide a common framework in which to judge the relative merits of various technical choices. This keeps the focus on the customer's needs instead of on the egos of the engineers or leaders involved.

Combine a vision-level scenario with quantitative data from your research, sprinkle in a few poignant, illustrative snippets from your qualitative research (direct customer quotes, a short video clip, photos, etc.) and perhaps a storyboard or sketch illustrating the customer problem, and you have a very powerful tool for aligning stakeholders.

Task-level customer stories

Each vision-level story is broken down into 5–10 smaller, task-level stories that represent the canonical customer situations the team will focus on solving. Note that task-level stories are still implementation-free; they just represent a more specific scope than a vision-level story, which is typically fairly broad. Task-level customer stories should be defined in such a way that together they cover the most important end-to-end path through the vision-level customer story—if a vision-level story is the plot line of a movie, task-level stories are the individual scenes that together make up the plot.

SFE in action: Windows Phone Cortana story hierarchy

Cortana team, Microsoft Corporation

Here is an example of a story hierarchy that shows how a theme can be broken down into several large scenarios, which can then be broken down into smaller scenarios.

Cortana is the world's most personal personal assistant.

- **Scenario 1**   Anna can see what interests Cortana is tracking for her and can modify them to her liking.

- **Scenario 2**   Anna gets suggestions for when to leave for appointments so that she can get there on time, even when there's traffic.

- **Scenario 3**   Anna can user her voice to set reminders so she can stay on top of her busy life.

  - **Subscenario 3a**   On her way to her car, Anna reads an email from Jill telling her she wants to come over and cook for Anna's family later this week. Excited about Jill's offer, and without looking at her phone, Anna tells her phone to remind her to speak to her husband Miles about which night would be best. Seamlessly, her phone hears what she says and adds a reminder. Anna is delighted at how quickly that was to do.

  - **Subscenario 3b**   Anna has been meaning to check in with her mom and tell her the latest stories about her young son Luca. But between her busy life and shuttling Luca around, the thought always slips her mind. Disgruntled at always forgetting, one day in the car she tells her phone to remind her to call Nana when she arrives at home. Her phone acknowledges the request and assures her it will remind her. Anna is confident that today she will not forget.

  - **Subscenario 3c**   Months after Anna has hosted a potluck, she realizes that she still has her friend Sara's strainer and baster in her kitchen. Anna doesn't frequently see Sara, but they are commonly in touch, so she tells her phone to remind her to make arrangements to return these items the next time she and Sara communicate. Her phone gives her a confirmation, and she's confident that she'll return these items promptly. She loves how her phone helps her stay on top of things.

Task-level stories typically have a size and scope such that a small, cross-discipline team of engineers can independently deliver a solution to the problems the story represents or orchestrate its delivery with a manageable set of dependencies. As their name implies, task-level stories usually correspond to a fairly discrete customer task that is described in terms of a specific customer in a specific situation with a specific outcome in mind. It is essential to pair task-level stories with a small set of specific success metrics that define what a successful customer experience would look like and that serve as criteria for declaring the story done. Teams should be able to complete the work covered by a task-level story within the next major release horizon and often much more quickly than that.

Task-level stories are where the SPICIER scenario narrative technique shines (see Chapter 6). Most teams write a SPICIER scenario at this level of the hierarchy, along with a 5–10 word title that is essential for tracking the scenario across the rest of the tools in the engineering system. Alternatively, teams can use an "I can" statement, an outcome, a user story, or another brief story format at this level in the hierarchy. Note, however, that either the vision-level stories or the task-level stories should be written as more complete narratives that capture the customer's situation and perspective in enough detail to evoke empathy for the customer. If task-level stories are presented in a briefer format, it is essential for the vision-level stories to be more fully developed narratives so that empathy can be created and shared. We have seen the best results when both levels are written in a full narrative format.

 MINDSHIFT

Scenario-mania: Stop the madness! You don't have to write scenarios for every single thing your software needs to know how to do. Remember that scenarios should represent the canonical cases that you will optimize for—the lighthouse cases that show the centers of gravity of the problems you are solving and who you are focused on. As such, your scenarios will not represent every single variant, user type, or edge case that is related to that situation. If you find that you are amassing thousands of scenarios, many of which seem to be variants of one another, you're probably overdoing it, no matter how big your team is. A portfolio of scenarios isn't supposed to be a replacement for complete specifications. Instead, scenarios are a way to capture the most essential customer-focused situations that you will optimize around.

Deliverables, work items, and reports

As each task-level story is iterated through the Fast Feedback Cycle, that task-level story is broken down into engineering deliverables and then into work items, the actual units of engineering work that are scheduled and tracked as part of the overall effort. For a particular story, the initial set of deliverables in the first few iterations of the Fast Feedback Cycle will likely look something like "Generate at least five viable solution alternatives," "Build wireframe prototypes," "Generate three architecture alternatives," or "Customer test on Friday." In later iterations, the deliverables will include items such as "Write the code for component Y," "Integration test pass," and "Deploy build 735 for A/B testing."

This part of the work-item hierarchy is typically very familiar to teams; it is generally not new. The new part is linking up work items to show which deliverables align to which stories so that progress can be tracked in the context of completing end-to-end stories, not just a pile of features.

Work-item tracking system

After you work out a story hierarchy, having the right tooling can make a huge difference, especially for larger teams of hundreds or thousands of engineers. Reflecting these new constructs and activities in the tools that a team uses on a day-to-day basis is second only to building new activities into the project schedule as a way to effectively change behaviors and build new habits. The tools should reflect the team culture that's desired and encourage the behaviors that you want to occur. Day-to-day visibility helps remind people what they should be doing, and the tools you use reinforce behavior, both good and bad.

Ideally, you have a work-item tracking system that allows you to represent the entire scenario hierarchy, from themes down to deliverables, work items, and bugs. However, it's equally important that this system be as automatic and easy to use as possible. If updating information is burdensome, information will be perennially out of date and therefore useless. Special effort needs to be made whenever a story is created to properly link it in the system so that subsequent deliverables and work items are filed correctly as the project progresses. As new vision-level stories and task-level stories are added, they can be prioritized alongside the current backlog of work. Also, all stories must be stack ranked, which lets the team know clearly which ones should be worked on next after a given story has met its success criteria.

 TIP

A few teams have had great success creating a scenario review council to provide oversight on their scenarios and help the team through the initial learning curve for these new techniques. This council is a team of champions that reviews all the scenarios to be sure they have all their components, are appropriately free of implementation details, and generally reflect SPICIER characteristics. The council also ensures that scenarios are reflected properly in the team's tools and are linked correctly in the story hierarchy.

Reports make new behaviors visible

While a robust and easy-to-use tracking system helps everyone gain clarity on what they should be working on at any given moment, reports are what bring you the full benefits of having such a system. The right reports make a team's current behaviors and priorities visible so that good behavior is noticed and encouraged and bad behavior and old habits don't fly under the radar. Nothing is as motivating as a poor rating on a very visible report to kick a team into high gear.

The most useful day-to-day reports account for task-level scenarios, but reports should ideally roll up status at the level of vision-level stories as well. The tracking system should be able to show reports like these:

- **How many deliverables (or work items) aligned to a scenario are complete vs. still in progress?** This is a much more informative view than looking just at the raw completion of deliverables by functional area or team. Status is very different if you have 10 scenarios that are each only 30 percent complete versus 3 scenarios that are 90 percent complete. If your goal is to drive scenarios to completion, publishing this report weekly with the expectation that a scenario be 100 percent complete before a new scenario is pulled off the backlog would be very helpful.

- **For each deliverable, which scenario (or scenarios) is it supporting?** This is a particularly important view when you find that a deliverable is at risk, may need to be cut, and you need to consider which scenarios rely on it. Figure 11-2 shows a sample of these relationships.

TIP

A single deliverable very often aligns to or supports more than one scenario. Representing this "one-to-many relationship" is a primary challenge in most work-item tracking software, which enforce strict parent-child relationships rather than multiple inheritance. In Team Foundation Server, you can use "related item" links to represent these relationships, but you still need to write custom reports to roll up this information properly. Whatever system you use must support the ability to indicate multi-inheritance—when you pull a report about completion status against one scenario, you need an accurate view of *all* the work that rolls up into that scenario.

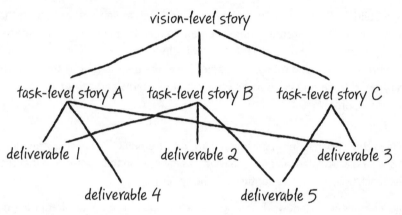

FIGURE 11-2 Deliverables often support more than one story.

- **Which deliverables are not aligned to a scenario?** You'll always have a certain amount of baseline work that doesn't roll up to a specific scenario (or, perhaps more accurately, is aligned to every scenario). Rather than polluting every scenario with these common work items, it's usually better to keep them separate. However, you should look over this list regularly to be sure that one-off feature ideas and other lower-priority work isn't hiding and being inadvertently prioritized over end-to-end experiences that have more impact.

- **Which scenario is next in line for iteration?** Reflecting the product backlog in your tracking system helps focus a team on the few items it is currently working on and puts a ready supply of scenarios and ideas on deck for the team to pick up as soon as it is ready. Building this ordering into your tooling helps honor the reality that you don't actually know how many scenarios you have time to build at any given moment, but you will work on them in priority order, one at a time, and see how far you get.

Track all work items, not just code deliverables

It's worth spending a moment to talk about the need to track the iteration work that happens before you write the first line of code and as you continue iterating and exploring (albeit at an increasingly finer level of granularity). You don't want to spend several iterations of work on a scenario and have nothing to show for it in the tracking system. The team is doing vital work in that time frame, and although the work outputs or artifacts are not yet specific code deliverables, it is still important to track, publish, and communicate these work artifacts.

 MINDSHIFT

> **Planning is not a phase, it is a continuous activity.** Some people label these precoding activities as the "planning" phase. We've come to dislike the term *planning* because it suggests a one-time linear push to understand the customer and figure out what you are going to build. It suggests a hard line between making a plan and executing that plan, which does not jibe with an iterative approach that alters the plan as you receive feedback along the way. Every indication is that the software industry is rapidly moving to a "continuous planning" mindset, and many companies have already made that shift. We think the shift is a very good thing and encourage you to build systems and tools that expect a continuous planning approach.

Some of this work happens before you have fully formulated a specific scenario, but as soon as you have a scenario articulated, all other deliverables involved in the iteration of that scenario around the Fast Feedback Cycle should be captured in the system.

Reflecting this important work among the deliverables in your work-item tracking system is a great way to legitimize these new behaviors and unequivocally communicate to the team that they are an expected part of the engineering team's work. It also gives managers a lot more information about the true status of a team in the early iterations of a project. These deliverables could include outputs such as customer research data, synthesized insights, defined metrics, solution ideas brainstormed, low-fidelity prototypes, customer feedback on prototypes, and so on.

Shift from ad hoc user testing to regular customer touch points

One of the biggest practical barriers to getting customer feedback is tracking down target customers you can interact with. It's time-consuming and expensive for each team to find its own customers to talk with or to work with user researchers to set up specific ad hoc testing sessions. When you wait to schedule user testing when you need it, you end up waiting around, because recruiting a set of customers who can all participate on the dates you need them and fit your screening criteria can easily take a week or more. In a Fast Feedback Cycle, a few days can be a long time, and wasting them creates a significant inefficiency in the system.

Teams can gain faster access to customers, especially to consumers, by going where their customers are—malls, coffee shops, train stations, trailheads, and so on. But while this is worth doing occasionally, especially because it can provide opportunities for more in situ observation, it's too expensive and time-consuming to use as the everyday approach to customer testing throughout the entire project. In addition, this approach doesn't work at all for some demographics of customers.

A better practice is to have dedicated staff set up a constant pipeline of customers who will come into your offices, usability labs, or so on, on a regular basis. This way, target customers are always available for teams to check in with. Having this infrastructure makes it drop-dead easy for teams to test with customers regularly so that the right behaviors can occur naturally in the course of the team's work. When you know that a customer is going to be available in just a few days, you tend to queue up more and more questions, ideas, sketches, and prototypes that you want feedback on. You keep the customer at the front of your mind, and the conversations and feedback you get during testing happen at the right time to immediately inform your thinking.

Most teams have found that the right cadence for customer testing is weekly. They specify a particular day of the week (usually Thursday or Friday) to bring in a few representative target customers. You can schedule customers at the same time of day or spread the schedule across the day. Teams typically try to bring in at least three customers per target segment (possibly more, depending on team and project size) to be sure that they can discern the patterns in the customer feedback versus the outliers.[1]

With this infrastructure in place, teams can count on getting feedback on a particular day. This regular, predictable opportunity really helps anchor an iterative cadence in the team. When the team knows that a customer will be there on Friday, the team naturally schedules its work to take advantage of that opportunity, and this encourages a fast iterative cycle.

Regularly scheduling customers for feedback also lets teams easily have a very quick customer touch point—often just 10 or 15 minutes is plenty to test out your latest ideas, where a full one- to two-hour dedicated user test would have been overkill. You get efficiencies by effectively sharing a pool of customers across the parts of the team that are working on different scenarios but focused on the same target customers and each needs only a portion of the customers' time.

The expectation is that most teams will be ready for customer feedback only every two weeks (say, at the end of a two-week sprint), but on any given week there are usually plenty of interim questions and artifacts that can benefit from a customer's view. We've found that putting effort into creating a steady and regular pipeline of customers is transformative in reducing barriers to team members getting customer feedback quickly and continually throughout the project.

Shift from bug counts to experience metrics

Many software teams are accustomed to gauging project status on the basis of how much code has been written and how much work remains. However, in addition to measuring project completion based on how many unresolved bugs you have or how many tasks you have completed, you need to hold yourself accountable to a much higher bar. Yes, you still want to track bugs and tasks and who is doing what, but if the ultimate goal is to deliver a product that customers really love, how will you know when you have achieved that? How do you know when you are done?

This is where the success metrics you identify in each scenario become vital. These experience metrics provide a clear goal that you need to meet and also act as the exit gate for that scenario. Simply put, if your scenario isn't achieving its success criteria goals, you're not done.

Altering the definition of completion to center it on the customer is a big shift for many teams that are used to thinking about "Code complete" and "ZBB" (zero bug bounce) as major milestones on the way to shipping. One of the structural pieces that needs to be in place to enable this shift is the regular customer pipeline we discussed in the previous section. Furthermore, teams need to establish the habit to check their top experience metrics regularly and to report on them during management reviews or whenever project status is communicated. At the end of this section, we discuss building scorecards, which are a great tool for tracking experience metrics and for keeping the customer at the center of the team's work.

Three kinds of metrics

You should be tracking lots of different metrics as part of any software project, and chances are that you're already tracking many of them. Although many teams tend to track metrics for business goals and technical completion and operational performance, many teams neglect to give the same attention to experience metrics, despite the fact that these are the lynchpin of defining and measuring overall product health.

Figure 11-3 shows a model that our colleagues Mike Tholfsen, Steve Herbst, Jeremy Jobling, and others have proposed that we find particularly helpful. This model presents a holistic view of the types of metrics that should be tracked for any software project. The model captures the fact that achieving business objectives (that is, getting people to pay money) depends on delivering experiences that customers value (that is, allowing customers to do things that are important to them in ways that are better than those offered by any available alternative). Further, delivering a good experience can only rest upon stable and performant technology.

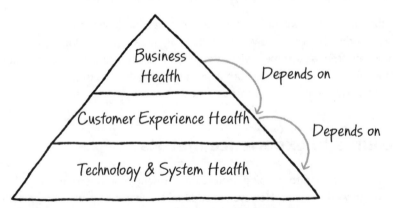

FIGURE 11-3 Business success depends on a great customer experience, which depends on solid technology and system performance. You must measure all three levels to have a complete picture of the health of your company.

As Steve Herbst asserts, "When populated with measurable, solution-free, data-supported metrics at all levels, the health pyramid provides a living 'thesis of success' that can be used to prioritize investments and drive overall product health."[2]

Working up from the bottom, measure the foundation of a successful product—solid technology that is operating with good performance, scalability, reliability, and so on. To provide a great customer experience, those basics surely need to be in place, and most engineering teams are adept at tracking and improving these technology and system-health metrics.

However, even the most complete set of system-level metrics doesn't tell you whether the customer experience is any good. It's entirely possible to have a perfectly functional, performant system but still have a lousy customer experience.

The next tier in the diagram relates to metrics that focus on assessing the experience from the customer's point of view. Are customers delighted with the product? Is it solving a real need for them? How satisfied are they with the solution you have provided?

However, knowing that you have a strong customer experience is not enough either. It's possible to have very happy customers but a failing business. For instance, perhaps your happy customers aren't coming back frequently enough, or aren't paying you enough to cover your costs, or aren't interacting with your advertisements. You need to have metrics specific to the business health as well.[3]

Customer-experience metrics are the ones most often forgotten. Most engineering teams are great at tracking their system metrics, and they find that business metrics are a necessity for staying in business. Customer-experience metrics can be overlooked, even though they may provide the missing link in learning why a terrific technology may not be translating into business success. If you want to build solutions that customers love to use, you need to actively track customer-experience metrics. In fact, many experts these days believe that optimizing for customer satisfaction is the single most important factor to manage. Monetization approaches can be fixed and technology can be improved, but if the customer experience isn't great, you'll never develop a loyal customer base, and the rest doesn't matter.

While it's important to track metrics at all three tiers to get a complete picture, we will focus the rest of this section on the center tier—customer-experience metrics.

Measuring customer experience

We discussed the importance of identifying the key metrics for your scenarios back in Chapter 6. As you consider what problem you are seeking to solve for customers, you identify what success for those customers would look like, along with a few metrics and specific goals that would best indicate whether the customer-experience goal has been reached. These metrics are typically easiest to manage if they are quantitative, but they can and should be a mix of both subjective (SAY data) and objective (DO data) metrics.

Here are examples of customer-experience metrics that you might find helpful to build into your scenarios and tracking system:

- **Performance metrics** that report on customer completion of a job. These can be measured during in-person testing with a stopwatch and careful note taking or online via your instrumentation or usage telemetry. You might capture performance metrics such as:

    How long did it take the customer to complete the task?

    How many errors did the customer make?

    What percentage of customers were able to complete the task without help?

- **Perception metrics** that report on a specific emotional state, positive or negative. This is most often captured by a question on a post-experience questionnaire, either online or in person. These perception questions can be used to measure a wide variety of emotions, such as satisfied, fun, magical, useful, or quick. Here are some questions that you might ask to measure perception:

    On a scale of 1 to 5, how satisfied are you with that experience?

    On a scale of 1 to 5, how confident are you that your document is saved and will be available for you the next time you need it?

- **Outcome-based metrics** identify a clear outcome and the criteria that customers require to consider their experience a success. This type of measurement is usually expressed in two parts: "Was the outcome achieved?" and "Did it meet the criteria?" Most often, criteria for success are based on time (eight seconds or less) or effort (less than two clicks). Examples of outcome-based metrics are:

    I find the media I want in no more than three clicks.

    My requested information is displayed in no more than five seconds.

    I trust that my data is more secure than the way I used to store it.

- **Global customer-satisfaction metrics** report on overall customer satisfaction. They are typically used to track customer satisfaction with a whole product, although they can be used at a smaller scope. Net Promoter Score (NPS) tracks how likely a customer is to recommend your product to a friend. Customer Satisfaction (CSAT) and Net Satisfaction (NSAT) track customer satisfaction. Loyalty metrics ask how likely your customer is to buy from you again. Brand metrics track the customer's awareness and attitudes toward your brand.

The science of summative data

When you want to know whether you have achieved your experience goals, you need to gather what is called summative data.

In contrast to formative data, which helps you figure out which problem to solve and identify the best solution, summative data tells you, with statistical confidence, whether you are meeting your success criteria and whether you are ready to ship. It's worth knowing a few things about the science of summative data to be sure that the way you are gathering metrics is actually giving you valid results and you are paying attention to statistical significance. The biggest factor to consider when you gather summative data is whether you have a sample size big enough to provide statistically valid data.

If you want to get data from a live service and you have instrumentation in place to capture your metrics, getting summative data is pretty straightforward. All you need to do is analyze the data you've collected because, by definition, you are collecting data on your entire population (which better be a big enough sample size; if it isn't, you have bigger problems to solve).

However, if you haven't shipped yet or don't have any working code, getting summative data is a bit more complex and nuanced. But don't let that stop you. It is important to check your experience metrics repeatedly and to track how well you are doing against them as you iterate your solutions. Capturing experience metrics is not something you should do only in the endgame when you are ready to ship.

In the absence of live usage telemetry or A/B systems, you can capture summative data in two main ways: benchmarks and trending metrics over time.

Capturing benchmarks

A benchmark is a specific, statistically valid measurement of user behavior or attitude that you can say with confidence represents an entire customer segment. For instance, you might conduct benchmark testing on a product to find out how long customers take to complete a particular scenario, how many errors they made, or how they felt about the experience afterward. You might do benchmark testing on your competitor's product as well and compare the results for your product against the results for theirs.

Usually, benchmarks are captured by using a formal usability test, where you measure as precisely as possible whatever key metrics you are trying to track. Exactly how a usability test is facilitated matters much more in a summative benchmark test than in a discount usability test. Variability and bias can be introduced into the data through inconsistent facilitation. In a discount usability study, if you are focused on uncovering problems and confusions, this variability and bias may not get in the way. But when you are gathering summative data, that bias and variability can dramatically alter the outcome, and that is definitely not what you want in summative data.

To get valid benchmark data, you need many more customers than you need for a quick discount usability test. For example, in a discount usability test (which is perfectly appropriate for fueling rapid iteration), you might test with five customers from the same target customer segment. However, to get statistically valid benchmark data, you need to test with at least 15–25 customers from the same segment.

Doing a benchmark usability test is worth the effort (such as after a release) to get a baseline measurement that can be used to judge future releases or to compare the customer experience of your product against a competitor's. Doing a true benchmark test to get an accurate "snapshot in time" is a case where you would be well served to engage an expert researcher to design the test, facilitate it, and analyze the numbers to produce the results.

However, throughout the bulk of the project you rarely need to have such statistically significant data. Usually it's enough to know whether the latest iteration made the key metrics worse or better or had no effect. Specifically quantifying the change or making it statistically bulletproof is overkill if you're just trying to see whether you're headed in the right direction.

Trending key metrics over time

Thankfully, most engineering teams can use a much cheaper and more pragmatic way to track their summative metrics. The basic idea is to identify the most important metrics you have set out to achieve and then collect data against those metrics in the same way every time you interact with a customer. Over time, as you talk with more and more customers, you will reach a statistically significant population, and in the meantime you'll develop a good idea (but not a guaranteed one) about which way the trendline is heading. (Because of its reliance on trending data, we like to call this the *trendline* approach.)

You can use different tactics for both perception and performance metrics. For perception metrics, you can develop a brief questionnaire and use that questionnaire as a follow-up to any customer touch point for a given experience. Capturing performance metrics accurately can be a bit more difficult because of the potential for variability. If your goal isn't ultimate precision, but is more about being good enough (for example, is the editing task taking five minutes or five seconds?), you can get performance data during usability tests or other customer interactions in a couple of ways. First, you can take careful notes that answer questions about the specific experience, such as "Did they complete the task successfully, or didn't they?" Or you can count and note specific metrics, such as the number of errors a customer hits or the number of times a customer clicks, or by literally using a stopwatch to time how long a user takes to perform a particular action. Keeping the prompts and measurement approaches as consistent as possible helps you minimize (but not eliminate) facilitation variability.

By asking the same questions and taking the same measurements over the course of multiple tests—each time bringing in a handful of people—you will accumulate the number of data points that is more statistically robust. In this way, you can get some initial data by capturing smaller sample sizes, and the more often you test with customers, the larger your sample size becomes and the more confident you can be that your results are valid. While the trendline technique doesn't fully replace the need to gather benchmarks (when you must know a specific statistic for a particular version of your product or service), you can use this approach as a pretty good way to track your experience metrics over time and see whether you are on track to achieve your goals.

TIP

Watch for regressions out of left field. One reason that you measure your metrics frequently is that it's quite common for an experience metric to regress because of an unrelated feature or because a section of code was added (often times by a partner team) that you didn't realize would have an impact. For example, an unrelated piece of code might introduce latency and slow down your feature's response time; or a new feature, integrated by another team, might make your features confusing when the features run side by side; or your very simple path through a scenario might become complicated when more options are added. When an experience tests well, you are not done. You have to test the experience over time to make sure that it doesn't regress.

By testing frequently, you get a good indication of a trendline and see whether you are heading in the right direction (are you slowly getting better or worse?). Based on that assessment, you know whether you are getting close to the original goals laid out in your framing or are a long way off. Often, the right balance between trendlines and benchmarks is to capture trendlines for all your metrics throughout the project but then, just before or just after you release your solution, switch to capturing benchmarks to get a formal set of stats that you can use to compare future versions against.

Experience scorecards

Most engineering teams are adept at tracking metrics on the progress of their project. We've all seen these reports and dashboards. We've created them and used them in decision making and in reporting status to management. All of us are familiar with tracking bug counts, bug trendlines, velocity, klocs (kilo—thousands—of lines of code), etc. And in leadership meetings, it's also typical to view, analyze, and make decisions based on business scorecards, which show data such as revenue, usage, growth (or lack of growth), costs, market penetration, competitors, industry movement, and similar measures. These engineering and business scorecards are used by leaders to run the business and to assess progress against goals. Teams should also include a scorecard that tracks the customer experience, or how the customer views a team's product, service, or device.

A great place to track customer metrics is on an experience scorecard. Instead of building a scorecard for each major feature area, component, or team involved, focus your scorecards on the end-to-end experiences you are building. Keeping a scorecard with customer-focused, end-to-end metrics is a key tool for keeping your focus on the big picture—for ensuring that you're really meeting the goals you aimed at and are solving the customer problem you intended to solve.

Many teams end up combining their metrics into a single dashboard that includes not only customer-experience metrics but also relevant system, technical, and business metrics for that area. Some also include execution progress, such as how much work is left to build the code and the number of active bugs, to give a holistic view of the state and health of the project. This dashboard should include an overall experience scorecard that rolls up top-line status across all the vision-level stories for a particular release time frame, and a way to drill into status for the task-level stories. The scorecard provides a foundation for regular project or executive reviews and can serve as a constant reminder of the vision-level scenarios that all of the team's work should be aligned to.

Scorecards might report status as specific numerical values, when those are available, or more often by using a red/yellow/green system. Usually scorecards report trendline data because full benchmarks or telemetry-based usage data (with stronger statistical significance) aren't yet available.

If this is true for your scorecard, it's best to show trends (up, down, no change) or sparklines alongside the raw metric and summarize that as an overall status (red, yellow, green, no data).

Figures 11-4, 11-5, and 11-6 show different examples of experience scorecards.

	Iteration 1	Iteration 2	Iteration 3	Iteration 4	Iteration 5	Iteration 6	Iteration 7	Iteration 8	Iteration 9	Iteration 10
Scenario 1	Not Rated	Not Rated	Poor	Poor	Fair	Fair	Good	Good	Good	Good
Scenario 2	Poor	Fair	Not Rated	Fair	Blocked	Good	Good	Good	Good	Good
Scenario 3	Blocked	Good	Good	Good	Good	Fair	Fair	Good	Good	Good
Scenario 4	Not Rated	Not Rated	Fair	Good	Good	Good	Good	Good	Good	Good
Scenario 5	Blocked	Blocked	Poor	Fair	Fair	Good	Good	Good	Good	Good
Scenario 6	Not Rated	Not Rated	Not Rated	Fair	Fair	Fair	Good	Good	Good	Good
Scenario 7	Not Rated	Good	Good	Good	Good	Good	Good	Good	Good	Good
Scenario 8	Poor	Poor	Poor	Fair	Fair	Poor	Fair	Fair	Good	Good
Scenario 9	Good	Good	Good	Good	Not Rated	Good	Good	Good	Good	Good
Scenario 10	Blocked	Blocked	Blocked	Good	Good	Good	Good	Good	Good	Good

FIGURE 11-4 A scorecard of the overall experience rating over multiple iterations.

	A	B	C	D	E	F	G	H	I	J	K	L	M
		Useful (cum.)	Useful (latest)	Useful trend	Usable (cum.)	Usable (latest)	Usable trend	Desirable (cum.)	Desirable (latest)	Desirable trend	Overall Satisfaction (cum.)	Overall Satisfaction (latest)	Sat. Trend
2	Scen 1	3.4	3.4		4.7	4.5		3.4	3.5		3.4	3.5	
3	Scen 2	3.2	3.8		3.3	3.8		3.8	3.9		3.7	4.2	
4	Scen 3	4.5	4.4		4.3	4.1		4.4	3.5		4.1	3.4	
5	Scen 4	4.9	4.6		3.4	3.5		4.6	4.5		4.4	4.5	
6	Scen 5	4.8	5		3.7	4.6		4.5	5		4.3	5	
7	Scen 6	3.8	4		4.1	4.2		4	3.2		4.3	3.5	
8	Scen 7	4.2	3.8		4.4	4.6		3.8	4		3.8	4	
9	Scen 8	4.6	4.5		4.5	5		4.5	4.2		4.1	4.8	
10	Scen 9	4.5	4.8		4.3	4.6		4.8	3.8		4.5	4.7	
11	Scen 10	4.9	4.7		3.8	4.5		4.7	4.8		4.8	4.8	

FIGURE 11-5 A scorecard of cumulative scores for useful, usable, desirable, and overall satisfaction, along with sparklines showing the direction of the trendline.

No matter which format you use, scorecards should be updated frequently, whenever customer feedback results in new metrics to report. Some teams invest in telemetry that feeds scorecards automatically, but be careful that the promise of future ease doesn't cause you to wait too long to start capturing your first metrics (some teams invest so heavily in the infrastructure to do this that they don't get around to actually capturing metrics until very late). And perhaps this should go without saying, but be sure that the metrics you are capturing come from actual target customers, not internal colleagues testing the system.

	Sponsor	Task-Level Stories	% Alt Docs Reviewed	% Specs Reviewed	% Work Items Completed	% Test Cases Run	Active Bugs	Active Experience Bugs	Active Blocking Bugs	Overall Test Rating	Overall Experience Rating	Overall Business Rating
Vision-Level Scenario 1	Leader a	11	95%	20%	0%	0%	0	0	0	No data	No data	On Track
Vision-Level Scenario 2	Leader b	18	75%	50%	10%	5%	2	0	0	On Track	On Track	On Track
Vision-Level Scenario 3	Leader c	5	100%	100%	80%	40%	23	3	1	Blocked	On Track	Risk
Vision-Level Scenario 4	Leader d	35	83%	30%	15%	5%	1	0	0	On Track	No data	On Track
Vision-Level Scenario 5	Leader c	9	100%	40%	10%	5%	2	1	0	On Track	Risk	Concerns
Vision-Level Scenario 6	Leader a	12	92%	66%	50%	33%	14	4	0	Risk	Concerns	On Track
Vision-Level Scenario 7	Leader e	23	92%	55%	20%	4%	3	2	1	Blocked	Concerns	On Track
Vision-Level Scenario 8	Leader f	7	90%	22%	0%	0%	0	0	0	No data	On Track	On Track
Vision-Level Scenario 9	Leader c	7	50%	0%	0%	0%	0	0	0	No data	Risk	On Track
Vision-Level Scenario 10	Leader g	15	30%	10%	0%	0%	0	0	0	No data	Risk	Concerns

FIGURE 11-6 A scorecard showing a mix of execution metrics along with overall test, experience, and business ratings for each vision-level scenario. Note that work on the lower-priority scenarios has been deprioritized until higher-priority scenarios are more fully on track.

Shift from building components to building experience slices

In Chapter 8, "Building prototypes and coding," we discussed the need to change how you sequence your coding work. Rather than build components one at a time in relative isolation, it's better to write code in vertical slices so that you always have an end-to-end experience you can test with customers at the end of each iteration. Slicing is originally an Agile technique and was intended to help engineering teams organize development work into chunks small enough that they could be coded within a single sprint but still provide customers with something for feedback at the end of the sprint to help inform the next one.

Writing code in slices instead of as components can be a big shift for teams in how code is written, how teams of software developers work together, and how work is assigned across developers. It's important to explicitly consider slicing in your schedule, tools, and other parts of your engineering system in order to support this approach to sequencing development work.

This section offers more guidance for how to think about coding experience slices and illustrates how a sequence of slices grows into a fully implemented end-to-end experience. As we mentioned, most projects start with a vision-level story, which is broken down into several task-level stories. For each task-level story, or scenario, you usually start with several noncode prototypes and iterate them based on customer feedback. Once you have identified a solution approach that is testing well with customers (and works for both the business plan and technical feasibility), it's usually time to start coding in earnest.

To start coding, the first step is to take the proposed solution for the task-level story and slice it into thin, vertical paths that represent a single, streamlined way that a customer might travel through the experience you're developing. Build the code for the most visible, most important, or riskiest slice, and then get customer feedback on it to determine whether you need to work more on that slice, thicken that slice with some additional functionality, or move on to a different slice within that story. Do this until you have implemented all the experience slices needed to complete the task-level story, and continue to iterate them using customer feedback until you create an end-to-end experience that meets your stated goals.

Let's work through an example to illustrate the details of how a slicing approach would work and to show how you might choose which slices to add based on customer feedback. Imagine that you're building a travel website. Here's a task-level story written in user-story format:

AS AN infrequent traveler

I CAN book a flight and rental car that meet my budget and schedule

SO THAT I can take my family to visit Grandma for her 60th birthday bash

First, you would make a few prototypes of your travel website and iterate them with customers until you land on a rough layout for a site that allows your customers to book both flights and rental cars. Now you're ready to start coding. However, this is a pretty big story, more than you can implement in one sprint or iteration. So you need to define the slices for this website and choose a slice to start with. The first slice of this user story might be very, very thin, maybe something as simple as giving the user a way to pick a destination city for a one-way flight. You might even limit this slice so that the user can select only a single city, say San Francisco, as a way to further simplify the problem at the start.

Figure 11-7 shows a conceptual view of this first thin slice, overlaid on your solution's architecture. Note that it goes all the way from the top presentation layer to the bottom platform layer. However, it does not necessarily touch every component in the architecture. It also doesn't completely build out any of the components of the architecture; rather, you are building a thin slice of an end-to-end experience that spans many of the solution's components. For this sprint, you are concerned with building only enough of each component so that the experience slice itself can be built. To achieve this, you may end up stubbing out or faking some parts of the platform to make it buildable in one iteration.

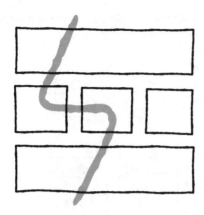

FIGURE 11-7 An experience slice that cuts vertically through your architecture.

Congratulations, the first slice is complete, and you have a very tiny experience: the user can use your site to reserve a one-way flight to San Francisco. The next step is to show your functional slice to customers and get some feedback to inform your next sprint.

Customer feedback may tell you that you're on the right path, so you can go ahead and add round-trip ticketing and the capability to select from many cities. In your next iteration, you "thicken up" your first slice to include this additional functionality. Next, customers inform you that the experience of selecting the flight is good enough for what they need, but what they really want to do next is rent a car once they get to their destination. In this case, you create a new slice that provides the smallest experience you need to enable the user to reserve a rental car. At first, you might not even do the integration work to connect this new slice to the existing flight reservation slice.

You continue getting feedback after every slice, looking for places where your implementation might be off the mark and identifying and prioritizing the most important pieces to tackle next, based on customer feedback as well as business and technology needs. But the key is that at the end of every iteration, whether you build a new slice or add functionality to an existing one, there is always a tangible customer experience that demonstrates the new functionality. This is good both for continuing to iterate the experience as well as for identifying technical integration issues as quickly as possible.

Putting it all together, Figure 11-8 shows how our travel website example might play out. After iterating prototypes to identify a basic design approach, the first code slice implemented the code to allow the user to pick a single, one-way destination. Based on the first round of feedback, the team decided to thicken up that slice in the second sprint by adding functionality: the user can select from multiple cities and get a round-trip ticket. At this point, the end-to-end experience of choosing the flight destination is sufficient for the target customers and the next priority is renting a car. The third sprint implements the capability to choose a rental car, based on designs that were sketched out in the earlier prototypes or possibly through a quick round of additional sketches or prototypes created at this point. The fourth sprint integrates the code for choosing flights and choosing a rental car.

The final code sprint adds more functionality to the car-rental slice to provide a choice of rental agencies and to be able to reserve car seats for the kids, completing the end-to-end experience for this task-level story.

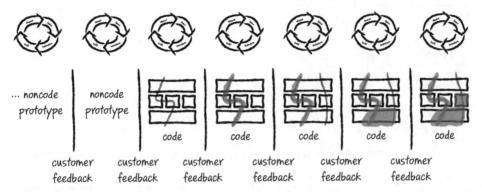

FIGURE 11-8 Progression of work artifacts from prototypes through multiple code slices, over successive iterations of the Fast Feedback Cycle.

Although this is a simplistic example, it illustrates the pattern of building up successive vertical slices to enable a full end-to-end experience that completes a task-level story. When you build code in experience slices rather than as discrete components, at each step you can get customer feedback to correct the course of your designs, capture data against your key metrics, figure out what features should be implemented next, and identify when you have gotten to a minimum viable product (MVP) that is complete enough and has high enough quality to ship to customers.

Shift from upfront specs to alternatives, prototypes, and documentation

This is a case where the shift is subtle. To be clear, we're not arguing that you should stop writing specs. However, the timing of when specs are written, what kind of specs to write, and the nature of the information in the specs may need to change to best align with an iterative approach.

The first issue is timing. It should be obvious to you after reading this far that writing a big, long document that details how a single solution idea should work without doing any customer testing is a nonstarter. The likelihood that your first idea is wrong is high. You may even be barking up the entirely wrong tree. Writing and rewriting a long document takes a huge amount of effort, all of which might be wasted, and developers don't like to read long documents anyway. The idea of writing a long, detailed specification and then handing it off to a development team for coding (over the course of many weeks or months) is quickly dying.

Teams have realized that pictures and prototypes are a lot easier than paragraphs to iterate. It is much more efficient to spend most of your planning effort doing some iteration with prototypes, trying different alternatives, and getting customer feedback that confirms you are on the right track.

Only after you have narrowed in on a pretty stable approach is it worth trying to document those ideas in any amount of detail.

Remember that the original goal of a spec is to communicate to the team what needs to be built so that everyone is clear on the plan and can do their part. To best achieve the same goal with an iterative approach, you effectively split what used to be the full functional spec into three different forms: the alternatives doc, the prototype, and the detailed specs or documentation for individual technology components.

The alternatives (alts) doc

The first document to write is sometimes called a one-page spec or a page-one spec (even though these documents are almost always longer than one page). Recently, we've seen teams begin to call this a scenario spec, or an alternatives, or "alts," doc.

An alts doc is written for each scenario during the first couple of iterations of the Fast Feedback Cycle. It's used to kick off a new project and communicate the scenario narrative along with a few proposed solution directions. It is a very helpful document because it provides just enough information to enable prioritization of which scenarios to work on when a team is forming or adding work to a product backlog. It also captures the latest proposed solution alternatives, which helps stimulate internal feedback on feasibility and business tradeoffs. In effect, the alts doc describes the assumptions and the hypotheses that the team is about to test with the iterative process and its current best guess about which avenues to try.

One of the biggest benefits of writing an alts doc is that it formalizes and enforces the expectation that teams actually consider several different viable alternatives before they decide on a solution path. Scheduling a project review to present alts docs to leaders is a good forcing function to make sure this work is done and taken seriously. Getting in the habit of writing alts docs whenever you start work on a new scenario is a particularly good practice to instill in a team that is just making the transition to using the Fast Feedback Cycle.

An alts doc typically contains the following:

- **Target customer** Describes the specific target customer for this scenario and any relevant data on segmentation, size, unique characteristics, etc.

- **Key insights** A short list of the key insights about this customer that motivated this scenario, originating from research.

- **Scenario narrative** The latest draft of the scenario narrative (or whatever other framing technique you are using).

- **Success criteria** The proposed success criteria and customer experience metrics that will define when a solution for this scenario is done and good enough to ship.

- **Alternative solutions** Describes three to five proposed solutions. These should be rough descriptions, not fully detailed. Using a storyboard, a few sketches, or a mockup for each proposed solution is often the best way to communicate these at this point in a project.

- **Customer feedback**   Includes top-line learnings from the first round or two of customer feedback as factors in deciding which solution path or paths to pursue.

- **Pros and cons**   A short list of benefits and possible problems with each solution direction, including customer experience issues, technical feasibility issues, and business issues. Writing this section encourages the team to think through these issues and invites feedback from reviewers on additional pros and cons that the team may not have noticed yet.

- **Key constraints**   A list of any notable constraints in available technical platforms, timing, partnerships, or other hard factors to consider.

The prototype

The utility of the alts doc—although it's highly valuable for kicking off a project and facilitating prioritization—is relatively short-lived. The workhorse of the iterative process really is a series of prototypes, as we have discussed at length in this book. As you iterate, the latest prototypes—whether they are simple sketches, grayscale mockups, click-through wireframes, functional code, or even production code—will typically be the best representation of the team's current progress. This means that the prototype itself, especially as you hone in on a particular solution approach and your prototype becomes more detailed, will serve part of the role that the functional specification used to serve.

Functional specs

Some teams find that a prototype is sufficient for describing the current plan in enough detail for team members to do their work and do not need to write additional specs. However, many times, you also need to document those nitty-gritty details for all the things that are nonnegotiable—that just have to get done—and document team decisions as they are made. This is often true for larger teams, for projects with larger scope, and for teams whose work is not fully visible in a user-interface prototype.

The functional spec should use photos or screenshots of the prototype wherever possible, but it should also include text, tables, and flow charts that describe edge cases, logic paths, exceptions, boundaries, underlying algorithms, and other architectural considerations that the team needs to follow as the code is fleshed out. This document might also describe or specify aesthetic details that may not be present in the prototype and may include a "redline" drawing of the interface that details fonts, colors, and spacing with precise pixel dimensions.

In the end, this document might look a lot like a spec that earlier was written at the very beginning of a project. However, this document should be written a lot later in the process than people are used to. When it is prepared too early, the plan has too much uncertainty, and the spec quickly becomes out of date—and often never gets updated. It's better to wait until the foundations are solid; then the document won't be as hard to maintain and will better serve the purpose it's intended for.

As we said, this spec is also a great place to park the list of requirements, the very specific and detailed items that have to get done but usually won't surface in the scenarios themselves. We don't mean to belittle these details. Often, it takes work to gather these details, and they offer a lot of value to the team. For example, your solution might need to account for a large and complicated set of relevant tax issues whose details are nonnegotiable. Discovering and documenting these details is important, but because there isn't room for interpretation, there's not much need for iteration or customer feedback. These details are what they are, so document them in the spec.

 TIP

> A number of teams now use a single OneNote notebook for their specs, using separate tabs for the functional spec, test spec, international spec, and dev/architecture spec so that all the information for a particular scenario is in the same place. Some teams also create tabs for the scenario, brainstorming lists, storyboards, and prototype artifacts. OneNote handles simultaneous editing by multiple users very gracefully and avoids the source control and explicit edit-and-track-changes rigmarole in Word that sometimes discourages team members from updating the docs right away.

Shift from component reviews to experience reviews

Team leaders play a pivotal role in helping cultural and process changes take root in the team. Many teams find that holding regular project reviews is a good way for team leaders to stay in touch with the team's progress and provide team members with ongoing coaching and feedback. Project reviews can act as another forcing function for taking on a specific new activity and reporting on it in the review, which makes reviews a powerful lever for driving behavioral change in a team. Reviews are also a time when leaders can encourage cultural change by clearly articulating their expectations, setting values and cultural norms, and holding teams accountable for new behavior they want to see.

Superformal project reviews are rarely efficient in today's fast-paced world. Thankfully, most teams are already shifting from formalized project reviews—infrequent dog-and-pony shows that take weeks to prepare for and that carefully present the team's work in the best possible light—to more frequent, informal conversations with leaders about status and issues. Project reviews work best when teams and leaders focus on sharing what's really going on, both the good and the bad, and openly discuss alternatives for dealing with problems or risks, taking advantage of the expertise of different people in the room. The ideal mindset in a project review is, "We're in this together, so let's put our heads together." Creating this kind of trusting, honest, open space requires leaders to act more as coaches and mentors than as judges and decision makers and to value failed experiments as learning opportunities that get a team closer to an optimal solution—not the result of poor team performance.

However, a further shift needs to happen. Instead of scheduling a project review for each product, component area, or functional team, schedule a project review for each vision-level story. Start focusing project reviews on your target customers and the end-to-end experiences that you are trying to deliver for them. These experiences typically cut across individual teams and require multiple teams to come together to fully represent the status of an end-to-end experience, a format that is much different from typical project reviews.

Yes, you need to continue to track and monitor how your project is progressing against the business and technical metrics you've used in the past. But it's important also to frequently check in on customers, to track how the end-to-end solution is progressing toward delighting them, and to make sure that all the pieces are coming together to make that delight a reality. These goals are best accomplished in the context of a review that focuses on an end-to-end experience, as opposed to splitting information across multiple project reviews for each team or functional component. You want to ship complete, end-to-end experiences, not individual components and not your org chart.

Here are some practices to consider when planning experience reviews:

- **Change the name**   To help send a signal to teams that this review is a different sort than perhaps happened in the past, rename it to emphasize the new scope and behaviors you want to see. Consider naming it something like "experience review" or "scenario review," and don't use terms such as "component review," "team review," or "project review."

- **Focus on vision-level stories**   Each review should focus on a vision-level story and show how all the task-level stories align and come together into an end-to-end experience. Always start the review with a reminder of the target customer, the specific vision-level story, and the task-level stories or scenarios that align with it.

- **Sponsor attends the review**   Each vision-level story should have a designated leadership sponsor, and it is essential for this sponsor to be at the experience review.

- **Cross-team attendance**   Leads or representatives from each team who need to contribute to a specific vision-level story should be present at the experience review. This means that many team leads likely need to attend multiple experience reviews. Keeping this overhead manageable is one reason not to be actively working on too many vision-level stories at any given time.

- **Everyone can listen in**   These reviews should not be private, closed-door affairs with only the leaders of the teams involved. Rather, anyone from the teams directly affected or from other areas of the project should be allowed to listen in and perhaps even participate. You can limit the people in the room to those who are directly involved with leading the relevant teams, but set up a video stream that others can watch from their desk and also provide a way for remote attendees to contribute questions or comments. Enabling a "side channel" of text conversation that takes place in parallel with the meeting is a great practice and allows the team to freely discuss, raise questions, and make suggestions without disturbing the main meeting. Have one person in the review room listen to the side channel and pull in relevant ideas, suggestions, and questions. Or, when possible, project the ongoing side conversation into the meeting room so that it is visible to all attendees and runs alongside the main content being reviewed.

- **Only report on full iterations**   Experience reviews are best done at the end of an iteration, when the team has gone through each stage of the Fast Feedback Cycle and can demonstrate the experience and report on customer feedback. You can also show progress against success metrics by using the latest experience scorecard. Report on the ideas you tried, what you built to show customers, how customers responded, and how far you are from being done.

This approach should create an open space to discuss possible next steps and whether you should continue in the direction you're going or try something new. It also helps bring to the surface any issues that are blocking the team from making further progress. In contrast, holding a project review in the middle of an iteration encourages teams (and especially leaders) to speculate about how customers will react, which just isn't productive. If you could predict what customers think, you wouldn't need an iterative approach in the first place.

- **Hold them regularly** An experience review shouldn't be a one-time event; experience reviews are most helpful if they happen on a regular basis. Many teams have found that a monthly cadence is about right, which for most teams means reporting on two two-week iterations. This pace avoids too much overhead but is frequent enough to ensure that cross-team alignment is being managed actively and that teams are not drifting away from one another.

- **Keep the content appropriate to the maturity of the project** If work on a vision-level story only just started, the first review should focus on the target customer, alignment to strategy, and how task-level stories align to the vision-level stories. Leaders should not press for details about engineering deliverables prematurely. This encourages teams to skip steps, which could result in costly mistakes. As you get further into a project, add technical and other details that are appropriate for the phase of the project. But do not focus the review on aspirational next steps. Rather, stay focused on the data you have at hand—what experiments you've tried, how customers responded, and what directions the team is planning to try next.

- **Demo the customer experience** As the project progresses, keep the focus of the review on what the experience looks like end to end, not on the guts and plumbing of how it is built. Keep it real and reality based—don't focus on abstract models, but what the actual product would look like. If the experience is an API, show the object hierarchy, the methods, and their signatures. If the experience is a user interface, show the latest storyboards or mockups, even if they are very rough. And if you have working code, by all means show that. We have been surprised to see even very technical, plumbing-oriented teams find that showing storyboards in project reviews was an extremely helpful way to communicate the experience to leaders.

- **Show the alternatives** Create an expectation for these reviews that teams should show not just their current "best" solution idea but also the alternatives. The reason to do this is twofold. First, it creates a forcing function to ensure that teams truly do consider alternatives and that those alternatives were meaningfully different from one another, not just variations on a theme. It's not crazy to ask to see the worst idea a team came up with because that idea will not only be entertaining but show the breadth of ideas that were considered. Second, sometimes an audience with fresh eyes will notice a "blend" that the team hasn't—a solution that combines ideas from multiple alternatives. Blends often show the way to powerful, innovative solutions.

How leaders can help

More than any other aspect of an experience review, the behavior of leaders is what helps a team make the shift to a customer-focused, iterative approach—or not. If, during the experience reviews, leaders reiterate the importance of the new approaches—the values and culture they expect—and hold teams accountable for acting this way, the team quickly gets the message that it is safe to try this new approach and that they will be rewarded for doing so. However, if leaders are ambivalent about the new approach—or worse, unintentionally undermine it by not adapting their own behaviors, language, and expectations for the team—that is a sure way to stall real change from taking place.

The biggest change leaders need to make is to stop speaking on behalf of customers. They need to stop using their personal knowledge and experience to purport to know which ideas will work best and what customers really want. One reason this shift is so difficult is that a leader's personal knowledge, experience, and smarts are likely what got the leader promoted to this position in the first place. Over time, these leaders have grown into the role of a HiPPO—the highest-paid person with an opinion—and the team has come to rely on their judgment for decision making. However, remember that when teams test their ideas through experimentation, teams correctly predict what will actually work for customers only a third of the time. The HiPPO is no different. (See the section "Why get feedback?," in Chapter 9 for more information about statistics on making successful predictions.)

Having a leader internalize this reality and stop making it a personal responsibility to be the decision maker can actually be quite freeing. Leaders no longer need to feel as though they should know all the answers, and their job becomes much more about making sure that the team is asking the right questions at the right time and is doing the due diligence with customers to answer those questions with high confidence.

Here are some essential questions that leaders should ask at experience reviews (if these questions aren't proactively addressed by the attendees):

- **Who is the target customer?**   Make sure that teams are focused on the target customers laid out in the original business plans. Listen for plans that sound like they are trying to be all things for all people (too generic or not focused, like peanut butter spread across a piece of bread), and redirect teams to focus on a specific end-to-end experience for a stated target customer, even though this might mean a compromised experience for other, lower-priority customers at times. Help teams understand that this tradeoff is okay and expected, and that it will actually produce better results overall. Listen to make sure that the same target customer is addressed across the task-level stories for a vision-level story or an end-to-end experience. Also listen to be sure that the target customer the team is using aligns to one of the targets chosen and communicated to the team as central to the business strategy.

- **Is this approach aligned with our business strategy?**   Be sure that teams aren't ignoring the realities of the business. It's easy for a team to get sucked into cool user experiences and technical details and forget monetization. Focusing on a target customer that is explicitly tied to your business strategy helps a lot, but it's not the only business aspect to worry about. Testing the visible parts of the monetization plan with customers is an important aspect of iterating an experience to be sure that it works.

- **What scenario is this focused on?**   Listen for scenarios that are thinly disguised feature ideas. Remember that scenarios should be implementation-free descriptions of a specific real-world customer situation. If teams seem off-track, remind them of which vision-level and task-level stories they are supposed to be solving, or ask what they've learned that tells them that they need to adjust those stories.

- **What are your success criteria?** Success criteria should be built into each vision-level and task-level story, and teams should be tracking and reporting metrics against those criteria, ideally on a scorecard. If success metrics haven't been met, the experience isn't done yet and needs more iteration. It's the leader's job to insist on meeting the quality bar.

- **When was the last time you got customer feedback?** Any team that comes to a review without recent customer feedback should be told that this isn't acceptable. Waiting until the code is written is almost always too late to get the first feedback from customers. Coach teams to get customer feedback from real customers *early*, before ideas are fully developed or directions are set. Postpone the first experience review until at least one round of customer feedback has occurred. Teams should continue getting customer feedback at every iteration. Risk grows as the time period between a team's customer touch points increases.

- **What do customers think about that?** Listen for teams that start sounding as though they are building a solution for the individuals on the team, not the stated target customer. Coach them to keep the focus on what customers like and dislike—the customers' perspectives, opinions, needs, wants, dreams, and pet peeves. If the team doesn't know this information or is making too many assumptions, these are good questions to ask at the next round of customer observation.

- **What course corrections have you made based on customer feedback?** This is a good question to ask to be sure that teams are actually listening to feedback and not just cherry-picking feedback that reinforces their personal opinions. Projects always have course corrections, at least small ones, and often a couple of bigger ones. A team that tells you that all their ideas have worked 100 percent the first time is highly suspect. Similarly, late discoveries and mistakes should be the topic of a postmortem—how could you have tested with customers to have discovered this problem earlier?

 TIP

A great phrase for leaders to use liberally is, "We reserve the right to get smarter." Stating this gives teams permission to pick a direction to move forward with and make progress, with the understanding that they might well change their mind or improve the plan based on customer feedback or other learnings, and that this is expected and good and supported by their leadership.

- **What alternatives have you considered?** Leaders should set a clear expectation for the minimum number of alternatives (typically three, five, or even nine) that a team should consider before making a decision. Whether deciding on a user-interface design or picking a technical architecture, better decisions result when teams do the due diligence to force themselves to generate and consider multiple credible options before narrowing in on a plan. Require that teams present these alternatives in their reviews.

- **What data do you have to support that decision?** Listen for teams that are making big decisions based on gut instincts, personal experience, or ego. Require teams to back up their decisions with data—customer data, technical data, business data—and to truly consider alternatives and not fall in love with their first good idea.

 TIP

Leaders should be cautious about asking "How exactly are we going to implement this?" too soon. Until the experience has been iterated and a viable direction is found that is good for customers, technically feasible, and sound businesswise, it's premature to expect teams to make specific technical decisions. Let the iterative process work through the technology and architecture decisions as well as the decisions about the customer's experience. Allow some time for the best approach to shake out. The question to ask is, "What alternatives are you considering for how we might implement this?"

Shift from individual focus to team focus

A pervasive but subtle shift that underlies everything we've discussed is to take a more collaborative approach to iterating ideas through the Fast Feedback Cycle. It's a subtle shift because you still want individuals who have particular expertise to take the lead at different times. But, generally, people need to be better plugged in to the overall work of the team, participate in key decisions, and be more aware of the work of others. Here are a few structural steps you can implement to help encourage teams to collaborate more:

- **Office space**[4] Creating an office layout that balances individual and group spaces can make a profound difference in how a team operates. Historically, Microsoft offices were designed as individual workspaces: each person was given a private office, complete with a door to close. Recently, buildings have been remodeled to favor open environments to promote more team collaboration. The team we work on has been part of a particularly interesting experiment over the past six years. We spent the first three years together in a team room, where we sat together, enjoyed peripheral awareness of one another's work, participated in numerous impromptu conversations, and scheduled collaborations and meetings regularly, all in our own space. Guess what? The extroverts on the team thrived, and yes, work was done in a more collaborative manner. But more introverted team members sometimes found it difficult to be productive (or they wore headphones most of the time). Then we moved to a different building and spent two years back in a traditional layout with individual offices. It's remarkable—with just a few walls in the way and even though our offices were adjacent to each other in the same hallway—how difficult it was to retain the collaborative approach we were used to. In the last year, we moved back to a more open layout, and it's been like a breath of fresh air. We were reminded of how much the physical architecture can encourage particular work styles. Our team room seats six people and also has several adjoining private spaces, called "phone rooms" and "focus rooms," that can be used for small meetings or time alone. The blend of team rooms and private spaces, and some specific, facilitated conversations about team-room norms (like taking phone calls outside and not eating smelly fish), created an environment that captures the strengths of an open plan and also fixes many of its weaknesses, especially for more introverted team members.

- **Broader, multidiscipline teams**   Most engineers are used to working on cross-discipline teams that include program, project, or product managers, as well as developers and testers. However, many of the activities that teams need to do to fulfill the promise of the Fast Feedback Cycle benefit from including experts in user research and design as well. For many projects, product planning, marketing, support, and operations are also highly useful. Resourcing multidiscipline teams that include these specialties as first-class members is essential.[5]

 MINDSHIFT

A designer is a designer is a designer, right? No, not quite. It's worth distinguishing between different flavors of designers because each can have quite different skill sets and backgrounds to contribute to the team. The three you're most likely to run into are interaction designers, graphic designers, and industrial designers. Interaction designers offer the most generally useful skill set and focus on creating smooth workflows to allow people to interact with software naturally and seamlessly. Interaction designers may not be particularly talented artists—their sketches may not look any better than yours—but they are probably great at quickly generating alternatives and thinking through sequences and customer experiences. They are also great at information architecture and at understanding human perceptual and behavioral strengths and limitations. In comparison,graphic designers create beautiful aesthetics that coordinate the form and function of a solution. Industrial designers create physical products that you can touch and that tend to have extensive manufacturing constraints to manage. There are other specialty disciplines as well, for sound, animation, information architecture, and so on. It's rare (but not impossible) for one person to have deep expertise in more than one area, so as you build your team, be thoughtful about what skill sets you really need.

- **Pairing and swarming**   Introduce the idea of "pairing"—two people working together on a task who take turns driving and observing. This is similar to the idea in extreme programming (XP) of pair programming, but it can be applied not just to two developers writing code together but also to two team members sketching storyboards, working through details of a spec, drafting a PowerPoint presentation, sorting through customer feedback, or any other task. Whether you are writing code or sketching new experiences, the interplay of two brains usually makes for a better deliverable with fewer bugs. When you have a big problem to solve or lots of data to analyze, swarming may help. Swarming is where the entire team drops everything and works together to focus on solving a single, urgent problem or to make fast progress on a particular scenario. Both pairing and swarming formalize the idea of collaboration as a natural part of the team's work and give the team a vocabulary for it.

- **Performance-review process**   If your performance review process emphasizes individual work and shipping code frequently no matter what (and deemphasizes teamwork and customer satisfaction), you will have a tough time getting the Fast Feedback Cycle to take root in your team. Building a performance-review system that factors in how well people collaborate as well as customer satisfaction can help align extrinsic rewards and motivations to the values you are trying to establish in your team's culture. For instance, you might align bonuses to the customer satisfaction of the solution that the entire team delivered or to how well the team met its stated scenario metrics at release. Keep in mind that social science research is clear that extrinsic rewards are not a particularly powerful motivator on their own. However, when extrinsic rewards are in direct conflict with the culture you are trying to establish, you are definitely going to run into problems. Be sure to align the team's performance-review process to the values and culture you intend to build, or at least make sure they are not in conflict.

- **Public spaces**   Using public spaces to unify the team and encourage collaboration is a great tactic. Hanging up posters of target customers, personas, key scenarios, success criteria/metrics, or other framing info helps to informally involve everyone in a set of shared goals. The museum approach we discussed in Chapter 5 also helps bring a team together. Whether you are covering the walls with customer research or the latest solution sketches, display the recent work artifacts in a place that is visible and frequented by team members. By doing this, you let the entire team gain a rough idea of the state of progress simply by walking the halls. Even better, you can encourage feedback by keeping a pile of sticky notes and a Sharpie pen adjacent to work that's in question and asking team members for their comments or feedback.

What doesn't change?

Despite what can feel like massive structural changes, many aspects of an engineering team's work don't need to change at all. Teams still need to write great code. They need a system to track bugs, profiling tools to measure performance, deployment tools to ship code to production, a fast and reliable build system, and all of the other sundry things that are used every day in engineering projects.

In fact, we didn't even begin to cover many, many aspects of managing an engineering team in this chapter, as well as various project management techniques. You can read piles of books on that stuff, and some of our favorites are listed at the end of the book in Appendix C. In particular, many Agile techniques—from scrum teams, daily standups, test-driven development (TDD), acceptance test-driven development (ATDD), extreme programming (XP), and more—are great techniques to include in your team's project management and engineering system and very compatible with the ideas in this book. Similarly, we've mentioned Lean Startup techniques throughout this book as great tools for various stages of the Fast Feedback Cycle. These are also very complementary.

As we wrote at the end of Chapter 2, don't forget what you already know. The focus of this chapter, and this book, is on the areas where we've found that teams need to amend their current systems and tools to bring more rigor into building great customer experiences. By and large, these are additions to current practices and not substitutes.

Notes

1. The description of the quick pulse study approach in Chapter 9, "Observing customers: Getting feedback," provides more details on how you can structure a schedule to prepare for, conduct, and debrief a customer touch point on a weekly basis.

2. Steve Herbst, private communication with the authors.

3. You can find a wealth of information about good business metrics. Some helpful sources beyond the basics of revenue and profit include average revenue per user (ARPU), cost of goods sold (COGS), and customer acquisition cost. Also consider Dave McClure's so-called pirate metrics—AARRR: acquisition, activation, retention, referral, revenue. Dave McClure, "Startup Metrics for Pirates: AARRR," *Master of 500 Hats* (blog), September 6, 2007, http://500hats.typepad.com/500blogs/2007/09/startup-metrics.html.

4. Some good books are available that discuss the importance of the workplace environment and its role in the creative process. One we like comes from the Institute of Design (d.school) at Stanford University: *Make Space: How to Set the Stage for Creative Collaboration*, by Scott Doorley and Scott Witthoft (Wiley, 2012).

5. Interestingly, we've noticed a pattern in which teams tend to make a business case for and hire additional user research and design staff within a year of training with our foundational workshop.

THE CHANGE IS BIGGER THAN YOU THINK

You can't overcommunicate

Teams with sustained focus from leaders make bigger changes

COLLABORATION ISN'T EVERYBODY DOING EVERYTHING TOGETHER

SEMANTICS MATTER **culture change**

Getting to aha isn't enough   CUSTOMIZE TO YOUR ORGANIZATION

LESSONS LEARNED   Don't overindex on scenarios

Recruit the trusted lieutenant   Drive culture change, not just process change   **champions**

Pilot with a small team first   YOU CAN'T FAKE A BUSINESS STRATEGY

Deceptively difficult to put into practice

You can't grow a foot overnight   **Design your own design process**

You don't have to do everything   Middle managers are the hardest to bring on board

HARNESS CHAMPIONS AS CHANGE AGENTS

CHAPTER 12

Lessons learned

The ideas in this book are easy enough to grasp, yet they are deceptively difficult to put into practice. In the last chapter, we talked about changing how you work, shifting from old ways of doing things to new ways. But beyond those mechanical and procedural differences, we've also been highlighting deep cultural shifts and mindset adjustments in the Mindshift callouts throughout this book— everything from understanding that your first idea is probably wrong, to truly believing that you are not the customer, to becoming comfortable with showing half-baked work to gather early feedback. These ideas challenge long-held beliefs about how we build software and the habits and practices that we have developed over the decades. Even if everyone involved truly believes in the power of Scenario-Focused Engineering and the Fast Feedback Cycle, adopting these practices in a team's daily work and getting them to stick is no small feat.

We have definitely seen teams encounter some speed bumps in adopting an SFE-inspired approach. We have also learned the hard way that some of our assumptions about what teams need and how best to make change happen turned out not to be true. Indeed, we made some mistakes in presenting these concepts to a few teams as we got started on this journey. For a couple of teams, critical errors in the team's rollout made the entire proposition so frustrating that people came to think of SFE as a four-letter word. We'd like to help others not make the same mistakes. This chapter focuses on the biggest lessons we've learned over the past six years and the mistakes we've seen teams and individuals make.

Getting started

These are some of the first lessons we learned while teaching SFE and while observing teams during their first months of adopting some of the practices.

Getting to aha isn't enough

We started the Scenario-Focused Engineering initiative with the conviction that if we just brought these powerful ideas to engineering teams in a way that they could understand and appreciate, the rest would take care of itself. We knew that Microsoft was full of brilliant, motivated, passionate people, and we figured that once people got the basic ideas, they would take them to heart and find the best means of incorporating them into their teams' work. Furthermore, we believed—and still do— that no single recipe would work for every team and that teams generally wanted to invent and create their own processes. So, we were reluctant to be prescriptive about what specific practices, processes, and schedules teams should use, since every team is different in its size, composition, scope, goals, constraints, and so on.

We focused our efforts on kick-starting teams to see the value in these ideas, bringing people to what we called the aha moment. To do this, we created an experiential workshop, designed for intact teams. The workshop was structured so that it would gradually rise to a climax by midafternoon, when most students realized that their first prototyped ideas didn't make sense to the person sitting next to them, never mind a customer. Students would realize that a bit more science and rigor than they thought was involved in figuring out what customers really want. A light bulb would go on in some new room in their head, and it was fun and exhilarating to be part of that experience for thousands of people.

Fascinatingly, after teaching hundreds of these classes, all of our instructors agreed that when this collective aha moment happened, the shift in the room was palpable. Most of the people who entered the workshop as skeptics agreed by the time they left that these ideas had merit. The whole class would spend the last hours of the workshop in deep conversation about how significant a change this was from their old ways of doing things and discuss plans for how they would overcome those challenges.

Looking back, it is remarkable how much ground we were able to cover in a single day. The feedback we received was very positive, and word of mouth traveled quickly. It sure seemed like it was working. We firmly believed that once we got leaders and their teams to that aha moment, the rest would be easy, and that with time, patience, and some iteration, these practices would naturally become part of a team's work.

We couldn't have been more wrong. After teaching more than 22,000 people, we can say with conviction that taking a team through a one-day workshop is a great way to start a team's transition to new practices, but on its own, it's not nearly enough. Despite the best intentions, old habits are strong, cultures and values are tough to change, schedules are tight, and institutionalized processes and tools deeply impact the way people think and work, often at a subconscious level. Until you address both the complexities and subtleties that are embedded throughout your formal and informal engineering systems, team culture, and organization, don't expect much to happen. We saw team after team start with enormous passion and motivation, but without strong, visible leadership support and a well-staffed effort to wrestle with how to operationalize these changes and make them real (or a supermotivated champion with the energy to move mountains), that momentum fizzled. Those teams still got some benefits, but the benefits were small in comparison with those gained by teams that really went the distance and had strong leadership support.

Many of the lessons we describe in this chapter detail specific aspects of the complexities and subtleties that we've learned over the years, which are vitally important for teams to pay attention to if they are to make this shift successfully.

This isn't paint by numbers

We've tried. We've tried really hard. But somehow, this message never quite comes through. Neither this book nor any other book can give you step-by-step, prescriptive guidance about how to put customers at the forefront of your thinking or how to create the next killer app that rocks your customers' world. If that were easy, wouldn't everybody be doing it?

To this day, teams say to us, "Just tell us what to do!" But, you see, we can't. Every situation is different. Every step of the way, critical variables involve the characteristics of the product, the type of target customer, the maturity and skills of the team, and the business opportunity you are going after. The same techniques and informal process that work terrifically for a 10-person team building a new game app for consumers clearly aren't the right ones for a thousand-person team building the next version of Office. The Fast Feedback Cycle has an underlying rhythm and includes many broadly useful techniques, but no single, complete formula works in every situation.

In our original workshop, we showed an image of the *Mona Lisa* made up to look like a paint-by-numbers page in a children's coloring book. The point we were trying to make is that you can't just blindly follow someone else's scheme and fill in the colors. You won't get your own masterpiece that way.

We then showed an image of an artist's palette and a set of brushes and tools. That's what we're trying to provide in this book—a palette of paints, plus tools, techniques, ideas, and mindsets that you can use to create your own masterpiece, as well as some guidance on which tools tend to be most helpful for different situations or phases of a project or different types of teams. The Fast Feedback Cycle is a toolbox, and you have to pick which tools make the most sense for your situation to help you reach your goals within the constraints you have to work with.

You may well find that the techniques you used on your last project don't work as well on your next project, perhaps because of differences in the team's skill set or in the type of problem you're trying to solve. Over time, as you gain more experience, you will develop your own favorite go-to techniques. But you also need to pick the right tools for the job at hand. Storyboarding, for example, is not likely to help much when you're designing a new API. In some cases, the choice of technique is fairly arbitrary, but the important point is getting the larger team aligned on the same approach—for example, whether you will frame the problem by writing scenarios or by sketching user journeys—so that you aren't comparing apples with oranges when it comes time to prioritize work. The bottom line is that you need a design process that makes sense for your team, your situation, and your goals and to be thoughtful about which techniques you use.

You don't have to do everything

We've seen a few eager teams try to make too many changes all at once—for example, large teams that try to implement the entire Fast Feedback Cycle on their first try, change the way they schedule, move to a cloud-based services technology stack, and adopt Agile techniques all at the same time. They bite off more than they can chew, and midway through they realize that they just can't keep up with it all. In the end, some of the changes they try to institute fade away without enough consistent success to build on.

We've learned that people consistently leave our workshops feeling like they have to do it all. Showing them the complete system made them feel as though there was really no hope unless they could do it all at once—and that, of course, was truly overwhelming. Teams need to understand the importance of choosing and adjusting the activities that work best in their current situation. We've seen plenty of teams make a ton of progress by implementing surgical changes or even just by adding a single new technique to their repertoire.

Over the years, we've been lucky enough to work with a few teams that had very strong leadership support from the beginning. These teams reaped huge value from the SFE workshop and were able to initiate a sustainable culture and shift to processes that capitalized on iteration and deep customer empathy. These leaders set clear expectations for change; established new tools, rhythms, and processes; and maintained that commitment to customer empathy over the long term.

But for the majority of the teams we've worked with, a holistic reset of their business, culture, processes, and tools was just not going to happen. For many teams, the complete set of changes we present in the workshop was simply too much work (and risk) to take on all at once. Every team has to do the hard work to find where and how it will incrementally shift its work toward the customer. All the changes we recommend are along a continuum and can be approached one bit at a time. For example, some teams first take on the task of learning to use scenarios, sketches, and storyboards to help align the team and partners and avoid being sucked into the rat hole of arguing over a myriad of implementation details and requirements. Other teams initially gain value from SFE by developing a handful of personas to serve as target customers for the team. Other teams find that they are already closely tracking to established business metrics and begin to develop and track experience metrics as well. It is essential to adapt the Fast Feedback Cycle to your specific situation.

You don't have to start at the beginning of the Fast Feedback Cycle diagram and do everything in order, perfectly. A better approach is to take a holistic look and decide which techniques and aspects will best align and energize your team toward understanding and solving your customers' needs. If you are already using an Agile project-management approach or have experimented with some of the Lean Startup concepts, you are probably already doing some of the things we've talked about. If so, there's no need to reinvent the wheel. If you already have elements of an iterative culture and a process to support that, start with that base and add from there.

The good news is that the concepts and techniques we present in this book are not monolithic and all of them are valuable on their own even outside the Fast Feedback Cycle. You can decide which techniques, and to some extent which mindsets, are most valuable to you and then focus on those. Does it help you most to change the team culture to understand that "you are not the customer" and build empathy for your customer based on research and data? Perfect—focus the team on doing that well, and it will serve as a good foundation to build on the next time. Is the team struggling with too many priorities and lacking focus? Then start by doing the work necessary to decide what the top customer and business problems are and come up with a well-crafted frame to get the team aligned. It may not be perfect, and it may not be the full Fast Feedback Cycle, but it's a step in the right direction. You get the idea.

As a matter of fact, you should feel free to adapt any of the individual techniques to your situation as well. If storyboarding with a software tool works better for you than paper and markers, go for it.

If you come up with a new approach for rapid prototyping or for getting quick customer feedback, great. Our goal is to show the bigger patterns and goals of each technique and how they fit into the Fast Feedback Cycle. This way, you have the background you need to safely riff on these ideas without losing the magic so that you can successfully adapt them to fit your specific situation.

Take a few of the ideas in this book and try them out in your work. Pick the activities that are best suited for your team today. Make some progress, adjust as appropriate, and do it again. And remember, you don't have to do it all. Just get started.

Don't overindex on scenarios

We've seen lots and lots of teams get started by focusing almost exclusively on customer research and writing scenarios (it probably doesn't help that we named our workshop "Scenario-Focused Engineering"). Many teams focus so much on the goal of writing SPICIER scenarios that they do great research, write tons of scenarios, spend way too much time trying to prioritize them, and completely forget about the rest of the iterative cycle. Once they achieve the goal of writing scenarios, they think they're finished with SFE and can go back to their old, linear approaches to building products. Often, they spend so much time working on scenarios that they really feel the crunch to start coding.

Until you start getting customer feedback on your ideas, you won't know whether you are solving the right problem. The longer you delay that, the more risk you carry and the bigger the waste if you indeed find you are pursuing a bad idea. Remember that the magic of the Fast Feedback Cycle is not in its individual activities and artifacts but in the repetition, iteration, and constant customer feedback. Optimize your approach to go around the cycle as quickly as possible, and constantly seek customer feedback to keep you iterating.

If you find that your team is overindexing on writing perfect SPICIER scenarios, here's a better way to think about it. A scenario is a useful way to communicate the customer's problem space. It can also be a useful place to park measurable outcomes. But, in general, think of a scenario as a tool for getting teams of people aligned on a customer goal or outcome and for developing customer empathy. We've seen teams achieve this goal a number of different ways, sometimes with SPICIER scenarios, sometimes without. But whichever framing tool you pick, the output does not need to be complex, and the resulting narrative does not need to be a work of art. Get it close enough, and let it fuel an iterative cycle.

Don't forget about the end-to-end experience

We've also seen teams iterate and develop a great end-to-end experience for their customers early on in their process but then lose sight of that experience's goals during coding and fail to actually ship that experience. Once they are coding, these teams tend to become distracted and forget about the end-to-end experience that they are targeting. They forget to get customer feedback and to measure against their experience goals. And as the team's codebase becomes more and more complicated and compromises have to be made, it's inevitable that the team's work diverges from the goals of the original scenarios, while no one pays enough attention to notice. Teams discover late in the project, usually during an integration phase, that they have built a set of components and features that almost, but don't quite, come together to form the end-to-end experience that they were intending. At that late date, it's often nearly impossible to fix. This is a very frustrating way to end a team's first foray into trying to build better end-to-end experiences.

We've seen teams combat this natural tendency in a few productive ways. First, it helps to introduce the Agile concepts of slicing and continual integration. Having regular team demos of the end-to-end experiences as they exist in the code is another forcing function that's very helpful for fixing integration bugs early and for keeping focus on the ultimate goal. Another crucial habit to develop is to consider the end-to-end experience when you make technology or business decisions or when a component or feature runs into trouble and is at risk. Making decisions to cut features on the basis of the impact they have on the end-to-end experience is essential. Finally, putting formal mechanisms in place to track progress against scenarios or experiences ensures that everyone keeps their eyes on the prize. You can do this through regular scenario checkpoints, project reviews, scenario reports from project-tracking tools, or by maintaining up-to-date scorecards that measure metrics and progress against end-to-end scenarios.

Team dynamics

Some of the biggest lessons we've learned have to do with people, teams, and behavior.

Engineers are natural skeptics

We had an inkling about the natural skepticism of engineers when we started teaching our workshops, and our experience working with lots of engineers has definitely reinforced this belief. Maybe it's in an engineer's DNA, or maybe people with that type of personality are attracted to engineering in the first place. Engineers like to methodically tease apart difficult problems and find root causes, and in the process they dot the i's and cross the t's and see that it all adds up. Most engineers have gone through lengthy and rigorous training to learn these skills, and they've been rewarded with grades, jobs, and money for achieving excellence. They are masters at precision questioning, finding holes in an argument, and solving complex problems.

Many of the ideas in our workshop and in this book strike engineers as unfamiliar, unintuitive, and not what they're used to doing. The first reaction from many engineers is to try to prove us wrong. And when you think about it, that's okay. That's a natural reaction. We learned quickly that we needed to be very thoughtful about how best to present these ideas for this target audience.

Over the years we've learned a few techniques to help appeal to the most skeptical of engineers and to get them over the hump so that they not only see the value in these ideas but are open to actually making a change:

- **Make it scientific** As you can see throughout this book, we take a logical, scientific approach to explaining these ideas. We take time to explain the reasons why a customer-focused, iterative approach works and what happens when you don't follow this approach. We describe the creation and iteration process as a system in which all the pieces are meaningfully interconnected. Even if a team uses only a few of the techniques, it helps for engineers to see how they fit into a larger whole that is systematic and thought through.

- **Make it experiential** We found that giving people a hands-on experience in our workshop went a long way toward opening the door to seeing the value in these ideas. By watching video footage of customers or, even better, having a handful of real customers answer their questions, people experienced customers saying surprising, unexpected things. By sketching out some ideas, building a paper prototype, and then finding that it didn't make sense to their colleague—never mind to an actual customer—people began to realize the need for customer feedback and iteration and that even if an idea made a ton of sense in their own mind, it may not make sense to anyone else. They were forced to generate multiple alternatives (and grumbled that doing so was pointless) and then realized that the best solution truly was a blend of several of the alternatives they had generated, not just their first good idea, which they probably would have stopped with.

- **Make it visible** It's really helpful for people to run into these ideas continually in their environment, which keeps the ideas visible and offers a growing realization that they are gaining traction. Teams do this by hanging posters on the walls, building museums of customer data, and posting sketches in the hallways. We also handed out bright-green plastic cards to workshop attendees that were printed with key SFE principles and perfectly shaped and sized to fit in a Microsoft badge holder. As people walked around, you would see a flash of green on the reverse side of their badge. This marked them as being part of the SFE "club" and created a sense of shared community. Over time, it created a visible movement across the entire company.

- **Show momentum** We found opportunities to demonstrate momentum across a team, making it evident to everyone on the team that people had bought in and were ready to make a change. At the end of every workshop, we asked everyone to write down, on separate cards, the six most important ideas they got out of the workshop that they thought their team should move forward with. We collected these and used them as the major focus of the debriefing session we held with a team's managers a week or two later. We worked with the managers to create an affinity diagram using the cards, taped them onto butcher paper, and hung the diagram in the team's hallway. Without exception, these diagrams showed a strong consensus about the value of these ideas and enthusiasm for adopting them. The handful of skeptical comments were called out separately, and it was obvious that they were outliers. This approach made the remaining skeptics realize that they were in the minority and helped the rest of the team realize that they were more aligned than they knew and were ready to make a change together.

Interestingly, a strong minority of the engineers we've worked with are not skeptical in the least. In fact, they longed to work this way and were frustrated with their organizations' current processes and approaches. Perhaps a quarter of the engineers we've encountered across nearly every team fall into this category. Without this largely invisible base of support, it may have been impossible to build consensus across a team. But with it, a small chorus in every group was saying "It's about time!" and many of them stepped up to become champions and leaders on their teams.

Collaboration isn't everybody doing everything together

Many teams find that when they work more iteratively and are focused on the customer's end-to-end experience, they require much deeper and more frequent collaboration across the team and among partners. By collaboration, we mean openly giving and receiving feedback, building trust across professional disciplines and partners, allowing (and expecting) ideas to marinate over time, and operating in a more network-oriented team structure rather than one based on a hierarchy.[1]

But when the pendulum swings to encourage more collaborative behavior on teams, we've seen a few teams swing a bit too far and interpret collaboration to mean that everyone does everything together, all of the time—for example, you can't have a meeting without every single team member, subgroup, partner, or discipline represented; developers need to put aside writing code in favor of going on lots of site visits; everyone must participate in writing scenarios and agree on the subtleties of each word; or that every member of the team must be part of every decision. Obviously, this sort of ultracollaborative approach simply doesn't scale, and it doesn't respect the unique expertise that different roles and disciplines bring to the table.

Design by committee doesn't work any better in software than it does in other domains. The point of collaboration is not for everyone to put their fingers in every pie, but to be more flexible about who does what and lean toward being more inclusive in day-to-day work. The goal is to operate as a team, with the common goal of delighting customers by solving their end-to-end needs completely. If you're going to build end-to-end experiences that cross organizational boundaries, clearly you're going to have to collaborate across those boundaries to get your work done. Collaboration is a means to an end.

The four crucial benefits that collaboration can deliver are the following:

- **Team alignment**   Getting buy-in from everyone involved is especially important in early activities, when you are deciding on the customer insights you will pursue, framing them in scenarios, and determining the metrics you will use to measure success. This is doubly important when multiple teams, organizations, or even external partners need to work together to build an end-to-end experience. Everyone on the team doesn't necessarily need to be involved in the scenario-writing process, but everyone should have a chance to review and understand where the team is headed.

- **Smoother integration**   As a project progresses, everyone needs to know how their piece will fit into the end-to-end experience and have direct access to the people they need to work with to smooth out any rough spots as integration progresses. Creating hierarchies or choke-points is often counterproductive and results in the telephone game, where the true message gets distorted the more people it filters through. Let the people involved talk to each other and work things out directly.

- **Harvest the power of many brains**   In many of the activities in the Fast Feedback Cycle, it is beneficial to have different disciplines work together, including developers, testers, program managers, business managers, designers, researchers, and others. There are three reasons for this. First, you are more likely to discover great ideas when a diverse set of people is involved. Second, a diverse working group helps prevent groupthink from occurring. Third, representation from each discipline helps bring more constraints, knowledge, and possibilities to the forefront, enabling better quality decisions.

- **Personal experience**   Some activities, like customer visits and usability tests, are highly experiential and provide direct benefits by having people other than researchers participate in them. The chances of discovering an aha moment or gaining deep personal empathy with a customer are substantially greater through personal experience than by reading the CliffsNotes reports from someone else. It's important that everyone on the team have an opportunity to partake in these experiences and not learn about them only from a report, an email message, or a presentation. This isn't to say that every team member should go on every site visit or usability test, but the majority of the team should go on at least one. If that is not possible, the next best thing is for reports to include photos, video, and audio and to convey as much of the real-life aspects of the experience as possible.

In the Fast Feedback Cycle, collaboration doesn't mean that everyone does everything all of the time. But it does mean that customer delight is everyone's responsibility. Collaboration is about holding the team accountable for working together to delight the customer. It's not about getting one piece of the system working and throwing it over the wall to someone else.

It's difficult to predict who will shine or where

During the final exercise in our workshop, we display a list of the major activities that we've introduced and practiced throughout the day. The list contains entries such as interviewing customers, writing scenarios, brainstorming, sketching, prototyping, and putting together a project schedule. We ask the class to take a long look at the list and to select the one activity that they enjoyed the most. We then go through each activity and call them out one at a time, asking the students to stand up when we call out their favorite.

Now, you might think that what happens would be quite predictable—that all project managers stand up for writing project schedules and driving decisions, program managers for writing scenarios, the marketing team for talking to customers, and designers for generating ideas. But that isn't exactly what happens. Instead, choices can be so unpredictable that the room begins to giggle when people stand up for their favorite part of the class. *"You liked that? You're kidding me, you are good at that? Cool, now I know."*

The distribution of who and how many people choose which activity is eye opening for the team. Usually, a strong contingent loves brainstorming (that particular exercise is very high energy), but among the other activities, the spread of preferences is quite unpredictable. Some teams clearly lean toward divergent activities, while other teams lean toward convergent activities. In some cases, certain activities are not chosen by anyone. We finish the workshop by talking through these balances, or imbalances, and then let the team consider how they would affect their work.

The lesson we've learned is that it's a mistake to stereotype people in the same role or discipline as being talented and interested in the same activities in the Fast Feedback Cycle. While one or two job functions might have a preponderance of interest in a specific activity, a number of people from other roles will also be interested—the tail of the bell curve. You just never know who is going to come up with that brilliant idea, or who is going to become the strongest customer advocate, the best identifier of latent needs, or the best person to help the team shift from diverging to converging.

SFE in action: Diversity, conflict, and creative output

Kent Sullivan, Principal UX Researcher, Microsoft, with Tonya Peck, Chief Talent Officer, POSSIBLE; Cofounder, Locomotive Partners

I have been a design researcher at Microsoft since 1989. Over the years, it has become more and more apparent to me that some teams work well together, seemingly through magic, while others do not. I have seen teams collaborate very easily, sharing work and accountability, while others stumble over basic communication and information sharing.

Recently, I've had the opportunity to investigate this question in depth. As part of that work, Tonya Peck and I created an experiential workshop with the intention of helping teams identify gaps in their behavior while learning about some approachable tools for discussing those gaps and making changes. We presented a short form of this workshop at the Design Management Institute conference in Seattle in 2011 (http://www.dmi.org/dmi/html/conference/designthinking11/DT11PEC.pdf).

A core element of the workshop uses the Basadur Creative Problem Solving Profile (CPSP; https://basadurprofile.com/). This tool assesses individuals' preferences for problem solving. Here's a brief description of the problem-solving styles in the CPSP model:

- **Generator**   Gets things started

- **Conceptualizer**   Puts ideas together

- **Optimizer**   Turns abstract ideas into practical solutions and plans

- **Implementer**   Gets things done

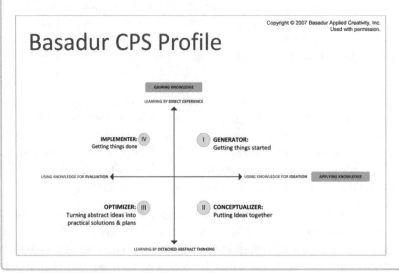

After using the CPSP assessment with a number of teams, we discovered something quite fascinating—the vast majority of people on the engineering teams we modeled had primary quadrants of implementer or optimizer, while a smaller portion of the people were identified as dominant generators or conceptualizers. We also found that the bulk of the generators and conceptualizers were user-experience designers, with the bulk of user-experience researchers distributed between conceptualizers and optimizers.

We noticed that the teams that reported having a high degree of difficulty in creating innovative solutions primarily included optimizers and implementers and had very few, if any, conceptualizers or generators. In contrast, the teams that had greater diversity within the CPSP quadrants (in other words, there were enough generators and conceptualizers to provide some balance to the majority of optimizers and implementers) described situations where innovative solutions came to fruition more easily.

On these more creative teams, we also saw an increased level of conflict. To visualize the type of conflict we're talking about, imagine a discussion between an energetic project manager who wants to account for undone work items and get them on a schedule (the implementer) and a creative designer (a conceptualizer) who comes up with a dozen new ideas every hour.

The teams that got the most benefit from these workshops were the ones that had a relatively balanced mix of styles and were experiencing a lot of spoken and unspoken tension and conflict that were getting in the way. By modeling the team makeup using the CPSP profiles, Tonya and I were able to identify where the greatest tensions most likely existed and were able to bring out those conflicts in a constructive way. No surprise, these tensions existed between the team members who are dominant in opposite quadrants. Specifically, the most conflict occurred between optimizers and generators and between implementers and conceptualizers.

For example, one of the teams we worked with was stuck reaching milestone commitments and deadlines, despite the fact that the team consisted of rock-star employees. We noticed great tension coming from a couple of teammates who crossed the conceptualizer and implementer diagonal axis. The conceptualizer thought that the implementer didn't respect the creative process and was pushing too hard to converge on a solution too early. The implementer thought the conceptualizer didn't respect deadlines and the looming milestones that were agreed to at the beginning of the project. Through an open, moderated conversation, each person started to recognize the assumptions and judgments they were making without checking on the accuracy of those assumptions with each other. The end result was that they realized how much they needed each other on the team and how important it was to give space for diverging and exploring possible design directions while also staying aligned with each other on possible schedule impact. The whole team acknowledged a physical change in the energy, and it went on to hit the deadline with a superhot solution.

We found (as the Basadur CPSP model advises) that the greatest conflicts lie between diagonally opposite problem-solving styles. The creative "magic" here is embracing those opposites and leaning in with attunement and respect rather than avoidance or contempt. The overarching goal is not a friction-free team, but one that consistently experiences healthy creative friction. We consistently found that introducing teams to this model and language accelerated the individual and collective creativity and performance.

Semantics matter

Are you a professional designer? Have you ever found that talking to an engineer about your craft was difficult? If so, you are not alone. One thing we learned, very early on, is that with engineers, the words you use matter.

In the very beginning, when we were experimenting with different content, formats, and instructional design patterns, we inherited a workshop titled "User Experience Design for Other Disciplines." Okay, we confess, it's a terrible name. As you might expect, the people who were attracted to that name were generally those who were looking to understand the design discipline at Microsoft. Some were considering a career change, and others already knew that they wanted to collaborate better with the designers on their team. But that was a relatively small number of people. And to be honest, the individuals who signed up for that course weren't the most senior or the most influential people in the company.

Because our desire was to immerse the engineering population at Microsoft into the world of design thinking and user-centered design, we knew we had to somehow reach a different audience. The early feedback we received on the workshop content told us we were heading in the right direction, all we had to do was get the right people interested and motivated to consider change. The content of the workshop wouldn't matter if we couldn't get the right people to attend in the first place.

We tested a lot of different names, many of which were some variant of "Design Thinking," "Design for Engineers," "User-Centered Design," and so on. Through those trials we discovered that *design* means a lot of different things to a lot of different people. We learned that many engineers have an allergic reaction to the *word* design. Associations such as "artsy, nonproductive, waste of time, and flower-shirted, pot-smoking creatives who are on a different planet and add no value to me" come to mind. Ugh. (And our sincere apologies to anyone reading this who is currently wearing a black turtleneck. Please read on.) What were we to do?

We eventually named the workshop "Scenario-Focused Engineering." This title proved to be much more acceptable to our audience of leaders and technical engineers. The idea of writing scenarios was enjoying a resurgence at the time, so that made the name naturally interesting. And people's general reaction to those words tended to be something like "I can guess what a scenario is, and I can see value in using one to drive an engineering project." The word *scenario* was something concrete they could immediately understand, with no ambiguity or magical fairy dust. In that way, we found our audience to be open to listening to what we had to say. The SFE title has worked well and has served as a Trojan horse of sorts for the meta-topics of user-centered design and design thinking that we introduce.

The title has also failed us in some ways. Once we put "Scenario-Focused Engineering" on the door, some teams tended to give too much weight to the importance of scenarios in the grand scheme. (We talk about this phenomenon specifically in a previous lesson in this chapter.) We never did find a perfect solution to this particular naming problem.

Another lesson we've learned is about the power of aligning a group of people on a shared context and new vocabulary. We learned this fairly early, both on our own team and by watching teams go through the SFE workshop. After the workshop, we would see the new vocabulary begin to emerge in teams. We began to hear words and phrases such as "scenario," "empathy," "diverge and converge," "less is more," "you are not the customer," "marinate," or "let's iterate one more time" as part of a team's vernacular. Even teams that did not make dramatic changes to their processes still found tremendous value in the workshop because it normalized terms and created a shared language across their team. The importance of using words to get a team on the same page and communicating more smoothly was evident. The new "language" that teams developed created a sense of tribe among team members and was an important part of establishing a culture around the iterative process that focused on deep customer empathy.

The role of leaders

In our ongoing work with teams, it's been clear that teams that make the biggest changes are those with strong leadership—with leaders who cared deeply about their customers.

Leaders: What got you here, won't get you there

Even though the leaders we worked with knew they had to change their behaviors, we witnessed over and over again how hard it was for them to step into a new relationship with their team and nurture a customer-focused, iterative approach. We believe that the root problem is that these leaders have spent many years acting as decision makers. If someone has a question, these leaders are supposed to have the answer. Leaders have probably spent many, many years in the industry. And, in fact, they probably became a leader precisely because they did have some customer empathy, business savvy, and the ability to come up with creative solutions. As we mentioned in the previous chapter, these successful leaders have spent many years living the life of a HiPPO.

And when you live the life of a HiPPO, you get used to people listening to you and doing what you say. The trouble is that if a team truly wants to operate in a customer-focused way, the HiPPO needs to let customer feedback, not his or her personal opinions, drive decisions at many points. The discovery of great solutions is most likely to occur in a trusted group where you encourage crazy ideas, build on the ideas of others, and say the words "Yes, and . . ." a lot. The value of an idea is judged by customer feedback and not by whose idea it is, regardless of whether it comes from the newest hire or the most senior team leader. The customer-focused culture you aspire to gets messed up when a HiPPO is continually asserting his or her opinion, making decisions, and trying to drive the ship in the same way as always.

It's not that leaders don't need to make decisions anymore, far from it. A good leader is still responsible for the team's business strategy and sets crucial guardrails and constraints within which the team must work. Leaders need to focus their team on a small set of target customers and make the bet on which customers and businesses are most lucrative. They may even act as tiebreakers from time to time when several solutions are available that seem equivalent or when a key tradeoff must be made. But for the bulk of the formation of detailed product plans and execution, leaders need to let go and trust in the iterative process. They must trust their team to talk to customers, listen to customer needs, come up with ideas, get feedback on those ideas, and iterate them until customers are delighted. A leader's role becomes one of coaching the team to ensure that the right steps of due diligence are followed and to hold the team accountable for delivering compelling end-to-end experiences. Leaders need to make the shift from knowing the right answers to knowing which are the right questions.

As former HiPPOs, we can tell you how difficult it is to let go, to think of our personal opinions as being no more and no less valid than anyone else's on the team, to accept that our instincts in knowing what customers want are not always accurate. Making the transition from being a person who is highly influential in the planning and creation of a product to being a coach, guide, and customer advocate who relentlessly tracks customer feedback and holds the team accountable for delighting the customer is very difficult. The pivotal moment in this change is when a leader realizes that her job is no longer to control the plan but to provide direction and to set the boundaries that enable the team to iterate the plan as quickly and efficiently as possible.

Here are specific areas where leaders have particular trouble or where they make mistakes that hamper their teams:

- Allowing early iterations to truly inform product plans proved tricky for many leaders. Some leaders insist that their teams develop complete, final plans before they have really done much iteration. It's tough for leaders to have the patience to allow a few iterations to happen without having a clear plan. It's even harder for them to realize that the initial plan might be wrong and might need to change, possibly drastically. While the rational side of your brain knows that it's better to allow iteration to happen up front—rather than find out much later that you built something no one wants or you have major issues to resolve—it's tough for leaders to have the patience to last through the ambiguity of the early iterations.

- It is also common for leaders to push teams to make decisions too soon, before the customer need and value are clearly articulated and validated with feedback. It's very difficult for a team to report on the feedback and progress of three solution ideas when the manager is demanding to know exactly what the team is building and becomes frustrated with what seems to be an ambiguous answer.

- One of the more unfortunate situations we saw involved leaders who empowered their teams to use a customer-focused, iterative approach but then imposed their own plan when what the team came up with didn't match what the leaders had expected. This created a huge amount of ill will on the team because it essentially made the customer-focused iteration a sham process that was ultimately ignored or greatly discounted. The lesson learned is "Don't disempower a team after you empower it."

- Letting go of a completely predictable schedule is one of the hardest cultural shifts that the managers of an Agile team need to make. Managers naturally want to know what you're going to build, how long it's going to take, how many people you need to do it, and what the end result is going to look like. We all know that it's impossible to know all of these things in advance, but still somehow we pretend that we do and make our best guesses, if only to satisfy the boss. The reality, of course, is that there will be plenty of gotchas and mistakes and miscalculations and improvements that need to be dealt with throughout the project. The only question is whether you plan for those up front, allow yourself to be surprised during the course of the project, or feel bad when your first ideas don't pan out as well as you thought they would. Seasoned managers know this, too: they know full well that the team will never ship what it originally intended to build, and usually leaders are quite happy as long as the biggest, most important investment areas land successfully. The rest is just extra. So stop fooling yourself, and instead of "committing" to a particular plan by a particular day, commit to getting a particular piece of the plan working to a high level of quality before you pick off the next major piece of work. This doesn't mean that you don't build a plan. Indeed, a plan is critical so that everyone can coordinate and be rowing in the same direction. But you have to have the humility to believe that your plan is imperfect and to leave space to make adjustments as you iterate.

The lesson learned is that leaders have to change, too, and their shift may be the hardest of all. They need to empower their teams to make decisions and not require teams to run ideas by the boss before they make a decision. They must embrace the iterative process and trust that it will lead to an optimal solution as quickly as humanly possible. You might be able to build a crummy solution faster, but is that really going to get you where you want to go?

You can't fake a business strategy

We can't count how many times we've talked with a bunch of group managers prior to running a workshop for their teams and found that they can't clearly articulate who their target customers are or just describe their target customer extremely broadly ("anyone with a computer" or "enterprise customers," for example). Digging a little deeper, it's often not entirely clear what their business strategy is either. Or, more likely, they have several reasonable directional ideas but haven't really done the work to test those ideas with customers or even to take the time to build consensus among the team's leadership about what direction they should try first. Without a clear strategy, it's no wonder that they have trouble identifying their target customers and crisply communicating that strategy to their teams.

Later, we'd hear from individuals on these teams that they didn't know who their target customers were and never got a straight answer when they asked their leaders, so they felt like they couldn't really use customer-focused approaches. The more industrious team members made up reasonable target customers on their own, thereby creating their own version of a strategic direction in the absence of an official one, which sometimes resulted in several competing customer targets across the team. Members of these teams commonly reported frustration about team politics and disagreement and confusion about what were the most important things to work on and how to make progress. Not having a clear direction certainly does make prioritization very difficult. Decisions become unstable and unwind when someone changes his or her mind or when different people are in the room. These teams eventually build something, but it is painful to watch and not very efficient, and none of the products they ship are particularly outstanding.

How you build a business strategy is outside the scope of this book, and we list several great references in Appendix C that we encourage you to read. But our lesson is that having a clear business strategy isn't optional; you can't fake it. A team needs a clear direction to make forward progress in an efficient manner and then either confirm that the direction is viable or to use data to instigate making a change. Leaders need to communicate that direction so that everyone is working toward the same North Star and with a shared mission.

You can't overcommunicate

Nearly all of the leaders we've worked with appreciate the fact that they need to communicate a huge amount of information to their teams as part of the shift to SFE practices. Whether it's announcing changes to schedules and tools or reinforcing behaviors they wanted to see, there is plenty to talk about. Leaders assured us that they were getting the word out.

However, when we talked to individuals on various teams later, the message we heard was invariably very different. Those folks felt like they still didn't know what's going on. They didn't know who their target customers are, what scenarios had been prioritized, or what they should be working on. In a more severe case, a schedule was created, but substantial portions of the team missed the first deadline because they had no idea there was even a deadline coming up.

When we've dug into a few of these situations, leaders were always surprised. They agreed that they could certainly do more to communicate, but they felt as though the major messages had been more than adequately communicated, in some cases multiple times, and didn't believe that the team felt so uninformed. In fact, leaders worried that they were going to start sounding repetitive, that the team was going to tune them out for saying the same things over and over again. Yet we never heard a single team complain about too much communication, too much repetition, or anything remotely like that. Sometimes, the problem was that the message was delivered only once, maybe in an all-hands meeting or in a long status email. But it often seemed that it was just a matter of not enough repetition, and the simple truth that not everyone reads every single email or attends every meeting.

Leaders who do a better job with communication realize that they need to rally the troops and be cheerleaders, not just relay information. Often they delegate this role to a key lieutenant who is in charge of beating the drum. Some teams create catch phrases or rallying cries. Others clearly articulate the team's directives or create a short list of principles. The best leaders found regular, predictable ways to get information out, whether through a weekly email, all-hands meetings, or demos at the end of every iteration. These simple, memorable, repetitive messages helped keep people on track and keep the organization's priorities and key milestones at the top of everyone's mind.

The lesson we learned is that you can't overdo communication. Overcommunicate, beat the drum.

The way to convince an executive . . .

How do you convince an executive that design is important? We have tried lots and lots of different approaches. Although some tech companies do have a culture and organizational structure that makes customer-focused design a leadership mantra, many do not. We've seen many talented people attempt to push inside their company the notion that design must be at the center and therefore you must place trusted designers at the highest levels of the organization so that they can implement a cultural shift toward design-centricity. That might be a great end goal for some, and may even be a recipe for success, but we have never seen that strategy work unless the top executive has already decided to drive that change.

Brute force and even logic will not work. The bottom line is that the leader who is going to drive change must have a sense of urgency that the long-term business is not as healthy as previously thought or that there is tremendous additional value that can be captured ahead of the competition. In class, we are very careful to frame the changes needed for customer focus as one leg of a stool. The other legs that you need are business and technology. So changing to a customer-focused approach is not about losing any of those existing assets or skills but about expanding your skills in developing team-wide customer empathy and then using that empathy to create compelling end-to-end customer experiences.

If you see advantages for your team in embracing some of the principles in this book, yet your leadership doesn't see it that way, is resisting, or is unwilling to change, here are a few things you can try. There's no single recipe for success, at least that we've been able to discover, but we have had a lot of success working with executives by using different combinations of these strategies.

Experiential approach   The best way to get someone to appreciate the power and potential of a good design process is to let them experience it firsthand. Among other institutions, the d.school at Stanford University has an excellent executive-education program that teaches professionals the techniques and values of design thinking using an experiential approach.

There are a number of interesting exercises that your team can do with a professional facilitator or just on its own. The "wallet" exercise provides an introduction to design thinking and is used at the Stanford d.school to experience how paper prototyping a new wallet for a colleague can be a productive approach for a difficult task.[2] The "marshmallow tower" challenge is another exercise used to help teams quickly experience the process of creativity and innovation.[3] In this exercise, teams are given a limited amount of time to build the tallest tower they can using only marshmallows, tape, string, and spaghetti. Invariably, the team that builds the tallest tower is usually the one that brainstorms, collaborates, prototypes, and iterates over many options.

The biggest blocking issue with these experiential approaches is the amount of time they require. From the point of view of an executive (who in this case is your customer, right?), these hands-on experiences are costly in terms of time, requiring anywhere from a half-day to a week. To take this much time out for something that is foreign and unproven (to them) is often a deal breaker. If it's improbable that you'll be able to convince an executive to invest this much time, perhaps you can identify a trusted lieutenant who can instead.

Recruit the trusted lieutenant   If you can identify someone who the executive trusts, it's usually easier to get this person's time and attention to turn him or her into a champion of design thinking. Often, these lieutenants are on the lookout for new and interesting ways to advance the business and their own careers, and they may be more motivated to take the time to hear what you have to say and perhaps even to attend an experiential workshop. The advice of a trusted lieutenant is a powerful way to build buy-in. It's even better if you can find several.

Start from the bottom up   One of the reasons the SFE workshop was adopted by so many teams at Microsoft is that we used a grassroots approach. The general pattern we followed was to first hold an open enrollment class, available to anyone. From that class, future champions would emerge. These were passionate people (albeit not particularly senior in the organizational hierarchy) who became enamored with the concepts we presented and who wanted to help their teams make a difference. They asked us if we would be willing to give the workshop to just their team. Our answer was always yes . . . but we told them that they first had to work from inside their team to develop the desire and sense of urgency up through the leadership ranks. We might offer to meet with a few other champions to help build a base of support in that team. Eventually, we would receive an email message several weeks or months later saying that the triad (program management, test, and development leaders) would like to speak to us about the SFE workshop and whether it would be appropriate for their team. During that first leadership meeting, we gave an overview of SFE and the key challenges of adopting it. For large teams, we arranged for team leaders to attend a half-day or full-day experiential workshop. In this way, the leadership team had the opportunity not only to learn about and experience Scenario-Focused Engineering but also to discuss which principles were more or less important for their team and to give us guidance so that we could customize the workshop to fit the team's specific needs. This leadership workshop was an essential way for leaders to be exposed to the depth of these ideas, get hands-on experience, and create consensus among the group of team leaders for how to move forward.

Data approach   Many executives respond well to data. They want to see proof that there is a favorable cost vs. benefit and ROI for whatever you are proposing. To be brutally honest, we never had great success with this approach. We were never able to put together the killer data set that categorically proved to an analytical person that if you embrace customer focus and iterative techniques, you will be better off. We showed some analyses that correlated companies known for good design with stock prices, revenue, or market share. But correlation isn't causation, there are always counter examples, and an analytical person can always poke holes in the data or the conclusions.

That said, we never went into a meeting with an executive without an ample supply of backup data. We just wouldn't necessarily start with the data, nor would we rely on the data to be the convincing factor. It just never worked for us.

Defog the vanity metrics   Data did help, however, when either us (or, more likely, the champion who had been working on the team) presented data about that specific team, its customers, marketplace, and competitors. The idea is to defog any and all vanity data that tells everyone how great the team is doing. The revenue, sales, and even survey data might all look quite positive. But show the leaders a multimedia presentation with their own customers displaying frustration, anger, or annoyance with their product, and then contrast that with customers showing love and loyalty for a competitor, and you may get some attention. In Chapter 1, "Why delight matters," we talked about how in the team workshop we spend a good amount of time having participants list products they love and discuss why that is so. And then, in stark contrast, we have the room discuss "What are people saying about your product?" For many, that discussion creates an aha moment.

Read a book   We've seen executives become curious and have a strong thirst for understanding why it is that some companies tend to continually design great stuff for their customers. Many will do their own research and reading. If you have the opportunity, you may be able to recommend one or two books that you find relevant to your team and situation. When Tim Brown's book *Design for Change* was first published, we gladly gave it to any leader who showed interest. We encountered some executives who read the recent biography of Steve Jobs to better understand the magic of Apple. A new book that we are recommending lately is *Outside In* by Harley Manning and Kerry Bodine.

And, of course, there is this book. Obviously, it hadn't been written when we developed the SFE workshop. But maybe it will be helpful for some. Part I is designed to be approachable as a quick introduction.

Just do it   We've discovered that grassroots efforts can go a long way. If you don't or can't get top-down support from leadership, do what you can at your own job and level. Pick some of the techniques in this book and use them. Enlist the two or three people you work most closely with. When you are successful, others will notice and want to follow. Of course, you are a bit limited alone. You can't get an entire engineering team to build prototypes and iterate quickly if they haven't bought in to everything involved. And you may need to be creative about how you manage your schedule. But it's certainly possible for you to quickly draw sketches and ask teammates opinions before committing to details. You can certainly raise your hand in a meeting and simply ask, *"Why are we building that? Is there a customer in mind or a particular need that is being solved? Oh, really? Would it be okay if we took a few minutes to quickly see whether we can think of any other possible options?"* Or you can go into the world to collect some qualitative and quantitative data on your customer. That data is often very interesting for a team, and once it exists, people will be curious. Share and keep referring back to that data to help drive daily decisions around you. Many have found that one of the easiest and most meaningful techniques to start using is to write a scenario describing a crucial customer problem, sketch a few storyboards, and use those as a tool to influence and align partner teams without getting into the weeds of arguing on implementation details.

Vote with your feet   This may not be practical for many people, and it is a last resort. But if you are deeply passionate about focusing on the customer, feel that your team and leadership have a different view, and are failing to lead them to a more customer-centered view, you always have the option to leave for a team with the same values and ideas about business, customers, and product development that you do. After all, business is business. Some succeed and many fail. If you discover that you are not on what you perceive to be a winning team, and you cannot affect the changes to make it a winning team, go find a winning team and join it. Everyone will be happier.

Managing change

Change is hard. We were often humbled by that fact. Here are some things we've learned about change.

Teams with sustained focus from leaders make bigger changes

Teams that have passionate, sustained, long-term support from their leaders are the ones that make the biggest changes, with broad adoption and large-scale changes to their culture. We figured out right away, when we started teaching teams, that team leaders needed to deeply understand and accept SFE ideas for a team to get anywhere. We learned over time that an initial burst of passion and buy-in was not really the important part. The teams that made the biggest leaps in their practices did so because their top leaders, often a vice president, director, or general manager, had strong conviction and drive about leading the team through this shift, and they sustained that focus over years, not just weeks or even months. They had long-term plans that counted on this shift and were able to create a sense of urgency on their teams that this shift was essential and must happen now. They proved the old adage that "you get what you measure," and used metrics, project reviews, and a focus on scenarios to keep their teams focused.

The best leaders reiterated their goals and expectations in nearly every communication—in email, at all-hands meetings, in project reviews, in one-on-one conversations with their direct reports—and they formalized those expectations in the schedule, in team goals, and in personnel review criteria. They kept their focus on the changes they wanted to see, kept it at the top of their mind, and they held the team accountable and gave it feedback when they saw behavior that wasn't aligned with their expectations. Leaders changed their own behavior in project reviews and other interactions with the team to ensure that they were practicing what they preached. When things got tough or there were bumps in the road, these leaders didn't abandon their goals. Instead, they helped the team see a setback as valuable learning on the journey and encouraged the team to iterate and keep at it. Most importantly, they were not distracted from their top-line goals by the next shiny object, whether it was a competitive wrinkle, a new technology, or less-than-glowing customer feedback on their latest iteration. Leadership focus on customers and iteration continued alongside whatever else was happening in the landscape. Leaders who did these things rocked it, and the results showed.

On the other hand, a few leaders we worked with treated the workshop day more as a fun "morale event"—after all, the workshop got rave reviews, was highly interactive, and had teams brainstorming and developing ideas based directly on the team's own target customers. Heck, their team might even come up with a breakthrough product idea right in class! These leaders believed the ideas we taught were all goodness, motherhood, and apple pie and wanted to expose their teams, hoping that some of it would rub off. Some leaders had the impression that their teams already worked this way, which was true some of the time, and saw the class mostly as a refresher. Overall, they thought that maybe their team would pick up and adopt some good changes, and the workshop certainly wouldn't do any harm. Unsurprisingly, what actually happened in these cases was that a team would see some incremental benefits, but their leader did not have huge expectations, so this was perceived as a successful outcome for many of them.

For only a couple of teams did their leaders truly not understand what customer-focused iteration was about, despite a conversation we held with them ahead of the training day. Those workshop days were painful—for instructors, for leaders, and for their teams—as the depth of the disconnects surfaced and became obvious to everyone over the course of the day's discussions. In those cases, we probably did more harm than good—stirring up a team to start thinking differently about how it went about building products—because its leadership had no intention to change their approach at all.

For the majority of teams, the top-level leaders had passion and a strong desire for driving a customer-focused change on their teams. They made the time and effort needed to take their management team through a special "leadership edition" of the SFE workshop a priority, and they supported the underlying principles we presented. They supported (and paid for) their entire team to go through the workshop. But problems came up weeks or months later, when those high-level leaders moved on to other urgent issues and stopped visibly following through on the changes they had initiated. In their minds, they had set the direction, delegated the responsibility for team-wide change to their middle-level managers, and assumed all was well. In these situations, it became difficult for the middle-level managers to drive change because the team did not see support for change coming from the top. The top leaders on these teams were the most disappointed: they had assumed big change was underway and were let down when they realized that the actual changes were smaller and slower than they had hoped for. They had underestimated the difficulty of change.

The bottom line is that sustained leadership, clear expectations, constant communication, and changing the way success is measured are major factors for successfully leading a team through this change. It takes a lot longer than you think to overcome old habits, and both managers and individuals need ongoing, clear signals from leadership that the effort and anxiety inherent in changing things is going to be worth it. If the leadership team isn't fully committed to adopting these ideas, the large-scale, long-term change you may be hoping for is not going to happen.

Middle managers are the hardest to bring onboard

It wasn't especially hard to convince rank-and-file members of each team to give Scenario-Focused Engineering a try. We quickly became pretty good at taking a room of (sometimes) skeptical engineers to the point where they could see that making changes might help them make better products.

It also wasn't that difficult to show the value of customer-focused practices to higher-level leaders. They tend to take a longer-term, strategic view of their products and business and saw the inherent value of getting closer to customers and using customer feedback to fuel creativity. Most already understood the customer-focused, iterative approach intuitively.

We noticed, however, that group managers (middle managers) had the most difficult time seeing the value of SFE. To be more precise, they had difficulty seeing the value with enough confidence to outweigh the inherent risk of change. After all, they were being asked to consider changing the processes, tooling, and culture of their team. That's a lot of change, and that made them weigh the risks very carefully. Change can be difficult and scary.

We realized that middle managers had the most to lose. They are the ones who feel responsible for executing the changes that are explored in the workshop. For them, embracing the iterative patterns of SFE represents a difficult and risky proposition, and if it didn't work and they still didn't deliver the right product on time, they were accountable. We found three important factors that helped middle managers get onboard:

- **Leader support** Middle managers need confidence that their own manager believes in these ideas and genuinely wants them to pursue changes to build products that resonate more deeply with customers. They need to know that if they make some dramatic changes in how the team goes about building products, that those changes will be rewarded and not punished, even if results are not obvious right away. Without hearing a strong message from their management, and without support and encouragement from key players on their team, middle managers are incented to keep up the status quo and not make any real changes. It's essential to ensure visible buy-in and support from higher-level leaders.

- **Active buy-in** It's not enough for high-level leaders to buy in and dictate that the team should adopt these ideas; team managers need to buy in as well. We began to require a preworkshop session with each team's set of group managers at which we presented the high-level concepts of the workshop and what would be required of them to make changes successfully. At the end of this session we asked them to make an informed go/no-go decision regarding the rollout of the workshop to their team. These manager meetings became a critical part of the rollout of the team workshop because they gave managers time to think about the concepts and make a conscious, active decision to move forward (or not). In fact, we learned this lesson so strongly that we refused to schedule a workshop for a team until we had a preworkshop meeting, the middle managers had actually shown up, and they agreed to support and participate in the workshop with their teams. Further, we made it a practice during the workshop to have one of these managers stand up about 45 minutes into the workshop and explain to the team why they have asked everyone to spend their valuable time with us on that day. (Why not have the managers kick-off the workshop? Because as many as 20 percent of attendees arrive a few minutes late, and it is much more important that everyone hear from their manager than from us.)

- **Support them with champions** Passionate champions were important in helping managers continue to see the value and need for change. These champions were typically highly respected individual contributors (perhaps an architect, a strong program manager, or a particularly influential developer). We supported these champions closely, and through these relationships we saw a healthy tension between the risk-averse middle managers, who were faced with executing change, and the optimistic influencers, who were able to rally the team around the value of customer-focused iteration and figure out how to make process changes happen.

Harness champions as change agents

Even when leadership support wasn't crystal clear, passionate champions were a powerful force for change. Almost all teams had champions with fire in their belly that deeply believed in customer-focused iteration and were driven to do whatever it took to get their team using these tools. Sometimes they were experts in some aspect of the process or a specific technique, but often they were just passionate people with a bent toward being change agents, eager to learn and figure it out on the fly.

Champions are needed to figure out the pragmatic steps for adoption: which techniques should be used by the team, what's mandatory and what's optional, and what are the implications for team systems such as schedules, tools, and processes. For this reason, we sometimes call these champions *operationalizers*, because they take charge of figuring out the practical details of how to operationalize Scenario-Focused Engineering on their teams.

The champion role is ideally served by an individual who is senior enough to have the trust and respect of top leaders and with sufficient authority to make decisions stick. Yet, they also need to be close enough to team members doing the work to understand the realities of day-to-day activities. They act as a critical liaison, translating the desires of leadership into an actionable plan for the rest of the team. They might have a formal leadership role, such as a lead or a manager on the team, or they may be an individual contributor who acts as a thought leader.

Often, champions provide the impetus that encourages top-level leaders to continue talking about customer-focused iteration after the workshop. They feed them key ideas to reinforce with the team as they see needs arise in their interactions with the team. Champions are particularly effective when they have a close relationship with their leaders and are also often pivotal in helping a team decide to sign up for the workshop in the first place. The best champions have a touch of salesperson in them—a dynamic personality that's fearless—as well as patience and a willingness to keep working with reluctant individuals or skeptics until they come around.

On some teams, this role is served by a single individual. On other teams, usually larger organizations, a group of people work collaboratively to coordinate and encourage changes across different parts of the team. Either way, these folks are essential for understanding the specifics of adopting this approach, for adapting it to their team, for helping explain these ideas in detail to all the members of the team, and for beating the drum to keep communication going and to keep people moving.

We've found that every organization already has change agents who are ready to go above and beyond for a cause they believe in. They fall into a few different categories. First, not all of them have the authority or depth of experience needed to be successful in their ambitions; these people are most effective when they are paired with a more senior person and can act as a powerful duo. Some have a lot of motivation but not a ton of direct experience with these new techniques, so while their learning curve is steep, their passion usually makes up for this, and they are still quite effective.

Some teams have passionate change agents in place who have been attempting to stimulate similar changes for years or are already deep believers in the tenets of a customer-focused, iterative approach. Some of these people have successfully gathered an enclave of like-minded individuals and are the thought leaders behind enormously successful teams or subteams, sometimes opting to fly under the radar or who call their approach the team's secret sauce. Other times these change agents have been frustrated, knowing what the team should be doing, but finding their attempts to influence reduced to tilting at windmills, feeling powerless to affect the depth of change they know is needed. Either way, these individuals are critical to identify and harness if broad, team-wide adoption of these ideas is to be successful.

In particular, we've learned that it is essential to identify these people when we first start working with a team and to bring them into the conversation early. After all, they have already been down this road and have experience on this specific team about which approaches work and which don't, what the roadblocks might be, and all of the intricacies of the team's existing culture, processes, and tools.

We learned this lesson the hard way. One of the first large organizations we worked with started by bringing its entire executive leadership team through a full workshop. They liked what they experienced and then asked us to start bringing their individual engineering teams through workshops. From our perspective, this seemed like a great start, with strong leadership support leading the way.

But from the perspective of the change agents already on the teams, this didn't look rosy at all. Think about it from the perspective of a person who has already been independently driving a very similar agenda. They start asking themselves, *"Doesn't our leadership know that we've already been pushing these ideas for years? Is this a not-so-subtle hint that we've been doing it wrong? Or is this confirmation that we're just not very effective? Why didn't they ask us to lead this training instead? We know just as much, more in some cases, than these people they're bringing in."*

Sure enough, many of the existing change agents became upset and angry, and some even started campaigning against the need for training or for team change. But once they attended the workshop, the majority realized that we were all aiming at the same goal, although they still had some pretty ruffled feathers. And these were the people who should have been the strongest supporters and the biggest assets on the team for figuring out how to put these ideas into practice on a team-wide scale. Yipes!

This lesson deeply informed our engagements with future teams. We've made sure that we always identify and include a team's natural champions from the beginning so that they fully buy in and can help direct and focus the change process for the team. Champions have ended up being instrumental in customizing the customer data used in the workshop as well as contributing and fine-tuning the workshop topics. Several were invited to serve as coaches during the training day itself to help answer questions in a visible leadership role. All of this adds up to making the training day that much more effective for a team. But, more important, it harnesses the passion and motivation of change agents to become visible, empowered champions for driving change throughout the team in the weeks and months afterward.

There is a limit to what champions can do on their own, however. When big conflicts come up— perhaps a more significant schedule change is proposed, or a long-standing process needs to be adjusted, or the need for a well-articulated target customer is questioned—sometimes even the most passionate champions hit the wall in what they are able to accomplish. As we discussed earlier, without visible, sustained support from top leadership, teams become confused about whether making the shift to customer-focused iteration is still a priority, especially as people begin to realize the more challenging implications of what needs to change.

You can't grow a foot overnight

We've developed a deep appreciation for how long it takes to shift behaviors, team culture, tools, systems, and institutionalized ideas about how to get things done. We've known from the beginning that this was going to be a long journey for teams we've worked with, but we have been surprised at the depth of the implications that stem from implementing these seemingly straightforward ideas and how long it takes to build these skills and mindsets on a team. Leaders and managers consistently underestimate what it takes to start working this way.

Early on, we noticed that many teams had unrealistic expectations about how much change would occur, how long the change would take, and how quickly they would see results in the quality of the products they shipped. The more passionate champions tended to downplay the magnitude of change needed and to be bullish about the team's ability to snap to a new way of doing things.

Looking back, as we've watched teams go through this transition, they've grown a lot more slowly than they (or we) expected. We've learned and observed that old habits die hard and that change takes a lot of work and sustained effort. Teams hoped to be proficient and comfortable with these new techniques by the time they started their next release cycle, but the reality is that several major release cycles were needed to make enough of the transition that the teams began to see clear results from this new way of working.

Appendix A details a list of the 10 most important capabilities we've identified as being central to adopting Scenario-Focused Engineering. We didn't see any team become good at all 10 capabilities at once—most teams followed a path through a set of stages.

SFE in action: One step at a time

Erin Chapple, Partner Group Program Manager, Microsoft Windows Server

In the technology industry it is not surprising to find people who are very passionate about technology. The defining aspects of engineers are often a combination of the passion for their domain, their pride in contributing to the industry, and their desire to deliver innovation to our customers. To deliver first-class, customer-focused products, the challenge is how to channel an engineer's passion, pride, and desire toward the customer. By focusing on specific customers and scenarios rather than on a collection of technologies or features, a product transforms into solutions that address real customer challenges. Over the last several releases, our team has been on a journey toward realizing this Scenario-Focused Engineering approach.

As part of the multiyear journey to embrace the principles of SFE, the team has undergone dramatic changes, both culturally and in our processes. In hindsight, while the changes seem to have taken longer than I would have expected when we began, given the size of the team (more than 1,000 engineers) and the size and complexity of the codebase (more than 25

---

distinct technology areas), we are actually quite happy with the consistent movement toward customers the team has achieved. At the beginning of this journey, we were perhaps a bit naïve, thinking that within a few months, or certainly by the end of our first release, the team would have transformed into a well-oiled, customer-focused machine. But in reality, that change has taken several releases and has followed a pattern that I believe is worthwhile describing here.

Step one: Pivoting from technology planning to scenario planning

The first step was to transform the way in which we planned. Historically each technology team would plan in relative isolation. They are the experts in their technology. They understand what was delivered in the last release, where the industry is going, how customers are using their technology, and from this they could easily create the next set of features to enable in the product. Often, this list was in part features that spilled over from the last release and in part new functionality. The end result was a solid plan for how to evolve the technology itself. What it lacked, however, was a focus on how the customer would use the technology. What was the end-to-end deployment experience? Operationally, what was the experience? Our first step in channeling the engineering passion was to define scenarios that captured the problems that our customers faced and the experience we could provide that would delight them with the next version of the product. This resulted in a plan focused on both the experience and the underlying features necessary to enable it. So we were done, right?

Step two: Extending scenario planning into scenario execution

While our plan improved dramatically, the end product did not. The challenge was that as we moved from planning to execution, the pull of the technology was simply too strong for our existing processes. We had the scenarios defined and in focus, but as development moved into full swing, the engineers fell back to talking about the features and the validation plan was focused on functionality and not scenarios. The second step in our journey was to put in place the necessary process to ensure that the scenarios were front and center throughout the development life cycle. Our regular project reviews ensured that we were reviewing the status of the scenarios. Our customer validation plans involved getting the customers to deploy scenarios and provide feedback. Our internal validation efforts focused around success metrics for scenarios. Because the organization was truly going through a cultural change, the focus on keeping scenarios front and center was critical in preventing the default wiring from kicking in and returning focus to the technology. So we were done, right?

Step three: Getting the scenarios right

While the product we delivered was by far the most customer-centric to date, the end product still seemed to be missing something. Upon reflection, we realized that the way we were planning was largely based on the original technology teams. While these teams were important internally for how we delivered the product, the customer didn't make these distinctions in their usage of the product. Each technology area had become more customer-centric, but we were still falling short on the scenarios that customers wanted to enable. The third step was to break out of our technology areas and think more from the point of view of why customers buy the product and what they want to enable. This meant that both planning and execution needed to happen across technology areas. This was a huge shift for the team, but given the foundation we had laid in the previous releases, teams now had more of a scenario mindset, and creating virtual scenario teams to define and then track the progress of development was a logical extension of how we had worked in the previous release.

At this point in our journey toward using Scenario-Focused Engineering, I believe we have started to realize the benefits of the approach. Our product is no longer defined by the technologies within it but by what scenarios it enables for our customers. I do not believe we would have reached this point had we not focused on the first step toward making this shift, reflected and learned from the results, and then refocused on the next step. We will continue this approach with the goal of always increasing the end result—a first-class, customer-centric product.

Pilot with a small team first

Several teams have found that piloting with a small "tiger" team is a great way to get started, gain familiarity with these ideas, and see how they land in their own environment. This approach is surprisingly productive and has lots of benefits:

- **Safe**   A pilot team can try things out in a contained environment, where it can fail without the risk of hurting larger business priorities.

- **Focused**   On a small pilot project, leaders have the ability to minimize the surface area of issues the team needs to deal with. A leader might even choose to protect the pilot team from some of the real-world problems that can arise on "normal" projects, such as resourcing, dependencies, firefighting, and (to some extent) the time pressure to deliver.

- **Experiential learning**   Pilot projects allow teams to gain experience in the practicalities of meeting with customers, iterating, prototyping, scheduling, and so on, and to develop a visceral, firsthand understanding of how these activities play out in the team's domain.

- **Inform broader adoption**   The pilot team can not only try out these new approaches but also translate how they will work with the team's existing tools and processes. Through this, the pilot team ends up developing a set of standards and examples that the broader team can reference and adopt, which makes for a smoother rollout to the larger team.

- **Confidence**   Seeing a pilot team succeed helps build confidence that these ideas will work for the larger team.

- **Build a stable of experts**   Finally, when it comes time for the larger team to adopt the Fast Feedback Cycle, a crew of well-informed and practiced champions will be in place ready to help. For this reason, it's worth being mindful when a pilot team is set up to choose people who will make good coaches later on.

For a variety of reasons, small pilot teams tend to perform extremely well. Perhaps they are more motivated because they feel like an A team. Or maybe it's just fun working on a team that is isolated from some of the issues of the daily grind. Small teams do tend to have an easier time building team-wide customer empathy, aligning on goals and success metrics, and developing a collaborative approach. Even when pilot teams have an extremely short time frame to operate in (one standout was a single "two week experiment"), they serve as a very helpful bridge toward a broader team rollout.

The change is bigger than you think

All the teams we've worked with have grossly underestimated the depth of change needed to adopt Scenario-Focused Engineering and how tightly wound they were in their habits, systems, tools, and processes. Cultural and attitudinal shifts are equally massive. They challenge core values about the "best ways" to do things, unwritten rules about how decisions are made, and other deeply held values and beliefs. Changing the engineering approach isn't only about changing the upfront design process. It affects every person on the team in every role, imposing new demands and expectations from leaders and managers. Even teams that are committed from the get-go remark that adopting these ideas takes longer and is more challenging than they had anticipated.

Months, or sometimes even years, afterward, we would check in with teams and hear back that putting these ideas into practice was much, much harder than they had thought. They had tried to make a big change, but only a few smaller aspects really stuck, or adoption was spotty, with some teams or subteams really getting great value from the approach, but others running into roadblocks and eventually settling back into old habits. Some managers were big believers, others were on the fence, and, unsurprisingly, their teams followed suit.

 MINDSHIFT

Learn the science of change management. People have studied the science behind driving change across large organizations (called "change management") for decades. Notably, pretty much every expert says that the vast majority of attempts to introduce change into an organization fail—as often as 95 percent of the time. Over the years we have developed a strong appreciation for John Kotter's work on the science of leading change in organizations. His eight-step model for leading change rings true with our experience, especially the need to establish a sense of urgency for change. We encourage you to read some books on this topic listed in Appendix C. Getting groups of people to collectively shift their behavior is dramatically harder than changing one person, and there is science and experience that you can use. There are lots of identifiable patterns and gotchas to know about. It's highly advised that you learn about them or risk learning the hard way.

If change is so hard, is it worth all the trouble? We believe that if you embrace these changes in a way that fits your team and business, you will see a high return on the investment over the long term. The promise is that you will deliver products that delight your customers, and we have seen that happen many, many times. But what may not be as obvious is what happens to the culture of a team that effectively aligns on its customer. Working on such a team is infectious. It is gratifying to see customers respond to your work mere days after you've created it. Making lightning-fast progress through rapid iterations is exhilarating. Working this way is fun, it is highly productive, it creates a strong sense among team members that their work really matters, and you deliver products that your customers truly love. Once you've experienced it, you'll never want to go back.

A call to action

Matt Kotler, Principal Group Program Manager, Microsoft Office

Congratulations! You are pages from finishing this book. If you picked up this book in the first place, you are probably already hooked on the idea of designing products that your customers love. And within these pages, I hope you've collected a set of tools that will help you tremendously along the way.

Either that or you are one of those people who likes to skip to the last chapter. No matter. This is really only the beginning. The hard work is ahead and, as they say, we've left that as an exercise for the reader. Your challenge is to take the tools and ideas presented throughout this book and apply them within your organization.

I have had the privilege to spend many years working with Austina, Drew, and many of the other people who contributed to this book (and countless others behind the scenes) to apply this shift in mindset to teams across Microsoft. If you have used a Microsoft product in the last several years, I hope you have been delighted by the experience. Unfortunately, it is possible that at some point over this same period one of our products disappointed you. Every day we work to ensure that that doesn't happen.

Scenario-Focused Engineering is a journey, and delivering amazing products doesn't happen overnight. Leading change across your organization and, just as important, to your organization's culture will take longer than you expect and certainly longer than you would wish. And even when you think you are making progress, a long road will lie ahead. Here are a few additional tips—a call to action—if you want to create a better organization in order to create better, transformative experiences for your customers.

Drive culture change, not process change

For some, especially for those of us who are engineers, it is tempting to read the chapters of this book and want to turn them into a recipe. At first, we tried to do just that. But the reality of design is that it is messy. A surprising amount of science can be applied to creating, evaluating, and delivering great designs, but at the end of the day, design is an art form that can't be broken down into a specific set of steps.

Take the tools from this book and experiment. Try them out and see how they work. Adapt them to your specific situation. But don't worry about applying every tool to every situation. You don't have to do it all to get good results. Instead, focus your energy on ensuring that cultural change is happening around you, that people are doing things with the right intent in mind.

If you are ready to take on the challenge of rolling this out across your organization, you may be about ready to find another book to read. Take a look at the references at the end of this book, especially the ones about driving culture change.

I would highlight three areas, already described in much greater depth in this book, that are at the essence of the Scenario-Focused Engineering culture shift. With every team I join and every project I work on, I focus on reinforcing these three areas over and over again:

- **Customer focus**   Never lose sight of the customer for whom you are designing your product or experience. And don't forget that you are not that customer. Even if you fit all of the demographic characteristics, the fact that you have been designing the product means that you already know all the answers, and it is extremely hard to step back and bring a fresh pair of eyes to look at your own designs every day.

- **End-to-end thinking**   Keep stepping back to look at what you are designing as a piece of a much greater whole. In design parlance, we have moved from a focus on feature design to experience design to—these days—service design. What is the experience that spans communicating why a user needs your product, the purchase of the product, long-term use and enjoyment of the product, and the end of your product's life?

- **Pride in craftsmanship**   Sweat the details. This is true all along the way, from ideation to first concept, but it is even more important at the very end. A great product can turn into a terrible product that is never used if it isn't delivered with high quality. And I believe the difference between a good product and a delightful product is hugely dependent on the final fit and finish. These are often the issues that are not fixed. "We'll get to them next time," but next time never comes around because of other priorities. Get it right the first time.

Customize Scenario-Focused Engineering to your organization

Every organization is different. What worked for us at Microsoft may not work in your organization. Similarly, things that we tried that didn't work because of our scale, culture, and even the type of experiences that we deliver may prove to be breakthroughs in your environment.

Don't even think about throwing out everything your organization does and replacing it with the tools and methodology described within these pages. Use the best of the tools, processes, and mindsets that you already have to build on. The culture change that I've described will be much easier if you can fold it into how your team or organization already works. You might just pick two to three things that you want to focus on for a period of time.

This chapter discusses the importance of driving change top-down and bottom-up. In fact, make sure that you are looking at all levels of your organization and identifying key influencers and key partners. Again, this will vary based on your organization. If you can get buy-in from a leader at the top, that may be critical to making the changes you need.

One of our senior vice presidents asked to have a regular meeting to review a scorecard of the most important scenarios that the organization was focused on. There were endless debates and an evolution of what scenarios to include, and more importantly what scenarios not to include. There were even more debates on how to measure each of the scenarios. A key part of driving culture change was getting the organization to embrace the fact that "red" on a scorecard was okay. At the end of the day, the meeting was not the target. The meeting forced a set of hard discussions at every level of the organization and was a key to getting the culture change to happen.

In organizations where there isn't support at the highest levels, you can still be successful in building a grassroots movement that has a huge impact on your customers. But don't forget about middle management. If you can get middle management onboard with the culture change that you want to drive (or, even better, if you *are* middle management), you will have a much better chance of influencing the people above you, the people below you, and all of their peers.

Also, don't forget to make use of the skills and perspectives from across your entire organization, depending on the size and role specialization. If you are an engineer and lucky enough to have a design and design research (or user research) team, they have years of training in most of the topics described in this book. If you are a designer or a design researcher, go find your kindred spirits in engineering.

Finally, and maybe most importantly, don't forget to apply what you learned in this book to rolling out Scenario-Focused Engineering in your team. Who is the customer? In this case, your team and your organization. How do you get to deliver great experiences that customers love? Iteration. Iterate on the process. Experiment and try new things.

Even as this book was going to press, we tried to cram in new things we had learned. Maybe you find that writing a SPICIER scenario is great for your organization. Or maybe there is a better way to frame the problem. In certain groups we now use scenarios alongside a short list of jobs that the product or experience is meant to accomplish with specific metrics that we can map to how well we need to deliver on those jobs to exceed user expectations. By the time you pick up this book, we will probably have evolved our thinking and best practices even more. Look for ways to evolve the concepts within this book and adapt them based on you and your team.

Be patient and don't give up

Creating experiences that customers love is very hard work. Changing the culture of an organization to be successful at creating experiences that customers love is just as hard, if not harder.

When we started working on rolling out Scenario-Focused Engineering across a large organization at Microsoft, we started with a team self-evaluation. This was a self-assessment for a group of leaders to rate how mature they were in becoming a Scenario-Focused Engineering organization. It was a 5-point scale. There was general consensus that the team was fairly mature in many ways with respect to designing for customers, but we rated ourselves at about a 2 to 2.5 on the scale. A couple of years later I gave a talk on lessons learned within our team and we rated ourselves about a 3.5.

Over those few years we had presented the workshop to thousands of employees and driven a shift in the organization. Teams were more focused on their customers, more focused on end-to-end thinking, and there was significantly more focus on the details. We had a lot to celebrate. But at the same time we had (and continue to have) work to be done.

This is not meant to scare you away from this journey. This is meant to simply communicate that this is a long path. I can say personally that being a small part of the culture change at Microsoft has been one of the most rewarding parts of my career. If you take this one step at a time, I hope that you will also find the same rewards. If you do nothing but improve how you personally design a customer experience, you have made a difference for your customers. If you can bring your team along, then you start to have an exponential impact.

Along the way, look for people to help. I mentioned the opportunity to work with so many folks across Microsoft, many who contributed to this book, and many more who contributed to this effort. These individuals were more than a group passionate about driving this change at Microsoft. They were a support network. We've bounced ideas and challenges off one another. We've leaned on one another when it looked like we weren't making any progress or when it felt like progress was glacially slow. Find your own support system. Find those people who are as passionate about delighting customers as you are. Heck, buy them a copy of this book or at least lend them yours. Say "Yes, and . . ." a lot. Keep learning. Be patient and enjoy the journey. And most importantly . . .

Go forth and delight!

Notes

1. John Kotter, *Accelerate: Building Strategic Agility for a Faster-Moving World* (Boston: Harvard Business Review Press, 2014).

2. "The Wallet Project," Design Resources, last updated October 10, 2013, https://dschool.stanford.edu/groups/designresources/wiki/4dbb2/The_Wallet_Project.html.

3. "The Marshmallow Challenge," http://marshmallowchallenge.com.

SFE capabilities roadmap

The Scenario-Focused Engineering capabilities roadmap is a tool that teams can use to assess their strengths and find opportunities for improving the way they build products for customers. The roadmap details 10 essential capabilities that teams need to most effectively apply the principles and practices of Scenario-Focused Engineering as presented in this book. No individual on a team will possess all the skills these capabilities entail. You need a collection of people with complementary skills to round out a team's capability map.

This roadmap is not intended to be used as a test. Its value is not in any "score" that results but in the deep conversations that come about when a team engages in an analysis of its current and future behaviors. Our hope is that you can use this roadmap as a framework for those conversations to help you think about the best ways to improve your practices today and to prioritize what specific skills and attitudes you should develop in the future.

It's worth noting that every capability has both behavioral (what you do) and cultural (team beliefs and attitudes) components. Although many teams have an easier time at first focusing on and implementing the behavioral components, they come to realize that they must also emphasize the cultural components for a capability to take hold. Teams should consider both the behavioral and cultural pieces in tandem.

Where did the SFE capabilities roadmap come from?

Teams have frequently asked us for more prescriptive guidance for what they should do, what skills they need to grow, and how to stage that growth to avoid taking everything on at once. This roadmap provides a perspective on the concepts, techniques, and examples behind Scenario-Focused Engineering by describing them in terms of the skills teams need to undertake a path toward growth.

To build the capabilities roadmap, we looked closely at teams at Microsoft that were executing really well in 2013–14 and reflected on their growth over the years. These teams provided examples of specific skills and cultural attributes that enabled them to drive a customer-first approach. In addition, we conducted extensive primary and secondary research about the leading practices at companies such as Amazon, Facebook, Google, JetBlue, Netflix, Samsung, USAA, and a dozen others. These findings were then interpreted through the lens of what was most relevant to engineering teams. (Capability development, research, and analysis was led by Jeanine Spence, www.jeaninespence.com.)

Specific business capabilities are not included because they are generally managed outside an engineering team. Complementary capabilities for business operations define skills needed to fully define a business direction and identify an opportunity. These capabilities are Articulate a Strong Vision and Strategy, Balance Continuous Planning and a Long-Term Roadmap, Analyze Market and Customer Opportunity, Define a Clear Business Model, Measure Business Goals Against Target Customers, and Build an Innovation Pipeline.

The 10 capabilities we describe are sorted into four categories:

- **Define direction**   Teams thrive under leaders who put customer experience first. Leaders who provide clear focus set up their teams to successfully deliver what is most important to their customers.

- **Customer focus**   Teams need to develop a deep understanding of their customers by gathering and analyzing various types of data and then use that data to drive decisions. As many of the examples in this book describe, paying attention to customers is not an upfront activity alone. It needs to occur consistently throughout development and delivery.

- **Complete experiences**   Understanding customers is the first half of the equation. The second half is for teams to be sure that they create the right experience. These capabilities describe the essential behaviors that enable teams to ship complete end-to-end experiences.

- **Iterative habits**   For teams to go from good to great in delivering innovative, high-quality products quickly and efficiently requires specific skills in iteration and experimentation.

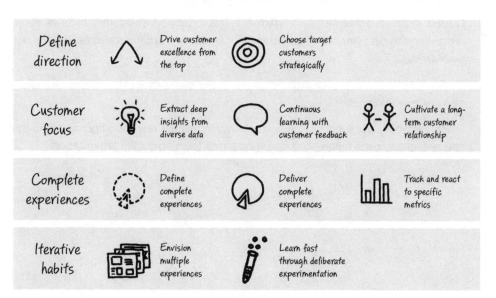

Define direction: Drive customer excellence from the top

Leaders must passionately believe that customer-focused iteration is essential to business success and take full responsibility for the customers' experience. By establishing a team culture that keeps customers front and center, leaders hold their teams accountable for delivering great experiences that delight customers.

What great looks like

- Leaders build a team culture that values customer focus, collaboration, and iteration.

- Leaders hire with the intent to build a team with skills that cover all capabilities and ensure that all members of the team are respected and utilized to their fullest.

- Leaders define and broadly communicate a clear strategic direction, including business opportunities and target customers.

- Leaders provide inspiration, space, resources, processes, tools, and support to enable their teams to put customers and their experience at the forefront of the team's work.

- Leaders expect consistent execution across all the capabilities and deliberately set improvement goals.

- Leaders create both implicit and explicit rewards to encourage the right behaviors across the team.

- Leaders empower individuals to experiment, try new ideas, and respond to customer feedback and not wait for approval to make decisions that benefit customers.

- Leaders negotiate agreements with partner teams to support a customer-focused, iterative process and to get commitments for delivering a seamless experience across organizational boundaries.

- Leaders pay close and regular attention to customer-experience metrics in addition to business and execution metrics.

- Leaders establish and support a dedicated position that has responsibility and authority to ensure alignment and follow-through on customer focus across the organization.

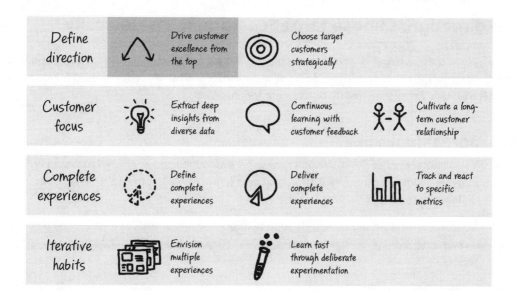

Define direction		Drive customer excellence from the top		Choose target customers strategically		
Customer focus		Extract deep insights from diverse data		Continuous learning with customer feedback		Cultivate a long-term customer relationship
Complete experiences		Define complete experiences		Deliver complete experiences		Track and react to specific metrics
Iterative habits		Envision multiple experiences		Learn fast through deliberate experimentation		

Typical roadmap

Basic   Leaders focus primarily on technology or the logistics of running the business and make important product or engineering decisions centrally. The team's culture generally does not reflect a high degree of customer focus or collaboration, and no leader is explicitly responsible for the customer experience. Success and team rewards are based on business and execution metrics and do not include specific customer-experience metrics.

Emerging   A handful of customer champions drive new customer-focused or iterative activities on the team. This effort is mostly bottom-up, with varied amounts of visibility and/or priority with top leaders. As the champions drive these activities, they gain some support and also experience some resistance. Some customer-focused tools, resources, reward systems, and other processes are put in place but may not be uniformly adopted by the team. These customer champions begin to realize that to make the deeper changes they think are necessary, the team culture needs to change.

Exemplary   A leader with authority and resources insists on a culture and practices that embrace customer focus and drives adoption broadly across the team and with partner teams. The leader empowers his or her team to iterate with customers and rarely vetoes a team decision once the initial strategy is solidified. The leader holds the team accountable to customer-experience metrics and creates rewards to encourage good practices. The leader sets the tone that all members of the team are respected and utilized to their fullest, including designers, planners, and researchers. A comprehensive set of tools, processes, and other resources are deployed and used consistently. The organization reflects a customer-driven culture, from top to bottom, and this culture sticks over the long term.

Define direction: Choose target customers strategically

Identify a few specific target customer segments that are aligned to your business strategy and brand and that give you the best chance for carryover to a broader market. If you try to build for everyone, you get a generic experience that isn't quite right for anyone.

What great looks like

- A small number of target customer segments are identified and prioritized based on their alignment with current business strategy. These segments reflect the most valuable or strategic customers that are driving the market.

- Target customers are segmented through behavioral characteristics (life cycle, level of knowledge/experience, job responsibilities, interests) and not just demographics (sex, age, geography).

- Customer segmentation is derived from a range of data, including telemetry to identify the specific customer behaviors that align to business goals and qualitative analysis to discern emerging trends.

- Identification of the target customer is based on and validated through research.

- Target customer segments are narrow and specific ("soccer moms" rather than "consumers").

- Definition of target customer segments also requires agreement about which customers are not targeted and why.

- Targets are chosen to maximize productive carryover into other market segments. The team tracks whether expected carryover actually occurs as the product is developed and shipped.

- Target customers are selected with an eye toward whether the customer is right for the brand.

- Target customers are understood and embraced by all partners and stakeholders (engineering, sales, marketing, support, operations, partners).

- All work is aligned and optimized for the chosen target customers.

Define direction	Drive customer excellence from the top	Choose target customers strategically	
Customer focus	Extract deep insights from diverse data	Continuous learning with customer feedback	Cultivate a long-term customer relationship
Complete experiences	Define complete experiences	Deliver complete experiences	Track and react to specific metrics
Iterative habits	Envision multiple experiences	Learn fast through deliberate experimentation	

Typical roadmap

Basic   A number of broad target customer segments are considered. The team has a basic understanding of these customer segments and how each is valuable to the business. Marketing, business strategy, and experience goals are developed in isolation and may be aligned to different target customers. The team resists tight prioritization of specific target customers in favor of a broad, general market approach.

Emerging   A comprehensive set of target customers is defined and often mapped by the customers' position on the value chain. Target customers are aligned to experience goals and business strategy and are compared with customers targeted by competitors. Adjacent customer segments and a carryover model are defined. Engineering teams consistently base their work on the needs of target customers, but these target customers may not be the same as those defined within the marketing and sales organizations.

Exemplary   A small set of well-defined and prioritized target customers is fully aligned with business goals, marketing plans, and all aspects of engineering work. Sophisticated carryover models are developed and validated through customer feedback and business results, and the choice of target customers and the carryover model are adjusted as needed. The same definition of the team's target customers is used for all touch points on the customer journey—from prepurchase through usage to support—and by all organizational functions—engineering, sales, marketing, support, and operations.

Customer focus: Extract deep insights from diverse data

Collect diverse types of customer data and synthesize that data into deep, actionable insights about unarticulated customer needs. Uncover the needs that your customers didn't know they had and that your competition hasn't noticed yet, and use those insights to drive differentiation and significant business results.

What great looks like

- Data is gathered from all four research quadrants: QUAL/SAY, QUAL/DO, QUANT/SAY, and QUANT/DO. This includes site visits, interviews, surveys, usage telemetry, customer support data, social media, sales data, competitive info, and so on.

- A team identifies unarticulated customer needs—what customers can't describe directly—especially needs not yet met by competitors.

- Key insights (the why behind the customer's needs) are identified. Often, these are deeply held beliefs, values, pain points, and root causes that explain the customer's motivation.

- Insights are shared with the entire engineering team, including partners and stakeholders.

- A team develops a strong sense of empathy for the customer.

- Customer research data consistently influences decisions in planning, engineering, and business strategy.

- A research portfolio covers all aspects of a team's customers and their environment, including needs, behaviors, emotions, market situation, competitive offerings, and trends.

- Research findings are broadly communicated and easily accessible by team members.

- When conflicting needs are identified in the data, the team has a process for making prioritizations.

- A consistent screener is used across all planning and user research to identify whether research participants are good representatives of a target customer segment.

- Data is gathered continuously to track the pulse of the dynamic marketplace and latest customer trends.

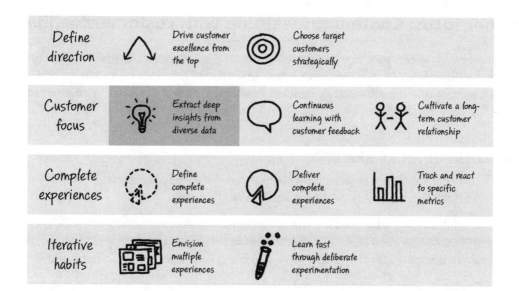

Define direction		Drive customer excellence from the top		Choose target customers strategically		
Customer focus		Extract deep insights from diverse data		Continuous learning with customer feedback		Cultivate a long-term customer relationship
Complete experiences		Define complete experiences		Deliver complete experiences		Track and react to specific metrics
Iterative habits		Envision multiple experiences		Learn fast through deliberate experimentation		

Typical roadmap

Basic   The team gathers limited customer research and has a surface-level awareness of customer needs, often biased by personal opinions. Research sources (including telemetry) are ad hoc, based on the usage of an existing product or service or competitive analysis. The understanding of customer needs is influenced by customer feature requests, stated needs, and required product fixes. Knowledge of the customer data resides in disciplines dedicated to research but is not shared widely among engineers. Decisions are often made based on personal experience and usage of the product, and not on customer data, research, or feedback.

Emerging   The team gathers customer data from diverse sources and consistently identifies unarticulated needs. The team analyzes the data to solve existing problems, generate new product features, and improve quality from release to release. Knowledge about customers is shared widely among engineers, and some engineers develop empathy for the customer. There is limited coordination between customer data used to drive business decisions and customer data used to drive product decisions, which can cause misalignment and conflicting priorities.

Exemplary   A portfolio of research is thoughtfully planned and executed at the right time to influence both business planning and engineering with fresh and relevant insights. The team's schedule allows enough time to wallow in the data for the discovery of insights. The team generates new insights about customer needs that competitors are not yet meeting and is able to make predictions about emerging trends. These insights use and integrate diverse data from marketing, planning, data science, and user research. They are clearly articulated to the entire engineering team and engender a sense of empathy for customers. The team is fluent in making tradeoffs when there are competing requirements among different customer targets.

Customer focus: Continuous learning with customer feedback

Use direct customer feedback to refine your understanding of customers and analyze how they react to your proposed solutions. Get feedback continuously throughout the product's lifetime. Relying on this feedback to guide your product decisions keeps you honest about what customers need and value.

What great looks like

- Customer feedback is collected continuously throughout the product cycle, from early concepts through delivery, release, and ongoing use.

- Multiple types of feedback are leveraged, representing all four quadrants: QUAL/SAY, QUAL/DO, QUANT/SAY, and QUANT/DO. Techniques include usability, A/B testing, focus groups, usage telemetry, instrumentation, surveys, informal interviews and observations, and others.

- The team has an innate curiosity and passion for the customer and looks for creative ways to get feedback.

- The team relies on customer feedback to get from its first idea to the right idea. The team understands that its first ideas are probably incorrect or suboptimal.

- Feedback is used to quickly influence product decisions and direction, typically in the next iteration.

- A pipeline of target customers is developed that makes gathering feedback easy for the entire team, with customers scheduled and available to provide feedback at least weekly.

- A consistent screener is used across all planning and user research to ensure that feedback participants are in the target customer segment.

- Social media and telemetry are constantly monitored for customer feedback. Feedback is interpreted according to its alignment with target customers. Emerging problems are discovered and fixed proactively rather than as the result of customer support calls.

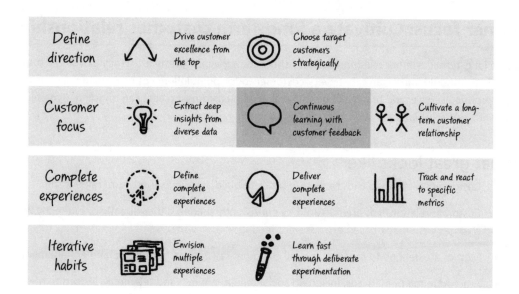

Define direction	Drive customer excellence from the top	Choose target customers strategically	
Customer focus	Extract deep insights from diverse data	Continuous learning with customer feedback	Cultivate a long-term customer relationship
Complete experiences	Define complete experiences	Deliver complete experiences	Track and react to specific metrics
Iterative habits	Envision multiple experiences	Learn fast through deliberate experimentation	

Typical roadmap

Basic   The team receives customer feedback occasionally, often close to shipping. The feedback is focused on validating that features work rather than on validating that the team is solving the most important customer needs. Changes based on feedback are usually made in the next release. Feedback is not consistently tracked or reported. The team relies on its intuition and judgment to make decisions (absent timely customer feedback). Teams directly implement what customers ask for instead of looking for and acting on deeper customer needs.

Emerging   A team gets customer feedback for every major integration milestone throughout the product cycle. Feedback is focused on target customers, defined by a screener, and is used to validate customer needs, the completeness of the solution, and customer delight. Team members are learning how to actively listen and interpret feedback. Changes based on the feedback are made quickly and consistently. Feedback and resulting actions are consistently tracked and reported. The team predominantly uses QUANT/DO data and might have trouble making decisions quickly, preferring to collect more data. The team might overlook QUAL data in favor of QUANT data.

Exemplary   The act of gathering customer feedback is integrated into a team's day-to-day work and is part of the rhythm of every iteration. The team is eager to get customer feedback frequently. Feedback is used to better understand customer needs but also to validate and fine-tune specific solution ideas. The analysis of feedback is triangulated among different data types and rationalizes conflicting findings. Heuristic methods are used successfully to find obvious problems not requiring direct customer input, enabling the team to iterate more quickly. Sources such as social media and telemetry are used proactively as means to identify emerging experience and operational problems. Results and analysis of feedback are shared with all partners. The team has struck a balance between data and judgment and knows when to stop collecting more data and make a decision.

Customer focus: Cultivate a long-term customer relationship

Value long-term customer relationships over short-term revenue or the efficiency of a single transaction. Teams should understand that every customer touch point influences how customers feel about their product, service, and brand. An honest dialog with customers creates an ongoing, dynamic, authentic relationship, not just promotion and marketing.

What great looks like

- Customers are treated with respect in order to build a positive, long-term relationship.

- Customer relationships are nurtured by consistently sharing either directly or indirectly which changes were made based on customer feedback.

- Metrics are defined to measure overall customer satisfaction, sentiment, and engagement.

- A broad range of methods, including social media, surveys, and telemetry, is used to track the overall customer experience at every stage of the customer journey, from prepurchase through ongoing use, to upgrade or abandonment.

- Customer satisfaction and sentiment are monitored closely because drops in these measures can be an early warning of a problem, and recovering lost ground takes a long time.

- The team understands which problems have the highest impact on customer satisfaction and focuses on proactively identifying and fixing those to minimize the impact on customers.

- Customer behavior is tracked and analyzed to determine which behaviors best predict customer loyalty, engagement, satisfaction, and future use of a solution.

- A detailed plan is created for prioritizing quick responses and resolutions of customer issues, even if a response or decision means delaying ongoing product development work.

- When a customer experiences a problem, the problem is fixed quickly and completely and steps are put in place to prevent that problem from occurring again. The highest customer satisfaction comes from having a problem fixed, not from having no problem at all.

- A service mentality pervades the team: customers must continually value the product, service, and brand to keep choosing your solution over competitive offerings and spend their time and money with you.

- The entire team has constant visibility to current customer satisfaction and sentiment scores and understands what factors most affect those scores.

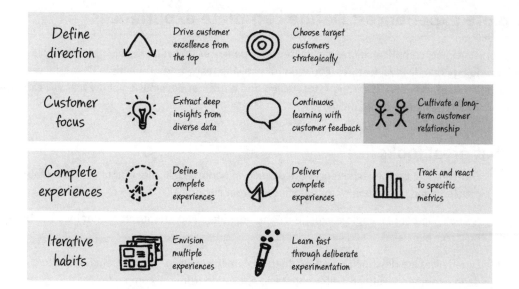

Define direction	Drive customer excellence from the top	Choose target customers strategically	
Customer focus	Extract deep insights from diverse data	Continuous learning with customer feedback	Cultivate a long-term customer relationship
Complete experiences	Define complete experiences	Deliver complete experiences	Track and react to specific metrics
Iterative habits	Envision multiple experiences	Learn fast through deliberate experimentation	

Typical roadmap

Basic   Overall customer satisfaction and sentiment is low or middling. Different disciplines (engineering, marketing, design, and so on) are isolated and customer-facing content is promotional in nature. The customer has difficulty contacting the company. Customer support and the resolution of customer issues are primarily reactive.

Emerging   The team tracks satisfaction measures appropriate to each channel (product satisfaction vs. customer support, etc.), which are optimized and aimed at verified target customers. The team responds to customer issues but does not follow through systematically and does not remeasure satisfaction after an incident. The team is aware of current brand equity and current levels of general customer satisfaction.

Exemplary   The entire team is able to view the customer experience from the outside in and knows not only the sentiment scores but specifically what drives those scores. A variety of customer satisfaction, sentiment, and overall experience measures are constantly monitored and are closely aligned to business goals. The team has developed a plan for prioritizing responses to customer issues and is able to investigate and respond to changes required. The team follows up on customer-experience measures to make sure that the team's actions and changes actually improve the score.

Complete experiences: Define complete experiences

Customers expect complete, seamless end-to-end experiences that solve problems, not bundles of technology or individual features. Focus on fully solving real-world problems in delightful ways. Describing these experiences through storytelling and outcomes develops empathy that will carry the team through the hard work of delivery.

What great looks like

- End-to-end customer experiences are defined to address customer insights and the real-world problems and opportunities for the chosen target customer.

- A small number of complete experiences are identified and prioritized so that they can be built to a high level of quality and detail.

- Experiences are described based on deep customer insights or unarticulated needs to create deep customer delight and differentiate your solution from the competition's.

- Storytelling, customer outcomes, and metrics (with goals) are used to create a structured frame that specifies the intended customer experience.

- Customer emotions are explicitly considered when a team defines end-to-end experiences.

- An end-to-end experience is clearly articulated and validated through customer feedback before a team makes feature, technology, or engineering decisions.

- All engineering, business, operations, marketing, and human factors are considered to coordinate a seamless, integrated end-to-end experience.

- As engineering, business, operational, and marketing deliverables are specified, each aligns to the priority end-to-end experiences.

- End-to-end experiences are prioritized over individual features, feature improvements, or optimizations.

- A long-term experience strategy is defined that spans multiple releases or even years.

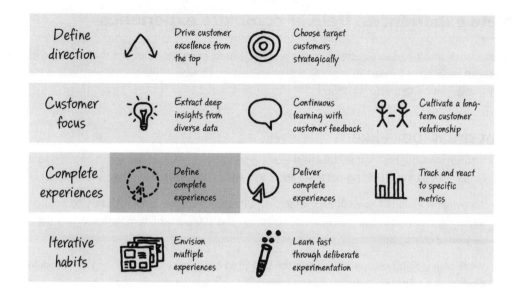

Define direction		Drive customer excellence from the top		Choose target customers strategically	
Customer focus		Extract deep insights from diverse data		Continuous learning with customer feedback	Cultivate a long-term customer relationship
Complete experiences		Define complete experiences		Deliver complete experiences	Track and react to specific metrics
Iterative habits		Envision multiple experiences		Learn fast through deliberate experimentation	

Typical roadmap

Basic   The team focuses on features and functionality with local optimization, low integration, and little immersion in customers' needs. Stories or scenarios describe a feature or a use case, include many implementation details, and don't describe the customer's motivation or problem. Planned solutions often focus on ad hoc features rather than a coherent path through the entire experience. The team tracks and manages work based on feature lists, which can be very long.

Emerging   The team uses storytelling, outcomes, and metrics, based on research, to focus engineering plans for a specific release and to articulate business, technology, and experience opportunities and constraints. Planned solutions are expected to be complete and smooth at the component level and to deliver high value seamlessly within a specific product. The team tracks and manages work using both experience framing and feature lists.

Exemplary   The team articulates and aligns experience plans to the long-term vision of many releases and uses that to make decisions on where to invest or divest. Experiences reflect deep insights about unarticulated customer needs and create opportunities for significant differentiation from competition. Planned solutions are expected to deliver high-value, seamless experiences across all customer touch points, including with partners and competitors. The team aligns all engineering work to experiences and uses these experiences to track and manage the project.

Complete experiences: Deliver complete experiences

Organize work and the team to effectively deliver integrated, seamless solutions that enable complete end-to-end experiences. Invest in systems and processes that support reliable delivery with a focus on quality and attention to craftsmanship.

What great looks like

- Solutions enable high-value, seamless experiences across all customer touch points and the larger ecosystem, including partners and competitors' platforms, services, and devices.

- An owner is assigned to each experience, who has the resources and authority to hold all dependencies accountable to smooth execution and 100 percent completion with a high degree of craftsmanship.

- Work plan is tightly scoped to deliver the designed experience on an achievable schedule. The work plan is based on a deep understanding of the intended experience.

- All work is tracked and organized to deliver a complete end-to-end experience. This includes all functionality as well as all resources, such as help and marketing materials.

- Each experience is defined with detailed success criteria, including task outcomes, sentiment metrics, and long-term engagement goals.

- Technology investments are prioritized according to how each contributes to the intended customer experience. Infrastructure and platform investments are scoped to the actual customer-experience requirements. Execution decisions and tradeoffs are based on empathy and customer feedback about customer needs and desires.

- Bug triage and design-change decisions are guided by the impact of the proposed change on the overall experience.

- The team is brutally honest about the state of the customer experience and whether the success criteria are being met.

- The team values shipping complete experiences and resists shipping partial solutions. Work that is not contributing to the overall experience is cut.

- Hard cuts are made early to maximize the resources available to finish the most important experiences with high quality.

- Tight integration with customer feedback verifies both the experience quality and the impact of any cuts.

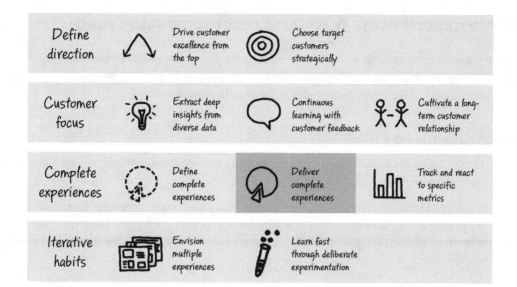

Define direction		Drive customer excellence from the top		Choose target customers strategically		
Customer focus		Extract deep insights from diverse data		Continuous learning with customer feedback		Cultivate a long-term customer relationship
Complete experiences		Define complete experiences		Deliver complete experiences		Track and react to specific metrics
Iterative habits		Envision multiple experiences		Learn fast through deliberate experimentation		

Typical roadmap

Basic   The team delivers incomplete or broken experiences and consistently attempts to do too much in a given release. The focus is on shipping features rather than on delivering a coherent whole. Experience quality is not tracked systematically. The team is easily distracted by exciting new opportunities.

Emerging   The team aspires to deliver complete end-to-end experiences. All experiences have clearly defined success criteria, and their completeness and quality are measured continuously. Bug triage and design-change decisions are guided by the current state of the experience and the assessed impact on the experience. Experiences that would be broken at the time a solution is shipped are cut from the release or the solution is held until these experiences are ready. However, the team might make cuts at the last minute that leave gaps in the overall experience.

Exemplary   The end-to-end experience is optimized across all customer touch points and is consistently high quality and polished. All engineering work is organized and tracked around delivering great end-to-end experiences, including resources such as help, marketing materials, product acquisition, and customer-support systems. An owner is assigned to each experience, and that owner has the resources and permission to hold all dependencies accountable to smooth execution. Triage ensures that all released solutions fulfill complete, seamless, end-to-end experiences with a high degree of craftsmanship. Hard cuts are made early to allow the team to focus. The team enables smooth integration with the entire ecosystem, including competitors' platforms, services, and devices. The team has a clear understanding of the customer's expectation for the experience and what it needs to do to deliver it.

Complete experiences: Track and react to specific metrics

Well-defined customer experience metrics, in concert with business metrics and technology performance metrics, set an explicit quality bar for all experiences. Carefully tracking these metrics holds a team accountable for delivering the intended experience to delight customers.

What great looks like

- Metrics are captured consistently at every iteration through instrumentation, customer testing, and observation.

- A metrics portfolio includes a balanced view across system-health indicators such as availability and page load; business-health indicators such as click-through rates, conversion, revenue, and adoption; and customer-experience-health indicators such as task success, discoverability, session abandonment, and continued usage.

- Standardized customer-experience metrics are defined across the team for both performance (task completion statistics and error rates, for example) and perception (measuring the useful, usable, and desirable dimensions of an experience).

- Vanity metrics are avoided, such as counting clicks or downloads when your business goals are based on usage.

- The team holds itself accountable to experience-metrics goals and does not ship until these goals are met.

- The team is able to evaluate the accuracy of measurements, align them with target customers appropriately, interpret them, and use them to drive decisions.

- Instrumentation is used strategically to capture defined metrics and is a regular part of code check-ins.

- Automated tools are developed and used to collate, track, and report on metrics.

- Interim builds are continuously validated against stated metrics and success criteria.

- Latest measurements are published broadly on a scorecard, a dashboard, or another format that is visible to the entire team.

- Metrics determining success criteria are reviewed regularly for how well they align to the customer experience and business goals and are revised if needed.

Define direction		Drive customer excellence from the top		Choose target customers strategically	
Customer focus		Extract deep insights from diverse data		Continuous learning with customer feedback		Cultivate a long-term customer relationship
Complete experiences		Define complete experiences		Deliver complete experiences		Track and react to specific metrics
Iterative habits		Envision multiple experiences		Learn fast through deliberate experimentation		

Typical roadmap

Basic   The team defines ad hoc technical performance metrics, with a general focus on system availability, performance, and reliability. Experience metrics are few and usually not actionable. There are no perception metrics.

Emerging   The team measures a range of technical, business, and experience metrics systematically. The team relies on this data to make decisions. Success metrics are measured and tracked for every experience. Experience metrics are used alongside technical and business metrics to determine overall readiness for shipping. The team publishes a scorecard to track and communicate experience health status.

Exemplary   All team members rely on knowing the real-time experience health status through dashboards and are skilled at evaluating the accuracy of the data, interpreting it, and using it to drive decisions. Telemetry is in place and data exhaust is analyzed for patterns of customer behavior. Perception data is considered equally alongside performance data.

Iterative habits: Envision multiple experiences

Discover the best ideas by exploring broadly, by encouraging wild ideas and playfulness. Deliberately diverge and consider multiple options for every decision to seek a globally optimal solution. Discover the best ideas by combining and recombining ideas in new ways to achieve a breakthrough.

What great looks like

- The team starts projects by generating a large number of diverse ideas in different modes, including written, physical, and visual.

- The team is proficient at brainstorming, holistic systems thinking, and sketching to visualize ideas.

- The team conducts facilitated brainstorming, lateral thinking, and idea-generation activities at the right time in the Fast Feedback Cycle, as well as informal idea generation individually and in small groups as needed.

- Throughout the entire project cycle, as the project progresses and more is learned, the team generates ideas at the appropriate level of scope in the iteration funnel.

- The team enforces a rule to not make any solution or design decision until at least a handful of credible, diverse ideas are generated.

- Ideas are combined and recombined to find new solutions that incorporate the best aspects of multiple ideas.

- A deep degree of trust exists across the team, enabling a safe environment for wild ideas to be floated and considered.

- Team members know how to give and receive feedback so that it is heard and considered.

- The team is aware of tunnel vision and has strategies to delay or mitigate its effects.

- The team takes time to marinate to enrich idea generation.

- The team recognizes when it has explored the problem space fully by generating and exploring enough ideas to move forward.

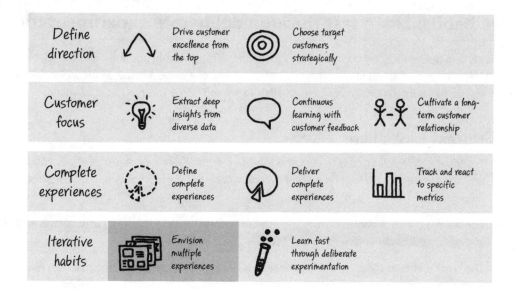

Define direction		Drive customer excellence from the top		Choose target customers strategically		
Customer focus		Extract deep insights from diverse data		Continuous learning with customer feedback		Cultivate a long-term customer relationship
Complete experiences		Define complete experiences		Deliver complete experiences		Track and react to specific metrics
Iterative habits		Envision multiple experiences		Learn fast through deliberate experimentation		

Typical roadmap

Basic   Ideation is focused mainly on brainstorming feature ideas that are based on the available technology, not on solving customer needs. Envisioning and ideation sessions occur sporadically, if at all, and do not yield changes in the technology-dictated direction. Relatively few ideas are generated before a decision is made. Team culture encourages picking an answer quickly.

Emerging   The team has a vanguard group that has responsibility for envisioning and ideation. Big-picture ideas generated by that group form the product roadmap for the broader engineering team. Ideation skills in the vanguard group are high, but those skills are not broadly distributed in the engineering organization. Managers of the vanguard group have high tolerance for ambiguity, but there is a natural tension with other managers, who press for locking down plans sooner. After the product roadmap is defined, the team switches to production mode and rarely ideates during decision making.

Exemplary   An entire team embraces diverging activities and ideation throughout the engineering process—at the right times and in rhythm with the Fast Feedback Cycle and the iteration funnel. The broad team and their partner teams understand that to find an optimal, innovative idea they have to start with many ideas. The team environment encourages consideration of wild ideas and unconventional approaches at appropriate times. The team routinely uses diverging activities to find creative solutions to problems and to solve customer needs.

Iterative habits: Learn fast through deliberate experimentation

Frequently and deliberately try out ideas with customers, testing your hypotheses, and use that feedback to inform the next iteration of your work. Iterations across a project follow a curved funnel shape as teams systematically winnow many ideas to a few ideas and finally reach an optimal solution.

What great looks like

- Experimentation (iteration with customers) is used to solve all types of problems, including product and service development, process and workflow improvements, and business model questions.

- The team is rigorous about forming hypotheses and validating them with customers as a core and widely practiced engineering and business discipline.

- The team is able to switch in unison between diverging and converging and maintain a rapid rhythm to enable consistently fast iterations.

- A smooth funnel shape of iteration is maintained throughout the product development process.

- The team expends minimum effort to produce rapid prototypes at multiple levels of fidelity, appropriate to the scope of the iteration funnel.

- The team intentionally keeps multiple solutions alive through several iterations until an optimal solution emerges.

- The team and its leaders recognize that failing fast enables a more efficient product development process.

- Team culture tolerates ambiguity and healthy risk and remains nimble in changing market conditions.

- Management actively discourages solutions that don't emerge from an iterative design process involving multiple alternative designs and customer feedback.

- The team has processes, schedules, and tools in place (including an A/B testing infrastructure) that allow time for and support iteration.

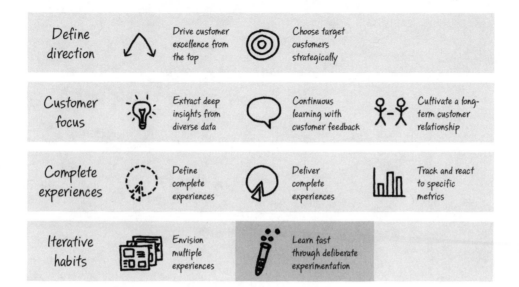

Define direction		Drive customer excellence from the top		Choose target customers strategically		
Customer focus		Extract deep insights from diverse data		Continuous learning with customer feedback		Cultivate a long-term customer relationship
Complete experiences		Define complete experiences		Deliver complete experiences		Track and react to specific metrics
Iterative habits		Envision multiple experiences		Learn fast through deliberate experimentation		

Typical roadmap

Basic   Experimentation is done ad hoc in pockets of the organization. A team consistently iterates ideas to improve them over time but rarely compares multiple viable solutions to a given problem. The team may revisit decisions or repeat debates because of a lack of either consensus or customer feedback that indicates which solutions are better. The team has difficulty abandoning ideas that don't test well. Most ideas and decisions come from a select set of team members who have a reputation for being visionaries. The team follows the visionaries' lead and does not feel much need for customer feedback to inform iterations.

Emerging   A team tests multiple solution options at regular intervals. The team uses low-fidelity methods to quickly build experiments and test proposed solutions with minimal investment. Experimenting with multiple prototypes for all significant investments is standard operating procedure for the team. Customer feedback is consistently used to inform decisions. Management regularly probes to understand how many solutions have been considered and embraces churn in the design phase because managers know that this diminishes much more costly churn during the implementation and stabilization phases and increases the likelihood of a successful release. The team is willing to abandon ideas that don't test well to focus on ideas that do. There is a system in place for A/B testing.

Exemplary   A team tests new solution ideas with customers often and regularly has multiple experiments in progress at any time and at many different levels of fidelity. The schedule allows ample time for iteration, and tooling is in place to support experimentation. The team uses experimentation fluidly to solve product problems as well as to iterate the business model, marketing plans, and process improvements. Failing fast is rewarded and carries no stigma. The team is able to scale up the volume and speed of experimentation and user feedback as needed. The team and the team's managers are very comfortable with ambiguity and allow projects sufficient design time to ensure that the team converges on the best solution. The team is driven by quality rather than by time.

The Fast Feedback Cycle

On the following page, you'll find a simple illustration of the Fast Feedback Cycle. Please feel free to print or copy it, and then give it to friends and colleagues or hang it on the wall as a poster. It's useful as a daily reminder of some of the principles we present in this book.

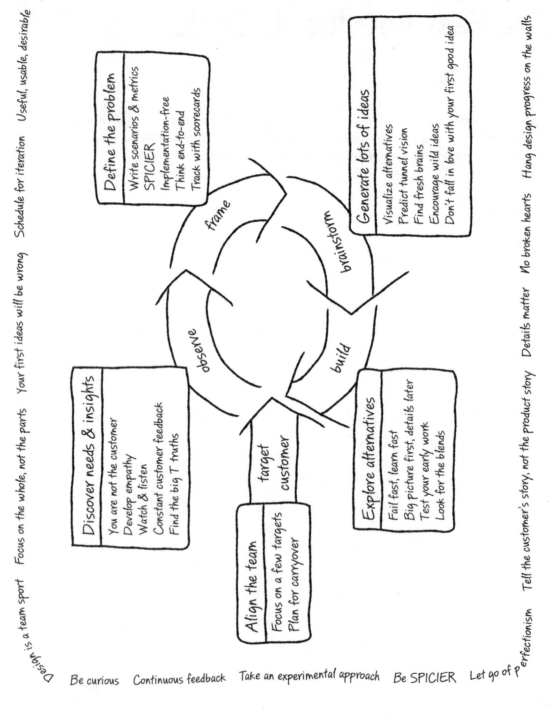

Team culture is critical   Diverge & converge   Time boxing is your friend   Discovering, not deciding

Useful, usable, desirable

Schedule for iteration

Your first ideas will be wrong

Focus on the whole, not the parts

Design is a team sport

Be curious   Continuous feedback   Take an experimental approach   Be SPICIER   Let go of perfectionism

Tell the customer's story, not the product story   Details matter   No broken hearts   Hang design progress on the walls

Define the problem
- Write scenarios & metrics
- SPICIER
- Implementation-free
- Think end-to-end
- Track with scorecards

Generate lots of ideas
- Visualize alternatives
- Predict tunnel vision
- Find fresh brains
- Encourage wild ideas
- Don't fall in love with your first good idea

Discover needs & insights
- You are not the customer
- Develop empathy
- Watch & listen
- Constant customer feedback
- Find the big T truths

Explore alternatives
- Fail fast, learn fast
- Big picture first, details later
- Test your early work
- Look for the blends

Align the team
- Focus on a few targets
- Plan for carryover

frame

brainstorm

observe

build

target customer

Further reading

This appendix lists books that can help you take the next step toward using many of the ideas and techniques we discuss in Scenario-Focused Engineering. Whenever possible, we've attempted to include what experts in each discipline would generally consider the seminal treatise on the topic, as well as our favorite practical guides for understanding and applying various techniques or for exploring a particular concept in more depth. Many more fine books are available on these topics. We limited this list to the books that we like a lot and think are worthy of a place in your personal library.

The categories we've used correspond to the big ideas in this book and are listed roughly in the order in which we introduced them. We could place many of these books in several categories because the books provide an integrated view of many of these topics. We made our best judgment about where they had the highest affinity.

Business strategy

Christensen, Clayton. *The Innovator's Dilemma: When New Technologies Cause Great Firms to Fail.* Boston: Harvard Business Review Press, 2013.

Lafley, A. G., and Roger Martin. *Playing to Win: How Strategy Really Works.* Boston, Harvard Business School Publishing, 2013.

Manning, Harley, and Kerry Bodine. *Outside In: The Power of Putting Customers at the Center of Your Business.* New Harvest, 2012.

Moore, Geoffrey. *Crossing the Chasm.* 3rd edition. New York: HarperCollins, 2014.

Osterwalder, Alexander, and Yves Pigneur, *Business Model Generation: A Handbook for Visionaries, Game Changers, and Challengers.* Hoboken, NJ: Wiley, 2010.

Sinek, Simon. *Start with Why: How Great Leaders Inspire Everyone to Take Action.* New York: Penguin, 2009.

Design thinking

Brown, Tim. *Change by Design: How Design Thinking Transforms Organizations and Inspires Innovation.* New York: HarperCollins, 2009.

Liedtka, Jeanne, and Tim Ogilvie. *Designing for Growth: A Design Thinking Tool Kit for Managers*. New York: Columbia University Press, 2011.

Lockwood, Thomas. *Design Thinking: Integrating Innovation, Customer Experience, and Brand Value*. New York: Allworth Press, 2009.

Martin, Roger. *Design of Business: Why Design Thinking Is the Next Competitive Advantage*. Boston: Harvard Business School Publishing, 2009.

Observation and customer research

Beyer, Hugh, and Karen Holtzblatt. *Contextual Design: Designing Customer-Centered Systems*. San Francisco: Morgan Kaufmann, 1998.

Goodman, Elizabeth, Mike Kuniavsky, and Andrea Moed. *Observing the User Experience: A Practitioner's Guide to User Research*. 2nd edition. Waltham, MA: Morgan Kaufmann/Elsevier, 2012.

Ladner, Sam. *Practical Ethnography: A Guide to Doing Ethnography in the Private Sector*. Walnut Creek, CA: Left Coast Press, 2014.

Pruitt, John, and Tamara Adlin. *The Essential Persona Lifecycle: Your Guide to Building and Using Personas*. Burlington, MA: Morgan Kaufmann, 2010.

Storytelling

Quesenbery, Whitney, and Kevin Brooks. *Storytelling for User Experience: Crafting Stories for Better Design*. Brooklyn, NY: Rosenfeld Media, 2010.

Simmons, Annette. *The Story Factor*. 2nd rev. edition. Cambridge, MA: Basic Books, 2006.

Metrics and measurement

Hubbard, Douglas. *How to Measure Anything: Finding the Value of Intangibles in Business*. Hoboken, NJ: Wiley, 2014.

Kaushik, Avinash. *Web Analytics 2.0: The Art of Online Accountability and Science of Customer Centricity*. Indianapolis: Wiley, 2010.

Tullis, Thomas, and William Albert. *Measuring the User Experience: Collecting, Analyzing, and Presenting Usability Metrics*. Burlington, MA: Morgan Kaufmann, 2008.

Innovation, creativity and brainstorming

Berkun, Scott. *The Myths of Innovation*. Sebastopol, CA: O'Reilly Media, 2010.

De Bono, Edward. *Lateral Thinking: Creativity Step by Step*. New York: Harper Colophon, 1990.

Kelley, Tom, and Jonathan Littman. *The Art of Innovation: Lessons in Creativity from IDEO, America's Leading Design Firm*. New York: Currency Books, 2001.

Prototyping and sketching

Buxton, Bill. *Sketching User Experiences: Getting the Design Right and the Right Design*. San Francisco: Morgan Kaufmann, 2007.

Roam, Dan. *Unfolding the Napkin: The Hands-On Method for Solving Complex Problems with Simple Pictures*. New York: Portfolio, 2009.

Savoia, Alberto. *Pretotype It*. 2012.

Synder, Carolyn. *Paper Prototyping: The Fast and Easy Way to Design and Refine User Interfaces*. San Francisco: Morgan Kaufmann, 2003.

Warfel, Todd Zaki. *Prototyping*. Rosenfeld Media, 2011.

A/B testing

Eisenberg, Brian, John Quarto-vonTivadar, Brett Crosby, and Lisa T. Davis. *Always Be Testing: The Complete Guide to Google Website Optimizer*. Indianapolis: Wiley, 2008.

Kohavi, Ron, Alex Deng, Roger Longbotham, and Ya Xu. "Seven Rules of Thumb for Web Site Experimenters." *EXP Platform,* http://www.exp-platform.com/.

Usability testing

Dumas, Joseph S., and Janice C. Redish. Rev. ed. *A Practical Guide to Usability Testing*. Exeter, England; Portland, OR: Intellect Books, 1999.

Dumas, Joseph S., and Beth A. Loring. *Moderating Usability Tests: Principals and Practice for Interacting*. Burlington, MA: Morgan Kaufmann, 2008.

Krug, Steve. *Rocket Surgery Made Easy: The Do-It-Yourself Guide to Finding and Fixing Usability Problems*. Berkeley, CA: New Riders, 2010.

———. *Don't Make Me Think, Revisited: A Common Sense Approach to Web and Mobile Usability*. Berkeley, CA: New Riders, 2014.

Nielsen, Jakob. *Usability Engineering.* Cambridge, MA: Academic Press, 1993.

Interaction and user interface design

Lidwell, William, Kritina Holden, and Jill Butler. *Universal Principles of Design, Revised and Updated: 125 Ways to Enhance Usability, Influence Perception, Increase Appeal, Make Better Design Decisions, and Teach through Design.* Rev. ed. Beverly, MA: Rockport Publishers, 2010.

Mullet, Kevin, and Darrell Sano. *Designing Visual Interfaces: Communication Oriented Technique.* Upper Saddle River, NJ: Prentice Hall, 1994.

Saffer, Dan. *Designing for Interaction: Creating Innovative Applications and Devices.* 2nd ed. Berkeley, CA: New Riders, 2010.

———. *Microinteractions: Designing with Details.* Sebastapol, CA: O'Reilly Media, 2013.

Agile development

Derby, Esther, and Diana Larsen. *Agile Retrospectives: Making Good Teams Great.* Pragmatic Bookshelf, 2005.

Rubin, Kenneth S. *Essential Scrum: A Practical Guide to the Most Popular Agile Process.* Upper Saddle River, NJ: Pearson, 2013.

Schwaber, Ken. *Agile Project Management with Scrum.* Redmond, WA: Microsoft Press, 2004.

Shore, James, and Shane Warden. *The Art of Agile Development.* Sebastopol, CA: O'Reilly Media, 2008.

Lean

Alvarez, Cindy. *Lean Customer Development: Building Products Your Customers Will Buy.* Sebastopol, CA: O'Reilly Media, 2014.

Blank, Steve. *The Four Steps to the Epiphany: Successful Strategies for Products That Win.* 2nd ed. K & S Ranch, 2013.

Maurya, Ash. *Running Lean: Iterate from Plan A to a Plan That Works.* Sebastopol, CA: O'Reilly Media, 2012.

Ries, Eric. *The Lean Startup: How Today's Entrepreneurs Use Continuous Innovation to Create Radically Successful Businesses.* New York: Crown, 2011.

Managing change

Heath, Chip, and Dan Heath *Switch: How to Change Things When Things Are Hard*. New York: Crown, 2010.

Kotter, John P. *Leading Change*. Boston: Harvard Business Review Press. 2012.

———. *A Sense of Urgency*. Boston: Harvard Business School Publishing, 2008.

Kotter, John P., and Holger Rathgeber. *Our Iceberg Is Melting: Changing and Succeeding Under Any Conditions*. New York: St. Martins, 2005.

Selected case studies

This appendix contains two case studies of teams that followed many of the concepts and techniques described in this book to deliver solutions to customers.

The first case study is a textbook account of how an expert used a design-thinking approach in a real-world situation. It details the process he used to discover the unarticulated need a company was hunting for, as well as the process he followed and the artifacts he created along the path to developing a final solution. It highlights how these techniques can be used quickly, with a full iteration completed in only one week.

The second is a good illustration of what the path more often looks like for teams that are embarking on a journey to delight their customers. This one is an account of implementing Scenario-Focused Engineering in a large team at Microsoft. This case study is written by an engineer who loved the ideas he was exposed to in the SFE workshop and was passionate about implementing them on his own team. The case study follows how he and his team worked through the speed bumps and challenges that ensued.

Case study: Scenarios set the course for a drifting project

Chris Nodder, Interface Tamer, Chris Nodder Consulting, LLC

Summary: Taking one week to plan a project by following a user-centered design process with a focus on common user scenarios stopped churn and led to the fast, focused delivery of a well-received social media product for hotel staff worldwide.

Hampton Hotels is part of Hilton Worldwide, with nearly 2,000 focused-service hotels in fifteen countries. Hampton prides itself on participation from hotel employees, or Team Members. A big differentiator from other hotel chains is Hampton's brand personality—summed up as "Hamptonality." The more engaged hotel Team Members are, the more likely they are to exhibit Hamptonality and thus delight guests.

A General Manager (GM) at each property is the focal point for questions from their teams and their management companies. They have formal channels to turn to for procedural advice, but at the point I got involved there was no common location for sharing tips and tricks on topics such as staff motivation or increasing customer loyalty—the kind of elements that make up Hamptonality.

To help GMs with these informal questions, the Brand team had planned a video-based tips-and-tricks site called Sharecast, which would be populated with both top-down content and grassroots Hamptonality suggestions.

The Brand team wanted to announce Sharecast at the GM conference, a massive annual event that was just seven months away. But the project had been stalled for months, partly because the team wasn't sure that it was the right direction to take.

To get the project back on track, we set up a one-week user-centered planning and design workshop with the business sponsor, user representatives, a project manager, a UX designer, and the primary developer.

Locking everyone in a room for a week was highly successful in getting them on the same page. We started by reviewing all the information we had about users of the system from site visits, user-testing sessions, and the personal experiences of the user representatives. This led to three personas: a sharer (knowledgeable, confident, posts best practices), a searcher (smart, curious, but lacks confidence, wants to gain knowledge), and a connector (isolated, hungry for community, wants reassurance).

To help project teams pull various information sources together, I normally create four headings for each persona: goals, conflicts, quotes, and attributes. You can see the resulting thumbnail persona sketch for the searcher persona in Figure D-1. In future design conversations, the persona names serve as a placeholder or shorthand for all of this information and for the discussions that led to each persona's creation. With this type of information written down, it's straightforward to work out how a key persona would want to use the system.

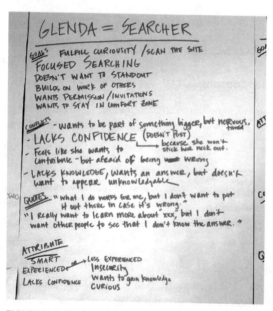

FIGURE D-1 Goals, conflicts, quotes, and attributes provide a quick summary of target personas.

We next wrote scenarios to work out how these personas would interact with each other and with the system. These scenarios played a pivotal role in reaching a way forward. Almost immediately, it became clear that the stories we were telling for these personas had very little to do with video, and no real need for company-produced content. The sharers, searchers, and connectors would create and consume content without any corporate assistance—in fact, they'd be more likely to use the system if it remained "corporate free."

This was a major turning point for the project team. Once we had the scenarios written, we performed some rounds of design charrette ideation exercises to identify creative ways of letting the different personas interact on the website. Although there were people from multiple roles in the room, the fact that in a charrette exercise everybody works individually before sharing ideas meant that everyone's voice was heard.

The project team was surprisingly creative, and several of these charrette sketches formed central parts of the final interface. Figure D-2 shows a charrette sketch of a profile page. This two-pane approach became a key design feature for the finished product.

FIGURE D-2 Design charrette output is normally just quick sketches to get across a key idea. We mined these sketches heavily for design ideas later in the process.

We created the first prototype interface using the scenarios as our guide. Although the scenarios themselves very clearly avoided defining interface components, it was easy to read through each one and find where an interaction was described. For every interaction, we then turned to the ideation sketches for inspiration on how we could create a suitable interface component. Pauses in the scenario coincided very well with the move to a new screen in the prototype interface.

We drew each component on paper with sticky notes glued to the back so that we could easily reposition each piece as the interface evolved. I find that this approach works really well as a way to keep the interface fluid. It bears no cost to rework the design, whereas when a design is drawn out fully on one sheet of paper, the designer may be more reluctant to make changes because it means redrawing the whole thing. Figure D-3 shows one of the screens that was developed in this way. I often get even more granular than this, creating individual pieces of paper for each design element.

FIGURE D-3 The profile view as a paper prototype. Note how the prototyped view compares with the original ideation sketch shown in Figure D-2.

On Thursday of this intensive week, we performed our first usability test to verify that we were on the right track. After just three participants, we had sufficiently consistent results to know what we needed to change before starting to code.

On Friday, we wrote high-level Agile user stories and prioritized them so that we could work out how soon we would have a sufficiently advanced product to be able to conduct alpha and beta tests of the interface with larger groups of users. We used a Story Map to prioritize the work items: we laid out each screen of the prototype interface on a long table and wrote user stories to cover every capability of each screen, placing the story cards directly below the screen they referred to.

It was then relatively simple to sort the user stories into must-haves (core functionality), essential experiences (what makes the interface workable for the personas), and nice-to-haves (which add delight). Or, to use a cupcake analogy—cake, frosting, and sprinkles. There is no point building sprinkles capabilities in one area of the interface if you still lack cake functionality in another area, but adding sprinkles at the end can really complete the experience.

Compared with a straight backlog, this two-dimensional approach, with interface components on the horizontal axis and priority on the vertical axis, lets you see the interaction between stories more easily. This quick prioritization exercise gave the developer enough information to estimate the effort involved, and the good news was that we could still be done in time for the GM conference.

Two weeks after the workshop, we visited two hotel properties and ran a more formal set of usability tests with computer-drawn paper prototypes to ensure that we were on the right track before coding. This provided the final set of tweaks to our assumptions. The capabilities we chose to build for our target personas ended up delighting the whole user base. The clean, minimal, focused interface provided just enough features beyond the basic set, and they were implemented in just the right way that users truly expressed delight with the system, even though it was still only a wireframe sketch on paper (Figure D-4).

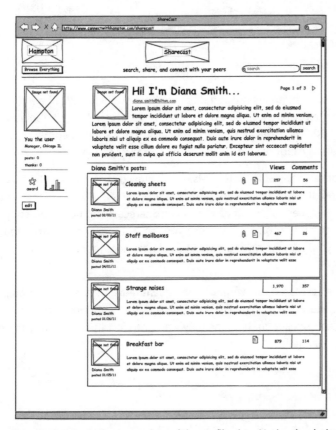

FIGURE D-4 A wireframe mockup of the profile view. Notice the design elements that have been carried through from the initial concept sketches but have been fine-tuned based on feedback.

When the alpha and beta releases rolled out to select groups of GMs, usage did indeed fit with our scenario predictions, so we felt confident gearing up to release the production version at the GM conference. User testing was a pleasant experience at this point because there were no big surprises. Early verification of the layout and functionality meant that there were only a few course corrections as we moved from wireframes to final design (Figure D-5).

FIGURE D-5 The final design that was released.

Alpha and beta participants were sufficiently engaged that they built out hundreds of entries for the community before release. At the conference, the launch was a big success. When the solution was announced in a room full of 1,800 GMs, the alpha and beta participants spontaneously cheered and applauded. There was immediately a lot of activity and energy on the site.

Today, Sharecast has been adopted not just by hotel GMs but by individual Team Members as well. One front-desk agent captured it perfectly in a note she sent to a GM she had never met, in a Hampton hotel five states away: "I've been following your posts on Sharecast and I just wanted to thank you. My goal is to be a GM of a Hampton Inn and I love your enthusiasm and the ideas you have shared. I've written many of your ideas in my journal so I can implement them at my own property."

And this wouldn't truly be a user-centered tale without some quantitative metrics to accompany the qualitative data. Today on the site, around 70 percent of views are from returning visitors, people spend an average of 15 minutes per visit, and in that time they view around 14 pages. That's a good set of engagement metrics by any estimation!

Case study: Visual C++ 2012

Mike Pietraszak, Senior Test Lead, Microsoft Visual C++

Summary: A large two-year project with limited customer interaction in the middle of the cycle was struggling, but after making short-term modifications to the scenario-focused techniques and through perseverance, the large team delivered a well-received product and began a long-term change in engineering practices.

In the summer of 2010, the various product groups that form the Visual Studio suite (Visual C++, Visual C#, Visual Basic, and others) started putting Scenario-Focused Engineering (SFE) techniques into practice. SFE would be used for the first time in the two-year development cycle for the Visual Studio 2012 suite, including for Visual C++ 2012. After completing SFE training, each product group took a slightly different approach to adopting SFE. I was a test lead in the Visual C++ group, and along with the efforts of many others, I played a part in the adoption of SFE for our group.

The Visual C++ group had spent several decades building expertise in feature-focused software development. The bug-tracking database, design specifications, milestone reviews, and even the organizational structure (feature teams) were all built around the concept of features. Over many years and many product releases, our seasoned group of engineers had also seen its share of new processes and procedures come and go. Some of these were viewed as flavor-of-the week fads, and we learned to be cautious and careful about investing in something that wouldn't be around for the next product release cycle. We wondered if our deep-rooted feature-focus would be an obstacle to the adoption of SFE.

Caution and enthusiasm

In May of 2010, Austina De Bonte and Drew Fletcher conducted an SFE training session for the entire Visual C++ product group, more than 90 developers, testers, and program managers (PMs). During the training, our product group showed a palpable degree of skepticism about the wisdom of pivoting from our proven feature-focused processes to a process that focused more on customer scenarios.

But Visual C++ management was enthusiastic about the promise of SFE, and so was I. Our group hired a user-experience expert and created a three-person subgroup. The SFE subgroup was not focused on a particular feature, as the other feature teams in the organization were. Instead, the subgroup had the unique charter to coordinate customer interactions and organize scenario-related test activities for all Visual C++ scenarios. I was thrilled to be the lead for the SFE subgroup.

Early on, the Visual C++ group chose a customer persona as our focus: Liam, a rising-star programmer who wants to develop and self-publish his own apps. My SFE subgroup planned, scheduled, and conducted interviews and focus groups. We turned our findings into large posters that were hung in the hallway, complete with photos of the customers we had met. The PMs made a healthy investment of their time in brainstorming. Together, we identified seven C++ scenarios for the 2012 product release, and we built end-to-end scenario walk-throughs and storyboards. As the product took shape in the very early stages, we conducted lab studies with customers. The development team reviewed this feedback and made product changes. We were on our way.

But as the product took shape, we had to make a tradeoff. We valued direct customer validation of our implementation, but we also wanted to prevent our new features and designs from leaking publicly too soon before product launch. We decided to halt customer lab studies until much closer to the product launch. Instead of customers, the Visual C++ testers took turns looking at different scenarios ("fresh eyes") and continued using Usable, Useful, Desirable (UUD) surveys to evaluate the scenarios at each milestone.

Struggles

But the following months were not exactly smooth sailing. In fact, adapting our historical feature-focused processes and "getting" SFE was very, very challenging. Milestone progress reviews were conducted, but they remained mostly feature-focused—with scenario reviews happening afterward if at all. Some scenarios were defined from the customer's perspective, but several were really just a collection of features that we called a "scenario" (for example, "Compiler toolchain fundamentals" and "Developer IDE productivity fundamentals"). The results of our first lab study UUD survey with customers did show an improvement over our 2010 baseline, but subsequent surveys weren't trending upward for 2012 as we expected. Our test team was now using UUD surveys to augment UUD survey data from real customers, but this data was trending downward. Was our product actually getting worse, or were we not using UUD correctly? (See Figure D-6.) We started doubting SFE and ourselves. Our confidence waned.

We should have expected this. Authors Paul Hersey (*The Situational Leader*) and Ken Blanchard (*The One-Minute Manager*) precisely capture this phenomenon in their situational-leadership model. It states that as teams take on a new skill (like SFE), they go through four phases, and leaders should engage their teams differently depending on the phase of maturity a team is in. Phase 3—when a team is proficient in the new skill but doubts itself—is particularly tenuous. At that point, a significant investment of time, energy, and money has been made, but the full impact of the results aren't very obvious yet. Bingo.

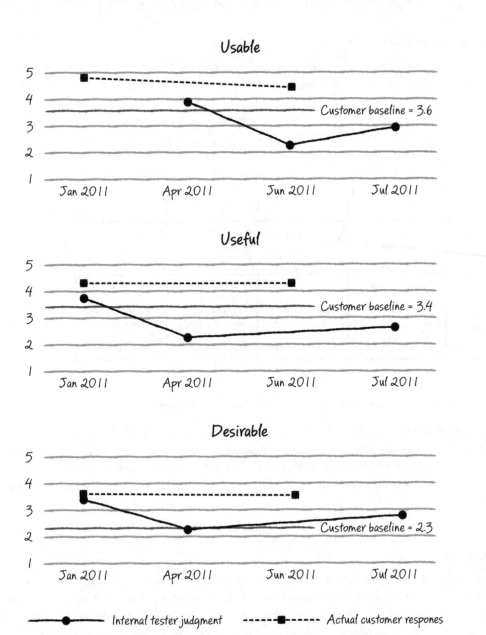

FIGURE D-6 Customer vs. tester survey data variance (for the scenario related to building a 3-D game in C++).

Waving the white flag

So we reached the summer of 2011, one year into our adoption of SFE. With all the effort we'd put into SFE, we did see some positive results, but our accumulated and persistent struggles—and doubts—hit us pretty hard. We were aware of the Hersey-Blanchard model, and as leaders we should have recognized where we were. We should have been supportive, encouraging our group to push forward. But it was precisely at this point that we buckled. (See Figure D-7.) At a scenario review that summer, a weary participant asked dishearteningly, "Why are we even doing this?" That turned out to be the last scenario review the Visual C++ group held for the 2012 product.

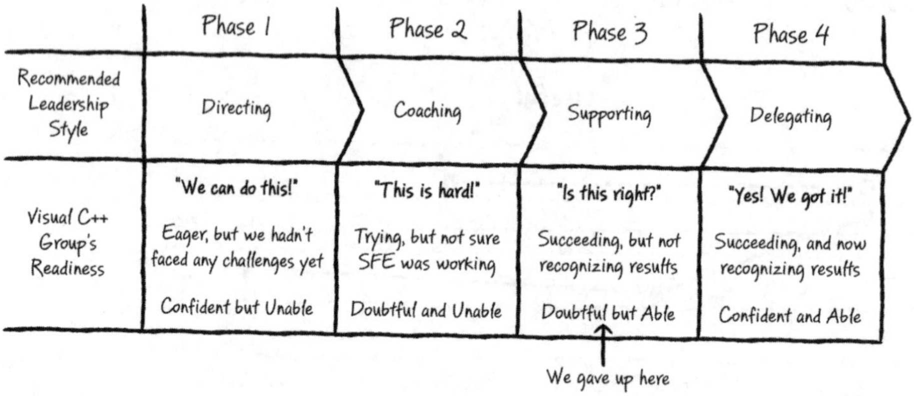

	Phase 1	Phase 2	Phase 3	Phase 4
Recommended Leadership Style	Directing	Coaching	Supporting	Delegating
Visual C++ Group's Readiness	"We can do this!" Eager, but we hadn't faced any challenges yet Confident but Unable	"This is hard!" Trying, but not sure SFE was working Doubtful and Unable	"Is this right?" Succeeding, but not recognizing results Doubtful but Able	"Yes! We got it!" Succeeding, and now recognizing results Confident and Able

We gave up here

FIGURE D-7 Visual C++ group's readiness and recommended leadership style

We reverted to a full-on feature-focus groove, effectively abandoning SFE. Testers stopped producing survey data for scenarios. We stopped scheduling customer lab studies. We shut down my SFE subgroup, reassigning people to other feature work. Our user-experience expert left the company. SFE was only a fad, just as our skeptical inner voices had predicted a year before. SFE had fizzled out.

Or had it?

Rebound

That same summer, independently of the Visual C++ group's efforts, the larger Visual Studio group began conducting new reviews for a small number of key scenarios across all languages in the suite. The Visual C++ group—which had merged with the Accelerated Massive Parallelism (AMP) group—was now responsible for representing four of these key scenarios at the Visual Studio reviews:

- Create high performance computing apps with C++ (AMP).

- Create a Windows Store application with HTML, JavaScript, and C++.

- Create a Windows Store application with XAML and C++.

- Create a Windows Store 3-D game with C++.

Our work began again, but with a different outlook and technique. Instead of our original seven scenarios and the AMP scenario, Visual C++ now focused on just four. Instead of having an SFE subgroup coordinating and advising all Visual C++ testers, the four key scenario testers now worked on their own but shared their best practices with peers. Instead of UUD surveys, our test team used a new evaluation method: customer experience values (CEV). The CEV rating system breaks a scenario into steps or "experiences." Each step is performed manually and is rated as Blocked, Poor, Fair, or Good. Bug reports describing the variance from expectations are required for any rating other than Good.

One group member, Gabriel Esparza-Romero, started and led the test-driven CEV effort as a way to quantify scenario progress and state, while also indicating what was needed to complete the scenario by highlighting gaps and areas for improvement. He was helped along by many others, and this methodology evolved and branched out throughout the release. In hindsight, this approach resulted in tester-provided ratings that were consistently lower than actual customer ratings. Later, in 2014, this was addressed by breaking test-provided CEV into three components: implementation quality rating, provided by the development team; design completeness rating, provided by the new "experiences and insights" team (more on that later); and a customer insight rating, provided by customer interviews and social media. While the CEV rating was invaluable, it wasn't a magic silver bullet. CEV ratings don't provide an automatic tripwire or mechanism to guide teams toward a change in course for the product when the data indicates a change is necessary. Teams must decide themselves how to detect and make those course corrections when using CEV.

Taking up the AMP scenario went smoothly for the Visual C++ team, despite a change to this scenario to support the C++ customer persona—Liam, the self-published, indie app developer. This scenario included the AMP language and library as well as the parallel debugger. The AMP group based its initial designs on the needs of technical computing customers, but it was able to adapt designs to also satisfy customers building consumer-facing parallel computing projects such as computer vision and general image processing. The parallel debugger was also adapted to this new focus, but it didn't require a significant change in design.

Recovery

We were very fortunate. The Visual Studio scenario reviews started precisely at the moment when we lost our gumption and had reverted to focusing on features. If we had truly abandoned SFE in the summer of 2011, it would have sent the message that SFE truly was just a passing fad. But by sticking with it in its new form through the rest of the cycle, it was clear that SFE was an important, sustained, long-term shift.

The Visual Studio scenario reviews also gave Visual C++ a consistent drumbeat and a forum for accountability and visibility. This, it turns out, was when the Visual C++ group found its SFE groove. SFE had taken on a new look, but it was back and here to stay.

Addressing scenario gaps

The Visual Studio scenario reviews proved to be particularly impactful. One example is the effect these reviews had on the 3-D game scenario. To complete this scenario, customers needed to use several new features:

- Create 3-D models with the *3-D Model Editor*

- Create preliminary C++ and HLSL code with the *3-D Project Template*

- Debug HLSL shaders with the *3-D Graphics Debugger* (Pixel History)

In this new era, with the SFE subgroup dissolved, I had changed gears and was now leading a small test team focusing on the 3-D game scenario. As we evaluated the scenario using CEV, we found that once a customer produced a model with the 3-D Model Editor (step 1), they could not use the new 3-D Project Template (step 2) to display the model in their game because the template did not include code to parse and render the model's file format. This was a *big* scenario gap. Reporting a "Poor" CEV rating for step 2 generated a lot of discussion during reviews and ultimately helped garner approval for the creation of the Visual Studio 3-D Starter Kit, which shipped shortly after Visual Studio 2012 was released in August of that year. The kit helped customers complete the full end-to-end scenario, and it was updated and rereleased for new devices, like Windows Phone 8. The kit consistently receives 4.5/5-star ratings from customers. Without the CEV reviews, customers might still be struggling to write their own code to overcome the scenario gap, but we caught the problem and were able to fix it.

Shipping Visual C++ 2012

Along with the rest of the Visual Studio suite, Visual C++ shipped in August 2012. InfoWorld did not evaluate Visual C++ on its own, but it rated the combined Visual Studio 2012 suite 9/10 for capability (utility), 9/10 for ease of use (usability), and 9/10 for value (desirability). Not bad. (See http://www.infoworld.com/d/application-development/review-visual-studio-2012-shines-windows-8-205971.)

The CEV evaluation method was time-consuming and took its toll on those providing regular evaluations, but using it on the reduced set of scenarios proved to be an effective technique. The 3-D game scenario, for example, saw a clear trend of improvement with each evaluation. The bugs we entered for each CEV evaluation were fixed incrementally as we went along, improving ratings and cumulatively piling up in number over the course of the release.

As the 2012 release ended, we didn't immediately recognize our own successes. The 2012 cycle didn't result in a rapid, seismic shift from features to scenarios. Instead, we gradually found a balance between the two. But we learned from both the successes and the painful aspects of the 2012 release, made iterative improvements in the 2013 release, and then made even more dramatic changes for our next release.

SFE process scorecard

Looking back at the 2012 release, how well did the Visual C++ group follow SFE principles and techniques? Here's a recap:

- **Identify target customers**   We defined a persona (Liam, the rising-star developer) for this release.

- **Observe** We used interviews, focus groups, and lab studies, but we could have "soaked in data" more to gain greater empathy and new insights. Our decision to restrict customer access of prerelease builds limited our ability to observe customers using our product, and we used testers as substitutes.

- **Frame** Product management made a healthy investment to create scenarios and stories, but we initially felt the need to treat all work as a scenario and mistakenly applied this term to some groups of feature work.

- **Brainstorm** We did brainstorm, but we didn't get customer feedback on many variations.

- **Build** We didn't create many prototypes but went right to production code.

- **Observe** We did use lab studies to guide us to make design changes (generative data). We struggled with UUD survey data as a means to track our progress (summative data).

- **Repeat** We didn't do frequent, rapid cycles. We spent about two months in each stage and then shipped in August of 2012.

So, what went wrong? In retrospect, we could have done several things differently.

- **Lost the faith** We gave up—but just temporarily. We were lucky that a white knight (in the form of the Visual Studio scenario reviews) appeared to help us restart. But we should have pushed through, adapted, and continued on our own.

- **Using testers for lab studies** We thought that by rotating the scenarios, we could use the "fresh eyes" of testers to act as the customer and rate our scenarios using UUD surveys. But as we should have known, we are *not* the customer, and the tester-generated survey data didn't show a good correlation to (or prediction of) what real customers thought. (See Figure D-6 earlier.)

- **Not everything needs to be a scenario** The Visual C++ 2012 release added great new functionality in the IDE and compiler (for example, support for the C++11 standard), and initially we tried to create a false wrapper around this functionality and call the work "scenarios," which was unnatural and unnecessary.

- **Didn't iterate designs with real customers frequently or consistently enough** We did meet with customers at the beginning and end of the release, but in the middle we used team members as proxies for customers to limit potential leaks. Our customer interactions were somewhat far apart, and we didn't always use them to validate changes we made in response to feedback from a previous interaction. We didn't do frequent, rapid cycles, and instead spent about two months in each SFE stage.

- **Overscoped** To be successful with SFE, you need to be able to modify your plans to adapt to feedback. We bit off a lot for this release and didn't make the necessary cuts to allow for unplanned new work.

What went right? A few key things really had a significant, positive impact on our scenario efforts.

- **Finished strong and adapted**   Midway through the product release, after we gave up, we dug deep, got back on the SFE horse, and shipped. Finishing this way allowed us to look back at our struggles and make iterative improvements to how we could use SFE in future releases (more on that later).

- **Interviews, focus groups, lab studies**   The data we collected from customers confirmed the directions we were already planning and helped us make adjustments. We turned this data into large posters—which included photos of the people we'd met with—that we hung in the hallways to remind us of what was important to customers. Our developers made good use of this data. With more iterations, we could have responded even better to this input.

- **Brainstorming**   Program managers deeply considered multiple approaches, which resulted in better designs.

- **Walk-throughs**   Our user-experience expert led the generation of detailed scenario walk-throughs and storyboards to help engineers visualize the product. The walk-through technique was very valuable and is still frequently used today.

- **Just a few scenarios**   Focusing on everything means you don't focus on anything. Reducing our focus to fewer scenarios helped us invest attention and resources in those scenarios and deliver a better product.

The importance of timing

When we started using SFE, we created a dedicated SFE subgroup. Doing this at the beginning, as we were all learning SFE, was probably a mistake. Forming an SFE subgroup created the unintended perception that it wasn't necessary for everyone to become more scenario-focused because that was the SFE subgroup's job. Also, my original SFE subgroup acted as consultants, but we were not scenario owners ourselves. Thus, we lacked credibility with other testers who were scenario owners and responsible for evaluating the scenarios they owned. In their book *Switch: How to Change Things When Change Is Hard*, Chip and Dan Heath stress the importance of "shaping the path" when making a difficult change, like the one from features to scenarios. You can desire change emotionally and intellectually, but when things get tough, you'll often fall back to a well-worn (feature) path. Having scenario owners provide guidance to other owners as peers proved to be far more effective than my "consulting" subgroup of nonowners. The owners of our four key scenarios cleared new paths themselves, sharing the processes that were working for them.

But in 2014, as of the writing of this book, the Visual C++ team has decided that the timing is right to reintroduce a similar "experiences and insights" team, similar to the initial SFE subgroup. The members of this team are unique—they created a new discipline—on par with traditional developer, tester, and PM roles. They visit, interact with, and poll customers. Then they analyze qualitative interaction data along with quantitative product usage data to ensure that customers' needs are fulfilled.

Using temporary stopgaps

As I mentioned, we chose to restrict customer access of prerelease builds and instead used testers as substitutes. Initially, our testers used UUD surveys, but then we switched to CEV. Neither using testers as substitute customers or using CEV instead of UUD surveys was the right long-term solution for us, but using them temporarily was good because they allowed us to move forward without abandoning SFE.

By using CEV to rate each step in a scenario, by filing bugs for gaps/defects in the scenario steps, and by reviewing the CEV ratings with peers and management, we shipped a better product. This system also proved to be consistent and a good summative metric for tracking and predicting progress. (See Figure D-8.) The testers also created detailed, end-to-end, manual scripts to follow when evaluating CEV data, which provided consistency during evaluation. These scripts were eventually automated, creating a great set of check-in tests that were run before developers committed product changes. The automation also reduced the cost and number of issues found during manual testing. The danger here was that CEV would just become another checklist of features rather than an evaluation of the customer experience, so it was important to switch back to UUD surveys and real customers.

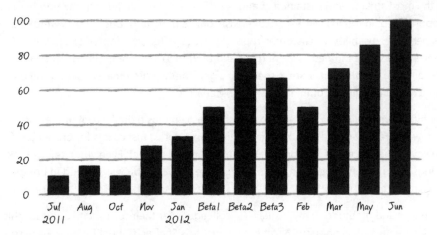

FIGURE D-8 Percent of scenario steps with CEV rating of Good or better

Temporarily using CEV also delayed our analysis and adaptation of how we used UUD surveys. It was great having a UUD baseline (from the 2010 version of our product), and we believed that by conducting future UUD surveys on incremental monthly builds of the 2012 product in development, we could track our progress toward being "done" (summative). However, our incremental data points didn't change much, even after six months of development. (See Figure D-6.) Before using UUD surveys again, we should better understand why this happened. Switching to CEV delayed our investigation of this situation.

Beyond 2012

SFE took root in the 2010–12 cycle, slowly at first, but it has continued to grow and flourish and has increasingly changed how we organize and produce software.

Work is still organized into features, but scenarios are driving the features that are implemented. The organization is changing and has restructured around the "experiences and insights" discipline and scenarios. Today, you'll more likely hear someone in the group ask, "What scenario are you working on?" than "What feature are you working on?"

With product updates shipping every three months instead of every two to three years, the group is building a fast (and positive) feedback cycle with customers. Through the team's agility and its willingness to make product changes based on feedback, customer engagement has increased. Scenario walk-throughs are now a core part of all milestone reviews. Product telemetry and customer data are now commonly used during planning and design. While independent prototypes are not common, the minimum viable product approach proposed by Eric Ries (in his book *The Lean Startup: How Today's Entrepreneurs Use Continuous Innovation to Create Radically Successful Businesses*) is often taken when we plan and brainstorm new product changes.

But one of the most striking and sustained changes from a test perspective is in the number and type of bug reports filed. In the Visual C++ 2010 release, only 6 percent of bug reports were related to scenarios/experiences, usability, or customer-reported issues. After we adopted SFE in Visual C++ 2012, bug reports of this type jumped to 22 percent and then to 31 percent in the Visual C++ 2013 release. This reflects the fact that the team is spending significantly more time evaluating the product from the perspective of delivering complete customer scenarios.

So while we hit a period of doubt one year in, the shift to scenarios did take root in the end. Scenarios are now a core part of the way the group thinks and works. Just as it is for products, iteration is the key to the success of SFE for your organization and project. Even when things look grim, keep going! If you experiment, listen, adapt, and move forward, you will succeed in bringing change to your organization.

My sincere thanks and gratitude to my Visual C++ colleagues for their review and input for this case study: Ale Contenti, Ayman Shoukry, Birgit Hindman, Chris Shaffer, Gabriel Esparza-Romero, Jerry Higgins, Jim Griesmer, Martha Wieczorek, Orville McDonald, Rui Sun, Steve Carroll, Tarek Madkour, and Tim Gerken.

Desirability Toolkit

The table below lists the words used on the product-reaction cards described in the sidebar "Desirability Toolkit" in Chapter 9, "Observing customers: Getting feedback."

The complete set of 118 product-reaction cards				
Accessible	Creative	Fast	Meaningful	Slow
Advanced	Customizable	Flexible	Motivating	Sophisticated
Annoying	Cutting edge	Fragile	Not secure	Stable
Appealing	Dated	Fresh	Not valuable	Sterile
Approachable	Desirable	Friendly	Novel	Stimulating
Attractive	Difficult	Frustrating	Old	Straightforward
Boring	Disconnected	Fun	Optimistic	Stressful
Businesslike	Disruptive	Gets in the way	Ordinary	Time-consuming
Busy	Distracting	Hard to use	Organized	Time saving
Calm	Dull	Helpful	Overbearing	Too technical
Clean	Easy to use	High quality	Overwhelming	Trustworthy
Clear	Effective	Impersonal	Patronizing	Unapproachable
Collaborative	Efficient	Impressive	Personal	Unattractive
Comfortable	Effortless	Incomprehensible	Poor quality	Uncontrollable
Compatible	Empowering	Inconsistent	Powerful	Unconventional
Compelling	Energetic	Ineffective	Predictable	Understandable
Complex	Engaging	Innovative	Professional	Undesirable
Comprehensive	Entertaining	Inspiring	Relevant	Unpredictable
Confident	Enthusiastic	Integrated	Reliable	Unrefined
Confusing	Essential	Intimidating	Responsive	Usable
Connected	Exceptional	Intuitive	Rigid	Useful
Consistent	Exciting	Inviting	Satisfying	Valuable
Controllable	Expected	Irrelevant	Secure	
Convenient	Familiar	Low maintenance	Simplistic	

Index

A

A/B testing
about, 312, 341–345, 362n
as complementary research approach, 109
prototyping with code, 298
abductive reasoning, 58, 62n
Abi-Chahine, Elie, 273
acronyms, inventing, 82–83
active listening, 323–324
affinity diagrams
about, 47, 137
brainstorming alternatives and, 251
creating, 141–148
finding patterns and insights using, 136–137
grouping considerations, 144
initial sorting, 143–144
looking for insights, 147–148
preparation, 142
reading out and re-sorting, 146–147
summaries, 144–145
taping it up, 147
Agile process, 58–59, 273, 368
all-hands meetings, 82
Amazon Kindle e-reader, 29–30
Amtrak case study, 30–31, 140
analysis paralysis, 54, 86
analyst reports, 133
animation, prototyping, 299
anomalies in data, 110–112
APIs (application programming interfaces)
design considerations, 32, 241–243
prototyping, 293–297
Apple (company), 208–209
application programming interfaces (APIs)
design considerations, 32, 241–243
prototyping, 293–297

Applied Imagination (Osborn), 253
architectural drawings, 241–243
Asch, Solomon, 329
assumptions, challenging, 226–228, 247
auditioning components, 300

B

Bach, Paula, 386
The Back of the Napkin (Roam), 235
Bacon, Kevin, 203
Bain & Company research, 16
Balsamiq tool, 265, 291
Basadur Creative Problem Solving Profile, 381, 452–454
BDUF (Big Design Up Front) philosophy, 368
Belfiore, Joe, 406
benchmarks, capturing, 423
Berkun, Scott, 257–258
biases
confirmation, 126
experimentation and, 263
functional fixedness, 218
groupthink, 131
introducing into data, 115
usability testing, 360–361
big data, 107–109, 344–348
Big Design Up Front (BDUF) philosophy, 368
big-T truths
about, 100
insights and, 104
motivation behind, 131
social media and, 206
Bing search engine, 97, 342–345
Blank, Steve, 59
blends, 210, 251
block diagrams, 241–243, 284
Bodine, Kerry, 17, 141, 347–348

About the authors

AUSTINA DE BONTE is a trainer, coach, consultant, and change agent. During her 16-year career at Microsoft, she was an intimate part of the company's first forays into online services. She led program management of the early versions of the popular MSN Messenger Service and experienced firsthand the value of a user-centered design approach. In 2008, Austina conceived and founded the Scenario-Focused Engineering initiative to help accelerate Microsoft's shift toward a more customer-focused, iterative approach to design and product development. Austina has bachelor's and master's degrees in computer science from MIT and did her thesis work in the Epistemology and Learning Group of the MIT Media Lab. She currently teaches with Labas, a children's Lithuanian folk-dance group in Seattle, and is also president of the board of directors of the NWGCA.

DREW FLETCHER is an educator, speaker, and consultant, currently living in the Seattle area. Following a career as a professional musician, Drew spent 20 years at Microsoft, where he led teams that delivered many innovative products, including the first versions of Visual Basic, Visual J++, Visual C++, and Visual C#. Known as a strong customer advocate, Drew joined Microsoft's Engineering Excellence team in 2008 as the director of program management. There, he teamed up with Austina to develop and champion the Scenario-Focused Engineering effort. Drew has a BSBA in international management from Boston University. As an avid backcountry climber and skier, Drew is an active field member of Seattle Mountain Rescue and serves on their board of directors.

Special contributor

DR. INDRĖ VISKONTAS has published groundbreaking work on the neural basis of memory and creativity and has won numerous research and teaching awards. She holds a PhD in cognitive neuroscience from UCLA and costarred in the television series *Miracle Detectives*, which aired in 2011 on the Oprah Winfrey network. Her 24-lecture series, "12 Essential Scientific Concepts," was released in audio and video formats by The Great Courses in 2014, and you can also hear her as the host of the popular science podcast, "Inquiring Minds." Defying traditional career boundaries, Dr. Viskontas spends much of her time performing as an opera singer. She has a master's of music degree from the San Francisco Conservatory of Music, where she also serves as a professor of sciences and humanities, and is an adjunct professor of psychology at the University of San Francisco, where she teaches biological psychology. http://www.indreviskontas.com.

Free ebooks

From technical overviews to drilldowns on special topics, get *free* ebooks from Microsoft Press at:

www.microsoftvirtualacademy.com/ebooks

Download your free ebooks in PDF, EPUB, and/or Mobi for Kindle formats.

Look for other great resources at Microsoft Virtual Academy, where you can learn new skills and help advance your career with free Microsoft training delivered by experts.

Microsoft Press

Now that you've read the book...

Tell us what you think!

Was it useful?
Did it teach you what you wanted to learn?
Was there room for improvement?

Let us know at http://aka.ms/tellpress

Your feedback goes directly to the staff at Microsoft Press,
and we read every one of your responses. Thanks in advance!